"UP SHIP!"

"UP SHIP!"

A HISTORY OF THE U.S. NAVY'S RIGID AIRSHIPS 1919–1935

By Douglas H. Robinson and Charles L. Keller

Naval Institute Press
Annapolis, Maryland

Library of Congress Cataloging in Publication Data
Robinson, Douglas Hill, 1918–
    Up ship!
    Bibliography: p.
    Includes index.
    1. United States. Navy—Aviation—History.
2. Air-ships—History. I. Keller, Charles L.
II. Title.
VG93.R6   358.4′00973   82-6374
ISBN 0-87021-738-0   AACR2

Printed in the United States of America

Dedicated to the memory of three great men we have known

Captain
Garland Fulton USN
1890–1975

Vice Admiral
Charles E. Rosendahl USN
1892–1977

Vice Admiral
Thomas G. W. Settle USN
1895–1980

Contents

Preface

This volume is the product of a joint effort by two friends of long standing. Twenty-five years ago Charles Keller, over a period of several years, spent a great deal of time in the National Archives pursuing and transcribing every available document relating to the U.S. Navy's effort to develop the rigid airship. He concentrated on the "era of experimentation"—the first tentative plans in 1916–19 to build such craft, and the procurement, construction, and operation of the Navy's first three rigid airships: the British-built R 38, which crashed in England before delivery to the United States; the American-built *Shenandoah*; and the German-built *Los Angeles*. Since the ships originated in different countries, the only three countries to seriously engage in rigid airship construction, the study of the era of experimentation actually encompassed the entire world's rigid airship expertise. The source material from the National Archives was supplemented by a quantity of documents generously made available by Captain Garland Fulton, who had played a leading role in planning and procurement of rigid airships in the Bureau of Aeronautics until his retirement in 1940.

When the research was essentially completed, Charles Keller became otherwise occupied, and his notes went into storage. In 1975, during a visit he made to Douglas Robinson, there was a discussion about Charles's historical studies and how unfortunate it would be if the results of his research never appeared in book form. At this point Douglas suggested a collaboration in which he would use the amassed records with the view of producing a book, and Charles agreed. Without the meticulous research and the early drafts that Charles had prepared, this book could never have been written. At the same time it was Douglas who spent several years in preparing several drafts of the text, the last of which was accepted for publication by the Naval Institute Press.

It seems appropriate that this book should be published by the United States Naval Institute. In 1956 Douglas Robinson, drawing on his earlier studies of the Zeppelin in the German Navy, prepared a pictorial article that was published in the Naval Institute *Proceedings* ("Zeppelins in the German Navy, 1914–1918," *U.S. Naval Institute Proceedings*, July 1956). The article was read by Charles Keller, who wrote to the publisher asking about the author. The letter was forwarded to Douglas Robinson, who answered it in person, thereby founding the friendship that ultimately produced this book.

The authors would like to acknowledge the assistance of several retired airship personnel of the U.S. Navy who provided oral information and who opened their private records—Ralph G. Pennoyer, Horace Dyer, James H. Collier, Norman Walker, Harry O'Claire, Frank Peckham, and John McCarthy; as well as John Shotter, formerly with the British airship service. Hepburn Walker, a former chief rigger in the U.S. naval airships of the World War II period, and a diligent student of the era of experimentation, read the operational chapters and provided information from his own archives. In England, Sir Victor Goddard and Lord Ventry read the chapters on R 38 and provided helpful comments and advice. Philip Edwards of the National Air and Space Museum provided rare photographs for the book. Others who offered valuable information on obscure matters were Captain Ralph Barnaby, Peter Grosz, Roger Pineau, Mrs. T. G. W. Settle, and Donald Woodward.

We are particularly grateful to the three men to whose memory this volume is dedicated—Captain Garland Fulton, Vice Admiral Charles E. Rosendahl, and Vice Admiral Thomas G. W. Settle. All three willingly made themselves available, answered numerous questions, and shared their archives. In particular, Admiral Settle closely read every one of the operational chapters, and his comments and suggestions were extremely valuable.

We are indebted to our publisher, the Naval Institute Press, and to our editors, Mr. Richard R. Hobbs and Ms. Constance M. MacDonald, for their patience and assistance. We appreciate the very particular favor extended by Mr. William Kerka, the expert researcher and draftsman who prepared the airship drawings in the text. We are indebted to the following publishers for permission to quote from their books: Dodd, Mead & Co.; Christian Wolff Verlag; Regent Press of Kansas; U.S. Government Printing Office; *Journal of the American Society of Naval Engineers*; *National Geographic Magazine*; W. W. Norton & Co.; Charles Scribner's Sons; and Yale University Press.

We are also grateful to Richard E. Byrd III for permission to quote from his grandfather's book *Skyward*, and to Robin D. S. Higham for permission to quote from his book *The British Rigid Airship 1908–1931*.

Douglas H. Robinson
Charles L. Keller

Introduction: The Rigid Airship's Place in the U.S. Navy

The year 1940 ended the era of the rigid airship, the giant aerial vehicle sustained in the sky by the lift of gases lighter than air. Today, with the everyday presence of jet aircraft, many with supersonic capability, the rigid airship seems a clumsy anachronism. Yet in the period from about 1910 to 1940 when the airplane was an undeveloped wood and fabric affair, short on endurance and load-carrying capacity, the rigid airship reigned as the conqueror of the oceans and "the battleship of the skies." Germany built over a hundred for World War I; to the Americans it seemed an ideal long-range scouting craft for possible war in the Pacific.

For the U.S. Navy, the rigid airship was but one example of rapidly changing technology in the two decades between the world wars. It was a period of changes in the probable enemy, of changes in the missions imposed on the Navy, and of changing weapons with which to fulfill the missions. The war with Spain in 1898 had made the United States a world power, while the capture of an overseas empire, particularly in the Philippines, expanded the responsibilities of the Navy and justified an increase in the fleet. Following the teachings of the American Captain Alfred Thayer Mahan, who preached that sea power depended on the possession of a strong battle fleet, all the major powers competed to outbuild each other in battleship strength. Upon entering World War I, the U.S. Navy possessed 14 dreadnoughts. Few of them were needed overseas, however, where the emphasis was on combating the German submarine war on shipping.

Following the Armistice in 1918, the U.S. Navy's major preoccupation became the possibility of war in the Pacific, in view of the aggressive ambitions of Japan, which, after victory over China in 1894 and czarist Russia in 1905, now aspired to dominate the entire Far East. Striving consciously to build "a fleet second to none," the United States was pushing for the completion of a 1916 program of ten battleships all with 16-inch guns, and six similarly armed 35-knot battle cruisers. While it was impossible to maintain in the Far East a fleet equal to the expanding Japanese Navy, now the third largest in the world, it was believed that with a 2 to 1 superiority in dreadnoughts, to be achieved by the 1916 program, Japan could eventually be defeated. The great weakness of the ORANGE[1] war plan was the defenselessness of the Philippines—8,000 miles from the West Coast of the United States, and less than 2,000 miles from Japan. Literally nothing could prevent the Nipponese from seizing them on the outbreak of war. At the same time, prestige and public opinion would demand the recapture of the Philippines—perhaps prematurely and with inadequate forces. War plans of this period anticipated at least a 60-day interval before the American fleet could appear in the western Pacific. Meanwhile Japan, having been granted a mandate over the former German-held Caroline and Marshall islands, could bring it to action at a time and place most favorable to itself.

The Washington Treaty, signed on 6 February 1922 as a result of a conference called by the United States, further undermined the American position in the western Pacific. The treaty established a 5–5–3 ratio in battleship tonnage among Great Britain, the United States, and Japan. Seven of the ten battleships building under the 1916 program and all six of the battle cruisers were to be scrapped (though two of the latter were completed later as the aircraft carriers *Lexington* and *Saratoga*). Worse yet, the United States agreed not to fortify further its possessions in Guam and the Philippines. With battleship strength reduced, the ratio of superiority cut from 2 to 1 to 5 to 3, with its western Pacific harbors defenseless, it seemed hopeless for the U.S. Navy to try to defend the Philippines or to defeat Japan in an ORANGE war.

The battleship was still the yardstick by which sea power was measured, and the U.S. Navy only gradually realized that naval aviation might be developed as a means of compensating for the unfavorable strategic situation in the western Pacific resulting from the Washington Treaty.[2] Naval aviation had played a prominent role in antisubmarine warfare in 1917–18, with large numbers of American-built flying boats operating from shore bases in France and the British Isles, but after the Armistice it had been cut back to a remnant flying from a few shore stations on the American East and West Coasts. Only in 1919 did Congress vote funds for the conversion of a fleet collier into the first U.S. aircraft carrier, the *Langley*, which entered service in 1922. Also in 1919 money was voted for the construction of an airship base, and for two rigid airships, one to be purchased abroad and the other to be built in the United States. But naval aviation, with control of its development divided among at least three bureaus of the Navy Department, and its advocates of junior rank, remained overshadowed by the battleship and battle cruiser programs.

Abruptly, however, beginning in 1919, the entire future of military aviation in the United States was catapulted into the headlines by the Army Air Service's Brigadier General William Mitchell, and his campaign to advance his unified air service theories by proving that his bombers could sink battleships, and that navies were therefore superfluous. "Billy" Mitchell's threat put the Navy on the defensive and caused it to close ranks and sink its differences. Operating in a constant glare of publicity, Mitchell commanded much public support for his air power campaign. In a joint Army–Navy bombing test in July 1921, on surrendered German vessels, Mitchell sent to the bottom the mislabeled "unsinkable" dreadnought *Ostfriesland*. Perceiving that Mitchell's agitation for a unified air service might rob it of the right to its own air arm, the Navy set to work to prove that aviation was necessary to carrying out its duties, and that aircraft could be operated at sea.

In July 1921, a separate Bureau of Aeronautics was established in the Navy Department. Under its first chief, Rear Admiral William A. Moffett, who served three terms until his death in the loss of the airship *Akron* in April 1933, BuAer was charged with "taking aviation to sea with the Fleet." This involved development of the aircraft carrier and its air group of fighters, bombers, scouting and torpedo aircraft; the light-weight, high-powered air-cooled radial engine; the long-range patrol flying boat; and the rigid airship for strategic scouting.

The rigid airship, if it could be developed into a reliable weapon, would have a uniquely effective place in the ORANGE war plans. Able to operate independently for days at a cruising speed of 40 knots, it could range far into the Pacific, to cover the ships of a fleet advancing against Japan or its island possessions. A scouting line of rigid airships, flying far ahead of the fleet, could give early warning of the approach of Japanese surface forces. No other aircraft in the early 1920s had the range and endurance to perform this mission. Last, whereas all previous airships had been inflated with inflammable hydrogen, a major reason for the elimination of the German Zeppelins as effective combat weapons after 1916, America possessed a world monopoly of a nonflammable lifting gas suitable for airships—helium.

Whereas the German Navy had as many as 20 Zeppelins simultaneously in operation in 1917, the U.S. Navy, existing on meager handouts by successive Republican administrations, procured only five rigid airships, and operated four, during the period 1919–35. The airship to be purchased abroad under the 1919 program was the British R 38, the last and largest of a series of rigids built during the war in imitation of German Zeppelins. In August 1921, and before her delivery to the U.S. Navy, R 38—known as ZR 2 in the American series—broke up in flight and burned, killing 28 British and 16 American airshipmen.

The domestic rigid airship, the ZR 1 *Shenandoah*, was entirely an American product, though her design closely followed that of German Zeppelins which had fallen into Allied hands. Over a two-year period she provided experience in rigid airship handling, and in the special techniques called for when flying with helium. Little time was spent in operations with the fleet; instead, Moffett used her for publicity flights intended to counteract Billy Mitchell's drive to take over naval aviation, and to stimulate enthusiasm in the country and in Congress for the Bureau of Aeronautics and its financially starved programs. It was on a flight to the Midwest, to show herself over a long itinerary of towns and state fairs, that the *Shenandoah* was destroyed with the loss of 14 lives.

The third craft, the ZR 3 *Los Angeles*, was procured from the *Luftschiffbau Zeppelin* as a replacement for the ZR 2, being the only craft ever built by the German firm to a foreign order. An advanced and original design, she fully came up to expectations and was in service for eight years with no major mishaps. She did much practical experimentation in connection with the next generation of American rigids, built specifically for scouting with the fleet in the Pacific.

No other comprehensive record of this "era of experimentation" of the rigid airship in the U.S. Navy has appeared, and the present volume has been made possible only by extensive research in the Navy's archives. A brief account of the subsequent *Akron* and *Macon*, built by the Goodyear-Zeppelin Corporation, is included here to carry to its conclusion the story of the rigid airship in the U.S. Navy.[3]

Why a history of an enterprise that failed, and is now generally forgotten? We hold that the tale is worth telling for its own value—a significant chapter in the early history of aviation in the United States, a fascinating technical romance involving the creation of a series of new industries for producing duralumin, helium gas, specialized power plants, and synthetic gas-proof materials. The American aircraft industry's dramatically successful development of all-metal aircraft was made possible by the Navy's encouragement of industry to produce duralumin for the *Shenandoah* and later airships, while helium production and utilization, on a vast scale today in the nuclear and space program, originated with efforts to make the nonflammable gas available for the big airships. Further, with many enthusiasts who never saw a rigid airship today advocating their revival for a large variety of missions, it is well to have on record factual information concerning the very real problems, difficulties, and frustrations that the pioneers experienced and attempted to overcome, hidden away heretofore in the archives.

Last, there is the ever-fascinating story of brave men, patriotic and dedicated, risking and giving their lives in a pioneering effort to perfect a new weapon for their country's defense. One hundred and five officers and men of the U.S. Navy perished in the accidents that ended the careers of the ZR 2 (R 38), *Shenandoah*, *Akron*, and *Macon*. May this work help to preserve the memory of their sacrifice.

"UP SHIP!"

1

The Foreign Influence

Though the U.S. Navy eventually made significant contributions to airship technology, in the beginning it was heavily dependent on the experience of foreign powers—Germany and Great Britain—in the design, construction, and operation of rigid airships.

Germany, in particular, was the spiritual home of the big rigid, and Friedrichshafen on Lake Constance, the home of the *Luftschiffbau Zeppelin*, was the Mecca to which the airshipmen of all nations looked for inspiration and enlightenment. And not without reason: of the 161 rigid airships built and flown, 139 had been constructed in Germany, 119 by the *Luftschiffbau Zeppelin* and 20 by the rival *Luftschiffbau Schütte-Lanz*, which failed to survive the 1918 Armistice. All rigid airships built in other countries owed a great deal to Zeppelin designs, and many were copies.

Count Ferdinand von Zeppelin, whose name is synonymous with the rigid airship, built his first craft in 1898–1900, and made three flights with her totaling 2 hours 11 minutes. There had been earlier airships—small affairs with fabric bags whose shape depended on internal gas pressure—but LZ 1 was different. A giant for her day, she displaced 399,000 cubic feet, was 420 feet long and 38½ feet in diameter. She embodied from the beginning all the essential features of all later rigid airships—enormous size and gas volume made possible by a framework of longitudinal girders and transverse frames fabricated of aluminum, in itself so novel as to be practically a laboratory curiosity; 17 separate drum-shaped gas cells filling the space between the frames, made of rubberized cotton and with automatic valves in the bottom and hand-operated maneuvering valves in the top; a

smooth outer cover of specially impregnated cotton fabric; and open boat-shaped gondolas fore and aft under the hull. Hydrogen was the inflation medium in LZ 1 and all later German airships.

LZ 1 was dismantled after Zeppelin's company went bankrupt, but the count, who had seen the big airship as a weapon of air superiority that would win the next war for Germany, persisted in his efforts to develop a viable military craft, and to sell it to the German Army and Navy, and, more important, to the German people. Attempting to make a 24-hour acceptance flight in a larger craft, the count met with disaster when his LZ 4, after a forced landing at Echterdingen near Stuttgart, was torn from her moorings and burned in August 1908. Six million marks, subscribed in the days after Echterdingen, put the Zeppelin enterprise on a solid financial footing.

With little encouragement from the old aristocrat, Zeppelin's business manager, Alfred Colsman, founded in the fall of 1909 a passenger company, the DELAG, with the aim of keeping the airship in the public eye. Carrying 20 to 24 people, the DELAG Zeppelins flew two-hour joy rides from sheds near the large German cities. More important, the experience of DELAG personnel enabled the German armed forces rapidly to train some 70 flight crews of roughly 20 men each after the outbreak of war.

Apprehensive about French superiority in military airships, the German Army in the three years before August 1914 procured ten Zeppelins. They were intended in the war plan to carry out long-range reconnaissance by day in the rear of the French and Russian armies. Proving far too vulnerable to anti-aircraft fire, the Army Zeppelins were forced to turn to night bombing, but the raids were infrequent, and owing to navigational errors, were generally ineffective. In June 1917 the Army airship service was inactivated, and its ships broken up for their duralumin.

The Imperial Navy, in the person of the all-powerful navy minister, Grand Admiral Alfred von Tirpitz, had been reluctant to take up the Zeppelin airship. The early craft were palpably too slow, too small, and too lacking in endurance to be of any use in operations over the stormy North Sea. Tirpitz continued to resist demands that he purchase Zeppelins until the spring of 1912, and when he did give in, it was because of the threat that the Royal Navy would have a large rigid airship first. The first German naval airship, L 1, was a slightly enlarged version of the DELAG craft, and only two more were purchased before August 1914.

Soon after the outbreak of World War I, the German Fleet Command realized that the conflict would not be over in a few weeks, and that the British Navy would not, as in the Napoleonic wars, make an immediate descent in force on the North German coast. The endless defensive patrols put an intolerable strain on the High Seas Fleet's cruisers and destroyers. Expanding the airship service was the answer—an airship could be built in six weeks, whereas a cruiser took over two years. Zeppelins were ordered as fast as the building works could turn them out. Exercising wartime powers, the German Navy took control of the Zeppelin works, sent its naval constructors in to act as inspectors and advisers, and saw to it that competent engineers were hired. Progressively larger designs were prepared throughout the war at the Navy's insistence, with refined and improved features developed by the Navy Department in collaboration with the Zeppelin Company's designers.

Though the Zeppelin raids on England were spectacular and affected morale, the U.S. Navy was more interested in the German use of airships for overwater reconnaissance, watching for enemy surface craft or submarines. In 1916–17 up to 20 Zeppelins were in commission, though because of weather-related problems, they would be out only one day in four. Despite shortcomings, the airship patrols gave the High Seas Fleet Command a feeling of security, while it was possible to limit the deployment of surface craft.

When Vizeadmiral Reinhard Scheer succeeded to the Fleet Command in January 1916, it was with a determination to use all of Germany's naval forces to the full. His aggressiveness culminated on 31 May in the Battle of Jutland. Owing to weather conditions, the naval Zeppelins played no part in the actual battle. Seven weeks later, however, on 19 August, Scheer set out to bombard Sunderland on the English East Coast. Two lines of U-boats were positioned across the probable line of advance of the Grand Fleet, and no fewer than eight Zeppelins were sent out for distant strategic scouting. Four of them formed a scouting line across the northern North Sea to detect and report the progress of the Grand Fleet south from Scapa Flow, and the other four were to cruise off the English East Coast, and over the waters off the Dutch coast, to report smaller forces proceeding against the High Seas Fleet. Units of the Battle Cruiser Force and of the Grand Fleet itself were sighted and reported by a Zeppelin flying off the Firth of Forth in low clouds and rain, but Scheer refused to believe the enemy main force could have gotten inside the circle of Zeppelins unobserved, and pressed on for Sunderland. What deflected him from his course, and saved him from a surprise encounter with the superior Grand Fleet, was a false report from L 13 to the south of an inferior force of cruisers and battleships. Failing to find the phantom dreadnoughts, Scheer kept on for home. For the Zeppelins it had been a promising beginning in strategic scouting in connection with fleet operations. The experience was never repeated because the German Navy turned to the submarine for an all-out assault on Allied shipping.

Very little information was made available to the Americans and British during the period 1919–39 on the operation of the German Navy Zeppelins, and in fact their story was not properly told until 1962, after extensive research by the author in the captured archives of the German Navy.[1] The first generally available account in English, by Ernst Lehmann, an experienced Army Zeppelin commander, was serialized in the *Saturday Evening Post*, and appeared in book form in 1927.[2] The German official history, which did not go beyond the Battle of Jutland, gave considerable space to the naval airship raids on England but dealt only very incidentally with routine patrols and airships in fleet operations.[3] In the chaotic period immediately after World War I, U.S. naval representatives in Germany commissioned a young naval airship officer to go through the German Navy archives in Berlin and prepare a report on the naval airship service. A brief summary rather than a comprehensive history, the report emphasized scouting and fleet operations, rather than the raids; devoted considerable space to Jutland and the Sunderland operations; and presented capsule histories of each naval airship.[4]

On the other hand, much technical information was made available to the victorious powers through the destruction of German airships over Allied territory, and from inspection of laid-up craft in Germany immediately after the war. Thus it was possible for the British and Americans to copy the latest combat craft provided to the German Navy, though with no knowledge of the underlying design methods and engineering principles involved. These had been evolved during the war years by the chief designer of the *Luftschiffbau Zeppelin*, whose formulae and methods were held as closely guarded trade secrets by the Zeppelin Company.

In March 1915, Dr. Karl Arnstein, an outstanding civil engineer with an established reputation as a bridge designer, was retained by the *Luftschiffbau Zeppelin* to investigate framework breakages in flight. After successful analysis of the cause, Dr. Arnstein was hired permanently. Rejecting the empirical methods of the company, Arnstein set out to develop a detailed mathematical procedure for the stress analysis of an airship framework with respect to aerodynamic as well as structural loads.

Arnstein's work was completed just in time, for in July 1915, the German Navy demanded that the Zeppelin and Schütte-Lanz firms produce a much larger craft than the million-cubic-foot ships just coming into service. It is to Arnstein's credit that not only did the first ship of the new class, L 30, make her first flight less than a year later on 28 May 1916, but also that she and her sisters were technically successful, even playing an indispensable role in the airship programs of other countries. In one leap, the gas volume nearly doubled, to almost 2,000,000 cubic feet. The basic L 30 design was repeated for the rest of the war in a total of 40 more ships.

After four of the original "thirties" were brought down over England in the autumn of 1916, it was obvious that performance would have to be improved. In February 1917 the first ship lightened to reach higher altitudes over England made her first flight in Friedrichshafen, attaining 19,700 feet in an altitude trial. Later craft were lightened still further, not only by introducing smaller and more streamlined gondolas, but also by lightening the hull structure through the use of progressively thinner gauges of duralumin in the girders. This of course reduced the strength of the hull and its resistance to aerodynamic and static loads, but the flight crews were cautioned not to attempt high speed maneuvers at low altitudes. One final Zeppelin design reached the "Front" before the end of the war—L 70, a lengthened high-altitude ship of 2,200,000 cubic feet with seven overcompressed "altitude motors" conferring on her a trial speed of 81 mph. The last raid of the war, on 5 August 1918, proved, however, that the land-based airplane had surpassed the performance of the Zeppelin. L 70, leading the attack with the Leader of Airships on board, was shot down in flames before reaching England.

The fourth "thirty," L 33, fell into British hands as early as September 1916, when she force-landed in England because of gunfire damage sustained over

London. Her crew set her afire, but a corps of Admiralty draftsmen were able to copy all her design features in great detail. L 49, one of the "height-climbers," as the British called the new high-altitude ships, provided information on the lightened hull with lighter girders when she was captured intact in France in October 1917. Detailed drawings, made by French naval constructors, were distributed to all the Allied powers. Last, in a secret salvage operation that was not revealed until 1958, quantities of wreckage from L 70 were recovered from the sea, giving the British much information on the very latest Zeppelin. It will be noted that both L 49 and L 70 were of the high-altitude type, lightly built with low factors of safety; the British and Americans copied them without being fully aware of the stringent restrictions on handling them at low altitude in the German service.

The Schütte-Lanz firm of Mannheim never found favor with the German Navy although the talented Professor Johann Schütte, the firm's chief designer, with a background in naval architecture, showed far more originality and competence than any Zeppelin Company engineer of the prewar period. His masterpiece, SL 2, completed in February 1914, was strikingly modern in appearance compared to her Zeppelin contemporaries, with a beautifully streamlined hull and many other features later introduced into Zeppelin designs during the war. Schütte, however, chose to build his girders of laminated plywood. Moisture absorbed in the damp North Sea air weakened this material, resulting in frequent girder breakages. American airshipmen were aware of Schütte's contribution, while the American Investigation Corporation, founded by American financiers to promote Schütte-Lanz designs, attempted unsuccessfully to market the firm's products in the United States during the 1920s.

A few days before the Armistice was signed, the seven "Front" ships in the North Sea bases were hung up in their sheds and deflated, together with three obsolete Zeppelins used for training. At Versailles the victorious Allies debated who should receive these Zeppelins, now prizes of war. As with the High Seas Fleet, the Allies were spared the trouble. On 23 June 1919, two days after German sailors scuttled their ships at Scapa Flow, the airship crew members still in the North Sea bases deliberately wrecked the five Zeppelins at Nordholz, and two at Wittmundhaven. A year later, in the summer of 1920, the three remaining Zeppelins, together with four older craft laid up in the Baltic in 1917, were flown to British, French, and Italian airship bases and surrendered. The United States, which had not ratified the Versailles Treaty, received nothing. American airshipmen showed a continuous interest in procuring a ship built by the Zeppelin Company, and this led to the construction of the ZR 3 *Los Angeles* as compensation for two of the destroyed wartime ships.

Impressed by the wartime Zeppelins, and by their alleged ubiquity over the North Sea, the U.S. Navy was determined to develop the large rigid airship for its own scouting requirements. Uniquely blessed with the nonflammable lifting gas helium, the Americans were sure they could succeed where the hydrogen-filled German Zeppelins had failed because of their vulnerability. Had the real operational story been known—the handicaps imposed by weather, the fact that scouting missions were flown on no more than one day in four, the uncertainty of navigation—it may be wondered if the Americans would have undertaken what in the end proved to be a losing endeavor.

Despite recognized German preeminence in rigid airship design and construction, the U.S. Navy made its first attempt to learn from the British. This was not surprising; following the Armistice, German builders and operators sullenly refused information about their airships, while the British claimed to have much information. Further, the Royal Navy and the U.S. Navy had developed a close, teacher–pupil relationship during the war, American airshipmen being trained in England to fly the numerous small "blimps" constructed for antisubmarine patrols.

Great Britain, which in the years 1908–21 completed 15 of the big craft, was second only to Germany in the building of rigid airships, the driving force behind the program being the Royal Navy, which, impressed by the German success with Zeppelins, desired a comparable long-range scouting arm to cover the North Sea. It was Sir John Fisher, who as First Sea Lord did so much between 1903 and 1910 to prepare the Royal Navy for World War I, who initiated the British airship program. The armament firm of Vickers undertook to design and build H.M. Airship No. 1; but, unfortunately, as with many prototype rigid airships, No. 1 came out much overweight—so much so that she could not fly when first brought out of her shed in May 1911. She was then rehoused for a drastic program of lightening, which included removal of the external keel between the two gondolas. This step so weakened the hull that No. 1 broke in two while being maneuvered out of the shed in September 1911.

A year and a half later, the successes of the DELAG Zeppelins, and the commissioning of the German Navy's L 1, caused concern that Britain might be left behind, and early in 1913 the Admiralty ordered a new rigid, to be known as H.M. Airship No. 9. Vickers again prepared the design, but this time with the assistance of drawings hurriedly made by the French when the German Army Zeppelin Z IV made a forced landing at Lunéville in April 1913. Again the ship

turned out overweight. Not until she had been extensively lightened did the Admiralty accept her in April 1917.

An expansion program was put in hand in the summer of 1915 comprising four ships of the No. 23 class—lengthened versions of No. 9, and again designed by Vickers. These ships did not enter service until the autumn of 1917. Stationed at the operational bases at East Fortune, Howden, and Pulham on the North Sea coast, they made a few coastal patrols and training flights.

These ships were also the last British rigid airships designed by Vickers to official specifications, for a rival design team had been created at the Admiralty from personnel of the Royal Corps of Naval Constructors, the commissioned shipbuilding technicians of the Royal Navy, who on 26 October 1915 were designated the official source of plans and designs. The head of the team was Constructor Commander Charles Ivor Rae Campbell, who of course had had no previous experience with airships, in spite of numerous assignments to naval construction during his 16 previous years of naval service. Campbell's responsibilities were enlarged, and he became more involved in administrative matters, when in September 1917 he was placed in charge of the Design Section of the department of the Director of Production (Airships) at the Admiralty. A conscientious civil servant, Campbell was not the brilliant investigator that Arnstein was, and extrapolated from German experience instead of conducting and utilizing original study and research.

Events in the summer of 1916 injected a new sense of urgency into the British rigid airship program. The Battle of Jutland, and more particularly the Sunderland Operation of 19 August 1916, heightened the Grand Fleet's feelings of frustration at being constantly watched by the German Zeppelins without being able to retaliate. Outdated British designs were shelved when L 33, the fourth 2,000,000-cubic-foot "super-Zeppelin," fell into British hands during her first raid on London. In November 1916, the Cabinet authorized production of two copies, R 33 and R 34. These were finally completed in the spring of 1919. Three modified and lightened versions of the R 33 type were ordered in January 1917—R 35, R 36, and R 37.[5]

Vickers played no part in this expanded wartime program of large airships, their rivals at the Admiralty freezing them out by the simple expedient of denying them the steel needed for a larger building shed. With no work in hand, Vickers's chief designer, the renowned Sir Barnes Wallis (as he finally became in 1968), characteristically proposed his own design for a 1,200,000-cubic-foot ship that could be built in the small 539-foot shed at Barrow. R 80 made her first flight on 19 July 1920.

It was unfortunate for Britain—and for America too—that Vickers was so coldly treated in the latter part of the war, for Wallis was a true genius in airship design. Instead it was Campbell who was solely responsible for the last British wartime prototype, R 38, intended to be larger than anything built by the wartime enemy and destined to be the American ZR 2. The genesis of the R 38 design (Admiralty "A" type) was a British naval staff requirement of June 1918, for a craft able to patrol for six days over the North Sea, to operate with cruisers of the Grand Fleet at low altitude, and to attain 25,000 feet to escape enemy aircraft. Calculations showed that the requirements could be met only by a 3,000,000-cubic-foot craft 750 feet in length. Because this was longer than any construction shed in England, the requirement was revised, and the ship finally measured 2,724,000 cubic feet with a length of 699 feet, a diameter of 85.5 feet, and a ceiling of 22,000 feet.

Many features of R 38, including her greatly lightened structure, derived from the very latest German "height-climber" Zeppelins. Indeed, even as the R 38 plans were being drawn, quantities of wreckage from the Zeppelin L 70 were being recovered from the North Sea. The latest reports from the salvagers must have been eagerly devoured by Campbell and his assistants, and the secretly acquired knowledge of the German "height-climber" incorporated in the new British giant.

R 38's highly streamlined hull, with only a short parallel portion amidships, was built on 13 main longitudinals and 12 intermediate ones. Twelve of the 14 gas cells were 15 meters long as in the latest German ships, and in the corresponding hull bays, there were two intermediate frames between the main ones. At the same time, the lightly built structure was heavily engined, with six V-12 Sunbeam Cossack engines of 350 h.p. each, intended to drive her at a maximum speed of 70.6 mph.

Campbell's most serious shortcoming in designing the light-weight high-altitude craft was his inability to calculate the aerodynamic loads—those imposed by the pressure of air when the ship was driven at speed by her engines. These loads increased with the square of the speed, and increased markedly when the airship deviated from a straight line, in turns or yawing, pitching up and down in the vertical plane, or flying nose up and "heavy" or nose down and "light." It was relatively simple to calculate the static loads on the framework—the shear and bending forces developed on the one hand by the lift of the gas, and on the other hand by the weight of the hull structure, engines, gondolas, fuel tanks and water ballast sacks along the keel, and the crew members, when floating motionless in the air. It appears that Campbell designed for the static stresses with a safety factor of 4, expecting that this would adequately resist the aerodynamic loads. Few studies had been done in England on aerodynamic loads on airships hulls—the R 38 crash taught the importance of fundamental research, but too late to benefit the 44 men who died.

One wind tunnel experiment on a model of R 29 seems to have seriously misled Campbell: the bending stresses as developed from the model came out so high that it was considered out of the question to provide for them in the actual ship by reason of the weight of the structure that would be required. Yet, in defiance of the laboratory data, R 29, a 23-class variant in which the strengthening keel had been omitted, flew successfully without structural failure. Campbell must have mistrusted model test figures thereafter. Today one can say that very little was known then about "scale effect," or the mathematical correction that must be made to obtain valid figures for aerodynamic forces on the full-size ship from wind-tunnel tests on a small model.

Summing up, German designers would have known, as Campbell did not, that it was impossible to meet the specifications for the R 38 design, which in order to reach 22,000 feet would have to have an extremely light, even fragile frame; while with 2,100 h.p. in six engines she was also expected to do 70 mph at low altitude in cooperation with the Grand Fleet, where rough air and control surface loads would impose stresses under which her light structure would collapse. Campbell's assumption that a safety factor of 4 with respect to the static loads would cover the aerodynamic loads was wishful thinking.

One competent airship designer did offer a second opinion of the R 38 design, long after Campbell had died in the ship he had created. Charles P. Burgess, the civilian expert in the U.S. Navy's Bureau of Aeronautics, visited England in connection with the inquiry into the R 38 crash, and related to his superiors in May 1922:

One of the primary objects of my visit was to go over the strength calculations of R 38 and learn as much as possible from them. They were scattered over some thirty work books, and were extremely confused with incomplete and tentative calculations. . . . It cannot be said that the R 38 calculations are likely to be of much more than historical interest. Only static conditions were considered, and but little ingenuity was shown in dealing with the peculiarities of the structural problems of rigid airships. . . . The inquiry into the loss of R 38 showed that in England, at least, there was a very serious lack of anything like adequate theory to deal with the strength problems of rigid airships.[6]

R 38 was ordered from Short Brothers of Cardington in September 1918, but work did not start until about February 1919. Despite the end of the war, the extreme requirements were not changed, nor was the design modified or the hull structure strengthened.

The British airship R 33 on the Pulham mast, summer 1921. The first mooring mast ever erected. Observations of R 33's operation from the mast inspired Maxfield, Hoyt, and Land to insist that the U.S. Navy had to have a similar mast at Lakehurst. R 33 was a sister ship of the transatlantic R 34. (National Archives)

Three sister ships were to be built, but were later canceled. In fact, with rigid financial restrictions being imposed on the British armed services, it was proposed that work be stopped on R 38 also. From this fate she was reprieved when the U.S. Navy approached the British with a view to purchasing a rigid airship. The Americans were delighted to be offered the largest airship in the world, while their former allies were happy to unload her for £400,000.[7]

British airshipmen must be given credit for a significant innovation: the development of the mooring mast. Resolved not to be handicapped operationally as were the Germans by their reliance on sheds and large parties of men, the British were determined to moor their craft in the open, where they could easily slip in any weather to take up their missions. For a period between 1917 and 1919, the "three-wire system" seemed the solution, and it was used by R 34

during her three-day layover at Mineola, Long Island in July 1919. In March 1918, Vickers was ordered to construct a girder work mooring mast 120 feet high to be erected at the airship station at Pulham. Not until 30 May 1919 was the mast ready at Pulham, with electrical and telephone leads, gas, water, and fuel mains to the masthead. Beginning in February 1921, R 33 made a large series of moorings to the Pulham mast, spending literally days fast to it, with no major problems. Difficulties were overcome and a mooring technique worked out that was used later for all "high" mast operations, by both the British and the Americans. The latter regarded the mooring mast as a great advance permitting operation in wide extremes of weather, and obtained all the information they could with the aim of using it for their own purposes.

2

Airship Background in the U.S. Navy

The U.S. Navy lagged behind the European powers in naval aviation. The first step in its development took place on 19 January 1911, when Lt. Theodore G. Ellyson, the first naval officer to take aviation training, reported to the Glenn Curtiss flight school on North Island at San Diego. He and other pioneers showed incredible daring and ingenuity in developing float planes for naval use, but two years later, when Woodrow Wilson was inaugurated as president, naval aviation consisted of half a dozen Curtiss and Wright pusher aircraft on floats based across the Severn River from the Naval Academy at Annapolis. Expensive airships for over-water reconnaissance were in the category of impossible dreams.

Wilson's secretary of the navy was Josephus Daniels; his assistant secretary was Franklin Delano Roosevelt. Daniels's aide for operations was Rear Admiral Bradley A. Fiske, a visionary who in 1911 had argued that 400 airplanes armed with torpedoes could successfully defend the Philippines against a Japanese invasion. It was Fiske who first took up the cause of the large rigid airship in the U.S. Navy. Impressed by a secret French report on the German Army Zeppelin Z IV, which had force-landed at Lunéville in April 1913, he pointed out to Daniels that the use of airships abroad "had reached a state of development that our Navy cannot ignore."[1] The General Board, a council of senior admirals advising the secretary of the navy on policy and strategy, should be requested to determine whether the airship had value for the fleet, and whether the Navy Department should take steps to obtain one for experimental purposes.

Contrary to the Billy Mitchell propaganda about hidebound battleship admirals, the General Board,

particularly its chairman, Admiral George Dewey, the victor of Manila Bay, were aware of the potential value of aviation to the fleet. In a memorandum dated 19 August 1913, the board reviewed aeronautical activity abroad; noted that Germany had ordered seven rigid airships since the Z IV incident, and recommended the prompt construction for training purposes of a nonrigid-type dirigible "of at least 7500 lbs. useful load capacity." Yet the secretary was not obliged to take the board's advice, while Fiske's ambition to be the first chief of naval operations incurred Daniels's wrath, and Fiske shortly found himself exiled to the Naval War College as its president.[2]

Far more effective in the long run as a friend of naval aviation was the new chief constructor of the Navy, Rear Admiral David W. Taylor, who served two terms as head of the Bureau of Construction and Repair from 1913 to 1922. A distinguished leader in the field of naval architecture, Taylor was also interested in aeronautics and had designed and built a wind tunnel at the Experimental Model Basin at the Washington Navy Yard. In July 1916 Admiral Taylor established an Aircraft Division in the Bureau of Construction and Repair. Its personnel included naval constructors Jerome C. Hunsaker, who played a prominent role in early American airship design; Garland Fulton, later to be head of the Lighter Than Air Section in the Bureau of Aeronautics; and Ralph D. Weyerbacher, later in charge of the construction of the airship *Shenandoah*. It was Admiral Taylor who fostered the wartime development of the Liberty V-12 engine, and who established the Naval Aircraft Factory in Philadelphia to mass-produce flying boats for the naval air stations in Europe in 1917–18. After the war it was Taylor who strongly supported the formation of the Bureau of Aeronautics, turning over to the new bureau the personnel of the Aircraft Division of his Bureau of Construction and Repair.

While the General Board's recommendation for procurement of an airship came to naught for lack of specific congressional approval, Admiral Taylor took some steps looking toward future airship construction: Hunsaker was sent to Europe in 1913 to study recent developments in naval aviation, succeeded in inspecting the outside of the DELAG Zeppelin *Viktoria Luise*, and made a flight in her over Berlin.[3] On his return he observed that "the principal function of the dirigible in naval warfare is to supplement the work of scout cruisers, and its offensive powers would rarely be called upon."[4] After World War I broke out, samples of metal girders from Zeppelins wrecked in France, Denmark, and Norway were made available by naval attachés in those countries and were determined by analysis to be duralumin as described in the 1909 patent application of Alfred Wilm of Düren, Germany, the original inventor. This finding aided the Bureau of Construction and Repair in persuading the Aluminum Company of America to commence production of the light alloy beginning in 1916.

The Naval Appropriation Act for fiscal year 1916, allocating one million dollars for naval aviation, led to a contract being awarded to the Connecticut Aircraft Company for an airship designated DN-1 (Dirigible, Non-Rigid, No. 1). The ship, of 150,000-cubic-foot volume, was scheduled to be completed by 1 October 1915, but it soon became painfully clear that neither the company nor its "experts" were competent to handle the task given them.[5] It was December 1916 before the DN-1 arrived at the air station at Pensacola, where its envelope was found to leak badly, its useful lift was minimal, and it was underpowered. After three flights, in April 1917 it was dismantled. Feeling that the Navy Department had been humiliated by the DN-1 episode, Admiral Taylor personally took charge of subsequent airship procurement. Before the United States entered the war, BuC&R had prepared a design for a small coastal airship of 77,000 cubic feet, of which 16 were built as the B class. Ten of the larger C class of 181,000 cubic feet were also delivered in 1918–19, regaining for Admiral Taylor and his Aircraft Divison the credit they had lost in the DN-1 fiasco.

In 1915, in anticipation of expanding lighter-than-air activity, a training program was set up at Akron, using a 19,000-cubic-foot balloon belonging to Goodyear. The senior officers were Lcdr. Frank R. McCrary and Lt. Lewis H. Maxfield, Naval Aviator No. 17. Maxfield had won his wings on the "bamboo tail" Curtiss pushers in the earliest days at Pensacola. Yet Maxfield, turning his back on heavier than air, went on to be the leading airship advocate in the

Navy, until his death in the ZR 2 disaster. His apostasy symbolizes one of the most damaging conflicts in naval aviation: Lighter than air and heavier than air from the beginning had little in common, drew wider apart, and in time became bitter rivals. Lighter-than-air men were more senior; flying their magnificent dirigibles, they could not help feeling patronizing toward the early aviators, reckless kids wearing ensign's bars. Later, as heavier-than-air flying expanded and its proponents gained in rank and influence, the hostility damaged the airship cause.

Maxfield, McCrary, and ten other officers were ordered to France in September 1917, to train and serve as personnel at two airship stations. They flew pressure airships purchased from the French on patrols over the Bay of Biscay. McCrary later turned against lighter than air when he recommended that airships be abandoned in favor of seaplanes. This change of loyalty made him a marked man when he became the first commanding officer of the *Shenandoah*.

By war's end there were a large number of naval personnel with lighter-than-air experience, so many in fact that the Navy's immediate problem was getting rid of them in the postwar demobilization. Those who stayed on, even though very few had had experience with the big rigids, would man the airships of the postwar program.

The year 1916 brought with it the first steps toward the construction of a rigid airship in the United States. On 24 June the General Board forwarded to Secretary Daniels the results of three months of study of "the possible naval use of aircraft . . . to enable the Department to undertake the orderly and systematic development of aeronautics in the Navy."[6] While noting the Navy's need for rigid airships after the example of the German Zeppelins, the board pointed out that the United States did not possess the engineering talent needed to design and construct such a craft. To gain experience, the General Board recommended that three small nonrigids for coastal patrol be procured at once, while one semirigid and one rigid should be designed and built for experimental work.

The Naval Appropriations Bill for fiscal 1917 specifically included one rigid airship. On 1 October 1916, Admiral Benson, the chief of naval operations, approved specifications for the rigid. It was to have a maximum speed of 60 mph and a ceiling of 4,000 feet fully loaded, and was to carry six machine guns, radio apparatus, and rations for its 20-man crew for four days.

The most important development of the year relating to the rigid airship was the establishment of the so-called Joint Army–Navy Airship Board. The initiative came from the U.S. Army's Lt. Col. George O.

Squier, the acting chief of the Army Signal Corps, which at that time included Army aviation. With the Army appropriation for fiscal 1917 providing funds for rigid airship development, Squier realized that a whole new industry would have to be created. "Will it not," he asked, "make for efficiency and economy of public funds if the Secretary of War and the Secretary of the Navy join in the production of this type of aircraft?"[7]

Secretary Daniels and Secretary of War Newton D. Baker concurred. Officers were promptly appointed to the new board, which was charged with the design and construction of the Zeppelin-type rigid airship under the direction of the chief constructor of the Navy. That the final responsibility for rigid airship design and production should fall on the broad shoulders of Admiral Taylor was a foregone conclusion. The Army possessed no personnel with the necessary background and experience, while the chief constructor and his dedicated assistants in the Aircraft Division were fully conversant with the principles and practice of naval architecture, which provided insights into the design and construction of rigid airships.

The first meeting of the Joint Army–Navy Airship Board was on 26 February 1917. The members' first idea was to acquire design knowledge by contracting for an airship from an experienced foreign builder. The board approached Vickers, only to be promptly rebuffed as the British government refused permission for Vickers to build an airship for the United States.[8] Britain was at war, the United States was still neutral, and the British government's attitude was understandable.

At the next meeting, on 26 March 1917, the board resolved to create its own airship design within the specifications laid down by Admiral Benson six months earlier. It was agreed that a civilian staff would be assembled to do the work, supported by Army funds although it would be located in Admiral Taylor's Bureau of Construction and Repair. A search began for a chief engineer for the Joint Army–Navy Airship Board; the man hired was Starr Truscott, a University of Michigan graduate previously employed on the Panama Canal. From the date of reporting, 1 May 1917, Truscott acted as project engineer on all rigid airship work.

Briefly the board enjoyed the services of a foreign "expert" who influenced it in the direction of Schütte-Lanz designs: none other than Hermann Müller, the Swiss Schütte-Lanz employee who had delivered to the British the plans from which they built R 31 and R 32. Hired by the Airship Board in May 1917, Müller, who in fact was merely a foreman in the girder-building shop, was soon proved incompetent as an engineer; but he was able to build 30-foot

wooden girder sections which were tested at the Bureau of Standards.

At the meeting on 26 July 1917, the board accepted the recommendation of the Bureau of Mines that nonflammable helium be used in airships, with the bureau asking the services to jointly provide $100,000 to build a plant to investigate helium production. The board also decided to construct for their airship a double shed measuring 720 feet long, 200 feet wide, and 100 feet high, clear inner dimensions. The shed was never built, but still later the board's design was turned over to the Navy's Bureau of Yards and Docks and served as the basis for a much larger hangar at the Lakehurst Naval Air Station.

On 12 December 1917, the board met to examine the airship design that Truscott and his staff had produced. The proposed airship was 500 feet long overall and 55 feet in diameter, with a gas volume of 888,715 cubic feet in 17 gas cells. The girder structure was of wood, showing Müller's influence. At the tail were thick cantilever section fins, a refinement not found in the Zeppelins until April 1918. Four 350-h.p. Liberty 12 engines, each driving its own tractor propeller on a bracket on the hull, were estimated to give the ship a speed of 50 to 60 mph. But unlike any rigid craft built heretofore, the engines were enclosed within the hull in engine rooms along the keel! As Truscott noted, "such a ship as this is an impossibility for any nation not possessing a supply of Argon."[9] Truscott's vision and originality are striking: here in the year 1917 was the first airship in the world designed specifically for helium.

The 500-foot wooden airship was not to be built, however. Significant advances had been made in fabricating duralumin sheet, while British drawings of L 33 featured the use of duralumin girders, which were seen as being superior to wood. Truscott himself recommended that the ship be redesigned. But the seven months' effort had not been wasted; the board had developed a degree of technical talent in Truscott's ten-man staff, while the chief engineer had been revealed as a bold and original thinker in the field of airship design.

To obtain up-to-date information on airship progress in the Allied countries, and to report on the use of duralumin in particular, the Airship Board sent four engineers to Europe in February 1918. The leader was Major J. H. Finney of the Army Engineering Reserve Corps, who in civilian life had been active in developing duralumin production for the Aluminum Company of America. The mission first visited England, inspecting the Short Brothers, Armstrong-Whitworth, Beardmore, and Vickers plants. They were told that sixteen airships were on order based on the L 33 design, three of which were under construction for delivery in the fall of 1918. In addition,

Vickers had two on order to their own designs, also for delivery in the fall. In France, they were acquainted with a program under which one rigid airship, the F 2, would be laid down immediately as a copy of L 49, to be followed by eleven more rigids, "practically copies of L 49." As for Italy, "while having designs for a rigid type, the difficulty of obtaining raw materials for hangars and ships have prevented a construction program up to the present."[10]

The American mission was too inexperienced to judge critically the optimistic forecasts of their hosts. In England the first two ships of the L 33 type, R 33 and R 34, did not fly till March 1919, while R 80, building at Vickers, did not make her first flight till July 1920. Nothing whatever came of the French rigid airship program.

Before coming home the mission met in London with Admiral William S. Sims, commander of U.S. Naval Forces in Europe. Sims's intervention, characteristic of his impulsive nature, was unfortunate. On 23 May he cabled the Navy Department to urge an immediate start on a rigid airship program and suggested doing the work in Italy because of a surplus of labor there. As the board well knew, the Italians, while possessing a considerable fleet of semirigid craft, had not built rigid airships or developed an industrial plant to produce them. The board disapproved Sims's proposal and ordered the mission to return home at once.

Finney and his colleagues presented their findings and recommendations at the final meeting of the Joint Army–Navy Airship Board on 19 July 1918. Subsequently, in their report to the secretaries of war and navy, the board advised that:

> The United States acquire in England any rigid airship needed abroad.
> Any rigid airship needed in the United States should be built in this country to establish the art.
> In view of the primarily naval use of the rigid airship, the Navy should undertake design and construction, furnishing full information to the Army. [This recommendation was later elevated by the Navy to a fixed policy, and put forward successfully whenever the Army sought to procure a rigid airship for itself.]
> The Navy should adopt a building program for four airships with necessary construction and station facilities.[11]

Feeling that its role was advisory, the board then voted that it be dissolved. The service secretaries approved, and the board disappeared from the scene on 21 September 1918. Most of the design staff, including the chief engineer, Starr Truscott, were transferred to the Aircraft Division of the Bureau of Construction and Repair. Their participation in the work of the board and the information they had accumulated were vital to their future responsibility for designing and building the first American rigid airship.

It may seem surprising that the Airship Board did not accomplish more, considering that there was a war on. Defeating the German submarine war on shipping took top priority, and the energies of BuC&R's Aircraft Division were largely absorbed in the quantity production of the large flying boats with which the overseas bases were equipped. There was no similarly urgent requirement for rigid airships overseas. The only way the U.S. Navy could have had a rigid airship flying before the Armistice would have been to acquire one of the obsolete craft of the British R 23 or R 27 class. Surely the Americans would have held out for one of the copies of the German "super-Zeppelin" L 33, the first of which was not ready until March 1919. The British would certainly have been cool to American requests to train personnel and to hand over one of their ships in wartime; and any American-crewed rigid, like the smaller blimps, would have been operating from a British base and under British orders.

Even more impossible would have been the construction of a rigid airship in the United States in time for the war. Even had the board committed itself to this goal from the day of the first meeting, and if it had received priority over more urgent programs, this could hardly have been accomplished before 1921. Realization of the Joint Army–Navy Airship Board's recommendations would have to await the coming of peace.

On 11 November 1918, the War to End War was over. Congress's wartime generosity was a thing of the past; at the Navy Department it was back to peacetime routine. Any new procurement request would follow a tedious path: the director of naval aviation would state the requirements for the coming fiscal year; the General Board would hold hearings at which officers connected with naval aviation would state their views; and the General Board would then make its recommendations to the secretary of the navy. He in turn would submit to the appropriate congressional committees his estimates for appropriations for specific programs to be initiated in the upcoming fiscal year. The committees, after further questioning, would then vote.

Two months before the Armistice the General Board had submitted a program for naval aviation in the fiscal year 1920 for a projected cost of $225,000,000! This sum was obviously excessive after the defeat of Germany, and Captain Noble E. Irwin, the director of naval aviation, hastily reduced the estimate to $85,649,300. This was to include 19 naval airship stations in the United States and its Pacific possessions, 114 small and 12 large nonrigid airships, and four rigid airships together with "an experimental field for lighter than air craft."[12]

The next step was to win congressional approval for appropriations for the program, and here naval officers, in 1918 and later, had to cope with the ignorance and suspiciousness of economy-minded congressmen, often from inland states, who knew very little about the Navy, and nothing at all about rigid airships. The Navy's airship advocates were hampered by a lack of information on the actual achievements of the German Navy's Zeppelins. Thus, when Representative Kelly, pointing out that the four rigids would cost $6,000,000, asked "Did the dirigibles figure much in the war?" Captain George W. Steele, the acting director of Naval Aviation, could only reply vaguely, "It is probable that the dirigibles saved the German Fleet at the Battle of Jutland."[13] When Admiral Taylor admitted that the experimental "Zeppelin station" would cost $8,200,000, the chairman of the Senate Naval Affairs Committee insisted it be eliminated.

The $85,000,000 budget for naval aviation was still too much, and Captain Irwin revised it downward to $46,000,000. The secretary lopped off $10,000,000 earmarked for air stations in the Pacific, and the Naval Affairs Committee reported out the naval aviation bill at $25,000,000. On the floor of the House this was further reduced to $15,000,000. Captain Irwin told the Senate Naval Affairs Committee that Secretary Daniels wanted the aviation appropriation restored to $36,000,000, and the committee did as the secretary requested. The rigid airship program was alive, if not thriving.

In the spring of 1919 the General Board held extensive hearings with the aim of establishing a peacetime policy for naval aviation. In these hearings the 35-year-old Commander Lewis H. Maxfield came to prominence as the Navy's leading airship advocate. Back from service overseas, where he had commanded the U.S. Navy's airship station at Paimboeuf near Saint-Nazaire, his experience made him an authority, and his enthusiasm was contagious. Maxfield urged the acquisition of land for an airship station, and on 21 April specifically mentioned Lakehurst, New Jersey for a construction station. At this early date, Maxfield's urging led Assistant Secretary Roosevelt to request that the secretary of war halt the sale of Army buildings at Camp Kendrick, the chemical warfare proving ground on the site of the proposed construction station. Maxfield further advised that negotiations be opened with the British for construction of two duplicates of R 34, a proven type, to fill the requirement for two ships to be built abroad. "It was largely due to his enthusiasm and energy," wrote Hunsaker later, "that the Department (and the

Commander Lewis H. Maxfield USN. Commanding officer of the U.S. Navy Rigid Airship Detachment, Howden, and prospective commanding officer of ZR 2. (National Archives)

General Board) agreed to approve a rigid airship program and the Lakehurst station."[14]

The General Board, on 6 May 1919, recommended to Secretary Daniels that rigid airship construction in the United States be established as an industry, with the government undertaking development and production as the costs would be prohibitive without government assistance. The board urged that immediate steps be taken to establish a rigid airship erection and testing station, and that two rigid airships be procured as early as possible for training and fleet use. The General Board specifically called for procurement in England of one rigid airship of the latest type, which would "give the United States the advantage of possessing one of the most advanced products in rigid airship construction. It would also give us one airship for training purposes."[15]

On 11 July 1919, Congress passed the naval appropriation bill for fiscal year 1920. Though both houses finally voted to reduce the funds for naval aviation to $25,000,000, the bill specifically allocated $3,000,000 for a construction shed for two large rigids; $2,500,000 for the purchase of one rigid airship abroad; and $1,500,000 for construction of a rigid airship in the United States. The first craft ultimately was to be the British R 38, procured in England and designated ZR 2 in American service; the second was designated ZR 1 and would be named the *Shenandoah.*

As if to emphasize the long-range capabilities of the rigid airship, and its potential usefulness in warfare at sea, the British R 34, one of the copies of the German L 33, made the first round-trip crossing of the Atlantic by air, and the first east-to-west crossing, early in July. Departing the air station at East Fortune on 2 July 1919, the airship arrived at Mineola, Long Island on 6 July, crossing in 108 hours 12 minutes. With following winds, R 34 returned to Pulham in 75 hours 3 minutes between 10 and 13 July. On the westbound flight she carried 30 persons including the U.S. Navy's Lcdr. Zachary Lansdowne, while 32 people made the homeward flight.[16]

R 34 failed by six weeks to be the first aircraft to cross the Atlantic, but whereas the crews of the U.S. Navy's three NC flying boats had faced incredible hardships in open cockpits flying via short stages from Far Rockaway on Long Island to Halifax to Newfoundland to the Azores to Lisbon, and two of them had gone down at sea, R 34 had crossed nonstop *both ways*. And the people on board had traveled in reasonable comfort, sleeping off watch in hammocks slung along the keel, able to move freely inside the giant hull, and enjoying three meals a day with tea and soup warmed on hot plates over the engine exhausts. To many on both sides of the Atlantic the R 34 crossing seemed to herald the dawn of transatlantic passenger service; but it was a false dawn, for not until 1936 were passengers regularly carried between Europe and North America by airship. Nonetheless the success of R 34 gave impetus to the U.S. Navy's own program, and made the rigid airship a reality for millions of Americans, not only those who had seen her on Long Island, but also for newspaper readers and newsreel viewers.

3

Naval Air Station Lakehurst and the Cape May Shed

The history of the Naval Air Station Lakehurst[1] is the history of the airship in the U.S. Navy. The last of the type was deflated and stored in 1962, but naval personnel and civilian visitors alike remember them in their days of glory. And although the ships in the sky are gone, the hangars remain as visible mementoes, particularly Hangar I near the main gate. The "big barn" housed them all—the *Shenandoah*, *Los Angeles*, *Akron*, and *Macon*, the *Graf Zeppelin* and the *Hindenburg*, the pressure ships of World War II, and the postwar craft that flew the early-warning missions over the Atlantic.

Once upon a time the Lakehurst site was a part of the New Jersey pine barrens. Then, in 1915, the Eddystone Ammunition Corporation leased the area as a testing range for ammunition being manufactured for the imperial Russian government. With America's entry into World War I, in April 1917 the U.S. Army acquired the proving ground area, named it Camp Kendrick, and developed it as a chemical warfare facility. However, following the Armistice Camp Kendrick was closed down, and the buildings were to be advertised for sale on 15 April 1919. In the nick of time Commander Maxfield and Starr Truscott arrived, on 7 April, to look over the area as a possible airship base. Railroad facilities and water were available, the location was within 1½ hours of Philadelphia, and less from New York. On 16 May 1919, Acting Secretary Franklin D. Roosevelt authorized the purchase of 1,700 acres of the Camp Kendrick site "for use as a dirigible field" for the sum of $13,088.

Why Lakehurst? The General Board, on 24 July 1919, had recommended airship stations to cover possible operational areas off either coast, specifically in the New York area, the Florida region, the

San Diego vicinity, and Puget Sound, as well as overseas. Certainly Lakehurst, with its flat, sandy terrain, was as suitable a site as could be found in the New York area. Accessibility to Philadelphia and the now-idle Naval Aircraft Factory clinched the decision; Maxfield had already foreseen the possibility of fabricating the airship structure and components in Philadelphia and assembling them in the Lakehurst hangar.

Only later did the meteorological disadvantages of the Lakehurst site become apparent. The anonymous author of the U.S. Navy *Rigid Airship Manual* of 1927 wrote of

> The unfavorable location of Lakehurst with regard to storm paths over and near the United States since practically all storms that cross the United States enter the Atlantic Ocean by the St. Lawrence Valley and the storms coming from the eastern part of the Gulf and the South Atlantic region move up the east coast before leaving the continent. The result of this is that practically every storm that passes over this country or along the Atlantic Coast exercises for a greater or less time an influence over the winds at Lakehurst. Thus, having a hangar with an axis 297° true, the percentage of winds parallel to the hangar direction is reduced by frequent cross-hangar winds that add to the difficulties of handling airships on the ground.[2]

The building of the Lakehurst shed was the legal responsibility of the Bureau of Yards and Docks, which drew plans based on the double-shed layout prepared by the Joint Army–Navy Airship Board. The final design was for a structure measuring 943 feet long, 350 feet wide, and 200 feet high overall, with clear inner dimensions of 804 feet long, 264 feet wide, and 193 feet high in the center. In principle the structure was a simple one, composed of ten girderwork arches supported on steel towers rising 63 feet above floor level, tied together with longitudinal girders and covered with corrugated asbestos sheeting. The four large doors, two at each end, rolling sideways on tracks, were 177 feet high, 136 feet wide, and 76 feet thick at the base. They were freestanding and held upright by 830 tons of concrete ballast, which, together with 350 tons of steel and asbestos sheeting, contributed to each door's total weight of 1,350 tons. Each door was opened or closed by four 20-h.p. electric motors which required 13 minutes fully to open it. Three sets of standard-gauge railroad tracks ran right through the hangar and for 1,500 feet beyond the doors—one set on the centerline of the hangar, the other sets on the centerline of the two berthing spaces—for taxying cars[3] on which rode the centerline gondolas of the airships. In addition, there were three docking rails of the same length, to which in German fashion the bow and stern of the airships were made fast by tackles and trolleys to port and starboard. Structures alongside the outer wall of the hangar contained offices, a joiner shop, a wire shop, a fabric shop, an engine repair shop, a machine shop,

and gas cell storage. A nearby hydrogen plant was to produce 75,000 cubic feet of gas daily. One large gas holder had a volume of 1,000,000 cubic feet, with two smaller gas holders of 25,000 and 10,000 cubic feet. A 16-inch main led to the shed, inside of which there were nine gassing outlets on each side.

After Congress had appropriated $3,000,000 for a construction shed able to house two large rigid airships, the Bureau of Yards and Docks solicited bids for the construction of the shed. The successful one, for $2,900,000, was from the Lord Construction Company. The contract having been signed on 8 September 1919, work was begun on the shed itself on 22 September. Bethlehem Steel Co. erected the steel girders, and the first of the ten shed trusses was hoisted into place on 17 May 1920, with one truss to be erected weekly thereafter.

Meanwhile a controversy had developed concerning the length of the shed. Yards and Docks felt it could not be more than 800 fcet with the allotted funds, while Maxfield argued from the beginning for 1,000 feet. Captain Craven, the director of naval aviation, called a conference on 20 December 1919 to discuss the shed length and question of doors. Craven insisted on two sets of doors for operational use; Con-

Lakehurst shed under construction, January 1921. All hangar arches are erected, and framework for the west door is in the foreground. (National Archives)

struction and Repair was willing to go along, but warned that the shed would have to be lengthened in three years; and Maxfield still wanted the shed lengthened immediately. In June 1920 Admiral Taylor, noting that a considerable sum from the 1920 appropriation remained unallocated, recommended that it be used to lengthen the Lakehurst shed to 1,060 feet. The secretary of the navy approved, but there was some argument as to whether the extension should be to the west or the east. As the west doors were already in place, the chief of naval operations decided that, because of the great cost of moving them, the extension would be made to the east, though this would leave only 1,700 feet from the east doors to the airfield boundary. On 5 October 1920, the secretary authorized $850,000 to extend the shed to 1,060 feet, but the contractor demanded $1,500,000— a figure that all felt was excessive. Yards and Docks recommended that the extension be canceled, and the secretary approved cancellation on 13 October.

Meanwhile it was clear that American officers training in England would insist on having a mooring mast at Lakehurst. On 2 February 1921 the British R 33 had been flown from Howden to Pulham for mast trials, and for six months thereafter she was constantly on the mast or flying to or from it. Maxfield and other officers, visiting Pulham, flew in the ship and observed mast landing procedures; they concluded that the mooring mast greatly increased the military usefulness of the rigid airship. Maxfield wrote with his usual enthusiasm:

Frankly the work at Pulham has been the making of airships, they have now become an assured, important factor in the Navy and in the near future their commercial value will be astounding. . . . On Thursday [7 April] at Pulham, a 25 mile wind was blowing. You know as well as I that no one would attempt to take a ship out of the hangar with that blowing. We got aboard R 33, one man knocked loose the pelican hook, and off we went. We came back to the mast with the same wind blowing. On Friday [8 April] R 33 left and returned with a 40 mile wind blowing. . . . Scott has done all this with a bunch of junk. We must have a mast and that right away. Try to use your influence and hurry it. Don't let Yards and Docks spend months designing something perfect. Let's have a mast of some sort and we will show the Navy what can be done with airships. . . . I used to think that airships were an extremely useful adjunct to the fleet, if you could get them out of the sheds and back again. Now I am convinced they are the whole show.[4]

With the coming of spring in 1921 there was a sense of urgency at Lakehurst, as in England the big R 38, which was to become the U.S. Navy's ZR 2, was approaching completion. After trial flights in British charge, she was to be turned over to the American

crew, which had been training in England, and would fly to the United States sometime during the summer. Obviously this could not be done until the Lakehurst shed was complete enough to house her.

On 11 April 1921 Captain Craven took the initiative in having a mooring mast erected for ZR 2. However, not until 5 August 1921 were the last of the drawings for the mast completed by the Bureau of Yards and Docks; so a British-style three-wire mooring was arranged instead. On 18 August 1921 Y&D advised the chief of naval operations that "since the flight of ZR 2 will not take place until 30 August, or later, Bureau reports all items under its cognizance ready for arrival of the ship." Obviously this date indicates the completion of the shed; but the station had already been in commission for two months. The Naval Air Station Lakehurst log states that on 6 June 1921 Lcdr. Joseph P. Norfleet reported and assumed command with five officers and seven enlisted men; but it was 28 June, the date that Captain Franck Taylor Evans assumed command, that was celebrated in 1971 as the fiftieth anniversary of the commissioning of the base.

The Naval Air Station, Cape May, New Jersey, was created specifically as an operational base for ZR 2. Its fate was sealed when, as related in Chapter 5, the big rigid plunged burning into the River Humber, carrying 16 American naval officers and men to their deaths. In a few tragic moments, practically all the experienced American airship officers perished, and the Navy's program was set back by two years.

While ZR 2 was being completed in England, the Bureau of Construction and Repair was developing the design for ZR 1 with the expectation that work would commence on her as soon as the Lakehurst construction shed was built. Clearly it would be impossible to house the big British ship at Lakehurst and work on ZR 1 in the adjacent berth at the same time. While drawings were being finished for Lakehurst in the summer of 1919, plans were being made by the Bureau of Construction and Repair, and the Bureau of Yards and Docks, to house ZR 2 at Cape May.

There was already an airship hangar at Cape May, built in 1917 for nonrigids flying coastal patrols. Of the standard "portable" type, the shed measured 250 feet long, with a clear door width of 100 feet and a height of 64 feet. ZR 2 measured 699 feet long, 85½ feet in diameter, and stood 93½ feet high on her gondola bumpers. The two bureaus, however, had some ingenious ideas for enlarging the Cape May shed at minimal cost to accommodate the big rigid.

Following the Armistice, many of the coastal airship stations were being closed, including the one at Montauk on Long Island. By re-erecting the Mon-

The Lakehurst hangar completed, from the south side. (Mrs. F. J. Tobin)

tauk shed in line with that at Cape May, by mounting the shed arches on towers and adding some more arches, a structure 687½ feet long, 114 feet wide, and 100 feet high at the door could be created. This would house a craft of the R 34 type. But when it became certain that the U.S. Navy would purchase the larger R 38, it was felt necessary to increase the height to 110 feet, while of course the length also had to be increased. On 10 November 1919 Secretary Daniels allotted $557,000 for the reconstruction, which included $32,000 for docking rails. These, it was argued, would make it easy to slide the ship into a hangar that looked like a tight fit.

Just when the Cape May shed was finished cannot be detemined, though the scheduled date was 1 April 1921. The shed then was to be 705 feet long, with door width of 106 feet and height of 109 feet 9½ inches. There would be only one door at the south end. The gas supply was a small silicol plant[5] with two gasometers holding 100,000 cubic feet each. The field extended about 2,000 feet from the single door, and was about 3,000 feet wide.

In retrospect, the idea of operating the big British "height-climber" from Cape May, with its tight-fitting shed, postage-stamp field, and derisory hydrogen supply, would appear thoroughly impractical if not downright dangerous. The director of naval aviation, Captain Craven, may have had these drawbacks in mind when on 18 March 1921, after visiting both stations, he suggested that their roles be reversed—that ZR 2 berth permanently at Lakehurst and oper-

ate from there, and that Cape May be used for construction of ZR 1. Admiral Taylor in his endorsement of 12 April concurred in the operational advantages of Lakehurst, even though he estimated it would cost $300,000 to $400,000 to outfit Cape May for construction.

Weyerbacher, already assigned to Lakehurst to direct the construction of ZR 1, was opposed to the move, having a vested interested in the matter. He acknowledged that the ZR 2 officers would complain about the Cape May shed, but he felt the criticisms would not be justified: "Although the hangar is small, the station is fitted with docking rails, and therefore before the ship enters the shed she is securely clamped to the docking rails, and the width of the shed is not so important." (Weyerbacher was a constructor; Maxfield, the operating expert, surely would have disagreed.) Last—was it intuition?—Weyerbacher wrote that "another thing I wish to call to your attention is that the ZR 2 has not arrived. Something may happen, so why not continue as planned?"[6] Something indeed did happen, on 24 August 1921, and there was no operational airship until ZR 1 was completed in September 1923.

On 1 August 1921, the chief of naval operations placed the Naval Air Station, Cape May, on a nonoperating basis. In 1931 some Lakehurst pressure airships were housed at Cape May pending completion of Hangar 4 at Lakehurst. The Cape May shed never housed a rigid airship, and it was dismantled in the winter of 1941–42.

4

The U.S. Navy Rigid Airship Detachment, Howden

Having obtained congressional authorization on 11 July 1919 for purchase of one rigid airship abroad, the U.S. Navy moved without delay to acquire it. There were only two possible sources—Great Britain and Germany.

The latter country, which had perfected the Zeppelin for the Imperial German Navy, was the acknowledged leader in airship design. Indeed, Captain Craven, the director of naval aviation, on 15 August 1919 wrote to Lcdr. Dewitt C. Ramsey,[1] in the London naval attaché's office, "another thing we desire is the obtaining of one of the latest type of German ships. . . . send officers and men to the station where this rigid may be housed in Germany; get instruction for these officers and men so that they could fly to the United States."[2] Such hopes depended on the U.S. Senate's ratifying the Versailles Treaty, but this did not come to pass;[3] and Admiral Benson's opposition to obtaining a German ship, and the destruction of seven Zeppelins by German naval personnel in the North Sea bases on 23 June 1919, further diminished the chances of U.S. acquisition of an ex-German ship.

So England it had to be; and in fact British airshipmen and airship designs were held in considerable respect by U.S. naval personnel who had served in England and flown in English craft. On 26 July 1919 a telegram from the Aviation Division in the office of the chief of naval operations to Admiral Knapp, the naval attaché in London, directed him to "make preliminary investigation with Air Ministry and Admiralty as to possibility of having constructed one of latest type rigid dirigible. Consideration must be given to the fact that this dirigible cannot be received in this country for 1 year."[4] Knapp officially handled the negotiations with British government depart-

ments, but the work was actually done by Ramsey, his assistant attaché for aviation, and Captain L. B. McBride of the Construction Corps, a member of his staff.

The British in turn were negotiating from weakness. The Lloyd George government's policy was one of deflation and economic retrenchment. Funds for the three services were drastically reduced; temporary and reserve officers and men returned in droves to civilian life; and dreadnoughts and battle cruisers that had fought at Jutland were sold for scrap. The future of the airship, an expensive peripheral weapon, looked doubtful.

Already the airship was an unwanted orphan in the postwar table of organization. Born into the Royal Navy, it had continued under the Admiralty even after the Royal Naval Air Service and the Royal Flying Corps had been amalgamated into the Royal Air Force on 1 April 1918. The Admiralty continued with design and construction; the Royal Air Force handled personnel; officers and men held naval ranks and ratings, and were housed and employed by the Admiralty, but were recruited, trained, disciplined, clothed, and fed by the Air Ministry. With the coming of the Armistice the Admiralty saw an opportunity not only to save money, but also to smother the infant Royal Air Force by dumping the expensive rigid airship program on the unwanted rival service. On 22 October 1919, the Air Ministry was made entirely responsible for airships. To carry the story further into the period when the Americans were in England training to take over R 38, the British Cabinet on 29 July 1920 agreed that the Air Ministry should either sell or give away the airships for commercial use, failing which they should be scrapped. In fact, the wartime British airships found no takers for commercial purposes, not only because of the deepening economic recession, but also because they were unsuited for passenger carrying.

The Air Ministry wanted nothing more to do with airships because of the expense,[5] and steps were taken, beginning in January 1921, to disband the service airship branch. In effect, certain segments of the British wartime airship operation were retained solely to provide needed training for the Americans.[6] On 31 May 1921 the government felt obliged in view of the serious state of the economy to order the closing down of the entire airship service by 1 August 1921.

The useless ships of the No. 23 class made very few flights after the Armistice, and were all scrapped in 1919. So was R 31, whose wooden framework had rotted beyond repair after storage in a shed with a leaky roof at Howden. While negotiations for the purchase of R 38 were being completed, Admiral Knapp wrote to the chief of naval operations on 24 October 1919, concerning the status of the remaining British rigids and the bases from which they operated:

> Under Treasury restrictions on expenditure, R 29 and R 32 will be broken up, R 34 will be retained for air service, R 33 will probably be turned over to commercial company which will also take R 80 and probably undertake to complete two of R 36, R 37 and R 39, the third being completed by Government. East Fortune will be abandoned. Howden will be kept in commission as a government station but may temporarily provide accommodation for two of commercial ships in addition. Disposition of Pulham not finally determined but would probably be closed if result of pending negotiations for commercial development are unsuccessful.[7]

In fact, R 36 was completed as a civil ship, R 37 was canceled in February 1921 after the hull framework was completed, and R 39 was likewise canceled in August 1919 after very little work had been done on her. As for R 32, she survived until the spring of 1921, as we shall see, and played an indispensable role in training the Americans.

Although the responsible political figures on the British side of the negotiations were Winston Churchill, the secretary of state for war and air, and his undersecretary, General J. E. B. Seely, Ramsey saw fit to deal in the preliminary stages with the Air Ministry's director of airships, General Edward Maitland Maitland. Fresh from the triumph of R 34's first round-trip crossing of the Atlantic by air (he had taken part as an observer "with special duties"), Maitland in fact was both the most influential and the most enthusiastic airship supporter in the Air Ministry. Only 39 years old at this time, he had taken up

balloning in 1907, had made his first parachute descent in 1908, had taught himself to fly on a Howard Wright biplane that he purchased in 1910, and had been assigned to the British Army's airship branch in 1911. Transferring to the Naval Airship Service early in 1914, he commissioned the rigid airship station at Pulham in the fall of 1916, and in November 1917 he became superintendent of airships at the Admiralty. The R 34 transatlantic flight represented a determined effort by Maitland, in the face of declining prospects for the airship, to demonstrate its superior capabilities in long-range commercial operations. A beloved leader possessing great personal charm, and a dedicated believer in the future of the rigid airship, Maitland was to be closely involved with the American airshipmen training in Britain, and to be loved and admired by them even as he was by his own countrymen.

Ramsey and McBride interviewed Maitland on 6 August 1919 concerning the American Navy's desire to purchase a modern British airship. "I am glad to say," wrote Ramsey to Craven, "that I know we have a very warm friend in General Maitland and he is in keen sympathy with our dirigible program. He will exert every effort to cooperate with us in this connection in every way."[8] Maitland's interest undoubtedly arose from the hope and expectation that the American desire to procure an airship might rescue the British program, or at least prolong its life. Maitland suggested that the Admiralty place an order on behalf of the Americans with a British firm, supervising the construction and the trial flights before the Americans took delivery.

As negotiations progressed during August and September 1919, it appeared that there were two possibilities: either to obtain one of the four Admiralty "A" type ships, of which R 38 was one, or to go a step further and procure something even bigger and better for two and a half million dollars—a 5,000,000-cubic-foot rigid with a gross lift of 152 tons and a useful lift of 50 tons.[9] As Admiral Knapp reported to the Operations Office on 20 August 1919, the British had no shed large enough to build one of these monsters, and enlarging an existing shed would mean an added charge to the Americans if they chose such a craft. Knapp advised "in view of probable cancellation of British contracts it would appear to be a favorable time for placing an American contract if the Department desires further steps to be taken. Request definite instructions."[10]

Secretary Daniels wired back on 30 August:

> Delivery of airship in U.S. is desired for Spring 1921. Obtain two definite proposals: First contemplates delivery of one ship of 2,700,000 cu.ft. Type A to shed in England in summer of 1920 and keeping ship there while American officers and men get training so

they can fly across Atlantic in Spring 1921. Second proposal is for design and construction of one five million cubic foot ship for delivery in U.S. in Spring 1921 by British crew or American crew trained in Britain. Desire training arrangements made independent of construction contract.[11]

The American representatives soon realized that the 5,000,000-cubic-foot ship was unlikely to be attained in any reasonable period of time, and that American funds would be tied up in a British experimental project that would not meet the U.S. Navy's need for a usable ship in the near future. Even General Maitland lacked enthusiasm for the projected big ship:

> He thought the proposition of placing a contract for a 5,000,000 cubic foot ship was a bad one, and he strongly advocated waiting, before considering this matter at all, for the trials of the new Admiralty "A" type, which is a ship of approximately 2,700,000 capacity. I [Ramsey] personally feel that one of our best propositions would be to purchase one of these "A" type ships and send over sufficient operating personnel to man it and at the same time negotiate for the services of experienced lighter than air operators in England to assist us until such time as our own personnel are qualified to take the job on their own.[12]

Knapp wired officially to Craven a few days later in relation to Secretary Daniels's proposal of 30 August:

> Due to fact Cabinet sanction is required for British proposals and pressure of urgent public business have prevented consideration, answer continues to be slow. However, . . . Air Council is ready to take action in accordance with first proposition and will offer to sell R 38, now under construction at Shorts, for £400,000. . . . Air Council opposed to second proposition for following reasons: first, inadvisable from technical point of view to construct larger ships until data obtained from R 38; second, no sheds of sufficient size available and no funds available for enlarging. Cost of enlarging existing shed estimated at £100,000 would have to be borne by U.S. Third, due to 2,700,000 cu.ft. and possible commercial interests taking over one or more of these contracts, considerable confusion in the industry would be caused by proceeding with a larger ship.[13]

On 17 October the secretary of the navy advised Knapp that the Navy Department desired to purchase R 38 for delivery in England in the summer of 1920:

> You are authorized to negotiate agreement with Air Ministry for purchase of R 38 complete with power plants and all equipment together with such spare parts as may be agreed upon between you and the Air Ministry with further understanding that purchase includes complete plans and specifications

and the right of U.S. Naval representatives to observe construction for a price not to exceed $2,000,000.[14]

The Air Ministry and the British Cabinet were agreeable to the sale of R 38 to the United States for this sum, and on 23 October Admiral Knapp drew up the agreement for the purchase of this ship. The document defined the ship, the conditions, time and place of delivery, and supervision of construction by U.S. officers, who were to participate in trial flights. Training of U.S. naval personnel was to be covered in a separate agreement. Liability in case of loss of the airship prior to delivery or during trials was discussed in one paragraph: this was to fall on the Air Ministry and the U.S. Navy in "such proportions as may be agreed upon in a conference to be held at an early date." (On 1 December it was agreed that the loss would be equally borne by both countries.) On 5 December Secretary Daniels approved the agreement with the Air Ministry on the sharing of possible loss and the inclusive price of $2,000,000.

The British airship R 38 thus became the property of the U.S. Navy. At this point everybody was happy: the British Cabinet at having sold an unwanted craft for £400,000, the Air Ministry at having got rid of an airship that would have been a financial liability, General Maitland at having assured that the finest and biggest airship in the world would be completed to the credit of Great Britain, and the Americans at starting their Navy's rigid airship program with what they thought was the latest and best example of the type. Nearly two years were to pass before they realized that as they trustingly accepted the role of pupil to the British teacher, their confidence had been betrayed at the cost of many irreplaceable lives.

The United States had long been interested in obtaining rigid airship training for its personnel in England, and during the war years a few of its officers, including Lcdr. Zachary Lansdowne,[15] had received such instruction. The purchase of R 38 implied that training for her personnel would likewise be made available, but the negotiations were separate from those for the airship, though carried on in parallel by the same officials.

The first training opportunity came in December 1918, when Admiral Sims forwarded to Admiral Benson, the chief of naval operations, an offer from the British to train six officers in rigid airships. Benson was unresponsive, commenting "I am opposed to rigid airship. Non rigids have proven of small value."[16] During the spring, and under pressure from the General Board's hearings on the Navy's need for rigid airships, Benson changed his attitude. On 19 April 1919 Captain Craven recommended to him that "a party of ten officers and fifty petty officers having non rigid training be sent as soon as possible to England for training."[17] In a letter of 15 August 1919, Craven advised Ramsey of the department's desire to have

> Technicists, pilots, and at least 50 enlisted men in England studying and flying rigids, so that within six months we would have a crew for one rigid. At present the British say they cannot take any of our officers. General Maitland, however, we believe to be a friend of ours and when opportunity permits will give us the opportunity to send these pilots over.[18]

One thing was clear, however, that only limited funds would be available: Congress had appropriated $2,500,000 for procuring a rigid airship overseas, the contract price for R 38 was approximately $2,000,000, and hence the training program would have to come within the $500,000 limit remaining. This negated dreams of British airshipmen of keeping their faltering program afloat with American funds.

As the R 38 purchase agreement became firm in October, Knapp wired to Craven:

> Air Council willing to make arrangements for training but cannot make definite proposal. Informal information says that they may be willing to place R 32 at our disposal and lease to U.S. Pulham and supply with sufficient experienced officers and men for definite lump sum to cover all expenses for this purpose other than maintenance and upkeep. . . . Air Ministry now have complete control of Rigid airships, and there is every indication that Air Council is not only willing but anxious to cooperate. Present position is extremely difficult due to necessity for strict national economy and future policy will be based largely on arrangements with U.S. on R 38.[19]

This is the first mention of possible use by the U.S. Navy of R 32, which in the end played a major role in training the Howden Detachment. Ramsey wrote to Craven:

> Col. Cunningham, General Maitland's first mate, told me yesterday that he thinks that the Air Council would be perfectly agreeable to turning over to us the R 32, which, while a wooden ship, is perfectly suitable for training purposes and was on the point of being destroyed when we opened up our negotiations. As a consequence, I think we could obtain the use of this craft free of charge and only pay for the incidental running expenses.[20]

The use of the wooden ship promised much more flight time for U.S. naval personnel in the face of severe cutbacks in the British program. As Knapp reflected officially a few days later:

> One full crew of U.S. officers and men with necessary alternates could be trained at Howden in conjunction with operations of R 34 but as this will be the only government ship during current year it will be handled with utmost care in operations with navy with result that amount of training that could be given to United States personnel would be limited. Alternative proposal put forward by Air Ministry . . . contemplates maintaining station at Pulham and keeping R 32 in commission for use solely as training ship for U.S. personnel. In this case we should assume the cost of operations of R 32, viz., hydrogen gas as necessary, fuel and oil and current repairs but U.S. would have no liability in case of loss. Furthermore . . . it would be desirable for U.S. to supply half the necessary personnel of the station, the total complement of which is seven hundred men. It is realized that three hundred fifty men is a larger number than the Department contemplated . . . but it appears highly desirable to meet generous spirit of Air Ministry by offering every possible assistance in a difficult situation.[21]

Knapp and Ramsey did not expect approval for such a large number of men, but wanted to sweeten the deal for the Air Ministry by making up their shortage of ground personnel.[22] Secretary Daniels replied immediately:

> Impossible to send unit for purpose suggested. Unit to be sent will be about fifty four and will not be sent for some months. Presently are sending observers for construction and operations, about six men. Essential our men assigned to an operating station manned by British at their expense rather than a station operated only for our accommodation.[23]

Daniels now took a direct hand in the negotiations. On 25 October he wrote to Vice Admiral J. S. McKean of the Office of Naval Operations, "with respect to Admiral Knapp's message about our personnel, and with reference to our buying the 'R' aircraft from Great Britain . . . please do not permit any action to be taken until I see you this afternoon." Underneath in the secretary's own handwriting was "I do not like some of the conditions which make this craft actually ask more than its figures and as at present advised I am unwilling to commit this Government to this expense. J.D."[24]

Meanwhile, Knapp had wired home requesting approval of the plan suggested in his 24 October message, that American personnel should train in R 32 and the Navy Department should assume operating expenses. The unexpected reply, undoubtedly dictated by Daniels himself, was that "the Department will not assume operating expenses of R 32 in training personnel,"[25] though it would be agreeable to paying for instruction of personnel. Apparently the secretary had taken literally an earlier Air Ministry proposal to "train a reasonable number of Officers and Men without cost to the U.S." until completion of R 38.

For Knapp, Ramsey, and McBride, this was a shock. Ramsey, in an unofficial letter to Captain Craven, wrote with unaccustomed feeling:

I have lately received a wire regarding your decision in the matter of the operating expenses of the R 32, and to be perfectly frank, Sir, we are all just a little bit up in the air. Captain McBride and myself have been on the heels of the Air Ministry about this ship and the training of the personnel, and we had hoped that the propositions which we outlined to you were the best that could be negotiated for at the moment. We have seen General Seely in person several times and he, as you know, is most desirous to grant every concession, and to cooperate with us in every way and it does not look as if our Department is meeting the British halfway.

The matter of the request for 450 or 500 men, I can readily appreciate, was a proposition that we expected to have turned down, but the proposition of utilizing the R 32 . . . was one which we anticipated would meet with your complete approval. I know that it is the Department's desire to have a flat price agreement drawn up for the expense incurred in the training, rather than to assume operating expenses which are more or less indeterminate at the present time, but it appears to me that the proposition as outlined would be more economical in the long run than the one we have been requested to investigate.

I sincerely hope that we may be able to come to an agreement which will be entirely satisfactory to the department, and to this end Captain McBride and I have an appointment with General Maitland this afternoon to go over again the situation in detail. We will draw up a wire immediately after this and let you know the findings, but I am frank in saying that the Air Ministry authorities, with whom we have been dealing, are, I feel, a little bit put out.[26]

Negotiations were at a standstill. Admiral Knapp, on 14 November, hopefully reminded Craven that

The Air Ministry offer in connection with R 32 amounts to practically a gift of the ship to U.S. and housing and handling it free of charge only asking us to pay actual costs of operation for which they have no funds available. They now repeat this offer and estimate as a maximum £5000 per month[27] which is based on ten flights of about five hours each. . . . I strongly recommend that Department accept offer of R 32 and assume exact cost of operations as being the best and only method by which adequate training can be obtained. Actual cost of operations should be considerably less than £5000 per month as in preparing this estimate ample allowance was made on each item.[28]

Meanwhile, Craven tried unofficially to explain to Ramsey the background of Daniels's mulish obstructiveness:

I can understand you being somewhat perturbed because of the situation, but you must have full understanding of the attitude of Mr. D. regarding this proposition. At the present time the policy here, as perhaps everywhere else in the world, is to save as much money as practicable. We want the R 38, but Mr. Daniels does not seem to be prepared to authorize any very great sum to be expended *in England*, for the training and operation of personnel in connection with rigids.[29]

Captain McBride's return to the United States early in December, and his representations as to the facts in England, served to bring the negotiations at the Washington end to a satisfactory conclusion. On 23 December the Secretary wired to Knapp:

Inform Air Ministry that I appreciate their offer of free training for our personnel . . . but in order to insure the safety of R 38 after delivery it appears necessary to obtain more extensive training than can be given on R 34 alone. It is desired therefore to accept their offer of exclusive use of R 32. In order to avoid further misunderstandings and any risk of over-obligation of funds, the following points should be covered in your agreement with the Ministry. First, U.S. cannot accept liability for value of R 32 in case of loss or extensive damage. Second, either government can terminate the arrangement at any time and all responsibility of U.S. for expenditures on account of R 32 will end at such termination. Third, U.S. will assume out of pocket expense in connection with use of R 32 for training purposes. Fourth, it is understood that this expense will not involve any charge for housing or handling and will cover only cost of hydrogen, fuel, necessary supplies and current repairs. . . . Fifth, accounts of expenditure should be made up each month and in time to be cabled to the Department for the fifteenth of the following month. . . . Sixth, the balance of $500,000 from appropriations for an airship abroad must cover both the cost of training on R 32 and all costs and handling on R 38 from the time of delivery until time of departure for U.S. . . . Seventh, it is understood that in case of termination of agreement in regard to R 32 by either government that the Ministry will continue to give such training as practicable to our personnel on R 34 or other airship which they may have in commission free of cost to U.S. Eighth, agreement will begin on March 1, which is the earliest date by which personnel can arrive in England.[30]

Knapp passed this on to the Air Ministry on 5 January 1920. Their reply of 20 February requested some amendments: "I am, however, to point out that it was not intended that the offer of free training should be as widely interpreted as it has in your letter." As for use of R 34, "it must be clearly understood that inasmuch as this airship will be the only one available for service purposes, she will at all times have to be in charge of a British crew, and that only such additional American personnel will be carried for training purposes as can be conveniently embarked on any given flight."[31] Last, the Air Council requested postponement of the date of the agreement to 1 April 1920 because of the problems of obtaining coke for the generation of hydrogen gas at Howden[32] (a coal miners' strike was in progress).

On 24 March the Air Ministry notified Admiral Knapp that "the Air Council are prepared to agree to a payment of £5000 per month to cover cost of hydrogen, fuel, necessary supplies, and current repairs instead of submitting monthly accounts as suggested."[33] Knapp replied a week later that £5000 per month was "the maximum that the Navy Department has permitted me to agree to." Because of the very limited funds available to the department for training purposes, "I should therefore greatly appreciate it if the Air Council could reconsider the matter and if possible, so modify their plan so as to cover the actual cost of hydrogen, fuel, necessary supplies and current repairs by monthly statements."[34] The Air Ministry agreed, adding that "The Council are glad to be in a position to arrive in this way at a satisfactory agreement with regard to this only matter hitherto remaining for decision."[35]

While the training agreement was later modified in detail from time to time, the Americans had obtained "their" airship on their own terms, thanks in part to the weakness of the British negotiating position. In fact, R 32, on 20 March 1920, was flown by a British crew from Pulham to Howden and there hung up in the shed and partially deflated, to await the arrival of the Americans. With a ship of its own, to be used solely in connection with its own requirements, the U.S. Navy could realize a coherent, continuous, and intensive training program while taking advantage of British direction and advice. Had the Americans been limited to occasional hops with a British crew in R 34, the only rigid remaining in the British military program, little of value would have been obtained.

As for personnel to go to England, Captain Craven had already decided in October to send about six officers and observers for construction and operation. On 26 November 1919 Maxfield, still in Washington, had drafted a memorandum for Craven concerning the officers to be sent ahead of the rest of the training detachment. Maxfield listed ten officers in the regular Navy who were designated "Naval Aviator, Dirigible," including himself (several more were overlooked). If six officers were sent to England, only four would be left in the United States. Many of the reserve officers were well qualified—Maxfield listed eight "whom I consider excellent material." Maxfield also wanted 38 enlisted men in various ratings—coxswains, riggers, radio men, and mechanics: "these calculations are based on the crew of R 34 with such additions as I think necessary."[36] Maxfield's suggestions about reserve officers were accepted, and several of them volunteered for overseas duty, certifying that they would remain in the service for three years.

On 22 January 1920 the Bureau of Navigation notified the commanding officers of all air stations of the need to send a crew to England to train in connection with R 38. A total of 38 men were to be sent in two parties, the first to depart about 1 March. The total was to include 18 mechanics ("should be excellent gas engine mechanics, preferably with previous LTA experience"), 12 riggers ("should be familiar with fabric, cordage, wire and cable splicing, valves and the use of hydrogen"), 6 coxswains ("should be qualified to perform duty of Quartermasters, D [dirigible]"), and 2 radio men. The men of course would be volunteers. "It is especially desired that commanding officers include only the very highest type in recommendations."[37]

Overseas duty, and the prospect of flying the Atlantic in the largest airship in the world, undoubtedly would have attracted the very best men in the naval air service; but considerable difficulty was encountered in assembling the necessary number. Although there had been many enlisted men with the necessary qualifications the year before, a large proportion had left the service for civilian life by January 1920. Those remaining were performing important duties at the airship stations at Chatham, Rockaway Beach, Cape May, Hampton Roads, Key West, Pensacola, and San Diego. The severe shortage of qualified LTA personnel was the reason that only 18 enlisted men left in the first draft, and it was two months before a second draft of 21 men could be gathered and shipped overseas.

Meanwhile the advance party of officers was proceeding to England. First was Maxfield, the commanding officer of the training detachment and prospective commanding officer of R 38, who left on board the Army transport Antigone on 20 February. Accompanying him was Lt. Ralph G. Pennoyer, who was Maxfield's choice for executive officer of the training unit and of the airship. Arriving in London, they participated with Admiral Knapp's subordinates in final negotiations with the Air Ministry.

Four airship pilots, Lts. Telford B. Null, Arthur R. Houghton, Charles G. Little, and John B. Lawrence, all reserve officers, left New York on 20 March on board the Army transport Mercury. They were followed by the 18 enlisted men of the first draft, who sailed on 5 April on board the transport Princess Matioka. The officer in charge of the draft was Lcdr. Valentine N. Bieg, designated as senior engineering officer of R 38, while the training unit's supply officer and medical officer accompanied the draft.[38] Landing at Southampton, England, they proceeded via London to Howden, arriving there on 20 April.

On 15 April, Maxfield had advised the Navy Department that "remainder of crew for R 38 should be sent as soon as possible. Air Ministry can handle remainder of crew at any time and the sooner these men are sent the more instruction they will be able to receive."[39] The date of this dispatch may be taken to indicate when Maxfield and Pennoyer moved from London to Howden.

To continue: The Bureau of Navigation on 27 April solicited the commanding officers of all naval air stations for men for the second draft. This was to consist of nine mechanics, six riggers, three coxswains, and two radio electricians. "No men should be recommended who are not excellent men, well above the average, and who are entitled to consideration in making up the detail for this attractive duty."[40] Notwithstanding which, certain commanding officers must have yielded to the common temptation to get rid of misfits, for 15 months later Maxfield recommended that two of the men of the second draft "be transferred to general service as their usefulness to aviation in General and ZR 2 in particular is negligible."[41] The 21 men selected (a chief yeoman was added at Maxfield's insistence) were to assemble at the Receiving Ship, New York, not later than 15 June.

More officers were to go to Howden with the second draft. At the weekly aviation conference held on 26 April 1920, the various bureaus of the Navy Department were directed to nominate representatives to accompany the second draft. Because radios were under the cognizance of the Bureau of Steam Engineering, the bureau chief, Rear Admiral Robert Griffin, was obliged to choose a radio officer for R 38. The only available officer qualified in LTA radio was Lt. Marcus H. Esterly USNRF, then stationed at Hampton Roads Naval Air Station. He received orders for England but did not actually arrive there until mid-July. Nonetheless he was considered to be part of the second draft, along with Lcdr. Emory W. Coil, who had been waiting in London to go into Germany to select one of the surviving Zeppelins for the U.S. Navy, but who, with the U.S. failure to ratify the Versailles Treaty, now proceeded to Howden for duty as engineering officer of R 38.

Other officers sailed with the enlisted men of the second draft on board the Army transport *Antigone* on 21 June. Three were dirigible pilots—Lt. Henry W. Hoyt, who was officer in charge of the draft, Ensign (T) J. W. Hykes, and Ensign (T) W. J. Medusky.[42] Chief Machinist (chief warrant officer) Shine S. Halliburton came as assistant engineering officer. The second draft reported to Howden early in July. In addition,

one officer, Lt. Joseph B. Anderson USNRF, reported in March 1921 as meteorological officer, and ten more enlisted men including four machinists' mates, three yeomen, two radio men, and one chief pharmacist's mate, joined at various times.[43]

The officers and men of the first draft were met at Howden by Maxfield and Pennoyer, and on the afternoon of 20 April the U.S. Navy Rigid Airship Detachment, Howden was formed. The base at which they found themselves was one of three erected by the Royal Navy during the war, the others being East Fortune on the Firth of Forth in Scotland, and Pulham in Norfolk. Howden, in Yorkshire about 20 miles west of Hull, had been opened in March 1916, and initially housed pressure airships used for coastal patrol and convoy escort. In December 1916 a large shed was completed for rigid airships, and in April 1917 the first British rigid airship to fly, No. 9, came to occupy it. Clear inner dimensions were 700 feet long, 150 feet wide, and 100 feet high. The shed was badly damaged when R 27 burned on 16 August 1918, but was later repaired, and, at the time the Americans arrived at Howden, it was occupied by R 32. In addition, a large double shed for rigids had been completed at the end of 1918, each bay of which was 750 feet long, 150 feet wide, and 130 feet high, the two bays being separated by steel girders supporting the roof. R 33, destined for civil employment, and R 34, intended to be the only military ship flying in 1920, occupied the two bays of the double shed. They were hung up and deflated, but their crews were still on the station and acted as instructors to the Americans. The commanding officer at Howden was the Americans' old friend General Maitland. No senior British airship officer more congenial to the Americans could have been found—confident, informal but sure of himself when dealing with subordinates, infecting everyone with his enthusiasm for the airship cause, Maitland won the devotion and affection of the "Yanks" just as he had won that of his own countrymen.[44]

The men of the Howden Detachment were split into engineering and rigger groups, and followed separate courses of instruction. The engineering group, led by Lcdr. Bieg, started by dismantling one of R 33's Sunbeam Maori engines under the supervision of Flight Officer William Edward James, R 33's engineering officer. Bieg, whose enthusiastic letters home to Sydney Kraus in the Bureau of Steam Engineering reflect his zeal for training his men thoroughly and for obtaining every scrap of information, formed a close friendship with both James and R 33's commanding officer, Flight Lieutenant Godfrey Maine Thomas.[45] In addition, there were field trips, Bieg's engineers visiting the Sunbeam works at Woverhampton, particularly at the time when R 38's

350-h.p. Cossacks were being initially tested, while the Royal Airship Works at Bedford, where R 38 was building, was also on their schedule.

Thanks to his friendship with the British, Bieg began flight training ahead of his men, accompanying the crew of a British SS Twin[46] pressure airship stationed at Howden. By 13 May, Bieg had made his first flight as engineer in charge of the blimp, with a decidedly mixed crew: Corcoran, an Englishman, as commanding officer; Onishi, a Japanese, as pilot;[47] Bieg, as engineer; and Houghton, another American, as coxswain!

The rigger group began their training under Flight Lieutenant Archibald H. Wann, the captain of R 32, as chief instructor. The training comprised theoretical lectures and actual instruction in the hangar on R 32. Some practical work was also done on R 33 and R 34, under direction of their officers. The subjects covered were: fabrics, wiring, automatic and hand-operated gas valves, tackles, repair and removal of gas bags, details of airship construction, and hull rigging. The rigger group likewise were taken on tour, to Bedford for two weeks' instruction in small groups on fabric work, goldbeater's skin laying, and duralumin work. They also spent four days at the airship station at Pulham in Norfolk, where the center of attention was the German Zeppelins L 64 and L 71, which had been surrendered there on 21 July and 1 July 1920, respectively. Here at last was an opportunity to study the ultimate in high-altitude operational design by the acknowledged experts of the Zeppelin Company, L 71 being the last airship commissioned by the German Navy before the Armistice.

A notebook, kept by one of the riggers, Harry H. O'Claire, CBM, testifies to the thoroughness of the instruction and the zeal and enthusiasm of O'Claire himself. There are many pages concerning R 32, the weights of equipment, design details, dimensions, mooring system, procedure for removing engine gondolas, gas cells, installation of same, inflation with hydrogen, maintenance procedures, and inspections. "Standing orders for R 33" were copied into the notebook ("There is to be no traffic in the keel other than for a specific reason. There is to be no running in keel except under special circumstances, or running on top of the ship. . . . No waving of hands or other friendly demonstrations is to take place" in flight.) Drawings and notes on L 64 and L 71 occupy 13 pages, well meriting the "excellent" endorsement by Lt. Pennoyer on 8 August 1920. The latter part of the book lists equipment and gear for R 38, four types of "three-wire moorings" for airships as evolved by Major Scott, notes on R 33 and R 34, and even gas bag information on R 37, half finished in the same shed as R 38 in Bedford, but destined never to fly. Today, airship rigging and maintenance is an even more forgotten and obscure art than that of the rigger on board the clipper ships; but much of it was captured for posterity in O'Claire's notebook.

To see the big rigids close at hand, and to be intimately acquainted with their innermost secrets under the tutelage of experienced British personnel, was thrilling enough, but all the Americans looked forward even more hungrily to actual flight experience. The gas cells of R 32, however, which had been in the ship for over a year, showed low purity of the hydrogen, and it was obvious that considerable work would have to be done on her before she would be airworthy. In addition, the shortage of coke for gas production prevented any flying by either R 33 or R 34, and it appears that the SS Twin was the only active training ship during the spring of 1920.[48]

In May further supplies of coke were made available, sufficient to inflate R 33 though not enough for R 32 or R 34. Though destined to be a civil ship, R 33 was used for flights in cooperation with the British Home Fleet, and specifically, on occasion, to train U.S. naval personnel by pairing them with the British crew of R 33 on a watch-and-watch basis. No accurate record of these flights survives,[49] though a dubious and incomplete summary exists of journeys with U.S. naval personnel on board, and Lcdr. Bieg's letters are informative.

Thus Bieg, in anticipation of the big ships' being inflated, wrote on 13 May: "I am getting all the men I can permanent stations on the R 33 and R 34. The C.O.s of these ships are very glad to get our men as they are shorthanded and our people are taking a pretty keen interest."[50] Maxfield, in his weekly news letter of 10 June, wrote that "it was intended to take the U.S. Navy personnel for a 24 hours flight in R 33 for instructional purposes, and R 33 was accordingly gassed, fueled, and prepared for flight, this work being done by the U.S. naval officers and men under the supervision of R 33's regular crew."[51] Owing to bad weather, he added, the flight had not been made; but the record makes it appear that on 8 June R 33 made a flight of 70 hours 30 minutes, covering 2,273 miles, with U.S. naval personnel under training.

R 33 was then slated to cooperate with the fleet— "for ordnance and photographic work. They are I believe to photograph salvoes and have thirty-six dozen plates aboard." Bieg added that "we are not allowed to go with them."[52] There followed three flights in R 33 for training of U.S. naval personnel on 27, 29, and 30 July, the first of which is confirmed by Bieg, for a total of 33 hours 5 minutes, and a distance of 1,188 miles. For training in operation and upkeep of R 38, this experience in R 33, with metal hull frame and Sunbeam airship engines, was invaluable.

Still, the Americans longed to be aloft in sole charge of "their" ship, even though it was the obso-

The wooden-girder R 32 flying at Howden in American charge. She was built from plans of the Schütte-Lanz "d"-type airship brought to England in 1916 by Hermann Müller, a former employee of the German firm. (J. H. Collier)

lete R 32 with wooden framework and Rolls Royce airplane engines. With the hull supported in the hangar from overhead tackles and with props under the main frames and cradles under the cars, ten of R 32's twenty-one gas cells were removed from the ship and spread on ground cloths on the hangar floor for inspection and repair. Bags in bad condition were returned to the factory, while lesser defects were repaired by the Americans, with the British riggers teaching them:

> The most common defect found is cracked skin or loose skin and bubbles [the gas bags were made of light cotton fabric with gold beaters' skin cemented to the inside with rubber solution, and then varnished]. To do repairs the right way, you would repair each defect as follows: for cracked skin, loose skin, cut skin or torn or bubbles: you remove skin a little. Be sure all old skin has been removed. . . . After this has been done you put a coat of varnish at the edge all around where the skin has been removed. . . . Then you put three coats of solution where old skin was removed, each coat being dry before the next coat is put on. When all has been put on you lay on the skin covering all with a good overlap where varnish was put.[53]

The bags when repaired or replaced were then hoisted up inside the ship, being inflated to about 50% of capacity, while the bags that had remained in the ship were deflated to remove the low-purity gas they contained and inflated to 50%. On 18 July 115,000 cubic feet of hydrogen was piped into the ship, and on the following day 100,000 cubic feet more; but with R 33 having priority, it was 11 August before R 32 was fully inflated and ready to fly.

On that day, Maxfield and his officers and men, under the eyes of their British instructors, proudly prepared the ship for flight, gassing each bag to 100% fullness. To keep the ship approximately in equilibrium, sandbags were removed from the gondola rails while fuel was piped on board to the tanks along the keel and over the five engine cars, and water ballast was released as necessary. With the crew at their stations, the ship was walked out by the handling party and onto the field. Taxying cars under the gondolas were detached, water ballast to the amount of 500 lb. or so was dropped to make the ship light, and at the command "Let go!" the men holding the gondolas shoved them skyward. The engines, idling unclutched to the propellers, were engaged, and the ship climbed slowly away.

Flight Lieutenant Wann was in command, but Maxfield certainly played a part from the beginning. An incomplete record shows three training flights in August for a total of 34 hours, and four in September for a total of 56 hours 10 minutes.[54] On the last flight, on 28 September, Maxfield took over from Wann for the first time as commanding officer on a flight of 9 hours 30 minutes.[55] R 32 made seven flights totaling 63 hours 58 minutes in October, but some of them, on 10, 13, and 14 October, may have been turning tests with National Physical Laboratory personnel on board. Maxfield certainly was in command for a flight of 21 hours on 11 October and on other occasions. There were two flights in November, two in December, two in January, and no fewer than five in February. Beginning on 9 February, Flight Lieutenant Wann was once more in command, Maxfield being in Bedford in connection with the completion of R 38. Wann continued in command to the end. The total flight time for the flights recorded between 11 August 1920 and 31 March 1921 was 203 hours 15 minutes; very probably there were even more flights, records of which do not survive today.

In April, R 32 was walked into the single shed at Howden for the last time. Her engine cars were removed, and her outer cover was stripped off. The bare framework, enclosing the gas cells, was supported by tackles from the overhead and shored along the keel. On 27 April 1921 the framework was tested to destruction by overpressurizing Cell 18 just abaft the control car. The hydrogen was turned on, and at a pressure of 20 mm. of water, the wooden framework began to crack. At 30 to 32 mm. there was a loud cracking noise and the walking way and several other longitudinals carried away at one or both ends. With the pressure remaining constant, after about ten minutes a rapid succession of breakages occurred until a total of 24 girder fractures were counted, with numerous shear wires pulled from their anchorages. The ship's gas cells were then deflated, and R 32's framework was dismantled.

Maxfield and his men had assuredly learned much in flying R 32—the recondite art of loading; trim and balance in the hangar; determining lift according to temperature of air, gas, and barometric pressure; undocking; flying heavy and light, with superheat and supercooling; navigation as it was then performed, by dead reckoning and pilotage, with crude radio bearings and perhaps sights of celestial bodies; the weigh-off before landing with engines idling, valving gas or dropping water ballast to bring the ship into equilibrium; and the landing itself, flying the ship down into the hands of the landing party in various conditions of wind. But she was a wooden ship with airplane engines, and the Americans had felt the need to train in a craft more like R 38. Now the opportunity was offered to them: with the airship service rapidly being run down in the name of economy, R 32 was to be deleted, and R 34 substituted for her. The Air Ministry wrote to Admiral Knapp on 21 January 1921:

> As a temporary measure the Royal Air Force will not maintain any airships in commission for service purposes after a date in the near future. . . . The existing agreement as to the terms and conditions of training provides that the initial stages shall be carried out on R 32 on the basis of repayment of the actual costs of hydrogen, fuel, necessary supplies and current repairs. It was further agreed that subsequent training could be given on the R 34 or other ship in commission, subject to the stipulation that a Royal Air Force crew should invariably be in charge.

As a result of a discussion on 13 January between Air Ministry representatives and Commander Emory S. Land (Construction Corps)[56] of the naval attaché's office, it was agreed further that

> a. The United States personnel should have the use of R 32 until February 15, 1921, after which date this ship will be scrapped. b. That from February 15 to May 15, the United States personnel should have the use of the R 34. This ship will be in charge of a Royal Air Force crew at first, but will subsequently be flown by United States personnel after sufficient experience has been gained. . . .[57]

The delight of the men of the Howden Detachment may be imagined—to have to themselves the only airship remaining in military service in Britain, the conqueror of the Atlantic, the fruit of research and knowledge of Zeppelin designers who had conceived

and built the 1916 prototype. Yet the prize was to be snatched from them in the worst accident to date in the British rigid airship program—although because there was no loss of life, and because of the impending demise of the British airship service, the event is little known or remembered today.

Shortly after noon on 27 January 1921, R 32 with the American crew under Maxfield and R 34 departed Howden on training flights. For the latter, preparing to train the Americans, it was the first flight since her transfer from Pulham to Howden on 20 March 1920, nearly a year before. By German standards, the crew could hardly have been considered proficient. Furthermore, owing to demobilization, there must have been many new faces on board—persons unfamiliar with the ship. One such was the commanding officer, Flight Lieutenant Hedley V. Drew, who had taken over only six days previously. The second in command, however, was Flying Officer Harold Luck, a veteran of the transatlantic crossing. Two errors—which would have been detected had the ship operated more frequently—prevented normal radio communication between Howden and R 34. Owing to a defective wave meter the airship was transmitting on the wrong frequency, while she also was using an obsolete call letter and did not recognize when she was being called up by Howden. Thus, R 34 failed to receive in good time an order to return to Howden because of deteriorating weather, and it was evening before Drew realized that he was supposed to return to base. However, the ship's course was laid out on the assumption that a light below was on Spurn Head, when it was actually on Flamborough Head some 40 miles to the north. R 34 was now fighting a strong head wind, flying at 1,200 feet to lessen its effects. Because of the navigational error, R 34 was not approaching Howden over flat land, but was a good 50 miles north and heading into the Cleveland Hills, which vary between 1,200 and 1,500 feet in height. Shortly after midnight the control car brushed the top of one of the hills, scooping up a quantity of heather, followed by the rear car striking also. Had the ship been flying only a few feet lower, she would have been destroyed on the spot; as it was, she drifted out to sea with her crew badly shaken, and three of her five engines disabled—the forward one through breakage of the propeller, the two after ones through the engine and gear shafts being knocked out of alignment.

With only the two wing car engines running, R 34 made slow progress back to Howden, and she did not arrive over the field until about 1300 on the 28th. The wind was now blowing at 18 mph gusting to 30, and an attempt to walk R 34 into her hangar resulted only in the control car being smashed as the ship tossed up and down in turbulence in the lee of the shed. The ship was now secured to a three-wire mooring on the field, but did not fly normally on it. Because of damage to the control car, the upper rudder was jammed hard left, while the maneuvering valve to one of the forward gas cells was pulled open. Gradually the ship became heavy, the wind blowing on top of the nose slammed her repeatedly into the ground, and the forward framework broke up. R 34 was a total loss, and during the next few days the hull structure was cut up with axes.[58]

The destruction of R 34, and the planned dismantling of R 32 on 15 February, created a crisis for the Howden Detachment, raising the possibility that Maxfield's partly trained men would be idle for four months awaiting the completion of R 38, when they needed further experience in flying a metal-frame rigid. Commander Land summarized the remaining prospects in a report to the secretary of the navy, and found them bleak. R 33 had been assigned to civil aviation and on 2 February 1921 had left Howden for Pulham, where she was to conduct experiments with the mooring mast there, the only one in existence. R 37 was not complete at Bedford, and probably would not be completed before R 38. Land considered the surrendered German Zeppelins, L 64 and L 71 at Pulham, both assigned to civil aviation; but their gas cells were at the end of their useful life, and it would take three to five months to put them in flying condition. Furthermore, two engine gondolas of L 71 had been removed and installed in R 36, then nearing completion at the Beardmore works at Inchinnan on the Clyde. Commander Land reported that:

> A number of conferences have recently been held with Air Ministry officials in an effort to ascertain whether training conditions could be improved. A specific request was made for the retention of R 32, and a further request was made for the use of L 64. We also requested that consideration be given to permitting some of our personnel to go on any flights of R 33. The desirability of expediting in every possible way the completion of R 38 was impressed upon Air Ministry officials. . . . It is believed that the Air Ministry officials realize the importance of the matter under discussion and it is believed that all practicable efforts will be made to meet us half way. The difficulties, however, are great, and it is not expected, under present conditions, that our training will go forward in anything like as satisfactory a manner as was anticipated [when R 34 was to be made available].[59]

The Air Ministry found nothing to scrape from the bottom of the barrel. They replied to Land:

> Under the circumstances the Council can only suggest that the R 32 should remain at your disposal until the date fixed for the completion of training, viz: May 15. They readily appreciate that some experience on a ship of a larger type and of metal construc-

tion would be welcome before the R 38 is taken over by the United States crew. The Council are exploring the possibilities in this direction and will address a further communication to you on the subject in due course.

> They regret that the L 64 on which you suggested at a personal interview with the Director of Training and Organization that some training should be given is unlikely to be serviceable before July 1st at earliest, owing to the necessity of constructing and fitting a complete new set of gas bags.[60]

Not surprisingly, the Air Ministry overlooked one metal-hull ship that might be available for training the American crew. At Barrow on the west coast of England, far from the centers of activity at Howden and Pulham, was Vickers, which in defiance of the Admiralty attempt to suppress it, had created its own design for a ship small enough to fit in its 539-foot-long building shed—R 80. She had suffered damage aft, due to excessive gas pressure, on her first flight in June 1920, and had been under repair since. In January 1921 she had been put in commission at Barrow and had resumed trial flights, but the controller general of civil aviation did not want her, partly because of her small size, and the chief of the air staff ordered her deflated and stored. However, the Americans apparently took the initiative in obtaining R 80, for Lcdr. Bieg visted Barrow on 8 February and inspected her in company with her designer, Dr. Barnes Wallis. Then, in quick succession, the controller general of civil aviation, General Frederick Sykes, on 12 February asked that she be preserved for use by the Americans as a training ship, and on 24 February she was flown to Howden by a British crew under Flight Lieutenant Ivor Cecil Little.

On 30 March the Air Ministry wrote to Commander Land: "I am commanded by the Air Council in continuation of their letter . . . dated 9 February to inform you that apart from R 80, which has now been placed at the disposal of the United States crew for training purposes until May 15th, no large airship of metal construction is likely to be available before the R 38."[61] A few days later Land desired "to thank the Air Council for their courtesy in placing R 80 at the disposal of the U.S. Navy crew at Howden for training purposes."[62] No other official correspondence remains concerning the assignment of R 80 to the Americans, but already she was flying out of Howden with Maxfield's men on board.

Walker and Collier's log books show seven flights with Americans on board between 26 March 1921 and early July, for a total of 29 hours 30 minutes, and Flight Lieutenant Little was always in command. However, John Shotter is probably correct in his assessment, that "the U.S. contingent did fly in her at odd times in Howden, but she was not used to any

R 80 in flight at Howden training the American crew of ZR 2. (J. H. Collier)

extent, she was more of a show off outfit."[63] And although the show continued, the leading actors were beginning to slip away—Maxfield, Bieg, and some of the leading chief petty officers—to Bedford, where R 38 was approaching completion and where she made her first flight on 23 June. Since only a handful of Americans were taken on R 38's early trials, flying in R 80 continued beyond the 15 May cutoff date. Her last ascent with Americans on board was a night flight of 5–6 July, almost certainly the one that John McCarthy remembered 50 years later in which General Maitland parachuted over Cardington. R 80 did not fly again until 20 September 1921, when she was ferried to Pulham. There she was laid up and dismantled in 1925.

The Howden Rigid Airship Detachment at play. The wedding of CMM F. F. Moorman at Howden, on 21 August 1921, probably saved his life, as he presumably was on his honeymoon when R 38 crashed three days later. (Norman O. Walker)

For the Howden Detachment it was not all work. America was just emerging from the Age of Innocence, and for youngsters from the small towns, the farms, the prairies, and the forests of the North American continent, it was an exciting experience to see the proud cities, the soaring cathedrals, and the ancient castles of the Old World, then the center of power and culture. Just as the American Expeditionary Force learned to love France and the French, so had the U.S. Navy learned to love Britain and the British during World War I, and the affection was reciprocated. Most of the officers of the Howden Detachment brought their wives to England and rented villas in the hamlet of Brough on the Humber 12 miles from Howden. Many were the good times there, particularly at the *Chateau de Bieg*. All hands were pleased with the abundance of good Scotch whiskey (the curse of Prohibition having descended on the home land). The enlisted men were initially quartered in barracks, but some of them brought their wives over, usually taking a house or apartment in Hull, about 22 miles from Howden via the North-Eastern Railway.

The good people of Hull and the surrounding area opened their houses to the men of the Howden Detachment, and many lasting friendships were formed. Lcdr. Coil, whose first wife had died during the influenza epidemic following the Armistice, married an attractive English girl, while at least ten of the men, including Broom, Steele, and Moorman, followed his example. Moorman's marriage at Howden on 21 August 1921 was reported in the weekly news letter, which advised that "a wedding breakfast was given to the happy couple by the other members of the crew of this detachment."

The training of the Howden Detachment was finished, and officers and men now looked forward to flying home to America in R 38, the big airship they had awaited for so long.

5

ZR 2: The Slaughter of the Innocents

The first American sent to England in connection with the acquisition of R 38 was not Maxfield, but Lcdr. Horace T. Dyer, representing the Bureau of Steam Engineering. For many months, from January 1920 until after the ship was lost, Dyer was the sole American naval representative in Bedford, where the airship was being built.

As early as 26 October 1919, and before Admiral Knapp had signed the agreement to purchase R 38, Captain McBride in London wrote informally to Admiral Taylor, the chief of the Bureau of Construction and Repair, to suggest that an engineering officer and a naval constructor be sent to England to observe her construction. "Present idea is that they should go right to Bedford setting up permanent headquarters and come to London from time to time to consult with either Air Ministry or Land, to whom I will turn over general supervision of the whole affair."[1] Knapp made a formal request to Craven along these lines on 11 November. The Bureau of Steam Engineering detailed Commander Dyer to act as engineering officer in connection with the construction of R 38, but Admiral Taylor was unable to detail a naval constructor, and requested that Dyer represent the Bureau of Construction and Repair as well as the Bureau of Steam Engineering.

Dyer's situation was analogous to that of the inspector of hulls and inspector of machinery in private shipyards at home building vessels to naval account, or the inspector of naval aircraft in the factory of a private contractor building to naval specifications. Yet there were important differences: In the United States, the Navy Department drew up specifications, invited bids, negotiated contracts with private firms, and sent its specialist officers into the contractor's premises to ensure that the specifications were being complied with. In the case of R 38, the bureaus in Washington, and Dyer, their representative, were not dealing with private citizens but with a sovereign power, the government of the United Kingdom of Great Britain and Ireland, and with an agency of the Crown, the Air Ministry. Obviously they could not be treated like private contractors at home, and Dyer had no authority, merely permission to observe, to forward progress reports and what data he could obtain, and to convey requests for information. Further, not being a naval constructor, Dyer was not qualified to criticize the R 38 design and structure, nor was he expected to do so.

Much later, Hunsaker wrote that "the United States was perhaps at fault in not detailing a competent naval constructor and an engineer to act as inspectors with the usual full authority."[2] But could this have been done? Suppose that Hunsaker himself had been detailed to represent Construction and Repair at Bedford (and surely, after the ultimate tragedy, Admiral Taylor must have wished he had sent a qualified officer to report directly to him). Within a month of his arrival, Hunsaker would certainly have come to the conclusion that R 38, with her light-weight high-altitude structure, was unsuited to the U.S. Navy's purposes, if not actually unsafe. His criticisms would have found support from the Aircraft Division in the Bureau of Construction and Repair, particularly from Charles P. Burgess, who saw with icy clarity the airship designer's dilemma: with hydrogen conferring a net lifting force of only 68 pounds per 1,000 cubic feet, the giant rigid framework had to be as light as possible and at the same time withstand virtually incalculable aerodynamic loads while being driven at speed in turbulent air. Admiral Taylor might have been expected to back up his subordinates, but what would have happened at higher levels? Would Craven and Maxfield, lacking the naval constructor's technical knowledge, have agreed? Would Secretary Daniels have listened? And what if he had? Cancellation of the contract with the Air Ministry, with serious repercussions for Anglo–American relations? Or a complete reworking of the design at American insistence, when the British experts were supposed to be the teachers, and the Americans the pupils?

Bedford, where R 38 was building, was then an industrial town of some 40,000 inhabitants 50 miles north–northwest of London on the River Ouse. The airship works actually were located in Cardington, a village three miles southeast of the town.[3] Here Messrs. Short Brothers, an aircraft building firm, had erected a construction shed for the Admiralty in 1916 on 2,800 acres of land. The shed, which measured 700 feet long, 180 feet wide, and 110 feet high, provided building berths for two rigid airships at once. On each side of the shed were lean-to type shops for construction of girders and gas cells, and for assembly of parts and small components. Here Shorts had constructed the wooden-hulled R 31 and R 32; and on one side of the shed in which R 38 was building was the naked but completed frame of R 37, with fabric-covered fins attached. Shortly after the Armistice the Admiralty had invoked the Defence of the Realm Act, and had seized the Shorts plant to use as a government airship works, paying £40,000 in compensation. Because of the chaotic state of the postwar airship program, and the transfer of airships from the Admiralty to the Air Ministry, it was not until April 1920 that the Royal Airship Works, as it was now called, was transferred to the Air Ministry. At the same time Constructor Commander C. I. R. Campbell, formerly acting in London as the head of the Design Section in the department of the Director of Production (Airships) at the Admiralty, was named superintendent of the Royal Airship Works and had to move to Bedford. His administrative duties (which involved sea voyages to the United States in December 1919 and September 1920 to consult with the Navy Department about the ZR 1 design) ensured that the responsibility for constructing R 38 was placed on his subordinates. The Admiralty of course had its own team of inspectors at Bedford, headed by Naval Constructor Payne. After April 1920, they continued to perform the same services for the Air Ministry with honorary rank in the Royal Corps of Naval Constructors.

On 5 and 6 January 1920, Dyer made his first visit to Bedford, with Commander Land and Lcdrs. Coil and Ramsey. This was the first time that any Amer-

R 38 under construction. The first section of the hull completed and in place on the cradles at the rear of the Bedford shed. From front to back: transverse frames 13, 13a, 13b, 14 in the stern of the ship. Photograph taken 15 December 1919. (Garland Fulton)

ican officers had seen the ship which their government had purchased two and a half months earlier. They saw two pairs of transverse main frames already aligned on the building cradles in the shed. British airship constructors, as did the Zeppelin Company, started construction by assembling the 13-sided main frames on wooden forms, or jigs, lying horizontally on the hangar floor at waist height. After the precut girders had been riveted, chord and radial bracing wires were installed and tightened. Next, a whole 15-meter section of the rigid hull was created in a vertical tower or jig at the end of the hangar, by sliding two main frames into the tower horizontally. Longitudinal girders were then inserted in vertical position around the sides of the tower, their ends mating with the corners of the polygonal main frames at top and bottom. Two sets of intermediate transverse girders were installed at 5-meter intervals, all joints were riveted, and diagonal shear wiring was installed in all the rectangular bays created by the longitudinal and transverse girders. There

Completed section of R 38 hull framework from Frame 9 to 10 being lifted out of the vertical construction tower. It will be turned horizontal and moved down the shed to be placed on cradles and joined to section 11–12 by longitudinal girders. (Garland Fulton)

now existed in the tower one complete bay of the airship 15 meters long, standing on one end. The next step was to lift the bay, rotate it to a horizontal position, and move it down the shed to rest on cradles which kept it in alignment with the axis of the airship hull. Two more main frames then went into the empty tower, and the next 15-meter hull section created was then placed on cradles with a 15-meter space between it and the nearest main frame of the preceding bay. The missing structure between the two sections of the ship was then filled in by lifting longitudinal girders into place, inserting the girders of the two intermediate frames, and installing shear wiring.

When Dyer and his party made their visit to Bedford, Bay 14–13 (with frames so designated) had already been completed and set on cradles, on 11 November 1919. Bay 12–11 was also in the cradles, and the longitudinal and intermediate frame girders were being installed to join the two hull sections together. Bay 9–10 was being constructed in the tower with completion expected on 16 January, and Frames 7 and 8 were being assembled in the jigs on the floor. Girders had been cut and fitted for Frames 5 and 6, and would be assembled as soon as the forms were free. In the lean-to sheds along the outside walls of the hangar, 1,727 of the 2,173 girders of the hull had been completed by riveting channels and lattices. A small force of skilled laborers, mostly women,

was working on 9 of the 14 gas cells required; 2 more were being constructed at the Beardmore works, and 3 had not been started. Two of the six power cars were practically complete as to structure, but nothing had been done about the cotton outer cover, or about radiators, gasoline tanks, piping, fittings, telephone and communication outfit, and radio. While work was proceeding slowly, Dyer was satisfied, as

First, the U.S. government having specified that delivery late in the year 1920 will be satisfactory, and second, as the British Authorities desire to retain the force which they have working at the present time, and which would have to be laid off if the construction were pushed and the ship completed in July, as they stated would be possible.[4]

Dyer's report contained the first up-to-date technical information and summary of progress on the erection of R 38, about which there was much interest in the Bureau of Construction and Repair, and in the office of the director of naval aviation. Taking with him Chief Yeoman James C. Burnett, formerly with the attaché's office in London, Dyer shortly moved to Bedford. Here the representative of BuSEng and BuC&R lived in almost complete isolation from his fellow American officers, seeing them only when duty brought them to Bedford.[5]

Work on the hull framework proceeded rapidly, with main frames being moved steadily into the tower, completed 15-meter sections being hoisted out and placed in the cradles, and gangs of men with ladders and scaffolding installing the intervening longitudinals. By April the hull framework was completed from Frame 3 in the nose to Frame 14 in the tail. Much remained to be done—completion of the bow with mooring gear, and the stern with the four big cantilever fins and rudders; the fuel, oil, and water ballast systems; control cables; gondolas; and outer cover. Progress here tended to appear slow, compared to the speed with which the basic framework had been erected.

Only on 22 October 1920 did Craven recommend that R 38 be designated "ZR 2," pointing out that "ZR" was the official designation of rigid airships, and R 38 was the second of the type, the one to be built in America—the later *Shenandoah*—being "ZR 1." The chief of naval operations and the acting secretary approved. On 21 January 1921 Dyer in Bedford requested instructions involving markings; it was planned to block out the outline for markings and insignia in the fabric shop before applying the outer cover to the ship. Because of the pressure to get R 38 flying in June 1921, only the insignia on the quarters were applied at the Royal Airship Works, but after her transfer to Howden on 18 July, she carried the ZR 2 number on both sides of the nose in

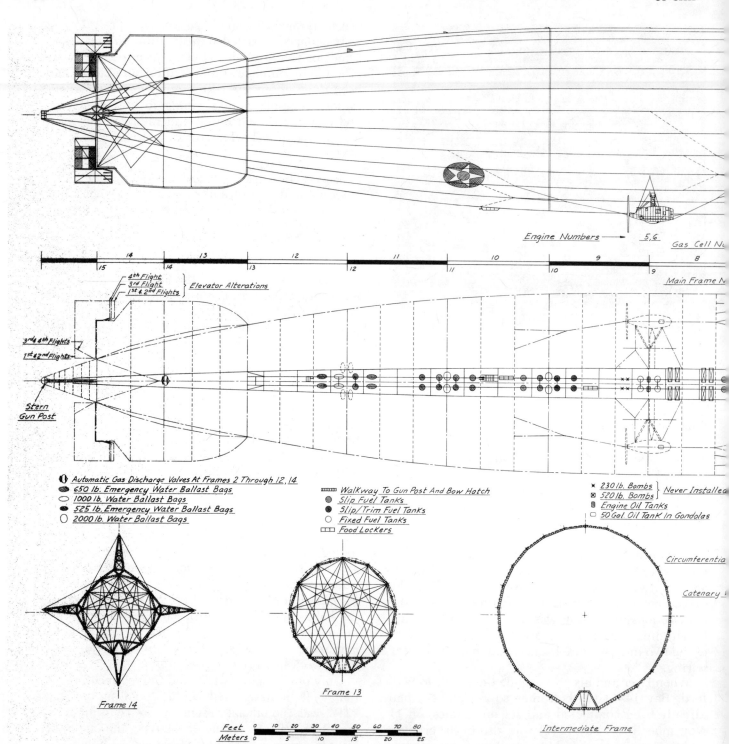

Engine Numbers → 5,6

Gas Cell Nu

14   13   12   11   10   9   8

15   14   13   12   11   10   9

4th Flight
3rd Flight   Elevator Alterations
1st & 2nd Flights

Main Frame N

3rd & 4th Flights
1st & 2nd Flights

Stern
Gun Post

Automatic Gas Discharge Valves At Frames 2 Through 12, 14   ⫿⫿⫿ Walkway To Gun Post And Bow Hatch   × 230 lb. Bombs ⎫ Never Installe
650 lb. Emergency Water Ballast Bags   Slip Fuel Tanks   ⊠ 520 lb. Bombs ⎭
1000 lb. Water Ballast Bags   Slip/Trim Fuel Tanks   Engine Oil Tanks
525 lb. Emergency Water Ballast Bags   Fixed Fuel Tanks   50 Gal Oil Tank In Gondolas
2000 lb. Water Ballast Bags   Food Lockers

Circumferentia

Catenary

Frame 14   Frame 13   Intermediate Frame

Feet   0 10 20 30 40 50 60 70 80
Meters 0   5   10   15   20   25

ZR 2

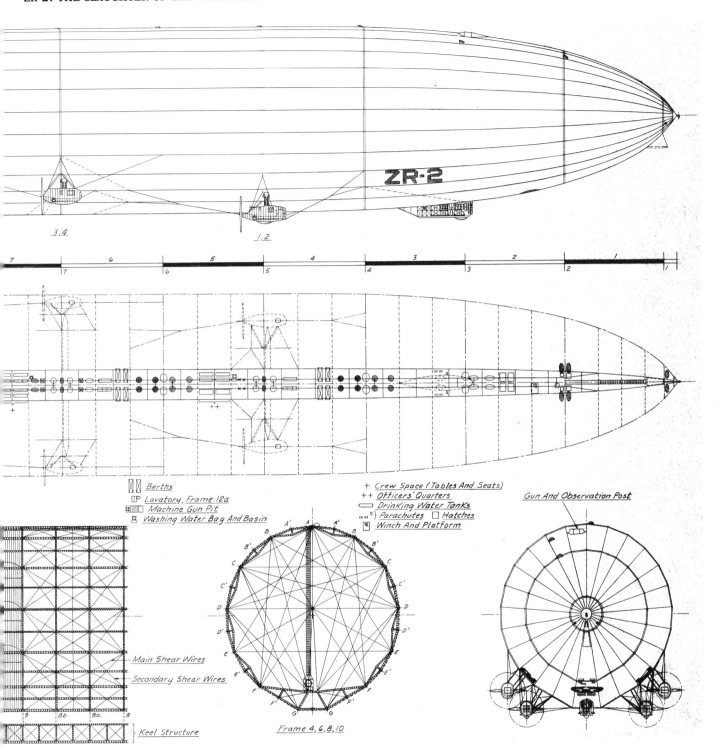

ZR-2

3,4   1,2

⊠⊠ _Berths_   + _Crew Space (Tables And Seats)_
⫴P _Lavatory, Frame 12a_   ++ _Officers' Quarters_
⊞▥ _Machine Gun Pit_   ◠ _Drinking Water Tanks_
⌾ _Washing Water Bag And Basin_   ▭◻ _Parachutes_ □ _Hatches_
                                        ▦ _Winch And Platform_

Gun And Observation Post

Main Shear Wires

Secondary Shear Wires

Keel Structure

Frame 4, 6, 8, 10

William F. Kerka

34

UP SHIP

letters 9 feet high, the U.S. Navy's white star with red center on a blue field 15 feet in diameter under the nose and on both quarters, and vertical red, white, and blue stripes on the upper and lower rudders.

One major modification was made early, during March 1920. For reasons that are obscure, R 38 was designed with two different types of engines—four 350-h.p. Sunbeam Cossack engines each weighing 1,200 lb. in the forward and midships engine gondolas, and two smaller 275-h.p. Sunbeam Maoris each weighing 920 lb. in the rear power cars, all with reduction gear. The Air Ministry proposed instead putting Cossacks in all cars, retaining the reduction gear for the smaller Maoris in the after gondolas and limiting the horsepower of the rear engines to 300 at sea level. BuSEng recommended on 20 March that the Cossack reduction gears be fitted, thereby reducing the number of spares, and in the end R 38 was equipped with six Cossack engines (three right-hand and three left-hand) with appropriate gears, four spare Cossacks (two right-hand and two left-hand), and two spare reduction gears. The added weight in the rear engine cars, due to fitting the larger power plants, was 1,290 lb., including extra wire bracing in main frame 9, from which they were hung.

In recommending the Cossack engines aft, the Air Ministry may have been making a virtue of necessity. R 38's original design was finalized in the autumn of 1918, and certainly did not include bow mooring gear, yet this was incorporated in the ship at completion and, with necessary stiffening of bow girders, must have added approximately 2,000 lb. right forward. Actually, nothing appears in the record about the shift aft of the center of gravity due to the engine change, but it would have had the effect of balancing the weight of the bow mooring gear.[6]

On 10 April 1920, Mr. Henry May, airship assistant constructor at the Royal Airship Works, drew up instructions for a so-called deflated gas bag test in Bay 8, the most advanced portion of R 38's hull frame.

Since the theories of stress analysis of the rigid airship structure were a matter of dispute, airship designers were eager to conduct actual load tests on the hull structure in the hangar. The deflated gas bag test was supposed to reproduce the static loads that would occur if one gas bag suddenly deflated while the ones in the adjacent bays were 100% full. Since the main frames at each end of the bay containing the deflated gas bag were braced radially and chordwise between the joints with taut steel wire, the pressure differential would cause the full bags to bulge into the empty bay, putting an increased strain on the transverse wiring of the main frames. The resulting compression loads on the main frames, to which the ends of the wiring were attached, increased as the cube of the diameter of the frame, and were much higher

than any loads imposed by the lift of the gas or the weight of fuel, bombs, or ballast in the keel (though with an axial cable, a stranded wire that in R 38 ran through all the gas bags connecting the central fittings to which the radial wires were attached, the compression loads were halved). The "deflated gas bag test" was thus a standard procedure in proving the strength of the hull of any rigid airship.

May's directive assumed that the structure between Frames 7 and 10 would be entirely complete with respect to girders and wiring, and that Cell 8 would be inflated in the bay between Frames 8 and 9. All diagonal and keel corridor wire tensions between Frames 7 and 10 were to be measured repeatedly as the test progressed, as well as all radial and chord wire tensions in Frames 8 and 9, and all gas bag wiring tensions in the bay between Frames 8 and 9. The deflection upward under gas pressure loads of the upper longitudinal girders in the bay between Frames 8 and 9 was also to be measured, as well as deflections in the keel corridor as weights were added to balance the lift of the gas. With Cell 8 being gradually filled with hydrogen, weights were to be added at

Deflated gas bag test with R 38, probably photographed on 16 June 1920. Cell 8 is installed between main frames 8 and 9 and is inflated to 100% fullness. Note how radial and chord wire bracing of main frame 9 shows on the face of the cell, also the diamond truss arrangement of main frame 10 in the foreground, and the light intermediate frames spaced 5 meters apart between the main ones. (AIAA)

the main frames 8 and 9 to a total of 3,000 lb. at each frame with 50% filling, and as filling continued to 90%, 4,000 lb. more weight was to be distributed in the corridor between Frames 8 and 8a, and 8b to 9. If possible, a further 1,000 lb. would be added as inflation progressed to 100%. May also directed that the axial cable segment in Cell 8 be connected as soon as possible during inflation.

On 28 May inflation of Cell 8 commenced, reaching 75% full by the end of the working day on 31 May. Weights were added in the corridor corresponding to the lift of the hydrogen. The cell was left in this condition overnight, and inflation was resumed on the morning of 1 June. Before any gas had flowed in, one of the diamond trusses of Frame 8 in the top of the ship, between the top longitudinal or A girder, and longitudinal B on the port side, collapsed, while the B longitudinal failed at its end attachment to Frame 8 and was pulled inward. The failure was blamed on a man standing on the A longitudinal at Frame 8, ready to deflate the bag in case of emergency. The bag was in fact deflated, and reinforcing plates were installed at the joints in the upper part of Frame 8, while the diamond truss was replaced. On 15 June, when repairs had been completed, the bag was filled to 50%. On the following day the bag was filled to 100%. It was allowed to remain in this condition for an hour, while measurements of radial wire tensions and girder deflections went on. Then a rigger slung from the shed roof in a boatswain's chair applied his full weight to the starboard A-B diamond truss of Frame 8, in order to reach a wire some 10 feet from him. Again the girders of the diamond truss collapsed under the load, and with the resulting increase of stress on the remainder of the structure, 15 longitudinal girders and 5 transverse girders buckled, not all in the bay between Frames 8 and 9.

Strangely in retrospect, the multiple girder failures caused no real anxiety among R 38's builders. Mr. Henry May even concluded that

> The result of test shows that the structure is amply strong and a sufficient margin of strength is obtained for any conditions which may occur in practice. The conditions imposed by this test give approximately 5000 lb. more direct loading on the chord and radial wiring of the transverse frames than would be obtained with a deflated gas bag and the adjacent gas bags 100% full at sea level.[7]

Reinforcing plates were installed at all the main frame joints with main longitudinals in the upper part of the ship from Frames 3 to 11, and the constructors emphasized that men should not stand on the girders.

Some of the Americans were not so easily satisfied. In Washington, particularly, the airship specialists in the Aircraft Division of the Bureau of Construction and Repair were only beginning to discover the characteristics of the big rigid they had bought sight unseen. On 25 March Admiral Taylor requested a complete weight statement for R 38, and on 17 May Truscott advised that the bureau had not obtained from Commander Land and Commander Dyer "calculations of Bending Moments in various conditions of load which would indicate the factors of safety, or calculations as to transverse strength with gas bag deflated or calculations to determine strength of the ship with rudders and elevators suddenly thrown hard over."[8] Hunsaker, visiting Bedford in June, sent some comments to Burgess on the girder failures in the deflated gas bag test. Both agreed that "the Admiralty method of making a stress calculation neglecting the chord wires gives results which are seriously in error," and while calculations showed that the load on the top joint of Frame 8 was well within its limits of strength, the added load from the chord wires "was more than the frame could have stood for even a short time." An added note from Burgess: "This investigation indicates that the transverses of the R 38 are only just strong enough, *and have no factor of safety*."[9] In other words, the structure could barely withstand contemplated static loads, not to mention dynamic ones. In connection with the failures it was disconcerting when Campbell, visiting Washington in September 1920, told Burgess that "they were still very much in the dark in England as regards the total force on the hull when turning and [that] he had asked the National Physical Laboratory shortly after the Armistice to make a thorough investigation into the question but to the present time no result was forthcoming." Operational experience had convinced the Admiralty that "the stresses were not nearly so great as calculations had indicated"[10] in turns, thus discrediting the advice of the constructors and leading Campbell to question the results of model tests.

Thus, doubts were beginning to arise, but only in the minds of personnel of the Aircraft Division in the Bureau of Construction and Repair. Burgess, who had the deepest misgivings, was a civilian employee and not in a position to shape policy. None of these doubts was communicated to Maxfield, who was then busy in Howden getting the training of his men under way, and the information probably would not have affected his faith in the airship, even if he had been aware of it.

On 3 November 1920 Admiral Knapp advised Craven that R 38 could be completed by 1 February 1921, and possibly, by expediting the work, by 1 January. The secretary's office advised that the 1 February date would be more acceptable—after all, Lakehurst would not be complete until the summer.

On 1 February, however, the ship was far from complete, and progress thereafter was even slower. Actually, the workmen at the Royal Airship Works were engaged in a slowdown, what was known in Great Britain as "ca-cannying." The cancellation in February of R 37 had been a blow to them: While working on R 38, they had expected that they would go on to complete the earlier ship. Now its bare framework on the other side of the hangar had become a literal skeleton at the feast. Knapp got nowhere with the Air Ministry, which advised him on 20 April that "the construction of the ship is at present being carried out under great difficulties owing to the fact that the Royal Airship Works is to be completely closed and the staff dispersed as soon as the R 38 is completed. At the present rate of progress it is hoped that the ship may be ready for flight trials by the end of May."[11] Knapp recommended that the Navy Department apply pressure on the Air Ministry through the British air attaché in Washington, and on the Foreign Office through the State Department and the British government, emphasizing "the urgent desire of the Navy Department and the international importance of having the airship completed and turned over to the United States at the earliest possible date."[12]

On 4 May, Campbell posted a notice offering the employees of the Royal Airship Works a bonus of one week's pay if the ship were completed by 31 May, or a half week's pay if she were completed by 7 June. She was still unfinished by the latter date, on which the director of research, Air Commodore Sir Robert Brooke-Popham, who was Campbell's superior at the Air Ministry, came to Bedford to inspect the ship, and presumably to indicate his displeasure. Campbell defended himself by pointing out that some necessary items had been delayed through the fault of outside contractors. Under the circumstances, and considering that the trades unions involved had made many concessions about overtime work, Campbell felt they had earned the bonus of a half week's pay and recommended Air Ministry approval.[13] The ship was considered complete by 7 June for flying trials, but as Flight Lieutenant Pritchard noted, "the work on the ship . . . owing to the rush was not up to the usual finish so far considered desirable in rigid airships, and although the main structure was completed, many minor items required considerable work."[14]

Flight Lieutenant John Edward Maddock Pritchard was officer in charge of airship flying trials. Thirty-two years old in 1921, he had joined the Royal Naval Air Service in 1915 and had had much flying experience in nonrigids. Showing a particular aptitude for the scientific side of airship operations, he was appointed in September 1917 to the Airship Department at the Admiralty, where he acted as accept-

ance pilot for the early rigid airships on completion. He also went out of his way to obtain information from German sources, himself interrogating captured German airship crew members, and translating captured technical documents. In December 1918 he went to Germany as technical airship officer in the British naval section of the Inter-Allied Armistice Commission, and brought back a quantity of information; and he participated in the R 34 transatlantic crossing in July 1919. Pritchard, alone of all the British and American officers connected with R 38, was familiar with German operating doctrine and methods. Above all, he was acquainted with the limitations imposed by the German Navy, on the advice of the Zeppelin Company, on low-altitude maneuvers in the lightly built "height-climbers" which were bombing England from 16,000 to 20,000 feet in the last two years of the war.

As early as 13 March 1921, Pritchard drew up a program of trials for R 38 calling for a total of 150 hours on the ship before she departed for America. This was to include one or two short flights from Bedford to test controllability and airworthiness, then a hundred hours further including rough-weather flying to prove the reliability of the ship. Pritchard anticipated that defects might be uncovered during this period (he pointed out that R 36, smaller and more nearly akin to the Zeppelin original, had just suffered collapse of two fins on her third flight), and he wanted a mooring mast erected at Bedford to facilitate repairs by factory personnel. Last, Pritchard advised that the American crew should have a further 50 hours on the ship for familiarization before they essayed the Atlantic crossing.

The extended trials program was not acceptable to Air Commodore Brooke-Popham, Pritchard's superior as director of research. He saw no reason why the 150 hours could not be reduced by two thirds, combining the rough-weather flying and the training of the American crew in 50 hours. Brooke-Popham's opinion became the official one of the Air Ministry and was communicated to Commander Land on 20 April.[15] Land was further informed that initially not more than four U.S. naval representatives would be allowed to accompany the British trial crew. Brooke-Popham, and the Air Council, were of course under pressure from both governments: the British Treasury demanding the shutdown of the entire airship establishment by 1 August on the one hand, and the American ambassador, George Brinton McClellan Harvey, pressing for early delivery on instructions from Washington. The lengthy trials program drawn up by Pritchard did not suit either nation's political leaders.

Air Commodore Maitland, who of course outranked Pritchard, was in effect in charge of the R 38 trials program and participated in all the flights. Some undated notes found in his effects after the final catastrophe state that "to properly try out an airship of a new type takes 150 to 200 hours. . . . she must be flown under all conditions of weather the most difficult of all being full speed under very bumpy conditions such as one is likely to meet with in the Atlantic." In principle, he would not be hurried ("the considered technical opinion in this country is that it is safer to fly an *airworthy* ship across the Atlantic in the *worst* month of the year than to attempt to fly an *unairworthy* ship in the best month of the year"). He was determined to test R 38 fully before handing her over to the Americans, who were considered too inexperienced to have valid opinions of their own ("we are in the position of instructors and the U.S.A. representatives are in the position of pupils and not in a position to say when the ship *is* or *is not* airworthy").[16] He urged that a mast at Howden would expedite the trials program. Yet Maitland was obliged to yield to political pressure: on 7 June, while still objecting that 150 hours was the minimum for trials, he was told to hand R 38 over to the Americans as soon as Brooke-Popham approved, and not to give any advice unless asked.[17]

Remarkably, Commander Maxfield also favored the abbreviated trials program. On 6 June an important conference took place at the Air Ministry to discuss the trials program. On the one side was the chief of the Air Staff, Air Marshal Sir Hugh Trenchard, in the chair, with Air Vice Marshal Sir Edward Ellington, the director general of Supply and Research and Brooke-Popham's superior; Air Commodore Philip Game, the director of Supply and Organization; and Mr. W. F. Nicholson, the secretary to the Air Ministry. On the other side, completely outranked, were Commanders Newton H. White, Land, and Maxfield. It was expected that R 38 would complete within a fortnight; after one short flight from Bedford and return to the constructor's shed for repairs if necessary, she could proceed to Howden and continue trials from there. Hydrogen, fuel, landing party, and two rigid airship captains would be supplied by the British, who predicted that the earliest date for the transatlantic flight would be mid-August. Maxfield took note of the Air Ministry desire for sufficient flights to carry out contract requirements; thereafter, he asserted, he would desire two more flights of 12 and 24 hours, being then ready to depart for America with only 50 to 60 hours on the ship.[18]

Why was Maxfield agreeable to the British plan to accelerate the trials program regardless of the advice of Maitland and Pritchard? He was of course aware that the program was behind schedule, and like the Air Ministry officials, was under pressure from Ambassador Harvey. Further, he was obsessed with the need to make the Atlantic crossing before stormy autumn weather arrived. Above all, Maxfield was unavoidably lacking in rigid airship experience and handling sense. By German standards, which called for two years of steady flying in command, none of the officers, English or American, responsible for R 38 was fully qualified to command rigid airships, and Maxfield, with probably 200 hours on R 32, was qualified least of all.

Even before R 38's first flight there were problems. As far back as May, Commander Land had been aware that the permeability of the gas cells was excessive, owing to an unsatisfactory process whereby the goldbeater's skin was laid on the cotton cell fabric while both were wringing wet. As drying took place, the skin shrank while the cloth stretched, so that the cloth wrinkled and broke away from the skin, which, being unsupported, ruptured when the cell was tensioned by gas pressure. Largely because of the resulting leakage, R 38 during her short life consumed a million cubic feet of hydrogen a month. Worse yet, the permeability of the cells worked both ways, permitting air to diffuse inward and creating a dangerously explosive mixture of oxygen and hydrogen. The purity figures obtained before R 38's last flight would never have been tolerated in German service, but were accepted in the general hurry to get the ship away to America before the end of the summer.

The first flight took place on 23 June 1921. In a flat calm at twilight (necessary to walking R 38 out of the Bedford shed, which was a tight fit) she was brought out at 2120, ascended at 2152, and landed again at 0430. On board was a crew of 40 Britishers, with Flight Lieutenant Archibald H. Wann as commanding officer, Flight Lieutenant Ivor C. Little as first officer, Flight Lieutenant Rupert S. Montagu as navigator, and Flying Officer Thomas F. Mathewson as engineering officer. Brooke-Popham, Maitland, Campbell, and Pritchard were along as passengers, and Maxfield, Bieg, Chief Machinist Halliburton, and Chief Rigger Aller were permitted on board as observers for the U.S. Navy.

The ship remained throughout in the vicinity of Bedford, rising to a pressure height of 2,500 feet, then descending to 1,800 feet, and operating at various speeds and with different combinations of engines. As speed was increased to between 35 and 40 knots, great difficulty was experienced with the rudders and elevators and their control cables. The latter became so slack that chains slipped off their sprockets, and the slack side of the control wire circuit wrapped around the taut side. The cause was the new "cruiser type" rudders and elevators, with large balancing areas ahead of the hinge line at the outboard end. It was in fact expected that the correct proportion of balance area would have to be determined by trial

ZR 2 being brought out of the shed at Bedford. The structure on the left, extending out from the hangar door, is a wind break, used only by the British and actually increasing turbulence at the shed entrance. (J. H. Collier)

and error. While the surfaces appeared to be in balance at low speed, they overbalanced as speed was increased. Pritchard felt that the center of pressure on the rudders moved forward with increasing speed. Maxfield's report to Craven commented on the control problems, and added: "it must be remembered that the atmosphere was stable and the ship practically in static equilibrium and trim. What she would do excessively light or heavy or in bumpy weather was not proved."[19]

At a conference on 24 June it was decided to cut a 14-inch strip off the leading edge of the balance area of the top rudder, which was the same in shape as the elevators, and to run a test as soon as possible. Guards were installed on chain sprockets of the control cables to prevent them from jumping off, and springs on the cables themselves to take up slack. On the evening of 28 June the ship was brought out for a second trial flight, with Dyer, Maxfield, Bieg, and Chief Rigger Aller as observers. The lower rudder was disconnected from the upper and clamped amidships, and with four engines running at 1800 rpm the speed was increased to 48 knots. Beyond this it was considered inadvisable to push her; the upper rudder still appeared slightly overbalanced, and the elevators very much so. There was disappointment that it had not been possible to work R 38 up to full speed. After landing, an inspection showed some distortion of the cruciform girders supporting the fins. These girders were reinforced with doubler plates, and further external bracing wires added to the cantilever fins at Frames 13b, 14, and the outer pintle bearing.[20]

The upper rudder, the two elevators, and the lower rudder all now had their balance areas reduced by removing 23 inches of the leading edge, while a triangular area was cut off the inboard trailing edge of each control surface. A number of other modifications and alterations were made at this time, principally the installation of a crew space amidships between Frames 7a and 7b, while the former crew space at 5a to 5b was converted into an officers' quarters. Frame 13 was also reinforced at the bottom transverse girder, where the leading edge of the bottom fin attached.

For the next flight, intended to last 48 hours and to terminate at Howden, an extensive test program was planned: Not only were the modified control surfaces to be tested, but fuel consumption data using different engine combinations at various revolutions were to be obtained to assist in planning the transatlantic flight. In addition, a team from the National Physical Laboratory was on board with equipment to monitor pressures on fins and rudders during turning tests: nine manometer holes had been installed in the upper and port fins, and ten on each side of the upper rudder. Pressure manometers were located in the keel at the cruciform girder, and motion picture cameras were to record air pressure during normal flight, turning trials, and rudder-maneuvering tests. R 38's turning circle was to be measured at different air speeds and rudder angles.

At 1930 on 17 July, R 38 lifted off at Bedford. In addition to the British crew, on board were the National Physical Laboratory team of three persons, four American officers including Maxfield and Bieg, four American riggers including Aller and Collier, and seven American mechanics. Fuel consumption tests began immediately and kept Bieg and his men busy. Engines 1, 2, 5, and 6 running at 1400 rpm gave a speed of 37 knots; 1600 rpm gave 43 knots. Arriving over Howden, the airship moved out over the North

Sea for the higher-speed tests. Advancing the four engines to 1800 rpm gave 48 knots. So far the ship had behaved well, and the control surfaces had not shown themselves to be overbalanced.

Shortly after midnight, with the ship at 2,000 feet and pressure height about 2,300 feet, Mr. John Pannell, the head of the National Physical Laboratory team, asked the permission of Flight Lieutenant Little to increase the engine speeds to 2000 rpm, which was their full power. Pritchard objected, pointing out that R 36, when her fins had failed at 50 knots on 5 April, had dived from 3,000 to 1,200 feet before she was halted by stopping engines, dropping ballast, and sending men aft, and he thought that R 38, a bigger ship, should be taken up to 2,500 feet before opening up the engines to full power. But he was overruled, Little pointing out that Captain Wann had ordered that the ship not be taken over pressure height.

At 0023 the four engine cars were signaled to give full power, and the air speed quickly built up to 50 knots. Within a minute the elevator man, Collier, found the wheel hard to handle, and the ship hunted up and down between 1,700 and 2,200 feet. The elevators, still overbalanced at the higher speed, were moving by themselves and inflicting heavy bending stresses on the hull. Little asked Pritchard to take over the elevator wheel, which he did, reducing the altitude fluctuations to about 100 feet. A few minutes later, Aller, whom Collier had relieved at midnight, and who was in the crew space at 7a and 7b, telephoned the control car to say that girders on the port side of the crew space had failed. Speed was immediately reduced, and the damage surveyed. While main frames 7 and 8 were intact, intermediate frames 7a and 7b had buckled between F and G longitudinal (the base girder of the keel), and F main longitudinal, F' intermediate longitudinal, and the GG transverse girder at 7a had also buckled. The decision was made to discontinue the flight. Although Campbell, Pritchard, and Wann preferred to return to Bedford to have the factory repair the damage, it was felt that it would be difficult to assemble a landing party on short notice before the morning breezes developed and made housing the ship impossible. So R 38 headed for Howden, where she landed at 0505. Some further fuel consumption tests were made en route.

While R 38 had been flying at only 50 knots at full power on four engines (it was estimated she might reach 60 knots at 2000 rpm on all six engines), she had experienced severe oscillations in her flight path over a range of 500 feet, due to uncontrolled movements of the overbalanced elevators, and had suffered significant structural failure. What was the cause? Surprisingly, Campbell, to whom everybody looked for an authoritative answer, promptly offered the opinion

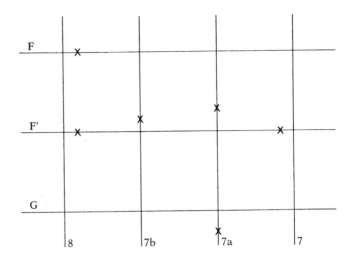

Bieg drawing of girder failures on third flight.

that the slipstream from the port forward propeller, beating on the large panel low in the ship between the main frames 7 and 8 forward and aft, and F and G longitudinals top and bottom, had caused the damaged girders to bend inward and collapse. (The port midships engine, located just ahead of the damaged area, had been stopped during the test.) Campbell thus ignored the possibility of the girders' failing in compression due to severe bending loads on the hull in the vertical plane. Whether he really believed what he said is open to question: The opinion, rendered during the flight to Howden, or just after the landing, was offered with little time for deliberation, to associates looking for reassurance, by the designer of the airship, who had at least an unconscious interest in justifying his work. R 38, bigger than any previous rigid, designed to outperform even the latest German Zeppelins, was Campbell's creation; he apparently had to conceal from himself the grave implications of the midships girder failures. So well did Campbell succeed in repressing his concerns that he continued to fly in the ship with no indication of anxiety, and only three days before his death in the disaster over Hull on 24 August, in a discussion with Commander Dyer, "he expressed himself most emphatically in regard to the strength of the ship and apparently there existed in his mind no question but that the trouble on the third flight had been caused by the slipstream and that the additional stiffening would entirely prevent the possibility of any further collapse."[21]

The port forward propeller was located a good 100 feet forward of the area of damage amidships, but Campbell was the engineering authority, and for the moment his views prevailed. In the Howden shed the lower part of the outer cover was unlaced, the lower portions of all the intermediate frames from 5a to 10a were reinforced by adding further material, doubling

40 UP SHIP

Repairs at Howden after the third trial flight. ZR 2 with the outer cover opened up amidships between longitudinals F and G, for replacement of damaged girders and reinforcement of those that did not fail. (J. H. Collier)

the strength of the sections between the F and G longitudinal, while F longitudinal between the main frames 5 and 10 was also reinforced. The balance areas of the elevators were further reduced by 6 inches, though the rudders, which had not given trouble, were not altered. The work was done under difficult conditions by personnel brought up from Bedford, and was completed on 30 July.

Maxfield was not troubled by the damage on the third flight: he accepted Campbell's opinion unreservedly, forwarding it to Admiral Twining in London, who on 21 July sent a RUSH telegram to BuNav advising that "some minor buckling" had occurred and "press reports re damage are exaggerated."[22] Maxfield's faith in the ship was unimpaired, and he was concerned primarily with the impending Atlantic flight, which he hoped could take place between 15 and 20 August. But the structural failure on the third flight raised grave doubts on both sides of the Atlantic.

Pritchard, on 20 July, prepared for Maitland a memorandum on the height at which future speed trials should take place, and urged that the air commodore make "a definite ruling before the next flight trial takes place." He reviewed the near-disaster to R 36 after the fin collapse on 5 April, and pointed out that under the approved program of trials* R 38 should be flown at 52 knots at an altitude of 3,000 to 4,000 feet, and at least 1,000 feet below pressure height, and at full speed she should be flown at 4,000

*This document was not available to us for verification.

feet, pressure height being 5,000 feet and the ship about a ton heavy.

Pritchard also called attention to the specially lightened structure of R 38 and the danger of overstressing her aerodynamically in high-speed flight at low altitude in dense air:

It should be clearly recognized that when R 38 was designed, she was lightened in every way to provide the very greatest performance which the British rigid airship design staff could achieve at the time of her design, and it therefore must be recognized that the factors of safety have been cut down in many directions. . . . the height at which it is the practice in Germany to carry out flight trials is also most significant, as in that country they have had plenty of experience with high performance airships, which they fly during the early trials at a height of from 2000 to 3000 meters (approximately 7000 to 10,000 feet).[23]

Unfortunately, Maitland did not heed the advice about maneuvering trials being made at higher altitudes.

In America, Admiral Taylor on 15 August endorsed Maxfield's optimistic report of 20 July to Admiral Twining: "Until further detailed information regarding this failure has been received it is not possible to form an intelligent opinion as to its cause. Pending receipt of such information it is believed that the ship should not attempt to make a trans-Atlantic flight until sufficient trials have been completed to demonstrate her airworthiness."[24] Even more explicit were the opinions of Admiral Griffin, the chief of the Bureau of Steam Engineering, who almost certainly

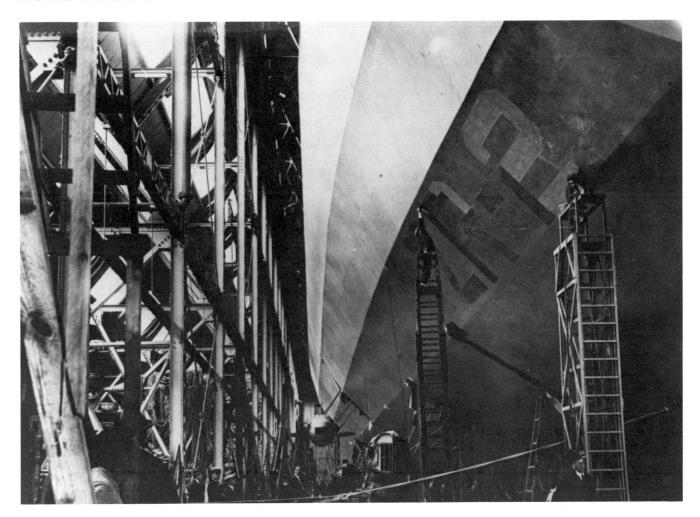

ZR 2 in the Howden shed, July 1921. While repairs were being made on the girders damaged on the third flight on 18 July, American crew members painted in the "ZR 2" letters blocked out on the cover underneath the bows. (National Archives)

had seen a letter from Commander Bieg with a sketch of the girder failures, and the opinion that "all failed in compression."[25] Griffin felt that on the basis of information at hand, the ship had not had adequate trials:

> A single satisfactory trial represents a too slender knowledge of the ZR 2's ability satisfactorily to negotiate a transatlantic voyage. In this connection it should be noted that the contemplated voyage to the United States constitutes a demand on the ship for a performance probably little, if any, less rigorous than any service the ship is likely to be called upon to perform during the remainder of its service life. . . . In the case of the ZR 2, attention is invited to the fact that the ship is of unique design, of a type whose history is not very extensive, and that knowledge of the hazards, practices, and technique of the voyage which she is to attempt are based upon history and experience of no great extent.[26]

In addition, Griffin was aware that, owing to the British economy drive, the ship might be sent across

the Atlantic with hydrogen of such low purity that her useful lift would be seriously degraded.

At the Bureau of Construction and Repair, Burgess was uneasy and alarmed. He was convinced that the midships longitudinals in the lower part of the hull, which in any case were under compression because R 38 usually flew in a hogged condition, had buckled under dynamic stress. Burgess had never liked the circumferential gas bag wiring of R 38, which ran around the ship from the bottom keel girder (G girder) on one side to the G girder on the other; for unlike the diagonal large mesh wire and fine mesh ramie cord gas cell netting in the Zeppelins, the circumferential wiring did not resist shear and bending loads. "In view of the undesirable system of wiring in the ZR 2 and the weaknesses disclosed in the early trials it is recommended that she not be allowed to attempt to cross the ocean until proof of adequate strength has been given by prolonged trials." To this, Starr Truscott had added some comments: "The criticism herein is justified. We have differed from the British on the matter of net wiring from the beginning. I think there can be no doubt that it adds very perceptibly to the strength when arranged as in the Zeps. There remains the fact that the longitudinals in R 38 are no larger than in R 33. In other words the limit of lightness may have been exceeded." Truscott felt that the adverse endorsements by Admirals Griffin and Taylor would ensure that ZR 2 be properly tested even if it meant keeping her in England until the spring of 1922. Later he changed his mind: "We must accept ship as per British practice, i.e., if acceptable to Air Ministry it must be to us. Question of starting flight is up to people in England."[27]

Already plans were going ahead for the reception of ZR 2 in America. As early as 20 October 1920, a board of five officers had been set up to plan for her arrival, with Weyerbacher as senior member and Lansdowne and Kraus as members. In a report of 18 March 1921, to the secretary of the navy, the board anticipated the ship's arrival about 17 July; noted that Maxfield had advised he would send an officer and two enlisted men on 21 June for duty to advise and train the landing party; and wanted the number increased to three officers and six enlisted men.[28] The board, after inspecting Lakehurst and Cape May, recommended the former as more suitable. Early in May, Weyerbacher realized that Lakehurst would not be sufficiently complete to receive ZR 2 by 17 July; but it was also apparent that the ship would not be ready for the crossing until early August at the earliest.

Other plans were set in motion from Washington. The chief of naval operations on 30 June advised the commander in chief of the Atlantic Fleet to be ready to assign vessels with suitable equipment for taking radio bearings to five stations along ZR 2's flight path, and indicated that the flight might be expected about 15 August. Eventually, the battleship *Utah*, already in European waters, was selected for Station A, the most easterly; and the oiler *Brazos* with a destroyer for Station B; with the battleships *Ohio* at Station C, *Wyoming* at Station D, and *Arkansas* at Station E.

Maxfield, looking forward to the flight to America, was a busy man. In response to a request from the Bureau of Navigation on 20 June for a crew list, he forwarded on 12 July the names of 9 officers including himself; 10 riggers; 16 mechanics; and 2 radio men for a total of 37. He was under great pressure to carry passengers, though as Bieg remarked, "I believe that violent opposition will be encountered from Maxfield in regard to taking these people to the States, as indications at the present moment tend to show that the lift available for petrol is not all that might be desired."[29] On 7 June, the chief of naval operations advised the Bureau of Navigation that the British Air Ministry had been invited to send two officers as observers, while the U.S. Army would send one

officer. The Air Ministry's two observers would have been Pritchard and Campbell, while the Army's Major P. E. Van Nostrand arrived in England before ZR 2 made her last flight. On 21 June 1921 the Bureau of Navigation directed Lt. Clifford A. Tinker USNRF to proceed to Howden for temporary duty as officer in charge of publicity in connection with the ZR 2 trials, and to make the journey to America in the ship (here one sees the hand of Admiral Moffett, who on 3 January 1921 had succeeded Craven as director of naval aviation, and on 10 August became the first chief of the new Bureau of Aeronautics). Commander Richard E. Byrd, the future polar explorer, had used his influence with Moffett to get himself assigned to the flight as air navigation expert and reported to Howden on 22 August to the displeasure of Maxfield, who wired Washington requesting that the passenger list be kept at four persons. Last, Captain Frederick E. Guest, who in February 1921 had succeeded Winston Churchill as the British secretary of state for air, requested on 12 August permission to make the transatlantic flight provided ZR 2 left by 24 August. The naval attaché in London, Admiral Twining, felt that Guest's importance justified making Maxfield leave a crew member behind in his place; but it was also clear that the flight could not commence before 24 August. Probably only Pritchard, Campbell, Tinker, and Van Nostrand would have been carried if the flight had been made.

Last-minute preparations were to include installing more 190-imperial-gallon fuel tanks, reducing weights, stationing guards to prevent unauthorized articles from being carried on board, having crew members assemble clothing for weighing and stowing, and organizing charts, books, and instruments. Just before the last flight Maxfield received from Henry May at Bedford a lengthy memorandum, with charts and diagrams, advising him to carry disposable loads (fuel, ballast, and personnel) in such a way as not to overload the very light "height-climber" framework:

> All disposable weights in the corridor should be situated as near the main frames as possible. No heavy weights should be placed between the adjacent intermediate frames. . . . Weights in the crew spaces should be kept as low as possible; not more than 15 persons should be allowed in the crew space at any time. . . . not more than seven persons should be allowed in the control car space at any time. . . . Under normal conditions not more than four persons should be allowed abaft Frame 13, and not more than two abaft Frame 15. . . . Not more than two persons should be allowed on any five meter length of the corridor walking way girder at the same time.[30]

Maxfield also had to worry about the permeability of ZR 2's gas cells and resulting contamination with air. For the Atlantic flight he expected a mean purity of only 93%; he would try to raise this to 96% just before the flight, presumably by purging the cells with fresh hydrogen; but the purity of the hydrogen manufactured at Howden was no better than 97%. "Fully realize that every point lost in purity means less fuel that can be taken aboard."[31]

Maxfield also thought he had to deal with a conspiracy by the British to prevent him from commanding ZR 2 on the transatlantic flight. After a meeting on 20 August with Pritchard and Maitland, he radioed via the USS *Utah* to Moffett: "The former officer appears to be the Air Ministry official mouthpiece. From statements and appearances at today's conference will force efforts on part of Air Ministry to delay turning over of ZR 2 to United States Navy until such time as offer to fly ship to United States with Royal Air Force personnel and under Royal Air Force command will meet with some possibility of acceptance by United States Navy."[32] There is no other record of this conference, and four days later Pritchard, Maitland, and Maxfield were dead. Probably the two Britishers urged Maxfield privately to delay the Atlantic flight in favor of more trials, and to take some experienced Royal Air Force airship personnel on the journey to America. What is clear is that Maxfield successfully demanded that the ship be turned over to him immediately after the next flight, to start to America as soon as possible thereafter.

On the contrary, at a conference at the Air Ministry on 10 August at which Tinker was the only American present, the chief of the Air Staff, Air Marshal Trenchard, and the director general of Supply and Research, Air Vice Marshal Ellington, had made the helpful suggestion that ZR 2 be flown to Pulham where the trials program could be expedited by the use of the mooring mast there. R 33 was still on the mast carrying out mooring tests, but would be taken off the mast (she in fact was flown to Bedford, deflated, and hung up in the berth vacated by R 38). After three or four days for adjustments to the mast, R 38 could either moor to the mast, or she could be berthed in one of the Pulham sheds measuring 712 feet long and 150 feet wide. At the end of the conference, Trenchard made "very confidentially" the following offer: "In addition to Mr. Campbell and Lieut. Pritchard, who are to take passage on the ZR 2, the Air Ministry will loan, if the United States should desire it, Pilots Thomas (captain of R 33) or Wann to act as advisors during the flight."[33] Far from wishing to take over R 38 for the transatlantic flight with British personnel, Trenchard was delicately suggesting the Air Ministry's concern that Maxfield and his men were too inexperienced to manage the crossing themselves. The final result of Trenchard's well-meaning offer was to engender in the harassed Maxfield an unjustified mistrust and suspicion of his British colleagues, and particularly of Pritchard, the only

man who realized the limitations of the lightly built "height-climber."

Although the original plan was for the Americans to make two familiarization flights after the turnover, Maxfield on 6 August argued that owing to various delays these flights should be omitted and the transatlantic flight made as soon as possible. But even Maxfield had to concede the need for a further trial flight before the ship could be handed over to the Americans at Pulham. Maitland's notes show his intention on the next flight to "test ship up to full speed provided nothing prevents this being done and then proceed to fly her through varying conditions of bumpy air at fast cruising speed, i.e. all engines 1800 revs. (full speed being 2000 revs.) Flight should last 10 hours to 20 hours."[34] But now, with the ship ready for trials on 3 August, the good weather broke. Day after day Maxfield had to cable home that the weather was unsuitable for the final trial flight; or if it appeared favorable during the evening, there would be a change for the worse by morning. Meanwhile the warships that were to man the ocean stations were idle in port. The delay made the Americans restless; as Bieg wrote on 21 August, "we are all packed up ready to decamp en masse for Pulham and are now living in suitcases and patiently waiting for some definite move." The three-week delay with little to occupy the men's minds was bad for morale—the more introspective brooded about the structural failures on the third flight, and whether the ship was really airworthy. Byrd, who had arrived in Howden on the evening of 22 August, tells of the anxieties of his friend Coil and adds: "strange to say the same spirit of apprehension pervaded the entire camp. Maxfield's face was drawn with strain, as were those of the other officers. The men were unusually quiet. There was little or no talk about the ship herself."[35]

At 0710 on 23 August, R 38 lifted off at Howden on what was to be her fourth and last flight. On board were the British crew, consisting of 6 officers and 19 men; 2 officer passengers, Maitland and Pritchard; 3 civilian passengers from the National Physical Laboratory, John Robert Pannell, Harry Bateman, and Cecil Duffield; Charles Ivor Rae Campbell and an assistant from the Royal Airship Works; and 6 American officers, including Maxfield, Coil, and Bieg, and 11 American enlisted men.[36] It was intended to carry out a considerable program of tests, and to land at the Pulham mast about 1800.

One American not making the flight was ACR James H. Collier, and he was worried. In the hangar, and while R 38 was being prepared for flight, he had taken the gas purity of all the cells and found several of them low, indicating a dangerously explosive mixture of air and hydrogen.[37] Some of the figures would have been quite unacceptable in German practice, but presumably there had been no purification of the

Marked for death: As ZR 2 is brought out of the Howden shed for her last flight, on 23 August 1921, CMM J. T. Hancock, on the ladder, and CMM L. E. Crowl (in window to the left), manning engine car No. 2, smile for the camera. Neither man survived the disaster the next day. Ground crew is Royal Air Force. (Norman O. Walker)

cells by purging them with fresh hydrogen because of the gas shortage.

During the morning, fuel consumption tests were made at various speeds, as well as controllability tests, with turns being made by Mr. Pannell, the head of the National Physical Laboratory team, at the helm. Pressure readings were taken with the manometer equipment on the fins, rudders, and elevators, and recorded photographically. The program lasted 40 minutes and was flown at a speed of about 44 knots with the after four engines running at 1600 rpm. Further pressure readings were taken during the morning, together with fuel consumption tests. In the afternoon, turning-circle tests were flown with 5 de-

grees of rudder, and at one time, 10 degrees. After tea, the NPL team made measurements of the air flow close to the giant hull by lowering an anemometer on a cable through the drogue hatch at Frame 2, alongside the ladder to the midships engine car at Frame 7, and at the machine gun position underneath Frame 10b. The measured velocity increased with the distance of the anemometer from the hull—an early demonstration of the boundary layer phenomenon. There were still more tests to make, and it was getting late. Flying at 700 feet in low cloud over Norfolk, the officers were unable to locate Pulham, and since the weather was fine, it was decided to stay in the air overnight and continue the trials the next day.

Further engine trials and fuel consumption tests were run the next morning, but as the low cloud persisted, Pritchard delayed the speed trials—the ship might be damaged, and he did not want to have to look for the airship base and have to land with the prevailing low ceiling. R 38 was approaching the Yorkshire coast, navigating on radio bearings from the station on Flamborough Head. The clouds were breaking up and the ceiling was rising; at about 1600, R 38 descended from 3,000 to 1,000 feet, sighted the Humber, and as the ship flew over Howden, Flight Lieutenant Little signaled with a flashing lamp that she would run speed tests and land about 1830. For the full-speed trials, R 38 ascended above the clouds to 3,700 feet, and the crew, on orders from Flight Lieutenant Little, distributed themselves around the ship to look for signs of damage.[38] Bateman went into the tail to photograph manometer readings, but as engine speeds were increased, Campbell asked him to come forward, fearing that Bateman might be injured if the fins failed (obviously Campbell was not thinking of a major structural failure). With all six engines opened out to 2000 rpm, a speed of 62 knots was achieved and maintained for ten minutes before

Last flight: ZR 2 rising statically at Howden for her fourth and last flight, at 0710 on 23 August 1921. Of 49 persons on board, only five survived the disaster the next afternoon over Hull. (J. H. Collier)

power was reduced. The ship handled well, it was clear that the elevators were no longer overbalanced, and Campbell, coming aft with Maitland, described himself as very pleased with the full-speed trial and with the steadiness of the tail structure.

Thinking that this was the end of the tests, Bateman walked forward through the keel, only to meet Pritchard and to learn that there was to be a further test involving rapid movements of the rudders, and that further photographs were desired. It was shortly after 1700, R 38 was now at 2,500 feet over Hull, and the air speed had been reduced to about 54.5 knots. What happened next is a matter of dispute between two of the five survivors of the disaster that followed: Wann, who was in the control car with Maitland, Pritchard, Thomas, Pannell, Maxfield, and Flight Lieutenant Little, asserted later that he did not order the rudders put over more than 15 degrees by the helm indicator (25 degrees was the maximum travel), and that with stretching of the control cables, he did not believe that the rudder travel was more than 10 degrees, while the rudders, even when moved from side to side, were briefly centered before being turned farther.[39] Bateman, however, who was in the lower fin at Frame 15 taking photographs, testified later that the rudders at the end of the 10-minute turning test "were being moved from hard over to hard over—a range of 50 degrees altogether," while "the movement of the controls was faster than under normal conditions." As for the elevators, "the movement . . . was greater than I would expect under the circumstances, and my impression was that an elevator test was being carried out at the same time." Bateman regarded the maneuvers as "a very severe test."[40]

R 38 was now directly over Hull, and large crowds had gathered on the banks of the Humber and elsewhere, enthralled by the beautiful sight of the huge silvery craft, her engines thundering, moving in and out of the clouds close overhead. Some of the spectators, who were members of the Howden Detachment living in the town, knew the ship well. What followed is generally agreed to by practically all the witnesses who gave testimony at the subsequent inquiry: The airship, on a southeast heading, turned sharply to the southwest, and the spectators were horrified to note a deepening diagonal wrinkle developing in the smooth outer cover on the starboard side, immediately abaft the rearmost pair of engine gondolas. The nose and tail went down, the hull opened up at the top, and the ship broke in two. The forward part fell rapidly, fire and smoke streaming from the ragged break at the rear. There was a thunderous explosion, heard 15 miles away at Grimsby, with a second violent blast occurring as the fore part struck the water. The shattered wreckage of the forward part then sank, leaving a huge pool of burning gasoline on

the surface of the river. At the point of rupture, the electrical cable and two petrol mains running the length of the keel were adjacent to each other beneath the walkway, and sparks probably ignited the fuel;[41] but the severe explosions surely involved some of the gas cells, which were filled with an impure mixture of air and hydrogen. Windows were shattered over a two-mile radius in Hull, and one woman died of shock. Had the tons of wreckage fallen in town instead of in the river, the destruction and loss of life would have been appalling. The broken tail portion did not catch fire and fell more slowly, alighting on a sand bar in four or five feet of water. All witnesses agreed that several parachutes were seen descending.[42]

Of the 49 souls on board R 38, only five survived, four of them in the relatively undamaged tail section. Bateman, busy with his cameras and manometers, was surprised to hear loud crashing noises forward and out of sight. He lost his balance as the tail drooped downward through 20 degrees, scattering his notebook, watch, and instruments in all directions. Realizing that the airship was going down, he resolved to jump with the parachute in the tail cockpit. Unlike today's free-fall seat or back-pack parachute, this was a clumsy affair enclosed in a fabric casing, from which it was drawn by the weight of the falling jumper. Bateman attached the 'chute to a harness he was wearing and went over the side, but in his haste snagged some of the shroud lines on a hook in the cockpit and dangled a yard below the rim, unable to climb back. As the tail fell, Bateman looked down on a scene of destruction—fuel burning on the water, floating gasoline tanks, pieces of fabric falling through the air, and 600 feet up on the port side, two parachutes tangled, one open and one unopened, with two men underneath.

Corporal Potter, Bateman's assistant, on hearing a crashing of girders forward, climbed down the ladder from the gun pit to run forward to his parachute station but found his way blocked by a tangle of girders at Frame 13, at the leading edge of the lower fin. Only then did he realize that R 38 had broken in two. Running back to the gun pit, he tried in vain to pull Bateman back up to the cockpit. ACR Norman Walker, who had gotten up from his bunk in the keel to enjoy the view from the tail gun pit, was in the lower fin at the time of the breakup. Just before the tail hit the water, he ran into the gun pit, jumped overboard, and found himself standing on a sand bar. Potter and Bateman climbed down to join him.

Lance Corporal Davies had the narrowest escape of all. At the time of the breakup he was going forward in the keel, and passing the gun pit beneath Frame 10b, he recognized two British airmen, who did not survive. Davies was between intermediate Frame 10a and main frame 10 when the girders collapsed "a yard" in front of him: "There was hardly any warning, only a slight shudder and creaking of girders. The ship buckled up under my feet and the stern and bows came down."[43] A few feet ahead of him, Davies saw Lcdr. Coil "stagger where he was standing," though he did not fall out of the ship. Within two seconds the forward portion, trailing smoke, was 200 feet away. The first explosion shook the tail fragment considerably; the second followed four to five seconds later. Within half a minute the forward part of the tail structure plunged beneath the river, and Davies, "swamped" in gasoline, had to fight his way clear of broken girders and swim to the surface.

Small craft put off from the Hull wharves. On board one of the first was ACMM Charles H. Broom of the Howden Detachment, who had seen R 38 breaking in two and had taken a taxi to the docks. Proceeding in a tugboat to the rear section, Broom took a small boat to the wreck, climbed on board through the rear gun pit, and made his way forward between the gas cells (the aftermost three were still full of hydrogen) and the outer cover. He found Lt. Montagu's body at Frame 12 and passed it out to the crew of the small boat, then had to jump clear as the entire stern section, pushed by the incoming tide, slowly rolled over. Meanwhile the tug had rescued Bateman, Walker, Potter, and Davies.

Other craft approached the forward section and picked up Flight Lieutenant Wann and the American Lt. Charles G. Little alive in the water, but Little died almost immediately. Wann, suffering shock and burns, only dimly remembered the breakup, the explosion, and diving out the control car window as the wreckage neared the water.[44] Presently, the boats recovered the body of Lt. Esterly, the American radio officer, but no other survivors were found, and indeed, there could be no hope of more, considering the circumstances of the disaster.

Early in the evening a telegram from Pennoyer to the American attaché's office in London reported the ship a total wreck as a result of an explosion over Hull, with Walker apparently the only survivor of the 17 Americans on board. At 1900 there was a meeting in the office of the acting attaché at which it was decided to send Byrd, who had been passing through London by train en route to Pulham, and Lcdr. White, to Hull to take charge of the salvage operations. Pennoyer, the senior surviving officer of the Howden Detachment, was named acting commanding officer at Howden.

Arriving in Hull at 0800 on the 25th, Byrd and White did their best to get salvage operations started, but were handicapped by lack of proper equipment and by the "ugly" tide in the river, which rose and fell 20 feet and flowed as fast as 5 knots, carrying quanti-

ties of sand which rapidly silted up the wreckage. Dragging operations located the forward section at midnight. Meanwhile the shipping community of Hull, led by Commander Regan RNR, the Admiralty representative, had brought forward a 90-ton floating crane and four tugs, and during the next few days portions of the wreckage were brought to the surface and carried ashore. Air Commodore Brooke-Popham arrived about noon on the 25th to act on behalf of the British Air Ministry, being relieved the next day by Air Vice Marshal A. V. Vyvyan commanding Coastal Area. The Americans were unfavorably impressed when Vyvyan announced that no work would be done on Sunday; he reversed his decison in the face of their insistent protests. Some bodies were recovered enmeshed in the wreckage; others washed ashore. Aller, the American chief rigger, Campbell, and Maitland were found in the remains of the control car, Maitland with his hands on the ballast releases, trying to the end to save the ship. Bieg's body was found in the keel abaft the control car. Maxfield's body was recovered at Hessel, three and a half miles upstream from the wreck, on the 31st, and the last American, CMM Julius, was found in the river on 3 September. Six of the British bodies still had not been found on 19 September: Pritchard; Flight Lieutenant Thomas, the captain of R 33 who was on board R 38 as mooring officer; and four enlisted men.

At noon on 31 August a deeply moving memorial service was held in the parish church at Howden. Three hundred eighty British and thirteen American airmen joined in singing "For All The Saints Who From Their Labours Rest," and the benediction was followed by the bugle call of the Last Post. On 6 September a funeral procession of British and American officers and men escorted the bodies of 15 of the American dead to the railway station at Howden.[45] Lieutenant Null accompanied the bodies on the train to Plymouth, where they arrived the next day and were carried on board the light cruiser HMS *Dauntless* for transportation to the United States, with Lts. Null and Tinker on board. Also on 7 September, an impressive joint memorial service was held at Westminster Abbey, attended by British and American notables including Air Marshal Trenchard, representing H.M. King George V; Ambassador Harvey; Rear Admiral Twining, the naval attaché in London; personnel of the Howden Detachment; and Admiral Niblack and a party of officers and men from his flagship, the USS *Utah*. The *Dauntless* was met off New York Harbor on 16 September by a division of destroyers and six big F5L flying boats of the Atlantic Fleet Air Force and escorted to the Brooklyn Navy Yard. Her sad cargo was offloaded, and after military funeral ceremonies, the bodies of the dead of the Howden Detachment were dispatched to their homes. Maxfield, Bieg, and ACMM Welch were buried at the National Cemetery in Arlington, Virginia. Coil, in accordance with an oft-expressed wish, was buried at sea from the destroyer USS *Breck*.

On 5 September, Pennoyer in Howden received orders from the staff representative in London to complete demobilization of what was left of the Howden Detachment by 20 September. By 16 September, all material had been loaded on board the oiler USS *Trinity* at Gravesend, including flying clothing and mess gear for ZR 2, the effects of the dead, and a set of blueprints for the airship. The *Trinity* sailed for New York on 12 October, being directed to transfer the aviation personnel of the Howden Detachment on board to the Naval Air Station, Lakehurst, on arrival in the United States. The chapter on ZR 2 and the Howden Detachment was closed; that on ZR 1 and Lakehurst was about to open.

Many questions remained to be answered concerning ZR 2, particularly the reasons for the disaster, which had taken 44 lives in the worst aviation tragedy in history. As early as 27 August a Court of Inquiry assembled at Howden "to enquire into the circumstances occasioning the loss of HMA R 38 on August 24, 1921, and to express an opinion as to possible causes of the loss."[46] Air Vice Marshal Sir John Salmond served as president of the court, which was composed of six Royal Air Force officers, of whom Wing Commander T. R. Cave-Browne-Cave was an expert on airship engines, and Squadron Leader N. B. B. Colmore had had extensive experience with airship operations.

The court heard a great many witnesses, including all the survivors of the crash except Captain Wann, who was too ill to testify; took evidence from many persons in Hull who were watching R 38 as she broke in two; and attempted to determine the views and opinions of Maitland, Campbell, and Pritchard, who could not testify in their own behalf. The transcript of testimony and the 63 appendices provide a mass of information on the R 38, her background, design, construction, and operation; but the court, possibly for reasons of state, merely attempted to assemble a narrative of events without offering opinions as to causes. Some of the evidence, however, was very disturbing to the Americans, particularly concerning British procedures, and influenced later American naval policy in airship procurement.

At the request of the president of the court, the secretary of the admiralty was asked to search the archives to determine if the Board of Admiralty had ever approved the design of R 38, a standard requirement in warship procurement that went back more than a hundred years. No trace of board approval could be found, though the witness lamely suggested

that "Mr. Green [the former secretary of the board] and Mr. Campbell might have obtained the *verbal* approval of the design from the Controller of the Navy at the time."[47] Thus, Campbell's design had not been examined and checked by the authority designated by the Crown. Nor was his work independently checked: the official inspection organization at Bedford, headed by Mr. Payne of the Royal Corps of Naval Constructors, actually participated in the work done, Payne being responsible for executing the modifications to R 38 at Howden after the third flight. Further, it was revealed that Campbell had his own personal and unofficial inspector, a Mr. J. Uren, who reported directly to him. Already the Americans saw Campbell, through flaws in the organization, proceeding with no supervision by responsible authority, with no independent checks on his work, and without support from competent subordinates in executing his lonely and burdensome task. Further, they were beginning to question his competence: the opinion was forming both in Washington and at Howden that Campbell was at fault for creating a ship incapable of resisting legitimate aerodynamic loads. Byrd, for instance, in a lengthy letter to Moffett from Hull on 27 August, wrote: "my own private opinion is that the disaster was caused by buckling from a sharp turn. It was well known that the ship was structurally weak along the 8th, 9th and 10th girders."[48]

Since the Court of Inquiry had not offered any technical opinions on the disaster, the director general of Supply and Research of the Royal Air Force, Sir Edward Ellington, requested the Accidents Investigation Sub-Committee of the Aeronautical Research Committee to carry out an investigation of the technical aspects. The committee was independent of the official establishment; its 11 members included in Professor Leonard Bairstow, Dr. A. J. Sutton Pippard, Sir J. E. Petaval, and Sir Richard Glazebrook the leading aerodynamic and structures experts in the United Kingdom,[49] as well as Major G. H. Scott, the leading airship operational expert in England, while the Bureau of Aeronautics assigned Commander Dyer and Charles P. Burgess to attend. Its report, published in March 1922, was a strong indictment of Campbell and of the design procedures in the case of R 38, and confirmed the Americans in their belief that she was structurally weak.

The committee traced the design history of R 38, and emphasized the lack of theoretical information in Britain on aerodynamic stresses and loadings. But while it noted that R 38 was designed for high-altitude operations, and even conceded that "the terms of the requirements laid down in time of war were drastic and imposed a severe task on the designers,"[50] it did not sufficiently emphasize that the alleged weakness in R 38's structure resulted from the requirement that she be built as light as possible to attain 22,000 feet with war load. It was properly critical of the fact that after the Armistice, when extreme high-altitude performance was no longer essential, the structure was not reinforced—the amount of material necessary to double the strength of the longitudinal girders, for instance, would have weighed less than four tons, with a sacrifice in ceiling of about 2,800 feet. Some calculations made for the committee by Professor Bairstow were shocking: assuming that R 38 was flying nose up at a 10-degree angle at 54 knots (an extreme case) with the elevators set at the corresponding down angle, as she might have done if flying heavy with dynamic lift, the bending moment would have been nearly enough to cause structural failure (i.e., the factor of safety would not have been 4, as Campbell thought, but only about 1). Turbulence, of course, could have increased the bending moment and caused structural failure. At the same time, the committee found that L 71, the last German naval "height-climber" Zeppelin, was weaker structurally than R 38, but considered that the former had not failed structurally because her control surfaces were not overbalanced and the controls in the Zeppelin would not permit rapid movements of the rudders and elevators.[51] In general, it may be said that there was a lack of awareness of German practice in flying the 1917 and 1918 "height-climbers" at high speed only in the thin air of high altitude, and handling them cautiously near sea level. It is true that even in 1921, the British had little information about German practice; but Pritchard was an exception, and his warnings had gone unheeded. In considering the girder failures during the third flight, the committee rejected Campbell's opinion of slipstream damage, and held that "the buckling then reported was significant as being the first indication of the existence of dangerous stresses and that the action of the late Flight Lieut. Pritchard who steadied the ship and relieved these before the failure spread, thus saved the ship." The committee remarked on the pressure manometer readings taken during the last part of the fourth flight, one of the cameras recording rudder pressures having survived, and declared that "during the last half hour of flight, there was at least one occasion when the rudder was moved fairly rapidly through an angle, the magnitude of which, as far as it affected the bending moment on the ship, was equivalent in straight flight to about 20° from the amidships position." However, "the movements of the controls were not in excess of those which might be required in the ordinary navigation of the ship."[52] The committee concluded that: "the accident must be ascribed either to inadequate strength of the ship or to stresses produced by an undue use of the controls. Since the Committee

are of opinion that the use of the controls was legitimate, they are forced to the conclusion that the structure possessed inadequate strength."[53]

In the light of my knowledge of German practice, I (DHR) must disagree with the findings of the committee. Because the ship's strength was marginal, the use of the controls was *not* legitimate, and therefore the immediate cause of the disaster was the misuse of the controls to produce violent changes of direction at high speed and at low altitude in dense air. Campbell had in fact succeeded in creating a light-weight, high-altitude craft to the Admiralty specifications which equaled if it did not surpass the performance of L 70, the latest product of Friedrichshafen which had inspired many of R 38's features. It was not his fault that she could not simultaneously satisfy the requirement for cooperation with the Grand Fleet at low altitude in turbulent 30- to 40-mph winds. The two requirements were irreconcilable, and the ship should never have been put through high-speed maneuvers at low altitude.

It therefore becomes necessary to determine who ordered the high-speed turns, and why. I have been unable to find the full schedule of planned trials to which Pritchard referred in his note to Maitland of 20 July 1921. Bateman at the Court of Inquiry testified that maneuvering tests with the rudder hard over in one direction, and then swung hard over in the opposite direction, were "in the preliminary program for R 38."[54] He did not believe that any definite scheme was laid down for rudder and elevator tests in R 38. In 1973 Sir Victor Goddard, who was acquainted with most of the important figures in the R 38 disaster, and who at the time was at Pulham as first officer of R 36, pointed out to me that it was an Admiralty requirement that all warships carry out turns under full helm at high speed during their trials, and the same was expected of airships. Wann, Pritchard, and others who knew the hazards of overstressing the lightly built hull protested in vain, Wann being told that if he refused to carry out the turning tests, he would be superseded by someone who would. Certainly such full-helm turning tests were carried out during R 32's trials. On the other hand, there is no evidence that anyone senior to Maitland was dictating to him how to carry out the R 38 trials, and the Air Ministry, not the Admiralty, was by then controlling the airships. Certainly Maitland was determined to prove in every way that the Americans were getting a sound ship, and the turning tests appear to have been part of his program. Why he refused to take Pritchard's advice—at the cost of his life—is obscure. Possibly it was the traditional contempt of the "practical man" for the "boffin."[55] Campbell, as I suggested above, was psychologically incapable of believing that his masterpiece was flawed, and for his unjustified faith he too paid with his life. If any individual was responsible for the high-speed turns causing the disaster, it would have to have been Maitland.

By now, with the report of the Accidents Investigation Sub-Committee confirming the Americans' worst fears about R 38, they had developed a permanent distrust of British designs and methods. In March 1922 the Air Ministry, at Scott's instigation, suggested that R 36, then about to be handed over to the Disposal Board, be given to the United States in lieu of R 38 spare parts with a book value of £15,000. The United States would have to bear the £30,000 expense of repairs to R 36, inflation, labor, and upkeep of Pulham after 31 March, and all risks of the transoceanic flight. The Air Ministry would not approve R 36 being flown across the Atlantic by an American crew, and Scott was to be the commander. Within three days of the forwarding of this offer by Admiral Twining's office, the Bureau of Aeronautics had politely declined, with the Air Service of the War Department following suit two days later. A further offer whereby Scott would form a commercial company to deliver R 36 to the United States for a lump sum apparently annoyed Moffett: "Navy Department not repeat not interested in purchase of R 36."[56]

The last official contact with the British Government over R 38 was a settlement of accounts. At the time of the disaster, three fourths of the $2,000,000 contract price had been paid, with the final payment of $500,000 being due on acceptance of the ship. Inasmuch as the agreement between the two governments provided that in the event of the ship's being lost before delivery, the cost would be shared equally, the Navy felt entitled to a refund. The attaché in London therefore presented a claim for $500,000 on 28 September. At the same time the Navy Department indicated it would prefer a cash payment instead of spares. On 14 March 1922 the British Treasury paid $500,000 for the wreck of the ship, and on 8 April $39,363 on account of uncompleted spares. The Navy, however, received $50,166 worth of spares shipped to the Naval Aircraft Factory, plus spare parts, goldbeater's skin and cotton fabric held in England on the Navy's account to the value of $26,373, leaving a net loss on R 38 and spares of $884,098. Together with the cost of training naval personnel—$98,069—the "total loss to Navy on ZR 2" as of 20 June 1922 was $982,167.[57]

There is some evidence in the archives as to what might have been done with ZR 2 after her arrival in Lakehurst. A memorandum from Commander Kenneth Whiting of the Plans Division to Moffett, while ZR 2 was flying her trials, looked forward to the year 1923 when both she and ZR 1 would be operating, the former from Lakehurst and the latter on the West Coast. Although they would be used particularly for long-range scouting at sea, they would also cruise over the continental United States "in order that an idea may be obtained as to the cost of airships operated by commercial concerns"[58]—and of course to stimulate public interest in the Navy's rigid airship program. Portable mooring masts at Puget Sound, San Diego, Pearl Harbor, Guam, and in the Philippines would facilitate these cruises, and it was hoped that municipalities would erect mooring masts at their own expense.[59]

The flying program outlined here for ZR 2 would have involved loading her with fuel for long range and endurance, flying her at low altitude to avoid valving hydrogen and losing lift, and probably operating her at 50 knots with four engines running at 1800 rpm, which was the "fast cruise" setting. For this type of operation she was not suited, being designed to attain high altitude with a large amount of water ballast and a small amount of fuel on takeoff. Ironically, considering all the sacrifices made to give her a ceiling of 22,000 feet, ZR 2 never made an altitude trial, and in her total flying time of 57 hours 35 minutes, she never appears to have exceeded the 3,700 feet at which she ran the speed trials just before she was lost. Had she been flown over the continental United States as planned, she would surely have broken up in turbulence at low altitude at an early date, taking with her a far larger number of Americans than died with her over Hull. The U.S. Navy would have done better to purchase a sister of the old R 34, as Maxfield had advised in 1919, in which the sturdy hull structure of Dr. Arnstein's original masterpiece, L 30, had been copied without alteration.

The U.S. Navy learned a great deal from the mistakes made in the ZR 2 program. The ship had been accepted on faith as the product of superior design knowledge and technology; the disaster had proved that the forebodings of Hunsaker, Burgess, and Truscott were justified, and henceforth the Americans placed full trust and confidence in their own experts. The purchasers had had no say in the original design, and no control over construction methods and procedures; in the future the U.S. Navy would lay down its own specifications, and ensure that they be met by the private contractors of its choice. Moffett was not about to deal with foreign governments for expensive craft not built to his requirements, whose design history he was not familiar with, regardless of giveaway prices. At the time the British were trying to sell R 36 to the Americans, the Bureau of Aeronautics was negotiating directly with the *Luftschiffbau Zeppelin* of Friedrichshafen for the construction to its specifications of the rigid airship that would become the ZR 3 *Los Angeles*. Henceforth the foreign influence in American airship design and operations would be German.

6

ZR 1: Creating A New Industry

The 1920 naval appropriations bill, passed by Congress on 11 July 1919, had allocated $4,000,000 for procurement of two rigid airships: $2,500,000 for the purchase of one rigid airship abroad, and $1,500,000 for construction of a rigid airship in the United States. The former appropriation was designed to obtain as promptly as possible—hopefully, as early as 1920—an up-to-date craft with which the U.S. Navy could begin immediately to train personnel and to gain operational experience. In the latter case, the Navy Department was planning for the future: to create an American airship-building industry, not only to provide long-range aerial scouts for the fleet, but to build commercial transoceanic craft to carry the American flag in the wake of the successful British R 34. This involved the development of native American designs, construction facilities, and the creation of several ancillary industries—for the production of duralumin, the light aluminum alloy that was the accepted material in both Germany and England for fabricating rigid airship hulls; for the manufacture of gas cells consisting of cotton fabric made gas-tight with goldbeater's skin, an intestinal membrane of cattle; and for the extraction in quantity of helium gas, the nonflammable lifting medium with 93% of the sustaining capacity of hydrogen, which was found only in the United States.

On 28 July 1919 Admiral Taylor, the chief of the Bureau of Construction and Repair, and Admiral Griffin, the chief of the Bureau of Steam Engineering, addressed a joint letter to Secretary Daniels:

> It is believed that a rigid airship can be constructed within the appropriation barring unforseen difficulties and accidents. The Bureaus have obtained

from abroad plans of the German Zeppelins L 33 and L 49, and have accumulated information regarding other German airships. In addition, the Bureaus have plans of the British rigid airship R 34, which is substantially similar, except in power plant arrangement, to the German airship L 33. Airships L 33, L 49, and R 34 are of 2,000,000 cubic feet displacement and while the Germans have constructed three ships of greater displacement, information regarding them is very incomplete.

> In view of the fact that our first rigid airship will be somewhat experimental involving not only new materials, and new construction, but new methods and unfamiliar practices, there is doubt whether it is advantageous in any case to attempt to design a ship larger than 2,000,000 cubic feet displacement, or to depart largely from previous designs. However, considering the limited appropriations it would not be practicable to construct a larger airship than 2,000,000 cubic foot displacement.

> The Bureaus, therefore, propose, and request the Department's approval to design a rigid airship of 2,000,000 cubic feet displacement, to be substantially similar to the British airship R 34 and the German airship L 49, except that it shall be adapted to use American power plants and American materials.[1]

On 9 August 1919 the secretary returned the letter with his approval. The Aircraft Division of the Bureau of Construction and Repair went into action, with Starr Truscott, who had developed an original wooden-girder rigid airship design for the Joint Army–Navy Airship Board, as project engineer. He was assisted by Mr. W. D. Clark in charge of the design work in Washington, and by Mr. Charles P. Burgess in making strength calculations. Already it was planned to fabricate the airship's structure at the

Naval Aircraft Factory in Philadelphia, and to assemble it at the Construction and Experimental Station at Lakehurst, whose completion was then expected in late 1920. Commander Ralph D. Weyerbacher (CC) was ordered on 23 August 1919 to report to the commandant, Fourth Naval District, as project manager, supervising the production of components at the Naval Aircraft Factory, and subsequently their assembly in the hangar at Lakehurst.

Because it was desired to start construction within a year's time, and the basic research needed to produce an original American design would take too long, it was decided to use Zeppelin models. The most detailed information was considered to derive from French studies of L 49, a German Navy "height-climber" Zeppelin which was captured intact in France after the "Silent Raid" of 19–20 October 1917. Truscott, visiting France early in 1918 with the Technical Committee of the Joint Army–Navy Airship Board, was promised a complete set of plans, but not until Hunsaker came to Europe late in 1918 did he receive the drawings for L 49 from Naval Constructor Sabatier. The bureau had some information from England, including drawings of L 33 and a book of photographs of the wreck, published by the British Admiralty in February 1917 as a classified document.[2] Further, Commander Campbell visited Washington twice, in December 1919 and September 1920, and since he was the designer of R 38, his advice was listened to with respect. In April 1921 Captains Ernst Lehmann and Hans Curt Flemming of the Zeppelin Company, in America on business, were invited to visit the bureau and comment on the design, but while polite, they were evasive. Actually, however, members of the bureau had opportunities to learn about Zeppelin practice at first hand, Hunsaker himself having been attached to the Inter-Allied Aeronautical Sub-Commission of the Naval Armistice Commission so that he could take part in the inspection of the German airship bases in the North Sea. Here he saw seven of the latest "height-climbers," an experience of the greatest value, though no notes or sketches could be made. In 1920 Hunsaker was again in Europe, visiting Friedrichshafen, and inspecting the small postwar passenger airships *Bodensee* and *Nordstern*. He was impressed by the thick cantilever section fins and the small, highly streamlined engine gondolas with fish-mouth radiators in the nose and simplified suspension. Hunsaker also received from M. Sabatier drawings of fins and structure of L 72, surrendered to France in July 1920. Weyerbacher was also in Europe in 1920, first observing British airship construction methods and then proceeding to Germany where he learned what he could of Zeppelin Company procedures. Here he made the acquaintance of Anton Heinen, a pre-1914 DELAG captain who during the war had commanded one of the two civilian acceptance trials crews of the Zeppelin Company. Dr. Eckener had not wished to retain him in the postwar DELAG organization, regarding him as a "worn-out pilot." Weyerbacher took a liking to Heinen, regarded him as a source of valuable information on rigid airship outfitting and operations, and invited him to come to the United States to assist in the American rigid airship program. Heinen accepted, and for a period, until the Americans gained experience, wielded great influence as an authority on German procedures and methods.

Truscott, on 29 August 1919, submitted a memorandum to Admiral Taylor asking that work on the design be commenced, with the assumptions that:

> a. This ship will have substantially the dimensions of the German L 49 as described in the French reports in the possession of the Bureau.
>
> b. The structure will in general be the same as in L 49, scantlings to be taken from the information in French reports so far as practicable.
>
> c. The cars will approximate, at least, those of L 49 but an attempt will be made to improve them, reducing the size and changing the interior plan to approach that of the cars of L 72.
>
> d. The materials will duplicate as far as possible those used in L 49.[3]

Truscott and his staff started work in September, and their initial design, known as FA-1 (Fleet Airship No. 1), closely followed that of the original. L 49 herself was a 1917 "height-climber" with main frames spaced at 10-meter intervals, measuring 644 feet 8 inches overall, 78 feet 5 inches in diameter, and with a capacity of 1,970,300 cubic feet of hydrogen in 18 gas cells. With her light frame, she weighed empty 55,500 lb., and had a useful lift of 87,200 lb. On her last flight she probably attained 19,000 feet.[4] Duplicating the hull structure would merely have involved copying the Zeppelin girders and assembling them, and the initial design would have approximated L 49 in performance, with an estimated weight empty of 66,720 lb., and a useful lift of 62,830 lb. when inflated 95% with helium.[5]

The machinery installation was something else. L 49 had been powered by five 240-h.p. Maybach HSLu 6-cylinder in-line engines built especially for airships, one forward abaft the control car, one each side amidships in small streamlined wing gondolas, and two in a large rear engine gondola geared to a single propeller. One engine turned right-handed; the other four were left-handed. All engines had reduction gearing, and the midships ones had reverse gear. Since there was no American engine especially designed for airships, the Bureau of Steam Engineering proposed to fit FA-1 with the ubiquitous Liberty 12-A. The Army version with a compression ratio of 5.42:1

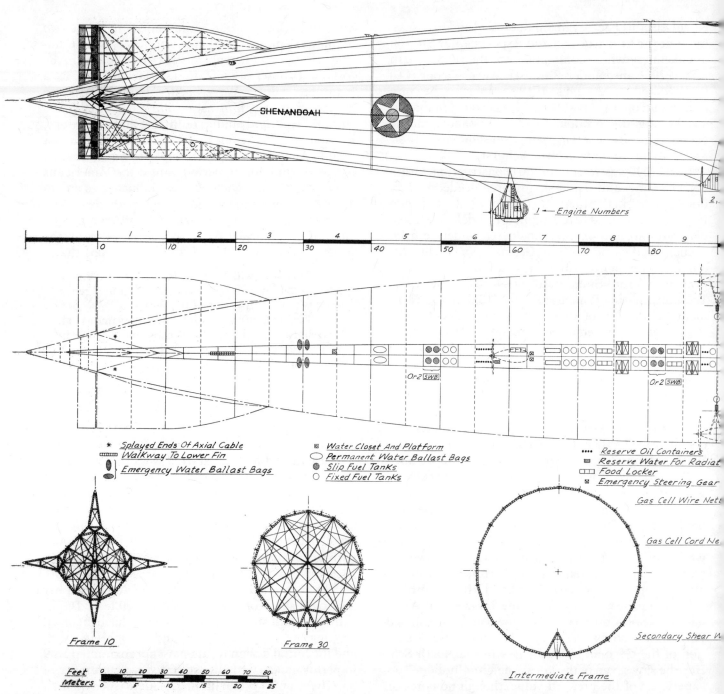

SHENANDOAH

1 ◄— Engine Numbers

	1		2		3		4		5		6		7		8		9
0		10		20		30		40		50		60		70		80	

Or 2 SWB   Or 2 SWB

✳ Splayed Ends Of Axial Cable   ▣ Water Closet And Platform   ···· Reserve Oil Containers
▥ Walkway To Lower Fin   ⬭ Permanent Water Ballast Bags   ▦ Reserve Water For Radiators
⬯ Emergency Water Ballast Bags   ◍ Slip Fuel Tanks   ▭ Food Locker
                                        ◯ Fixed Fuel Tanks   ▨ Emergency Steering Gear

                                                                             Gas Cell Wire Net

                                                                             Gas Cell Cord Net

                                                                             Secondary Shear W

Frame 10   Frame 30   Intermediate Frame

Feet   0 10 20 30 40 50 60 70 80
Meters   0   5   10   15   20   25

ZR 1

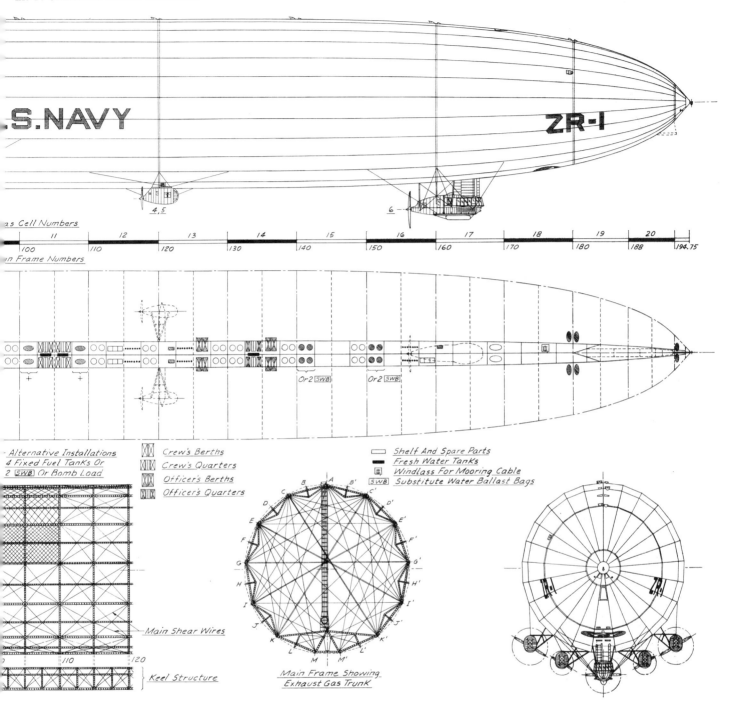

as Cell Numbers

11	12	13	14	15	16	17	18	19	20
100	110	120	130	140	150	160	170	180	188	194.75

n Frame Numbers

Or 2 SWB   Or 2 SWB

Alternative Installations
4 Fixed Fuel Tanks Or
2 SWB Or Bomb Load

⊠ Crew's Berths
⊠ Crew's Quarters
⊠ Officer's Berths
⊠ Officer's Quarters

⬭ Shelf And Spare Parts
▬ Fresh Water Tanks
Ⅲ Windlass For Mooring Cable
SWB Substitute Water Ballast Bags

Main Shear Wires

110   120

Keel Structure

Main Frame Showing
Exhaust Gas Trunk

William F. Kerka

delivered 420 h.p. at 1700 rpm; the Navy version had a compression ratio of 5:1. Initially the Liberties in FA-1 were to be de-rated to 250 h.p. for greater reliability, but to improve the ship's chances of fighting her way back to Lakehurst in a head wind (and unlike the Germans, the Americans had no alternate sheds) the power was increased to 275–300 h.p. The Liberties were longer and heavier than the Maybachs, ensuring that the gondolas would have to be changed accordingly.

An even bigger headache was the reduction-gear problem, four different types being required for the five engines in L 49.[6] In the German Naval Airship Service, with up to 20 similar craft in service simultaneously, it would be feasible to keep spares on hand for so many types of gear drive. For the single American ship this would be extravagant. Further, American firms equipped to manufacture reduction gears were reluctant to try to duplicate the German spur gear drive, and persuaded the bureau to allow them to manufacture planetary or epicyclic gearing. This type, which changed the alignment of the engine crank shaft and propeller shaft, introduced another variation in the gondolas as planned for the American ship. Pending the development of gear design, the power car configurations were left in abeyance. Ultimately, they resembled, not those of L 49, but the later engine gondolas in L 72 and the Bodensee, with nose radiators with hemispherical doors and an exhaust aperture at the rear. In the end, the American ship had two centerline engines with simple reduction gears, and two port and starboard engines with reversible reduction gears, all driving propellers 17 feet 6 inches in diameter; and two port and starboard engines directly driving propellers 11 feet 6 inches in diameter—which were lighter and less complicated than the larger ones, but also less efficient at low speed.

Another headache resulted from the decision to follow metric dimensions as in the original French drawings. This proved impractical when it came to rivet size and riveting tools, which were instead the next larger size in English figures; while the duralumin sheet manufacturer was unwilling to install metric-gauge rolling machinery and instead rolled it to the nearest English measurement.

In December 1919 Commander Campbell arrived in Washington for consultation with Truscott and his associates, in accordance with a provision of the R 38 contract. Unfortunately, as a result of a change in policy on the part of the U.S. Navy on exchange of information with the Royal Navy, Campbell was forbidden to give any information on British airships, though he was allowed to criticize and comment on BuC&R's plans for the FA-1. Some of his suggestions were eventually followed: that the flat wire-braced fins of the L 49 be replaced by thick cantilever-section fins with a minimum of wiring and decreased drag; and that the fins be made larger in area to improve stability relative to R 33 and R 34, which were considered unstable by the British. Also he advocated the fitting of bow mooring gear; but since no extended experiments had yet been made with this equipment in England, the bureau was not convinced that the advantages would outweigh the disadvantage of adding some 2,000 lb. in weight. Campbell also offered advice by letter: In June 1920 he was writing to Hunsaker about the latter's plan to substitute two single-engine cars aft for the large twin-engine gondola with single propeller, an arrangement the Americans regarded as a mechanical nightmare.[7] The drag of two single cars, with two sets of ladders, struts, and so on, would be greater, and more mechanics would be needed. Campbell's suggestion was to use fewer engines of higher power—four instead of five—one forward and one aft on the centerline, and one each to port and starboard amidships.[8]

With the end of the fiscal year on 30 June 1920, only $811,000 of the $1,500,000 appropriated had been allocated. The remaining $689,000 was allowed to lapse. But the 1921 appropriation included an additional $1,500,000 "to continue authorized construction of one rigid airship."

Whereas it had been hoped that FA-1 would be completed in the spring or summer of 1921, it was now clear that there would be a considerable delay. In fact, the Lakehurst shed was not completed until the late summer of 1921, and not until the following spring could erection of the hull framework be commenced. To Truscott and his colleagues, it was apparent that there was time to elaborate the design further and to include up-to-date refinements. Hunsaker's trip to Europe in May and Campbell's second visit to Washington in September 1920 were particularly fruitful. Campbell was not handicapped this time by any restrictions on what he could divulge. He suggested that the design be lengthened by two gas cells for an increase of 20 meters. It was known that L 71 and L 72 had two more cells and were 30 meters longer than L 49, and were fitted with six or seven engines; so it seemed practical that FA-1 should be so altered. In fact, three modified designs were submitted on 15 October 1920. FA-1a had 20 gas cells and a length of 710 feet 3 inches with five engines, two in a large rear gondola with one propeller. FA-1b had only 19 gas cells and a length of 677 feet 6 inches, but her six engines were in individual gondolas—one forward abaft the control car, one aft at Frame 55, and two pairs at Frames 80 and 120. FA-1c again had 20 gas cells and six engines distributed much as in FA-1b, and FA-1d of 29 October 1920 was likewise 710 feet long with 20 cells, but the six engines were in

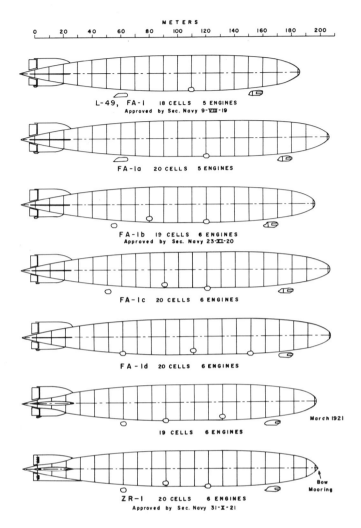

METERS
0   20   40   60   80   100   120   140   160   180   200

L-49, FA-1   18 CELLS   5 ENGINES
Approved by Sec. Navy 9-VIII-19

FA-1a   20 CELLS   5 ENGINES

FA-1b   19 CELLS   6 ENGINES
Approved by Sec. Navy 23-XI-20

FA-1c   20 CELLS   6 ENGINES

FA-1d   20 CELLS   6 ENGINES

March 1921
19 CELLS   6 ENGINES

Bow
Mooring
ZR-1   20 CELLS   6 ENGINES
Approved by Sec. Navy 31-X-21

Evolution of ZR-1.

pairs at Frames 60, 110, and 150, with a separate control car forward as in R 38.

Charles P. Burgess was responsible for the calculations of stresses and balance in the modified designs. With this step forward, he began to eclipse his chief, Starr Truscott, who left the Bureau of Aeronautics about 1924 to join the National Advisory Committee for Aeronautics at Langley Field. Burgess, who was to remain a Civil Service employee of the Navy Department until his death in 1951, had been born in 1888, a brother of W. Starling Burgess, the noted naval architect and yacht designer. He studied naval architecture at the University of Glasgow, but returned to America in 1917. Found physically unfit for military duty, he joined the Aircraft Division of the Bureau of Construction and Repair. Burgess taught himself airship stress analysis from his knowledge of naval architecture (with some advice from Professor William Hovgaard of M.I.T., a world authority on warship design), and was able to discuss airship design on equal terms with Campbell during the latter's American visits.

C.P. was nominally under Truscott but C.P.'s work assumed a somewhat independent status as *Shenandoah* progressed. . . . C.P. developed into quite a remarkable project-design man. An exceptionally competent draftsman was assigned to work with C.P. and the pair could take an idea, put it on paper, and come up with a first approximation to an answer in a remarkably short time. His series of "Design Memos"— some 300 in number—constitute a running historical record of practically all problems that figured in the technical history of airships.[9]

Burgess was sent to England in 1921–22 to participate in the investigation of the R 38 crash, an event that had a profound effect on his professional outlook. Shocked by the realization of the fragility of the light "height-climber" hull when driven at high speed, he wrote home from England:

The fact that the German rigid airships and the British airships of the R 33 class have shown themselves strong enough for service conditions, although the factor of safety was undoubtedly very small, has been accepted as proof that the outer cover must very largely relieve the structure from stress due to gas pressure. Although justified by experience up to the time of the loss of the ZR 2, *there was actually little more than a blind faith that an incalculable source of strength offset an equally incalculable source of strain.*[10]

Burgess co-authored a 1924 paper that reflected his concern about rigid airship structural strength, and was a milestone in airship design theory.[11] He drew up specifications for Bureau of Aeronautics Design No. 60, which led to the later *Akron* and *Macon*, and wrote the only textbook on airship design to appear in the United States.[12] Burgess was one of the very small number of fully qualified and instructed rigid airship designers, the others being Dr. Karl Arnstein, Dr. Johann Schütte, and Sir Barnes Wallis.

Burgess's comments to Admiral Taylor, accompanying the 15 October design revisions, were that with five engines the ship would be difficult to balance with one additional 10-meter bay, but a good balance could be obtained with two additional bays, as in FA-1a. Adding bays without adding engines would increase the static bending moment on the hull by 20% at maximum altitude in the light condition. With one additional bay, six engines, and a rearrangement of cars, the balance was satisfactory, and bending moments hardly changed over those of L 49 (FA-1b). With two additional bays and six engines the solution was better (FA-1c). The FA-1d design was criticized because the maximum static bending moment would be higher—108,710 kg. meters at Frame 90—than in the original FA-1 (102,270 kg. meters at Station 90).

Admirals Taylor and Griffin, in a letter to the secretary on 5 November, plumped for the FA-1b design which "will compare favorably with the latest German and British airships of equal displacement." Presumably they regarded the other designs with two added gas cells as too great a step into the unknown. The altered design would involve eliminating the large twin-engine gondola aft with single propeller; substituting two wing cars of standardized design driving variable pitch propellers directly without gearing at Frame 120; slinging two wing power cars high on the hull aft at Frame 80 so that their propellers, driven by reversing gears, could be run on the ground; and adding a further 10-meter gas cell, which would permit carrying a sixth standardized engine gondola with geared propeller aft at Frame 55 (the original engine abaft the control car with geared drive would remain).

> In the North Atlantic, the cruising speed should be at least 53 knots in bad weather which will require four engines. For FA-1 this leaves but one engine in reserve, and if the gear in the after gondola is out of order the two engines in that car are thrown out, leaving but three engines operating—and cruising speed cannot be maintained. The proposed modification gives always two engines in reserve. . . . Approval of revision of design in accordance with this letter is requested, and if approved, it is recommended that the fact and nature of such revision be held confidential.[13]

Secretary Daniels forwarded the letter to the General Board, which on 22 November 1920 reported favorably. On the following day the secretary approved the revised FA-1 design. Only it was no longer FA-1b, but ZR 1, this designation having been proposed by the acting secretary on 28 October 1920.

The ZR 1 design of course presented the same flat, wire-braced fins as in the original L 49. The Aviation Division was interested, however, in fitting the new ship with thick fins with minimal bracing as in the later German ships. In a conference at the Bureau of Construction and Repair on 24 June 1920 it was decided to construct the parallel center body, then work forward, while delaying the final design of the fins. Hunsaker, then in Europe, was to bring back information on thick fins, after which the design for the tail would be drawn up. In fact, Hunsaker's information on the *Bodensee* fins and rudders, and, more particularly, the L 72 drawings which he obtained from M. Sabatier, enabled the bureau to design thick cantilever fins, of which the upper and two horizontal ones were virtually copies of those of L 72. Weyerbacher, who was responsible for construction, objected to the bureau's plans as stated by Burgess to leave the stern till the last: "Stern erection requires so much more time that it should be started first and continued during remainder of hull work and avoid having completed structure awaiting tail like R 38."[14]

The cantilever fins appeared in a modification approved in March 1921, together with a single centerline engine gondola aft at Frame 60, ungeared direct drive engine gondolas on each side on Frame 90, and the two heavier geared and reversible engine gondolas high on the hull forward at Frame 130, thereby balancing the heavier fin structure aft.

These gondolas were likewise much influenced by those on the *Bodensee* and L 72. A mockup of the new standardized engine gondola was inspected at the Naval Aircraft Factory by Truscott on 7–9 March 1921. He reported that "this car is so surprisingly accessible that it is recommended that the lines be approved as they are and that structural plan be changed only in the minor details which have been recorded."[15]

A final change in the fins resulted from a suggestion by Professor Hovgaard that they be carried well forward to contribute to the longitudinal strength of the after body. This was done with the bottom fin which ran forward as a triangular girder to Frame 30. The final rudder form derived from wind tunnel tests by Dr. Albert F. Zahm at the Washington Navy Yard on a model of ZR 1: six different types of rudders were tested, the one chosen being hinged in three places at the after end of the fins, and balanced with small surfaces on each side ahead of the hinge line, carried on the control quadrant and on struts.

Late in the day, the bureau accepted the suggestion that Commander Campbell had made two years earlier—that ZR 1 be fitted with bow mooring gear. The decision was made by the enthusiastic reports received from Maxfield, Hoyt, and Land in March and April 1921, after they inspected the mooring mast at Pulham, watched R 33 moor and unmoor in winds up to 40 knots, and, in some cases, flew in the ship herself. It was clear that the mooring mast would greatly increase the utility of ZR 1, and a mast at Lakehurst was placed on order (see page 15). On 26 October 1921 Moffett at BuAer requested the approval of the secretary of the navy (who since the inauguration of President Warren G. Harding on 4 March 1921, had been Edwin Denby, a figure in the later Teapot Dome scandal). The modifications to the nose would not only involve adding a solid nose cap and mooring cone, but several other changes: heavier girders in the hull forward; the division of Cell 19 in the nose into two smaller cells, with a braced main frame at Station 188; a light walkway from the forward end of the heavy keel girder at Frame 180 into the nose, with hoops and netting to hold off the forward gas cell; a hinged gangway in the extreme nose at Station 194.75 to give access from the mooring mast; and winches for the main mooring cable and yaw lines. Further, leads were fitted to enable water ballast, gasoline, and electricity to be piped on board from

ZR 1 under construction, April 1923. Hull framework completed, fins being added. The starboard horizontal fin is in the foreground. The thickness of the cantilever section fins is apparent in this photograph. Note the special design of the outer boundary girder of the fin to the right: it was this girder that failed in the port fin on the return from the St. Louis flight, 2 October 1923. (Navy Department via National Archives)

the mast through the nose hatch, and a fabric tube 2 feet in diameter was rigged the length of the keel under the apex girder to enable gas to be piped from the masthead to each of the gas cells. The total added weight was about 2,000 lb. Burgess did the strength calculations for the modified hull structure. He found that the added ton of weight in the nose could be balanced by shifting the control car aft by 5 meters, and by interchanging the wing gondolas so that the heavier ones with reverse gearing were aft at Frame 90, while the light direct drive ones went forward, but to Frame 120 instead of 130. But with the added weight, the ship's fuel load would be 2,000 lb. less at takeoff. Moffett claimed that "the advantage of being able to moor the airship to a mast will outweigh the slight decrease in performance and approval of the change is requested."[16] However, the ship's range with hydrogen at a cruising speed of 53 knots would be decreased from 3,860 nautical miles to 3,705.

It was fortunate that Moffett, inaugurated as chief of the new bureau on 10 August 1921, was as great a friend of the rigid airship as Admiral Taylor, for he found himself forced to defend it immediately. By the end of the fiscal year 1921, only $330,000 of the $1,500,000 appropriated for ZR 1 in the previous year had been spent or obligated, the remainder being allowed to lapse. The erection of the airship had not been started, though design work was well along, and contracts had been let for duralumin and gas cells. Not surprisingly, congressional appropriations for fiscal 1922 made no specific provision for further expenditures on ZR 1. Funds for "aircraft in course of construction" and for "procurement of aircraft" could have been diverted to the big rigid, but Moffett, acutely sensitive to political forces and currents, wanted explicit approval of the airship program.

Seeking support in the Navy Department, Moffett addressed an eloquent plea to the chief of naval operations, pointing out that the future of both military and commercial rigids depended on the completion of ZR 1, that $10,850,000 had already been spent on Lakehurst, Cape May, ZR 1, and ZR 2, and for training of personnel, with over $7,000,000 in addition to develop helium production.

> To fail now to complete the ZR 1 will dissipate the organization of skilled technical personnel which has been built up and allow much of the material which has been assembled to deteriorate. Not only the money spent directly on ZR 1 herself, but this entire outlay of seventeen million will become a loss instead of an asset to the United States, if the rigid airship art is permitted to die in this country. . . . THE COMPLETION OF THE ZR 1 IS AN ECONOMIC NECESSITY.[17]

Undoubtedly representations were made at the same time to members of Congress, and on 16 August the secretary's council approved the expenditure of the funds cited above for ZR 1.

Moffett had salvaged the airship program just in time, for the storm broke eight days later with the crash of ZR 2 and the loss of 16 American lives. The opponents of the airship had a field day, and editorials protested the cost of the program in lives and money. The airship cause, however, found support within the aviation community, notably from the National Advisory Committee on Aeronautics, which on 17 September 1921 sent a resolution to the president and the secretaries of war and navy:

> That the development of rigid airships should be continued in this country; that sufficient funds should be devoted to experimental work for the obtaining of definite information regarding the strength qualities of materials and girders used in the construction of airships, and for the development and checking of the theories used in the general design of airships; and that the present program for the construction of the airship ZR 1 and for the production of helium be prosecuted with renewed vigor.[18]

Burgess had gone to England on behalf of the bureau to report on the technical aspects of the ZR 2 disaster, and his letters were disquieting. It was clear that little was known about aerodynamic loads in flight, and much investigation would have to be done to ascertain the true nature of these loads and forces, and the design of structure to withstand them. Reports from Burgess in England suggested that the ZR 1 design, like ZR 2, was too light to withstand the bending loads imposed by the rudders in high-speed turns. Various steps were taken in the spring of 1922 to mitigate the problem: The rudders were made relatively small compared to those of L 49, the next to narrowest of the six examples tested in the wind tunnel being chosen. Although the control surfaces could be moved 30 degrees in each direction, stops were put on them to limit their travel to 15 degrees for the rudders, and 13.5 degrees for the elevators. These were not removed until the first trial flights

had been completed. The controls were altered: where previously ten turns of the wheel had been required to put the surfaces hard over from 30 degrees one way to 30 degrees the other way, the gearing was altered to require 18 turns (six turns were all that were required in L 49). The hull structure was also strengthened: The three lower intermediate longitudinals on both sides, H, J, and L, and H', J', and L', were increased in dimensions, from the size in L 49 to those of L 71. The larger intermediate girders ran nearly the full length of the ship, from Frame 20 aft to 188 forward, and increased the resistance of the lower part of the hull to failure in compression under bending loads in the vertical plane. Calculations showed a "discontinuity" in hull strength at Frame 20, where the intermediate longitudinals ended and the fins began. This meant in fact that the structure at this point was weaker than elsewhere in resisting bending loads. The solution was to fit heavier longitudinals from Frame 10 to 40, and in most of the longitudinals from 40 to 60, while the keel was extended 5 meters farther aft from Frame 15 to 10.

How much stronger was ZR 1 than the prototype "height climber" L 49? One answer may be found by comparing structural weights of the two rigid hulls. The figures may not be fully comparable, but one reference gives the total weight of hull structure (without fittings or fins) of L 49 as 23,803 lb.,[19] while for ZR 1 the same figure was 30,363 lb.[20] The latter rigid of course had an extra bay compared with L 49; subtracting the weight of a midships bay of ZR 1, 1,616 lb., the result is 28,747 lb. The difference, nearly 5,000 lb., indicates a heavier and therefore stronger structure. Yet Weyerbacher, years later, declared that tests on the structure of ZR 1 as it approached completion indicated a factor of safety of only 1.1! "Naturally we had to fly it. How could that have been explained to Congress?"[21]

Mindful of the fact that the design of R 38 had never been checked by a competent and independent commission, Moffett resolved that this should be done, and addressed himself to the prestigious National Advisory Committee for Aeronautics (of which he was an ex officio member), which had adopted the resolution advocating the continuing construction of ZR 1 after the ZR 2 crash. Advising that the design was now complete, and that a quantity of technical information would be available on ZR 1 by 1 July, Moffett on 20 April 1922 recommended that the NACA appoint a technical committee.

> To pass upon the design and calculations of ZR 1. . . . It is suggested that this technical committee include no personnel from the Bureau of Aeronautics, but that such personnel be called before it for ex-

planations and information as may be required. It is further suggested that the committee include Prof. Wm. Hovgaard of the Massachusetts Institute of Technology, who is an expert in indeterminate structures and has undertaken independently an investigation of the theory of longitudinal strength of rigid airships. The Committee should further include an expert in aerodynamics in order to properly judge the dynamical stresses when manoeuvring, and such other persons of sound engineering judgment as may be considered competent to judge the evidence submitted and the reasonableness of the conclusions drawn.[22]

The committee formed at Moffett's request included not only Professor Hovgaard, but also Henry Goldmark as chairman, a consulting civil engineer from New York; W. Watters Pagon as secretary, a consulting civil engineer of Baltimore who was co-author of a technical volume on pressure airships; Dr. L. B. Tuckerman, engineer-physicist of the Bureau of Standards; and Dr. Max Munk, technical assistant to the NACA, an aerodynamicist destined for later fame in his profession. The first meeting was on 18 June 1922 in Washington.

Starting with the foreign material on L 33, L 49, and L 72, and handbooks for the British airships No. 9 and No. 23, the committee held many conferences with the design staff of the Bureau of Aeronautics, and examined the calculations on which the ZR 1 design was based. Two hundred full-size girders and other materials built for the ship were tested for strength. Fifteen meetings of the committee were held, and in addition there were field trips to the plant of the Aluminum Company of America at New Kensington, Pennsylvania, in June, and to the Naval Aircraft Factory and to Lakehurst in August, where by this time the erection of the ZR 1 hull structure was well under way. Recommendations made by the committee were accepted by BuAer and incorporated into the design: Thus, in October the committee stressed the need for adequate hull ventilation to equalize static pressures and to avoid the implosion accidents that had seriously damaged the German L 49 and L 51. Spring-loaded hatches were installed along the keel, to open either inward or outward. Another recommendation, not publicized, was that ZR 1's maximum speed at low altitude be limited to 50 knots to minimize the aerodynamic stresses on the hull, which increased as the square of the speed. This restriction, on top of the limited range due to helium, was a blow to operating personnel: the anticipated maximum speed with six engines developing 1,800 h.p. had been 62.5 knots, and a cruising speed of 53 knots had been considered essential to overcome head winds. Only 1,050 h.p. was required for 50 knots—a fact that contributed to the removal of one of the six engines in the spring of 1924.

On 4 December 1922, the committee approved the ZR 1 design. It endorsed the decision to work from the L 49 prototype while checking its strength by detailed calculations, as "the only wise policy." The committee approved the bureau's methods of calculating stresses, praised the quality of material and workmanship, and concluded:

The ZR 1 is shown by comparative calculations to be measurably stronger than the British airship R 38, which failed on a trial trip, while other possible reasons for the failure, besides structural weakness, have been guarded against in the ZR 1.[23]

Judging the design of the ZR 1 as a whole, the committee has been very favorably impressed by the thorough studies made by the engineers in charge, and the good judgment shown throughout in applying their results, and also the great care shown in executing the plans. It sees no reason whatever to doubt that the ZR 1 will prove a complete success in service.[24]

Moffett's actions in obtaining NACA endorsement of the ZR 1 design, so much in question since the ZR 2 disaster, had been an astute political move to placate congressmen, newspaper editors, and the general public. Furthermore, the committee had done its work conscientiously, and it could be said that with ZR 1 the possibility of major structural failure in high-speed maneuvers at low altitude had been eliminated. Therefore it was all the more shocking to the experts when the American ship, like her predecessor, broke in two in flight—though this time, still another new and unanticipated danger was encountered, namely turbulence of unprecedented severity.

While the ZR 1 design was being developed, the ancillary industries were playing their part.

Thanks to encouragement and support from Admiral Taylor and the Bureau of Construction and Repair, the Aluminum Company of America was prepared for the contract awarded to it on 4 December 1919 for the duralumin metal of the airship. Admiral Taylor had been diligent in obtaining from abroad samples of metal from Zeppelins brought down over Allied territory, and analysis had shown that this material was duralumin as patented by Dr. Alfred Wilm in Germany in 1909. This alloy was rendered as strong as mild steel, while being much lighter than steel, by combining 94% aluminum with 4% copper, and small amounts (less than 1% of each) of magnesium, manganese, silicon, and iron—ingredients that nonetheless were important in giving the material its strength. The Aluminum Company, which had been founded in 1886 to exploit the Hall process of electrolytic refining, was invited by Admiral Taylor in 1916 to attempt manufacture of the alloy and to roll and stamp it to make Zeppelin-type girders for test purposes. The subsequent ZR 1 contract was the first large production contract issued in the United States, and called for the preparation of both narrow and wide sheets, shapes, lattices, and rivets. Although the Aluminum Company was the low bidder and chief supplier of duralumin for ZR 1, a small amount of sheet was purchased from the Bausch Machine Tool Company of Springfield, Massachusetts, in 1920.

The Aluminum Company initially had trouble in providing acceptable rolled angle sections as well as lattice stampings, but problems were eventually solved with the help of the Navy Department. Commander Dyer in Bedford, for instance, sent home a report on British rolling and heat-treating equipment, while Hunsaker, visiting the Zeppelin works at Staaken and Lindau in 1920, reported on the German practice of straightening duralumin channel sections by stretching them in draw benches. Finally, by February 1921 the Aluminum Company was able to start preliminary deliveries of material to the Naval Aircraft Factory for assembly into test girders, with detail material delivery to start 15 May for full-scale production of girders for the ship.[25] As in Germany, where the first duralumin structure airplanes were built as early as 1914 by Claudius Dornier at the *Zeppelin Werke Lindau*, the development of duralumin in the United States for ZR 1 paved the way for its general use in aircraft, starting with the Stout Metal Plane Company of Detroit, whose all-metal thick-winged 2-AT "Air Pullman" monoplane of 1924 was the ancestor of the Ford Trimotor.

The Goodyear Tire and Rubber Company of Akron, Ohio, with much experience in creating rubberized fabric envelopes for the earlier B, C, and D class of U.S. naval nonrigid airships, was the source of the ZR 1 gas cells. In the late summer of 1920 Goodyear received a contract, for the price of $459,650, to fabricate and deliver to Lakehurst 18 gas cells, one complete set for the ship as designed at that time, plus 14 additional cells as spares (in the end, because the ship completed with 20 gas cells, there were a total of 36 including 16 spares).

While rubberized fabric as used in the American nonrigids had relatively low diffusion rates for airship gases, and was even used on occasion in the German Zeppelin gas cells, its weight was unacceptably high. Further, it was suspected that the fires that destroyed some of the early Zeppelins were caused by the rubberized fabric creating static electrical discharges. For these reasons the Zeppelin Company in 1912 fostered the development of gas cells made of goldbeater's skin, the outer membrane of the cecum of cattle, which was superbly gas-tight but also ex-

pensive, each animal yielding only one skin not larger than 10 by 40 inches. The early cells were made of six layers of goldbeater's skin shingled together, but because of their fragility and expense, a change was made early in 1914 to "skinned fabric" (*Stoffhaut*) in which two or three layers of goldbeater's skin were glued to light cotton fabric, varnished inside and out, and waterproofed on the outside with a coat of soft paraffin wax. The weight of this material was 145 grams per square meter, compared with 240 grams for the rubberized fabric.

L 49 of course revealed to her captors the composition of her gas cells, but the British were unsuccessful in copying them. In particular, the secret of the glue or cement used in attaching two layers of goldbeater's skin to the cotton fabric eluded them. Instead, they used a rubber solution to attach the skins to light cotton fabric that had previously been proofed with a thin coat of vulcanized rubber. A coat of varnish was then applied to the inside. The resulting gas cell material had a weight of less than 160 grams per square meter.

Although Goodyear had had no previous experience with goldbeater's skin, they obtained the secret of the British process by hiring a British subject, Mr. Norman Meadowcroft, who formerly had been superintendent in charge of gas bag manufacture at Beardmore's at Inchinnan, and earlier had done similar work at Vickers. As early as the spring of 1920, Meadowcroft was working in a special laboratory at Akron making up sample lots of skinned fabric for testing. A memorandum that he wrote following a visit to the Chicago packing houses on 7–8 February 1922 is a classic on the complicated process of separating the goldbeater's skins from the intestinal tract of slaughtered cattle, and the method of cleaning and preserving them. The #1 skins were the largest, measuring 30 inches or more long; #2 skins were 20 to 30 inches long. These were salted, packed 25 to a bundle, then placed in casks "thoroughly paraffined inside and tamped down," 2,500 #1 skins or 4,000 #2 skins to a cask. The skins were stored at a temperature of 35 to 40 degrees Fahrenheit and kept moist until they were needed to make up gas cells. Meadowcroft estimated that the Chicago packers would together slaughter 6,000,000 cattle per year: "with 75 to 80 per cent of skins available there will be between 4,500,000 and 5,000,000 skins per year, divided to give about 2,750,000 to 3,000,000 grade #1 and 1,750,00 to 2,000,000 grade #2 skins."[26] On the other hand, some 50,000 skins were needed to make one large gas cell in Germany during World War I, at a cost of $10,000.

Meadowcroft's attempt to transplant British know-how in gas bag construction to America was successful. Since the useful life of gas cells with gold-

Interior view of ZR 1 gas cell inflated with air for inspection. Note the transparency and fragility of the material, made up of separate longitudinal gores of light cotton fabric, with goldbeater's skins shingled on. Black object overhead is the conical sleeve for the axial cable. (AIAA)

beater's skin was roughly two to three years, after which the diffusion rate of gas outward, and of air inward, was unacceptable, the bureau did not want them delivered too early before completion of the ship. At Lakehurst they could be damaged by being stored too long in a folded condition. They were delivered beginning in the spring of 1922, with the last ones on 23 January 1923. One cell, Regular #15, was rejected for being overweight. Not until the ship was completed, in August 1923, were the gas cells installed and inflated.

Gas valves were manufactured at the Naval Aircraft Factory. On 17 November 1920, the factory agreed to fabricate 15 large automatic valves (10 plus 5 spares), 12 small automatic valves (8 plus 4 spares), and 14 maneuvering valves (9 plus 5 spares) for FA-1 in case the bureau was unable to obtain satisfactory proposals outside.[27] The automatic valves, spring-loaded to open at pressures of 8 mm. of water, allowed gas to escape as it expanded through heating or a rise to higher altitude; the maneuvering valves, actuated by wires from the control car, enabled the release of gas when necessary to make the ship less buoyant, as in landing. As completed, ZR 1 had 18 automatic valves in the bottom of each gas cell (the two smallest ones at the ends of the ship communi-

cated with their neighbors) and 16 maneuvering valves in the tops of the gas cells.

The axial cable running through the center of the ship from end to end, and connecting the center fittings of the radial wires at the main frames, was not actually a continuous wire. Each gas cell contained a 10-meter segment, connected up to the central ring fitting when the gas cell was inflated and installed. In ZR 1 the axial cable was one-fourth inch in diameter, nonspinning, breaking strength not less than 10,000 lb., and proofed with pure rubber to protect the gas cells in case of fraying.[28]

ZR 1 when completed was the first rigid airship to fly with helium; but her designers and prospective operators had expected to fly her with hydrogen, until their plans were overtaken by a ground swell of public opinion following several airship disasters accompanied by hydrogen fires. Considerable work had already been done on helium production in the United States; but at the time of ZR 1's completion, output was so limited as to seriously handicap the operators of the ship; while a marked decrease in useful lift and range, and the need to evolve special techniques to minimize the loss of expensive helium, involved further operational handicaps. Trained in hydrogen flying, ZR 1's personnel almost certainly would have preferred the advantages of the cheap though flammable gas, and its employment in wartime was advocated because of higher performance, greater weight-carrying capacity, and higher ceiling.[29]

A great effort had been made during 1917–18 to make helium available for military use, the British being particularly concerned to obtain the nonflammable gas for their rigid airships intended for operation in the North Sea. First discovered in the solar spectrum in 1868, and isolated in the laboratory by Sir William Ramsay in 1895, the rare, inert gas continued to be a laboratory curiosity even after its identification in natural gas from a well in Dexter, Kansas, in 1905. Attempts to discover helium in other parts of the world have been unsuccessful, significant amounts being found only in the United States, where "about 90 per cent of the helium is concentrated in a small area within 250 miles of Amarillo, Texas."[30]

As late as the year 1917, scientists and chemists were investigating the properties of the new gas— which cost $2,500 per cubic foot when produced in minute amounts in the laboratory—with no idea that it might have a practical application. It was Ramsay, acting on behalf of the British Admiralty, who first drew attention of officials of the U.S. Bureau of Mines to the possibility of procuring helium for airship use from sources in the United States. Following America's entry into the war, the Joint Army–Navy Airship Board on 26 July 1917 took up a proposal by the Bureau of Mines to set up an experimental helium plant, and $500,000 of military funds were approved for the project.[31] Subsequently, and largely at British insistence, the program was greatly expanded. Under the direction of the U.S. Navy, two separate experimental plants were erected in Fort Worth, Texas, to extract helium from the natural gases of the Petrolia field. Plant 1 (designed by Linde Air Products) was completed on 6 March 1918, and Plant 2 (by the Air Reduction Company) on 5 May 1918. In both facilities, the extraction process involved liquefaction of the major constituents, methane and nitrogen, while the helium, still gaseous, could be recovered in a 70% pure state. Further purification improved the figure to 90%. By Armistice Day the two Fort Worth plants had produced 150,000 cubic feet of helium. A contract for a large production plant was signed with Linde on 22 October 1918, but with the severe cutback in military appropriations following the Armistice, it was not completed until March 1921. Running at two-fifths capacity because of defects in the compressor equipment, the Fort Worth plant between 28 March and 30 November 1921 produced 2,000,000 cubic feet of helium, and then suspended operations for lack of funds. The total amount in storage when the plant closed was 2,400,000 cubic feet. Thus, even if it had been desired to inflate ZR 1 with helium, barely enough had been produced for one filling.

The R 38 disaster caused concern about the use of hydrogen: though it was not the cause of the breakup of the ship, the explosions of impure hydrogen in the forward gas cells were responsible for much of the heavy death toll. Immediately the Plans Division of the Bureau of Aeronautics recommended to Admiral Moffett that ZR 1 be inflated with helium. A few days later, on 31 August 1921, the Navy's new nonrigid D 6 was destroyed in a hydrogen fire. Gasoline ignited in the gondola set fire to the bag, and also burned the airships C 10 and H 1, and the shed in which they were housed at the Rockaway Naval Air Station.

In pursuit of the Plans Division's recommendation, Fort Worth shipped 250,000 cubic feet of helium to the Naval Air Station, Hampton Roads, where the Navy's only operational airship, C 7, was based. On 2 December 1921, she made two flights, the first ever made by a helium-inflated craft, under the command of Lcdr. R. F. Wood, with Lcdr. Lansdowne and Lt. Charles E. Bauch from BuAer on board. On 5 December, under Lansdowne's command, she flew to Washington, circled the Washington Monument and landed at the Anacostia Naval Air Station, to the accompaniment of favorable publicity for the bureau's plans to use "safe" helium in its airships. Fifteen flights in all were made before C 7 was deflated at the end of three months. The gas was recompressed into cylinders, and forwarded to Langley Field to be sent through the purification plant. Of the 204,000 cubic feet used, only 12,500 cubic feet had been lost, and the purity had dropped from 93% to 89.9%.[32]

Then, on 21 February 1922, came a tragedy that decided the issue in the minds of congressmen and the public: the U.S. Army's Roma, a large Italian-built semirigid of 1,204,000 cubic feet, which was still running trials out of Langley Field, suffered a structural failure in flight and dove into high tension wires; 34 of the 45 persons on board died in the ensuing hydrogen fire. Three days later at a Cabinet meeting in the White House the question of whether the government should resume the production of helium for airship use was informally discussed. The Department of the Interior was ready to increase helium production through the Bureau of Mines, and even to erect new plants if necessary, but funds were not available. Yet the Bureau of Aeronautics was increasingly leaning toward a helium policy for airships. "To educate and bring to the attention of the public the safety and practicability of helium in lighter than air work," Commander Joseph P. Norfleet participated in the 13th National Balloon Race held at Milwaukee on 31 May 1922, with his

76,000-cubic-foot "Navy Helium" balloon inflated with the nonflammable gas. This stunt sacrificed nearly 100,000 cubic feet of the Navy's scarce supply of helium, but had its effect on public opinion.

Notwithstanding the *Roma* crash, the Army Air Service continued to use hydrogen. This was painfully brought to public attention when the nonrigid C 2, a former naval craft, while returning east after the first airship crossing of the American continent, burned at Brooks Field, San Antonio, Texas, on 17 October 1922, fortunately without loss of life. The press, having been fed the unending helium propaganda for too long, began to question why C 2 had not been inflated with helium. It was suggested that the Army and Navy between them had only enough helium to inflate one C-class airship. Although this was not quite so, it was closer to the truth than the overstated helium production figures the services had been releasing in the past. As a result of the C 2 controversy, Secretary Denby stated that he hoped it would be "unnecessary to send any of the big dirigibles up without helium gas"[33] in the future. And on 2 October 1922, the Fort Worth helium plant had resumed production, though at only three-fifths of capacity owing to low pressure of the natural gas supply and frequent freeze-up of equipment. Nonetheless, by the end of the 1923 fiscal year, 4,069,941 cubic feet had been produced. Theoretically this was to be shared equally with the Army, but more than half went to ZR 1.

Already the Bureau of Aeronautics was studying the implications of filling the big rigid with helium instead of hydrogen, while the prospective commanding officer, on 16 November 1922, understood that the bureau had "definitely decided to make at least the first charge of the ZR 1 with helium."[34] A memorandum by A. D. Micotti of the bureau's Design Department showed how the substitution of helium, lifting 60 lb. per 1,000 cubic feet, for hydrogen lifting 68 lb. per 1,000 cubic feet, would reduce the cruising range by roughly 40%—a serious drawback for an aircraft being sold to the fleet as a long-range aerial scout for covering vast ocean areas. For example, with hydrogen 82.5% full to attain 6,000 feet altitude, the ZR 1 had a range at 40 knots, using reserve fuel, of 3,760 miles. With helium 82.5% full for a ceiling of 6,000 feet, the total fuel that could be carried would suffice for a range of only 1,790 miles at 40 knots. By removing the forward engine, the added fuel would increase the range to 2,200 miles. Here was another reason for the later removal of #6 engine.[35]

To most American men and women, nonflammable helium may have appeared an unmitigated blessing, but to American airshipmen it must have often seemed a curse. The marked impairment of performance, range, and ceiling, the expense ($120.22 per

thousand cubic feet vs. $2 to $3 per thousand cubic feet for hydrogen in fiscal year 1922), the actual scarcity due to low output at the Fort Worth plant, and the resulting need to avoid valving it at all costs, must frequently have made them wish they had been flying with hydrogen. The cheapness of the latter meant that it could be valved as needed, and the ship kept in equilibrium at all times. The remarkable expedients to which American airshipmen had to resort to conserve helium—taking off with superheat in the morning, landing with supercooling in the evening, driving the ship dynamically light or heavy to maintain constant altitude, and the use of water recovery apparatus, heavy and drag-producing—compromised the performance of the ships, and at times threatened their very safety.

The actual construction of ZR 1 may be credited to the manager of the Lakehurst Construction and Experimental Station, Commander Ralph D. Weyerbacher, Construction Corps, USN. Born in Indiana in 1888, he graduated from Annapolis in 1909 and transferred from the line to the Construction Corps in 1912, at which time he was taking postgraduate instruction in naval architecture at the Massachusetts Institute of Technology. While there he became interested in aeronautical engineering. After receiving his master's degree in 1914, he went to the Philadelphia Navy Yard where he made significant contributions to rationalizing and improving the management of the yard. When the Naval Aircraft Factory opened late in 1917 on navy yard property, Weyerbacher was assistant to the manager, Naval Constructor F. G. Coburn. Here he gained much experience in progressive assembly techniques of aircraft production using inexperienced labor in turning out nearly 200 large twin-engine H 16 and F5L flying boats, the parts for which were manufactured by furniture builders and other outside contractors. Following the Armistice, Weyerbacher took lighter-than-air training at Pensacola, and in May 1919 was designated Naval Aviator (LTA).[36] With the Navy Department's decision to have ZR 1 constructed by the Navy itself, using the now redundant facilities of the Naval Aircraft Factory, Weyerbacher was put in charge of the project in August 1919.

Thus, Weyerbacher was exceptionally qualified to be project manager for the construction of ZR 1. In addition, he had other unusual qualifications: Family connections gave him access to members of Congress, whereby he could speak for appropriations and obtain advance information. At the same time he was forthright and direct in dealing with artisans, with no superiority of manner, and he ably executed his duties in building ZR 1 although he was working with employees completely inexperienced in airship procedures. He had unlimited energy and enthusiasm, was aggressive, and possessed the somewhat arrogant self-confidence of the person who expects results and gets them. A fault in his character was that he needed to lead and command, which was generally the prerogative of the line officer. The Construction Corps officer could, however, command a navy yard or similar construction facility; so for personal reasons, Weyerbacher fought to have Lakehurst designated a Construction and Experimental Station, rather than an operational Naval Air Station. As a result, during the building and early flight testing of ZR 1, Weyerbacher was in complete control, totally overshadowing the line officer nominally in command of the air station, and during the first six months of ZR 1's existence, he was the de facto commanding officer of the airship, assisted by his protégé, Anton Heinen. It was a severe blow to Weyerbacher's pride when, during the personnel "shake-up" following the airship's breakaway from the mooring mast on 15 January 1924, he was himself ordered away—to be chief engineer of the Naval Aircraft Factory.

In order to obtain information on foreign methods, Weyerbacher had sailed for England in March 1920, to study the erection of the R 38 hull framework. Writing home to the bureau, he proposed building the bow, stern, and three bays at a time of the midships section in towers, according to British practice.[37] Proceeding to Germany, he inspected the Zeppelin plants at Friedrichshafen and at Staaken near Berlin, and became a convert to German construction methods, which he followed in erecting ZR 1.

Back in the United States before the end of the year, Weyerbacher chafed at the delays that steadily put back the expected completion of ZR 1 early in 1922. The Lakehurst shed was far behind schedule, while the Aircraft Division at the Bureau of Construction and Repair delayed getting out drawings because they felt correctly that they had time to investigate and introduce modifications and improvements in the FA-1 design, particularly in the power cars and the tail. Until early in 1922 Weyerbacher remained at the Naval Aircraft Factory, where the sheet duralumin ordered from the Aluminum Company of America was being delivered. He supervised processing of the alloy, which was worked into channels and lattices using different thicknesses of metal depending on the strength required of the different kinds of girders, after which these components were riveted up into the hundreds of triangular girders required for the main and intermediate frames, main and intermediate longitudinals, and keel structure of the 680-foot hull.[38]

In December 1921 and January 1922, Weyerbacher submitted schedules for the work on ZR 1. All con-

struction at Lakehurst necessary to erect the ship was to be completed by 1 March 1922, and he wanted to begin assembly not later than that date. He felt that the entire work of erection could be completed in 52 weeks (i.e., by 1 March 1923). While the Naval Aircraft Factory had followed Zeppelin practice in preparing a 13-sided radial jig for assembling the transverse frames of the ship, Weyerbacher wished only to have an assembly table at Lakehurst on which the frames, precut and fitted at the Naval Aircraft Factory, could be riveted up and the chord and radial wires could be installed. He anticipated that the frame assemblies for the parallel midships portion of the ship could be completed by 15 March, the intermediate frames for bow and stern by 1 June, and the main frames for bow and stern by 30 June 1922. Power cars were to be completed by 1 August 1922, engine installation by 16 October, and the control car by 1 November 1922. Ninety main fuel tanks, each of 100 gallons capacity, would be required.[39] At the end of January, the Naval Aircraft Factory announced that the first shipments to Lakehurst would start in a few weeks, about a third by truck and two thirds by rail.[40]

Not until the latter part of April did the first frame arrive at Lakehurst. This was intermediate frame 105, which was quickly assembled and riveted, and on 24 April hoisted up under the roof, supported below on a cradle, as was the German practice. A pleased Weyerbacher wrote to Hunsaker in Washington: "it is surprising the amount of elasticity there is in this frame. We had very little difficulty in hoisting it and our rig was most simple."[41] More frames followed rapidly. By the end of May, 1,450 of the 2,189 girders required for the frames from 30 to 188 were completed. Three main frames and four intermediate frames of the midbody were assembled complete, while two more, 80 and 120, were on the radial jig. By the end of June, 11 gas cells had been shipped to Lakehurst. At the end of July, 8 frames, 90 through 125, were hung in position in the shed. Yet the keel of ZR 1 had not yet been laid! Originally Weyerbacher had planned this occasion for April, then for the end of July with Admiral Moffett doing the honors, but the admiral found himself unable to get away from Washington. The ship was not being delayed structurally, for the keel-laying ceremony as Weyerbacher envisaged it would only involve placing the first walkway girder at the bottom of the keel. On 26 July he wrote to Hunsaker: "if Admiral Moffett takes no action in regard to laying the keel I suggest that you come here some time next week and during the lunch hour I will have you go through the ceremony of laying the keel, for I firmly believe the ship should have some sort of keel laying ceremony."[42]

Two foreign-trained airshipmen assisted Weyerbacher by acting as inspectors—a Mr. Farlam, a Brit-

Two thirds of the material for ZR 1 was shipped from the Naval Aircraft Factory to Lakehurst by rail. In this time exposure, the engine crew of the Central Railroad of New Jersey Camelback loll on the footboards at the rear of the tender, while the train crew poses at the front. Note the gondola with large box at the far end of the track. ZR 1, seen here in the early summer of 1923, has almost the entire outer cover in place, with #3 engine gondola being attached. (Robinson)

ish Admiralty overseer familiar with rigid airship work, hired by arrangement with the Admiralty, and Anton Heinen, who had left Germany for America in April 1922. Interestingly, the two former enemies worked well together. Heinen, however, had the greater influence, representing German methods and procedures that Weyerbacher had chosen to follow, and here there was an immediate and growing source of conflict. Although Lakehurst, in the firm grip of Weyerbacher, followed German examples, all of the U.S. Navy's rigid airship personnel had been trained in England to follow British procedures—this group including the members of the Howden Detachment now serving at Lakehurst, and Lansdowne and Lawrence at the Bureau of Aeronautics. There were of course differences in opinions and methods; and when Heinen, backed by Weyerbacher, got his way, there was resentment. For example, in German airships, the elevator man's station was on the port side of the control car, with the commanding officer's chart board, instrument panel, and engine telegraphs

to starboard. The opposite was true in British rigid airships. Flight Lieutenant Wann, on visiting the bureau in May 1922, criticized "the German scheme of putting the altitude pilot on the port side of the car. This was contrary to British practice and contrary to his own ideas as to the proper position of altitude coxswain."[43] Some months later, however, Heinen insisted that the handling and trail rope releases be mounted on the starboard side, along with the commanding officer's instrument board, "as this is the proper position of Commanding Officer during landing." Someone in the bureau added "if you are German trained."[44] A year later Heinen disapproved of a new and improved engine telegraph dial suggested by Lawrence, prompting someone in the bureau to write on the correspondence, "A. Heinen wants it so and it is so!" Admittedly Heinen played an indispensable part in the early trial flights, as no living American officer had ever commanded a rigid airship, and none of those at Lakehurst had had any rigid airship experience. But basking in the glare of newspaper

Frame assembly jig on hangar floor, with frame complete. Extra girders at lower left and right show this is either Frame 90 or 120, reinforced to support power cars to port and starboard. (AIAA)

publicity apparently went to his head, particularly after his prominent role in the "breakaway flight" in January 1924, and Heinen's publicity consciousness irked many people at Lakehurst. He made no further flights in ZR 1 after February 1924, when Lansdowne assumed command.

On 1 November 1922 the hull structure of ZR 1 was 75% complete, with 29 frames in place comprising fifteen 10-meter bays. The structural work had progressed far enough to allow the installation of detail fittings. Four fuel tanks were hung in the keel between quarter frame 97½ and main frame 100 and filled with water, while stresses were measured in the surrounding girders and wires.

With completion of the central part of the hull, it was possible on 23 November to perform a "deflated gas bag test." (This could have been done earlier but for a delay at the Naval Aircraft Factory, which was providing the axial cable.) Initially Burgess had suggested that the test cell be inflated with hydrogen. Weyerbacher wanted to use helium, but BuAer re-

plied that 150,000 cubic feet of helium would be needed, which was about all that the Navy possessed, and with recompressing and purifying it afterward, the cost would have been excessive. Actually in this first "deflated gas bag test," Cell 11, between Frames 100 and 110, was inflated with air to 100%, under a pressure of one-half inch of water. Tensions in the wires could not be taken, but those in the main frame trusses were found to be less than expected.

At the first of the year the structure was complete from Frame 25 at the leading edge of the fins to 188, the last main frame abaft the bow cap. The stern structure and the four fins were now built on, and the nose extended to the bow cap, though the bow mooring gear was not installed. This work was completed by 1 April 1923. Meanwhile another "deflated gas bag test" had been run with Cell 11 between 19 February and 3 March. This was the first use of helium in a rigid airship. Three carloads of helium, each comprising 500 cylinders containing 140 cubic feet each, were ordered from Fort Worth on 28 December 1922; they

ZR 1 deflated gas bag test, 23 November 1922. Cell #11, located between Frames 100 and 110, is inflated with air. Note gas shaft running vertically up the center of the cell head, and radial and chord wire bracing of Frame 100 showing on the face of the cell. Fire ladders, shown prominently here, were much used for work high on the airship hull. (AIAA)

arrived in Lakehurst early in February. Of this supply, 1,175 cylinders were used to fill the bag with a total of 164,500 cubic feet of helium. At the end of the tests the helium was piped into the large gas holder on the station.

It was time to start assembling and training a crew for the new ship. As far back as the spring of 1922, Moffett had begun looking for a prospective commanding officer. Hunsaker particularly considered it advisable that he be at Lakehurst while the ship was under construction so that he could be thoroughly familiar with it technically. Curiously, previous LTA experience was not considered necessary, as he could obtain such training after being detailed. It was thought that a submarine or destroyer officer might be especially suited, but the main thing was that he have "sound judgment with capacity to absorb an immense mass of detail and to impart it to others in a clear form."[45]

Admiral Moffett's first choice was an excellent one—none other than Commander Ernest J. King, the future fleet admiral and commander in chief, United States Fleet, who led the U.S. Navy to victory over Japan and Germany in World War II. King had a background of staff duty in World War I under

Admiral Mayo, the commander in chief, Atlantic Fleet. Later he was to go into submarines and be in charge of the salvage of the S-51 and S-4; qualify as a naval aviator in 1927 at the age of 48; command the carrier Lexington; and in 1933 succeed Moffett as chief of the Bureau of Aeronautics. On 25 May 1922, when Moffett wrote to offer command of ZR 1 and of the Air Station at Lakehurst, King was captain of the storeship USS Bridge undergoing repairs at the Norfolk Navy Yard. Had King accepted, the history of the rigid airship in the U.S. Navy might have been different, and certainly the history of Lakehurst would have been different. The pattern of feuding and conflict between Weyerbacher and the line officers continued throughout the 1920s and into the 1930s, involving airship officers vs. station officers, staff corps vs. line, Shenandoah vs. Los Angeles crews, military vs. civilian personnel. Wives frequently added fuel to the flames, and many officers and men came to Lakehurst "solely for flight pay and desired to fly to the minimum extent possible and then only on hand waving missions."[46] Successive commanding officers of the air station appeared helpless to deal with the continuing feuding, and Moffett in Washington, though having some knowledge of the problems, was unable to resolve them from a distance. By contrast, Ernest J. King, a "sundowner" notoriously strict both with himself and with subordinates who gave less than their best to the Navy, would have exercised the firmest sort of control over the time servers and the empire builders at Lakehurst, ruthlessly sending to sea those who failed to meet his high standards. Yet King, whose goal was to become chief of naval operations, was not about to compromise his career by identifying himself with a peripheral weapon with an uncertain future. In any event, he demonstrably could not have gotten along with Moffett: named assistant chief of the Bureau of Aeronautics in August 1928, King asked to be relieved the following May after disagreeing with his chief over the latter's favoritism toward certain "prima donna aviators"—notably Lt. Alford J. Williams, Jr.[47] King's refusal of the offer of command of ZR 1 is not to be found in the records; probably, as Captain Fulton suggested, it was given orally during one of his frequent visits from Norfolk to the Navy Department in Washington.[48]

Still looking for an officer with rank who would give prestige to the rigid airship program, Moffett approached Commander Frank R. McCrary, who accepted and reported to Lakehurst for duty in October 1922. The choice was a poor one: McCrary had indeed had LTA experience before America's entry into World War I, but later had turned against the airship and was on record as favoring flying boats. A passive personality, he accepted the command against his will, did not have the confidence of his

ZR 1 under construction. View from under shed roof. Hull structure complete, horizontal fins and rudders being built on. Jig for frame assembly near the east door. (AIAA)

subordinates, and was easily dominated by Weyerbacher. He was even agreeable to the proposal that he might function as "administrative" commander while Heinen, in the position of "pilot," would operate the ship. In the "shake-up" in January 1924, McCrary was happy to be put in command of a submarine tender, and never returned to lighter than air, though he spent the rest of his naval career through World War II in aviation.

Formal training for the ZR 1 crew was scheduled to commence on 1 February 1923, with 17 enlisted survivors of the Howden Detachment as a nucleus. In addition to the commanding officer, the ship would require one commander or lieutenant commander as executive officer; two commanders or lieutenant commanders as navigators; and four lieutenant commanders or lieutenants as watch officers. Moffett actually wanted 18 officers in order to train a second group for ZR 3, then under construction at Friedrichshafen.[49] In December 1922 a request was made for volunteers for rigid airship training; 41 officers responded, of whom 9 were selected—Commander Jacob H. Klein, Jr., Lcdrs. Maurice R. Pierce, Joseph M. Deem, and Lewis Hancock, and Lts. J. C.

Arnold, Charles E. Rosendahl, Herbert V. Wiley, Earle H. Kincaid, and W. O. Bailey. Eight Army Air Service officers were also sent to Lakehurst to take the rigid airship course, though they would not participate in flight training until the two naval crews had graduated. The ground school opened on 15 March, with lectures and demonstrations by Captain Heinen and survivors of the Howden Detachment. A number of the selected naval officers had not yet reported, the last of them, Commander Klein, not arriving until 24 April, while Lt. Bailey changed his mind and did not go. Besides ground school, apparently there was practical training in free balloons (using hydrogen), the bureau having approved the shipment of three of these with volumes of 35,000, 19,000, and 9,000 cubic feet to Lakehurst on 12 December 1922.[50] Still later, and after ZR 1 had been completed, the nonrigid J 1, of 174,880 cubic feet, was made available for training, making her first flight from Lakehurst on 16 May 1924.

By 15 June the hull of ZR 1 was complete including outer cover and bow mooring gear, and only the power plant installation remained. The control car and engine cars #1 and #2 were already at Lake-

hurst, and the remaining four power cars were shortly sent on from the Naval Aircraft Factory.

Although the Liberty 12-A had been the intended
power plant for ZR 1, another engine was fitted in the
completed ship. While ZR 1 was in the early design
stage, two private firms had shown an interest in
developing an engine specifically for airship use, and
one, by the Packard Motor Company, was accepted
by BuAer as being superior to the Liberty. The Packard Model 1A-1551 was the brain child of Jesse C.
Vincent, the vice president of engineering of the Packard firm and the co-designer of the Liberty engine.
Like the German Maybach, the Packard was a 6-
cylinder inline water-cooled power plant.[51] Its superiority for airship use compared with the Liberty was
in its rugged construction and more favorable fuel
and oil consumption—.45 lb./h.p./hr. and .02 lb./h.p./
hr. vs. .509 lb./h.p./hr. and .037 lb./h.p./hr. in the
Liberty. In an airship, where the weight of fuel for a
long flight might well exceed the weight of the engines, the heavier (and more durable) power plant
with lower fuel consumption would be a better tradeoff. Designed for airship use, the Packard could easily
be changed from right-hand to left-hand operation by
reversing cylinders and shifting parts and accessories
to the other side.[52] A governor automatically closed
the throttle to idling speed if the oil pressure dropped
below 25 p.s.i. or if revolutions exceeded 1500 rpm.

While the four experimental engines could be run
on straight gasoline, the nine high-compression engines initially required a mixture of 30% denatured
alcohol and 70% domestic aviation gasoline to prevent detonation or "knocking" at the higher compression ratio. There was trouble with absorption of
water by the alcohol, and the mixture did not cure the
detonation problem. Only in 1922 was it discovered
that tetraethyl lead would eliminate knocking in
high-compression engines. The alcohol was eliminated, and it then became the practice to carry liquid
tetraethyl lead in small containers. When detonation
occurred at high power settings, the anti-knock fluid
was measured into graduated glass containers and
poured directly into the gravity fuel tanks in the hull
over the engine cars. While the Packards could be
hand-cranked, small water-cooled 2-cylinder opposed engines were fitted in the power cars to provide
950 foot-lb. of starting torque at 50 rpm.

Following inspection of the experimental 1A-1551
engine at the Packard plant, and conferences at the
Naval Aircraft Factory and BuAer in March, the
bureau decided to fit the Packard instead of the
Liberty.[53] The first experimental Packard was delivered to the Naval Aircraft Factory in September 1922,
followed by two more in October. Truscott was somewhat unhappy over the greater weight of the 1A-
1551—"returned weights indicate cars with reduction gearing will be 300 pounds overweight and cars

with reversing gear 350 pounds overweight."[54] One
solution was to omit the gearing in two of the power
cars, #4 and #5. When the modified high-compression 1A-1551 arrived, Truscott changed his mind:

> We are particularly happy about the Packard en-
> gines. The redesigned engine is fitted with compres-
> sion reliefs which make the job of cranking it much
> easier. However, it has a personality and it is almost
> amusing to see the way in which chaps who do not
> have the knack of starting it can work their heads off,
> accomplishing nothing, while the man who knows
> how can have the engine roaring away in a very few
> moments. It really is a beauty of an engine and a most
> delightful thing to watch and listen to. The noise of
> the exhaust is not a rattle nor a harsh noise but a
> distinct mellow boom comparable to the whistle of a
> large steamer.[55]

Nonetheless, only 13 of the Packard 1A-1551 engines were manufactured. (The four experimental engines were rebuilt with high-compression pistons
and other improvements to bring them up to the
standard of the production power plants, and thereafter served as spares.) No commercial airship market developed as Moffett and others had so optimisti-
cally predicted. While the Packard was certainly
much more reliable than the Liberty would have
been, two of ZR 1's Packards failed her in her final
agony. Yet they were being stressed beyond their
limits, as was the ship herself. Subsequently the U.S.
Navy used German 12-cylinder VL-1 and VL-2
Maybachs exclusively in its rigid airships, not only in
the *Los Angeles* but also in the American-built *Akron*
and *Macon*.

Not until the new year, after delivery of the modified high-compression engines, did the Naval Aircraft Factory begin installing them in the six engine
cars under construction. The acceptance test involved a trouble-free 24-hour run of the engine in the
power car, and the #2 engine car was the original
guinea pig, with tests being made at various times
beginning on 23 January 1923. Assorted "bugs" were
revealed and eliminated, and finally #2 car passed
the 24-hour test on 16–17 May. The #1 engine car
completed its 24-hour test on 7–8 June, followed by
the other two geared power cars, #3 and #6. There
was trouble with the direct-drive cars #4 and #5; at
low speeds (500–900 rpm) the long propeller shaft
vibrated badly, turned blue with heat, and finally
deformed. A heavier shaft and flexible coupling cured
the vibration problem; the direct-drive cars finally
passed the 24-hour test and were shipped to Lakehurst late in July.

Various hull details were taken care of at appropriate times, often at the end of construction. The plywood walkway along A girder at the top of the ship,
intended to permit inspection of the maneuvering
valves in flight, was to have a safety rope running

from Frame 30 to Frame 180. Exhaust heating cookers were installed in the four midships engine cars. A closed trunk and ladder from the after end of the control car to Station 162½ in the keel was fitted after the decision to inflate the ship with helium. The Sperry Gyroscope Company modified a small gyro compass originally developed for Army tanks for installation in ZR 1; 23 inches in diameter, 18 inches high, and weighing 90 to 100 lb., it was the first gyro compass carried in any aircraft. There was much correspondence between BuSEng, responsible for radio equipment, BuAer, the Naval Aircraft Factory, and Lakehurst about installation of a radio compass coil of battleship type six feet in diameter: Should it be on the top platform, in the tail cone, or in the keel? Actually it was carried only after the removal of #6 engine early in 1924, and the substitution of a small, wooden-structure radio car abaft the control car which was roomy enough to house the rotating directional antenna. It is interesting that ZR 1 was completed with no gun armament or bomb racks, though there was a top platform at Frame 170 forward. Later, during operations with the fleet, two Lewis machine guns were briefly mounted in the control car windows, though newspaper photographers were forbidden to take pictures of them. Such was the strength of pacifist opinion in the United States in 1925!

Shed tests began as the ship approached completion. On 14 May the electrical bonding of the metal hull was tested, traditionally of great importance in a hydrogen-inflated craft, and also desirable to prevent damage from lightning strikes. At night, and with all lights extinguished, high voltage electric current was turned into the framework, and all hands looked for sparks where the bonding might be incomplete. In July the elevators and fins were statically loaded while the stresses were measured in the girders and wires. On 30 July, after the engine gondolas had been installed, the fuel system was pressure-tested for leaks.

On 12 July, McCrary advised BuAer that the ship would be ready for inflation at the end of working hours on 31 July. This, however, depended on the arrival of ground crew personnel in time for two weeks of training. McCrary recommended that 411 men be made available by 1 August, else the installation of gas cells and inflation would be delayed. The Bureau of Navigation was requested to make the men available, while McCrary was advised to use the civilian station personnel as a ground crew until the regular Navy men arrived.

There was a slight delay when, on 2 August, the brakes of an overhead crane failed, sending it crashing into the top girder of the hull at Frame 180. Three girders were damaged and had to be replaced.

Finally, on 13 August, inflation commenced. Over the next four days, 13,000 cylinders of helium were emptied to fill the 20 gas cells to 85% capacity, for a total of 1,783,000 cubic feet of gas.

On 20 August the official "launching" of ZR 1 took place. General quarters were sounded; 278 men were stationed at the handling lines along the length of the ship, and on the handling rails of the control car and the after engine car. In the ship were two men in each of the six engine cars; seven men distributed through the length of the keel; and two men in the control car along with Lcdr. Pierce and Anton Heinen. All overhead suspension lines were cast off, 18,400 lb. of water ballast was released, and the bow lifted four inches off the shoring, which was removed. A further 2,400 lb. of ballast was released aft, but the stern still failed to lift. Five men were ordered out of the after power cars, but the stern did not rise until two men in the keel at Frame 40 walked forward. The men around the after engine car then lifted it and removed the cradle. At 1434 hours the ZR 1 was floating clear of the cradles and shoring, with a launching weight of 103,320 lb. She was then walked from the north side of the shed, where she had been built, to the south side and placed on cradles under the control car and engine cars #1 and #6.

Shed tests continued, including engine trials. The bureau had unrealistically demanded that all six engines be run simultaneously at full power in the shed. Weyerbacher insisted that only two be run at a time, citing Farlam's experience with British practice, and he got his way.

On 24 August a disquieting mishap occurred, when ACR Frank L. Peckham, walking on the upper walkway looking for leaks, slipped and fell into Cell #11. A replacement cell was installed and inflated the next day, but 164,000 cubic feet of precious helium had been lost. On 25 August there was a further threat: at 0300 personnel on watch in the hangar discovered that the maneuvering valve in the top of Cell #4 was leaking. The accordion-pleated sleeve from the cell to the valve was tied off and the valve removed.

With the completion of shed tests of the various systems, ZR 1 was ready for her first flight. On 14 August BuAer had requested that she be ready for flight tests by 1 September. The deadline had been met. America at last had a rigid airship, four years after passage of the naval appropriations bill that provided for the procurement of two such craft, and two years after R 38, intended to be ZR 2, plunged blazing into the River Humber in England, taking 16 Americans with her. This time it would be different: the design of the silvery beauty had been painstakingly researched, she would be handled with greater knowledge, and she would be the first to be lifted into the air by safe helium.

7

Shenandoah: Learn to Run Before You Walk

Three months before ZR 1's first flight, Weyerbacher had written a memorandum on the flight tests he would propose for the ship. He recommended that the tests be conducted in seven stages, starting with familiarization flights not longer than two hours, in good weather in evening calm, and progressing through tests of the following: rudder and elevator deflections with gradually increasing speed and altitude; turning trials; machinery endurance; fuel and oil consumption (flight of about 24 hours' duration); air speed calibration; dynamic lift at low altitude on a calm day with inclination up to 11 degrees; and dynamic lift at night at high altitude (10,000 feet). In addition, Weyerbacher proposed a flight of 72 hours' duration, and various mast landing trials, ground landings, and tests with a drogue at sea. The early flights, Weyerbacher argued, should be carried out without the knowledge of the public and with the station closed to outsiders so that handling of the ship would not be handicapped by visitors. The program reflected Weyerbacher's professionalism and was appropriate in view of the completely novel nature of the enterprise; it would have provided many useful data on the new airship. Weyerbacher wanted the same crew of 27 to participate in each flight: the officers to include the station commander (McCrary), the manager (Weyerbacher), and the test pilot (Heinen). The test pilot was to be responsible for the operation of the ship, but the manager was to determine if the flight was satisfactory.[1]

The question of who should be responsible for the ship sparked immediate controversy. McCrary, forwarding the plan to the bureau on 2 June 1923, approved the test pilot being responsible, but *only* during test flights, after which the commanding

officer should be in charge. The bureau withheld approval for the time being, later directing that two builder's trials should be made under the manager's direction, after which the schedule of trials should be carried out by the commanding officer.[2]

Weyerbacher's program was never carried out, largely because of Moffett's obsession with using the ship for publicity purposes. On 30 August Moffett advised that on the very first flight, scheduled for 4 September, he wanted to have present representatives of the movie newsreel companies, newspapers, and so forth. Only two more brief flights were made before the big rigid started on a round of "hand-waving" publicity flights, well advertised in advance, intended to show the silvery giant to the big cities in the Northeast. The careful trials program was forgotten. Thereafter, and until the ship met her end two years later, all her triumphs, and many of her troubles, were bathed in the kleig-light glare of radio, newspaper, and magazine publicity. Only 13 of the 59 flights recorded in her log book could be considered related to her intended function as a fleet unit in operations at sea, and the initiative of her commanding officer played a part in scheduling them. Nineteen involved showing her off inside the continental United States, the remainder being local flights, often related to mast mooring. In the end, Moffett became a prisoner of his own campaign for publicity for the airship: the powerful chief of naval operations, Admiral Edward W. Eberle, took a direct interest in the ship and her operations, and issued orders to her commanding officer for flights sometimes beyond her capabilities. Eberle of course had no aviation operating experience, but appears to have felt that the airship should live up to the exaggerated promises of her supporters, while having doubts that she could do so. When ZR 1 was lost in Ohio on her last flight, 400 miles from the sea, she was following orders originally issued by Eberle three months earlier in response to insistent demands from the people and congressmen of the Midwest that she should show herself over a large number of towns and county fairs en route to Minneapolis and Detroit.

Indeed, press coverage was all that Moffett could have desired (he was present but not on board), and 15,000 excited civilians were on the station, when on the late afternoon of 4 September 1923, ZR 1 was walked out of the Lakehurst shed for the first time by a ground crew of 320 Marines and sailors, and 100 civilians. At 1720 she took off with 29 persons on board, and cruised in the area for 55 minutes with only four engines running at half speed, before landing and being returned to the shed. McCrary, Weyerbacher, and Heinen exercised joint command—the latter, because of his experience, giving all the orders for ship handling. In a postflight press conference, Moffett made several enthusiastic statements including a prediction of a journey to the North Pole in the following year.

There followed an evening flight of 1 hour 10 minutes on 6 September, in which all six engines operated, and one of 1 hour 13 minutes on 10 September. On the very next day came the first publicity triumph, in which ZR 1 showed herself first over New York City, and then over Philadelphia. Taking off at 0618 from Lakehurst, she remained in the vicinity of the air station until about 1000, climbing to 7,000 feet to test the automatic gas valves and doing turning tests at 50 knots. Then, having announced by radio that she would be over New York at 1130, McCrary brought the silver airship up the North River to Manhattan precisely on time. Three escorting Army Air Service De Havilland D.H.4B airplanes were suitably dwarfed by the Navy's pride. Circling Manhattan and proceeding down the East River, the ZR 1 went on to Philadelphia, where she arrived about 1430. After a flight of 11 hours 28 minutes the ship landed at Lakehurst in the early evening, somewhat delayed by waiting for the helium to cool. The sensation was all that Moffett could have wished, with huge crowds out in the streets to see the beautiful ship pass over. The newspapers provided full coverage, the New York Times facetiously alleging that the purpose of the flight was "to allow New Yorkers a chance to see Lieut. Bauch take his constitutional walk on the spacious walkway atop the airship."[3] Weyerbacher even wrote an article for the New York Tribune on the flight, emphasizing the existence of an odoriferous layer of what today would be called "smog" over the city.

A similar flight to Washington was scheduled for 18 September, but was postponed because cross winds rendered undocking hazardous. McCrary proposed trying again on the 20th, but Moffett advised him to wait until Saturday the 22nd, on which date the Army Air Service was to execute an air show over the capital. Moffett, advising General Mason M. Patrick, the chief of the Air Service, of the big rigid's participation in the Air Carnival, requested that his pilots be directed not to fly over, under, or within 1,000 yards of ZR 1 to "avoid possibility of accident or distraction of the crew." Departing Lakehurst at 0927, the ship flew in thick weather all the way to Washington where she arrived at 1400. With the air show canceled because of the weather, the Navy's giant drew all the attention and applause.

Now, with only 25 hours on the ship and trials not complete, came a bold tour de force—a journey a third of the way across the continent. The publicity benefits were great; the wisdom of risking the unproven sky giant, with her inexperienced crew, would appear questionable.

On 6 September, after the second flight, Moffett had promised that ZR 1 would go to St. Louis for the International Aeronautical Congress on 1–3 October, and for the National Air Races, which were being held in the first week in October. A naval racing team led by Lcdr. Marc A. Mitscher was to participate in the prestigious Pulitzer Trophy race on 6 October, flying Navy-developed Curtiss R2C and Wright F2W biplane racers.[4] As early as 27 August, Senator Selden P. Spencer had pressured Moffett to send the ship to St. Louis: "It will mean so much in aeronautics if this great ship can at least sail over Saint Louis on each of the three days of the international congress." In replying, Moffett pointed out that the airship's first flight was scheduled for 4 September, and he doubted that test flights could be completed in time. "I can only say that if the trials of the ship are successful, and it is possible to do so with safety, she will be sent to Saint Louis."[5] There was no doubt of Moffett's desires: on 24 September, he asked McCrary for a list of cities and routes he would follow "provided trip is made," while next day Lcdr. Pierce and ACR F. J. Tobin were sent to St. Louis to direct the ground crew. On 26 September the chief of naval operations approved the flight. On the 29th, Pierce and Mitscher received a suggestion from Assistant Secretary of the Navy Theodore Roosevelt, Jr. and from Moffett that "mayor and other authorities of Saint Louis be requested to act as honorary volunteer ground crew for landing ZR 1."[6] The departure from Lakehurst was now scheduled for the morning of 30 September, but McCrary postponed it because "existence of thunderstorm area vicinity of Saint Louis considered unfavorable."[7]

Finally the ship was off at 0659 on 1 October with 42 persons on board. Initially she encountered strong

ZR 1 at the National Air Races at St. Louis on 2 October 1923. A view of the control car and forward engine car from close underneath, as they must have frequently appeared to the Lakehurst ground crew as the airship slowly descended toward them. Note the 18-foot-diameter propeller, geared down to move a large amount of air efficiently at low speed. The control car and radio compartment to the right and the engine car to the left are actually separated by a 3-inch gap, which is faired over with a clearly visible strip of white fabric. (NASM A 4166A)

head winds—over Mount Holly, New Jersey, air speed was 47 knots but ground speed only 17 knots. As she proceeded westward the head wind dropped. For Weyerbacher it must have been a solemn moment as he flew over his home town of Booneville, Indiana, at 0100 on 2 October, and dropped a box of flowers and a greeting for his parents. At 0330 the airship was over St. Louis and circled the city until 0745, when she landed at Lambert Field. For slightly less than two hours she was held on the ground by soldiers while loading fuel and water, and the crew were fed a hearty breakfast of ham and eggs.

ZR 1 being held on the ground at National Air Races, St. Louis, Missouri, 2 October 1923. (U.S. Air Force)

Moffett came on board for the return flight, by way of Chicago (which the airship circled for nearly two hours), Toledo, and Cleveland. With a tail wind, the 725 miles from Chicago to Lakehurst was covered in 12 hours. In all respects but one the gamble had paid off, and the trip was a triumph for the airship, her crew, and the Bureau of Aeronautics. Nothing was said, however, about a failure in the outer boundary girder of the port fin which occurred while the ship was flying over the Alleghenies during the afternoon:

> The ship had been pitching pretty badly and apparently rapid changes of pressure inside the fin had caused some alternating local compression forces which buckled the lattices of this member. It was repaired in flight by lashing a couple of spruce planks in place. Watching this part of the ship afterwards indicated that there was a bulging in and out of the fabric of the fin, presumably caused by air pressure inside the fin. Holes were cut which appeared to stop it. . . . As the interior of this fin is open to the interior of the entire ship, it would appear impossible for any considerable pressure to be built up here, but the fact remains that there is a fluctuation in pressure sufficient to cause difficulties.[8]

The damage was discovered by Lt. Roland Mayer, the ship's first lieutenant and repair officer, whose duty it was to check the hull structure continually for damage in flight. Burgess, who participated in this flight and some of the earlier ones with strain-gauge equipment on board, felt the tail surfaces would require strengthening.

The ship having proved herself, the time had come, in Moffett's opinion, to give ZR 1 a name. Before the St. Louis flight, Moffett had asked McCrary if 10 October would be a suitable date, how many passengers the ship could carry after the christening, and "do you consider it practicable and desirable to take ZR 1 on a flight to London England and return any time during October?"[9] McCrary agreed to the date, but nothing more was heard of the fantastic suggestion of a transatlantic flight.

The naming of the ship was actually the prerogative of Secretary Denby, who on 24 September advised Moffett that the ZR 1 would be christened the *Shenandoah*. The ceremony in fact took place on 10 October—Secretary Denby, his wife, Marion Thurber Denby, who was to act as sponsor, and a party of admirals and dignitaries including Moffett, being received at Lakehurst with full military honors. At 1430 the ceremony took place in the hangar. With the airship floating lightly above the cradles, Marion Denby proclaimed, "I hereby christen this ship the *Shenandoah*, which in Indian language means 'Daughter of the Stars,' "[10] while a number of pigeons, symbolizing peace, were released in the hangar. Rear Admiral Archibald H. Scales, commandant of the

Fourth Naval District, read the orders commissioning the ship, and Commander McCrary read his orders assuming command. The airship, which previously had in effect been in the hands of the builders running trials, was now a unit of the U.S. Navy, and her log book commenced on this date. She also came under the jurisdiction of the chief of naval operations, who on 12 October advised all commands that "the *Shenandoah* is added to the Navy List and assigned for special duty to the Naval Air Station, Lakehurst, New Jersey."[11]

While the distinguished guests looked over the *Shenandoah*, the crew departed to their quarters to change into flying gear. The airship was then undocked and took off for a 1-hour 15-minute flight with the christening party, Mrs. McCrary, Mrs. Klein, and reporters and newsreel cameramen on board. McCrary was now commanding officer, Commander Jacob Klein was executive officer, and Weyerbacher and Heinen, no longer members of the crew, were carried as "advisors to the Commanding Officer." They continued, however, to participate in all further flights, sometimes being listed as "aides."

Navy Day, 27 October, the birthday of Theodore Roosevelt, the "big Navy" advocate of the early years of the century, was of course to be an occasion for another publicity cruise. On 18 October McCrary sent Moffett a list of six possible flights: Lakehurst to Boston and return; Lakehurst to Boston to Syracuse and return; Lakehurst to Syracuse and return (McCrary had been under pressure to visit Syracuse); Lakehurst to Buffalo via Syracuse and return; the Shenandoah Valley; and Lakehurst to Norfolk to Savannah and return. Moffett chose the Shenandoah Valley trip, and on Navy Day the airship made the journey in a leisurely 15 hours 40 minutes, taking the opportunity to show herself over Harrisburg, Richmond, and Washington.

McCrary and the ship's company, however, were becoming impatient with the steady diet of publicity flights. As early as 24 September he had protested to the bureau: "the trials have not progressed as fast as I would desire. . . . personnel are getting rather restless to have training started, as there are a number of officers under training who have not yet made a flight in the ship." To which Commander Emory S. Land, the head of the Material Section of BuAer, remarked: "I don't blame him. He is right to insist on stopping this circus stuff until the trials are completed, and then she should be placed under the commander of the Fleet."[12]

There was for instance the matter of the mooring mast, an issue not to be neglected as there was increasing talk of an Arctic expedition, during which the ship would have to be kept on masts for long periods. Yet nothing had been done to date with the

The *Shenandoah* on the high mast at Lakehurst showing the six-sided house between the mast legs. Photo taken prior to the "breakaway" flight on 16 January 1924. (*Aero Digest* via NASM 81-14798)

Lakehurst mast, completed in May 1922 and dominating the field from a position a quarter of a mile directly out from the west door of the big hangar.

While different in appearance from the Pulham mast, the Lakehurst mast was designed on British principles, and the mooring equipment at the masthead was a copy of that designed by Major Scott for the mast at Pulham. The Lakehurst mast was a stout three-legged steel tower measuring 148 feet to a large lower operating platform, and 160 feet high overall to the gimbals supporting the female cup into which the male cone on the bow of the airship fitted, to be held by heavy clamps. Between the outspread legs at the base was a six-sided building housing winches and pumps, with bunks for 4 officers and 20 men. An elevator ran to a height of 136 feet above ground, with a ladder to the operating platform, whence access to the ship could be had by the nose gangway. Up the center of the mast ran electric cables and piping. A 12-inch gassing main was capable of delivering 300,000 cubic feet of helium per hour to the operating platform under 1 inch of water pressure; 1,500 gallons of fuel per hour could be supplied from an 8,000-gallon underground storage tank, as well as 13,000 lb. of water per hour, via 2½-inch piping to the operating platform. In a circle of 500-foot radius around the mast were 48 snatch blocks at 7½-degree intervals to take the airship's yaw lines regardless of the direction of her approach.

The bureau certainly intended that mast mooring should take place according to British methods, as set forth at length in reports by Land, Maxfield, and Hoyt on operations with R 33 at Pulham in the spring of 1921. This involved laying the main mooring wire from the masthead out along the ground for about 600 feet in the direction from which the ship was approaching at an altitude of 500 feet. The ship dropped the end of her own 450-foot mooring wire, which was coupled to the mast wire on the ground, and she then released 500 lb. of water from an emergency bag forward and rose to about 1,200 feet, approximately two tons light and trimmed down by the tail. She was then hauled down by the winch at the base of the mast reeling in the main mooring wire. At an altitude of 500 feet or so, the ship released two 450-foot yaw lines made fast to the nose. These were coupled to the mast yaw wires and led to snatch blocks bearing approximately 60 degrees from the wind direction, and through the snatch blocks to the yaw winches at the base of the mast. All three lines were reeled taut; then, while the main mooring wire gradually hauled down the ship's nose toward the masthead, the taut yaw lines ensured that she would not swing from side to side, or worse yet, move forward to impale herself on the masthead. A heavy responsibility rested on the mooring officer, directing the entire operation from the operating platform—invariably a member of the ship's company detached for the purpose. Even when the ship's bow cone was secured in the mast cup, much work remained to be done, for "the ship is never safe until in all respects ready to take the air instantly."[13] The ship's main mooring wire and the yaw lines had to be hauled back into the ship, and water ballast and fuel loaded, while the cells would be topped up with helium as necessary. At the mast a skeleton crew consisting of about four officers and one watch of enlisted men[14] was on

board at all times to handle the rudder and elevators, to add or release ballast depending on changes in lift, and to fly the ship if she were forced to slip from the mast in an emergency.

Yet when McCrary finally attempted a mast mooring, he rejected the well-tried British method and instead followed a procedure dreamed up by his German advisor, Anton Heinen, who had had absolutely no experience with mast mooring and had never seen it done! This should have occasioned no surprise, for even before ZR 1 had completed, Heinen had seen fit to write a paper on "The Operation of Securing an Airship to the Mooring Mast." He proposed that the ship approach the mast "not more than 50 feet above the mast cone" and then check her way by running two engines in reverse. The *yaw* lines (not the main mooring cable) were then to be dropped and rove through the snatch blocks, after which the main mooring cable was to be dropped. During the process the ship, already dangerously close to the masthead, was free to move forward into the mast unless restrained by the engines running in reverse. One can only conclude that Heinen, the German Zeppelin expert, suffered from an exaggerated view of his own omniscience in airship matters, while the outcome underlined the degree to which he and Weyerbacher dominated the *Shenandoah*'s commanding officer.

The moment of truth came on 5 November, when McCrary made his first attempt to moor to the mast using the Heinen method, and experienced total frustration. Late in the afternoon, at 1645, the ship took off after being carefully weighed off on the field. McCrary anticipated that she would become heavy with the approach of sunset, but in two attempts to moor to the mast, the *Shenandoah* proved to be light and rose as the engines were set on "idle." The only way to land her would have been to valve helium, which McCrary was not willing to do, and he finally abandoned the attempt owing to the onset of darkness. "The failure to accomplish the mooring on these attempts was not due to any material failure or design," wrote McCrary. "No, it was the method!" wrote Truscott on the cover sheet.[15]

For too long the British-trained airship operators in BuAer, Lansdowne and Lawrence (who on ZR 2's last flight was to have acted as mooring officer at Pulham)—not to mention the veterans, Truscott, Hunsaker, and Burgess—had swallowed their resentment over Heinen's dominance, through Weyerbacher, of operations and procedures at Lakehurst. In most matters they could not second-guess his authority as an expert on German methods. Now that he had ventured to pontificate in an area where he had no experience, and had suffered failure, they could not restrain their sarcasm. Worse yet, there was the fear that the trio commanding the *Shenandoah* would damage the precious ship through reckless disregard of established procedures.

Noting that McCrary and his advisors preferred their method to the proven British one, the bureau stated its belief that it was inferior, and pointed to the failure on 5 November. Had McCrary been using the British method, it was argued that he would have been successful. The British method had been developed over a period of five months with R 33 at Pulham by Captains George H. Scott and Godfrey Maine Thomas, two airship pilots "believed to be as experienced and capable as any." The bureau disclaimed any intention to "impose limitations on the Commanding Officer," but invited "attention to the fact that at present the Navy has but one rigid airship; consequently experimental or untried methods of handling should, at least for the present, be avoided as far as possible."[16]

On the same day, 16 November, the *Shenandoah* was finally moored to the mast using the Heinen method. The entire procedure took over 45 minutes in a light wind of only 4 mph, which McCrary considered a disadvantage. Approaching the mast from two miles out at an altitude of 1,000 feet, the ship was 500 to 600 lb. light and in trim, gradually descending to 500 feet above the ground. With two engines running at half speed, the ship was forced down by the elevators to 350 feet. About 1,000 yards from the circle of snatch blocks the elevator was put hard down and #2 and #3 engines run full astern, thus stopping the ship just inside the circle of blocks. Here she started to rise, but was checked when the starboard yaw line was dropped and connected up. She was then sailed to port with the engines and the port yaw line dropped and connected up, after which one emergency ballast bag was dropped forward to put a strain on the yaw lines. Fearing that the ship, at low altitude, would surge forward into the mast, McCrary kept #2 and #3 engines running full astern until they overheated and had to be stopped—no air was flowing through the radiators in the gondola noses! The main mooring wire was finally dropped, but it was 25 minutes more before the nose was made fast in the mast cone. Again the comments in the bureau were critical—"totally wrong in principle" (Lawrence); "Concur" (Truscott); "in my opinion the method of first mooring with yaw guys close to the top of the mast is not only wrong but dangerous except in favorable weather as the ship should first go to 1000 feet or more on the main cable at least 1 ton light and trimmed down by the tail at least 3°" (Lansdowne).[17]

Meanwhile, to add to his troubles, McCrary on 8 November was ordered to make a flight over the New England states on the first day after 11 November that weather and other conditions would permit. Only the order came, not from Moffett, but from the

chief of naval operations, Admiral Eberle. McCrary scheduled the flight for the 13th, but had to postpone it because of high winds. The same problem occurred on the 14th and 15th. Meanwhile the newspapers had been announcing the flights that could not be made. On the 16th McCrary canceled for the next day—"the clouds are so low that the ship could not be seen and the object of the flight would have been destroyed thereby." The *New York Herald* published an editorial on "the Delicate Zeppelin" commenting on the cancellation of the Boston flight—"for the fourth time because of unfavorable winds and the reappearance of storm threats." The airship was labeled slow and helpless in comparison with the airplane: "for war service the gas bag is to the plane as the circus fat man is to Jack Dempsey."[18] McCrary believed the *Shenandoah* was being criticized as a "fair weather ship," yet in St. Louis he had told newspapermen, "you people . . . were lucky to have the clear weather that you had today, after your storms, or we couldn't have come."[19]

Finally, on 20 November, the *Shenandoah* took off at 0648 for the Boston flight with a crew of 38, four press representatives, and four of the Army officers under training. Passing over Brooklyn and out over Long Island, she proceeded via New London, Fall River, and Providence to Boston. On the return flight over Worcester, the ship, now light from consumption of fuel, was allowed to ascend to 6,950 feet, her pressure height, blowing off 5% of her helium through the automatic valves.[20] At 2115, after a flight of 15½ hours, the ship was back on the field at Lakehurst in the hands of the ground crew, but the weather was unfavorable for housing her as the wind was blowing almost directly across the entrance to the hangar with gusts up to 17 mph. For two hours the *Shenandoah* was held on the ground in the open in hopes the wind would drop, but instead it worsened. McCrary rejected the idea of taking the ship to the mast because of insufficient training of personnel "and other probable damage to the ship resulting from mooring her to the mast in the face of the weather forecast."[21] Knowing that the gondola struts might be damaged, McCrary ordered the ship walked into the hangar. A down draft forced the stern to the ground, the suspension struts of the rear engine car collapsed, the car rotated aft through 90 degrees and was forced up into the hull, while the gondola's nose was damaged. The *Shenandoah* was laid up and under repair until 12 December. McCrary tried to blame the damage on weakness in the car suspension, claiming that if further struts had been fitted as previously recommended by Lakehurst personnel, there would have been no damage. But the bureau was not impressed: since on 16 November, McCrary had held that the light wind was a disadvantage in mooring to the mast, why on 20 November, when he had the wind, did he try to house her in the shed instead of taking her to the mast? Had the ship been taken into the shed within half an hour of her landing, everything probably would have been all right. Instead she was held on the ground for three hours before going into the shed.[22]

On 15 December the ship was out for a training flight, but there was no intention of mooring her to the mast. A landing attempt at noon failed because the ship was too light; to make her heavy the *Shenandoah* was taken to 8,400 feet, her pressure height, to valve helium.

Three days later, in the evening, the *Shenandoah* was taken from the hangar, flown to the mast, and moored by Heinen's method in a light wind. At takeoff, 4,930 lb. of ballast was on board; during the mooring, 4,900 lb. was discharged—to the consternation of Lawrence and the airship people at the bureau. The ship stayed on the mast overnight, and by 1345 on the following day had loaded 6,100 lb. of water ballast. At 1515 she left the mast and landed on the ground. A strong cross wind was blowing at the hangar, however, and remembering the criticism that followed the Boston flight, McCrary chose to put the *Shenandoah* back on the mast. But instead of being flown, she was walked to the mast by the ground crew and let up on the handling lines. The Heinen method thus was not tested in a strong wind; the consequences might have been disastrous. At 0630 on 20 December, the ship was unmoored, descended to the ground, and at 0730 was secured in the shed. A report forwarded by McCrary on 29 December was characterized as "a fine lot of no information" by the bureau, which asked for more data on the use of ballast. Instead, McCrary described the Heinen method, claiming that "Captain Heinen had most remarkable control over the ship at all times, and it is believed that the manoeuvres were carried out in the most adverse conditions, that is, with very little wind and at a time of day when the lift was being decreased by the loss of superheat." Lansdowne noted contemptuously: "still using the wrong method of mooring ship. Operation was performed in almost a calm. Therefore any method is safe."[23]

Moffett's patience with McCrary, Weyerbacher, and Heinen was exhausted when, early in January 1924, a copy of Heinen's "The Operation of Securing an Airship to the Mooring Mast" came into his hands. The German's procedure was compared unfavorably with that set out in Hoyt's and Maxfield's reports on the actual operation of R 33 at the Pulham mast in March and April 1921: "In these references the method of mooring is described in detail, not from theoretical study but from actual observation of the operation. . . . Ample opportunity for this study was

had and the final method cannot be said to be tentative or subject to probable improvement by inexperienced personnel." By contrast, Heinen's method had only a "theoretical foundation" and "reflects the ideas of an individual who is, as stated in its first paragraph, without experience in the handling of rigid airships around mooring masts." In particular, "to proceed to the mast . . . at an altitude of not more than 50 feet above the mast cone . . . invites disaster. No matter how perfect the control or preparations, a failure to stop the ship might easily bring her on the mast. With this altitude of approach it is apparent why the securing of the guy lines first is proposed." In summary, "the Bureau has come to the conclusion that the method of mast mooring described is based on an unsound analysis of the problem which, made without experience in such operations, has resulted in incorrect conclusions. It is believed that the method proposed is dangerous to the ship." Moffett directed that at as early a date as practicable the *Shenandoah* be moored to the mast five times using the British method. "On the completion of these five moorings a report is to be submitted to the Bureau describing the operation. With this report recommendations are to be forwarded as to the method of mast mooring to be followed in the future but until the Bureau's approval has been given the general method followed in the five moorings is to be adhered to."[24] Anton Heinen, though he did not know it, was on his way out, while the bureau viewed McCrary's uncertain handling of the ship with misgivings.

The *Shenandoah* had made her last flight of the year. Meanwhile, serious planning was going ahead for the polar flight.

To be the first to reach the North Pole by air—and in an American rigid airship—was Admiral Moffett's most dramatic and persistent idea for publicizing the Bureau of Aeronautics and its various projects. As early as 6 March 1923, in a radio broadcast over Station WJZ in New York, Moffett had promised that the ZR 1, when completed, "will be sent on trips around the world and to the North and South Poles."[25] There can be little doubt that he believed the ship would be capable of such performance. He repeated the prediction of a flight to the North Pole in a press interview after the first flight on 4 September, and the success of the St. Louis journey stimulated Moffett to proceed with planning for the expedition in the following months. An excuse for pushing the project at this time was the publicly announced intention of Captain Robert A. Bartlett, the commander of Admiral Robert E. Peary's ship the *Roosevelt* in the successful polar expedition of 1908–9, to purchase the *Roosevelt* from her then-owners and fit her out for another polar expedition. There was also an element of international rivalry: Roald Amundsen, the Norwegian discoverer of the South Pole, who had taken a German Junkers monoplane to Alaska for a flight from Point Barrow to Spitzbergen, only to lose it in a crash in June 1923, was planning another aerial attempt on the pole with the financial backing of the wealthy Lincoln Ellsworth.[26] Proceeding through the secretary of the navy, Moffett secured the approval on 20 November of the president, who since Harding's sudden death on 2 August 1923, had been Calvin Coolidge. In eloquent prose uncharacteristic of "Silent Cal," the president wrote to Denby: "as it fell to the Navy to achieve the final goal, through the efforts of Admiral Peary, it is eminently fitting that the Navy should continue the work, and I believe that the expedition that you have in view will be of great practical value."[27] Denby immediately appointed Moffett as senior member of a board to "prepare a detailed plan for the exploration of the North Pole region."[28] Robert Bartlett was given a commission as Lieutenant Commander USNRF and added to the board. Though nothing was said in the secretary's directive about the means of exploring the polar region, the designation of Moffett indicated that it was to be by air. The ancient *Roosevelt* was forgotten in enthusiasm for the *Shenandoah*.

The board held its first meeting on 5 October, and submitted its report on the 13th. "Semiportable" mooring masts—160-foot poles of steel tubing 16 inches in diameter and braced by three sets of guy wires, with operating platform and masthead as on the Lakehurst mast, and 24 snatch blocks for yaw wires, on a circle of 500-foot radius—were to be erected at Fort Worth, San Diego, Camp Lewis (Washington), and Nome, Alaska, the first two having already been authorized. Two vessels were to be converted as tenders for the expedition, each with a mooring mast on the fantail, accommodation for three seaplanes, helium in cylinders, and gasoline stowage. One was to proceed to Nome, which was to be the Alaskan headquarters of the expedition, the other to Spitzbergen to provide an alternate base during exploration flights, or in case of a transpolar flight. The ship in the Nome area was to carry, in addition to her regular complement, 12 officers including a rear admiral (Moffett on 10 January 1924, was named commander of the polar expedition) and 57 enlisted men; while the vessel at Spitzbergen would carry 6 lieutenants and 32 enlisted men. On 22 December Secretary Denby approved the report, and three days later he announced the expedition to the press.

Immediately after President Coolidge approved the flight, Lakehurst and the bureau began considering how to increase the *Shenandoah*'s range. One attractive modification, advocated by Weyerbacher

and Heinen, was to inflate the ship with hydrogen while inserting an extra 10-meter bay amidships to increase her length to 710 feet and volume to 2,263,000 cubic feet; but Secretary Denby stated that helium was to be used. Truscott contemplated a 3,000-mile flight from Teller to the North Pole and return.[29] With not more than 20,000 lb. of fuel on board (gross lift would be greater than usual in the Arctic, owing to low air temperature), she had sufficient range at 40 mph to do it, but at 60 mph she could not do so safely. The fuel capacity could be increased by reducing the ballast loaded from 4,400 to 1,100 lb.; this was feasible only with water recovery. Removing the #6 engine, gearing, and propeller abaft the control car would gain 2,000 lb. Although 1,000 lb. could be saved with a new and lighter set of gas cells, Truscott did not believe this was feasible in time for a flight in the summer of 1924, but a new cover should be applied before the flight, and if it were made of lighter material, 500 lb. would be saved.[30] In fact, the #6 engine was removed and a new, light-weight gondola of wooden construction substituted (so as not to shield the radio compass), which at the same time provided room for powerful long-range radio sending and receiving equipment needed for scouting with the fleet, as well as a radio compass, a motor-generator for the radio equipment, and a tiny galley with two-burner gasoline stove.

On 24 December, Lansdowne was named project manager at the Bureau for the polar expedition, with Bartlett and Truscott to assist him. Lansdowne's room was promptly labeled "the igloo," someone even recommending that "all radiation be removed from Room 2244 to make it suitable for use as an igloo."[31]

After a study of all ships suitable for the tender role, the fleet oilers *Ramapo* (AO 12) and *Patoka* (AO 9) were recommended; the secretary approved their conversion on 11 January 1924. The *Ramapo* was already at the Mare Island Navy yard for overhaul, where the modifications could be carried out at the same time; she was intended to serve as the expedition flagship at Nome. The *Patoka*, then in the Mediterranean, was to report to Norfolk about 5 February for conversion, and would be the base ship at Spitzbergen. Both tenders were to receive a mooring mast aft similar to the one at Lakehurst with mast cone 141 feet above the waterline, with hinged 80-foot booms that could be extended horizontally to handle the yaw guys. Further modifications included: construction of a deck house for quarters for personnel; installation of 6,900 flasks of helium with manifolding and piping; gasoline storage for 32,500 gallons in drums; and cutting down of foremast, top of mainmast if necessary, and some of the superstructure. On 14 February the two vessels' commanding officers were placed under Admiral Moffett for temporary duty with the Naval Arctic Expedition. A "very approximate" schedule of movements, drawn up by Marc Mitscher in the Plans Division at the bureau, had the *Ramapo* arriving at Nome on 15 May 1924, "or as soon thereafter as ice conditions permit," and the *Patoka* arriving at Spitzbergen on 20 May. The *Shenandoah* was to depart Lakehurst 1 June, or upon the *Ramapo*'s arrival at Nome; and to arrive at Fort Worth 2 June, San Diego 6 June, Seattle 8 June, and Nome 15 June, followed by "Exploration Flights: Flights to Spitzbergen. Return by same route."[32]

An important meeting on 5 January brought together Moffett, Land, Lansdowne, and Truscott of the bureau, and McCrary, Weyerbacher, and Heinen from Lakehurst. Here it was agreed to remove #6 engine and install the radio equipment in the new car. Moffett believed that because the president had authorized the trip, there would be no difficulty getting needed helium from the Army. McCrary, however, was pessimistic: Much training remained to be done, but owing to the need to purify the helium in the ship, she could only operate until 15 March, when she would have to be put in the shed. He did not think the *Shenandoah* could get away before 1 June, and she would take a month to get to Nome. Following the meeting, however, he took a more optimistic view: "Since my return from Washington I have been thinking and dreaming of nothing but the Polar exploration flight and contrary to the usual experiences, the difficulties seem to lessen in importance as the investigation proceeds." But he still wished to hangar the ship for two months starting 15 March for a thorough overhaul including deflation, installation of the new forward car without the engine, and water recovery apparatus. After recommissioning 15 May, two weeks would remain for tests and mooring trials with the *Patoka*.[33]

Already, however, the expedition was in deep trouble. Moffett, remarkably for him, had failed to do his homework with Congress, whereas McCrary, allegedly backed by Weyerbacher and Heinen, had caused alarm by telling the press that "the *Shenandoah* is not suited for the Polar flight and that if she is sent out she will never return."[34] He later denied the pessimistic pronouncement, but the press, now hot on the scent, claimed that he had disagreed with Heinen and Weyerbacher concerning the route to be followed in approaching the polar regions. The papers expressed doubt about the ship's capabilities and the safety of the flight, and increasing pressure in opposition to the expedition was brought to bear on Congress. Moffett in an interview claimed primary interest in exploring the "Pole of Inaccessibility," the area 400 miles from the pole toward Alaska which no living being had ever visited; and he claimed that success

was certain as the longest flight would be only 2,000 miles, while the airship's range was now 4,000 miles.[35] Nonetheless, Representative Taylor of West Virginia introduced a resolution to determine whether the flight was feasible, and the House Naval Affairs Committee held hearings. Moffett testified, as did Secretary Denby on 19 January, stating that the *Shenandoah* might fly over the pole to Spitzbergen and go on to England before returning home. A skeptical Representative Butler of Illinois remarked, "I received information that members of the crew have agreed among themselves that in case McCrary retains command when the *Shenandoah* heads for the north, they will refuse to volunteer." Denby could only reply that "nothing has been decided upon the personnel for the expedition and I have not heard of the report."[36] In February the Naval Appropriations Sub-Committee started hearings on the matter: there was much criticism of the $350,000 estimated cost of the expedition, and the fiscal year 1925 appropriations bill was voted out with no specific appropriation for the expedition.

President Coolidge, himself a more astute politician than Moffett, noted the storm signals with alarm. Much of the criticism of the previous administration in respect to the Teapot Dome scandal was that the naval oil leases had been transferred to private interests without congressional knowledge or approval. Should the *Shenandoah* suffer a disaster in the Arctic, the blame would be placed squarely on the president. With increasing indications that congressional approval would not be forthcoming, Coolidge on 15 February ordered that planning for the expedition, and expenditures in connection with it, cease. Already an advance party for Nome had left the East Coast, and it had to be recalled from the Bremerton Navy Yard. Alterations to the *Ramapo* were canceled, but because the *Patoka* was designated a permanent fleet airship tender, her conversion proceeded; while work went on with the Fort Worth, San Diego, and Camp Lewis masts. Although other airships—the Italian-built *Norge* and *Italia*, and the German *Graf Zeppelin*—made well-publicized flights in the Arctic in the 1920s and 1930s, no American airship crossed the Arctic Circle until after World War II.

Meanwhile a serious accident to the *Shenandoah* had made her the center of public attention, with mixed results. As discussed earlier, Admiral Moffett on 9 January had ordered McCrary to make five mast moorings following the English method. As a result, the *Shenandoah* on the evening of 12 January was walked from the hangar to the mooring mast, and stayed there for 42 hours, when she was unmoored for a local flight and landed to the mast. Another mast mooring was made on 15 January. McCrary had no trouble with the English system, except for slowness of the yaw winches. So far the weather had been fine, but McCrary and Weyerbacher wanted to test the ship at the mast in bad weather, Weyerbacher holding that a wind of 45 mph would be the maximum she should be subjected to at the mast, while McCrary wanted to see what she could actually stand. Strain gauges had been installed at Frame 160 to measure stresses on the longitudinals in the nose, and C. P. Burgess was on board to read the results. It was McCrary's intention to keep her on the mast for a week, but with a partial crew on board and ready in all respects to slip from the mast if the wind were too strong.

A change in the weather occurred on the 16th as the sky clouded over and the wind freshened from the south–southeast. In the early afternoon moderate rain began to fall, and at 1500 a slight rolling motion was continuous. At 1600 when the watch changed, it was raining and blowing with gusts up to 63 mph. At 1700 McCrary, who had been on board all day, went ashore, believing that the weather was moderating. Remaining at his house nearby, he was ready for duty whenever called. Of the 9,000 lb. of ballast on board at noon, 3,400 lb. had been dropped by 1800 to compensate for the weight of rain on the outer cover. Personnel on board at 1800 included Lcdr. Pierce as senior officer, Lcdr. Deem, Lts. Mayer and Kincaid, and Anton Heinen, with ten members of the regular crew, four Army enlisted men under training, and Burgess. Each engine car had at least one man standing by for orders. A relief watch was also in the building at the base of the tower, ready to board if the officers decided to slip from the mast.

Instead of moderating, the wind and rain became ever more violent. Burgess wrote that:

so much water came down the exhaust trunk at Frame 160 and fell upon the strain gauges that it was necessary to cover them with a piece of canvas, and observe their movements by lifting a corner of the canvas, and peeking under it with a flash light. . . . From about 6.15 p.m. . . . the noise, jar, and vibration in the ship were truly terrific, far more than anything I ever experienced in the ship in flight. . . . The maximum stresses observed during this period . . . were large, but not such as to indicate any danger of the ship breaking in two at Frame 160 where the most severe stresses were expected.[37]

At 1830 the winds reached a peak of 64 mph at the Aerology Building and 71½ mph at the top of the mast. Heinen and Mayer had just come from the Aerology Building, the former having decided to leave the mast to ride out the storm in the air. McCrary had been called at his home, and while waiting for him, Heinen asked Mayer to go aft and inspect the tail.

The covering on the top fin being loose, I first climbed out on the ship to investigate this. The cover was very loose, the flapping of the cover running like waves from the forward to the after ends with each gust. It was impossible to get into this fin. I therefore went into the port horizontal fin, this being the one with which we had trouble on the St. Louis flight. The cover of this fin was acting very badly, the gusts whipping it back and forth with terrific force.[38]

As he started forward, Mayer "heard two metallic clicks indicating wires or lattices breaking." Returning aft, he crawled into the port fin and there was an explosion and gust. Climbing to the upper fin as rapidly as possible, Mayer found the fabric from Frame 5 to 0 had been blown off and the girders broken. As he started forward, the ship went down sharply by the tail—but Mayer did not realize that she had broken away from the mast until he reached the control car.

Neither did the control car personnel—Pierce, Deem, Heinen, Kincaid, Chief Rigger Masters at the rudder wheel, and Army Sergeant Brown on the elevators—until they saw the masthead lights disappearing upward. It was 1844, and a gust of 77 mph striking the ship on the starboard bow had destroyed the top fin, causing the ship at the same time to roll so sharply that the nose cap and foremost Frame 194.75 were wrenched right out of the ship. Realizing what was happening, Kincaid, Pierce, and Heinen seized the ballast toggles, dumping 4,200 lb. of water from forward, midships, and aft, while Deem called all engines to start via the engine telegraphs. Heinen shouted for everyone in the keel to run aft and took the elevator wheel, and the Shenandoah, driving across the field stern first, rose just in time. Gasoline slip tanks at Frames 80, 150, and 151 were dropped through the cover, followed by a spare generator, repair tools, reserve oil tanks, and spare parts. With the engines running, and the ship rising as she was carried north–northwest, the situation was under control. Going forward to inspect the damage, Mayer found the foremost cell, #20, rapidly deflating and #19 with many holes. To protect Cell #19, #20 was torn down and pulled over #19, and several holes in #19 were tied off, but when the engines were set on cruising speed to reduce the sternway, Cell #19 collapsed and was tied up to protect Cell #18.

Badly damaged forward, unable to run engines at full power, the Shenandoah made sternway toward the northwest. At 2000 the officers estimated their position over New Brunswick, with the wind velocity exceeding the ship's speed by 16 knots. Meanwhile the radio operator, Gunner Robertson, was frantically working to reassemble his set, which at the time of the breakaway was in pieces being worked on. At 2100 he broadcast his first message, "we think we are over New Brunswick," and was surprised to read, "you are over Newark," the home of Station WOR, which was talking to him. While other stations went off the air in order not to interfere, WOR relayed the *Shenandoah*'s messages until 2200, when she made direct contact with Lakehurst. After crossing Newark the wind shifted to 260° and with the ship still heading into the wind, she was being driven over Manhattan and Brooklyn. Now the wind was dropping, and bringing it on the starboard bow, the airship made leeway to the south and west, arriving over South Amboy at midnight.

Here Lt. Kincaid, who was handling the rudder wheel, became involved in a quarrel with Heinen—a trivial matter, but one destined, because of Kincaid's arrogance, to have far-reaching consequences. A favorite of McCrary, who had not punished him for stowing away on the first flight, Kincaid had developed a grudge against Weyerbacher and Heinen after the former had reprimanded him. Though only a student naval aviator, Kincaid was not about to take orders from a civilian, and chose to argue when Heinen found him steering the ship into the wind instead of holding the wind on the starboard bow. Heinen won, but Kincaid had his revenge a little later when Pierce gave him a position report to send by radio: "Over Keyport making some headway to south cruising speed all engines please tell families not to worry." To which Kincaid chose to add "control car is delightful for first time because of not being overcrowded,"[39] and signed his name. The message was received not only by Lakehurst but by all the commercial stations listening in. Reporters sensed a good story.

With airspeed about 50 mph and ground speed about 4 mph, the *Shenandoah* gradually approached the air station; at 0330 she landed on the east field and was walked into the shed. Over the next few days the ship was inspected by a board of investigation appointed by Rear Admiral Scales, commandant of the 4th Naval District, to inquire into the accident; and repairs commenced, which obviously would take considerable time. Joy and relief were universal: Heinen was praised and applauded, quite justifiably, for having saved the ship by his skill and resolute action, while Pierce, the ranking officer on board, was commended by his superiors. Admiral Moffett praised the ship as "the best and strongest rigid in the world." But the reporters could not leave Heinen and Kincaid alone. Kincaid was quoted as saying that Heinen was employed as a consulting engineer at a salary of $500 per week; Heinen was furious. Other people talked—the *Shenandoah* crew members, station personnel, civilian employees. The line officers' resentment of Weyerbacher, the Construction Corps officer who arrogated to himself the privilege of com-

Bow damage to the *Shenandoah* after breaking away from the mast on 16 January 1924, photographed in the Lakehurst shed on the following day. Note that the bow mooring fitting has been wrenched right out of the ship. The two foremost gas cells #19 and #20 have collapsed, and the head of cell #18 is visible through the tear in the outer cover. (AIAA)

mand, was out in the open, together with McCrary's lack of confidence in the *Shenandoah*, and his crew's lack of confidence in him. A report by Lcdr. Victor Herbster, Naval Aviator #4, was critical of personnel and operations at Lakehurst:

> [there] seemed to exist rather contradictory ideas as to the authority and reponsibilities of the personnel at Lakehurst relative to the *Shenandoah*. It was apparent that the Construction and Repair manager attached to the station and the civilian personnel had ideas as to the management and operation of the *Shenandoah* which were at variance with the ideas of the line. The situation was further complicated by the fact that no officers qualified as rigid airship pilots were attached to the *Shenandoah*.[40]

Moffett had to act. The polar expedition was still the *Shenandoah*'s next mission, McCrary's lack of leadership qualities was apparent, he was not qualified for command, and it was intolerable that the ship, on a flight on which the eyes of the world would be fixed, should be the responsibility of Weyerbacher and Heinen. Last, the latter two had become persona non grata in the bureau by their arrogant insistence on running matters at Lakehurst in their own way, particularly after the mast mooring controversy demonstrated that they were not infallible.

On 8 February BuAer proposed orders for the officers at Lakehurst: McCrary to be relieved of duty as commanding officer of the *Shenandoah* and of NAS Lakehurst (later going to command the submarine tender *Canopus* at Mare Island). "I am tickled to death at this opportunity to be relieved from duty here," he told reporters.[41] Commander Klein was relieved of all duties on board the *Shenandoah* and as executive officer at Lakehurst, and assigned duty as commanding officer of NAS Lakehurst. Commander Weyerbacher was detached from all duties at NAS Lakehurst and the *Shenandoah*, and proceeded to Pensacola for flight training, later becoming chief engineer at the Naval Aircraft Factory. Having set his heart on going on the polar flight, he went to Washington to protest in person, but in vain. Nonetheless, he left behind at Lakehurst a strong clique of supporters and admirers. Kincaid was punished by having his student naval aviator designation revoked and being detached from all duties at Lakehurst and with the *Shenandoah*. Transferred to the Receiving Ship at New York, he went on to spend two years on board the cargo ship USS *Kittery*, an ancient tub that was built in Germany in 1905 and was seized upon America's entry into World War I. Heinen was not further employed at this time, and his contract was not renewed when it ran out on 1 July 1924.

Looking for a qualified commander for the polar flight, Moffett found the man he needed right at hand—none other than the project manager for the expedition, Lcdr. Zachary Lansdowne. Rank did not matter as much as experience, and Lansdowne in fact had had more rigid airship flight time than any other officer then in the Navy. After training in R 23 and R 25 at Pulham and Howden during the war, he had made the westward transatlantic crossing of R 34 in 1919, and more recently had been in Germany in connection with the construction of ZR 3, then building at Friedrichshafen. Events would prove his officer-like qualities, his skill as a ship handler, and his ability to command the loyalty and devotion of his men. Above all, he saw the need to operate the *Shenandoah* with the fleet and to demonstrate her naval capabilities, and while always deferential to Moffett, he attempted to oppose the latter's publicity mania through channels.

On 16 February 1924 general quarters were held in the hangar at Lakehurst and Lansdowne read his orders to relieve McCrary as commanding officer of the USS *Shenandoah*.

Three months would pass before the ship flew again. Not only was it necessary to rebuild the nose, replace the two foremost gas cells, reconstruct the upper fin, strengthen the other fins, and replace damaged longitudinals in the tail; but all the changes planned for the polar flight had to be carried out. One decision altered the *Shenandoah*'s appearance, and for the better: on 22 January Moffett directed that the huge "ZR 1" letters on the bow be removed. Engines were torn down by the crew and given a top overhaul. The new commanding officer made his presence felt. Even though he had no opportunity to demonstrate ship-handling ability, his manner was self-assured; and had the polar flight not been canceled, Lansdowne would gladly have undertaken it, probably successfully.

It is noteworthy that Lansdowne made very little change in the team of officers and men under him. Lieutenant Lewis Hancock stepped into Klein's place and proved a thoroughly loyal and competent executive officer to the end. Lieutenant John Lawrence, who had been close to Lansdowne at the bureau, reported on board as watch officer on 15 April, while Lt. (j.g.) Carlton D. Palmer had joined as radio officer on 15 February.

A new installation in the ship during this period was a water recovery apparatus on #1 engine car. Even with earlier operation of hydrogen-inflated rigid airships, when it had been customary simply to valve gas to compensate for the weight of fuel burned on a long flight, there had been some interest in compensating for the weight of fuel consumed by condensing water from the engine exhausts. The first British rigid airship, H.M. Airship No. 1 of 1911, was fitted with condensers, and it was claimed that 70% of the weight of fuel consumed could thus be recovered. Theoretically, for every 100 lb. of gasoline burned, 145 lb. of water was formed. Only the Americans, however, made a serious and consistent effort to take advantage of this possibility—having little choice, for the nonflammable helium with which their airships were inflated was too scarce and expensive to be wastefully valved off at the end of a flight.[42] While the theory was simple, the practice was not, and some of the problems were never solved.[43]

Prior to 1920 a water recovery apparatus was developed at the Washington Navy Yard; but the equipment installed on board the *Shenandoah* was the work of an Englishman, Humphrey F. Parker, at the Bureau of Standards in 1921. Three thousand feet of aluminum tubing 1 inch in diameter and 0.022 inch in thickness was wound into a package measuring 20 × 4 × 3 feet and weighing about 450 lb. The exhaust gases entered the tubing, and were cooled and condensed by the atmospheric air; the condensed water was drained off at suitable points. Power plant efficiency was of course reduced by the back pressure of the condenser; so when full power was required, the engines were "run atmospheric" (i.e., disconnected from the water recovery apparatus).

The *Shenandoah* bow being rebuilt after the "breakaway" flight. Note how cells #17 and #18, about 70% full, have "risen" to the level of the helium inside. Black spot on the head of Cell #18 is the axial cable fitting. Note two emergency ballast bags on the port side of Frame 180. (Garland Fulton)

In September 1923, Parker, now an employee of the Aeronautical Engine Laboratory at the Washington Navy Yard, was assigned the task of designing water recovery equipment for the *Shenandoah*. The units were wanted in a hurry, and Parker, forced to choose between "eliminating the worst defects from the Bureau of Standards type and equipping the ship with a minimum of delay, or of designing more efficient apparatus which probably would not be ready for this summer's operation" (1924),[44] felt obliged to follow the former course. The largest dimension of the new unit was reduced to five feet, though the weight was still 450 lb. Parker admitted that the unit was overdesigned and experimental, and because of drag, "*will* detract from the performance of the ship to an appreciable extent."[45] In November, with the design complete, Parker moved to the Naval Aircraft Factory to supervise the detailed design and manufacture of the six units required. The first was completed in January 1924, and with the *Shenandoah* laid up, tests were run at the factory using the #6 Packard engine formerly installed abaft the control car, with a Liberty engine providing an air flow through the condenser. In tests

at the factory between 24 March and 3 April, the recovery rate ran between 63.5 and 84% at 60 mph air speed with a gasoline/benzol mixture, while with straight gasoline recovery was 102 to 112% at 150 h.p., the higher value occurring at higher air speeds (60–70 mph).[46] A few days later the bureau ordered immediate installation of the unit on board the *Shenandoah*.

Indeed, by the time the *Shenandoah* was ready to fly again, helium conservation was very necessary, becoming, in fact, an obsession with Landsdowne, and with reason. Unlike McCrary, he knew he could not afford to valve helium to make the ship heavy during or at the end of a flight. While the helium plant at Fort Worth was increasing its production during fiscal 1925, only half went to the Navy,[47] and the *Shenandoah* had to share this with the J 1 training ship at Lakehurst, while the new ZR 3, with a volume of 2,624,000 cubic feet when 95% inflated—nearly 25% greater than the *Shenandoah*—was expected shortly from Germany. And there were accidental as well as operational losses: On 28 February 1924, 457,000 cubic feet of precious helium—a quarter of the amount needed to inflate the *Shenandoah*—

A photograph of the *Shenandoah* officers in the summer of 1924, showing the five who died (*) in the later disaster in Ohio. Left to right: Lt. (j.g.) Edgar Sheppard*; Lt. Roland Mayer; Lt. John Lawrence*; Lt. Charles Rosendahl; Lcdr. Joseph Norfleet; Lcdr. Zachary Lansdowne*; Lcdr. Lewis Hancock*; Lt. (j.g.) Charles Bauch; Lt. Arthur R. Houghton*; and Chief Machinist Shine Halliburton. (NASM 81-14809)

escaped from the station's 1,000,000-cubic-foot gasometer. The upper portion of the tank apparently failed to lift to allow the necessary expansion from the sun's heat, and the gas blew out through the water seal at the bottom. No wonder Lansdowne made every effort to make water recovery work: before long flights, putting the ship on the mast the night before to accumulate superheat in the sunshine the next morning, enabling him to get away with more "false lift" at departure; and usually landing after dark when the gas would be supercooled, thus averting the need to make the ship heavy by valving helium. In flight he avoided release of ballast as much as possible, though this meant stressing the structure by flying heavy much of the time. Further, to avoid loss of gas through valve leakage, Lansdowne greatly reduced the number of maneuvering and automatic valves, in the face of reservations by the bureau due to the limit set on the ship's rate of ascent in an emergency. "Jampot" covers were used to seal the valves in the shed, and then, after a time, were left on the automatic valves in flight to eliminate the seepage of contaminating air into the bottom of the cells. The keel watch was instructed to rip the covers in the event of a sudden rise.

Inflation of the *Shenandoah* commenced on 14 May 1924, and continued, with addition of ballast and fuel, to 82% on the afternoon of 15 May. At 1630 she

was launched and docked on high cradles. On 22 May she was brought out for an evening flight of 1 hour 13 minutes, and "landed slightly light, no ballast used or gas valved." On the evening of 30 May, she was walked to the mast, where on the following day she was the center of attention during a Memorial Day open house. Thousands of persons were thrilled by the day-long succession of events—Marine Corps squadrons flying in formation and making simulated strafing attacks, parachutists jumping from a kite balloon and a Martin bomber, the J 1 taking off and landing with passengers, and a dogfight between two crack racing pilots, Lts. Alford J. Williams and David Rittenhouse. The sensation of the day was Al Williams's flight through the empty hangar in a Vought VE-7, not written up as such in the station log![48] During the day 10,000 numbered miniatures of the *Shenandoah* were sold, from which lucky numbers were chosen entitling 13 winners to a flight on board the ship. Only two persons came forward, however, for the flight, which left the mast at 1400—Charles E. Garrod of Port Richmond, Staten Island, and Oscar Spitz, a reporter for the Newark *Star-Eagle*. A third passenger was Lansdowne's eight-year-old son, Falkland McKinnon. A good time was had by all, as the airship cruised in the vicinity of the field, until 1835 when she landed on the east field and was walked into the shed.

The *Shenandoah* on the high mast while an airplane leaves a smoke screen across the field. Taken from the top of the big Lakehurst hangar during the air demonstration, at about 1410 on 31 May 1924. (AIAA)

Yet on this afternoon the aggressive and ambitious Jacob Klein, the station commanding officer, and Lansdowne

broke over an insignificant matter; this fire was fanned by wives and immediately the station was broken up into two "armed camps," the Lansdowne and Klein factions respectively; officers would refuse to speak to those in the opposite camp, wives would snub the opposite ones. This situation persisted until the loss of the *Shenandoah* in September 1925.[49]

Klein, the former executive officer of the *Shenandoah*, had expected to succeed McCrary as commanding officer, and found it intolerable to be sent ashore in favor of Lansdowne, who was junior to him in rank.

The first long cruise of the *Shenandoah* under Lansdowne's command was on 3–4 June. Admiral Eberle, on instructions from Assistant Secretary of the Navy Theodore Roosevelt, Jr., ordered Lansdowne on 20 May to make a flight on those dates, weather permitting, via New York City and Poughkeepsie to Albany and thence westward over Syracuse, Rochester, Niagara Falls, and Buffalo, before returning to Lakehurst. Securing the ship to the mast at 0434, Lansdowne hoped that superheating after sunrise would enable him to get away with more fuel, but he was disappointed by the weather, which brought rain squalls at Poughkeepsie. As the ship passed over Niagara Falls at 1,500 feet, considerable spray was felt in the control car. Lansdowne apologized to Moffett for not passing over Binghamton on the homeward flight: "Thunderstorms were brewing in our vicinity and there were a number of threatening cloud banks as well as considerable lightning. Consequently my object was to avoid these condi-

tions and the courses steered were with this end in view. . . . I have been in three thunderstorms myself and am of the opinion that one cannot be too careful to avoid them."[50] Arriving over Lakehurst at about 0330, Lansdowne found his plans to land foiled by a ground fog which persisted until two hours after sunrise. By this time the ship was 5,000 lb. light. Twice Lansdowne tried unsuccessfully to land the ship before valving helium, and when the third attempt failed, valved more for a total of 40,000 cubic feet. The ship was landed on the fourth attempt about 3,000 lb. light, after 23 hours 21 minutes in the air. The water recovery condenser on the #1 engine car had, however, recovered 1,150 lb. of water for an expenditure of 967 lb. of fuel, though only 800 lb. of water was conveyed to the ballast bags in the keel. "We can operate without any valving if we plan our schedules to leave with superheat and return in the evening, particularly with three water recovery units on board," wrote Lansdowne.[51] The bureau, noting that a paltry 50,000 cubic feet of helium remained at Lakehurst, directed that water recovery apparatus be installed on the other *Shenandoah* power cars, and that care be taken to valve as little helium as possible. This would probably limit the length of flights, but was considered desirable in view of the acute shortage of the gas.

Lansdowne proposed installing units only on engine cars #4 and #5 initially; he suspected that there would be "a balance between installed weight and reduced speed." This proved to be the case on the ship's next flight on the night of 24 June, for the purpose of running engine tests with engineering representatives of BuAer on board. Lansdowne was disturbed to find the ship's standard speed had been reduced from 42 to 36 knots and refused to add further water recovery units on engine cars #2 and #3; and the ship flew for most of her career with only the three engine cars so equipped. In bringing the *Shenandoah* into the hangar in a cross wind of 10 mph, the after taxying car jumped the track, and a strut was broken on the after gondola, with some hull damage. Remembering his own criticism of McCrary, Lansdowne felt obliged to justify his having taken the ship into the hangar:

> It would have been ill advised at this time to have put the airship on the mooring mast as thunderstorms were predicted for that day. Actually, the worst storm of the season—a line squall extending from the Carolinas to New England—passed over the station. The force of the wind during this squall rose to 60 mph and was accompanied by heavy electrical disturbances and rain. Owing to the scarcity of helium and consequent lift the ship had only a small amount of fuel on board and the weather conditions which occurred would have to a certain extent jeopardized the safety of the ship had she been in the air or at the mast.[52]

Lansdowne need not have worried. Nobody in BuAer ever criticized his handling of the *Shenandoah*, and he enjoyed Moffett's unlimited confidence to the very end.

On 28 June the ship made a brief flight over New York City and Philadelphia; 800 lb. of loudspeaker equipment had been installed at Frame 170 ahead of the control car, and over Philadelphia the commanding officer broadcast an address by the president of the United States. On 24 July the *Shenandoah* made a flight to Binghamton, New York, the city that had failed to see her on the earlier New York State flight because of thunderstorms. This time the airship, held on the ground for two hours before takeoff, acquired considerable false lift due to superheat. The flight was uneventful, but the return 12 hours later was not. At 2217 the ship landed on the east field, but wind conditions precluded bringing her into the hangar. Instead of moderating, the wind suddenly freshened at 0015, and a few minutes later the ship took off, the air speed being 38 knots and the ground speed 1 knot. Course was changed to avoid thunderstorms, and while approaching the station at 0515, the ship had to run from violent thunderstorms. The ship was taken out to sea and did not return and land until 0745. Then, having loaded fuel and ballast, and having replaced one of the two watches on board with the third standby watch, the *Shenandoah* took off at 1018 to cruise in the vicinity for six hours. At 1628 she landed on the east field and was walked into the hangar.

The next step forward with the *Shenandoah* would be mooring trials with the fleet airship tender *Patoka*, whose conversion had been proceeding since February, and which on 1 April 1924, was ordered to report to the commander, Scouting Force, for assignment to Aircraft Squadrons, Scouting Force, to serve as a tender for the *Shenandoah*. On 1 July the *Patoka*, now renumbered AV 6, was recommissioned, and between 6 and 10 July, Lansdowne and Rosendahl, who was designated as mooring officer on board the *Patoka*, were in Norfolk inspecting her airship handling facilities. On 9 or 10 July, the *Patoka* sailed for Newport, Rhode Island, for duty with the Scouting Force.

Meanwhile the bureau took note of the fact that while the *Shenandoah* had been moored to the mast three times by Lansdowne, she had been walked to the mast, not flown. The bureau suggested that he get as much mooring practice as possible before the *Patoka* trials. On the evening of 14 July Lansdowne made his first flying moor to the mast, using the English method. The wind was steady at 15 mph, and the ship was at all times under perfect control. The time from the dropping of the main mooring wire until the *Shenandoah* was secured to the mast was 46 minutes, a delay being caused by the failure of the port yaw guy winch to function. Thirty minutes more were required to retrieve the ship's wires and to make ready to leave the mast, after which the *Shenandoah* cast off, to cruise over the area for six and a half hours. She then landed on the field, and was walked into the shed.

On 11 July the chief of naval operations ordered the *Shenandoah* to report to the commander of the Light Cruiser Division about 1 August for mooring experiments with the *Patoka* in Narragansett Bay. Following the mooring experiments the airship was to be available for scouting problems with the Scouting Force until the end of the calendar year, except for the month of October, when she was to fly to the West Coast. The *Patoka*, however was not ready to receive the airship at Newport until 4 August.

Lansdowne advised the commanding officer of the *Patoka* that he would proceed to Newport on 6 August, but in fact postponed the flight two days because of the threat of evening thunderstorms. He did not feel concern about them as such, but was in an almost impossible position because of the helium shortage. The *Shenandoah* having been inflated to 85% fullness (Lansdowne would have preferred 90% to carry more fuel), the helium supply at Lakehurst had been exhausted, though five carloads of helium totaling 350,000 cubic feet were due to arrive from Fort Worth later in the week.[53] Nor was there any helium on board the *Patoka*.[54] The flight had to be carefully planned to ensure that no helium whatever would be valved, while the ship would be able to carry enough fuel for scouting 400 miles to sea. With the help of water recovery Lansdowne believed it

Aerial photograph of the *Shenandoah* approaching the *Patoka* in Newport Harbor. The "Bird"-class minesweeper USS *Rail* in foreground. (National Archives)

could be done, but only by taking off with superheat and landing to the *Patoka* in the evening. Should thunderstorms prevent this, and delay the landing until the following morning, the *Shenandoah* would almost certainly experience superheating problems and have to valve helium; and since that gas could not be replaced, her ability to carry fuel for the flight home would be impaired. Lansdowne realized his determination to wait for ideal weather conditions might be misunderstood: "I do not know whether or not the Commander Aircraft Squadrons[55] and the C.O. *Patoka* are becoming restless, but we will not proceed to Newport until such time as we think conditions are perfectly satisfactory and suitable for the first mooring unless directly ordered to do so."[56] Having become aware of the *Shenandoah*'s limitations, Lansdowne with good reason followed a cautious policy:

> If we possessed 60 or more airships as did the Germans the loss of a ship now and then would be of little consequence. In time of peace, however, and in the present critical period in the history of airships, I believe the *Shenandoah* should not fly except when in all respects in first class condition. . . . The policy I have attempted to carry out in flying the *Shenandoah*, and the only policy I believe justified, as long as the Navy possesses but one airship, and this ship is so prominently featured in the press, is to play safe and be conservative.[57]

There was no direct order. Moffett had too much respect for Lansdowne ever to overrule his judgment.

Shortly after midnight on 8 August, the *Shenandoah* was brought out of the hangar and put on the mast. Superheating enabled her at 0921 to slip from the mast with 12,204 lb. of fuel and 5,850 lb. of water ballast, 8 officers, 29 men, and 1 passenger on board. In the *Patoka* were Lt. Rosendahl, Lt. (j.g.) Palmer, the radio specialist, and three *Shenandoah* crew men to assist with the mooring, while Truscott and Burgess had come from Washington to observe the operation. At 1500 the ship was over Newport, but not until 1730 did the *Shenandoah* descend and approach the *Patoka*, which was steaming south at 3 or 4 knots against a surface wind of about 10 knots. At 1745 the airship dropped her main mooring cable; this was picked up by the *Patoka*'s gig and coupled to the mooring mast cable at 1802. The *Shenandoah* now should have been reeled in slowly to the mast, with the yaw guys being dropped and made fast to the 80-foot booms, but to everyone's consternation, instead of riding astern, she veered far out on the port beam, a position in which it was impossible to continue the operation. It appeared that while the wind at the surface was from the south, it was from the west at the airship's altitude. Lansdowne requested Captain Meyers to turn to starboard, but he could not because of the proximity of Prudence Island on the starboard beam. Meanwhile, owing to Lansdowne's

88

The *Shenandoah* moored for the first time to the *Patoka* at Newport, Rhode Island, 8 or 9 August 1924. Note 80-foot booms extended horizontally to port and starboard to handle yaw guys. Recently fitted water recovery condensers can be seen on #1 and #5 engines. (Garland Fulton)

reluctance to drop water ballast, the main mooring wire went slack, jumped the sheave at the base of the mast, and kinked so badly that it later had to be replaced. Lansdowne then released ballast, the ship rose enough to make the main wire taut, and the yaw guys were slid down the main wire by means of a messenger and coupled. The *Patoka* was now able to turn to starboard, and the mooring proceeded in straightforward fashion, being completed at 1910.

The *Patoka* then steamed slowly to her anchorage off Jamestown, towing the airship on the main wire because it was found that the locking plungers in the airship's nose cone would not line up with the grooves in the mast cup. Temporary lugs made in the machine shop of the aircraft tender USS *Wright* secured the two cones together. Through the night, and during the following day, the *Shenandoah* was on the mast with no trouble, experiencing fresh breezes to calm, and swung in a complete circle around the *Patoka*'s masthead, safely clearing all top hamper. The duty watch found that even with daytime superheating, it was much easier to keep the airship trimmed and ballasted than when on the mast at Lakehurst, with convection currents rising from the hot sand. Though Lansdowne had hoped to make scouting flights to sea from the *Patoka*, he changed his mind because of the uncertainties of operating without helium supplies. After loading 1,356 lb. of fuel, and receiving official visitors from the Scouting Force, the *Shenandoah* slipped from the mast at 1506 on 9 August. Thunderstorms developing in the area were avoided by running the engines at standard speed, and setting a course out to sea. The airship landed at Lakehurst at 0406, and was hangared half

an hour later. No helium had been valved, and the ship was still 83% full.

Lansdowne, Rosendahl, Truscott, and Burgess submitted lengthy reports on the experience, the first time a rigid airship had been moored to a surface vessel. All agreed that the airship had been endangered flying on the slack main mooring wire to port of the tender; in the future, the British practice would be strictly followed, and after the main wire was coupled up, the airship would drop ballast forward and ascend to keep the wire taut. Because the entire problem resulted from the *Patoka*'s not steaming into the wind, Rosendahl felt the tender should use pilot balloons to determine the wind aloft. Small problems such as the incompatibility of the two mooring cones were taken care of, and the procedure was followed with little change in further moorings by the *Shenandoah*, the *Los Angeles*, and even the *Akron*. Only Burgess was pessimistic:

> The mooring of the *Shenandoah* to the *Patoka* is undoubtedly a much more difficult and dangerous operation than mooring to a land mast because of the unsatisfactory spread of the yaw guys; and it is recommended that plans for operation of the *Shenandoah* be based as much as possible on land masts rather than on the *Patoka*. It may be said that the first operation was accompanied by "*Shenandoah* luck," but it seems wise not to tempt the gods too often.[58]

The ship's crew was in no way intimidated by Burgess's opinion. In fact, they gleefully embraced the phrase "*Shenandoah* luck," and used it as a password among themselves.

With the arrival of the five cars of helium, it was possible for the *Shenandoah* to make one flight from

Lakehurst in connection with Scouting Force exercises. Four of the battleships of the Scouting Force were to simulate forces approaching Boston, Newport, New York, and Hampton Roads, and Commander Aircraft Squadrons, Scouting Force, ordered the *Shenandoah* to fly between four designated points about 300 miles east of Lakehurst on 16 August. On 14 August the airship was gassed to 91% fullness, that evening she was placed on the mast, and at 1022 the following morning she slipped from the mast with at least 6,000 lb. of superheat, enabling her to load an additional 1,000 lb. of fuel and 500 lb. of water. On departure she was carrying altogether 18,186 lb. of fuel and 4,975 lb. of water. En route to the scouting area, where she was to arrive at 0600 on the 16th, the *Shenandoah* ran through some heavy rain squalls over the Gulf Stream, and had to drop 2,700 lb. of water at various times, some of it water-recovery water, to compensate for the weight of rain on the outer cover. Once on station, Lansdowne found he could complete the search pattern only by going full speed on the last leg: "high fuel consumption would make ship light as water recovery apparatus is on only three engines and operates best at cruising speed. To save helium the track was altered."[59] Through the day the *Shenandoah* flew in a 25- to 30-knot northeast to north wind: "The cold breeze blowing over the water in addition to the low clouds and rain squalls made the atmosphere very unstable, and we felt considerable vibration. This, together with the rain, loosened up the outer cover appreciably."[60] Not until completing the box search at 2145 did the airship sight any surface vessel, when the battleship USS *New York* was found and reported by radio. "Had full water recovery apparatus been installed, or helium valved at will, the *New York* could have been followed since *Shenandoah* had consumed only 49% of her fuel at time of landing."[61] As it was, Lansdowne had to break off contact in order to land at Lakehurst before dawn. Finding a cross wind too strong to enter the hangar, he had the ship walked to the mast and moored at 0530. On the evening of 17 August the *Shenandoah* was released from the mast and taken into the hangar, for a total of 72 hours since her leaving Lakehurst on the evening of 14 August.

Lansdowne was proud of the fact that this was the longest flight ever made by an airship, both in duration and distance, without loss of gas:

> Only a mishap, or an unforseen emergency, will cause me to pull the top valves. This was demonstrated by our last 40 hour flight, and was due, in large measure, to the successful operation of the water recovery apparatus. I do not remember the figure now, but offhand, I should say that we recovered about 6000 pounds of water during this period. We are now keeping the jampots, or covers, on the man-

oeuvring valves[62] in flight. This, of course, in the days of hydrogen, would have been looked upon as bad practice, but by fitting a rip panel to the jampots I have no hesitation in doing it.[63]

More to the point, Lansdowne deserved credit for his skillful execution of a long scouting flight to sea in unfavorable weather, which succeeded in locating a major fleet unit. If only the *Shenandoah* had been involved in more such missions—in sight of the seagoing Navy—rather than the publicity flights over inland cities so dear to Admiral Moffett!

Early in August the chief of BuAer had directed Lansdowne to make plans for a flight to Des Moines, Iowa, on 20 August, by way of the Army's Scott Field airship base near St. Louis. Fortunately Moffett decided now to postpone it, which pleased Lansdowne as it would save helium, and he wished to make another *Patoka* mooring. It was time, however, to start planning and preparing for the West Coast flight, and the *Shenandoah* was not again airborne for a month and a half.

The journey to the West Coast and back, using mooring masts at Fort Worth, San Diego, and Seattle, was a long-standing dream of Admiral Moffett, particularly after the cancellation in February 1924 of the polar flight, which would have had the *Shenandoah* proceeding to Alaska by this route. As early as May 1923, Lcdr. Mitscher in the Plans Division at BuAer had prepared an itinerary for such a flight. Mitscher predicated his scheme on the existence of a mooring mast at Chicago, from which the *Shenandoah* could make three 24-hour local flights over major cities of the Midwest and upper Mississippi Valley before proceeding to Forth Worth and thence to San Diego via El Paso, Tucson, and Yuma. "By mooring at Chicago and Fort Worth, the Navy could fly across the continent being entirely independent of Army fields or Army activities."[64] McCrary, in November 1923, made some comments pointing out that the ship, if required to climb to a high altitude early in the flight, as in proceeding from San Diego to Lakehurst, could not carry enough fuel for a long flight, and that the mast at Fort Worth would be absolutely essential for the eastward journey.[65]

On 11 July 1924 the chief of naval operations forwarded to the commander in chief, United States Fleet, Admiral Robert E. Coontz, an itinerary for the October flight as proposed by BuAer: Lakehurst via Fort Worth to San Diego, 7 days. San Diego to Pearl Harbor (where a mooring mast was under construction at Ewa), 3 days. Operate with the Battle Fleet based on the *Patoka* and Pearl Harbor, 10 days. Pearl Harbor to Seattle, 5½ days. Seattle to San Diego, 1½ days. San Diego to Lakehurst via Fort Worth, 7 days. Admiral Coontz felt that the *Shenandoah* should be allotted more than 10 days in Hawaiian waters, and on 18 August offered a schedule for her to operate for three and a half months out of Pearl Harbor. This was to involve her with the Battle Fleet in a strategic problem to be played from 25 February to 12 March 1925. From 12 March to 15 April, the *Shenandoah* was to parallel the fleet schedule; then she was to participate in a joint Army–Navy exercise between 20 and 27 April, with the fleet approaching the islands from the east. She was then to continue in Hawaiian waters until 7 June during the period of fleet concentration.[66]

All of this was far more than Lansdowne and Moffett wanted, and impossible to fulfill without a hangar on Oahu. In two pages of arguments that Lansdowne submitted to Moffett on 2 September, he pointed out that the *Shenandoah* would be required to operate for six months 6,000 miles from her base without proper and adequate repair facilities, and that the only precedent—R 34's transatlantic flight in July 1919—had kept the ship away from her base for only 11 days. The West Coast flight as planned was

> The most extensive flight that a rigid airship has attempted in distance and duration, being upwards of 10,000 miles and requiring 15 to 20 days. It is believed that this flight is an important step in the development of the rigid airship, will test out the new masts and facilities recently erected at these points and make available the information necessary in order to advise the Commander in Chief more accurately as to how long it is reasonable to expect a rigid airship to operate 6,000 miles away from a proper base.[67]

Further paragraphs emphasized the experimental character of this prototype rigid airship, its limited cruising radius with reserve fuel of 2,000 to 2,500 miles, the handicap of flying with helium conservation methods, and the need to improve water recovery equipment. A decision on operating in Hawaiian waters should be deferred until completion of the West Coast flight:

> The rigid airship will always present a special problem in operating and handling and may not be regarded as or forced to conform to the requirements of surface vessels. A bird cannot be made to conform to the requirements of a fish, but this does not prove that the bird runs any greater risk of extermination under the law of the survival of the fittest.[68]

Moffett forwarded Lansdowne's comments to Admiral Coontz on 18 September, and the chief of naval operations endorsed Admiral Moffett's letter on 27 September, directing that decisions on future employment of the *Shenandoah* be deferred until all experimental work contemplated had been completed. Following the West Coast flight, Admiral Eberle advised Admiral Coontz that the *Shenandoah*

would not make the trip to Hawaii to participate in the winter maneuvers because of her lack of cruising radius.[69] The mast at Ewa (not completed until July 1925) was never used.

The West Coast flight as planned was a sufficiently strenuous test of the airship, destined to keep her away from her base for a total of 19 days 19 hours. Careful preparations had to be made, and the ship brought into first class condition. Lansdowne could not help worrying about helium, as usual, and asked Moffett to provide 600,000 cubic feet for Lakehurst, 300,000 cubic feet for Fort Worth, 300,000 cubic feet for San Diego, and 200,000 cubic feet for Seattle.[70] "Naturally, we do not expect to expend this helium, but I have made the figures high in order to certainly cover the situation. That is if we can get it."[71] On 3 September, Rosendahl departed by rail to inspect the masts at Fort Worth, San Diego, and Camp Lewis; he was to meet the ship at Fort Worth and serve there as mooring officer.

Lansdowne on 26 August requested permission to overhaul the ship, with emphasis on a new outer cover to replace the one that he claimed had been on the airship for 15 months. BuAer approved three days later, but Truscott insisted that large parts of the cover were brand new, and in fact only certain panels were replaced. During the next month a new after section to the forward car was built on, with weight reduced to a minimum; the engines in the ship were removed and replaced with five spare Packards; a redesigned water recovery separator was installed on Parker's advice; and 11 gas cells were removed and replaced by spares.

On 25 September the chief of naval operations issued orders to Lansdowne to proceed on or about 3 October to San Diego via Fort Worth, and thence at his discretion to Seattle. For the return he was "authorized to select the route you deem best to proceed to Lakehurst at your discretion."[72] At the last minute Moffett wrote to say he would be on board for the flight from Lakehurst to Seattle; Lansdowne's expression of pleasure was undoubtedly genuine. There would also be one other passenger: Junius B. Wood of the *Chicago Daily News*, with a skillfully argued letter to Moffett playing on his desire for maximum publicity for the flight, won himself a berth in the airship as a representative of all the newspapers:

> Both the Secretary and yourself are as interested as any newspaper man in publicity, and the right kind of publicity, for the voyage. . . . The Navy and the public want, and are entitled to, full discussion of this history making voyage. Unless a newspaperman is aboard, I doubt whether the maximum amount or the best will be secured.
> At every stop, the local newspapermen will be among the thousands who will meet the ship. Each of them will want to see the Commanding Officer and

get his impressions of the flight. Obviously he has been too busy with the technical operation of the ship to retain colorful impressions, will have many details requiring attention at the brief stops and will have little time and less inclination to give out interviews. . . . The reporters will then get what they can from anybody and everybody who comes down the mooring mast. The results will be a hodge podge of stories in the local newspapers and distributed over the wires to the rest of the world.[73]

Wood's dispatches on the front pages of the nation's newspapers secured the public's attention on every day of the cruise, while he left a more durable memorial—a classic magazine account of the entire voyage, splendidly illustrated, which today is a collector's item.[74]

On 26 September the *Shenandoah* was gassed to 78% fullness, and on the morning of 1 October there was a six-hour test flight. On 6 October, the ship was gassed to 85% fullness. At 0700 the following morning, she was secured to the mast and, over the next few hours, gained 6,000 lb. of lift from superheating. An additional 1,700 lb. of fuel was loaded, while the crew, followed by Admiral Moffett and Junius Wood, boarded. At 1000 the ship left the mast with 11 officers and 27 men on board, 19,488 lb. of fuel, 2,500 lb. of water ballast, 895 lb. of oil, and 948 lb. of spare radiator water. The *Shenandoah* climbed to 1,500 feet and then proceeded southwest. With a huge high pressure area centered over the Midwest, Lansdowne proposed to reach Fort Worth by a course through the southeastern states whereby he would be speeded on his way by following winds around the southeastern and southern edges of the "high."

For the first time the cities of the South and West were to see the big airship. The flight route and times had been communicated by BuAer to the press services, and the information was passed on by local newspapers and broadcasting stations to those who had the battery-powered superheterodyne radios of the day. Thus, there were crowds on the streets as the *Shenandoah* shortly after 1400 appeared above Washington, setting her course over the capital, down Pennsylvania Avenue, and between the White House and the Washington Monument. Darkness fell as she proceeded over Virginia, and running lights came on—white on the forward and after gondolas, red on the two port-side engine cars, and green on those on the starboard side. Thus she was visible in the sky to those who ran out of their houses at the distant humming sound of the big Packards. Colored flares burned on the ground in greeting at High Point, North Carolina, and locomotive whistles shrilled through the night at Salisbury. Shortly after midnight the *Shenandoah* reached South Carolina. Since leaving Lakehurst, 1,825 lb. of water had been recovered from the engine exhausts. In the early morning

Atlanta loomed through the autumn mists, with a surprising number of people on the streets, up early to see the silvery craft. The novelty was all the greater as even one of the contemporary wood and fabric biplanes was a rare sight in the sky in 1924. For today's younger generation, who never saw one of the graceful sky giants, it is difficult to impart the fascination they evoked: "It was not, as generally described, 'a silver bird soaring in majestic flight,' but rather a fabulous silvery fish, floating quietly in the ocean of air and captivating the eye just like a fantastic, exotic fish seen in an aquarium. And this fairy-like apparition, which seemed to melt into the silvery blue background of the sky, when it appeared far away, lighted by the sun, seemed to be coming from another world and to be returning there like a dream."[75]

The *Shenandoah* crossed the Mississippi River at 1300, "air extremely rough, clocks set back an hour." At 2145 the airship approached the brightly floodlit Fort Worth mast and dropped her main mooring cable, but not until 2305 was she secured to the mast—the winch engine at the base of the mast refused to start, and relays of sweating sailors cranked her down by hand.

The next leg, through the mountains of West Texas, New Mexico, and Arizona to San Diego, brought the severest test of airmanship of the crew, and airworthiness of the *Shenandoah*, that either had yet been subjected to. Designed for operations at sea level, the big rigid lost considerable lift, and much helium, in rising to clear the Continental Divide, while the need to conserve the precious lifting gas meant that she flew through the mountain passes, rather than over them.

At 0946 on 9 October, the *Shenandoah* slipped from the Fort Worth mast. With superheat, she was carrying 17,016 lb. of fuel, 900 lb. of oil, 2,500 lb. of water ballast, and 948 lb. of reserve radiator water. The ship was 87% full of gas. Rosendahl, who had acted as mooring officer at Fort Worth, had come on board for the flight to San Diego. Climbing to 1,500 feet above sea level, the ship was 1,000 feet above the ground, and headed west to follow the railroad to Pecos, Texas. At 1100, with superheat dissipated the ship was 2,500 lb. heavy and flying 3 to 4 degrees up by the nose to carry the load dynamically. At 1816 the *Shenandoah* had climbed to 4,000 feet over Odessa. At 2000 she was over Pecos, 3,500 to 4,000 lb. heavy with supercooling after sundown and flying 7 to 8 degrees nose up. All day Lansdowne had been following the "iron compass," and he now continued along the Texas and Pacific tracks to El Paso, to take advantage of the mountain passes through which the railroad led.

Bright moonlight made it easy to follow the shining tracks below. At 2020 the airship reached pressure height of 4,400 feet, at 2035 she dropped 1,600 lb. of water, and at 2130 she was at 6,000 feet. Twenty minutes later she was over Van Horn, about 5,000 lb. heavy, 9 to 10 degrees up by the bow. Still the ground rose beneath. At 2200, passing through Sierra Blanca Pass west of Van Horn, the control car personnel got a shock when the streamlined lead weight on the radio antenna carried away by striking the ground: the weight was only 300 feet below the ship, less than half her length! An additional 1,000 lb. of water was released, and the ship rose to 6,600 feet, her maximum altitude on the flight, losing 40,000 cubic feet of helium in her ascent above pressure height. As she flew at standard speed through the passes, the air was extremely turbulent and the ship difficult to control. At 2330 she was over El Paso, and the clocks were set back an hour. The *Shenandoah* was now following the Southern Pacific Railroad into New Mexico.

Past Deming the airship flew, 5,000 lb. heavy, 9 degrees up by the bow, and 12,210 lb. of fuel still on board. By 0300 the ship had reached Bowie, Arizona. Ahead lay the Dos Cabezas Pass, with Dos Cabezas Mountain, 7,300 feet high, to the south and the 10,000-foot Pinaleno Range to the north; and the moon was now obscured by clouds. In the black darkness, the *Shenandoah* hurried on between narrow, twisting walls by a tail wind, there came a dramatic moment of crisis when the ship, her engines running at full speed and her rudders hard aport, drove straight toward a mountain wall! At the last moment some eddy off the mountain forced the bow to the left, and she went on. "Dos Cabezas!" from that day forth was "a pass word amongst *Shenandoah* personnel and good for a recollective thrill any time."[76] Shaken by the experience, the watch in the control car waited for daylight before heading through the next defile, the Dragoon Pass. Now, with the sun rising and the ground falling away, the ship passed over Tucson at 5,800 feet. At noon of 10 October the airship was over Colfred with 8,600 lb. of fuel, flying 1,500 lb. heavy and 2 degrees up by the bow. At 1400 she was two miles north of Yuma at 6,500 feet.

Over the mountains between the *Shenandoah* and San Diego a stiff head wind was blowing, so Lansdowne turned onto a northwest heading to pass up the Imperial Valley via the Salton Sea, Indio, and Banning. With evening came another close call as the ship headed west through the San Gorgonio Pass to reach Los Angeles. The lights of Riverside and San Bernardino suddenly vanished in a heavy snow squall. Lansdowne descended to 3,000 feet in an attempt to get under the snow cloud for a sight of the ground, and at this altitude above sea level the antenna weight carried away again! Climbing to 3,600 feet, the ship was 6,000 lb. heavy owing to loss of superheat and accumulation of 3,000 to 4,000 lb. of

wet snow on the outer cover, and was flying at 12 degrees nose up, developing her maximum dynamic lift. After 15 minutes she was in clear air. At 2115 she crossed the Pacific coastline at Seal Beach, and proceeded down the coast to the San Diego naval air station where she arrived at 2300. Because there was no experienced ship's officer on the ground to direct a mast mooring, the *Shenandoah* was weighed off for a landing on the ground. In warm air close to the ground the ship became heavy. The inexperienced ground crew caught the control car and checked its descent, but aft the men stood back and allowed the rear gondola to strike the ground with such force that six girder joints failed in the keel structure above the car. Fuel on board on arrival was 4,122 lb. At 0030 *Shenandoah* was let up on trail ropes and walked to the mooring mast, where she was secured at 0100 on 11 October. Nearly 40 hours had passed since the departure from Fort Worth, and after the nightmare passage through the mountains in the dark, all hands must have been exhausted.

Over the next five days the ship's crew and station personnel, working in very cramped quarters in the keel, cut out and replaced the damaged girders with others on hand at the station. The skeleton crew on board was very busy around the clock: by day as superheat built up, water had to be piped on board; at night with supercooling, and heavy condensation of moisture on the outer cover, first water ballast, and then fuel, had to be dropped.

On 13 October, Lt. Rosendahl flew north with Lt. Ben H. Wyatt in a naval DH4B to act as mooring officer at Camp Lewis, Washington. On 16 October the *Shenandoah* followed. At 0915, after waiting for sufficient superheat to give her positive buoyancy, she departed the mast at San Diego. In addition to Admiral Moffett and Junius Wood, the big ship carried Captain Moses, the commander Aircraft Squadrons Battle Force, and an aide; and Mr. W. J. Johnson, a Pathé News moving picture photographer. The ship carried 16,500 lb. of fuel, 822 lb. of oil, 948 lb. of reserve radiator water, and "motion picture gear 175 lb." More at home over the ocean than passing through the Continental Divide, the *Shenandoah* did not exceed 3,000 feet on the flight up the California and Oregon coasts. She was at 2,000 feet as she passed over two divisions of the battle force at gunnery practice off San Pedro, and Admiral Moffett exchanged greetings with Admiral Samuel S. Robison commanding the battle force. Struggling against a head wind, the airship was off Point Arguello at 1900, looking down on the wrecks of seven U.S. naval destroyers which had driven ashore in fog a year earlier. Low fog moved in over the coast with the onset of darkness, but the mountains inland loomed above the white undercast. At 0615 on the 17th the light on the Faral-

The West Coast flight: the *Shenandoah* on the mast at the Naval Air Station, North Island, San Diego, California. The similarities and differences between the "expeditionary" pole masts and the permanent mast at Lakehurst may be noted. Only at San Diego were colorful pennants attached to the mast guys because only at North Island were naval HTA aircraft flying off a field with a dirigible mooring mast. Note that the outer cover has been unlaced abaft the rear engine gondola to deal with the damage sustained in landing on the night of 10–11 October 1924. Admiral Moffett's personal flag (two white stars on a navy blue field) is flown below the control car. (NASM 78-4650)

lon Islands was abeam, but San Francisco, 30 miles to the east, was not seen. At 1450 the airship was off Cape Mendocino, and at 1600 off Eureka. Not until 1935 did the *Shenandoah* reach Oregon, being abeam of Brookings. The head wind now freshened, and at 0030 on the 18th Lansdowne turned inland at the Suislaw River, proceeding north down the Willamette River via Eugene and Corvallis. At 0416 the airship was over Portland, which was hidden in fog. At 0800, 47 hours after departing San Diego, the big rigid was approaching Camp Lewis. Low fog covered the ground, and the mast was not visible from the *Shenandoah*, though Rosendahl, on the operating platform 160 feet above the ground, could see the airship and directed her toward the mast by radio. Already, however, the airship, delayed by head winds, was picking up superheat, and Lansdowne saw himself obliged to wait until evening to land, in order to avoid valving a considerable amount of helium.

For nearly ten hours the *Shenandoah* cruised monotonously in the vicinity of the mast with only

#1, #4, and #5 engines running at two-thirds speed, while the ship, which was 3,500 to 4,000 lb. light, was being held down by flying 12 degrees nose down. At this marked angle it was difficult to keep the engines running because of lubrication problems and overheating, and at times an engine had to be stopped and #2 or #3 cut in, even though they did not have water recovery units. Even so, the ship at 1500 ascended to 4,000 feet, her pressure height, going on up to 5,300 feet and venting gas through the automatic valves. Heavier now, the ship was brought down to 2,300 feet, but "although descent was made slowly gas took up 6 degrees adiabatic heat" through compression during the descent.[77] Not until 1830 did the *Shenandoah* approach the mast. Because a developing inversion, with cold air temperatures near the ground, would make the airship still more buoyant, Lansdowne broke his self-imposed rule and valved gas for three minutes through the maneuvering valves. At 1910 the ship was secured to the mast and commenced taking on helium and fuel. Only 1,740 lb. of fuel remained on board at the landing. The total time

The *Shenandoah* with the Battle Force, Pacific Fleet, in the Santa Barbara Channel on 16 October at the start of the flight to Seattle. The dreadnought in the foreground is the USS *California*, flagship of the Battle Force. The aircraft on her stern catapult is a Vought UO-1. (*Aero Digest* via NASM 81-14807)

in the air was 57 hours 55 minutes—longer than the time (in 1924) for a journey by train from San Diego to Seattle. Admiral Moffett went ashore, and Lt. Rosendahl boarded the airship.

The situation was reversed next morning at 0800 as Lansdowne prepared to get away for San Diego. The airship at the mast was enveloped in heavy fog, in which engine cars #4 and #5 sometimes were not visible from the control car. Condensation on the outer cover was very heavy, the gas bags were wet, and the ship was 5,000 lb. heavy with moisture. There was nothing to do but wait for the fog to burn off and sufficient superheat to develop for the ship to get away. Not until five minutes after noon was this possible, with 17,514 lb. of fuel and 3,100 lb. of water ballast on board.

After the head winds of the flight north, Lt. J. B. Anderson, the ship's aerologist, now forecast a storm for the flight south. ("He always prophesied head winds. There were no pleasant surprises. He was always right."[78]) The worst of the storm came on the following morning. Off Point Cabrillo at 0500 the wind was east-southeast at 30 mph and the ground speed 18 mph. At 0600 the gale had freshened to 40 mph. At 0900 the *Shenandoah* crawled past Point Arena doing 15 mph over the ground, but by noon the head wind had dropped to 30 mph. At 1500 the ship was approaching San Francisco, and circled the city. As the airship proceeded south, the head wind dropped further; off Point Arguello at 2232 the wind was northwest at 5 mph. Approaching San Diego at 0500 on the 21st, the airship was flying on top of fog extending up to 1,200 feet, with wireless towers visible at Chollas Heights and San Diego. The ship was already getting very light because of superheat, and water recovery on the flight south had been poor because the tubes of the apparatus were coated inside with carbon, there having been no opportunity to clean them. Lansdowne had to let the ship go through her pressure height, 3,500 feet, and on to 4,500 feet to blow off gas through the automatic valves, then down to 600 feet at 0945 with the fog breaking up. At 1046 the airship dropped her trail ropes to the ground party on the air field, but again Lansdowne had to valve gas for 4½ minutes—and, even so, the ship was still 2,500 to 3,000 lb. light. At 1055 the *Shenandoah* was on the ground; 35 men climbed on board to serve as ballast, and she was walked to the mast and secured at 1140 on the 21st, nearly 48 hours after slipping from the mast at Camp Lewis. Water and fuel were started aboard, and small repairs undertaken. One hundred fifty thousand cubic feet of helium was piped in, filling the gas cells to 88%.

At 1107 on 22 October the airship left the mast for Fort Worth, carrying 18,000 lb. of fuel and 3,000 lb. of ballast. Captain Moses and his aide had gone ashore, and in their place the *Shenandoah* bore the commanding officer of the San Diego naval air station, none other than Captain Thomas T. Craven, the former director of Naval Aviation, in 1919–21. The eastward flight was an even more severe test of the ship than the westward journey, for she was heavily laden with fuel, and the mountains were immediately ahead of her. By noon the *Shenandoah* had already climbed to 4,500 feet over Sweetwater Lake (pressure height was 4,000 feet), flying at 7 degrees up by the bow and 4,000 lb. heavy with all engines at standard speed. An hour later over Jacumbo she was at 5,500 feet in very bumpy air and 12 degrees up by the bow, so that Lansdowne was forced to drop 1,000 lb. of water. Engine #1 was on standard speed, the other four at full speed. At 1510 Yuma was beneath, the

Shenandoah continuing east along the Southern Pacific Railroad toward Gila Bend and ultimately Tucson. With loss of superheat after sunset, the ship at 1815 was flying 13 degrees up by the nose and making only 41 knots. Two tanks of fuel were jettisoned and another tank an hour later. At Benson the *Shenandoah* was 6,000 lb. heavy and 11 degrees up by the bow. Here, instead of going on through the Dragoon and Dos Cabezas passes, Lansdowne chose to follow the El Paso and Southwestern Railroad to the south, through Bisbee and Douglas. Another slip tank was dropped south of Bisbee, the ship climbing to 7,300 feet. This made a total of 2,770 lb. of fuel dropped as ballast. Lansdowne had had some hopes of flying all the way to Lakehurst with the prevailing westerly winds; now it was certain that he would have to land at Fort Worth for fuel and helium. Fortunately, the remainder of the journey across New Mexico and West Texas was uneventful, and at 0241 on 24 October the *Shenandoah* was secured at the Fort Worth mast.

The return to Lakehurst was anticlimax. Fueling and gassing continued throughout the night at the mast, to be completed shortly after 0900, with 16,926 lb. of fuel on board the ship, and an added 220,000 cubic feet of helium, the gas cells being 87% full. At 1030 the *Shenandoah* left the mast. The route home was direct, through Arkansas, Indiana, and Ohio. One town overflown was Greenville, Ohio, Lansdowne's birthplace and the home of his mother. At 2300 on 25 October the *Shenandoah* was over Lakehurst, but again she was approximately 2,500 lb. light owing to a 10-degree temperature inversion extending up to 1,000 feet. Helium had to be valved for 1½ minutes, and the ship driven down with engines #4 and #5 running at standard speed. By midnight she was on the field and being walked into the shed, 3,348 lb. of fuel remaining on board. The long-awaited German Zeppelin ZR 3 was already in the shed, having arrived from Friedrichshafen on 15 October with Dr. Hugo Eckener in command.

Congratulations poured in from all sides, Eckener and his officers being among the first to extend them. Whereas more experienced German and British airshipmen had regarded the American effort with skepticism, the 19-day flight demonstrated that the Americans were serious in their desire to develop the rigid airship and were learning their trade thoroughly, and that their innovations including the use of helium and water recovery were practical. Furthermore, they were going much further than the British in developing and using the mooring mast. The secretary of the navy[79] commended Lansdowne for: "the successful completion of the longest journey ever made by an airship. It is believed that this has demonstrated the ability of the rigid airship to remain away from its base for a period much longer than has been thought possible and will undoubtedly have notable influence on the development of this type of airship for both military and civil purposes."[80] Indeed, the flight aroused great excitement and interest in the American public. In the year 1924 there was no transcontinental air passenger service—this began only in 1929 with Ford trimotors whose passengers flew by day and rode in Pullmans by night; and only mail was being flown from New York to San Francisco, by the Post Office Department in rebuilt World War I open-cockpit De Havilland biplanes. Thus it was easy to see the *Shenandoah*'s transcontinental flight as the precursor of commercial passenger service. Yet Lansdowne had to call attention in his report to the *Shenandoah*'s actual unsuitability for the flight:

> As the weather conditions were severe on the Westward mountain leg, gusts were experienced in Dos Cabezos Pass in Arizona that exceeded the ship's standard speed and full speed was required to check the drift of the ship into a mountain wall. On the Southward leg, down the West Coast, the airship made no headway at standard speed for nearly the whole of one watch off Pt. Arena, California, and practically no headway was made for a time in rounding Point Reyes, California. Full power was required for approximately two hours in crossing the mountains in Southern California after leaving San Diego, due to the extreme heaviness of the ship, at the time 12 degrees down by the tail. These instances are cited to show the need for providing future airships with greater power and higher speed.[81]

Burgess was much concerned about the stresses on the ship while she was being flown with extreme heaviness to save helium. While coming east from San Diego at 12 degrees nose up at 41 knots and 6,000 feet, he estimated the bending moment was about 190,000 meter lb. sagging between Frames 70 and 90, giving—with allowance for bumps, gas pressure, and so on—a stress of about 75% of failing in girders. Since this was the first time the ship had been flown so heavy, Burgess recommended that when she was deflated, the structure between Frames 50 and 100 be carefully checked for buckled girders, as well as slack or broken wires in the top of the ship.[82]

Another dark side of the picture was that 640,000 cubic feet of helium had been expended in the flight—three quarters of it because of the need to ascend to high altitude in the mountain crossings. The annual production from the Fort Worth plant between June 1923 and June 1924 was 7,709,924 cubic feet,[83] but the Navy received only half of this, or 3,854,962 cubic feet.

Clearly it was impossible with this annual supply to operate both the *Shenandoah* and the new ZR 3 *Los Angeles* simultaneously, particularly as the former, merely sitting in the hangar, lost 150,000 cubic feet per month, while the latter, whose German-made gas cells were becoming porous, was found to require 250,000 cubic feet per month.[84] In any case, under the terms of the contract with the Zeppelin Company, part of the German crew was to train U.S. naval airship personnel in flying the new craft until 10 February 1925. So in the hour of her triumph, the *Shenandoah* was required to take second place to her glamorous new sister, and give up her helium. The resulting hibernation was to last eight months, ending only with the *Los Angeles*'s being laid up and returning her helium to the *Shenandoah*.

Shenandoah: "No European Designer Could Possibly Imagine the Violence of Weather Conditions in the American Midwest."

Laying up a rigid airship was a time-consuming process, which could occupy the ship's company for the better part of a week. The complex structure of the hull, no longer lifted by the gas in the cells, had to be carefully supported otherwise. A yoke was attached to each main ring at three points to suspend the hull from the hangar overhead, while long poles, cut to the proper length, shored up the keel structure from below. The *Shenandoah* was then gradually deflated, beginning transfer of her helium to the *Los Angeles* via the purification plant on 13 November. The #1 engine car was removed, as well as the reduction gear in #3. On 14 November Cells #1 to #18 remained 15% full; Cells #19 and #20 were removed for inspection and repair. No fuel or water ballast was on board. At the end of November, 24 of the *Shenandoah*'s crew were transferred to the *Los Angeles*, and four more to the Naval Air Station, Lakehurst.

Lansdowne was not idle—on 6 November he appeared before the General Board, led by Admiral Eberle and including Admirals Strauss, Phelps, Williams, and Jones. After describing the West Coast flight, emphasizing the performance handicaps under which the *Shenandoah* operated and the need for larger and faster airships with greater cruising range, Lansdowne made a pitch for the construction of a West Coast hangar at San Diego. During the following question period, he insisted on the need for hangaring the ship for overhaul and repair. "We have to live in a hangar. We can't live in the Fleet. If you are

going to look at the airship in the light of surface craft, it can't be done." The admirals found this unpalatable, and accused Lansdowne of wanting a hangar at every overseas location, which he denied. Yet Lansdowne was the only person in the United States fully acquainted with the capabilities and limitations of the helium-filled rigid airship; and regardless of the disillusionment of the General Board members, nourished too long on airship propaganda and fantasy, he insisted on giving them the facts.

Back in Lakehurst, with the expectation that not until March 1925 would there be enough helium to inflate the *Shenandoah* as well as the *Los Angeles*, Lansdowne was free to consider how to improve his ship's performance. If she were to operate in the Pacific by June 1925, as he hoped, an increase in range and fuel capacity would be necessary, while the West Coast flight had shown the need for increased power and speed. He offered a table of present fuel load and normal cruising radius with one third reserve depending on air temperature, ranging from 22,426 lb. and 2,730 miles at 30°F to 11,040 lb. and 1,344 miles at 90°F. Although the hull structure could not be lightened, weight could be saved in renewable items such as outer cover and gas cells, and by improvement in power plant and cars. For example, 1,200 lb. could be saved by fitting a new cover of cotton weighing 1.8 oz. per square yard and having the same strength as the older material, which weighed 2.5 oz. per square yard. Similarly, the lighter fabric could save 800 lb. in gas cells. Claiming

Two rigid airships at Lakehurst, but only one flying! Because of the helium shortage, the *Shenandoah* (left) is deflated, with framework suspended from the overhead and supported from below. The *Los Angeles* (right) has received her helium and is tied down in the shed. Taken in 1925 before 26 June. (R. S. Clements)

that reliability of engines would permit a reduction in the number of power plants, Lansdowne proposed that the five 350-h.p. Packard 1A-1551s in the ship be replaced by three Packard 1A-2500s, V-12 power plants delivering 800 h.p. at 2,000 rpm, weighing 1,100 lb. with a weight/h.p. ratio of 1.37, compression ratio of 5.5 to 1, and specific fuel consumption of .50 lb./h.p./hr. Three power cars instead of five would reduce weight and drag, giving a speed increase of 10 knots and saving 5,000 lb. in weight, plus 800 lb. saved by eliminating four mechanics. The total weight saving of 7,800 lb., converted to fuel, would increase the cruising radius by 1,000 miles. In addition, and after seeing the *Los Angeles* control car built onto the hull, Lansdowne suggested a similar one built onto the hull structure. "This change would provide for a further saving in head resistance without any additional weight increase and possibly some saving."[1] For reasons of economy, the bureau refused to replace the fabric, but in the following spring a preliminary layout for a new power car with reverse gear as previously used and Packard 1A-2500 engine was circulated in the bureau. Yet when she was lost, the *Shenandoah* still had the control car and engine car layout with which she was completed two years earlier. The modified control car, if it had been im-

plemented, might have saved eight lives in the ultimate disaster in September 1925.[2]

Lansdowne's concern with conserving helium also led him, during the long lay-up, to advocate and carry through a considerable reduction in the number of valves in the ship, a step much criticized in certain quarters after she was lost. Not only had she been completed to German specifications with 16 maneuvering valves in the tops of her 20 gas cells, opened by wires leading from the control car, and 18 automatic valves in the bottom of them, which opened when gas pressure exceeded that of the surrounding air, but also the cells were connected by a fabric inflation manifold two feet in diameter designed to enable the ship to be gassed through the nose hatch while at the mooring mast. Having developed the practice of flying the ship with the gas-tight jampot covers in place on the automatic valves, Lansdowne relied on the inflation manifold to equalize pressure in the gas cells. On the West Coast flight all the automatic valves were covered until reaching the Rockies, when three of the jampot covers were ripped—one forward, one amidships, and one aft. As the ship rose above 6,000 feet on this flight, the expanding helium was exhausted through the manifold to the favored cells. Lansdowne was pleased with the scheme, while aware that if the ship was carried rapidly over pressure height, the keel watch would have to rip more of the jampot covers.

Already before the West Coast flight Lansdowne, with bureau approval, had removed 8 of the 16 maneuvering valves in the top of the ship for a weight reduction of 228 lb., while the leakage of helium from them was halved. Now he recommended that automatic valves be removed from cells still retaining the maneuvering valves, and suggested that "future cells should have smaller automatic valves as helium practice does not require them to handle the volume necessary in hydrogen practice."[3] Further, for future construction, Lansdowne recommended the elimination of the automatic valves from individual cells: all would be connected to a large permanent manifold with an automatic valve at each end, with a few maneuvering valves in the top of the ship. The bureau was doubtful, fearing that the two automatic valves could not accommodate the expansion of helium in a rise of 800 feet per minute. Another scheme was a combination automatic and maneuvering valve in the top of the cells. Such a Gammeter Automatic Gas Valve, 20 inches in diameter and manufactured by the B. F. Goodrich Co., had been installed in Cell #16 in May 1923, and had functioned perfectly since; but the valve was inaccessible in flight unless a man was sent to the top of the ship, and there was always the fear that it would stick open and release a quantity of helium.[4]

Finally, in the spring of 1925, Lansdowne forced the removal of 10 of the 18 automatic valves. Though his alleged goal was to conserve helium, he pointed to the saving of 400 lb. in weight and the slight increase of volume due to eliminating five of the nine exhaust trunks, each of which served two gas cells.[5] The bureau had doubts, and with good reason: Lansdowne argued that the large valve capacity of the German Zeppelins was designed to enable them, if attacked by airplanes, to drop a quantity of water ballast and ascend at the rate of 2,000 feet per minute, while the Shenandoah, when taken over pressure height, was "eased up so that a minimum amount of gas is valved. During this operation the present automatic valves barely open, observation showing the opening never to be more than ¼ of an inch."[6] The bureau, however, considered that every gas cell should have its own automatic valve, with a capacity to deal with a rate of ascent of 800 feet per minute:

> The modified arrangement of valves proposed for the Shenandoah is not as fool proof as the original installation. . . . If for any reason the ship gets out of control and drives above pressure height the consequences will be serious. However, on the assumption that the operating personnel realizes and accepts the operating practice which is involved and will take the

necessary precautions the rearrangement of gas valves and trunks as proposed . . . is approved by way of experiment.[7]

Still later, Burgess, for the bureau, warned that with only eight automatic valves functioning, 400 feet per minute was the maximum rate of ascent that could be accommodated without dangerous overpressure of the gas cells:

> The Bureau notes the argument . . . that a very small gas valve capacity was found to be sufficient on the West Coast flight. In this connection the Bureau invites attention to the fact that in that flight no very rapid ascents above pressure height occurred. It is considered that the maximum valve capacity is likely to be required only in the event of the airship being suddenly carried upward in a vertical current of air during a squall. It is understood that Shenandoah has never been subjected to this condition although it quite conceivably may occur, and the total gas valve capacity must be sufficient to provide for it.[8]

Lansdowne's reply was that if the rate of ascent exceeded 400 feet per minute, the control car personnel would open the maneuvering valves to increase the rate of escape of gas. But in the final event in Ohio, as Burgess had warned, the ship, for the first time, was carried up uncontrollably at the rate of 400 feet per minute, finally reaching 1,000 feet per minute.

It had been expected at the time that the Shenandoah was laid up, that by March 1925 there would be enough helium to fly both her and the Los Angeles, with the Shenandoah to operate from the Patoka with the fleet in southern waters in April; but by February it was apparent that this hope would not be realized. Actually during fiscal year 1925 the Fort Worth plant produced 8,889,051 cubic feet of helium (which had to be shared with the Army), a little more than a million cubic feet in excess of the production in fiscal 1924.[9]

On 18 May 1925, Garland Fulton at the bureau examined the helium situation in the light of flights desired in the near future. These included two important publicity cruises, to Annapolis during "June Week," 1–3 June, and to Minneapolis on 8 June. A scouting problem was planned for 20 June, and antiaircraft target practice with the fleet between 15 June and 1 August. On the Fourth of July a visit was to be made to Bar Harbor, Maine, during the Governors' Conference, to carry the visiting dignitaries on passenger flights. The problem was that with the Los Angeles restricted to "civil" flying, by order of the Conference of Ambassadors which had authorized her procurement from Germany, only the Shenandoah could fly the military missions, while the Los Angeles was the obvious choice for the passenger hopping at Bar Harbor, an occasion of transcendent political importance. Yet the *Los Angeles* was experiencing excessive helium loss from her German-made gas cells, and repairs were necessary. Fulton proposed that the *Shenandoah* be inflated with whatever helium was available at Lakehurst by 10 June, and after that date, following the *Los Angeles*'s return from Minneapolis, enough of her helium be transferred to the *Shenandoah* to enable the latter to operate. The *Shenandoah* would undertake the fleet missions and the Bar Harbor flight; only a few of the 25 governors could be given a ride in the military ship—the others would have to be disappointed. Yet Fulton, adding up the helium at Lakehurst, plus anticipated shipments from Fort Worth, less monthly losses from each ship, found that only 3,524,800 cubic feet would be on hand on 1 August, not enough for two ships. Four million cubic feet was needed with monthly shipments of at least 350,000 cubic feet.[10]

The *Shenandoah*'s turn actually came sooner than expected. The *Los Angeles* made the Annapolis flight on 2–3 June, and on 7 June set off for Minneapolis. Thirteen hours later, near Cleveland, one of her German-built Maybach engines failed, and her captain chose to return. The *Shenandoah* was then ordered on 10 June to inflate with helium transferred from the *Los Angeles*, which was to commence overhaul at once with special attention to engines and gas cells, while the *Shenandoah* was to make a preliminary flight, the Minneapolis flight as outlined for the *Los Angeles*, and the Bar Harbor flight by 5 July if possible. Replying the same day, Lansdowne estimated that his ship could make one preliminary flight and be ready for operations by 1 July.

Obviously the Minneapolis flight would have to take place after the one to Bar Harbor, but Admiral Eberle was insistent about its being undertaken as soon as possible, regardless of plans for joint operations with the battleship *Texas*. On 16 June Eberle ordered Lansdowne to make the Bar Harbor flight in sufficient time to arrive by the afternoon of 3 July; specified that he was to pass over Providence, Rhode Island; Boston, Cambridge, and Lawrence, Massachusetts; Portsmouth, New Hampshire; and Portland, Maine, en route. He was to "make a 4 to 6 hour flight on the forenoon of the Fourth taking as many of the governors of states who will be assembled there and on this flight visit Eastport, Maine, and as many other Maine cities as possible."[11] The *Patoka* would be in Bar Harbor 1–4 July, and would serve as his base. He was also ordered to make the Minneapolis flight, with no date specified. On 19 June, Eberle ordered Lansdowne "immediately upon return from Bar Harbor" to "prepare for a flight to Minneapolis and return as rapidly as possible so as not to miss any favorable weather." He was "to follow as closely as possible the following itinerary," which listed 23

cities and towns en route to Minneapolis; 12 en route from Minneapolis to the Army's Scott Field near St. Louis, where the ship was to land and refuel; and 8 between Scott Field and Lakehurst on the homeward leg. "C.O. *Shenandoah* is directed to provide on the schedule giving the approximate number of hours after leaving Lakehurst of passing over the above cities. . . . Operations with USS *Texas* will be held in abeyance until completion of the above flight."[12]

Lansdowne must have been exasperated at the rigidity of his orders, and the unreasonable expectations concerning times and places, as if he were operating an express train on schedule. Obviously the briefing at the General Board meeting on 6 November had gone unheeded: Eberle was showing no regard for the experimental nature of the *Shenandoah* and of the entire rigid airship program, and he was not asking for Lansdowne's comments and advice. Knowing that what he had to say would be unwelcome, Lansdowne drafted a reply that put him on a collision course with the powerful chief of naval operations:

The *Shenandoah* has been ordered to make a flight to Minneapolis and return. . . . The length of this flight is approximately 3000 statute miles. The beginning of the flight includes a mountain range requiring a minimum altitude of 3500 feet so that leaving Lakehurst the ship should be only 89% full without superheat. A flight towards westward will probably be made against headwinds. The temperature conditions prevailing in July are hot, reducing cruising radius to a minimum. The prevailing weather conditions in July in the upper Mississippi Valley include many and severe thunderstorms, the type of weather the airship must avoid, and this procedure requires additional fuel.

Such an itinerary requires one or two landings and it is understood Minneapolis has been selected as one landing point and Scott Field another. As the airship is required to leave Lakehurst without superheat, these landings should be made without superheat, or otherwise an indeterminate quantity of helium will be valved. . . . Any delay, therefore, due to unfavorable weather, requiring a landing during the heat of the day, is serious unless arrangements for gassing are provided. Should occasion arise, and such occasions are frequent, that a heavy rain or severe thunder squall arrive at the landing field during the fueling operation, the ship must take to the air for safety and ride out the condition in the air. This procedure is satisfactory if the airship has sufficient fuel. If the ship may be safely held on the ground the heavy rain will make it necessary to hold the ship continuously until sufficiently dried out to take on additional weight in fuel. It is doubtful if the Minneapolis landing party is prepared to meet such a situation. . . . Adequate and proper facilities should be provided at landing points, including a mooring mast and a supply of helium. . . . It is pointed out that should the Department desire to make this flight without the facilities referred to, that such a course is reasonably safe later in the season after the thunderstorm period has passed (September), provided freedom of action with respect to the exact date the flight is scheduled be permitted. It is, therefore, recommended that the Minneapolis flight be postponed.[13]

Captain George Steele, the commanding officer at Lakehurst, and commander of the *Los Angeles*, loyally backed Lansdowne with an endorsement: "The experience of the *Los Angeles* on her attempted flight to Minneapolis on June 7 indicates that there is considerable hazard in a voyage to Minneapolis at this season of the year."[14]

Eberle's second endorsement, addressed to Moffett, was critical, unreasonable, and even unfair: "It is not the policy of the Department to erect mooring masts at the various points selected for refueling on a cruise of this nature. If the limitations and *apprehensions* outlined in this letter and those in the first endorsement are sound, it would appear that our airships are of little military or commercial value, and that the great cost of their upkeep and repair would not be warranted." Lansdowne and Steele had not been expressing fear, but merely pointing to the hazards of attempting a long journey over the mid-continent of North America in the thunderstorm season with inadequate facilities. Was Eberle now turning his face against the airship, even intending to put an end to the program? No—"the CNO is not ready to concur in these opinions and believes that these ships can be operated safely with the exercise of care and judgment within the discretion of the Commanding Officer, and within reasonable limits of time."[15] However, the storm signals were flying, and Moffett urged his superior to see reason: Lansdowne was simply pointing out difficulties that Eberle was not aware of; both airships were handicapped in performance by using helium instead of the hydrogen for which they had been designed; while the fact that Henry Ford had erected a mooring mast at Detroit which would be ready for use after 7 July would change the picture considerably. Moffett backed up Lansdowne: "The C.O. *Shenandoah* should still have latitude in choosing the time of starting, as well as changing the route." He recommended that the decision as to whether the *Shenandoah* should make the Minneapolis flight be based on the relative importance of the trip as compared with operations with the USS *Texas*.

Surely it was Moffett, recognizing the need for the principals to reach an understanding, who arranged a conference between Lansdowne and Eberle at the Navy Department on 30 June. Moffett of course was present, as was Captain Gatewood C. Lincoln, director of Ship Movements under the CNO, who was responsible for the orders issued to the *Shenandoah*. Unfortunately no record exists of this conference, perhaps because some of the remarks were better forgotten. In the end, however, Moffett's backing of Lansdowne prevailed; Eberle held the orders he had drafted the day before for the *Shenandoah* to fly to Minneapolis as soon as possible after the Bar Harbor flight,[16] and accepted Lansdowne's advice that the journey be made in the latter part of August or early September. Henceforth Eberle showed more understanding of the problems of the big rigids, and even after his term of office expired, his successors gave the airship commanders much more discretion as to time and routes than had earlier been permitted.

Meanwhile, between 10 and 24 June, the *Shenandoah*'s crew and the station force had gradually inflated the ship to 88% full, the time consumed being necessary to run the *Los Angeles*'s helium through the purification plant and into the station gasometer. Water recovery units of a new design were installed, with weight said to be reduced by 50% and resistance by 75%. Initially the three available were on engine cars #1, #2, and #3, but by 15 August, an additional two-stage unit had been installed on #5.[17] On 26 June the *Shenandoah* was walked to the mast and secured at 0412, leaving after sunrise for a test flight of 9 hours 4 minutes. Over Bayonne, New Jersey, Rigger L. H. Ford made a successful parachute jump.

On the evening of 2 July the *Shenandoah* was put on the mast, and at 0813 next morning set off for Bar Harbor. Rosendahl was already on board the *Patoka* to serve as mooring officer, but there were a number of passengers in the airship, including Lcdr. Joseph P. Norfleet from BuAer, a Pathé news cameraman, Mr. H. MacCracken, and two student airship officers. At 1930 the airship was over the *Patoka*, and after one attempt during which the *Patoka* cast off the main mooring wire as the *Shenandoah* was drifting dangerously over the tender, the airship was secured to the mast at 2145. On the following morning, Independence Day, both vessels played host to visitors from the Governors' Conference. At 1018 the airship left the mast carrying Governors E. P. Jackson of Indiana, E. L. Trinkle of Virginia, and M. E. Trapp of Oklahoma, as well as G. E. Torrey, aide to the governor of Maine. After flying for about two hours in the vicinity of Bangor and Bar Harbor, the *Shenandoah* landed to the *Patoka* mast to disembark the distinguished guests. Fuel and water were loaded, Rosendahl boarded the airship, and at 1353 she departed for Lakehurst, where she arrived the following morning after sunrise. No helium had been lost, except for a small amount leaking from two holes in Cell #6, which had lost 8% in fullness.

It was now time for the *Shenandoah* to undertake

some missions with the fleet, to experiment with new equipment, and to train her personnel in the purely naval duties for which she had been built. These missions had been evolved in BuAer during the spring of 1925, in cooperation with the chief of naval operations and fleet personnel. They included search problems with the battleship *Texas* of the Scouting Force; towing outsize sleeve targets for anti-aircraft gunnery practice; experiments in refueling at sea from vessels not equipped with mooring masts; towing of the *Shenandoah* by a surface vessel in smooth and rough water; and complete calibration of the radio compass installed in the radio gondola abaft the control car. The most intriguing BuAer idea was the hooking on of a small airplane in flight to the *Shenandoah*, dropping it, and recovering it. These desires were forwarded to Lansdowne over Moffett's signature on 16 April 1925. While the *Shenandoah* never progressed to hook-on experiments, Lansdowne had some definite ideas on the subject which he forwarded to BuAer: Eight-foot vertical struts, suitably braced, should be installed below the keel at Frame 120 between engine cars #4 and #5, with a cable between the ends of the struts to take the airplane. The plane hook he suggested foreshadowed the fitting on the later "hook-on" aircraft of the *Akron* and *Macon* era. Lansdowne suggested a two-seater plane of about 3,000 lb. weight with a self starter so that it did not have to dive to start the engine. It was necessary that the plane be taken aboard and released at the captain's will so the operation would not be classed as a stunt.[18]

Between 9 and 11 July a towing winch was installed in the tail just abaft Frame 0, the cruciform bearing the rudders and elevators. On the morning of 13 July the *Shenandoah* was gassed to 90%, and in the evening she flew for three and a half hours testing the towing winch with an ordnance sleeve, put over on 1,200 feet of cable. With the engines on standard speed the sleeve carried away and the ship returned to Lakehurst, landing to the mast. Just after 0800 the next morning the *Shenandoah* left for Narragansett Bay where the *Texas* and the *Patoka* were anchored. Before arriving, the *Shenandoah* put over a target sleeve on 5,000 feet of cable while she steered on various courses near the Brenton Reef Light Vessel. After two hours the sleeve was dropped on Gould Island in Newport Harbor, and the *Shenandoah* stood out toward Block Island, steering various courses to calibrate her radio compass and that on board the *Texas*. A grapnel was used for the first time to connect the airship's main wire to the *Patoka*'s, an innovation that speeded up the landing operation, and 20 minutes later the *Shenandoah* was secured to the *Patoka*'s mast. Leaving the mast the next morning, 15 July, the *Shenandoah* spent two hours completing calibration

of her radio compass, and then proceeded to Lakehurst where she landed to the mast.

Without hangaring the ship, Lansdowne left the mast eight hours later, on the early morning of 16 July, for a search problem with the battleship *Texas*. Once more carrying an admiral, the *Shenandoah* was flying the flag of Rear Admiral Charles F. Hughes, director of the Division of Fleet Training. As she proceeded toward Nantucket Light Ship, a freighter was seen, but not until 1732 was the elusive *Texas* sighted. A contact report was transmitted by radio on three different frequencies, and received by the *Patoka* despite heavy static and jamming by the *Texas*. As the *Shenandoah* passed abeam, the battleship fired a 13-gun salute in honor of Admiral Hughes. Shortly afterward the *Shenandoah* headed for Lakehurst, skirting thunderstorms. Lansdowne in fact made special note of the severe electrical display over New Jersey on the flight home. The radio compass was constantly taking bearings, and during the night it was found that bearings could be taken on static, thereby obtaining the location, direction, and movement of the thunderstorms. Arriving at Lakehurst in midmorning, the airship made two attempts before landing on the field, valving helium for a total of three minutes.

On the morning of 23 July, the *Shenandoah* left the mast and headed for the Southern Drill Grounds off Hampton Roads. The radio compass gave the bearing of the *Texas*, and shortly after noon the battleship was sighted off Cape Charles and the towing sleeve streamed on 5,000 feet of wire. After several practice runs, the airship made a firing pass down the starboard side of the *Texas* while the four 3-inch anti-aircraft guns of the starboard battery fired for three minutes; then it was the port side's turn. Afterward the *Shenandoah* returned to the Naval Operating Base at Hampton Roads, where she dropped the target to be checked for hits. She then proceeded to moor to the *Patoka* off Cape Charles City, the maneuver taking only 19 minutes ("they are getting good. Practice helps!" minuted Truscott on the *Patoka*'s report to BuAer[19]).

The next morning the *Shenandoah* again proceeded offshore and streamed another target for the *Texas*, making three firing runs. After dropping the target ashore, she continued up the coast via Cape May and Atlantic City to Barnegat Light and landed on the field, being secured in the Lakehurst hangar just before midnight. Admiral Hughes later commented favorably on the advantage of having an anti-aircraft target larger than could be towed by contemporary airplanes:

We fired 835 shots at it, and there are 807 holes in the target, of which 12 are holes where a full shell had gone through. This was towed at about an altitude of

5000 feet, and was a large sleeve, 10 feet in diameter by 45 feet long. The speed was only 30 knots, but that was because the wire was not strong enough to hold it at any other speed.[20]

There followed another search problem with the *Texas*, with the airship ordered to be at Nantucket Shoals Light Ship at 0500 on 28 July. To take advantage of daytime superheat, Lansdowne took off at 1824 on the evening of the 27th, and cruised up and down the New Jersey coast at low speed until 2300 when he set a course of 58 degrees. At 0400 the airship was on her station, but was hampered by thick fog, which prevented her from commencing the search until about 0900 when the fog thinned somewhat and No Man's Land was sighted. The visibility was poor all day, never better than 12 nautical miles, with haze and rain squalls in the late afternoon. Radio silence was maintained, and the radio compass was used for navigational purposes and to listen for the *Texas*, but she was not sighted, and at 1900, with the search pattern completed, the *Shenandoah* headed for Lakehurst. Her landing at 0001 on 29 July was delayed by a line squall, the ship flying through the southern end of it.

At 0453 on 30 July, the *Shenandoah* was again walked out of the hangar and secured to the mast. At 0758 she cast off, steering south. At 1220 the airship was passing Hog Island, 25 miles north of Cape Charles, and a few minutes later the *Texas* was sighted ahead in Lynnhaven Roads. For the exercise, the battleship had embarked two Vought UO-1 seaplanes from the naval operating base, but as she lacked a catapult, there was a delay while the planes were hoisted over the side and took off from the water. Flying at 2,500 feet, the *Shenandoah* was over the battleship before the planes could climb to her altitude, much too late to prevent the sending of a contact report.[21] The UO-1s then made a series of simulated attacks from astern and underneath on each quarter. After they landed near the *Texas*, the airship set a course for Lakehurst.

Lansdowne believed that both planes could have been shot down if machine guns had been mounted on the airship, but a greater number of airplanes "will increase proportionately the chances of their successfully disabling an airship." Machine gun mounts were provided only in the port and starboard windows of the control car. For adequate defense, Lansdowne recommended two machine guns in the control car; four in the side engine cars; two in the centerline engine car aft; a three-pounder on the top platform; two machine guns on the tail platform; and one machine gun atop the ship at Frame 100, one at Frame 40, and one in the nose.[22]

On 4 August, the chief of naval operations forwarded a schedule for the *Shenandoah* for August.

During the week of 3 August she was to install machine guns and train gun crews. During the week of 10 August she was to carry out towing experiments in rough and smooth water, test refueling at sea, and complete calibration of her radio compass, flying from the *Patoka* based at Newport. In the week of 17 August she was to continue gunnery training and machine gun exercises. Lieutenant Houghton in fact was designated the ship's gunnery officer, and on 8 August two machine guns were mounted in the control car windows, but they were removed the same day at the insistence of the Navy Department, which did not want them appearing in newspaper photographs. Denied the chance to practice gunnery in the air, the *Shenandoah*'s crew got their machine gun practice on the ground at the firing range.[23]

On the evening of 14 August, the *Shenandoah* departed Lakehurst for Newport, where she moored to the *Patoka* at 0105 on the 15th. At 1035 she stood 15 miles to sea off Newport for towing exercises. Dropping a sea anchor—actually a canvas drogue or bucket—at the end of a 450-foot yaw line made fast at Frame 180, the *Shenandoah* rode quietly with her engines stopped, drifting very slowly with the wind, simulating an airship out of fuel. The *Patoka*, steaming out of the harbor, now picked up the sea anchor and attached the yaw line to the main mooring line, led down from the masthead through a block on the stern, and started towing her. Small pressure airships had occasionally been towed by surface vessels particularly in the British service during World War I, and airshipmen had discussed the possibility of towing the big rigids. This, however, was the first time it had actually been done, and though the wind and sea were quite moderate, the three-hour experience was unexpectedly unpleasant. With the *Patoka* on a northerly course, and the wind southerly, the *Shenandoah*, trying to head into the wind, several times veered right round through a complete 360-degree circle on the end of the wire. When the *Patoka* changed course into the wind, the tension on the wire pulled the *Shenandoah* down toward the surface so that emergency ballast had to be dropped forward. The *Patoka*'s pitching and rolling, and the resulting constant whipping of the wire, which was violent at times, continuously jerked at the airship's structure. Lansdowne's opinion was unfavorable, and he recommended that towing be considered only as an emergency maneuver.[24]

Once in Newport Harbor, the *Shenandoah* was reeled down to the *Patoka*'s masthead at 1822, and fuel and water were piped on board. Four hours later she departed for Lakehurst, where she arrived before sunrise after a flight of about six hours. A week later, on 22 August, she made a four-hour flight for deceleration tests. These provided direct information on the actual drag of the airship, which could only approximately be measured with wind tunnel models. Proceeding at a steady speed, the engines were simultaneously stopped at once, and the ship's speed as she decelerated, and the distance traveled, were measured at short intervals. Obviously the more rapid the deceleration, the higher the skin friction drag of the big hull, and the parasite drag of fins, rudders, cars, supporting struts and wires, and propellers.

There remained the Midwest flight. The conference of 30 June involving Lansdowne, Moffett, and the chief of naval operations had not canceled it, but merely postponed it at Lansdowne's request to late August or early September. Admiral Eberle's operating schedule of 4 August 1925 had specified that the Midwest flight was to take place about 1 September, and the August operations should be completed in time to allow preparations for that flight. As early as 20 July, Eberle had forwarded to Lansdowne a list of state fairs scheduled to take place in the last week of August and the first week of September, and the Shenandoah's commanding officer was directed to prepare an itinerary for visiting Columbus, Des Moines, Minneapolis, Milwaukee, Detroit, Indianapolis, and other towns, while the Detroit mooring mast, erected by Henry Ford and completed about 7 July, was to be tested. Moffett, noting the latter directive, suggested that a separate trip be made to Detroit first. Rosendahl, sent to inspect the new mast, reported that it was much more complex than the naval masts, with modifications that permitted the airship to be lowered to the ground after mooring to take on passengers and cargo. Rosendahl therefore recommended a special flight to Detroit to test the mast.[25] In a letter to the chief of naval operations, Lansdowne proposed an itinerary from Lakehurst to Scott Field, Scott Field to Detroit via Minneapolis, and Detroit to Lakehurst. He proposed a preliminary flight to Detroit in the last week of August to test the mast—in the event of a malfunction, the Shenandoah would have sufficient fuel to return to Lakehurst, while such would not be the case at the end of the long leg from Scott Field via Minneapolis. Lansdowne also recommended that the flight be made in the second week of September to give Scott Field and Detroit more time for preparations.[26] Eberle disapproved this recommendation—BuAer had advised that Scott Field could easily be ready by the first week of September, and the state fairs at Columbus, Des Moines, and so on, would be over by the second week. Subsequently it was contended that Lansdowne wanted the delay because of the greater likelihood of thunderstorms in the first week in September, but there is no reason to believe that he did not mean what he said in the original request. Further, his orders embodied a so-called prudential clause:

Should the dictates of safety and the weather conditions existing make it advisable, the commanding officer of the Shenandoah is authorized to make such modifications in the above itinerary as he deems necessary, remembering, however, that this route will be published in the press and that many will be disappointed should the Shenandoah fail to follow the approved schedule.[27]

As for the preliminary trip to Detroit, Eberle replied that "in view of the present schedule of the Shenandoah the Department is reluctant to undertake the extra trip unless the commanding officer is convinced of its necessity."[28] When Lansdowne visited Washington on 18–19 August, he agreed to drop the separate flight to Detroit, and seemed satisfied with the plan for the flight in the first week of September. He insisted, however, on having a carload of helium (100,000 cubic feet) available at the Detroit mast, and this was shipped from Lakehurst on 18 August.

It is noteworthy that Lansdowne was being given greater latitude and discretion than in the past, as a result of his conference with Eberle on 30 June. Another indication is his handling of successive requests from the chief of naval operations for the Shenandoah to fly over cities and towns of the Midwest. The first two times Lansdowne simply added them to his itinerary, but the third time he objected, pointing out that the added cities would take him too far from the direct route: Des Moines, Iowa, would for instance have to be overflown on the Lakehurst-to-Scott Field leg of the journey. Eberle concurred and altered the itinerary to that previously agreed on. When a further list of cities was forwarded on 28 August, it was merely "for information." Later it was contended that Lansdowne was forced to undertake a flight he feared during the thunderstorm season; but as Rosendahl pointed out at the later court of inquiry, if he had feared for the safety of his ship, it was his duty as commanding officer to make proper representations to his superiors concerning his apprehensions. This he had done successfully in June; he would surely have done so again if he had felt it necessary.

The route as finally drawn up by Lansdowne and accepted by Admiral Eberle and Captain Lincoln was: First leg—Lakehurst via Zanesville to Columbus, Ohio; Indianapolis and Lafayette, Indiana; Springfield, Illinois; and Scott Field, to be reached on the evening of 3 September, 941 miles. Second leg—Scott Field to St. Louis, Kansas City, Des Moines, Minneapolis, Milwaukee, Kalamazoo, to the Henry Ford mast at Detroit, 6 September, 1,330 miles. Third leg—leaving Detroit on the morning of 7 September, the airship first to pass over Flint, Bay City, Owosso, and Lansing, Michigan, before proceeding to Lakehurst, 671 miles, for a total distance of 2,959 miles. The final order from the chief of naval operations concerning the Midwest flight authorized Lansdowne to carry Henry Ford and his subordinate William B. Mayo on a local flight at Detroit or from Detroit to Lakehurst.

In the late afternoon of 1 September 1925, the *Shenandoah* was once more walked out of the Lakehurst shed and put on the mast. On the following morning, as superheat accumulated, additional fuel was piped on board. The crew ascended the elevator, climbed the ladder to the operating platform, crossed the gangway at the nose, and went down the keel to their stations. The junior officers boarded first; so Lcdr. Lansdowne was still on the ground at the foot of the mast, talking to Captain Steele, the commanding officer of the naval air station, when Lansdowne's young wife drove up to say good-bye. Actually there was little to say, for her husband had not hidden from her his concern about the Midwest journey, and the clash with Admiral Eberle, the chief of naval operations, concerning the original July departure date. Though the flight had been postponed at Lansdowne's insistence, neither husband nor wife was looking forward to it. Betsy Lansdowne consoled herself with the knowledge that this would be Zach's last scheduled flight in command of the *Shenandoah*—he had requested orders to sea duty to obtain the two years necessary for promotion to commander, his service in command of the airship being regarded as shore duty.

There were a few words, Betsy revealing her anxiety by remarking that she did not like the looks of the local weather. Zachary Lansdowne saluted Captain Steele, saying "Shove off with your permission, sir." A few minutes later he appeared at an open control car window, and ordered the masthead crew to cast off. The clamps holding the nose cone inside the mast cup were released, and at 1452 the *Shenandoah* lifted from the mast, carrying 41 crew, 2 passengers, 16,620 lb. of fuel, 860 lb. of oil, and 948 lb. of reserve radiator water, the gas cells being 91% full. After release of 2,225 lb. of water ballast in getting away from the mast, 6,850 lb. remained on board. The next stop would be Scott Field.

Betsy Lansdowne walked to her naval car without looking back and told the driver to take her home to Lakewood. In the early days of aviation, when every takeoff was a venture into the unknown, the educated as well as the ignorant were superstitious. Most Lakehurst wives believed it was bad luck to watch their husband's ship out of sight.

Shortly after 1600 the *Shenandoah* was over Philadelphia and headed west across the Alleghenies. As usual, the jampot covers were on the automatic valves, but before reaching the mountains they were removed from the valves on Cells #8 and #9, and #16 and #17. The valves on Cells #4 and #5, and #12 and #13, were still covered. Between Chambersburg and

Connellsville, Pennsylvania, the *Shenandoah* ascended to her pressure height of 3,600 feet. Passing over Wheeling, West Virginia, at 0145, Lansdowne set a course for Zanesville, Ohio. The ship was then flying at 2,500 feet, 6 degrees heavy, and making an airspeed of 36 knots. The mountains having been crossed without loss of helium or water ballast, it might have seemed that the worst of the flight was over.

Lightning was flashing in the distance ahead and to the north, however, and at about 0230 Lcdr. Hancock, the navigating watch officer, called Commander Lansdowne and the aerologist, Lt. J. B. Anderson. It had been known on the morning of 2 September that there was a large low-pressure area in Canada north of Minnesota, and a small secondary at Moorhead, Minnesota, which the evening weather map, drawn in the ship at 2000, showed to have moved to Green Bay, Wisconsin. This secondary was expected, however, to move due east and remain clear of the *Shenandoah*'s track. The ship was steered on various courses, mostly south of west, to avoid the electrical display to the north, which at 0345 Central Standard Time extended from slightly forward of the starboard beam to a little on the starboard quarter.[29] Meanwhile, though the air continued smooth, it was clear that a stiffening head wind from the southwest was markedly retarding the *Shenandoah*'s progress. With standard speed ordered on all engines, Lt. (j.g.) Edgar W. Sheppard, the engineering officer, requested permission to "dope" fuel, and men were roused out along the keel to pour tetraethyl lead liquid into the gravity tanks over the engine cars. The ship at this time was over Cambridge, Ohio, and though different headings, altitudes, and engine speeds were tried, she made very little progress over the ground from this point. At this time the airship was 1,200 lb. heavy, 2½ degrees nose up, flying at 1,800 feet (altimeter setting at zero at the Lakehurst mast, 200 feet above sea level), and making 38 to 40 knots with standard speed on all engines. Thanks to water recovery, 9,600 lb. of water ballast was on board. There was no feeling of danger to the ship at this time. Hancock, however, though he had been relieved by Rosendahl at 0400, continued in the control car to be of assistance to the commanding officer.

At about 0420 Rosendahl, who was taking drift measurements, observed on the starboard bow

> a streaky cloud forming, and although it did not seem threatening, I turned to call Lieutenant Anderson's attention to it. However, he was sitting in the after end of the control car and watching out of the window to starboard, so that I was sure that he saw this cloud. Shortly thereafter the Captain came over to the starboard side and it was apparent to him that this new cloud was either coming towards us or building up very rapidly.[30]

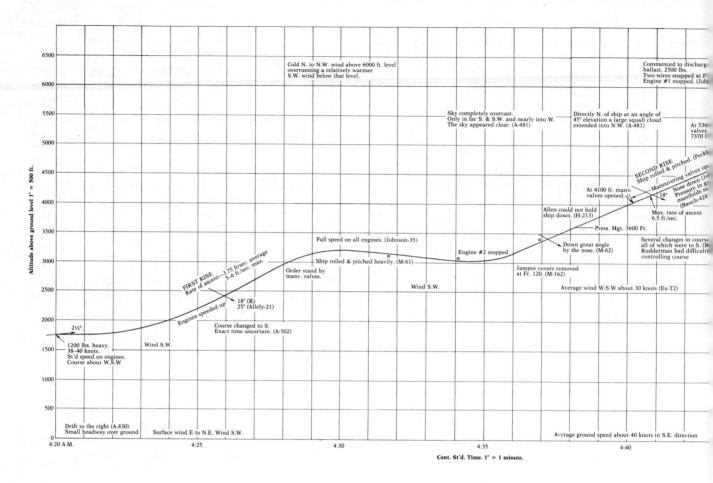

Barograph tracing, redrawn by Professor William Hovgaard, 19 December 1925, for the *Shenandoah* Court of Inquiry, annotated from testimony before the Court. A = Anderson, H = Hall, M = Mayer, R = Rosendahl. Adapted from ASNE, p. 630.

At this point the elevator man cried a warning that the ship had started to rise a meter a second (200 feet per minute) and he could not check her. The control car personnel were astonished—"it seemed so unnecessary that the ship should rise at this rate with no warning whatever,"[31] Lieutenant Mayer recalled; but, indeed, the big airship had entered an upward current of more than 1,000 feet per minute, an experience unprecedented for her ship's company, or indeed for any airship personnel of any country.

Lansdowne ordered the appropriate countermeasures—the elevators to be put down, and the engines set on full power. The nose-down angle exceeded that which the elevator man's inclinometer could register, but Rosendahl several times read 18 degrees on the large inclinometer mounted on the chart board on the starboard side of the car. Lansdowne ordered that the angle not be exceeded lest the ship stall upward and lose the dynamic downward force on the top of the hull. Yet despite these measures, the *Shenandoah* continued to rise for seven minutes at an average rate of 225 feet per minute, the variometer sometimes showing a maximum of 300 to 360 feet per minute. At 3,100 feet the ascent was checked, and the control car personnel believed the ship would now descend. Nonetheless, as she was approaching pressure height of 3,600 feet, Lts. Mayer and Bauch, who acted as keel officers for the forward and after portions of the ship, saw to it that the jampot covers were ripped on the automatic valves at Frame 40 (Cells #4 and #5), and Frame 120 (Cells #12 and #13). With Lt. Bauch's knowledge, ACR Carlson tied the inflation manifold between Cells #8 and #9, for with the marked nose-down angle, helium was rushing aft to the high end of the ship, and tying the manifold was considered a routine measure to prevent overpressure damage to the after gas cells.[32] The nose-down angle was too much for the lubrication system of two of the Packard engines: #2 overheated and failed at this point, and #1 followed shortly afterward.

The air became turbulent, the ship pitching and rolling. After about six minutes the *Shenandoah* be-

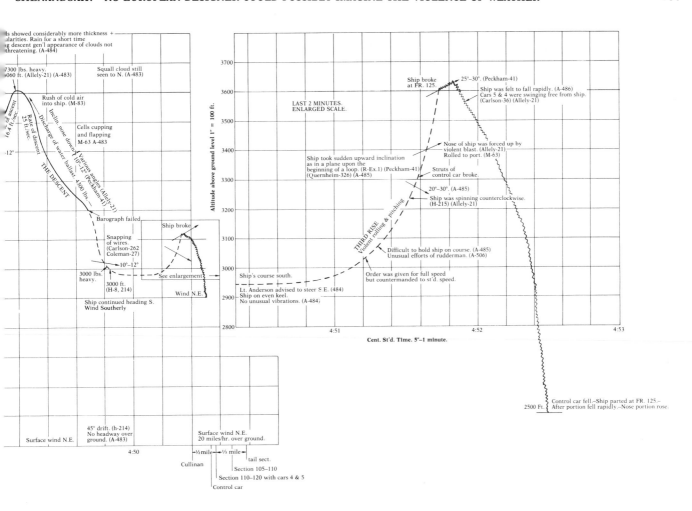

gan rising more rapidly than before, despite being held down at an angle perhaps as great as 25 degrees—the average rate being again 225 feet per minute, and the maximum being just under 400 feet per minute. Later calculations indicated that the upward velocity of the vertical current in which she found herself was 2,100 feet per minute. She rapidly passed through pressure height, and Lansdowne, recognizing that the eight automatic valves could not vent the expanding helium fast enough, ordered the maneuvering valves to be opened. For five minutes the valves were open, as the ship rose from 4,100 to 5,360 feet. After the valves were closed, the airship continued to rise even more rapidly to a peak of 6,060 feet at a rate of nearly 1,000 feet per minute. The second ascent had lasted about 11 minutes, the vertical current carrying her up measuring 2,700 feet per minute. With the venting of helium through the automatic and maneuvering valves, the ship at peak altitude had lost 8,600 lb. of lift.[33]

Whether the *Shenandoah* sustained structural

damage due to gas overpressure at peak altitude was a hotly debated matter in the subsequent investigation: personnel in the keel insisted that the cells and inflation manifold were not at undue pressure to touch, but it was also a fact that sounds were heard in the upper part of the hull as of wires breaking, and even crashing noises as of girders collapsing. It was now clear that the *Shenandoah* was in grave peril, and that if she escaped from the region of severe atmospheric instability, the Midwest flight would have to be abandoned owing to shortages of helium, fuel, and water ballast. Suddenly a blast of cold air through the keel hatches indicated that the ship had reached an overrunning cold air mass, and she started down. Even before reaching peak altitude, Lansdowne had ordered the release of 2,500 lb. of water ballast, reducing the ship's heaviness to 7,300 lb. The fall was rapid, the average rate being 1,500 feet per minute, the ship still nose down at 10 to 12 degrees. An additional 4,300 lb. of water ballast was dropped, but the ship was still 3,000 lb. heavy after

3½ minutes when her descent was arrested at just under 3,000 feet by another ascending air current. All the way down the gas cells, their helium contracting, were flapping and cupping up, and it is probable that some of them had been damaged, for just before the final break Cells #9, #10, #11, #12, and #13 were seen to be rapidly deflating.

Realizing that the ship might again be carried upward, and that only 2,500 lb. of water ballast remained, Lansdowne sent word to the keel watch to stand by to drop fuel tanks as the only way to save the ship in another descent. Rosendahl was asked to go up into the ship to see that they were actually ready to drop fuel. "As I stepped upon the ladder leading into the keel the ship took a very sudden upward inclination which seemed to me very much the same condition that exists in a plane upon the beginning of a loop."[34] A violent gust, possibly as high as 4,800 feet per minute, striking on the underside of the bow from starboard, was forcing the whole ship upward at an angle of 30 degrees, and as Lt. Mayer, then at Frame 180 in the nose, later testified, the whole ship rolled over to port. "This manoeuvre was accompanied by a terrific vibration of the whole structure, the sensation being akin to that experienced upon putting a plane in a spin. It was necessary for me to hold fast to the keel strut to keep from being thrown into the netting on the port side of the keel."[35] This was more than the structure could tolerate: the inertial load on the control car suspensions caused some of the struts to break. ACMM Coleman, on top of Car #2 pouring water into the radiator, was horrified to see Car #4 ahead of him break free from its attachments at Frame 120 and swing down under the hull, though still hanging by its after suspension wires. There was a loud crashing roar high in the ship on the port side, and the giant hull broke in two, opening up at the bottom at Frame 125.

Hearing the noise of breaking struts and girders, Lt. Lawrence in the control car said, "She's gone." "Everybody out!" cried Colonel Chalmers G. Hall, an Army observer, as he started up the control car ladder, followed by Lt. Anderson. The time was 0452, and the ship had been carried up to 3,600 feet before breaking up.

Mute evidence on the ground graphically depicted the sequence of events as the *Shenandoah* disintegrated and fell to earth. Four men had the misfortune to be standing in the keel at the very spot where the break occurred, and only one of them survived. Aviation Pilot Cullinan was thrown immediately through the opening, and his body, marking the spot where the breakup took place, was found half a mile to the northeast of the main wreckage.

For a minute and a half, drifting with a 20-mph northeast wind, the two halves of the broken hull were held together by the massive rudder and elevator cables leading from the control car into the tail. The four elevator and four rudder cables ran aft from sheaves immediately above the control car on the port side; and soon the tremendous pull exerted by the after part of the broken hull caused the sheave foundations to carry away, tearing out some of the keel structure. The control car was now pulled aft by the cables; the suspension wires broke one after the other, first those leading forward and then those on the port side; and the car rolled over to port, still held by the control cables and some of the starboard suspension wires. The end links of the chains leading up from the control car to the wires in the keel then opened under the strain,[36] and the control car fell away, trailing the two lower rudder cables and tossing out its occupants—Lansdowne, Hancock, Lawrence, and Houghton; ACR Everett P. Allen, the elevator man; and AR1c Ralph T. Joffray, the rudder man. The rudder cables, being dragged up the keel, broke and damaged girders, and tore away the outer cover under the keel forward of Frame 110. For 15 to 20 seconds the separate radio car must have been carried along on the hull before it fell with CRM George C. Schnitzer and AMM1c James A. Moore, Jr. inside.

With the final separation of the hull, a further break occurred at Frame 110, hurling to the ground the two engine cars at Frame 120, #4 with ACMM Charles H. Broom, and #5 with AMM1c Celestino P. Mazzuco and AMM1c William H. Spratley. AMM1c Bartholomew B. O'Sullivan, one of the unlucky quartet caught at Frame 125, also fell to his death in the wreckage. The after portion of the hull at first fell rapidly 30 degrees up by the tail, but after engine cars #4 and #5 broke away, it leveled off to about 5 degrees and descended more slowly, landing about a third of a mile from the control car and engine cars #4 and #5. Eighteen men survived uninjured in the stern section, while four more lived, one slightly injured, when the "crew space" at Frame 105 was brushed off as the tail section dragged through trees.

Lightened of the weight of the control car, the 210-foot bow section of the *Shenandoah* ascended possibly as high as 10,000 feet. Seven persons were on board—Rosendahl, Mayer, Anderson, Colonel Hall, Chief Machinist Shine S. Halliburton, ACR John F. McCarthy, and AMM1c Joseph Shevlowitz, who would have gone down in #4 engine car with Broom if he had not been sent forward to Frame 125 to assist in doping the fuel. Hall and Anderson, the last men out of the control car, were lucky to have made it: Hall had taken only a few steps aft when the catwalk seemed to be pulled out from under him, but he grasped a girder and pulled himself up atop the apex girder of the keel. Just as Anderson reached the top of the ladder, the control car fell away, leaving him, soaked in gasoline, precariously astride the catwalk, which spanned the huge hole left by the control car's tearing out much of the keel structure and outer cover on the bottom. Only by holding on to some wires with both hands was Anderson able to stay in the ship, as it was some time before Mayer could pass a manila line with a loop in the end to him. At last Anderson placed the line around his body, and he was hauled up into the structure.

Briefly the bow section carried an eighth passenger, for the ship's engineering officer, Lt. (j.g.) Sheppard, who was standing at the break at Frame 125, managed to grasp some wreckage as he fell. Shevlowitz, a few feet forward in the remains of the keel, tried to reach Sheppard and heard him say "Never mind me—look out for yourself!"[37] just before the structure he was clinging to pulled free under his weight. The engineer officer's body, still clutching in one hand a piece of girder and in the other a wire, was found hours later by Lt. Bauch in the woods a quarter mile southwest of the wrecked tail section.

Finding that there was 1,600 lb. of water ballast in one of the forward bags, as well as two nests of fuel tanks aft that could be drained, and that the maneuvering valve on Cell #18 could be operated by pulling on the control wire in the keel, Rosendahl was confident that he could free-balloon the derelict nose section to a landing. Observing the progress of the bow from the open end at the break, Rosendahl shouted orders to Mayer, standing by the ballast bag, and Colonel Hall, working the valve wire. The trail ropes and trail rope hatches in the nose were intact, and the ropes were dropped in hopes they would catch on the ground. The first attempt at landing was abandoned owing to a high ground speed, estimated at 25 mph, but not before the bow section struck a large walnut tree, the branches of which pulled McCarthy out of the ship; he was seriously injured in the fall to the ground. Half a mile farther, the valve was pulled, gas cells were slashed open as high as the men could climb in the ship, and the trail ropes caught and held the bow on a hill near Sharon, Ohio, some 12 miles south of the remainder of the wreckage, which had fallen near Ava. The time was 0545 Central Standard Time.

Shocked and shaken, their leader taken from them, the Shenandoah survivors, far from the sea and alone in a hilly and sparsely settled area of Ohio, rallied themselves with the help of tradition, discipline, and, above all, their pride in themselves as the elite of naval aviation. At the crash site near Ava, Lt. Charles Bauch, the senior survivor on the spot, mustered the living, picked up the crushed bodies of the 14 dead, all of them killed by falling from a great height, and prepared a list of the dead, the injured, and the survivors in his area. Posting lookouts to follow the flight

of the forward section, he sent two chief petty officers with the list when he saw it had landed. Rosendahl, the senior survivor, had the list in his hands about 0700 and dictated a telephone message to be telegraphed to Lakehurst from Caldwell, the nearest town. He then proceeded to Caldwell where he made his headquarters for the remainder of the day. The bodies of the dead, wrapped in blankets, were trucked to the nearest undertaking establishment at Belle Valley. Here the Shenandoah personnel took custody of their valuables and assisted the undertaker, and half a dozen other men he had called in, in embalming the dead and preparing them for shipment in coffins marked "not to be opened." Meanwhile, with a county fair in progress at Caldwell, swarms of sightseers descended on the crash site, providing in the hot dusty sunlight a Roman holiday atmosphere which the survivors long remembered with loathing. A handful of sheriff's deputies could not prevent looters from making off with whole girders, yards of gas cell fabric and outer cover, articles of equipment, personal effects, instruments, log books and other documents, and even canned goods from the lockers in the crew space.

At 1500 on 3 September the majority of the 29 Shenandoah survivors entrained for Lakehurst, while Rosendahl, Bauch, Mayer, ACR Carlson, and ACMM Russell stayed on.[38] Later in the afternoon assistance arrived in the form of the naval recruiting officer from Cincinnati and three naval medical officers. On the morning of 4 September a board of inquiry arrived, consisting of Commander Jacob Klein, the executive officer of the air station, Commander Sidney Kraus, and Lcdr. William Nelson (CC), all from Lakehurst; and Lt. William T. Merrick (MC) from the Naval Recruiting Bureau at Pittsburgh. Rosendahl and his aides stayed on until the evening of the 5th, and then departed for Lakehurst. Numerous other persons, including Burgess and Fulton from the bureau, participated in the investigation. Klein contracted with the Aluminum Company of America to purchase the wreckage for 20¢ a pound on condition that none of it be sold for souvenirs. By 13 September, 40% of the wreckage had been cleared away, and the cleanup job was completed by 16 September. The salvaged scrap totaled 27,500 lb., five carloads going to Pittsburgh to be melted down at the New Kensington plant and three to Lakehurst as salvage and exhibits for the coming Court of Inquiry. On 7 September, Lansdowne, Hancock, Lawrence, and Sheppard were buried at Arlington National Cemetery with military honors; the other ten dead were buried by their families in their home towns.

The Shenandoah crash, an unprecedented event in North America and the most spectacular aviation disaster in the country to date, was of course a news-

Wreck of the stern section of the *Shenandoah* at Ava, Ohio, on 3 September 1925. Photo taken in the late afternoon after looters had stripped much of the outer cover fabric from the wreckage. (National Archives 80-MS-11)

paper sensation for days. This was hardly the kind of publicity that Moffett had intended, and to add to his woes, a big Navy PN-9 flying boat commanded by Commander John Rodgers, Naval Aviator #2, which had left San Francisco on 31 August in the first attempt to fly to Hawaii, was missing with all hands.[39] A storm of criticism of the Navy Department and of BuAer exploded in the press, led by the apostle of air power, Brigadier General William Mitchell, who from his exile in San Antonio, and with typical exaggeration, claimed that the loss of the PN-9 and of the *Shenandoah* were "the direct results of incompetency, criminal negligence and almost treasonable administration of the national defence by the War and Navy Departments." This accusation led to his court-martial and the martyrdom he sought.

Lesser figures made the headlines. Lansdowne's attractive 23-year-old widow, Betsy, was "good copy": On the day of the disaster she was quoted as saying that she blamed Secretary Wilbur personally for her husband's death, as he had forced Lansdowne to make the flight for political reasons: "he had long felt a premonition that the flight would end disastrously and had used every honorable means to avoid making it."[40] On the following day Wilbur denied that the flight was made for political purposes, while the widow denied having made the accusation. There was a further sensation when Betsy charged that personnel at Lakehurst had broken into and rifled her husband's safe; in fact, it was the official ship's safe, which in the absence of the *Shenandoah*'s officers in Ohio, was forced open on the day of the disaster on the order of Captain Steele, commanding the air station, to obtain the "death envelopes" deposited by the crew directing the disposition of their property and effects (curiously, Lansdowne had not deposited a death envelope for himself).[41] Clearly, Mrs. Lansdowne had intended to emphasize her naval officer

husband's disgust with the *Shenandoah*'s being prostituted for political purposes instead of being operated as a unit of the Fleet, but in the end she created the impression that he was afraid to make the flight before mid-September because of the thunderstorm danger—a charge refuted by his recorded desire to fly to Detroit, over much the same route as that followed on the last flight, in the second half of August.

Anton Heinen, unemployed for 14 months, reveled in the role of "Zeppelin expert" suddenly conferred on him by the press. He criticized the reduction in gas valves, claiming the accident was caused by gas overpressure at the end of the second rise to 6,000 feet, and that the reduced valve capacity could not handle the expanding helium. Secretary Wilbur saw fit to argue that "it is manifest that the accident to the *Shenandoah* was in no way due to the change in the escape (sic) valves. The gas bags did not explode and were intact at the time the *Shenandoah* broke up."[42] To which the German replied in a letter:

> Never did I say for one instant, as it seems to appear in your statement, that the gas bags did explode. A simple extended rip in one or more of the bags could release the dangerous overpressure, but certainly not before the structure was dangerously overstrained. . . . Doubtless such a rip would develop in the upper part of the bag where the highest pressure would be and where no human eye could see it. Therefore, I challenge the possibility of any truthfully convincing testimony that the gas bags were intact when the ship broke up.[43]

Heinen's accusations were difficult to refute in the light of German operating practice, but since the dead commander of the *Shenandoah* was himself responsible for the reduction in the automatic valves, the survivors, led by Rosendahl, strove assiduously to refute any testimony supporting Heinen's contentions. Meanwhile the talkative German discredited himself by making even wilder accusations: "the condition of the ship was very well known and very much feared by the crew"; "in my opinion the ship ran deliberately into the center of this storm. For at least half an hour danger signs were shrieking out loud"; etc.

On 14 September, Secretary Wilbur appointed a court of inquiry to investigate the loss of the *Shenandoah*, to be headed by Rear Admiral Hilary P. Jones of the General Board, and former commander in chief of the U.S. Fleet, assisted by Captain Lewis B. McBride (CC), who had worked on the ZR 2 negotiations in England, Captain Frank H. Clark, aide for navy yards, and Commander John T. Towers, of the Bureau of Aeronautics. Captain Paul Foley was the judge advocate, with Lcdrs. Ralph C. Pennoyer and Maurice Pierce, both experienced airship officers, as advisers to the judge advocate. Later, on 26 September, Professor Hovgaard was added as technical adviser to the court. The first meeting was to be held at Lakehurst on 21 September.

Rosendahl, the senior survivor, was the first witness on the opening day. His report to the secretary of the navy on the loss of the *Shenandoah*, which he read into the record, at once focused attention on himself. Lucid, comprehensive, and dramatic, it made him a public figure overnight, a role in which he was to continue until more than 50 years later as the leading American advocate of the rigid airship. During the next few days the other survivors testified—all except the injured McCarthy, who had not fully recovered by the end of the inquiry. Colonel Hall, the Army observer, closed his testimony with a moving tribute to Lansdowne and his men:

> While I was in the control car there was perfect order and discipline and the several duties of the officers and enlisted men were performed as calmly and efficiently as in normal flight. . . . I am sure that Captain Lansdowne with his officers and men in the control car went to their death attempting to keep control of the ship, which they had not lost until the actual breaking occurred. In making this statement I do so with the desire that the bravery of these men be made a note of in the record of this court, and that their conduct be recorded as upholding the best traditions of the Service.[44]

Commander Klein offered his theories on the disaster, together with 200 photographs of the wreck. Although it had been suggested that the fall of the control car had led to the breakup of the ship, it was clear from the testimony of at least four witnesses that the control car tore away only after the hull broke in two at Frame 125. ACR Allely, who was in the crew space at Frame 105, saw the sequence of the breakup just forward of him, particularly as the outer cover was torn off ahead of Frame 110—this permitted him to see engine cars #4 and #5 hanging down after the break at Frame 125. The structure then broke at 110, permitting the section from 110 to 125, or at least its bottom portion, to fall free with the power cars. A final break through the bomb hatches, between 95 and 100, occurred just before the after section landed.

ACR Collier presented damaging testimony supporting the argument that some at least of the gas cells might have ruptured because of overpressure: he stated that he awoke just before the break in his bunk forward of Frame 85, saw Cell #9 deflated to about 70% capacity and going down rapidly, while he saw other cells forward deflated to some extent though he could not say how much. On the other hand, he described Cell #8 as being up to high pressure, bulging through the netting and wires. He stuck to his story then and later, despite severe cross examination by Rosendahl, and a complaint by Commander Kraus: "to my mind, that Cell 8 should have been full after having descended some 3000 feet from the earlier altitude is, in effect, an almost physical impossibility."[45] AMM1c Quernheim testified concerning Cell #10, farther forward, that "the lower part of this gas cell cupped up, and the whole cell dropped down after that through the axial cable," though this might have happened after the break at 125.[46] Collier's and Quernheim's testimony was not followed up, and though it was made to appear that several midships cells were deflating rapidly as the *Shenandoah* fell from 6,000 feet, no explanation was offered. Did they rupture from overpressure, or were they damaged by girder breaks in the top of the ship?[47]

Heinen had his day in court on 30 September, and again on 1 October. Ignoring the feelings of naval officers, and acknowledging that he was aware of their hostility toward him at Lakehurst, he insisted that Lansdowne was solely to blame for the accident because of his having reduced the number of automatic valves to the point where they could not accommodate the *Shenandoah*'s unprecedented rise. He was severely critical of the use of the jampot covers, and claimed that on the West Coast flight the ship had gone over pressure height with the jampot covers in place, and all the maneuvering valves had to be operated by hand. Nor, he contended, were these valves uniformly effective at pressure height: When they were operated in the hangar, the gas cells were less than 100% full and not under pressure, and the main frames, up which the maneuvering valve control wires led from the keel to the top girder, were to a degree oval instead of round. At pressure height, however, the pressure of the gas cells, bulging outward, caused the frames to be more circular in shape.

The vertical height of the frame was now less, and the relative slack in the control wire might mean that the valve would not open as far as it did in the shed. "I know that you moved the hand valves, but you did not open the valves. You only opened part of the valves," the German shouted at Rosendahl. The only remedy, according to Heinen, was to make the hull stiffer in the vertical plane by following Zeppelin practice and fitting shear wires to run down through the midships gas cells from the top longitudinal to the keel—and the *Shenandoah* did not have them.[48]

The ship's company, and the experts who appeared later, contradicted Heinen's accusation of excessive gas pressure and insisted that Lansdowne's reduction of automatic valves had not endangered the ship. Mayer asserted that four automatic valves were uncovered on the West Coast flight and handled ascents of 400 to 600 feet per minute. In rebuttal to Heinen, he claimed that the radial and chord wire bracing of the main rings would prevent any distortion, and he was satisfied that all the valves were operating properly. Lieutenant G. V. Whittle (CC), who had performed various tests of the valves and their discharge rates with helium at Lakehurst, even argued that with the reduced number of automatic valves, and hand operation of the maneuvering valves, "the gas pressures at all points along the rise are less than would have occurred with the original valve installation."[49] Burgess also concluded from his calculations that there had been no excessive gas pressure in any cell at any time, but he still did not like the reduction in automatic valves. Given hypothetical questions concerning the second rise, he replied:

> I think the whole hypothetical story proves that that system of valving is not as good as systems of proper automatic valve capacity in each cell. . . . I am sorry to say that I think the event showed the disadvantage of that kind of valve system; because by the hypothetical questions the ship is supposed to have risen 700 feet at the rate of 1000 feet a minute with the hand valves closed, which I think was bad.[50]

Hovgaard, too, felt it was "safer to rely primarily on the automatic valves. If every cell is provided with an automatic valve, we avoid the complete dependence on the human element." He also found the use of jampot covers in flight "objectionable. The fact that they were removed in time on board the *Shenandoah* does not prove they will always be so removed."[51]

Both experts felt that the breaking of the hull in two resulted from severe aerodynamic loads:

> It appears that the principal cause of the breaking was a great sagging moment at frame 120–130, due to an upward gust, directed obliquely from the starboard towards the port side, and due to the speed of the ship through the air, at a considerable angle to the transverse plane. This is consistent with the fact that the nose was turned violently upwards and to port and that the ship was set turning counter-clockwise, while she was carried bodily upwards some 500 to 1000 feet.[52]

With the midships gas cells #9 through #12 deflating, "an extra sagging moment would exist, which together with the effect of the gust, would amply explain the breaking of the ship."[53] Lieutenant Commander Nelson (CC), a member of the Board of Inquiry at Ava, testified that the *Shenandoah* broke first at the top of the hull on the port side.

Much attention was given to the possibility that the girders of the hull were weakened in advance by corrosion, particularly after Lt. Havill of the detachment that salvaged the wreck testified that salvage crews found metal in the girders near the break "to be noticeably brittle and were able to 'work through them' with ten-inch pliers."[54] A large number of samples of duralumin from the wreck, including some from specimens marked "brittle" by the salvage crews, were tested over a period of months at the Bureau of Standards, with negative results. "No single specimen was found which had deteriorated sufficiently to lower the resistance of the structure of the ship to static or aerodynamic loads, nor was any evidence found that fatigue failure had contributed to the wreck of the ship." General corrosion was found in the duralumin channels of the girders, but "at the time of the wreck the corrosion of the duralumin in the *Shenandoah* had not proceeded far enough to weaken the structure of the ship."[55]

The most significant testimony on the loss of the ship came from Lt. Joseph B. Anderson, the *Shenandoah*'s aerologist, who had been so miraculously saved after being the last man to escape from the control car. Not until 29 September did he appear before the court in Lakehurst, having spent the period between 19 and 24 September in a personal investigation in Ohio to uncover every bit of information available on the weather on the morning of 3 September.

The destruction of the *Shenandoah* is often ascribed to a line squall, but Anderson's testimony indicated that a massive flow of cold air from the northwest, overrunning warm air flowing from the southwest, abruptly created severe atmospheric instability over a wide area of Ohio:

> The instability increased to the point where thunderstorms were formed in the north, a condition which spread rapidly farther to the south, where, possibly, the instability was not so great, hence formed detached clouds first, as was noted from the *Shenandoah* about 0330, in the north and northwest;

then these gradually merged into a solid sheet, as observed from the ship for some time before the time of the disaster, then the thickening of this sheet, in places, into rolls, and later, squall clouds, which appeared about the time the *Shenandoah* was caught in the ascending current.[56]

The steep temperature gradient, or lapse rate, between the warm air at low altitude and the cold air above 6,000 feet ensured the development of high-velocity vertical currents exceeding in intensity those encountered by any airship in the past. What Anderson did not emphasize was that such extreme super-adiabatic conditions were characteristic of the eastern half or two thirds of continental land masses where intense solar heating of large land areas and the existence of mountain ranges with resulting orographic effect would combine to produce violent thunderstorms with powerful ascending currents. By contrast, previous airship operations in England and Germany had taken place in a maritime environment with cool winds off the ocean and relatively little heating of the air over the adjacent coastal areas. With these phenomena little known or understood in 1925, even Lansdowne, with his Ohio upbringing and familiarity with the summer thunderstorms of the Midwest, could not have envisaged the severe, unpredicted disturbances that destroyed his ship and cost him his life.[57]

Dr. Karl Arnstein, who had recently arrived in Akron from Friedrichshafen to act as chief designer of the Goodyear-Zeppelin Corporation, and who had been consulted about the disaster, summed up the *Shenandoah*'s destruction years later with the observation: "No European designer could possibly imagine the violence of weather conditions in the American Midwest."[58]

On 5 October, the court closed its sessions in Lakehurst and adjourned to Washington, to take testimony from senior officers. Its proceedings became entangled with the concurrent Billy Mitchell court-martial, Mitchell himself testifying before the naval tribunal against the advice of his counsel, but contributing nothing, while Rosendahl, Mayer, and others testified at the Mitchell trial. Admiral Eberle appeared before the Court of Inquiry, claiming that Lansdowne was willing to make the flight in July, and it was postponed to permit operations with the USS *Texas*! Captain Lincoln told of the conference on 30 June with Lansdowne and the decision to postpone the flight to September, and the correspondence between Lansdowne and Eberle was read into the record.

On 21 December Professor Hovgaard offered a lengthy, lucid, and objective "Technical Argument" on the design of the *Shenandoah*, the events leading up to her loss, the possible reasons for the structural

failure, and the possible effect of the reduction in valve capacity. He offered ten recommendations for future airship design, many of which were followed in the later *Akron* and *Macon*: (1) a smaller fineness ratio for the hull—i.e., making it fatter and therefore stronger in resisting bending forces (in the *Shenandoah* the ratio was 8.6 to 1, but it was only 5.9 to 1 in the *Akron* and *Macon*); (2) control car to be built integral with the keel structure; (3) engines located inside the hull; (4) higher speed; (5) research on design of higher-strength duralumin girders; (6) automatic valves on every gas cell, and hand valves as in the original outfit for the *Shenandoah*; (7) in the future, ships to be built of 5,000,000 cubic feet for war service and long-distance commercial operations, and one of 1,000,000 cubic feet for training and research; (8) additional mooring masts at strategic locations; (9) weather service especially adapted for aerial navigation; (10) a systematic policy to be followed in development and operation of rigid airships.

On the following day Rosendahl presented to the court a "Brief Submitted By Interested Parties," a vigorous refutation of charges that Lansdowne feared to make the Midwest flight and undertook it under protest; that the reduction in automatic valves made by Lansdowne was ill-judged and contributed to the loss of the ship; that removal of the sixth engine made it impossible for the ship to outrun the storm;[59] and that lives would have been saved if the crew had been wearing parachutes.[60] It also attacked the competence of hostile witnesses including General Mitchell, Captain Heinen, and ACR Collier. The brief argued that the loss of the *Shenandoah* due to extreme weather conditions of which Lansdowne had no warning placed the disaster in the category of "Inevitable Accident." It closed with the ringing declaration that "although we are survivors of one of the worst air accidents that has ever occurred, we nevertheless have not lost faith in rigid airships and are still of the opinion that rigid airships are of a great deal of value for naval and commercial purposes as well."[61] Most of the *Shenandoah* personnel continued in rigid airships, and when the USS *Akron* went down at sea eight years later, five of the 73 dead were *Shenandoah* survivors—Boswell, Carlson, Quernheim, Russell, and Shevlowitz.

On 24 December 1925, the report of the *Shenandoah* Court of Inquiry was completed and submitted to Rear Admiral E. H. Campbell, the judge advocate general of the Navy. The court found that:

> The final destruction of the ship was due primarily to large, unbalanced, external, aerodynamic forces arising from high velocity air currents. Whether the ship, if entirely intact and undamaged, would have broken under the forces existing, or whether prior

minor damage due to gas pressure was a determining factor in the final break-up are matters which this Court is unable definitely to determine.[62]

The actions of individuals were "without negligence or culpability," though errors of judgment were noted:

> The practice of leaving any valve covers in place at any time after an airship takes the air is considered unsafe and inadvisable. . . . The change resulting in a reduction of the number of gas valves was inadvisable. The initiation and urging of this change by the commanding officer of the *Shenandoah*; the recommendation for its approval by the commanding officer of the Naval Air Station, Lakehurst, and its final approval as an experimental installation by direction of the Chief of the Bureau of Aeronautics appear, in the light of subsequent events, to have been errors of judgment, but were arrived at after full and careful consideration by the most experienced officers of the Navy in the operation and design of rigid airships.[63]

The court did not hesitate to criticize Moffett's policy of publicity flights:

> While recognizing the propriety and necessity of the legally constituted authorities in the naval service being the sole judges of the sufficiency of the reasons actuating all orders to naval craft and further recognizing that the practice of ordering movements of naval vessels for the purpose of complying with public requests is in accord with long-established customs, it is considered that such movements should be limited to essentially naval and military operations in so far as possible, especially in the case of new and experimental types.[64]

Now Lansdowne could sleep more peacefully in his grave.

Years ago my professor of pediatrics advised, "Have five children and throw away the first one; you will have made every possible mistake with it." The U.S. Navy had five rigid airships, and with the *Shenandoah*, the first to operate, many mistakes were made:

Owing to financial stringency, over which BuAer and the Navy Department had no control, too much was attempted with too little. The single ship in service was overburdened with a plethora of experimental programs, while there was only one adequate base with a hangar at Lakehurst (the Army's Scott Field offering the only other hangar in the country big enough to house the *Shenandoah*). A mooring mast was no substitute for a hangar, as the Germans knew, and in retrospect, excessive risks were involved in mooring away from Lakehurst, particularly on the West Coast flight. A hangar in the San Diego area would have enabled the ship to work with the main body of the United States Fleet for an indefinite period, in favorable weather conditions.

Undue emphasis was placed on publicity flights, with resulting neglect of training and operations with the fleet. This policy impaired acceptance of the rigid airship in the eyes of the Navy generally, and ultimately led to the loss of the *Shenandoah*. Moffett must bear the blame for this policy, though he was abetted and even instigated at times by the chief of naval operations, Admiral Eberle, who might have been expected to give priority to the development of the airship for naval purposes.

It was a mistake for Moffett, Eberle, and the General Board to assume that the *Shenandoah* could cruise inland over the continental land mass, with its powerful thermal convection currents, turbulence, and even thunderstorms, with the same safety and assurance with which she operated in the stable air over cool ocean waters and adjacent coastal areas.

It was a mistake to attempt large-scale operations with inadequate supplies of helium. The result was a series of questionable practices designed to conserve the gas at all costs—flying the ship excessively heavy to avoid discharging ballast, with severe bending loads on the hull; reducing the number of automatic valves; and most dangerous of all, keeping the jampot covers on the automatic valves in flight. German criticism of all these techniques was fully justified.[65]

Lcdr. Zachary Lansdowne. (National Archives 80-G-459068)

That so much was accomplished before the disaster at Ava stands to the credit of Lcdr. Zachary Lansdowne. It is noteworthy that of the 740 hours put on the ship to 3 September 1925, 605½ hours were flown after Lansdowne assumed command. Only a combination of the highest officer-like qualities, inspired leadership, superb ship handling, and a sixth sense for all the arcane variables of weather, static lift, dynamic lift, superheating, supercooling, and loading and weight distribution, made it possible for him to accomplish succcssfully the 235-hour West Coast flight and other impressive feats. Nor should it be forgotten that he had the moral courage to stand up to senior officers on matters of principle. In the succeeding years, few commanders equaled him and none surpassed him. Lansdowne's death was a tragedy for the rigid airship cause, for the U.S. Navy, and for his country.

The *Shenandoah*'s two-year career had many consequences for the U.S. Navy's rigid airship program, which had been initiated by the General Board in 1913. On the positive side, she had gotten the program started, trained a number of personnel, and demonstrated the possibilities of such American innovations as helium and water recovery. Owing to Moffett's mania for publicity, only a minimal amount of work had been done with the fleet, and she had not been able significantly to show her qualifications as a long-range scout. Moffett regarded her as successful, and despite the adverse effects of the disaster in Ohio, was able in the following year (with the assistance of Paul W. Litchfield of the Goodyear Company, who wanted to establish an airship industry in the United States) to obtain congressional approval for the construction of two large rigid airships, the later *Akron* and *Macon*, and a West Coast airship base, which was eventually located at Sunnyvale near San Francisco.

The extravagant expectations of 1919–22 had not been realized, however, and the *Shenandoah* had also demonstrated several disadvantages: high unit cost, low availability, limited range with helium, low speed, and vulnerability to weather.[66] Comparisons with the airplane were inevitable, and here the airship was at a disadvantage because of its cost. Moffett had failed to act as he should have to show the airship's unique advantage over the airplane—its range and endurance for strategic scouting at sea. Increasingly, his brilliant and imaginative subordinates in BuAer regarded the admiral's fascination with the rigid airship as a defect of judgment on his part, while they saw the aircraft carrier with its attack group of aircraft as the decisive aerial weapon at sea. The millions spent on airships, they argued, would better be allotted to fighters, dive bombers, and torpedo planes, and the specialized vessels needed to carry them. While the airshipmen at Lakehurst, struggling with helium supply problems and procurement delays, became an increasingly isolated minority in naval aviation, the new carriers, the *Lexington* and the *Saratoga*, captured the imagination of the public, being highly visible in fleet exercises. Last, remembering the 14 dead at Ava, the public was beginning to regard the rigid airship as an expensive death-trap, an attitude that gained many supporters after the flaming crash of the British R 101 in 1930, the loss at sea of the USS *Akron* in 1933, and the *Hindenburg* disaster in 1937.

One lesson had been learned: for the *Los Angeles*, *Akron*, and *Macon*, there were fewer publicity and "county fair" flights. Rarely were they seen inland, and they operated much more in the environment for which they were best suited—over the sea and coastal areas.

9

ZR 3: Inspector of Naval Aircraft, Friedrichshafen

The last of the three rigid airships of the U.S. Navy procured in the Era of Experimentation, the ZR 3 *Los Angeles*, was not a Zeppelin copy, but an authentic original from the *Luftschiffbau Zeppelin* of Friedrichshafen, LZ 126 in that company's series. The preeminent position of the German firm in the rigid airship field made it inevitable that the U.S. Navy should seek to obtain one of its products. Once again, the U.S. Navy was dealing with a foreign supplier—but, unlike the procurement of ZR 2, the former British R 38, nothing was to be taken on faith; and the Bureau of Aeronautics was determined to have inspectors with full powers, as in contracts negotiated in the United States. Yet the negotiations that were involved, not only in preparing the contract, but even more so in the execution, were infinitely delicate and complex. In particular, the inspector of naval aircraft stationed for two years in Friedrichshafen, and charged with obtaining the Zeppelin Company's design secrets, had to proceed with the greatest tact and circumspection in order not to offend his opposite numbers, sensitive, secretive, and smarting from Germany's recent defeat in the Great War. Commander Garland Fulton (CC) USN, to whom this formidable task fell, deserves great credit for the final success. But even his astuteness, patience, and tact would not have sufficed to overcome German suspicion and pride if he had not been met halfway by the chairman of the *Luftschiffbau Zeppelin*, Dr. Hugo Eckener, who realized that the Zeppelin enterprise could not survive in the postwar world without American support and involvement.

As early as 1919, the director of naval aviation, Captain Thomas Craven, had desired to obtain a wartime German naval Zeppelin (see Chapter 4). His interest led nowhere, partly because of the destruc-

tion of seven of the surviving craft by German naval airship crews at Nordholz and Wittmundhaven on 23 June 1919, and partly because of the refusal of the U.S. Senate to ratify the Versailles Treaty. It was in fact not the Navy but the U.S. Army Air Service that in the same year entered into a contract with the Zeppelin Company to build an airship of 3,500,000 cubic feet. While the orders and directions went out over the signature of Colonel Charles de Forest Chandler, the chief of the Army's Balloon and Airship Division, he certainly was not in a policy-making position. The subterfuges employed, the indifference to established legal procedure, and the disregard of operational realities point to the chief training and operational officer, the flamboyant Brigadier General William Mitchell, who had taken office on 1 March 1919. Having elaborated his theory of air power as a means of winning the next war, Mitchell was determined to influence public opinion in favor of a single air service, which would be coequal with the Army and Navy. Though there were occasional vague references to troop carrying,[1] and to night bombing,[2] it is clear that the Army's rigid airship would have been part of the headline-seeking razzle-dazzle of the Mitchell years, which included the first transcontinental air race in 1919; the first nonstop transcontinental flight in 1923; the first successful flight around the world in 1924; participation in the Pulitzer and Schneider Trophy races; and, most spectacular of all, the bombing tests of 1921 in which Army Air Service aircraft sent the "unsinkable" German dreadnought *Ostfriesland* to the bottom off the Virginia Capes.

When Mitchell made his move in the summer of 1919, it was in the face of the following realities, which he chose to ignore:

1. The Joint Army–Navy Airship Board opinion of 19 July 1918, that the U.S. Navy should undertake design and construction of rigid airships, furnishing information to the Army, was still in effect.

2. The Versailles Treaty, signed by representatives of the Allied powers as well as Germany on 28 June 1919, stated in Article 201 that "during the six months following the coming into force of the present Treaty, the manufacture and importation of aircraft, parts of aircraft, and parts of engines for aircraft, shall be forbidden in all German territory."

3. Owing to the refusal of the U.S. Senate to ratify the Versailles Treaty, a technical state of war between the United States and Germany continued until 28 October 1921, when the Senate ratified a special peace treaty with Germany.

4. No hangar existed in the United States, in either Army or naval hands, large enough to house a Zeppelin-type airship. The naval hangar at Lakehurst was not finished until August 1921, and the large hangar at Scott Field, Belleville, Illinois, the Army's big lighter-than-air base near St. Louis, was not completed until January 1923.[3]

Mitchell's chosen instrument was Colonel William N. Hensley, a 1905 West Point graduate commanding Langley Field, who during the war had been commander of the Army Balloon School at Pasadena, California, and who was a qualified free balloon, kite balloon, and airship pilot, though he of course had had no experience in rigid airships. His orders were "to acquire as much information as practicable concerning airships and airship stations in England. . . . If the opportunity occurs this office has no objection to your securing airship information in Germany, France and Italy."[4] However, it is clear that Hensley had confidential instructions to get in touch with the Zeppelin Company.

Hensley was speeded on his way by being detailed to the British R 34 as the U.S. Army's representative on her return voyage to England. Arriving at Pulham on 13 July, he spent over a month visiting building works at Bedford (Shorts), Barlow (Armstrong), Inchinnan (Beardmore), and Barrow in Furness (Vickers). On 27 July he flew in R 34 from Pulham to her home base at East Fortune on the Firth of Forth. General Maitland even promised to give him rigid airship training.

Meanwhile, Colonel Edward Davis, the military attaché at The Hague, had been approached on 1 August by a Dr. Dumreicher, representing the Zeppelin Company, with an invitation to Davis and any American Army airship expert to visit Friedrichshafen and inspect L 72 at Löwenthal. This ship, whose contract the German Navy had canceled when she was almost complete, was considered by the Zeppelin Company to be its private property. Davis's report to Washington was referred to the Joint Army–Navy Board on Aeronautics, which advised that no action be taken, as L 72 clearly fell under the provisions of the Peace Treaty, which provided for the distribution of the surviving naval Zeppelins among the victorious powers. The decision was signed by the director of the Army Air Service, General C. T. Menoher, who at the same time was chairman of the board. Yet behind his back, someone on 20 August cabled orders to Hensley to report to The Hague "for the purpose of carrying out confidential instructions with reference to the original Zeppelin Airship Corporation." Hensley's British hosts, heretofore friendly and cooperative, became decidedly cool, which Hensley attributed to the orders being cabled in clear text. Two days later he left for The Hague.

On 5 September Hensley and Davis proceeded to Berlin to discuss sale of L 72 with Zeppelin Company representatives. The two officers learned that the Zeppelin Company, faced with the prospect of having its activities halted and its hangars demolished under the Peace Treaty, was eager to develop a liaison with some American corporation. Ironically, on 5 September the Interallied Aeronautical Commission of Control had decided on the distribution of the surviving Zeppelins, awarding L 72 to France and her sister L 71, then laid up at Ahlhorn, to England. Hensley still hoped to purchase L 72 from France, while his deluded partner, back in The Hague, wired home: "we now have tentative plans to fly airship L 72 from Berlin across Asia to Philippine Islands thence across Pacific via Honolulu to the United States and afterwards back to Berlin if desired. This is an opportunity to promote science under American auspices."[5] There were of course no facilities for mooring or servicing rigid airships in Asia, the Philippines, or Hawaii.

Seeing an opportunity to rescue their enterprise through the interest of the U.S. Army, Zeppelin Company representatives rolled out the red carpet for Hensley. In his first ten days in Berlin, the colonel made two round trips between Berlin-Staaken and Friedrichshafen in the small commercial Zeppelin *Bodensee*, which had initiated a demonstration passenger service between the two cities on 24 August. Further, Hensley was promised a round trip each week for training purposes. In Friedrichshafen he learned of the "America Ship," a reworking of the big L 100 of 3,800,000 cubic feet, which had been ordered for the German Navy in September 1918, and canceled a month later. *Commerzienrat* Alfred Colsman, the business director of the *Luftschiffbau Zeppelin*, offered to build such a ship for the Army Air Service for 8,000,000 marks, equal to $360,000 at the prevailing rate of exchange, which reflected the rapid inflation in bankrupt Germany. Through Davis, Hensley sent Chandler on 3 October a request for $500,000 with which he proposed to purchase *two* of these huge craft—one for carrying mail and one for passengers—"these to be delivered two months after expiration of six months' limitation stipulated in Peace Treaty or in other words next autumn."[6] In reply, the adjutant general placed at Hensley's disposal the sum of $360,000 for the purchase of one Zeppelin. With Colsman protesting that he had not realized the inflated price of raw materials, and that 12,000,000 marks would barely cover expenses, Hensley was authorized to sign a contract at that price.[7] Having been promised by the Germans that he could be the commanding officer (surely they knew that he was not adequately trained and experienced!), Hensley wired home for 13 officers (5 listed by name) and 37 men to form a crew. On 26 November 1919 Hensley and Colsman signed a contract for construction of the airship, to be known as LZ 125, and to be 774 feet long, 97 feet 11 inches in diameter, with 3,532,000 cubic feet of gas in 16 cells and twelve 240-h.p. engines in eight single-engine and two twin-engine power cars. The contract was to take effect on the date the state of war between the United States and Germany was declared to be at an end; but the *Luftschiffbau Zeppelin* began work immediately on the new craft, though expressly forbidden to do so by Article 201 of the Versailles Treaty. Later the Germans claimed that Hensley had orally directed them to do so.

Abruptly Hensley's dream was shattered when he was advised on 1 December 1919 that the secretary of war, Newton D. Baker, had ordered the project abandoned and that no further expenditures were to be made. Hensley protested in vain that the contract had already been signed, while the Zeppelin Company threatened to bring a claim for damages, alleging that a number of girders and a twin-engine gondola had been built during the period between 26 November 1919 and 6 January 1920, when Hensley advised the *Luftschiffbau Zeppelin* that the contract was rescinded.[8]

Though the U.S. Navy had had some inkling of the Army's negotiations with the Zeppelin Company, it was Brigadier General Mitchell himself who gave the secret away by boasting to the Senate Committee on Military Affairs: "We negotiated and, in fact, we had almost bought the biggest airship in the world in Germany at a very small cost, a cost of less than one-half million dollars due to the exchange."[9] Secretary of the Navy Daniels immediately pointed out that the War and Navy departments had jointly placed cognizance of the rigid airship in the hands of the Navy Department, and requested more details. Secretary of War Baker, in his reply, referred to the unsuccessful attempt to obtain L 72, and added:

Early in October, 1919, the matter of purchasing a large dirigible abroad was again brought to my attention and under an erroneous assumption that the dirigible referred to at that time was one to be procured under conditions similar to those which would have brought about the purchase of L 72, I permitted negotiations to be entered into. . . . When I became fully acquainted with the facts in the matter and realized that we were entering into negotiations with nationals of a country with which we were still at war . . . I therefore promptly gave instructions to cancel the contract and to drop the matter entirely.[10]

Thwarted in his attempts to obtain a giant Zeppelin, Mitchell compensated himself by procuring from Italy the semirigid airship *Roma*, of 1,204,000 cubic feet, which, with a length of 410.1 feet, was small enough to fit in the Army's 420-foot-long shed at Langley Field. Completed late in 1919, the *Roma* was purchased for the Army Air Service on 9 June 1920, and was dismantled and shipped by sea to the United States. On her arrival at Langley Field it was found that the fabric envelope had been attacked by mildew and was in bad condition. The ship was assembled and inflated, and she made her first flight in America on 15 November, 1921. Persistent troubles with the Italian Ansaldo engines caused them to be exchanged for Liberties. However, on her first flight with these engines, on 21 February 1922, she suffered structural failure, dived from a low altitude into electrical wires, and burned, with the loss of 34 of the 45 persons on board. Although this was the worst disaster in the history of the Army airship service, the Army, as we shall see, continued to try to obtain ZR 3—until February 1925 when, as punishment for his intemperate attacks on senior Army and naval officers, Mitchell was demoted to his permanent rank of colonel and exiled to Fort Sam Houston in San Antonio, Texas.

The repudiation of the Army contract for LZ 125 created a crisis for the Zeppelin Company, and led to a bitter struggle for power behind the scenes. Naively expecting to do business as usual, the board of directors, immediately after the Armistice, had drawn up plans for the "America Ship" and had ordered the small commercial airship *Bodensee*, which in fact had flown between Berlin and Friedrichshafen between August and December 1919, as well as a lengthened sister ship, the *Nordstern*, which was intended to extend the service to Stockholm. Abruptly, in December 1919, both commercial craft were seized by the Entente; the Versailles Treaty forbade the construction of any kind of military aircraft in Germany; and the later London Protocol limited the volume of commercial airships to 1,000,000 cubic feet—too small to fly the Atlantic. Worst of all, the treaty called for razing the building hangars and destroying the Zeppelin works.

Though Count Zeppelin's nephew, Baron von Gemmingen, had become chairman of the company on his uncle's death in 1917, he was suffering from a fatal illness, which led to his death in 1924. Colsman, who had continued in Friedrichshafen as business director throughout the war, was in the strongest position to control the company, whereas his rival, Hugo Eckener, had been in North Germany for four years acting as director of training for the Naval Airship Division and as technical advisor to Fregattenkapitän Peter Strasser, the Leader of Airships. But having signed the contract for LZ 125 with Hensley, Colsman was blamed for its cancellation. Further, a journey that he made to the United States in the spring of 1920 to seek financial assistance not only failed to obtain the support and interest of either Henry Ford or Paul W. Litchfield of the Goodyear Tire and Rubber Company; but also, with his stiff-necked manner and narrow provincial outlook, Colsman managed to offend the more informal American industrialists. By contrast, Eckener had the vision, which Colsman lacked, to see the role of the Zeppelin in world commerce; and Eckener possessed a cosmopolitan outlook that appealed to the Americans and made him an international figure.

Meanwhile the Zeppelin Company had found a friend in America—Harry Vissering, a Chicago manufacturer of railroad equipment who happened to fly in the *Bodensee* during a visit to Europe, spent considerable time in Friedrichshafen, and on his return home acted officially as the company's agent in the United States. Yet Vissering's ties with the company were not through the business director, Colsman, but through the operators—Eckener, the flight director of the DELAG which was managing the *Bodensee*, and his right-hand subordinate Ernst Lehmann. A brilliant airship pilot who had commanded the *Sachsen* in 1913–14, flown with the German Army during the war, and, after the dissolution of the Army airship service in 1917, provided technical liaison between the *Luftschiffbau* and the German Navy, Lehmann also spoke good English, being more fluent in that language than any other officer of the Zeppelin Company. In 1921 Lehmann accompanied Vissering to America, returning with a broader vision, a respect for American methods, and the conviction that future relationships with American business—to which the Zeppelin Company had to look for political and financial support—could not be left to Colsman.

The awareness of Colsman's parochial outlook toward America intensified the struggle between him

and Eckener. Weyerbacher, who was in Friedrichshafen in late 1920, recalled: "it was about the moment when Eckener stabbed Colsman in the back and tossed him over the side. Everything was charged with suspicion. . . . He had great respect for Eckener as an airshipman—a shrewd, cautious operator—but as a person he [Eckener] was just plain rotten."[11] Eckener's ruthlessness, however, sprang not from personal ambition, but from *raison d'Etat*—the need to ensure the survival of the Zeppelin concern. By late 1921 Eckener had wrested control of the company from Colsman, and eventually became chairman after Gemmingen's death three years later.

With the Versailles Treaty taking effect on 10 January 1920,[12] the Allies commenced to implement its provisions at the expense of defeated Germany. The Air Clauses, among other provisions, included Article 202:

> All military and naval aeronautical material . . . must be delivered to the governments of the Allied and Associated Powers. . . . In particular, the material will include all items . . . which are or have been in use or were designed for warlike purposes. Dirigibles able to take to the air, being manufactured, repaired or assembled. Plant for the manufacture of hydrogen. Dirigible sheds and shelters of every kind for aircraft. . . .

The agency charged with enforcing the Air Clauses of the treaty was the Inter-Allied Aeronautical Commission of Control (IAACC), headed by Brigadier E. A. D. Masterman R.A.F., the leading figure in the British Navy's rigid airship program from the earliest days when the *Mayfly*, H.M. Airship No. 1, was building at the Vickers plant in Barrow. The IAACC numbered over 500 members representing all of the Allied powers, but with none from the United States because of the latter's failure to ratify the Versailles Treaty.

From information obtained immediately after the Armistice by the Allied Naval Armistice Commission, whose Aeronautical Commission had inspected the German naval airship bases in the North Sea and the Baltic, Masterman on 5 September 1919 had drawn up a list of the surviving Zeppelins and prepared for their distribution.[13] The plan was in two parts: The two latest naval Zeppelins, L 71 and L 72, were to go to France and Great Britain (the former had first choice and naturally picked L 72, then lying nearly complete in the building shed at Löwenthal). In the second list, each power made one choice, starting with the newest ships, and continuing until all of them were allotted. At the time it was not known that on 23 June 1919 five of the allotted Zeppelins had been destroyed by the naval personnel at Nordholz, and two more at Wittmundhaven. When this act was discovered, the two small commercial airships *Bodensee* and *Nordstern* were seized in their sheds at Friedrichshafen. Eventually the surviving naval Zeppelins were distributed to Italy, Great Britain, and France in the summer of 1920, while the *Bodensee* went to Italy, and the *Nordstern* to France, in the summer of 1921. Next, the IAACC ordered the demolition of the airship sheds in the North Sea, the Baltic, and the interior of Germany. This was carried out by German contractors during the year 1921–22; some of the larger sheds were disassembled and delivered to France, Italy, and Japan, but only the latter went to the trouble of re-erecting the Jüterbog double shed, at the Japanese naval air station at Kasumigaura, where it housed the *Graf Zeppelin* in August 1929, on her flight around the world.

Early in March 1920, Masterman met with the German government to discuss the question of compensation for the seven Zeppelins destroyed in the North Sea bases in June 1919. The Berlin authorities refused to accept responsibility, arguing that the flight crews had acted on their own initiative. Masterman passed the problem back to the Commission on Aerial Clauses, which ruled that the German government was fully responsible and would have to provide compensation. Eventually, on 2 October, the Conference of Ambassadors, meeting in Paris, ruled that the *Bodensee* and the *Nordstern* should be confiscated to replace two of the destroyed naval airships, and that the German government should pay for the other five destroyed Zeppelins either in gold marks,[14] or by constructing a civil-type airship in lieu of cash payment for those powers desiring this option. The protocol was signed by the Conference of Ambassadors and the German minister in Paris on 30 June 1921.

The Zeppelin Company's rival, the *Luftschiffbau Schütte-Lanz*, which had completed 20 rigid airships for the German Army and Navy, failed to survive into the postwar period, the chief reason being that their building sheds at Zeesen-Königswusterhausen near Berlin, and at Mannheim-Rheinau, were demolished in 1921–22 in accordance with Article 202 of the Versailles Treaty. The possibility that the hangars in Friedrichshafen, particularly the big Factory Shed II measuring 787 feet long, 138 feet wide, and 115 feet high, might suffer the same fate, caused great concern to the directors of the *Luftschiffbau Zeppelin*: without the building plant the company could not possibly have been resurrected in the impoverished Germany of the 1920s. Perceiving that their salvation depended on building an airship for the Americans, the Zeppelin Company began to press for the execution of the Hensley contract. On 13 June 1921, Colsman wrote to Major Benjamin Foulois, an aviation

assistant to the U.S. military observer in Berlin, to call his attention to the possibility of providing an airship of the LZ 125 type for 3,560,000 gold marks ($837,000):

> The reason why we would effect the order at this extraordinary price is that we consider this the only way to save our big shed from demolition. Of course it is supposed that in this case the Government of the U.S.A. uses its influence that the big shed in Friedrichshafen would be saved from demolition until the trial trips between the American port and Friedrichshafen have been terminated.[15]

In Washington, the chief of the Air Service promptly advised the secretary of state, via the secretary of war, of the Air Service's desire to obtain one of the compensation Zeppelins. On 1 July the American ambassador in Paris, Myron T. Herrick, acting on instructions, advised the Conference of Ambassadors of his country's desire to obtain an airship in lieu of cash payment for the two wartime Zeppelins to which it was entitled. Further, the airship was to be of 3,500,000 cubic feet, essentially the one described in the Hensley contract of 1919. Since only the Factory Shed II at Friedrichshafen was large enough to construct such an airship, Herrick asked that the shed be kept intact if possible. While the U.S. request was referred to the Allied Military Council for its consideration, the Conference of Ambassadors on the same 1 July instructed Masterman to take no steps toward the destruction of the Friedrichshafen sheds while the question was being studied.

The eagerness of the American government, led since March 1921 by President Warren G. Harding, contrasted sharply with the attitude of the previous administration under President Wilson. In fact, Harding personally was influenced in favor of procuring a compensation airship from the *Luftschiffbau Zeppelin* through his friendship with Harry Vissering. It was through the latter's enthusiasm and advocacy that Harding was persuaded to embrace the unusual opportunity to acquire a new airship without expense to the United States, and to give appropriate instructions to the secretary of state, Charles E. Hughes.

The U.S. request encountered unexpectedly rough sledding in the various Allied councils, and it was unpleasantly apparent that the British and French representatives particularly had been instructed by their governments to oppose the request, or at least to whittle down the size of the compensation airship[16] to 1,000,000 cubic feet, useless for long-distance operations and incapable of flying the Atlantic. On 26 July 1921, the Allied Military Council reported adversely on the American desire for a 3,500,000-cubic-foot ship. Herrick was then instructed to compromise by reducing the size to that of the lengthened L 70 type, about 2,400,000 cubic feet. He was also authorized to state that "it is not the intention of the Government to use this airship for military purposes but rather for commercial purposes."[17] This was not in accordance with the Army Air Service's intentions, and opened the way for the Navy to make a claim for it. The Navy, being invited by the War Department to concur in the latter's desire to acquire the airship for itself, called attention to a 1920 Joint Board decision giving responsibility for the development of the rigid airship to the Navy, and the Aeronautical Board on 8 September recommended that the approved policy be followed. Henceforth the procurement of the compensation Zeppelin would be in naval hands.

On 17 August the Conference of Ambassadors voted against the U.S. request for a 3,500,000-cubic-foot ship. Herrick then submitted a request for an L 70-class airship, which was referred to the Military Council with the same adverse opinion as before. The council suggested that the United States order two airships of 1,000,000 cubic feet each. This figure was then held to be suitable for "commercial" airships, while any higher volume would designate the craft as "military."

Two days before the Military Council's decision, on 24 August 1921, the disaster to R 38 in England killed 16 U.S. naval airship personnel, and threatened to set back the American rigid airship program by years. Thus procurement of the replacement airship from the Zeppelin works became a matter of the greatest urgency. But the British, aspiring to monopolize prospective world air routes with a postwar commercial airship program, dominated the Allied councils and conferences; and it was the British who led the opposition to the American acquisition of a compensation airship from Germany. Furthermore, Great Britain was, in a sense, to blame for the setback to the American program, as R 38 was in British charge at the time of the disaster, and the impression was developing both in England and in America that the airship's design was faulty. As Secretary of the Navy Denby outlined the American position to Secretary Hughes:

It might be pointed out to the British Foreign Office that anticipating the satisfactory delivery of ZR 2 by the British Government, the United States has organized and trained a large airship personnel, and invested heavily in airship sheds and gas plants. This investment exceeds $12,000,000. Due to the disaster to ZR 2, the opposition of the British representatives to our acquiring a substitute for ZR 2 from Germany appears to be untimely. . . . In conclusion, my dear Mr. Secretary, I wish to impress on you first, the embarrassing position in which the loss of the ZR

2 has placed the Navy Department and second, and consequently, the urgent necessity for pushing this negotiation for a German Zeppelin as a replacement for ZR 2 in our program through and, in spite of Allied opposition, to a successful issue.[18]

On 14 October, Denby reiterated his arguments:

In view of the good faith that has characterized all dealings between the United States and Great Britain concerning rigid airships, the fact that the British themselves have taken over Zeppelins L 71 and L 64, and particularly since the embarrassing position in which the loss of the ZR 2 has placed the Navy has been pointed out, the Department is at a loss to understand the British attitude of attempting to prevent the United States from securing a German-built airship. . . . On account of the fact that the United States was in no way responsible for the loss of the ZR 2, it was expected that the British Government would welcome the opportunity to assist in securing this replacement.[19]

These arguments, conveyed by the secretary of state through the American ambassador in London, George Brinton McClellan Harvey, undoubtedly caused His Majesty's Government to instruct its ambassador in Paris, Lord Hardinge, to alter his attitude. Sensing that the British and French were opposed to the United States obtaining a military airship, Hughes advised Herrick on 9 November 1921:

Navy Department will be delegated to act on behalf of this Government in all matters dealing with construction, acceptance, and maintenance of the airship, and for that reason the airship will be incorporated in the naval establishment of the United States. *The airship will be used for experimentation to determine the feasibility of rigid airships for commercial purposes.*[20]

At last the American plea was successful, with the Conference of Ambassadors, in their 157th meeting, on 16 December 1921, approving the American request for the construction at Friedrichshafen of "a dirigible of the L 70 type (about 70,000 cubic meters)." The German government, however, was to be informed that this was an exceptional circumstance, and following the completion of the American compensation airship, "all the material and the shed which were used for its construction shall immediately be destroyed and dispersed and the personnel employed in its construction shall be dispersed so as to insure the complete execution of the treaty." The British ambassador remarked on "the assurance of America that this airship is to be devoted to purely civil purposes,"[21] thus insuring that the United States would so employ it. On 6 January 1922 General Masterman was instructed to issue the necessary orders for the Zeppelin Company to proceed.

Since the U.S. Navy had been designated by the U.S. government as the agency to handle procurement and construction of the compensation airship, Captain Frank P. Upham, the naval attaché in Paris and the senior attaché on the European Continent, was ordered to handle the negotiations. In this he was assisted by the attaché in Berlin, Commander W. P. Beehler, who spoke fluent German and had many German contacts, and who took a continuous interest in the ZR 3 project. Commander Horace T. Dyer and Mr. C. P. Burgess, having completed their participation in the R 38 inquiry in England, arrived on the Continent in January 1922 to offer technical assistance to Captain Upham in negotiations with the Zeppelin Company. Majors Benjamin Foulois and Harold Geiger of the military attaché's office in Berlin participated in the early conferences.

Upham had been provided by BuAer with general requirements for the airship desired by the U.S. Navy:

> 1. The airship is to be non military without armament, but otherwise of approximately the displacement of the type L 70.
> 2. The airship may be more rugged structurally than the L 70 and of substantial decrease in length–diameter ratio.
> 3. To be provided with a bow attachment to fit the mast at Lakehurst.
> 4. The maximum speed at 3000 feet to be greater than 70 miles.
> 5. The airship is to be delivered at Lakehurst by a German crew.
> 6. There shall be accommodations for twenty passengers, to be symmetrically disposed about the center of buoyancy, these accommodations to be removable for the transatlantic flight.
> 7. There shall be a reasonable quantity of spare parts and repair material.
> 8. The airship to be constructed in accordance with plans and specifications approved by American inspectors stationed at the builders' works.[22]

Only the last provision was to cause serious difficulty between the Navy and the Zeppelin Company. It did not make clear to the Germans that the Navy was determined to have complete access (on a confidential basis if necessary) to the German design methods, theoretical aerodynamic and structural calculations, stressing procedures, and the basis for the use of particular structural items throughout the airship. Many Zeppelin Company personnel were violently opposed to giving up their "trade secrets," which they considered to embody a unique fund of knowledge attained through the exercise of German scientific genius.[23] Only the far-sighted vision of Dr.

Eckener, and the threat that the U.S. government might cancel the contract, an action that would lead to the immediate demolition of the Friedrichshafen hangars, sufficed to obtain this information for the U.S. Navy Department.

Several meetings took place early in January 1922 between Upham and Eckener. Whether the Americans would have accepted a copy of the lengthened L 70 with a passenger cabin amidships is not clear. Fortunately for all concerned, Eckener had a vision of something far more significant. Not only would the ship—possibly the last ever to be built by the Zeppelin Company—be as sound and perfect as she could be made, with a view to leaving a lasting impression on the aeronautical world; but with the limitation that she would be designed for commercial work, she would demonstrate the Zeppelin Company's advanced ideas for a transoceanic passenger carrier. ZR 3 in fact was a milestone in the history of rigid airships, the prototype of the famous *Graf Zeppelin*, and in the opinion of many, the most beautiful and gracefully proportioned craft of her type ever built.

In a conference with Dr. Eckener on 14 January, Captain Upham discussed the tentative requirements and found the *Luftschiffbau* in general agreement except for the arrangement of the passenger quarters. Dr. Eckener, drawing on his experience with the small commercial airship *Bodensee*, argued that they should not be amidships: "Accommodations for 20 passengers (besides the crew) will be built in the forward part of the ship. According to our experience, it is neither practicable nor in consideration of the stability of the ship, is it necessary to arrange the passenger rooms symmetrically around the center of buoyancy."[24] Eckener further proposed that the main frames be 15 to 16 meters apart with only one intermediate frame between. He contemplated fitting eight of the wartime 245-h.p. six-cylinder high-compression Maybach MbIVa engines—four in two twin-engine centerline power cars forward and aft, each pair of engines driving one propeller through reduction gearing; and four more in four single wing cars port and starboard.[25] With the recent crash of ZR 2 in mind—a ship with 15-meter main-frame spacing with two intermediate frames, which nonetheless had failed structurally—Admiral Moffett, in his written instructions to the prospective inspector of naval aircraft, Friedrichshafen, criticized the single intermediate frame as not appearing sound. On the other hand, the inspector was authorized to agree to the Zeppelin Company proposal that the passenger cabin be forward, provided that the inspector agreed.[26] On 19 January, Captain Upham was able to report "all general contract requirements accepted by the Zeppelin Company."[27]

Two matters had to be resolved, however, before a contract could be drawn up between the U.S. Navy and the Zeppelin Company. One was the matter of how much the German government would have to pay for the compensation airship. The other was the need for the German Reichstag to pass a law authorizing the construction of ZR 3 as an exception to an earlier law, passed at the demand of the Allies, forbidding the construction in Germany of rigid airships larger than 1,000,000 cubic feet (the larger ships being considered to have military value).

On the one hand, the Zeppelin Company had suggested in conversations with Captain Upham a price of 4,000,000 gold marks ($941,000) for the compensation airship; on the other hand, it was in the interest of the German government to pay as little as possible for its construction. Clearly also the U.S. government expected the German compensation figure to cover the cost of ZR 3, and was not prepared to spend any of its own money. The decision as to the German payment rested with General Masterman and the IAACC, which had previously estimated the value of the five destroyed ships at 8,250,000 gold marks (L 63 and L 52, which had also been destroyed, having been made good by awarding the *Bodensee* to Italy and the *Nordstern* to France). Allotting one of the five destroyed ships to the United States, Masterman figured that only 1,650,000 gold marks was due for it. Ambassador Herrick, arguing before the Versailles Committee on 13 February, claimed that the United States was entitled to the value of two ships (L 65 and L 14 in the original award, both destroyed at Nordholz on 23 June 1919). "This discussion lasted an hour and a half. The British, French and Belgians during this made remarks decidedly adverse to us. The Italians were more favorable, and the Japanese were silent. Hostility to our contentions was the general attitude. The question seemed almost prejudged and there was no indication of an open mind on the Committee's part."[28]

The State Department accordingly made representations in London, Paris, and Rome, reminding the British particularly of their responsibility in the ZR 2 disaster. As a result of these efforts, Upham was surprised on meeting with Masterman and the IAACC on 9 March to discover that while Masterman still valued the five destroyed Zeppelins at 8,250,000 gold marks, he was willing to award the Americans 2,000,000 marks for L 65, more than for any of the other airships; and for the obsolete L 14, commissioned in August 1915, and to which Majors Foulois and Geiger had awarded a value of NIL, he assigned a valuation of 1,000,000 marks. While Upham would have liked more, he felt sure he could not obtain it. The Versailles Committee and the Conference of Ambassadors approved Masterman's figures, and Upham was authorized to negotiate with the Zeppelin Company on the basis of the 3,000,000 gold marks figure.

Eckener and the *Luftschiffbau* were of course in a weak position. On the afternoon of 9 March, Upham met with Eckener and Dr. Dürr, informing them that their price of 4,000,000 gold marks was excessive, that 3,000,000 was the maximum sum available, and that with the recent loss of ZR 2 and the U.S. Army's semirigid *Roma*, the U.S. Congress would not add more. Upham suggested that if the sum were not acceptable to the *Luftschiffbau*, there would be no contract, and the sheds in Friedrichshafen would promptly be demolished. Eckener replied that an exact copy of the L 70 type could be built for 2,500,000 gold marks, but the Zeppelin Company was planning a much superior type of ship with advanced streamlined form and 400-h.p. engines of a new design, the cost of which, with spares, would be 3,500,000 gold marks, delivered in Friedrichshafen. To save the airship industry, he would be willing to take a loss and charge 3,200,000 marks with delivery in the United States, the 200,000 marks being for insurance to cover the transatlantic flight. The problem was finally resolved by Upham's accepting Eckener's suggestion of a separate contract to pay 400,000 gold marks for "turning over" the ship after her arrival in the United States, the contract to cover training of an American crew by the Germans. In the end, the German government's payment for the compensation airship was 3,031,665 gold marks, and on 23 June Upham signed contracts with the Zeppelin Company representatives to build the ship for that sum;[29] to pay an additional $150,000 for three months' instruction of the American crew by the Germans at Lakehurst; and to acquire as many spare airship engines as funds would allow.

The passage of the law authorizing the Zeppelin Company to build an airship larger than 1,000,000 cubic feet was of course a foregone conclusion, though Upham expected opposition in the Socialist Reichstag, not so much because of hostility to the United States, but from resentment of the favoritism being shown to "the rich Zeppelin Company where smaller companies are not to be accorded similar relaxation of the law."[30]

Meanwhile the inspector of naval aircraft, Friedrichshafen, had arrived in Germany. Upham, having met Dyer, wanted him for the post, and indeed, Dyer and Burgess, accompanied by Major Geiger, were the first Americans to visit Friedrichshafen in connection with the construction of ZR 3. Over a three-day period, 19–22 January, they were taken by Captain Lehmann on a tour of the Zeppelin plant and the

Maybach engine works, and met Baron von Gemmingen, Dr. Eckener, Dr. Dürr, and Dr. Maybach. Dyer later reported that:

> All of these gentlemen were most courteous and pleasant, but it soon became obvious that they did not propose to give us the slightest bit of information in regard to the proposed airship, as far as structural details were concerned. . . . As a result of our various conversations during some three days, it became evident that they were simply stalling and proposed to show us nothing.

There followed a "very frank conversation" with Dr. Eckener and Captain Lehmann, in which the three Americans spoke directly about the difficulties in dealing with the Zeppelin Company. The chief one involved the Navy's requirement for submission and approval of all design data. Not only would the Navy Department expect, but

> Would insist on being shown such plans, drawings and figures as would permit them to satisfy themselves that what was proposed would meet the required performance and would, in addition, have the safety desired, and further, that the construction having been started our inspectors must have such access to the work that was going on to assure themselves that the work was being carried out in accordance with the design plans.

This was an obvious shock to the two Germans, who even in dealing with their own Army and naval representatives had not been required to produce such information. They suggested that the Americans might propose what tests they desired after the ship was completed, but this idea was promptly rejected. Dyer and Burgess were certain that the Germans now understood the American position, but were doubtful that the Zeppelin Company would produce any figures, as "their methods of design and their experience are really the only thing they have left at the present moment."[31]

Dyer and Burgess were also made aware for the first time of the closeness of Harry Vissering in America to the Zeppelin Company, and of his activities on their behalf in dealing with the Navy Department. Dyer warned of the complications that might ensue if negotiations for the construction of ZR 3 were carried on simultaneously by the Navy Department with Vissering in America, and by Upham and his assistants in Germany.

Dyer, however, was not to get the inspector's post. While he had held a comparable position in the building of ZR 2 at the Royal Airship Works at Bedford in England, he represented the Bureau of Steam Engineering and had no qualifications in aeronautical engineering. Returning to Washington, he spent several months attached to BuAer before being sent to sea as engineering officer of the battleship *Arkansas*, thus disappearing from the airship scene.

As early as 23 December 1921, Commander Land had written to Captain Upham to advise that Lcdr. Garland Fulton (CC) USN and Lt. Ralph G. Pennoyer USN would be sent to Germany as inspectors in Friedrichshafen. Pennoyer, the former executive officer of the Howden Detachment and the senior surviving officer after the ZR 2 crash, had had considerable rigid airship training and was well qualified to advise on operational matters.[32] Fulton, however, had the chief role, from both the technical and the diplomatic point of view. Born in Mississippi in 1890, he was a Naval Academy graduate in the class of 1912, and between 1914 and 1916 had earned a master's degree in naval architecture at M.I.T. Early in 1918 he had joined the Aircraft Division of the Bureau of Construction and Repair as assistant to Commander Hunsaker, and soon specialized in the design, construction, and repair of pressure and rigid airships. By the end of 1921 he was the best informed officer in BuAer on technical airship matters and Moffett's obvious choice for the Friedrichshafen post.

Accompanying Fulton and Pennoyer when they sailed for Europe late in February 1922, was Lcdr. Zachary Lansdowne, under orders to Berlin as assistant to Commander Beehler, the attaché. Following his return from Europe in July 1919, on board the British R 34, Lansdowne had served as lighter-thanair assistant, first to the director of Naval Aviation, and later in BuAer. Serving in Berlin until October 1923, he advised Beehler and assisted in the negotiations for procurement of ZR 3.

The three officers arrived in Berlin on 8 March. On the following day, Fulton and Pennoyer conferred with General Masterman; and they participated in conferences with Zeppelin Company representatives beginning on 12 May, and continuing until 26 June. Both attended the signing of the contract for ZR 3 on 23 June.[33] With these negotiations out of the way, Fulton and Pennoyer, with Chief Yeoman A. J. Boutin, proceeded to Friedrichshafen where they opened the inspector's office on 6 July 1922.

The Americans were assigned two rooms on the second floor of the Administration Building of the *Luftschiffbau Zeppelin*, with Captain Lehmann on the same floor, and Dr. Eckener downstairs.[34] Later the U.S. Army observers had a room across the hall. Fulton began by calling on the various officials of the company: Baron von Gemmingen, the chairman; Colsman, the head of the Business Office; Dr. Eckener, the head of the Operations Department; Dr. Dürr, heading the Construction Department; Dr. Maybach, head of the *Maybach Motorenbau*; and Captain Lehmann, the *Luftschiffbau*'s front man in dealing with the Americans. In time, Fulton discovered that Dr. Arnstein, the chief calculator, was the source of design information. As Weyerbacher remarked: "there was no two ways about it that Arnstein was the brains of the outfit, though the Zep people took pains to hide this. In fact, when he was there in 1919 and 1920, they even hid Arnstein's person."[35]

In some "Notes on Personalities," Fulton recorded his impressions. Baron von Gemmingen, possibly overrated, was: "A very fine cultured German. Cordial and pleasant. He is often consulted and takes a more active part in affairs than appears on the surface. When trouble and friction arise he steps in with a club and straightens things out."

Colsman was: "Typically German (Prussian) in his attitude and manner. Following his visit to America in 1920, where he created a none too favorable impression, a campaign was started to oust him from active interest in the plant here. This has been accomplished, and while he is consulted frequently, his impulsive head-strong ideas no longer control."

Dürr was: "A typical 'Schwäbischer'—i.e., provincial native of South Württemberg. Unmarried and lives almost a hermit's life. Has never travelled and has very narrow views. Believes implicitly in German theory of absolute secrecy about work. . . . He has never quite accepted the ZR 3 contracts Eckener signed and it was rumored he declined to affix his name to a contract that 'sold' the Zeppelin 'birthright.' Is a very difficult man to deal with. . . . Have had scant opportunity to size up his technical ability. It appears to be based on long experience rather than superior brains. . . . He is 'the old man of the sea' as far as we are concerned."

On Dr. Eckener: "Realizing that Colsman's handling of affairs was hurting the Zeppelin Company he was instrumental in having him shoved aside. For this, and for other reasons, he is sometimes criticised by people here. There is really the 'Colsman faction' and the 'Eckener faction' with possibly a third 'Dürr faction.' The Eckener faction is in the saddle and the Dürr faction pulls very well with it. Dr. Eckener is a very fine type and the most broad minded and reasonable man in the organization. He creates an excellent impression and is very highly regarded throughout Germany. He is an excellent negotiator—sizes up a situation and makes decisions quickly."

Of Lehmann: "At present he is Dr. Eckener's first assistant and is specially charged with keeping track of matters of interest to Zeppelin in America and England. . . . He is very highly regarded by Dr. Eckener (and Baron von Gemmingen)—so much so that his ideas are generally taken up at once. He is also very well thought of throughout the organization (except by Colsman) and is consulted frequently."

Of Dr. Arnstein: "Is now head of the mathematical and structural section where he seems to be doing excellent work. Appears to be an exceptionally capable bridge mathematical engineer, who has switched to airship work. . . . Personally he is very pleasant and cordial but, evidently acting on instructions, shows some reluctance about giving detailed information. . . . Appears to be broad minded and would like to leave Friedrichshafen, which he considers has a very narrowing influence."[36]

To the end of his long life in 1975, Garland Fulton held Dr. Eckener in the highest esteem, regarding him as one of the great men of his day, the greatest airshipman who had ever lived, and a firm friend of American airshipmen whose projects commanded his interest and encouragement. His opinion of Lehmann, on the other hand, deteriorated; in later negotiations he found the little captain to be two-faced, devious, and even obstructive while offering protestations of cooperativeness and friendship. Fulton found it unforgivable that when Eckener's outspoken criticism of the Nazi gangsters led to his being kicked upstairs and declared a "nonperson" by Joseph Goebbels, Lehmann was all too ready to toady to the Brown Shirt leaders and take Eckener's place as manager of the Zeppelin Reederei.

Almost immediately, Fulton and Pennoyer were involved in conferences with Zeppelin Company personnel concerning the design and construction of ZR 3, which was numbered LZ 126 in the company's series.[37] On 12 July there was a meeting with Lehmann, Dürr, and Jaray, the Zeppelin Company aerodynamicist and project engineer, concerning the passenger gondola. The company proposed a roomy car about 16½ feet wide and 70 feet long, comparable to a Pullman car with berths for 20 passengers and seats for 30, with toilets and galley, the control car and radio room placed in the forward portion of the gondola—substantially the passenger accommodations in the completed ship. The weight was estimated at four tons. Fulton accepted the passenger gondola's being located forward. While the company did not want to make the car detachable, they were persuaded to proceed on this basis until more evidence became available to show impracticability or undesirability of this scheme.[38] On 20 July the conferees discussed what Fulton later called "a Lehmann brainstorm"[39]—an idea for building a small 1,000,000-cubic-foot "civilian" airship, an enlarged Nordstern. The proposed 400-h.p. Maybach VL-1 engine which the Americans were told would be created for ZR 3 could be tried out in the small ship, while eight of the 245-h.p. wartime high-altitude MbIVa Maybachs would be obtained as a reserve. In fact, the eight Maybach MbIVas were somehow obtained from German naval storage and reserved for the Zeppelin Company at Cuxhaven, but progress with the 400-h.p. engines resulted in the MbIVas' never being used.

In any case Dr. Maybach felt they did not have the durability and dependability for the transatlantic flight. The 1,000,000-cubic-foot ship was not built.

Fulton at this time was entitled to believe that the ZR 3 design was proceeding somewhere in the remote recesses of the *Luftschiffbau*, but he felt increasingly that he was being put off with excuses. On 24 July he spoke to Lehmann about progress on the design: Lehmann appeared to be unfamiliar with the design process. To save time, Fulton proposed that information be fed to him piecemeal as it became available, rather than that he should be overwhelmed with a mass of material when the design was complete. Lehmann said he understood, and that "probably in a week there would be something to see."[40] On 17 August the preliminary balance schedule was presented for discussion. On 1 September Fulton again requested information to be sent to Washington—performance curves, general airship drawings, data on engines, and so forth. For INA approval, two copies of all plans would be sent to Fulton's office, one to be retained, the other to be signed or commented on and returned to the Design Section. After final approval, a third copy would be sent over by the Design Section. On 7 September Lehmann delivered a general profile of the proposed ZR 3 design. It is noteworthy that Dr. Arnstein, the actual designer, was not present at any of these conferences, and Fulton's first meeting with him, according to his diary, was on 11 November.

Meanwhile a crisis occurred over the presence of Army observers in the Zeppelin plant at Friedrichshafen. Majors Foulois and Geiger in Berlin had been helpful in early negotiations to obtain the ZR 3, and Fulton respected them. Both were continuously involved with heavier-than-air matters, however, and Foulois soon dropped out of the picture; but Geiger maintained an interest and made a number of visits to Friedrichshafen. On 30 June 1922 he was designated the senior Army Air Service observer by the chief of the Air Service. But there were also reasons for disquiet: In Washington, General Mason M. Patrick, the chief of the Army Air Service, egged on by Mitchell, now assistant chief, pressed for complete information on the new airship, while an assistant observer was to be sent from the United States to take up residence in Friedrichshafen. This observer was Major Frank M. Kennedy, who was detached from duty at the Army's airship base at Scott Field, Belleville, Illinois, on 31 July 1922, and ordered to proceed on or about 15 September to Berlin and Friedrichshafen. Kennedy, tactless and ignorant, and incapable of understanding the sensitivities of the Zeppelin Company's leadership, was to be a constant source of annoyance to the INA during the one and a half years he was in Friedrichshafen.

Moffett had already foreseen the problems and complications that might ensue in Friedrichshafen if the Zeppelin Company found the Army aggressively competing with the Navy for the firm's design secrets. Early in May 1922, the admiral wrote to Commander Beehler in Berlin of his concern that the Inter-Allied Aeronautical Commission of Control might interfere (it did not), and that problems might be created by

> our own good friends the Army. As you may know there is an element in the Army Air Service, which is sincerely and zealously advocating an independent air service, and use anything they can lay their hands on as material to advance their arguments.... There will be, no doubt, a discussion when this ship is finally delivered as to whether it is to be turned over to the Army or Navy for operations.... in the meantime it is a NAVY ship and a NAVY project. The Army may and should keep in touch with it by means of such observers as they care to send, but there is no question of any joint control and in my opinion joint control will be fatal to getting results.[41]

A few days later, Moffett wrote officially to General Patrick urging that Army observers not be sent to Friedrichshafen until the contract was signed and plans were completed. A month later Moffett warned:

> If any attempts are made to tamper with or obtain through devious channels information from employees of the Zeppelin Company, they will probably have a serious effect upon the confidential relations which it is hoped to establish and maintain under this contract.[42]

Now the Zeppelin Company was becoming agitated about the number of American visitors going through the plant. On 21 August, three Army officers, headed by Major Oscar Westover, appeared in Friedrichshafen and presented orders from the secretary of war stating that the purpose of their visit was for them to become familiar with the latest practice in airship construction and operation. Geiger had frequently visited from Berlin, and Kennedy was due to arrive shortly. Lehmann protested to Fulton that the Zeppelin Company considered that admitting the Army personnel was a concession on their part; he requested that their number be kept to a minimum; and he stated that the company would recognize their presence only through the naval inspector's office. Fulton was particularly concerned that the Zeppelin Company might take advantage of the Army observer's presence and appetite for information to try to create a division between the two services and thereby gain the upper hand in interpreting the contract in their favor.

Dr. Eckener loyally supported Fulton by sending a letter to Geiger advising that Kennedy wait until the end of March or early April before coming to Friedrichshafen permanently:

At the moment there is very little to see and residence in Friedrichshafen during the winter months offers no particular attraction for anyone who is not settled here with his family, so that there would be little satisfaction and a great deal of discomfort and boredom should he arrive in the near future.[43]

Kennedy postponed his arrival until February 1923.

The dispute concerning design information came to a head in the fall months of 1922. The design of ZR 3 was well along, but the Zeppelin Company continued to evade supplying the information needed by Fulton to approve the design, and to enable the Zeppelin Company to proceed with construction. In the shops, Fulton found work continuing on fabrication of material, and warned that this was at the company's risk. There was evidence of a conflict within the leadership of the Zeppelin Company—Eckener undoubtedly intending to live up to the contract; Lehmann professing willingness but stalling or evading unless pressed or threatened; Arnstein still out of sight though later showing cooperation and even friendship; and the remote and seclusive Dürr undoubtedly representing the attitude that it would be better to forfeit the contract than to surrender one iota of the company's "birthright."

On 20 September, Lehmann turned over copies of the specifications for ZR 3, and a few plans forming part of the specifications. Fulton found the material incomplete, lacking clarity, and not in agreement with earlier decisions. He complained formally to Lehmann that the first test in getting design information from the Luftschiffbau Zeppelin was not satisfactory, and that the design staff was unwilling to cooperate and live up to the spirit of the contract. Fulton asked to confer directly with personnel of the design department. Lehmann as usual agreed that there was cause for complaint and that he would speak to Drs. Eckener and Dürr about providing more information. During a visit by Vissering on 16–21 October, Fulton tried to impress upon him the need to persuade his principals to take a more cooperative attitude. Conferences followed with Drs. Eckener and Dürr, and, in November, Arnstein finally appeared at discussions concerning the passenger gondola and hull strength. At a 1 December conference Fulton was given a glimpse of Arnstein's data and design methods, and felt matters were progressing satisfactorily. But in January, Fulton found himself right back where he had started on the question of strength data. Either the company would reveal its "trade secrets," or the contract would be terminated. "The fundamental question," Lehmann argued, "is to which extent is the Navy Department entitled by the contract to obtain information about the methods of the Luftschiffbau Zeppelin in constructing

airships."[44] The contract of course read "data such as plans, specifications, weight estimates, balance diagrams, calculations, reports of tests, instructions for operation, etc., for which approval is required shall be submitted to the Inspector of Naval Aircraft in duplicate as they are completed." Lehmann was persuaded that the Zeppelin Company had been very generous with the Navy Department, and then argued:

1. The *method* of strength calculations is one of the most *vital business secrets* of the *Luftschiffbau Zeppelin*.
2. A secret held by more than one or two individuals is in continual danger.
3. In the opinion of the *Luftschiffbau Zeppelin* it is *not at all* necessary for the Navy Department to have these calculations for any reason in connection with this ship.
4. The *Luftschiffbau Zeppelin* is *not obligated* under the contract to *surrender* these *calculations unless the ship is accepted.*[45]

At one point Lehmann contended that

It is not the duty of the *Luftschiffbau Zeppelin* to convince the Inspector of the soundness of the ship, but the task of the Inspector to convince himself. . . . It is not an obligation for the *Luftschiffbau Zeppelin* to submit a stress analysis, but it is up to the Inspector to make one of his own. . . . it is not a duty of the *Luftschiffbau Zeppelin* to show why the parts shown on the drawing are reasonable, but it is expected that he will approve them without further procedure and delay, unless he can prove them to be unreasonable.[46]

Such arrogance provoked the ordinarily even-tempered Fulton to ask:

Has the Zeppelin Company ever before seriously held the idea that the Navy Department proposed to make its own stress analysis of the LZ 126 based on data obtained from drawings alone or drawings supported merely by general data?[47]

Fulton also denied Lehmann's contention that the company need not submit strength data until 60 days after the airship was accepted by the Navy Department.

Needless to say, Fulton's reports, and correspondence describing his difficulties in getting design information from the Zeppelin Company, had been read with great interest in the bureau in Washington. Moffett himself was seriously concerned and felt it necessary to make it clear to the Zeppelin Company that they could not evade the terms of the contract. On 24 February 1923 he addressed a strong letter to Harry Vissering:

As representative in this country for the Zeppelin Company, you may be in a position to make that concern realize that its apparent evasiveness and lack of good faith in carrying out the terms of the contract agreed upon with Navy Department are considered by this Bureau so serious as to throw doubt upon the wisdom of continuing this contract. The contractor persists in constructing the ship without the Inspector's approval, as specified in the contract, continues to delay submission for approval of the factors of safety and loading specifications, which the ship is designed to meet and, in general, appears to be trying to force the Department's hand by manoeuvring for a position where the ship is built before its strength is revealed, or to accomplish the evasion of certain contract requirements as to evidence of strength. You can appreciate that there is absolutely no hope of any outcome favorable to the contractor in such a policy. The Bureau is fully prepared, as soon as convinced of the determination of the contractor to continue to evade contract requirements, to request cancellation of this contract.

Naturally, the Bureau in the interests of the development of airships desires to see the Zeppelin Company to make a great success of its undertaking and is prepared to cooperate in every legitimate way. However, the Bureau cannot cooperate unless good faith and good will are evident and cannot tolerate a continuance of the present condition. It is possible that the Zeppelin Company does not realize the American prejudice against a slippery contractor nor does it appreciate the reasons for the very tolerant attitude of the Bureau. This attitude was taken with the hope of establishing mutual confidence and a harmonious working agreement. Apparently, the time has come for a change in policy.

In view of your repeated assurances of interest in American airship development, and of your interest in promoting an American connection for the Zeppelin Company, it is suggested that you use your good offices to make it very clear to your principals that they are entirely misjudging their position and doing themselves serious damage as to their future reputation and good will in this country, as well as making it doubtful whether the present ship will ever be built.

These are the points to be made clear:

(a) Zeppelin appears to be evasive in living up to his contract.

(b) The Bureau will not accept the ship unless built as per contract.

(c) The Bureau will never be in the position of letting Zeppelin build and fly a ship which the Bureau must refuse to accept when presented.

(d) The only alternative to (c) is to denounce the contract at an early stage of construction and recommend to the Allied authorities the destruction of shed and fabricated parts.[48]

Though Moffett undoubtedly felt it necessary to strengthen Fulton's hand, the situation had altered by the time Vissering got in touch with the Zeppelin Company. Thus, there was consternation when Vissering cabled on 2 March to report receipt of Moffett's letter with the threat that the contract would be can-celed and the Navy Department would recommend to the Conference of Ambassadors the destruction of the building shed and parts already completed.

Part of the blame can be put on the delays in communication by letter. There was no commercial air service across the Atlantic, nor would there be one until the *Hindenburg* commenced flying on schedule in 1936. The fastest ocean liner took five days from New York to Europe, and mail from Washington to Friedrichshafen could take two weeks. At this particular time, in the winter of 1922–23, communication was delayed even further by the chaotic political conditions in Germany. Unreasonable Allied demands for reparations payments, the flight of German capital abroad, and the obstacles to revival of foreign trade led the German government to issue paper money to pay off its debts, fueling a runaway inflation with catastrophic consequences for the middle class. Ordinary postage stamps sold for 50 million marks each—nearly 12 million dollars at the prewar rate of exchange! In January 1923, French troops with tanks and artillery occupied the industrial Ruhr and enforced a blockade that cut off the occupied Rhineland from the rest of Germany with disastrous economic results. Sabotage and guerilla warfare broke out, and civil war threatened. Not until the autumn was some stability restored by the drastic actions of the Stresemann government, and meanwhile, on 8–9 November 1923, Adolf Hitler made his unsuccessful *Putsch* in Munich. These troubles echoed only faintly in remote Friedrichshafen, but were watched with concern by Fulton and his fellow Americans.

At the request of the Zeppelin Company, Fulton wrote to Moffett:

I was not satisfied either with the way things were going and during November, December, and the first part of January had several discussions with the Zeppelin Co. The last of these talks resulted in an understanding being reached that I believe will yield results satisfactory to the Bureau. These results are still slow in being delivered but will be forwarded to the Bureau just as promptly as I can get them from the Zeppelin Company. It is a fact that some of the data we require has intentionally never before been put on paper or compiled in understandable form. . . . To get an accurate picture of conditions it should be realized first that German psychology, methods, habits and language are all different from our own. Secondly that the Zeppelin Company is a peculiar organization. They always enjoyed very special privileges from the Government, their only previous customer, and have therefore had a free hand in regard to building airships. This independence coupled with secrecy carried to an extraordinary length even for Germany, and a somewhat narrow viewpoint about certain matters, coming mainly I think from the isolated position in Friedrichshafen, has created a state of mind which requires a process of education and time to dispel.[49]

An admirable psychological evaluation, revealing yet another of Garland Fulton's many talents. In a private letter to Moffett the next day, Fulton put his finger on the Zeppelin Company's deepest apprehension: "If we were inclined to cancel the contract they wondered whether we would not wait until we had all their data and then cancel the contract leaving them in a hole. They have been afraid of this all along."[50] There were more hurt feelings when a copy of Moffett's letter, forwarded by Vissering, arrived in the mail late in March (Fulton did not receive his own copy until 3 April). In a lengthy argument addressed to Fulton, Eckener complained of the "grievous and threatening letter" and of the accusation that the *Luftschiffbau Zeppelin* was a "slippery contractor." Fulton replied unofficially that "there is yet time to avoid having this appellation apply. I've told them to forget it and deliver the goods but they are disposed to 'discuss' it when there is plenty else to get done."[51] From Moffett's point of view, the incident was closed with a letter to Fulton expressing his relief at the assurance that the Zeppelin Company was prepared to cooperate in bringing the ZR 3 contract to a successful and creditable conclusion. Fulton was commended on "the tactful conduct of your very difficult position," but also requested to "use the cable somewhat more frequently, say at least monthly, to keep the Bureau informed as to the general situation and rate of progress."[52]

Fulton had won, but skilled diplomat that he was, he kept a smile on his face and his iron hand concealed in a velvet glove. He was accepted, and even liked, by Eckener and Arnstein, and much worthwhile information came from lengthy discussions with the latter. "The real values, whatever they were, lay not in a few volumes of strength data, but in the week to week reports, getting into provocative discussions, posing problems to draw the *Luftschiffbau Zeppelin* out, etc."[53] In Washington the data were evaluated by C. P. Burgess as they arrived, some data being applied to the *Shenandoah*, then in the process of erection. Hunsaker congratulated Fulton on the material derived from interviews with Arnstein—"a glowing testimonial to your powers as a diplomat"— and added: "I have not tried to puzzle out the calculations but the general method is ingenious. I suspect it will give about the same results as ours but it will take a long time to find this out."[54] The insiders in the bureau, including Fulton, believed that their own independently evolved methods of stress analysis, for which C. P. Burgess deserved most of the credit, were just as sophisticated as those of the Zeppelin Company, if not more so.

One more crisis arose before BuAer and the Zeppelin Company could get on with the construction of ZR 3—another attempt by the Army Air Service to obtain control of the ship on her delivery. The technique chosen was to plant inspired articles in the press; and though the battle was fought in the United States, it had its echoes in Friedrichshafen.

Appropriately, it was Major Frank Kennedy who was chosen to open the campaign. In an interview with *Aviation* magazine on the eve of his departure for Friedrichshafen, he was said to be going to Germany for 18 months:

> Supervising the construction of a great Zeppelin Airship being built for the United States by Germany. "The object of the trip, and in fact, the object of having Germany construct the airship for us, is to obtain the latest developments they have made in airship design and improvements." ... Ten months is the estimated building time, and thus, the ship should be ready for delivery in the fall of 1923. It is possible that it will be used by the Navy for some time after it is acquired, but it is expected eventually to arrive at Scott Field.[55]

In February 1923, Fulton in Friedrichshafen heard the rumors of the Army wanting a decision on the ultimate allotment of the ZR 3. Fulton was concerned first about the effect of the Army's intervention on the attitude of the Allied powers, who had been skeptical about the airship's employment for commercial purposes, and second about the effect on the Zeppelin Company and its relationship with the Navy Department. As he wrote to Moffett:

> ZR 3 is a civil type. The State Department commitments at the time of getting authorization for the ZR 3 must be upheld, possibly to the extent of assigning ZR 3 to commercial work. Allied governments were a bit sarcastic over the Navy acquiring a civil type. Discussion now about the allocation to another military service will certainly be known; will bring outside troubles and may embarrass the State Department. With France and Germany technically at war agitation of any kind is highly injudicious. . . . Give Germany the slightest chance and we would be included in her repudiation of the Treaty of Versailles.

As for the Zeppelin Company:

> Discussion now will awaken doubt in the minds of the Zeppelin Company as to who is their ultimate consumer, weaken our hand, and give them a fine chance to play the Army against Navy, or vice versa, also to be more evasive than they already are and to procrastinate. In case ZR 3 is assigned to the Army, it certainly places "acquirement" by the Navy in an equivocal status.[56]

Fulton, visiting Paris for his examination for promotion to commander, had discussed the problem with Captain Upham, who expressed his official concern in a cable to the Navy Department. Undoubtedly Upham spoke also to Ambassador Herrick, who alerted the State Department to the evils that might result from the Army's meddling. To Moffett, Captain Upham wrote:

> It must be kept in mind that the building of this ship was granted us on the express condition that it be a "civil" airship. If we do not stick to that proposition we *will* have the Inter-Allied gang after us. Moreover a row between the Army and Navy as to allocation of this ship would certainly destroy any illusions as to its being a civil airship.

As for the Zeppelin Company's reaction:

> We now have three officers on the job down there and I should say that the situation is at the saturation point; if any more go down there, whether Army or Navy, I can see old Dr. Dürr closing up like a clam and blocking the whole works. I have encountered that bird in the conference room and have noticed that for unadulterated, square-headed resistance, he wears a gold medal, or if he don't, they ought to give him one. . . . Your choice of Fulton for the job could not have been better, but he has got to have the fighting support of the Navy against the Army.[57]

Prodded by Ambassador Herrick and certainly also by Moffett and the Navy Department, the State Department entered the quarrel by sending identical messages to BuAer and the chief of the Army Air Service:

> The State Department has received advices from their sources abroad from which the Department understands that the fewer officers of the War and Navy Departments hanging around Friedrichshafen the better. . . . Also questions between the Army and the Navy as to ultimate allocation should be postponed in view of the fact that discussion as to ultimate allocation may revive interest in the Military Control Committee who have the right to make inspection of the ship, and such an inspection at this time may produce consequences which cannot be foreseen.[58]

This warning did not halt the Army campaign. An article in *Aerial Age*, headed "Army May Get ZR 3," went on to say:

> It is quite within the bounds of probability that the Army Air Service may be the recipient of the ZR 3. . . . In the summer of 1919 the Army instituted the first negotiations for a rigid German airship. In January, 1920, the Joint Army and Navy Board allocated the development of rigid airships to the Navy. . . . However, the operation of an airship is not necessarily *development*. The Army has needs for a rigid ship apart from those of the Navy. The Army wants a rigid ship as a means of transportation of personnel and supplies. . . . The airship is a long distance bombing and reconnaissance instrument with capabilities entirely different in extent from those of the airplane.[59]

An article in the *Washington Post*, datelined Paris and headlined "Army–Navy Rivalry May Lose Zeppelin: Their Claims Show Ship Built In Germany Is Not For Commercial Use," commented:

> Certain of the Allied Powers are watching the row with interest, preparing to take measures to prevent the completion or delivery of the ship on the ground that its construction was authorized as a commercial dirigible and not as a military machine, whereas the activity of the American Army and Navy proves that it is not aimed at peaceful purposes.[60]

Shortly afterward Secretary Denby wrote to Secretary of State Hughes calling attention to the press articles about the Army–Navy competition for ZR 3:

> I am sure that you will agree with me that it is very undesirable that there should be any grounds for public statements of this character. . . . I suggest, if your opinion is in agreement with mine, that a public statement be made that will set at rest all rumors questioning the good faith of this Government, and making it clear that after this ship is accepted, there will be no change whatever in its status, and that the Navy will retain this ship for experimental purposes in determining the feasibility for commercial use of rigid airships.[61]

The concurrence of the State Department, and the resulting pressure brought to bear on the chief and the assistant chief of the Army Air Service, finally put an end to General Mitchell's agitation to obtain ZR 3 for the Army.

The final ZR 3 design was for a craft with a nominal displacement of 2,471,000 cubic feet. This figure corresponded to the 70,000 cubic meters authorized by the Conference of Ambassadors: the actual gas volume with 100% inflation was 2,599,110 cubic feet. The weight empty was 77,836 lb., the gross lift with hydrogen 179,266 lb., and the useful lift 101,430 lb. The fully streamlined hull was 658.3 feet long including the bow mooring fitting; the maximum diameter was 90.7 feet. Main frames had diamond trusses and were spaced 15 meters apart, with two intermediate frames. The keel was unusually sturdy, constituting an upright V with stout lateral bracing at each main frame, which projected slightly below the inscribed circle of the hull. There were 14 gas cells, and with Frame 5, carrying the rudder post,[62] some 55 feet ahead of the extreme end of the tail cone, there was a cell (#0) in the tail cone with a volume of 15,892 cubic feet. The fins were of thick cantilever construction with two cruciform structures at Frames 5 and 15. The five engine gondolas were arranged conventionally—one on the centerline aft at Frame 55, and the others in pairs at Frames 85 and 115.

As early as 7 November 1922, it was announced that the keel of ZR 3 had been laid and that completion of the ship was expected in August 1923.[63] Actually, however, the keel-laying ceremony involved the passenger gondola and not the ship's hull![64] At the same time, in the old 1909 Ring Shed, the frames for the midships structure—main frames 100 and 115, and intermediate frames 105 and 110—were partially completed, and work on the five power cars was beginning.

By 10 January 1923, Frames 85, 95, 100, 105, 115, 120, and 125 were under construction. Main frame 100, the first completed, was moved into the big Factory Shed II, fitted with 5-meter longitudinal girders, and intermediate Frame 105 was mounted atop it. On 19 January the assembled frames were hoisted into a vertical position in the center of the shed, supported by cables from the overhead and cradles underneath. The hull structure was then extended fore and aft by erecting further frames at 5-meter intervals and tying them together with longitudinal girders and shear wiring. Fulton noted that 16 men were employed on this work, and that assembling and wiring each 5-meter section took about 24 working hours.

By 30 January, the midships bay from main frames 100 to 115 was completed; section 95–100 on 2 February, and 90–95 on 6 February. Simultaneously, Frames 85, 120, 125, and 130 were completed in the Ring Shed and ready for installation, and work was in progress on Frames 80, 75, 55, 50, and 40. By 13 March the hull framework was completed from Frame 50 aft to 130 forward. Frames 40 and 45 were ready for installation, while 135, 140, and 145 were under construction. In his monthly progress report, Fulton noted that the French Army's blockade encircling the Ruhr was causing difficulty in procuring duralumin from the Düren Metal Works, though progress on the ship was not being held up.

On 8 March there was an air inflation test of Cell #8, installed between Frames 100 and 115. Without an axial cable (which Dr. Arnstein felt was not necessary in view of the greater strength of the hull structure) the cell stood up well to a pressure at the top of 16 mm. of water; the wartime ships with the axial cable were tested at 13 mm. By 11 April the hull was completed from Frame 40 to 160. Frame 165 was ready for installation; the bow frames 170, 179.5, and 183.25 were under construction. The passenger gondola was to be completed in ten days, and the rear power car was 50% complete. The outer cover was being made up in panels tailored to the lines of the ship and was about 60% complete.

By 17 May the hull was complete from Frame 30 to 170. The nose section from 170 forward was being assembled vertically on the floor of the adjacent Factory Shed I and within two days was to be ready to be moved into Shed II for hoisting and attachment to the hull. Frames for the tail cone—Frames −3.5, −7, and −10—were completed, and the tail cone likewise was to be assembled vertically on the hangar floor. Frame 5, embodying the cruciform supporting the rudder posts, was under construction, but the frames forward of it—10 and 15—were delayed by the Ruhr blockade holding up the raw material. The passenger cabin was complete and secured to the hull; the rear engine gondola was 90% complete, whereas the other four were 15% complete.

By 13 June, Frames 20 and 25 were ready for installation, but frames further aft were still delayed by lack of material. The keel was complete from Frame 30 to 160, and all gas shafts and maneuvering valves were installed, as well as some fuel tanks and ballast bags. By 14 July, the hull was complete all the way aft to Frame 10, and the tail cone was ready for hoisting. The ballast system was complete except for the rear emergency "breeches" at Frame 25. Sixty fuel tanks had been installed, and two engine gondolas had been fitted to the hull. Within ten days Fulton expected the hull would be complete, and fitting of the outer cover panels could commence. The Zeppelin Company subsidiary, the *Ballonhüllen-Gesellschaft* at Berlin-Tempelhof, had completed 8 of the 14 gas cells.

By 18 August the hull framework was complete except for the fins. The upper fin was being attached to the hull, and the two horizontal fins, building on the hangar floor, were about 75% complete. The lower fin was about 10% complete. Outer cover panels had been laced on from the bow to Frame 55, and two coats of clear dope had been applied from the bow to Frame 100 (a third coat would have half a pound of aluminum powder added per gallon of dope, and a fourth and final coat with aluminum powder would be put on after sealing strips had been applied to cover the lacings that attached the outer cover to the girders). The fuel system was practically complete. "Fitting out the ship is trial and error. Drawings are not used to any extent."

By 19 September, the hull was complete except for the fins, which were to be completed in seven to ten days. The gas cells were to be shipped from Berlin on 23 September. By 16 October, Fulton reported the hull 98% complete; however, a photograph dated 20 October 1923 shows that the outer cover did not extend abaft Frame 25, nor were the fins covered. On 20 November, Fulton was able to announce the completion of ZR 3 in all respects—except that she did not have her engines! Nine frustrating months would pass before they could be installed, while Fulton would learn that Carl Maybach could be even more

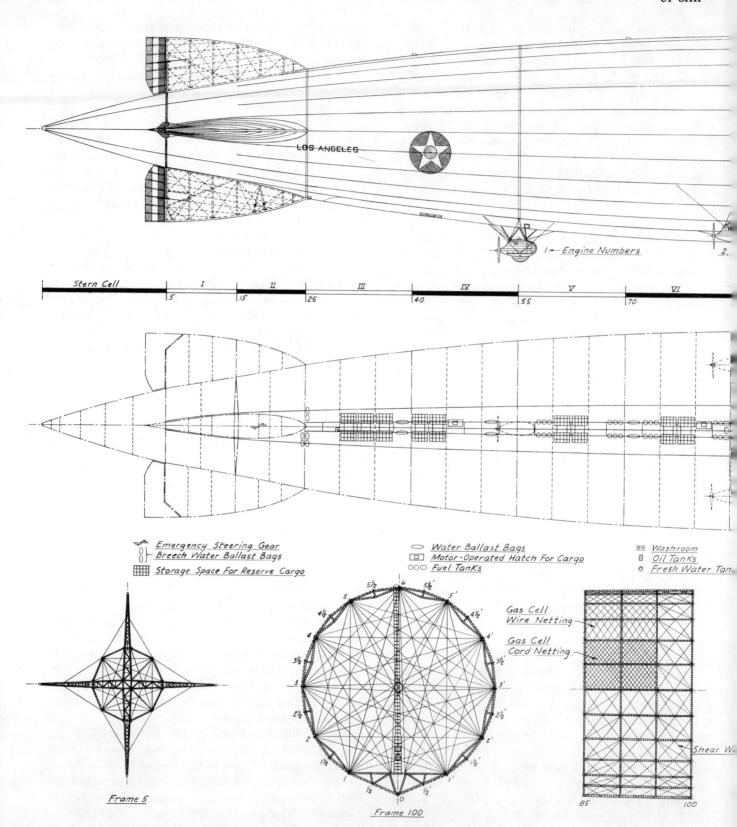

LOS ANGELES

1 ← Engine Numbers   2.

Stern Cell	I	II	III	IV	V	VI
	5	15	25	40	55	70

⊞ Emergency Steering Gear   ⬭ Water Ballast Bags   ⊡ Washroom
0|0 Breech Water Ballast Bags   ⊡ Motor-Operated Hatch For Cargo   ▯ Oil Tanks
⊞ Storage Space For Reserve Cargo   ooo Fuel Tanks   ⊙ Fresh Water Tan

Gas Cell
Wire Netting

Gas Cell
Cord Netting

Shear W

Frame 5   Frame 100

85   100

The *Los Angeles*

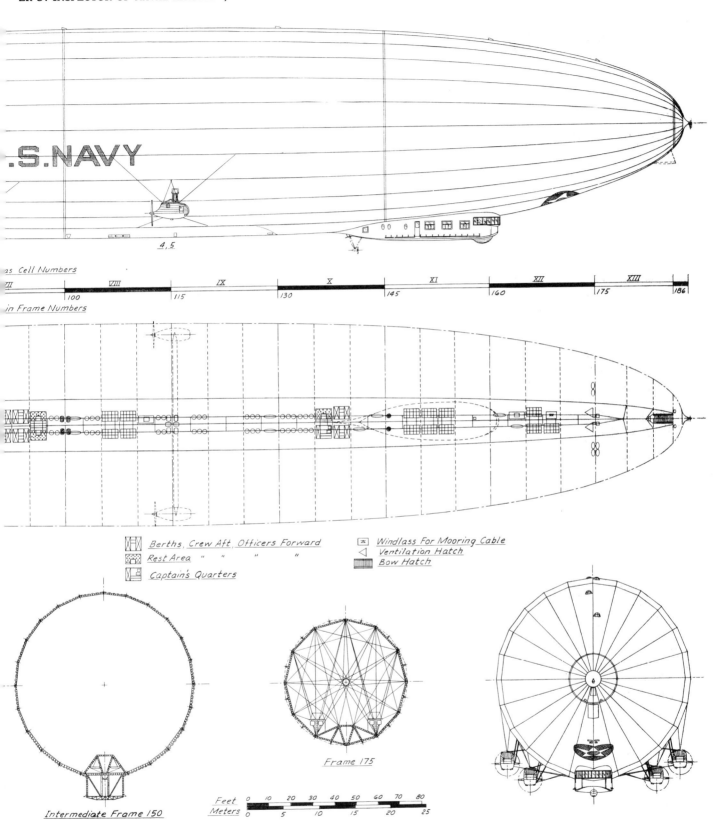

as Cell Numbers

III	VIII	IX	X	XI	XII	XIII
100	115	130	145	160	175	186

in Frame Numbers

Berths, Crew Aft, Officers Forward   Windlass For Mooring Cable
Rest Area   "   "   "   Ventilation Hatch
Captain's Quarters   Bow Hatch

Intermediate Frame 150

Frame 175

Feet   0 10 20 30 40 50 60 70 80
Meters 0   5   10   15   20   25

William F. Kerka

ZR 3 nearing completion at the Zeppelin works in Friedrichshafen. Photo, taken 20 October 1923, shows framework complete, both hull and fins, while the outer cover has been attached as far aft as Frame 25. (Luftschiffbau Zeppelin)

stubborn and secretive than that "old man of the sea" Ludwig Dürr.

The *Maybach Motorenbau*, a subsidiary of the *Luftschiffbau Zeppelin*, directed by Dr. Carl Maybach, the son of Wilhelm Maybach, who had collaborated with Gottfried Daimler in constructing the first practical automobile in the 1880s, had a great reputation among airmen and engineers of the Allied powers. As early as 1909, Carl Maybach had developed a 6-cylinder in-line water-cooled engine especially for airships, which had exceptional reliability for its day and a relatively low specific fuel consumption. Both properties were essential for airships, which, in contrast to airplanes, might have to stay airborne for days, carrying large amounts of fuel. The heavier engine with greater reliability and low fuel consumption would be a better tradeoff than a light-weight, low-endurance engine with higher fuel consumption. From the beginning, the Maybach engines featured a floatless carburetor in which the fuel level was kept constant by an overflow mechanism, eliminating the possibility of backfiring and carburetor fires which could be fatal in a hydrogen-filled airship. A clever starting system saved weight: the valves were lifted,

a hand suction pump drew a fuel–air mixture into the cylinders, and this was then ignited by a hand magneto.

German airship engine practice was to increase the number of individual power plants, rather than the horsepower, because of the frequency of engine failure on long flights. Thus, the Maybach C-X, in service in 1914, was rated at 210 h.p., and the lighter HSLu, which was introduced in 1915, at 240 h.p. The MbIVa of 1917 could produce 300 h.p. at full throttle at sea level, but in fact was limited to 245 h.p. up to 5,900 feet as it was designed for high-altitude operation. The MbIVa was a success from the beginning. Without a supercharger (which none of the belligerents succeeded in getting into service during the war) it developed more power at high altitude than its predecessor through being overdimensioned with a bore of 165 mm. and a stroke of 180 mm., compared to 150 × 180 mm. in the earlier HSLu; and by developing the unprecedented compression ratio of 6.7 to 1 in the 1918 version with aluminum pistons. The engine handbook asserted that either gasoline or benzol could be used as fuel; very probably a mixture was used to eliminate preignition and detonation at the high compression ratio used.[65] Though only 110 MbIVas were built for airships, many more were used in airplanes, particularly in the high-flying Rumpler C VII *Rubild* photographic aircraft with a ceiling of 24,000 feet.

Though a 400-h.p. Maybach engine had been proposed for ZR 3, and though Dyer, in his January 1922 visit to Friedrichshafen, believed that such an engine was already in existence and had been thoroughly tested, such was not the case. True, a 12-cylinder MbVII of 520 h.p. had been developed at the end of the war, but this power plant, consisting of two 6-cylinder MbIVas mounted vertically side by side on a common crank case, and geared to a single propeller shaft, had been a failure and had not been continued. Nonetheless the Zeppelin Company personnel were confident that a new V-12 design would be completed and tested by the time the airship was finished. In fact, Dr. Eckener urged Maybach to start work on the new power plant, to be known as the VL-1, as early as March 1922. Eleven were in the original order—five for ZR 3, two as spares, and four more for the 1,000,000-cubic-foot ship briefly advocated by Lehmann in July 1922.

It soon became apparent that the design of the VL-1 had not been completely worked out in detail, though probably it had been in concept. As weeks passed and the engine data failed to appear, Commander Fulton began to feel concern over whether the power plants would be available when the ship was due to complete in August 1923. As his repeated attempts to get information failed, he gradually became aware that the *Motorenbau* was in effect an *imperium in imperio*, over which Carl Maybach reigned as supreme autocrat, negotiating on his own terms with the *Luftschiffbau Zeppelin*. As Fulton later wrote:

> The secretiveness of the Maybach organization and their general distrust of everyone has hampered I.N.A. and *Luftschiffbau Zeppelin* in finding out the exact situation at any time. Even now (May 1924) the ship contractor (*Luftschiffbau Zeppelin*) does not know the exact situation.... It is therefore completely in Maybach's hands so far as theoretical or design questions are concerned.[66]

From July to October 1922 Fulton questioned Zeppelin Company personnel about progress with the VL-1 engine, with little result. Even Eckener and Lehmann expressed annoyance that Maybach would not deliver installation drawings and dimensions. Repeatedly, they expressed confidence in Maybach's organization, asserting that Maybach was always conservative, always met promised delivery dates, and the engines would be delivered "in time." On 16 November 1922 Fulton managed to talk to Carl Maybach in a conference attended by *Luftschiffbau Zeppelin* personnel and Harry Vissering. Maybach asserted that work was proceeding as rapidly as possible, the first engine would be ready for testing in May or June 1923, and five engines would be available for ZR 3 in September 1923. Various suggestions by Fulton were brushed aside, Maybach's attitude, according to Fulton, being "let me alone. I know what I am doing. You don't and I object to your making suggestions"[67]—an attitude that included *Luftschiffbau Zeppelin* personnel as well as the inspector of naval aircraft. For the time being, Fulton was rebuffed in his attempts to get information from Maybach, but Eckener and Lehmann assured him that Maybach would have an engine ready for testing by May 1923. Only in January 1923, and after many requests, did Fulton receive an installation drawing.

With the prospect that the ship would be completed in the late fall of 1923, both Fulton and the bureau in Washington were concerned that the Zeppelin Company might telescope trials and rush the delivery of ZR 3 in the winter months. Pennoyer, remembering that the mad dash to fly ZR 2 to the United States in the late summer of 1921 led to trials being abbreviated, wrote to the attaché in Berlin, Commander William F. Halsey, the future fleet admiral, to ask that Lansdowne be sent to Friedrichshafen to dissuade Dr. Eckener from trying to fly the Atlantic in winter. After all, in spite of Eckener's greater experience, Lansdowne had flown the Atlantic in R 34, and Eckener had not.[68] Moffett wanted the flight delayed until the spring of 1924 to ensure that the engines were properly tested; in windy winter weather there would be danger in putting the ship in the Lakehurst shed, and the training contract could not be executed in winter.[69] On the other hand, with Germany on the brink of civil war, the *Luftschiffbau* feared that ZR 3 would be sabotaged in her shed. But, as Pennoyer observed, this would be preferable to having her lost en route to America.

They need not have feared. Only in July 1923 did the first VL-1 arrive at the factory for use as a mock-up to fit connections and to lay out power-car equipment around it. To the disgust of Fulton, who pleaded in vain that the engine should be tested immediately under load, the mock-up engine remained idle at the factory for nine days. Only on 21 August was a VL-1 run under no load; the run was reported very satisfactory and Zeppelin Company personnel were elated, confidently expecting to have all engines installed in the ship by 1 November 1923. Yet the original engine design was full of defects, and as the months went by, the inspector of naval aircraft gradually became aware of the following:

Serious carburetion and distribution problems existed, leading to three redesigns of carburetors and intake manifolds. Continuous lubrication problems led to overheating, piston seizures, and piston pin seizures. After a piston broke, wrecking a cylinder and manifold and damaging the crankcase, connecting rod, and crank pin bearing, all pistons on hand were scrapped because of defective material due to faulty castings. "Defects were apparent to superficial examination," wrote Fulton, "and seemingly *Maybach Motorenbau* had been doubtful of safety of pistons at some previous date but used them anyhow."[70] After two cylinders failed by cracking around the base flange, the design was changed, and all cylinders on hand were scrapped. A camshaft housing broke, allegedly due to having been dropped; later it appeared that the cause was elongation of the camshaft with temperature increases, and the problem was solved by making the camshaft in three parts. After these problems had been dealt with and eliminated, Maybach proposed to get approval for his engine with a test run of only 20 hours. Fulton dismissed this as "entirely inadequate" and insisted on 20 hours at full power plus 70 hours at reduced power. Fulton reluctantly considered substituting American engines—Packard 1A-1551s or Wright T-2s—in place of the unattainable VL-1s. In the end, however, Moffett insisted on German engines, one reason being that the Germans would blame all problems with ZR 3 on the American power plants.[71] On 2 May 1924, during a "more or less formal test," the engine was started several times but had to be stopped each time as it would not come up to revolutions. "There appeared to be dangerously high friction. Disassembly showed all pistons of one bank had been badly overheated and much under-lubrication, one cylinder was scored. Low initial oil pressure is reported as the cause."[72]

Swallowing his pride, Carl Maybach admitted he needed help and called in Professor Alexander Baumann, of the Technical College at Stuttgart, who during the war had headed the Zeppelin design department that produced the four- and five-engine "Giant" bombers at Staaken. On his advice, a new connecting rod design was utilized. On 19 May 1924, using the rear power car of ZR 3 as a test stand, engine #110003 successfully passed a 20-hour full-power test. The engine was disassembled and inspected, and after reassembly, passed the 70-hour reduced-power test on 28 May. But when it was disassembled, it was found that one of the main bearing housings had cracked. A further 40-hour test on 17 June with engine #110001 resulted in crankcase failure at two main bearings. All crankcases were then scrapped, and new ones cast from "Silumin," an alloy that Maybach felt would solve all his problems. Yet in a 65-hour test with engine #110001 and one of the new crankcases on 7 July, the crankcase at 63 hours was found to have four cracks visible from the

outside, with one more found inside at disassembly. Fulton wrote to Burgess:

Maybach has a world's record on engine troubles—also on breaking crank cases and still having his engine run. His last 300 hours of running have been practically without forced interruptions (two or three stops for minor repairs), and yet he has busted some four or five crank cases. His engine certainly seems to like to run under difficulties.[73]

Maybach now consulted Professor Kutzbach of the Technical College at Dresden, with the result that he was persuaded to fully balance his crankshaft. As a part of his peculiar design philosophy, heretofore only half of the rotating weights were balanced by counterweights. Maybach had been able to get away with this concept on the smaller wartime engines, but it did not work with the VL-1.

As soon as the new and fully balanced crankshaft was ready, the type tests were run again. The 90 hours were run with only two interruptions, both due to minor problems. On 4 August 1924, inspection of the disassembled engine was completed. All parts were satisfactory! After two years of trial and tribulation, Carl Maybach had succeeded in producing one of the most successful airship engines ever built.[74] With a dry weight of 2437 lb., and a compression ratio of 5.3 to 1, the VL-1 produced 400 h.p. at 1400 rpm, while its fuel consumption of 190 grams per horsepower hour was the lowest of any Maybach yet built. Each bank of cylinders had a floatless carburetor at each end, the engine was started by compressed air, and it was reversed by stopping the engine, shifting cam shafts by compressed air, and restarting in the opposite direction, a method that saved weight compared to conventional electric starters and reverse gears. The VL-2, a modified VL-1 with a heavier crankshaft, aluminum pistons, and a compression ratio of 7 to 1 producing 550 h.p. at 1600 rpm, powered the later *Graf Zeppelin* and the U.S. Navy's *Akron* and *Macon*; and many of ZR 3's VL-1s were returned to Germany and rebuilt to VL-2 standards by the factory in Friedrichshafen.

Three more weeks sufficed for workers to fit the five engines, install the gas cells and inflate them with hydrogen, and attend to a multitude of last-minute details before the trial flights.

In addition to Fulton, Kennedy, and Schmidt, two more American officers were now in Friedrichshafen and expected to participate. On 14 April 1923 Admiral Moffett had written to the Bureau of Navigation (which handled the assignment of officers) concerning a commanding officer for ZR 3. In view of previous airship disasters including the loss of ZR 2, Moffett felt that the commanding officer of the new rigid should be the very best available, of the rank of captain, and a qualified naval aviator, so that in the event of a future catastrophe the Navy would be able to say that it had selected the very best officer that could be found. As he would have to deal with foreigners, he should be "an officer of tact, fine bearing, and personality." Moffett's choice was Captain George W. Steele, who in 1918 had been assistant to Captain Irwin, the director of naval aviation, and who in 1919, as commander, Air Detachment, Atlantic Fleet, had conducted early experiments with flying boats and shore-based aircraft from the tender USS *Shawmut* at Guantanamo. Soon afterward Lcdr. Sidney Kraus was designated engineering officer of ZR 3. In the expectation that the ship would be completed in the late summer of 1923, both officers departed shortly for Germany, Kraus sailing on 9 June and reporting at Friedrichshafen on 22 June. With the delay in completion of the airship, there was no urgency in their reporting to Friedrichshafen, and Steele, having recently married a charming heiress, Mrs. Lily DuPuy, delayed for several months in Paris and on the Riviera. As early as August 1923, Steele, Kraus, and Kennedy were accepted by the Zeppelin Company as observers on the transatlantic flight. At the last minute a fourth was added—Commander Jacob Klein, the commanding officer at Lakehurst, who undoubtedly aspired to command the new airship. Klein sailed from New York on board the *Mauretania* on 10 September 1924.

Zeppelin Company personnel were in charge of the ship until her arrival at Lakehurst, and Eckener was quite frank in desiring to use ZR 3 to create favorable propaganda for the rigid airship, to demonstrate the capabilities of the rigid airship in transoceanic commerce, and to counteract the adverse effect on public opinion of the ZR 2 crash and the loss of the French *Dixmude* in the Mediterranean in December 1923.[75] The trial flights, ostensibly to prove the ship and engines before the ocean crossing, were also deliberately planned by Dr. Eckener to cover the length and breadth of the *Reich*, and to remind his fellow countrymen of German predominance in the lighter-than-air field.

Eckener purposely chose a threatening day for the first flight, which took place on 27 August over Lake Constance and lasted 2 hours 47 minutes. Among those on board were Steele, Fulton, Kraus, and Schmidt. Controls tested satisfactorily and the ship handled well in going through a turbulent squall line with rain and hail. At full power on all five engines she developed 79½ mph, and 70 mph at cruising speed with 300 h.p. from each engine. The full-speed run, however, caused a crankshaft counterweight to break loose in one of the engines and go through the crankcase. All bolts in the crankshaft and counterweights were strengthened.

The second flight, on 6 September, lasted 9 hours 32 minutes and covered 475 miles over Munich, Regensburg, Nuremberg, and Stuttgart. Eighty-six persons were on board. The Americans included Fulton, Kraus, Commander John H. Towers of BuAer, and Majors Kennedy and Geiger. Two movie cameramen were on board as well as many German and foreign newspaper correspondents, all generating favorable publicity for the Zeppelin airship. The enthusiastic crowds on the streets of the German cities were all that Dr. Eckener could have wanted; in fact, ZR 3 was rapidly becoming a focus of nationalistic pride and enthusiasm.

Because of many letters and inquiries, the third flight, on 11 September, was intended to show ZR 3 to the various cities in Switzerland. Eighty people were on board, including many reporters. Initially dynamic lift was measured over Lake Constance, the ship climbing from 2,000 to 4,200 feet in ten minutes without release of ballast. ZR 3 then proceeded over Konstanz, Schaffhausen, Basel, Lucerne, and Zürich before landing after a flight of 8 hours 25 minutes. During the flight the rear engine had to be shut down. A defective thrust bearing in the crankshaft had been found, and Maybach engineers requested time to change all thrust bearings.

The fourth flight, on 13 September, presumably with only four engines operating, took the ship over the lake for calibration of the radio compass, and practice in blind flying by bearings from Friedrichshafen to the radio station at Konstanz and return.

Thus it was not until 25 September that the final long trial flight could be undertaken. Great excitement prevailed throughout Germany over the planned *Deutschlandfahrt*; rumors had the ship going as far as Königsberg, Stockholm, or Copenhagen. Thousands of requests came in for the ship to fly over the writer's home town, or even his house! Eckener decreed that as many as possible of these wishes would be fulfilled. With 71 persons on board, ZR 3 spent an hour running tests over the *Bodensee*.[76] Then Eckener ordered the ship flown over Tübingen, Heidelberg, Frankfurt, and Kassel, "to show the last Zeppelin to the German Fatherland, and to say farewell."[77] During the afternoon the cities passed below—Hannover, Bremen, and Hamburg, where the airship arrived promptly at 1700 as previously announced, six hours after departing Friedrichshafen. Via Schleswig, Kiel, and Lübeck the airship reached the Baltic, where during the night her crew practiced overwater navigation with radio bearings, compass bearings on lighthouses ashore, and drift measurements with acetylene-filled smoke bombs on the water. Heavy rain squalls causing the flight to Königsberg to be abandoned, ZR 3 touched the Swedish coast, then at dawn came inland over Stettin. On schedule the airship arrived over Berlin at 0830 on 26 September, to cruise for 45 minutes over the capital, the streets and housetops packed with excited citizens. Then home via Potsdam and Dresden to land after a flight of 33 hours 32 minutes. Engines, controls, radio set, all systems had functioned perfectly, and Eckener and his crew felt ready to undertake the journey to Lakehurst.

Privately, however, Eckener viewed the ocean crossing with some apprehension. Not only had it never been flown by a Zeppelin airship, but with the limited gas volume of ZR 3, the range and fuel endurance were somewhat marginal. With a useful lift of 43 tons, some 33 tons of fuel could be carried, which would confer a range of 5,400 nautical miles in 70 hours at full power. Since Eckener had to expect an average head wind of 13 to 15½ mph on the westward crossing, it was decided to cruise at reduced power, which would enable the ship to go 5,350 miles in 96 hours against such a head wind.[78] This would suffice to reach Lakehurst from Friedrichshafen via the Azores. In fact the flight was made over a distance of exactly 5,000 miles in 81 hours' flying time at an average speed of 61½ mph.

As the day of departure drew near, excitement in Germany rose to a fever pitch. Crowds of reporters and ordinary citizens converged on Friedrichshafen, and every hotel room was filled. A handful of die-hard nationalists vowed that no foreigner would ever possess ZR 3, the supreme example of German genius. Eckener's life was threatened.

There was an angry reaction when on 11 October the departure was canceled. The fully loaded ship did not lift owing to warming of the air, and Eckener was accused of having "lost his nerve." Yet he was not about to sacrifice fuel as well as ballast to please the crowd. On the following morning, by starting an hour earlier, ZR 3 got away with 33 tons of fuel, 2.2 tons of oil, and 7,300 lb. of water ballast. The crew numbered 27, six of whom—Lehmann, Flemming, von Schiller, Wittemann, Pruss, and Sammt—later held command. The observers included Steele, Klein, Kraus, and Major Kennedy.

Eckener had decided to cross by the southern route, via Cape Finisterre to the Azores, as the northern part of the Atlantic was dominated by low-pressure areas offering nothing but head winds. The flight across France was uneventful, ZR 3 leaving the country at the mouth of the Gironde River. Toward midnight the ship was passing north of Cape Finisterre, and by noon of the 13th she was in sight of San Miguel in the Azores.

Now, however, there was a check to the ship's progress, for a sight of the ocean below indicated that a strong southwest wind had sprung up—blowing at 31 mph, and reducing the ship's ground speed to the same figure. Under these circumstances it would have taken 70 hours for the airship to reach New York, and fuel for only 50 hours remained on board. Weather reports from two U.S. naval cruisers, sent out to aid ZR 3, indicated the presence of a low-pressure center south of Newfoundland. Boldly Eckener set a northwest course for Cape Race, to go around the north side of the low, and was rewarded by finding a strong northeast wind on the afternoon of the 14th. Making 78 mph over the ground, the airship was steered direct for Boston. In the early dark hours of 15 October, Boston was sighted, and after sunrise ZR 3 passed over New York. At 0937 the ship settled on the field at Lakehurst, and on entering the hangar, she became the property of the U.S. Navy.

Eckener and his crew were feted and acclaimed in the press, and welcomed at the White House by President Coolidge, as was their due. Steele, Klein, Kraus, and even Kennedy received their share of attention. In faraway Friedrichshafen, Commander Garland Fulton, who deserved as much credit as anyone else, was ignored; he was too modest to demand a place in the airship, and came home a month later on board the S.S. *George Washington*. He had what he wanted: the respect of his superiors and associates, and the awareness of a difficult job well done. As he later wrote:

> All these problems were certainly present and were part of the picture, but I would hope that any narration of them is not allowed to cloud the fact that we did get a good airship and at the end all was sweetness and light with the *Luftschiffbau Zeppelin*. This I attribute to Eckener who I feel was a good guy and tried to do right.[79]

So was Fulton himself, and the achievement would not have been possible without the respect and affection that these two remarkable people, the one German and the other American, felt for each other.

10

Los Angeles:
The Rosendahl Years

The U.S. Navy, after a two-year wait, had its Zeppelin airship with all the latest and advanced ideas of the master builders of Friedrichshafen; but with her had come a problem—what use to make of a craft restricted by international agreement to commercial operations? Even with ZR 3 safe in American hands, there was still concern about the possible reaction of the Allied powers to any suggestion of military employment, while pacifist public opinion in the United States would have protested against such use. To many in the Navy, the restrictions on the ship's operation led to the understandable conclusion that she would be an unjustified drain on the Navy's tight operating budget, and therefore she should be decommissioned or sold. Such naturally was not the view of BuAer, or of the airship advocates at Lakehurst.

One approach was for the Navy to operate ZR 3 as a model commercial vehicle, with the expectation that business interests would be attracted, would take her over, and would procure further rigid airships for regular passenger service. Garland Fulton put down some ideas before the craft was completed, advocating a special accounting system to maintain a record of costs after the fashion of a commercial firm. He foresaw that expenses would have to be paid by the Navy Department as not enough paying passengers would be found to materially reduce operating costs. Fulton suggested a number of possible routes, pointing out that "an airship service will show up to the best advantage over a water route":

1. New York (Lakehurst)—Palm Beach (landing only)—Guantanamo (mast)—Panama (mast)—Callao, Peru (mast). Return via Panama—New

Orleans (landing only)—Fort Worth (mast) for replenishment of helium—Lakehurst. A shed at Panama would be "a great help and a safety factor."
2. San Diego or San Francisco, California (mast)—Sand Point, Washington (mast)—Honolulu (mast or the *Patoka*). Here again a shed on the West Coast would be very desirable.
3. Demonstration flights around the rim of the United States—Lakehurst—Washington—New Orleans—Fort Worth—San Diego—Seattle—Omaha—Chicago—New York (this was written before the loss of the *Shenandoah*). "It would serve to show ZR 3 to the greatest number of people. The political aspect of the Navy Department operating an airship over land is pointed out."
4. Lakehurst to England. "This is a possible route but with ZR 3 filled with helium there is none too much margin for the west bound trip. Lengthening ZR 3 is feasible but may not be a desirable thing to do—certainly not in the immediate future."[1]

On 14 November 1924, Commander Klein, the commanding officer of the Lakehurst Naval Air Station, convened a "Board on Employment of ZR 3" consisting of Lcdr. Kraus, Lcdr. Maurice Pierce, Lcdr. Lansdowne, and Lt. Anderson. They recommended (a) training flights, (b) practice moorings to land masts and the *Patoka*, (c) long flights to test cruise radius at various speeds over water, (d) extended cruises to evaluate commercial value, (e) considering advisability of carrying passengers, and (f) considering advisability of lengthening ship by one or two 15-meter sections.[2] In fact, the ship never carried paying passengers, though her very comfortable quarters were appreciated by her crew and by the prominent guests who were frequently on board. Neither did the potential commercial operators appear.[3] ZR 3's real mission, particularly after 1929, was to train personnel for the giant *Akron* and *Macon* ordered in 1928, and to pioneer many of the innovations to be introduced in these ships—synthetic gas cell material, improved water recovery apparatus, mechanical mooring and ground handling equipment, and airplane hook-on procedures and material.

Meanwhile there was the practical necessity to get the ship flying. A priority consideration was the training contract involving the German crew members which Captain Upham had negotiated along with the construction contract for ZR 3; the Germans' obligation would run out on 10 February 1925, and Moffett and the bureau were pressing to get in as many flights as possible before then. At the same time, and to the Navy's embarrassment, there was not enough helium on hand to fly both the *Shenandoah* and the new ship; so ZR 3 received priority.[4]

ZR 3 was suspended from the hangar roof and shored up from below, so that on 18 October her hydrogen could be valved off into the atmosphere. The gas cells were then filled to 5% volume with helium to support their weight in the ship and to reduce the load on their overhead attachments. After the *Shenandoah* returned from her West Coast flight on 25 October, her helium, as well as part of her crew was transferred to the new ship. U.S. naval insignia—the red, white, and blue star in a circle under the nose and on both quarters, red, white, and blue stripes on the rudders and elevators, "U.S. Navy" in black letters amidships—were painted on.

By 24 November, the new ship was inflated and ready in all respects for the next event—the christening. Secretary Wilbur advised on 21 November that ZR 3 would be christened during the week of 23 November by Grace Coolidge, the wife of the president, and would be named the *Los Angeles*. Earlier, at a luncheon in Washington for Dr. Eckener and his officers, Wilbur referred to ZR 3 as an "angel of peace," but she was certainly named for the city.[5] The christening ceremony was originally set for 24 November, but three days before then was changed to the 25th.

On the morning of the 25th, ZR 3 was walked out of the Lakehurst hangar and ascended for her first flight in American charge, the destination being the Naval Air Station at Anacostia, D.C., near Washington. Captain Steele was on board, but his executive officer, Commander Jacob Klein, exercised command, Steele being unwell at the time. The airship carried 39 people, including Flemming, Wittemann, and nine of the German crew. A handling line parted as the ship tried to land at Anacostia without valving helium. With the ground crew, directed by Lt. Rosendahl, holding her, she was christened *Los Angeles* by Mrs. Coolidge with a bottle of water from the River Jordan (prohibition forbade the use of more appropriate champagne). Mrs. Coolidge presented to the ship an autographed portrait with the inscription "To the good ship *Los Angeles* from her sponsor mother. 'Go forth under the open sky and may the winds of Heaven deal gently with thee.'" The commandant of the Washington Navy Yard placed the ship in commission, and Captain Steele read his orders to command. President and Mrs. Coolidge, and about a dozen distinguished guests, boarded for a quick tour of the forward gondola; it was necessary to get away promptly for Lakehurst. The president's flag was briefly displayed, the only time this was ever done on board a U.S. naval airship. Klein relieved Steele of command, and Admiral Moffett boarded the ship for the return flight to Lakehurst, together with seven passengers including Commander Richardson and Lieutenant Rosendahl. At 1704 the *Los Angeles* rose statically and headed for Lakehurst with all engines on standard speed.

Remarkably, in view of the shortage of helium, the new airship had not been fitted with water recovery apparatus. In spite of arriving at Lakehurst after dark, the *Los Angeles* was still light through consumption of fuel, and made several unsuccessful attempts to land, not getting down until the maneuvering valves had been open for a total of 6 minutes 20 seconds.

The need of course had been foreseen; and Klein, himself, as early as 11 June 1924, had written to BuAer to ask that steps be taken to design and manufacture water recovery units for ZR 3. The work had been assigned to the Naval Aircraft Factory, the units to follow those produced earlier for the *Shenandoah*, with the same castings and tubing. The NAF apparently was in no hurry to prepare units for a ship still in Germany, but with the news that ZR 3 was starting trials, BuAer on 16 September pressed the factory to give 100% priority to the first four water recovery units, saying that "the fifth can probably be delayed."[6] A month later, on 22 October, the bureau was insisting that two water recovery sets should be installed by 15 November. The factory actually claimed it would have two sets ready to ship to Lakehurst on 10 November, while advising that two spare *Shenandoah* sets could also be installed by 15 November. Yet it turned out that Lakehurst did not want the units installed yet, an attitude "due to desire for speed data without the apparatus."[7] Not until 6 December were the spare *Shenandoah* sets installed on

Water recovery unit on engine car #4 of the *Los Angeles*. Obviously the drag caused by this type of unit was high. Actual tests in September 1927 with and without water recovery units showed that they decreased the air speed by 5 to 10%. (U.S. Air Force)

power cars #4 and #5; the remaining two sets from the NAF were delivered 6 and 10 December and would be installed immediately.

On 15 December, the chief of naval operations approved the bureau's recommendation for employment of the *Los Angeles* and the *Patoka* over the next six months—for the airship, training flights until the contract with the Germans expired on 10 February, then the *Los Angeles* and the *Patoka* to practice mooring in Chesapeake Bay in late January and early February. Next, the "*Patoka* was to proceed to Panama for a series of trips by *Los Angeles* to simulate commercial operations between New York and Panama."[8]

Yet in spite of pressure from the bureau, and Klein's undoubted ambition and drive as acting commanding officer, attempts to get the *Los Angeles* flying were largely defeated by winter conditions and unforeseen mechanical problems. The Americans had had little experience with winter airship operations with the *Shenandoah*. It was foreseen that the water ballast would freeze unless an antifreeze was added: calcium chloride was chosen for its cheapness, with disastrous results that became apparent only months

later when it was found that many keel girders were badly corroded and required replacement. The miserable winter weather for which the northeastern United States is noted frequently confined the ship to her hangar, not to mention snow and ice on the field hampering the ground crew. Above all, the water recovery units gave continual trouble, demonstrating that with the higher power and exhaust temperatures of the Maybachs, the *Shenandoah* condensers would crack and warp, requiring frequent replacement. Only two short flights were made in December, on the 22nd and 30th; on the first one the apparatus on cars #4 and #5 tested satisfactorily, but the water pipe in the keel froze, and the recovered water could not be saved. On the second flight 583 lb. of water was recovered from the condensers on cars #2, 3, 4, and 5, for expenditure of 638 lb. of fuel. On 9 January 1925, with the ship practicing mast mooring for the first time, the water recovery distribution froze again, while the flexible exhaust lines on cars #2 and #4 broke, filters clogged, and water lines and pumps froze. Zeppelin Company personnel were on board on these short flights, but it is doubtful that they were able to give much training.

On 15 January, the *Los Angeles* made her first mooring to the *Patoka* in the Patapsco River below Baltimore. A near accident in undocking delayed the takeoff by two hours: as the ship was being walked stern-first out of the east door, the starboard after trolley jammed in the crossover, and the tackle was tripped and released. The wind then started to swing the stern to port, the ground crew slipping on the solid ice on the field, unable to hold her. By running all four side engines full speed ahead for 15 seconds the airship was forced back into her shed undamaged.[9] There was trouble with the water recovery condensers on the later flight—#2 unit froze outside, could not be repaired under way and was disconnected. The #3 unit also froze. Subsequently the heads of three of the condensers were found badly warped by excessive heat. These were replaced by three condensers removed from the *Shenandoah* for the long overhaul, but after the next flight, the so-called eclipse flight of 24–25 January, which carried 25 scientists offshore to the track of a solar eclipse near Nantucket, only two condensers remained serviceable. New welded steel headers, finned connections between the engine and condenser for additional cooling, and four new separators designed for 400 instead of 300 horsepower, were installed by 16 February, and eventually metal double primary and secondary condensers especially designed for the *Los Angeles* took care of the overheating problems.

Captain Steele resumed command on 19 January, but continued to leave the handling of the *Los*

Angeles, and her internal administration, to his executive officer, Commander Klein. Faced with water recovery problems, bad weather, and a need to overhaul the engines, Steele resolved to make every effort to fly by 16 February. He was right to do so, for the next part of the program involved long overwater flights to simulate commercial operations. The goal, however, would be Bermuda rather than Panama. The Navy Department's interest was shown by the participation of the assistant secretary of the navy, Theodore Douglas Robinson, whose flag was displayed; Admiral Moffett; Captain Land of the bureau; and Commander Robert L. Ghormley.

The takeoff was made at 1520 on 20 February, with 39 persons on board including Colonel Hall and Captain Kepner of the U.S. Army and four Army enlisted trainees, the ship carrying 18,673 lb. of fuel and 14,850 lb. of water ballast, and the gas cells 84% full. Barnegat Light on the starboard beam was the last sight of the United States. During the night the *Los Angeles* proceeded southeast cruising on four engines at 52 knots at various altitudes up to 3,000 feet. Accurate navigation by Commander Pierce resulted in the Grassy Bay lighthouse on Bermuda appearing nearly ahead at 0255, with Gibbs Hill lighthouse in sight five minutes later. The *Patoka*, which had arrived in Bermuda 14 February, was seen under way at 0550 from Great Sound to Murray Anchorage. At 0745 she was ready for the mooring operation, but the weather was deteriorating, with successive black squalls with heavy rain and gusty winds. Because of the weather, and the fears that the airship, soaked with rain, could not get away from the *Patoka*'s mast with sufficient fuel for the return flight, Klein canceled the mooring and at 0958 departed Bermuda on a northwest heading. At 0036 on 22 February the *Los Angeles* landed on the field at Lakehurst with two hours' fuel in her tanks, after a flight of 33 hours 16 minutes—a creditable feat in itself.

Now another problem grounded the ship—excessive helium loss from the gas cells. These cells, which had been made by the Zeppelin subsidiary the *Ballonhüllen-Gesellschaft* of Berlin-Tempelhof (see Chapter 9), had been delivered in the spring and summer of 1923 when it was expected that ZR 3 would be completed in the autumn of that year. Hence the gas cells were nearly two years old and approaching the end of their useful life. Cells #2 and #13 were so leaky that they were removed from the ship. Numerous loose and fatty goldbeater's skins were found, and under a German patch that showed signs of lifting, a hole was found in #2 cell that was an inch long, while there were small holes in the valve sleeve on #13. Though Steele urgently recommended procurement of a spare set of cells, BuAer refused on the grounds of expense; instead, goldbeater's skins were relaid and

The *Los Angeles* on the *Patoka* mast at Bermuda, 22 April 1925. This photo underlines the concern felt for the damage that might result if the airship were carried over the tender, with the risk of striking some part of the superstructure. Later the mast was heightened by 30 feet. (NASM 80-7739)

revarnished in the two defective cells. By 10 April the cells were reinstalled, and the ship was ready to fly, but weather delayed the post-overhaul test flight until 16 April. On coming in to land the engineers of three power cars did not have time to remove the atmospheric plugs of the water recovery condensers, which as a result became very hot. The header of #4 unit was badly warped and had to be replaced, while that of #5 was also warped and would require replacement in the near future.

Five days later, on 21 April, the *Los Angeles* was off again for Bermuda, this time carrying no important guests. At 1435 she was under way, sighting Gibbs Hill Lighthouse on Bermuda at 0100 next morning. The wind was fresh and gusty, blowing up to 40 mph, and an hour passed before the airship was secured to the *Patoka* at 0636. "Time and again during the operation gusts drove her below the mast and perilously near the water. Often the mooring wires literally lifted the ship to safety."[10] The wind blew hard into the afternoon, but the *Los Angeles* remained on the *Patoka*'s mast for 26 hours 21 minutes, slipping from the mast at 0857 on the 23rd. At 0537 on the 24th the airship landed at Lakehurst and was walked into the hangar. She had spent 16 hours 1 minute on the outward flight, and 20 hours 37 minutes on the journey home.

The next cruise was even more ambitious, taking the *Los Angeles* to Puerto Rico, where the *Patoka* was anchored off Mayaguez on the lee side of the island. On the evening of 27 April the *Los Angeles* had been put on the high mast, but not until 0958 on 3 May did she cast off. Forty persons were on board, together with 25,383 lb. of fuel and 2,750 lb. of water ballast. With the ship cruising on four engines, the air speed was 49 knots. On the first evening 2,420 lb. of ballast had to be dropped, but the water recovery units were working, and after midnight, 6,720 lb. of water ballast was on board. By late afternoon on 4 May, the *Los Angeles* was approaching Puerto Rico; at 1707 the course was changed 9 degrees to starboard on receiving a radio compass bearing from the *Patoka*. At 1740 land was sighted on the port bow. The ship was light at landing, gas being valved for a total of three minutes, and not until 2215 was the airship secured to the *Patoka*'s mast. The flight from Lakehurst had taken 36 hours 17 minutes. Fuel and water ballast were loaded, the latter being released to compensate for the added fuel. On the afternoon of the 5th, the ship began taking on helium from the *Patoka* to a total of 21,500 cubic feet. Meanwhile, to the alarm of the *Los Angeles* personnel, the airship showed a tendency to swing over the tender with fluctuations in the light wind. The airship's engines were backed or run ahead to counteract the swings, and on one occasion the *Patoka*'s small boats were used to move the tender's stern. The watch on board the airship, consisting of 16 persons, changed every four hours.

On 6 May, the *Los Angeles* cast off from the *Patoka* to make a leisurely ten-hour flight around Puerto Rico in a clockwise direction. On the following day, the 7th, there were even more close calls as the *Los Angeles*, in gusty weather with strong vertical currents, swung over the *Patoka*. During the morning watch, two main ballast bags in the keel ruptured,

unexpectedly dumping 3,740 lb. of water. Heated by the tropical sun, the hot water pumped on board from the *Patoka* softened the seams of the rubberized fabric bags. In the afternoon watch the *Los Angeles* first took an extreme up angle by the stern due to gusts, and then her stern descended until an aft emergency ballast bag was pulled, releasing 550 lb. of water. The stern rose to an up angle of 14 degrees, then settled until the rudder touched the water. Still later the airship swung directly over the *Patoka*, and as her stern settled, another aft emergency bag was emptied to prevent her from impaling her hull on the *Patoka*'s cargo mast.

At 1433 on 8 May the *Los Angeles* slipped from the *Patoka* mast and headed for Lakehurst via Florida and the East Coast carrying 41 persons, including Lcdr. Charles E. Rosendahl, who had been acting as mooring officer on board the *Patoka*. At 0431 on 10 May the airship landed at Lakehurst after a flight of 37 hours 58 minutes.

This was the first time that an attempt had been made to use the *Patoka* as a mobile base for an extended period, and it was a creditable achievement for the *Los Angeles* to maintain herself at the mast in Puerto Rico for a total of 78 hours 2 minutes—slightly over three days. On the other hand, the obvious danger to the ship from swinging repeatedly over the tender had caused concern. True, the *Shenandoah* had swung over the tender more than once during the nearly 20 hours she had spent at the mast in her first *Patoka* mooring at Newport in August 1924. But the *Shenandoah*'s diameter was only 78.4 feet, whereas the *Los Angeles*'s diameter of 90.7 feet left far less clearance. The commanding officer of the *Patoka* recommended on 19 May that either the mast height be raised by 20 feet, or bridges and masts be cut down. BuAer, questioning the practicability of lowering the bridge, suggested that the mast height be increased

The *Los Angeles* moored to the *Patoka*. This photo was taken some time after early 1926, when the mooring mast was raised by 30 feet (white painted lower portion), providing ample clearance for the airship to swing over the tender. (AIAA)

by 30 feet. The bureau was reluctant to recommend an increase in height because of the cost, but eventually, in order to safely accommodate the future 6,500,000-cubic-foot ships, the height of the *Patoka*'s mast was increased by 30 feet, early in 1926. This took care of the *Los Angeles*'s problems, but ironically, the *Akron* used the tender only twice in her two-year career, and the *Macon* not at all.

BuAer's operational plan of 19 May for both the *Shenandoah* and the *Los Angeles*, approved by the chief of naval operations on 22 May, anticipated that by 1 August there might be enough helium to operate both ships. The *Los Angeles* was to make local passenger flights, and to be in Annapolis on 1–3 June for "June Week"; and on or about 8 June, the *Los Angeles* was to make a flight to Minneapolis. Thereafter she would deflate and begin an overhaul, with her helium going to the *Shenandoah* in the expectation that after 1 August, when the necessary helium might be available, the *Los Angeles* would make a flight to Hawaii. As it happened, the Hawaii flight was not made, owing to the shortage of helium and the loss of the *Shenandoah*; but Captain Steele's comments had led to second thoughts before that tragic crash. The return flight from Honolulu to San Diego in the tradewind season would require that the *Patoka* be available, either to tow the airship part of the way or to refuel her at sea. In the winter months the Honolulu–San Diego journey could be made in 44 hours without fuel problems, but it would be extremely difficult to cross the Rocky Mountains in winter.[11] These opinions were the reason for the *Shenandoah*'s towing experiments off Newport on 15 August 1925.

After the trip to Puerto Rico, three local flights were made later in May. One, on 15 May, with 33 distinguished passengers, was an obvious publicity gesture. With Moffett as host, the guests included two future commanders in chief of the United States Fleet, Rear Admirals Charles F. Hughes and Claude C. Bloch; one future chief of naval operations, Rear Admiral Hilary P. Jones; Graham McNamee, the famous radio announcer; the chief of staff of the U.S. Army; the assistant secretary of war; the presidents of the DuPont Company, the Victor Talking Machine Company, the Midvale Steel Company, the Atwater Kent Radio Company, the Bethlehem Steel Company, the University of Pennsylvania and Lehigh University; two editors of the *Saturday Evening Post*; and many others. Three naval cooks and two Filipino mess attendants were carried to cater to the passengers, who presumably enjoyed themselves and the *Los Angeles*'s elegant accommodations during a 7-hour 8-minute flight up the Delaware River to Easton, Pennsylvania, and home via Reading, Pennsylvania, Wilmington, Delaware, and Philadelphia.

A flight on 26 May served to calibrate the Lakehurst radio compass station, while C. P. Burgess was along to check on the performance of new recording strain gauges. A disquieting event occurred when #2 engine burned out a connecting rod bearing, after 359 hours of operation. With only four engines operating, the *Los Angeles* on 27 May flew to West Point via New York City with 12 newspaper men, and then was hangared to exchange the damaged engine for one of two spare Maybachs which had arrived at Lakehurst from Friedrichshafen on 12 December 1924.

On the morning of 2 June, the *Los Angeles* proceeded to Annapolis, where she remained for two days based on the *Patoka*. The first mooring involved a new method devised by Lcdr. Rosendahl as a substitute for the previous procedure whereby the *Patoka*'s launch, carrying the end of the mast mooring line, had to pursue the airship's main mooring wire and couple the two in the boat. On 2 June, the *Patoka* steamed 90 degrees off the wind with 500 feet of mooring line streamed astern to a launch. Heading into the wind, the *Los Angeles* dragged her main mooring line, with a small grapnel on the end, across the tender's line. When the grapnel caught the *Patoka*'s wire, the launch released its end. As the airship rose with engines throttled, the *Patoka* reeled in her wire, and the grapnel caught on a cross-shaped stopper at the end of the wire. When the grapnel arrived at the mast cup, a preventer was thrown on the main wire to take the load, the cross and grapnel were removed, the two wires were coupled, and the airship was reeled in. With this technique, the *Los Angeles* was secured in the mast cup only 28 minutes after the grapnel caught on the wire. In a second approach to *Patoka* later in the day, the grapnel failed to pick up the *Patoka*'s wire in four attempts, and the two wires were finally coupled in the boat as before, the operation taking 1 hour 47 minutes. After some further practice, however, the procedure with the grapnel became routine.

At 1728 on the evening of 3 June, the *Los Angeles* landed on the field at Lakehurst after a flight home via Washington, Baltimore, and Wilmington. The next operation was the flight to Minneapolis. This of course was a publicity trip pure and simple, laid on in response to countless requests from congressmen and public officials in the Midwest, but it was also intended to test the airship mooring mast erected by Henry Ford at his own expense at Dearborn, Michigan. Ford's mast, however, was not ready in time for the flight.

If Steele felt any of the doubts that Lansdowne expressed about flying over the Midwest in early summer, when he was shortly ordered to make the same journey, they do not appear in the record.

Arrangements were made with the War Department to use Scott Field if necessary, and to land at Fort Snelling south of St. Paul for fuel. Three hundred soldiers were requested as a ground crew.[12]

Shortly after midnight on the night of 5–6 June, the hangar doors were opened and the *Los Angeles*, with 17,600 lb. of fuel and 11,560 lb. of water ballast on board was walked out and put on the mast. There she remained for nearly 24 hours while an interesting experiment was carried out for the first time with a so-called tail drag, designed to minimize the angles assumed by the ship at the mast, depending on whether she was heavy or light. A 90-foot length of anchor chain weighing 540 lb. was attached by a manila line to Frame 25 of the airship. With the ship down 3 degrees by the stern, the chain was all on the ground. At 6 degrees up, the chain was clear of the ground, the end being about 20 feet in the air. The day was rather windy with gusts up to 25 knots. Before the drag was attached at 1050, the maximum inclination of the ship was 15 degrees up and 6 degrees down; afterward it was limited to 6 degrees up and 3 down. The chain appeared to dampen all motion, both vertical and horizontal. Steele recommended the use of the tail drag as standard practice, felt it should be longer and heavier, and believed that without the drag on 6 June, the stern would have gone up as much as 30 degrees, or down to 12 degrees, at which the tail would strike the ground.[13]

At 0130 on 7 June, the *Los Angeles* slipped from the mast carrying 37 persons, including two Army officers and three enlisted men, and an officers' cook second class, as well as 18,693 lb. of fuel and 3,960 lb. of water ballast. The ship proceeded west via Mount Holly, New Jersey, and Norristown and Reading, Pennsylvania, reaching pressure height of 2,950 feet at 0440. She crossed the Alleghenies between Sunbury and Clearfield, Pennsylvania, and went on west via Brookville and Clarion, never exceeding 3,000 feet. At 1010 the *Los Angeles* crossed the Allegheny River near Lamartine. Four minutes later engine #5 had to be shut down with a burned-out connecting rod bearing, the same serious injury that had occurred to #2 engine on 26 May. The engine had logged 390 hours in operation. Steele felt concern about two of his other engines, #3 and #4, which had 440 and 406 hours respectively. The #1 engine in the rear car had only 293 hours but did not have a water recovery unit, whereas the new #2, installed after 27 May, had only 86 hours. While Steele went on via Youngstown and Akron to Cleveland, he had already decided to abandon the flight to Minneapolis. After circling Cleveland he returned via Pittsburgh, Lock Haven, Sunbury, Reading, and Philadelphia. At 0135 on the 8th the *Los Angeles* was over the air station, but heavy fog extending up to 900 feet prevented her from attempting a landing until about 0900. By then the sun was warming the helium, increasing superheat defeated one landing attempt after another, and not until the eighteenth try, and after valving 125,000 cubic feet of helium, did the ship land at 1342, still 5,000 to 6,000 lb. light.

Steele felt the *Los Angeles* could not fly again without a long overhaul:

ONLY ONE SPARE ENGINE AVAILABLE STOP OCCURRENCE OF TWO VERY SIMILAR FAILURES INDICATED EITHER REAPPEARANCE AFTER A YEAR OF OLD TROUBLE ENCOUNTERED BY BUILDERS OR THAT RELIABLE OPERATING LIFE OF ENGINES WITHOUT MAJOR OVERHAUL HAS BEEN REACHED STOP IMPERATIVE EXAMINE AND EFFECT MAJOR OVERHAUL OF AT LEAST TWO ENGINES REQUIRING NOT LESS THAN THREE WEEKS COMMA REMAINING SPARE ENGINES IN OPERATING CONDITION TO BE INSTALLED DURING OVERHAUL PERIOD LONG TIME REQUIRED FOR OVERHAUL NECESSITATED BY VERY SMALL NUMBER OF MEN AVAILABLE WHO HAVE HAD EXPERIENCE IN COMPLETE OVERHAUL THIS TYPE ENGINE TOGETHER WITH ENTIRE LACK OF TESTING FACILITIES STOP[14]

The teardown of the two engines with burned-out crankpin bearings revealed carbon deposits in the bearing assemblies. Steele and his associates at Lakehurst decided that the crankpin bearings should be inspected every 150 hours, a procedure that required complete disassembly; subsequently there were only two failures involving burned-out crankpin bearings, of the engine in #2 car at 482 hours during a 65-minute run to adjust carburetors on 17 November 1925, and of the engine in car #3 on 26 April 1927, at 688 hours, with damage beyond repair. Though Steele asked for purchase of four more Maybachs on 17 September 1925, the bureau refused on grounds of economy. Two further engines were ordered in January 1926 and delivered in September; two more were purchased in 1927 and received on 9 November and 5 December 1927; and one was bought in 1930.[15]

On 10 June 1925 Lakehurst received orders from BuAer to concentrate efforts on getting the *Shenandoah* ready for flight on the earliest practicable date. The *Los Angeles* was to commence overhaul at once with special attention to engines and gas cells. On 11 June deflation of the German ship's gas cells began, with helium being transferred to the *Shenandoah*, and by 15 June the gas cells were being removed from the ship for overhaul. Thus commenced a lay-up that was expected to last only until mid-September 1925; but owing to a number of unforeseen circumstances, particularly the disaster to the *Shenandoah* with the loss of two million cubic feet of helium on 3 September, the *Los Angeles* would not be ready to fly again until April 1926.

A thorough inspection of the deflated ship revealed the extensive corrosion of keel girders caused by the use of calcium chloride antifreeze in the ballast bags the winter before; and through the summer girders were replaced wholesale with spares supplied by the *Luftschiffbau Zeppelin*. Subsequently, alcohol was the preferred antifreeze despite the greater expense. The German gas cells, when removed from the ship, proved to be in far worse shape than had been realized. Even before the lay-up it was known that some of the cells were losing helium in excessive amounts. On 13 April 1925, #2 and #3 were deflated for inspection, and on 4 June, in preparation for the Minneapolis flight, #2, 8, and 13 were deflated and reinflated with high-purity helium. Cell #2 was deflated and removed ahead of the others on 10 June. Initially, Steele thought that only cells #0, 1, 2, 8, and 13 required extensive reworking, but the bureau felt that all cells should be repaired and reworked during the overhaul. Eventually cells #3, 4, 6, 7, 8, 9, and 10 were shipped to the Naval Aircraft Factory for reworking, while the remaining seven were reworked by the *Los Angeles* crew members at Lakehurst. Thousands of new goldbeater's skins were laid and glued by hand, and the cells revarnished, but when the ship was reinflated in March 1926, "it was found that the repair had accomplished nothing, and if anything, the cells were worse from the handling."[16] Particularly after the loss of the *Shenandoah*, her spare gas cells were available for re-tailoring for the *Los Angeles*, though when these were put to use, it was found that they leaked because of their age. A new Cell #13 was ordered from Goodyear, of experimental paraffined rubber. Yet on 17 April 1926 all cells in the ship except #13 were original German cells.

A determined effort was made by BuAer and the Bureau of Standards to find a cheap and impermeable substitute for goldbeater's skin, which was expensive and came in relatively small sizes that had to be laid by hand. Further, in contrast to German experience, American airshipmen found that goldbeater's skin cells did not last for their expected life in the Lakehurst climate, with high temperature and humidity in summer. Cellophane, a cellulose-based transparent and gas-tight film manufactured in the United States by the DuPont Company, seemed a likely substitute, and in July 1925 BuAer approved the manufacture at the Naval Aircraft Factory of an experimental cellophane gas cell for position #13 in the extreme bow of the *Los Angeles*. The cell material consisted of rubberized HH cotton fabric, pale crepe rubber cement, #400 clear cellophane, and Valspar varnish, the whole weighing 4.8 oz. per square yard. The cellophane cell was never delivered, however, and the *Los Angeles* flew after overhaul with a Goodyear rubberized fabric cell in the #13 position. Early in September 1926, Naval Aircraft Factory personnel swabbing a portion of the #13 cellophane cell with glycerin to soften it found that this caused the cellophane to blister, and it had to be replaced. During an air inflation test of the cell at the NAF in February 1927, a seven-foot tear developed at a pressure of 0.4 inch of water, and the bureau authorized the destruction of the experimental cell. A gutta cellophane cell for the #2 position in *Los Angeles*, authorized in August 1926 and built by Goodyear, was flown in the ship after 3 January 1930, but no further development took place. By 1928, however, a substitute for goldbeater's skin had been developed by the Bureau of Standards—fabric impregnated with viscose latex. The *Los Angeles* obtained a first experimental cell of this material, built at the NAF, on 23 April 1928. A year later the bureau came up with a gelatin latex compound that was much more durable than viscose latex. Several of the *Los Angeles*'s cells were of gelatin latex, as were half those of the *Akron* and all of those of the *Macon*.

The anticipated recommissioning of the *Los Angeles* in the spring of 1926 brought with it a personnel crisis comparable to the "shake-up" following the *Shenandoah* breakaway flight in January 1924, though with none of the attendant publicity. It was apparent that Captain Steele would have to be replaced as commanding officer. On the one hand, he had not truly exercised command of the ship's operations since her commissioning, partly from reasons of health, and the ship had been flown and handled by his ambitious executive officer, Commander Jacob Klein, who had also acted in Steele's place as de facto commander of the air station. On the other hand, Steele himself had lost interest in lighter-than-air duty. His wife, particularly after the *Shenandoah* disaster, urged him to get out of airships, while like Lansdowne before him, Steele required sea duty to be eligible for promotion. Early in 1926 Steele did in fact apply for sea duty.

The obvious possibilities from Moffett's point of view were to promote Klein officially into the positions he was already occupying, or to bring in another officer of high rank, give him some training, and place him in command of the *Los Angeles*. Such use of high-ranking officers was Moffett's basic policy, with the aim of having lighter than air "draw more water"— i.e., exercise more influence and authority by virtue of the higher rank of its personnel—despite the discouraging effect on qualified junior officers who had spent years in lighter than air and saw their chances of advancement being blocked. In fact, as the *Akron* and *Macon* program unfolded, it became Moffett's policy to award command only to officers of commander's rank or above.

Klein, however, had made enemies by his aggressiveness and ambition, and had incurred Moffett's displeasure by demanding to be included in the transatlantic flight of ZR 3. Further, with Steele himself having failed as an operator, it appeared urgent to put in charge someone who was fully qualified, regardless of rank, and who would not be afraid to fly the ship at every opportunity. If the *Los Angeles* were inactive as before, there would be increasing pressure to decommission her as an economy move. Maurice Pierce, the *Los Angeles*'s navigator, was the senior lieutenant commander, had had extensive experience, and had demonstrated skill and ability, but he was suffering from severe and progressive deafness. "After much soul searching on Moffett's part,"[17] Rosendahl was chosen. On 15 March 1926, he was ordered to the *Los Angeles* as executive officer, with the expectation that he would succeed Steele when the latter was ordered to sea duty. Klein, whom Rosendahl replaced, received orders to command the 950-ton "Bird"-class minesweeper *Chewink*, then serving as a submarine tender—an obvious indication of official displeasure. Shortly thereafter Klein resigned from the Navy, to pursue a successful career as a stockbroker in New York. Lieutenant Roland Mayer (CC), who was close to Rosendahl, was ordered to the *Los Angeles* on 20 January 1926. Captain E. S. Jackson became commanding officer of the air station with Lcdr. Pierce as his executive officer.

With adequate helium finally accumulated at the station for inflating the *Los Angeles*, her gas cells were installed during the month of March, with small amounts of helium in each cell to support its weight in the ship. By early April the ship was completely inflated, and she was weighed off on 8 April. A post-repair flight of 2 hours 35 minutes took place on 13 April, during which a hole was found in the outer cover near engine car #2, as well as three holes in the adjacent Cell #6, which were repaired after the cell had lost 2% of its helium—about 5,300 cubic feet. BuAer in March had advised Steele of a desired schedule of operations, which included flight testing of a cellophane gas cell (which was never delivered), tests of towing the airship at sea, and "experiments along practical lines with picking up, carrying and releasing airplanes from airships."[18] Yet only a few short local flights were made for the National Advisory Committee for Aeronautics, measuring air pressures over the hull with pressure leads installed in February during the long overhaul. Already the gas cells were giving trouble: On 21 April, Cells #2, 3, and 8 were deflated because of low purity, and they were

inflated the next day. Between 3 and 6 May the helium in the ship was repurified. It was determined that the *Los Angeles* was losing 26,000 cubic feet of helium daily from her porous gas cells, while only 12,000 cubic feet per day (on an average) was being delivered from the Fort Worth helium plant.[19]

Such was the situation when, on 10 May, Rosendahl succeeded Steele as commanding officer. In the traditional ceremony, Steele read his orders detaching him, while Rosendahl read his orders (dated 20 March 1926) to assume command. On that same date, Lt. Charles E. Bauch, the last of the *Shenandoah* triumvirate, reported aboard for temporary additional duty. Lieutenant Commander J. C. Arnold succeeded Rosendahl as executive officer, while Lcdr. Herbert V. Wiley, who had been with the ship since her first commissioning, continued as navigator, as he had been since April 1926. For three critical years Rosendahl would continue in command, with interludes during which Wiley, shortly promoted to executive officer, would take Rosendahl's place while he participated in the first transatlantic flight of the *Graf Zeppelin* in the autumn of 1928, and in her flight around the world in the summer of 1929.

Moffett's decision to promote Rosendahl to command was now to be justified. A lesser man would have been totally discouraged by the problems he faced—hopelessly deteriorated gas cells, inadequate helium supplies on a hand-to-mouth basis, reliability of engines suspect, the rigid airship itself poorly thought of in the fleet, and even in some circles of BuAer; and with the restrictions on military operations, it would be difficult to find missions for the *Los Angeles* to justify her being kept in commission. Nor would there be any easing of the ship's precarious status until roughly three years later, when with the *Akron* and *Macon* under contract and the helium supply improved, more personnel were ordered to Lakehurst for training, and the *Los Angeles* was involved in many experimental projects testing and developing new equipment and techniques for the big ships. In the meantime, Rosendahl's unquenchable optimism and unshakeable faith in the rigid airship kept the *Los Angeles* flying—in calibrating radio stations, publicity flights, and experiments with new ground handling equipment (particularly the short stub mast, Rosendahl taking the initiative in its development). And in spite of jealousy and opposition, both at Lakehurst and in Washington, Rosendahl's influence and authority grew steadily. Already a public figure in the aftermath of the *Shenandoah* crash, he increasingly sought and obtained national attention for the rigid airship.

After one flight in command on 13 May, Rosendahl made the unavoidable decision that because of the excessive daily loss of helium, the *Los Angeles* should be laid up until new cells could be provided, and until a supply of helium could be accumulated. On 15 May 1926 the ship was shored up in the hangar, and overhead suspensions were installed preparatory to partial deflation and purification. Cell #12 was removed and replaced, and work started on rebuilding Cells #0 and #1, from used *Shenandoah* material. On 1 June, Cells #2, 3, 9, 12, and 13 were out of the ship; #4, 5, 6, 7, 8, 10, and 11 were in the ship approximately 3% inflated; and #0 and #1 were totally deflated. By 1 July, Cells #7 and #8 were also out of the ship. Cells #2 and #8 were regarded as unfit for further use, #9 generally good but needing overhaul, #12 capable of being repaired at considerable cost. Rosendahl pushed for an immediate contract for a complete set of goldbeater's skin cells for the *Los Angeles*, but nothing was done because of financial stringency. A new #8 was made up from old *Shenandoah* cell material, but did not last beyond mid-October. When reinflation commenced on 12 July, only six of the 14 gas cells were original German goldbeater's skin. Six were re-tailored *Shenandoah* spare cells, and two were goldbeater's skin cells ordered from Airships Inc. of Hammondsport, New York, as *Shenandoah* spares, then modified in construction for the *Los Angeles*. Two new cells (#4, 12), to be built from used *Shenandoah* cell material by Airships Inc., were ordered at this time, along with at least three rubberized cells (#6, 9, 11) from Goodyear. Daily loss of helium was now 10,000 cubic feet, compared to 23,000 cubic feet (sic) before replacement cells were installed. Each week about 120,000 cubic feet of helium arrived from Fort Worth, barely keeping ahead of the loss rate and leaving little margin for valving or accidental losses.

By 25 July 1926, inflation was completed, and on 26 July the *Los Angeles* made a post-repair flight of 11 hours 37 minutes, calibrating the radio compass stations at Manasquan and Sandy Hook. This involved flying the ship in a circle of 15-mile radius around the station while the latter compared actual bearings of the airship, obtained visually, with those derived from the radio compass equipment tuned to the airship's frequency.[20] Meanwhile the chief of naval operations approved a schedule of post-repair flights in July and August, with training and experimentation including calibration of radio compass stations; weekly flights to land on the *Patoka*; and, in September, weekly flights to the *Patoka* at Newport and Bar Harbor. Such were the activities of the *Los Angeles* during this period, with no unusual problems. Guests were sometimes on board—on 3 August, Edward P. Warner, assistant secretary of the navy for air, and his aide, Lcdr. Bruce Leighton; on 9 August, Admiral Moffett. On 4 August the airship made her first mooring to the *Patoka* at Newport under Rosendahl's command, taking 32 minutes with the grapnel method. A water drag, analogous to the chain drag at the Lakehurst high mast, was tested attached to Frame 25. On the 5th, the airship slipped from the *Patoka* for a 14-hour 13-minute flight for calibration of the radio compass stations at Price's Neck, Rhode Island, Fourth Cliff in Massachusetts, and Deer Island near Boston, landing back on the *Patoka*. With mast height now increased by 30 feet, there was no concern about the airship's swinging over the tender.

On 19 August, though there was no flight, the *Los Angeles* was mounted on new type taxying cars under the forward gondola and rear engine gondola, to which was attached temporary bracing laterally upward to Frame 55 to withstand side loads. The ship was brought out on the new cars, the trolleys were disconnected, and the cars rolled back into the hangar. The ground crew then walked the airship to the three-point mooring, and she was let up on the yaw guys, then hauled down with a winch and returned to the hangar. The taxying cars, which ran on rails through the centerline of the ship's berth in the hangar, were pronounced a success and enabled the ship to be handled on the ground with fewer men. Increasingly instead of taking the airship to the high mast before a flight, it was Rosendahl's practice to walk her to the three-point mooring before take off, hold her on the ground while superheat accumulated, taking on board the flight crew and added fuel and water ballast from the hoses at the three-point mooring.

The frequent short flights for calibration of radio compass stations certainly provided much training for the crew in ground handling, takeoff, and landing procedures, and management of the various systems of the airship in flight. Between the date of taking command and the end of the year 1926, Rosendahl had put 284 hours on the airship, nearly doubling her total time in the air. On 1 September, and again on 7 September, the *Los Angeles* moored to the *Patoka* at Old Plantation Flats, close to Cape Charles, Virginia. On 10 September there was a publicity flight, with the airship landing at the Model Farms field near Philadelphia where the National Air Races were being held. There were moorings to the *Patoka* in Narragansett Bay on 20 September and 7 October, following a practiced routine that included the use of the grapnel. On 12 October a "training flight" was made to Philadelphia where an American Legion parade was in progress. The Army's pressure airship TC 5 and two squadrons of airplanes were seen circling the city. A formation of three U.S. Army Martin bombers passed under the ship, cutting off the *Los Angeles*'s streamlined radio antenna weight.

Rosendahl at this time was under orders to make a flight to Detroit to test the Ford mooring mast at

Dearborn, but he was allowed to choose his weather for the journey. In view of the destruction of the *Shenandoah* in September 1925, while flying approximately the same route, there was some concern, but the superior performance and structural strength of the *Los Angeles* enabled her to overcome somewhat similar meteorological conditions.

With Admiral Moffett, Captain Jackson, the commanding officer of the Lakehurst Naval Air Station, and Colonel T. A. Baldwin, Air Service, U.S. Army, on board, the *Los Angeles* was put on the high mast on the morning of 13 October. The sky was overcast, and after three hours the airship slipped from the mast and stood out to sea to avoid the threatening weather. Through the afternoon and evening she flew under heavy cumulus clouds and through rain squalls, returning to Lakehurst as the weather improved and making fast to the mast at 2352. Next morning, with the sky clear and visibility excellent, the ship was topped up with helium and fuel to 20,354 lb. and cast off from the mast at 1107 on the 14th. The route westward led via Philadelphia, Lancaster, and York, with a maximum altitude of 4,000 feet going through a pass in the Alleghenies from Gettysburg to Chambersburg. At 1820 the *Los Angeles* reached Pittsburgh and circled the city for 22 minutes before heading for Youngstown. A mile south of the Ohio city, heavy clouds were sighted ahead, signaling a front extending from Canada to Texas—an ominous reminder of the earlier disaster. Now, however, all engines were put on full speed, and the *Los Angeles* plunged through the squall line at a spot that appeared somewhat lighter than the rest. Again the air was very unstable; but unlike the conditions that had destroyed the *Shenandoah*, there were no extreme vertical currents. A few men were thrown from their bunks in the brief turbulence. To the rear of the wind shift line the air was smooth and the sky clear. Encountering no more difficulties, at 2300 the airship passed over Akron, and at 0030 on the 15th she reached the shores of Lake Erie at Lorain, Ohio.

Finding the air turbulent once more over the lake, Rosendahl proceeded along the shore westward, and at 0335 was over the Ford airport. During the approach to the mast the main wire fouled in the treetops, and the ship was not moored until 0538. Though the mast was designed to enable the airship to be lowered to the ground while moored, this was not done. After taking on board fuel to a total of 17,312 lb., plus 48,000 cubic feet of 93% pure helium, and after landing AMM1c E. J. Riley for treatment of pneumonia, the *Los Angeles* slipped from the Ford mast at 1542 on 15 October. The flight home via Cleveland, Buffalo, Rochester, Syracuse, and New York City was uneventful. At 0700 on the following day, after a flight of 15 hours 18 minutes, the ship was

The *Los Angeles* departing the Ford airship mast at Dearborn, Michigan, on the afternoon of 15 October 1926. The Dearborn mast was much more complicated than that at Lakehurst. The track running down the left side of the mast was to permit the airship to be lowered from the masthead to the ground if desired. It was not used on this occasion. (*Detroit Times* via NASM 81-14804)

on the ground at Lakehurst. An inversion and sunrise caused the *Los Angeles* to be very light, and 45 men and considerable sand were taken on board as ballast. After taking on water ballast at the three-point mooring, she was walked into the shed. This was the only time that the expensive, privately owned Ford mast at Dearborn ever serviced a rigid airship.[21]

Only a few more short flights were made to the end of the year, including a mooring to the *Patoka* off Old Plantation Flats in Chesapeake Bay. A double crisis made it impossible to continue flying the ship. Again some of the gas cells were found to be leaking excessively: #8, made from old *Shenandoah* material and removed and varnished during the repurification period ending on 4 October, was found on 20 October to be losing purity at an alarming rate due to a breakdown of goldbeater's skin on the after head. The ship was laid up, and with the delivery of three Goodyear rubberized fabric cells on 29 October, a new #9 cell was installed in the #8 position, while the other new cells were installed in the #11 and #13 positions. The old #11 cell tore during deflation, and 16,000 cubic feet of helium was lost. At the end of the year a hodgepodge of cells of diverse origin were in the ship: #0, 2, 3 built at Lakehurst from *Shenandoah* material; #1, 7, 9, and 10 original German cells; #4 and #12 built by Airships Inc. of Hammondsport from *Shenandoah* material; #5 built at the Naval Aircraft Factory from *Shenandoah* material; #6, 8, 11, and 13 Goodyear rubberized cells. Replacement cells were on hand for #1 and #7, and had been requested for #0 and #9.[22]

Worse yet was the helium shortage, which was to severely limit operations for the next year. The basic difficulty was the exhaustion of the Petrolia natural gas field near Fort Worth: during fiscal 1926 (1 July 1925–30 June 1926) 8,805,204 cubic feet of helium had been produced; in fiscal 1927 this dropped to 6,021,531 cubic feet; in fiscal 1928 it was 6,352,654 cubic feet, and only 3,373,072 cubic feet in fiscal 1929,[23] half of this going to the Army and the other half to the Navy. In desperation, the Navy Department turned to private industry: In March 1927 the Kentucky Oxygen–Hydrogen Company formed a subsidiary, The Helium Company, and began to build a helium plant at Dexter, Kansas. During 1927–29 this plant, processing natural gas obtained from wells in Kansas and Colorado, produced over 8,250,000 cubic feet of helium for both services, first delivery being on 1 October 1927. About 35% of the Navy's 1928 helium supply came from The Helium Company, and in 1929 about 65%.

Supply did not keep up with the demand, however, in November and December 1926. The Army, in a rare burst of generosity, handed over its November, December, and January allotments, starting on 8 November, but this was not enough. The flight to the *Patoka* on 21 November was for the purpose of piping all her helium into the *Los Angeles*: none was in reserve at Lakehurst, and the shipments from Fort Worth were meager. A shipment of 634 cylinders from Fort Worth was due to arrive 5 December. Because of the helium crisis and bad weather, BuAer felt obliged, on 27 November, to recommend laying up the *Los Angeles*. The chief of naval operations concurred on 10 December, and the lay-up period commenced on 17 December.

By early March 1927, there was 2,471,160 cubic feet of helium available at Lakehurst, with 110,840 cubic feet due to arrive, and Rosendahl suggested to Admiral Eberle, the chief of naval operations, that inflation of the ship might began about 14 March. Inflation was completed by 26 March, but on that very day a train backed into the hangar at Lakehurst to carry away 187 marines—the bulk of the ground crew—for duty in China! Unable to take the *Los Angeles* out of the shed, Rosendahl was obliged to spend the following two weeks on static experiments such as docking with spring devices on the hold-down lines to continuously indicate buoyancy. On 5 April, 100 recruits arrived and commenced training in ground handling; but for some months, Rosendahl had to operate cautiously as the ground crew was under strength. The post-repair flight on 12 April was intended to be a mooring to the *Patoka* at Old Plantation Flats; but the airship was unable to do so as the *Patoka*'s main mooring cable had fouled her propeller and immobilized her. The flight to the *Patoka* was made on 15 April; after her return the *Los Angeles* was held on the field at Lakehurst because winds were unfavorable for going into the shed, and finally she was put on the high mast.

On 23 April, with Admiral Moffett and Commander Garland Fulton as passengers, the *Los Angeles* flew to Pensacola in 22 hours 58 minutes, mooring to the *Patoka* in Pensacola Bay. The commanding officer of the Naval Air Station, Captain F. P. Upham, who had taken the leading part in negotiations in Europe for the procurement of the *Los Angeles*, came on board for a two-hour visit of inspection. The flight home to Lakehurst on 25–26 April took 33 hours 8 minutes, and was not without adventure. Upon arrival over Lakehurst at 0930 on the 26th, a gusty 40-knot wind was blowing from the south, so Rosendahl cruised along the coast, heading into the wind. At 2300 engine #3 had to be shut down with two connecting rod bearings burned out and the crankcase damaged. At 0122 on the 27th the *Los Angeles* landed on the field during a lull and at 0150 was inside the hangar. During the next two days the #3 engine was replaced.

On a 15-hour 17-minute flight to Washington on 7 May the airship had a close call. At 0415 the *Los*

Angeles rose from the field statically to 100 feet before engines were started. The surface wind was north-northwest; at the higher level it was northeast, and the ship drifted toward the hangar. Frantically the engine telegraphs signaled to the mechanics to start their engines, but two of them balked, and the other two could not check the drift in time (the #1 after centerline engine was not used at takeoff as it tended to pull the tail down). Only by releasing 2,900 lb. of water ballast was the *Los Angeles* enabled to rise clear of the hangar; this required the later valving of 48,000 cubic feet of helium before landing. Three days were spent in investigations of why the engines refused to start before "the decision was made to charge failure to eccentricities of the gasoline engine."[24]

The late spring of 1927 saw a whole series of trans-atlantic flight attempts to win the Raymond Orteig prize of $25,000 for the first nonstop crossing between New York and Paris. The first try was by Charles Nungesser, a 45-victory French World War I ace, and François Coli, who on 8 May departed Paris for New York. When they failed to arrive, a massive search was organized in the western Atlantic. The *Los Angeles* participated, making a flight of 14 hours 30 minutes on Friday 13 May beyond Nantucket Shoals lightship. The airship spent 12 hours searching over water but in vain: the two brave Frenchmen had vanished forever. But on the airship's next flight, to Hartford on 21 May, the radio brought the thrilling news that an unknown air-mail flier, Charles Lindbergh, had made the crossing from New York to Paris in his *Spirit of St. Louis* monoplane. Returning to New York City, the *Los Angeles* appeared in the sky just as the celebration of Lindbergh's triumph started on the streets below.

Once again, gas cell problems and shortage of helium were handicapping the *Los Angeles*'s operations. Cells #2, 3, 9, and 10 were losing gas at an unacceptable rate, while helium deliveries were so meager and variable that Rosendahl could not plan ahead. At his insistence, the bureau had ordered gold-beater's skin cells from Germany through Goodyear for the #3, 4, and 6 positions, but these cells would not arrive for some time. Orders were placed with Goodyear for cells for locations #0, 1, 2, 3, 5, 8, and 10, these to be made of goldbeater's skin by the British method. On 1 June the *Los Angeles* commenced deflation with the intention of removing the four leaky cells, but on the following day BuAer requested that the ship be prepared to meet the cruiser USS *Memphis* at sea on 10 June and escort her with Lindbergh on board to the Washington Navy Yard. The airship was reinflated and flyable on 9 June, but high winds kept her in her shed. Although Rosendahl was ready to take her out on the following day, his officers persuaded him not to: with low gas purity, and a high

percentage of inflation, the ship could not ascend above 3,000 feet; the wind was such that the ship could not make headway without running the engines at cruising speed or higher, while their condition was such that half speed was the maximum possible. In the end, the *Los Angeles* participated in the Lindbergh reception by meeting the *Memphis* in the Potomac River on 11 June and escorting her the last few miles to the Washington Navy Yard. Some of the gas cells were full at 2,000 feet, but Rosendahl was unwilling to ascend to pressure height and blow off helium, as he feared that the deteriorated gas cell fabric could not stand the slight superpressure involved.[25]

Back at Lakehurst, the *Los Angeles* began deflation for purification on 17 June. During the two-month lay-up that followed, the bureau made a determined effort to improve the supply of helium. Production was to be increased at Forth Worth, The Helium Company was to start delivery of 100,000 cubic feet per month in July, with the option of increasing helium production to 300,000 cubic feet per month, and the Army would turn over its monthly helium allotment in May and June, less one tank car per month for itself.[26]

Some of the Goodyear goldbeater's skin cells were delivered during the lay-up, the first of these, #2, on 20 August. Water recovery units were removed and overhauled, but not replaced, as the bureau desired that deceleration tests be done to determine the effects of changes in the ship and propellers since her arrival from Germany. The *Los Angeles* was inflated and ready for service on 24 August. Since Rosendahl planned a five-hour high-altitude flight to 10,000 feet, she was only 70% full of helium and carried only eight hours' fuel. At 0440 on 25 August, the airship was undocked and placed on the high mast, and a 2,200-lb. tail drag was attached aft. The sky was clear, the wind light and variable, and the *Los Angeles* accumulated a great deal of superheat. Rosendahl planned to slip from the mast about 1400, but weather conditions caused him about 1300 to plan an earlier takeoff and to start getting the crew on board. In the light wind, the ship swung continually in azimuth while superheating fluctuations caused the stern to oscillate up and down, at times lifting the end of the tail drag chain 50 feet off the ground. The nonrigid J 3 had just made a hard landing, reporting a steep temperature gradient with very cold air flowing over the warm air on the ground.

At about 1330, with the *Los Angeles* headed north–northwest, the stern started up, but instead of checking at 8 to 10 degrees and starting down again, it continued to ascend. It was evident that a wind shift was taking place. The control car personnel, with Lt. T. G. W. Settle in charge of the watch of 24 men, felt a sudden gust from astern which threw the rudders violently to port (at first it was believed they had jammed) and, acting dynamically on the under side of the horizontal fins, lifted the tail before the *Los Angeles* could start swinging around the mast to head in the new wind direction. As the stern ascended into the colder air at higher altitude, she rose even faster. Settle ordered all available men aft, trying to get more men on board from the masthead and to add water ballast. Seven men boarded, but it was impossible to load water ballast. As the up angle steepened, the men found it increasingly difficult to climb upward through the keel. The ship was not released from the mast, nor did the senior officer on board order it to be tripped. An attempt was made to cast off, but the bow cone would not lift from the mast cup. As the crew members held on for dear life, and Rosendahl and others watched incredulously from the ground, the *Los Angeles* reached an up angle of 85 degrees and was standing on her nose atop the mast. Then, swinging gradually to port, the airship began to settle toward the horizontal, while 2,500 lb. of water ballast was dropped to check her fall. The *Los Angeles* had rotated through an angle of 150 degrees, and was now heading approximately southeast. Miraculously, although much gasoline had spilled in the keel from the vents in the tops of the tanks, none of the tanks themselves, nor the heavy water ballast bags, had torn loose and fallen down the keel, even though their supports were not designed to withstand loads in the longitudinal direction. Rosendahl, relieved that a major disaster had not occurred, ordered the ship down from the mast and she was housed in the hangar for a thorough inspection. This revealed that several wires had snapped, puncturing #10 cell in two places; four gasoline slip tanks had gotten adrift from their guides, but were held in place by their suspensions; and four girders in the stern of the ship had been damaged by falling tools and parts. In retrospect, the *Los Angeles* could have flown immediately after her spectacular head stand, and all damage was repaired on the following day.

A naval photographer had recorded the entire episode in a series of snapshots: planning to get pictures of some parachute jumpers with the *Los Angeles* in the background, he realized that an unusual event was occurring, and took five photographs showing the ship with her tail going up, standing on her nose, and then settling to head in the opposite direction.[27] Rosendahl sent the photographs with a long letter of explanation to Admiral Moffett, but was dubious about the effect they might have on public opinion:

> We have been very careful not to let any of these pictures get off the station and the set I am mailing to you is the only set that will leave the station without authority from the Bureau. I rather doubt the advisa-

The *Los Angeles* head stand, 25 August 1927. Heading northwest, her tail goes up as a sea breeze sets in from the southeast. Note elevators put up in a vain attempt to keep the tail down. (U.S. Navy via Dr. Smith de France)

Starting down toward the horizontal. The 2200-lb. tail drag made fast at Frame 25 shows well in this photograph.

The *Los Angeles* starts to rotate around the mast to the left. Though she appears to be vertical, the up angle is about 85 degrees.

The *Los Angeles* settles on a southeast heading, having rotated through 150 degrees. Elevators have been put down to check her descent.

bility of releasing them, but if they are released, I think there should be an accompanying promise to use only the captions which the Bureau might assign such as "Remarkable demonstration of strength of rigid airships," or "Airship construction proves equal to any occasion," or something on that order.[28]

In the event, the incident was not publicized, and the photographs were suppressed, not being published in the United States until after World War II, though one of the set appeared in a 1938 book by Hans von Schiller, one of the *Graf Zeppelin*'s officers and a friend of Rosendahl.

This dramatic experience sealed the fate of the "high" mast. Rosendahl used it for mooring the *Los Angeles* only seven more times; Wiley used it twice in 1928, and only once in 1929. The *Akron* and *Macon* never moored to it, and it was dismantled in 1935. Not only did the ship have to be "flown" at the mast by the crew standing one watch in three; not only was the ship inaccessible except through the bow hatch; but, more particularly, Rosendahl had "pictured and so stated a number of times that in severe thunderstorms or line squalls the ship might be turned over on her back,"[29] though he had never expected that she would turn over as she had done in light airs on this occasion. He had already decided that it would be safer and more practical to moor the airship to a short stub mast, with the rear engine gondola on a riding-out car which would enable her to swing around the mast on the ground. The ship could be ballasted heavy to ensure that she would not lift off in gusty winds, and the keel would be accessible throughout its length.

Rosendahl now went ahead on his own at Lakehurst with a discarded wooden radio mast, 60 feet high with guy wires and a mast cup on top, while a wheel from a heavy bomber was attached under the rear engine gondola. The stub mast was first used on 5 October 1927. Brought out on the field by the ground crew on taxying cars which rolled on railroad tracks running through the hangar, the *Los Angeles* was walked to the mast and then slipped from it to rise statically for takeoff. On returning from a flight, the airship landed in the hands of the ground crew and was walked to the stub mast. A circular track for the rear gondola wheel was built and first used on 17 July 1928. Only on 21 November 1929 and two occasions thereafter, did the *Los Angeles* make a flying moor to the stub mast, dropping her handling lines and the main mooring cable, which was coupled to the mast cable, with the airship winched down to the masthead. Some later moorings were made by the *Los Angeles* to stub masts at Parris Island, South Carolina, and Guantanamo Bay, Cuba.

Rosendahl, obsessed with the shortage of ground handling personnel at Lakehurst, and with the need

to substitute mechanical aids for manpower, conceived a bold extension of the stub mast concept—a mobile version, which could be used to tow the airship on its taxying cars right out of the hangar to the takeoff point, and on completion of the flight, to tow it back into the hangar. Only a small number of men—60 instead of 250—would be needed to man the tackles of the four trolleys which ran on the docking rails to port and starboard, and to handle the mobile mast and the taxying cars. On 9 May 1927 the Bureau of Aeronautics requested the Bureau of Yards and Docks to prepare plans for a mobile mooring mast to weigh 184,000 lb., to have a telescopic head adjustable through a range of 20 feet in height, and to withstand a 20,000-lb. horizontal pull in any direction at 80 feet above the ground. It was described as:

An awkward looking structure, comprising a mast whose height can be varied from 70 to 90 feet, mounted in the center of a 60 foot triangular frame. Under each corner of this frame is a wheel of the self-laying track or caterpillar type. At first this contrivance, weighing about seventy tons, will be towed by a tractor. A self-contained drive can be included when the practicability of the device is assured. Hauling in winches, ballasting and fuel facilities, and other desirable equipment are mounted on the mobile mast so that it will be in every way as complete as the high mast is now. While the auxiliary equipment is not necessary for towing across the field, it is necessary to the operation of mooring to the mast. During mooring, tractors will be used to handle the yaw guys. During the manoeuvre of towing across the field, the stern of the airship will be supported on a "taxi car" provided with a castering wheel and ample shock absorbing ability.[30]

Not until the spring of 1929 was the first mobile mast ready at Lakehurst. During March and April, Rosendahl experimented with towing the mast without attempting to attach the *Los Angeles* to it. A 35-ton Army Mark VIII tank was used initially for towing, but did not prove fully practical, because its metal tracks could not be used on hard surfaces such as those in the hangar. Later, tractors were tried: a Monarch 75 and a Cletrac 100 were compared late in 1929. Both were able to haul the mast over firm ground, but tended to dig in and bury themselves in soft earth. In March 1930 Rosendahl was trying to motorize the mast. Its first use with the *Los Angeles* was on 22 June 1929, when the ship, attached to the mobile mast, was moved out of the shed and back in with the help of tractors. On 25 September the airship was moved out onto the field on the mobile mast and took off for a flight of 6 hours 38 minutes over New York Harbor. On landing, the airship was walked into the hangar by the ground crew. On 10 October, after landing from a short flight, the *Los Angeles* was for the first time walked to the mobile

The *Los Angeles* moored to the original stub mast, with a large airplane tire under the rear gondola. This is supported against lateral loads by a pair of detachable A-frames extending up to Frame 55 as it rolls around the mast. (Fred Tupper-Hepburn Walker collection)

mast and moored to it to be taken into the hangar. This routine was followed for several months until, on 23 April 1930, the airship made a flying moor to the mobile mast, dropping trail ropes and main mooring wire as for moorings to the stub mast; the yaw lines were handled by spider parties, in contrast to the high mast mooring, where they were taken through snatch blocks to yaw winches.

In April 1930 the bureau conceived the idea of a mobile mast on railroad tracks. Rosendahl argued heatedly in favor of the mobility of the mast on crawler feet, asserting that the railroad tracks would be vulnerable to damage and a danger to ground handling crews. He was overruled, and on 24 June 1930 a contract was awarded for a quadrupod mobile mast riding on two pairs of railroad tracks, the tracks being 64½ feet apart. This was used by the *Akron* for all her operations at Lakehurst, and undoubtedly was the best solution for the 6,500,000-cubic-foot ships. A

developed version, with telescopic head, was completed in 1933, and in fact the massive telescopic quadrupod mast was the standard motive power for the *Macon* at Lakehurst, and also at Sunnyvale. The *Los Angeles*, however, never was moored to either railroad mast, and enjoyed the exclusive use of the crawler-feet mast to her decommissioning in 1932. Further, the *Graf Zeppelin*, during her 1930 "triangle" flight from Friedrichshafen to Rio de Janeiro to Lakehurst to Friedrichshafen, was taken into the Lakehurst shed on the mobile tripod mast. On the other hand, the *Hindenburg*, in her 1936 transatlantic flights, made fast to the railroad mast.[31]

Returning to the events of 1927: Though the *Los Angeles* was serviceable the day after the "nose stand" at the high mast, bad weather prevented the altitude flight. The cells were inflated to 80% fullness, and fuel was added. Speed and deceleration tests

Operations with the mobile mast on crawler feet at Lakehurst, with the *Los Angeles*. The rear gondola is mounted on a taxiing car with lateral bracing up to the hull at Frame 55. Note two women standing under engine car #4. (NASM 81-14802)

were run over a triangular course 14 miles to a side, first on 2 September without the water recovery units, then on 6 and 7 September with the units added. Speed was reduced 5 to 10% with the water recovery equipment installed. As usual, Rosendahl was concerned with publicity for the airship: On the 7th, the *Los Angeles* made an appearance over Atlantic City for the beauty pageant parade. Together with a division of destroyers, and the Navy blimp J 3, the *Los Angeles* on 10 September escorted the giant liner *Leviathan*, carrying a large number of American Legionnaires traveling to a convention in Paris, from her pier to beyond Ambrose Light Ship. On this flight #2 engine failed with a wrecked connecting rod. *Patoka* moorings were made with the tender at Old Plantation Flats near Cape Charles on 8, 16, and 22 September; at Newport, Rhode Island, on 13 and 25 October; and again at Old Plantation Flats on 15 November. After the stub mast became available on 5 October, the high mast was used only twice more, for flying moors on 14 and 27 October.

Gas cell problems caused the *Los Angeles* to be laid up during the week of 21 November for partial deflation and repurification. Cell #9, the only remaining original German cell, split in two while being lowered from the ship. The replacement cell from Goodyear, expected at this time, had not arrived, but a rejected overweight rubber cell by Airships Inc. of Hammondsport was made available by BuAer and

installed by 28 November. Two of the three new German goldbeater's skin cells were installed in the #3 and #6 positions, while the third, for the #4 position, was on hand as a spare.

Bad weather kept the *Los Angeles* in the shed most of December. Short training flights were made on the 22nd and 23rd, and holiday leave was granted for most personnel. Then, on the morning of 26 December, came a request from the chief of naval operations that the *Los Angeles* search for the Sikorsky S-36 amphibian *Dawn*, in which Mrs. Frances Grayson, aspiring to be the first woman to fly the Atlantic, had gone missing with a crew of three after leaving Roosevelt Field for Newfoundland on Christmas Eve. Rosendahl rose to the occasion: The *Los Angeles* was gassed and fueled, eight men returned from leave at 1200, a ground crew was organized from local civilians, and at 1700 the *Los Angeles* took off with 8 officers, 27 men, 3 passengers, 24,624 lb. of fuel, 7,150 lb. of water ballast, and 3,614 lb. of alcohol on board. At 0100 the ship was over Chatham Light on Cape Cod and headed out to sea on a course for Sable Island, following the assumed track of the missing Sikorsky. With dawn at 0600, and visibility 10 miles, an active search commenced for wreckage. Two hours later, having covered nearly 200 nautical miles toward Sable Island, the airship reversed course, continuing her search. Nothing was sighted, and at 0040 on 28 December the *Los Angeles* landed in the hands of the

Rear view of stern engine car of the *Los Angeles* resting on a taxiing car rolling on railroad tracks leading out from the hangar. Temporary duralumin girder A-frames take lateral loads up to main frame 55 while on the ground. At the stub mast, the rear gondola will roll around on a large airplane tire. (AIAA)

ground crew and was walked into the shed. No airplane of the period could have made such a flight, lasting for 31 hours 40 minutes and covering 1,062 nautical miles. At least 15,000 lb. of water had been recovered during the flight, to which 961 lb. of alcohol had been added.

The very next flight of the *Los Angeles* in the new year, 1928, provided much favorable publicity, but made no real contribution to airship technology and employment with the fleet. Naval aviation had taken a giant stride forward with the commissioning of the aircraft carriers *Saratoga*, on 16 November 1927, and *Lexington*, on 14 December 1927. Converted from battle cruiser hulls, they measured 888 feet over all, displaced 40,000 tons at full load, carried up to 90 aircraft on their broad decks, and with the original battle cruiser power plant, the *Lexington* on trials reached 34.5 knots with 210,000 h.p. It is not too much to assert that the techniques and doctrine that won the sea–air war against Japan were developed aboard these vessels during the period 1928–41.

Rosendahl wanted the *Los Angeles* to share the publicity generated by the new carriers, and on 2 January 1928 proposed to the chief of naval opera-

tions a landing on board one of them to prove their suitability as refueling and regassing stations. Queried by the chief of naval operations, the commanding officer of the *Saratoga*, Captain Harry E. Yarnell, replied that he was willing to attempt the experiment if it would not interfere with the carrier's itinerary: lying then at Hampton Roads loading her air group, "Sara" was to sail for Newport on 21 January, and would be available for the exercise then or on the following day. The weather through most of January was "exceptionally poor," however, and the *Los Angeles* was confined to her hangar until the end of the month. On 27 January the weather improved, providing the airship with her last chance as the carrier was departing Newport that day for the Pacific. At 0354 the *Los Angeles* took off from Lakehurst and proceeded to Newport, where she arrived at 1200 to find the *Saratoga* at anchor. Twenty minutes later the carrier was under way with the airship following at slow speed. At 1430, with the carrier on a heading of 95 degrees, making 10 knots into a gusty 10-knot wind and rolling and pitching moderately, the airship made a rehearsal approach to within 100 yards on the port beam at masthead height. At 1440

Rosendahl valved helium for 1½ minutes. At 1453, with the *Saratoga* now making 15 knots, the airship began her landing approach, reducing altitude to 225 feet. Helium was valved for 45 seconds, trail ropes were dropped, and as the *Los Angeles* descended toward the flight deck, a downdraft forced the airship stern downward and to starboard. A thousand pounds of emergency ballast was released forward, soaking the handling party on the flight deck. At 1535 the control car touched down on the flight deck. Conditions were very different from what Rosendahl had anticipated—the carrier was rolling and pitching, the stern rising and falling; the control car was in constant motion despite the best efforts of the holding party; and at 1542 a sudden upward gust wrenched the control car out of the hands of the holding party and parted the port trail rope. Rosendahl had had enough and cast off, leaving behind Lcdr. Wiley, the executive officer, who had disembarked to supervise the handling party. Course was set for Lakehurst where the *Los Angeles* landed at 1910. An inspection showed minor damage to the control car bumper bag and duralumin girders in the bottom of the gondola. Moffett was enthusiastic: the experiment "greatly increases the possibilities of refueling dirigibles at sea, and thereby means a tremendous increase in the radius of action of such cruisers of the air."[32] A dramatic photograph of the *Los Angeles* descending to the carrier's deck appears in all standard airship histories. Yet the experiment had been a fiasco, the *Los Angeles* had narrowly escaped serious damage, and the constant relative motion of the two different vessels in their respective elements would have made resupply dangerous if not impossible. The stunt was never repeated with rigid airships, though carrier landings were made 20 years later by the nonrigids of the post–World War II period.

On 28 January the chief of naval operations, now Admiral Charles F. Hughes, directed the *Los Angeles* to make one flight to the *Patoka* at Old Plantation Flats about 10 February, and as soon as the tender arrived at Guacanayabo Bay on the south side of Cuba, to make a flight to her there. The *Patoka* mooring at Old Plantation Flats was made on 11–12 February, but in place of the flight to Cuba, Rosendahl had a more ambitious idea—a journey all the way to Panama, which at the same time would demonstrate the utility and convenience of the new stub mast. The *Patoka* in Cuban waters would serve as an intermediate fueling point. Admiral Moffett of course responded enthusiastically, and arranged a meeting for Rosendahl with Secretary Wilbur and Admiral Hughes. The secretary's initial response was noncommittal, but two days later Rosendahl was agreeably surprised when he gave his consent.

France Field, the Army's air base at the Atlantic end of the canal, was generously made available to the *Los Angeles* as the Navy's Coco Solo field was too small to accommodate the airship moored out. Lieutenant Scott E. Peck was dispatched by sea along with the 60-foot wooden stub mast and the stern wheel device, and a few days after his arrival reported that all was ready. February, however, is deep winter in New Jersey, with blustery winds heralding the coming of March; while the weather map was favorable on 25 February, high winds confined the *Los Angeles* to her shed. It was very gusty still on the following morning, but around sunrise, with one section of the flight crew on board, and the rest holding the ground lines, augmented by a volunteer group of civilian employees, the *Los Angeles* was walked out on the field. The remainder of the crew boarded, and at 0656 she took off carrying 9 officers, 2 student officers, 30 men, and 29,192 lb. of fuel. Proceeding north, she took her departure from New York City, where the air temperature was 6 degrees above zero.

All day the *Los Angeles* proceeded south along the coast with a following wind, through snow, sleet, rain, and fog. At 0105 on the 27th the lights of Nassau in the Bahamas were seen through a hole in the clouds. At 0515 Cuba was beneath, and at 0632 the *Patoka* was seen at anchor. But with the northeast trades helping the *Los Angeles* on her way, Rosendahl chose to continue on to Panama. At 2130 the airship was circling France Field, and at 2200 she landed in the hands of the ground crew. She was walked to the stub mast, the mooring cone was locked in the mast cup, and the taxying wheel and tail drags were attached. The first nonstop flight from New York City to Panama was an impressive achievement by the small *Los Angeles*, inflated with helium, involving a journey of 2,250 land miles in 39 hours 51 minutes. The tired crew members went ashore by sections to clean up, and 21,441 lb. of fuel was loaded.

On the following morning, 28 February, the crew again boarded, the after taxying wheel was removed, and at 1012 the *Los Angeles* lifted off from the stub mast with a fuel load of 28,454 lb. Before heading for Cuba the airship toured the Canal Zone at low altitude, finding the air turbulent over the hilly country. At 1213 she was once more over France Field and took a heading of 358° true for Roncador Reef. With the trade wind now ahead, there was no question of a nonstop return flight to Lakehurst; in fact, 26 hours 50 minutes passed before the *Los Angeles* was secured to the *Patoka*'s mast, at 1303 on 29 February. While fuel was piped aboard, the crew rested in the tender.

At 1040 on 1 March the *Los Angeles* lifted off from the *Patoka* mast carrying 29,474 lb. of fuel, though 778 lb. had to be released to bring the ship into equilibrium. An hour later the airship was about 6,000 lb. heavy from loss of superheat, and 800 lb. of water ballast was released. Steering west, the *Los Angeles* then headed across the island to appear above Havana at 1800. During the evening the airship proceeded on a course for Tampa, and at 0115 on 2 March had the lights of Sarasota beneath. Heavy ground fog having forced the ship up to 2,500 feet, Rosendahl after dawn tried various altitudes seeking a more favorable wind. In the afternoon a following wind sped the *Los Angeles* on her way at a ground speed of 90 mph.

The airship received a dispatch from the Navy Department advising that a Loening amphibian aircraft carrying Commander Theodore G. Ellyson, the Navy's aviator #1 and executive officer of the carrier *Lexington*, together with two other officers, had gone missing on a flight from Hampton Roads to Annapolis on the evening of 27 February, and the *Los Angeles* was directed to take part in the search. But as darkness had set in before the airship reached Chesapeake Bay, Rosendahl decided to land and refuel at Lakehurst, and be ready to search at daybreak on 3 March. He was aware that the strong southwest wind speeding the airship on her way was a harbinger of an approaching cold front, due to pass Lakehurst within a few hours, but he believed he could moor to the high mast and refuel before it arrived.

Just after midnight, the *Los Angeles* started her approach to the high mast with 16,275 lb. of water ballast and 11,190 lb. of fuel on board, and the ship 1,500 lb. heavy. The average wind velocity was about 35 mph, but the air was very turbulent with gusts up to 50 mph. Not only did the ship pitch heavily, but she also yawed widely from side to side, and the rudders and elevators were in constant motion. At 0014 the airship dropped her main mooring wire, followed by the yaw lines, and these were coupled to the corresponding mast wires. The rudder jammed, preventing the *Los Angeles* from correcting for a gust from starboard, and the starboard yaw cable parted. The ends were quickly knotted together by the ground crew, and the wires were reeled in. At 0120 the nose cone was only some 50 feet from the mast when a fierce gust slammed the bow downward, followed by an upward blast which snapped the 9/16-inch steel main mooring wire. There was no way that the mast mooring could be successfully completed. Rosendahl ordered the yaw lines cut, ballast dropped, and the ship rose rapidly to 1,000 feet. The wind had shifted to northwest! "We had been caught on the mooring wires at the worst possible moment of the wind shift!"[33] While the *Los Angeles*, with engine #4 running at half speed, hovered over the field, the ground crew was assembled. Around 0335 the radio brought

word that the surface wind had dropped to 12 mph, low enough to permit the *Los Angeles* to be walked into the hangar. At 0358 the airship settled into the hands of the ground crew, which started walking her across the field to the end of the docking rails extending from the east hangar door. The wind was west, at 11 mph. Rosendahl described what happened next:

> I had disembarked Wiley and two other officers to assist on the ground, but some sort of intuition kept me in the control car, contrary to my usual practice. My "hunch" was certainly a correct one this time. When just short of the hangar, a sudden blast of cold air with a velocity jumping up to 35 miles per hour almost instantly as a passing snow squall swept by in the inky darkness, struck the ship about at right angles. Immersed suddenly in this ocean of 10° colder air, the ship acquired several thousand pounds of instantaneous and momentary additional buoyancy and tried to rise. Simultaneously, before she could pivot her length into the new wind direction, she was being carried broadside across the field towards the scrub pines, the crunching noise of the heels of some three hundred clinging determined men digging into the gravel surface standing out like that of a stampede of wild horses. A blinding curtain of snow let down at the same moment. Once more, the safety of the ship lay in the free air above. My order to "let go everything" was echoed first by officers near the control car and then by others throughout the ground crew. After a few moments, in which the men should have been able to get clear, I called for the engines. In perfect unison the five engines boomed back their message that they were with me. Rapidly into the blinding squall we rose. The door to the control car snapped open. An officer sprang through breathless. "My God, Captain, we've carried a bunch of men up on the hand rails. We've got to get them in at once, sir."[34]

Two men had failed to let go of the after engine gondola rails; one did so at 15–20 feet and sprained a toe, while the other, BM2c Bruce J. McClintock, a member of the *Los Angeles* crew, hauled himself to safety inside. Four men hung by their hands from the control car rail—Sea2c Robert N. Dils, Cox Earl W. Kirkpatrick, Sea1c George L. Smith, and a civilian painter named Murphy. Murphy was able to throw a leg over the rail and reach a window that crew members had knocked out. They assisted him inside.

Young Dils said he could no longer hold on and was going to let go. Kirkpatrick urged him to hold on and even let go with one of his own hands to pull Dils up until he could hook an elbow over the rail. In the radio room directly above, CRM Cesare P. Cavadini managed to grasp Dils by the wrists, and he was pulled up with the help of Lts. Mayer, Thornton, and Settle. Sea2c Donald L. Lipke, who had boarded while the *Los Angeles* was on the field, crawled out of one of the windows, walked along the rail 500 feet in the air, and while holding by one hand to a window frame, reached down and helped Smith and Kirkpatrick to get their feet on the rail. Lipke was the last man back into the ship, and only then did he realize the danger in which he had placed himself. Rosendahl recommended that Lipke receive the Life Saving Medal or an equivalent award, but inasmuch as regulations covered only the saving of life at sea, he merely received a letter of commendation from the secretary of the navy, as did Kirkpatrick.

At daybreak the *Los Angeles* landed on the field, now covered with several inches of snow, and was walked again toward the east end of the hangar, the wind being west–southwest at 10 mph. When the ship was almost halfway into the hangar, the wind shifted to north, 15 mph, very gusty with snow swirling around the stern. Two after emergency ballast bags were released for a total of 1,100 lb., and the airship rushed on into the shed. The flight from Guacanayabo Bay to the Lakehurst high mast had taken 41 hours 18 minutes, the emergency ascent with the men on the hand rails 2 hours 18 minutes. The exhausted flight crew and ground personnel collapsed in their bunks; the search for Commander Ellyson was forgotten. Some wreckage of the Loening amphibian was found near Cape Charles on 2 March, and over a month later the sea gave up the body of Naval Aviator #1.

There was a long pause after the Panama flight. The weather was too bad for flying through the month of March, and the airship was laid up for overhaul and installation of new gas cells. Not until 2 May was the *Los Angeles* out, for an 8-hour 35-minute flight over the New Jersey coast. A few more ascents were made, including a mooring to the *Patoka* at Newport on 16 June. Then, on 6 July 1928, came a change of command, as Rosendahl departed for Europe. Dr. Hugo Eckener, the chairman of the board of the Zeppelin Company, in return for the U.S. Navy's making the hangar at Lakehurst available, had invited one of its officers to make the expected transatlantic flight of the new 3,707,550-cubic-foot passenger airship *Graf Zeppelin*, then under construction. Thus began for Rosendahl a lifelong close friendship with the great German airshipman, based on mutual respect and the sharing of identical views on the future of the rigid airship in world commerce. Arriving in Germany in mid-July, Rosendahl found that the *Graf* would not be ready for her trial flights for two months, so he proceeded to England to confer at Bedford with the builders and designers of the 5,000,000-cubic-foot R 101, being constructed for the Empire route to Canada and India; and with the rival organization building R 100 of similar volume at Howden in Yorkshire. Back in Friedrichshafen Dr. Eckener paid Rosendahl a special compliment by

inviting him to take part in the trial flights of the new airship, commencing on 18 September 1928, and Rosendahl was treated as a member of the ship's company on the transatlantic flight 11–15 October.

By virtue of his close relationship with Dr. Eckener, and with his subordinates, Captains Lehmann, Flemming, and von Schiller, Rosendahl came increasingly under the influence of German ideas and procedures. Insofar as these related to ship handling and operation, and weather expertise, the U.S. Navy's rigid airship program benefited. The same cannot be said of Rosendahl's fixation on the scouting methods of the German Navy's Zeppelins in World War I: Operating independently over the North Sea, the German ships not only made the original contact with enemy surface units, but they shadowed them from the leeward position as long as possible, reporting ship types, course, and speed. Rosendahl's attempts to imitate this procedure in the early 1930s were anachronistic and would have been suicidal in wartime, given the presence of high-performance aircraft on cruiser catapults and carrier flight decks. His successors, Dresel and particularly Wiley, were correct in keeping the airship in the background while her ship-borne airplanes did the scouting.

Wiley, left temporarily in command of the *Los Angeles*, made two flying moors to the high mast, but thereafter preferred the stub mast, and spent considerable time developing its usefulness. A new carriage was now used under the after car, riding on a circular railroad track around the mast. After sunrise on 17 July, with the wind calm, the *Los Angeles* was walked by hand 360 degrees around the mast while the crew checked for discrepancies in the track. On 7 August the ground crew was reduced by a draft of 50 men; the remainder was insufficient to handle the ship on the ground, and replacements did not arrive until 14 August.

Meanwhile Wiley found himself charged with the responsibility for a flight to Texas. As early as 28 February 1928, the chief of naval operations had authorized a trip to San Antonio as part of a schedule of operations, but nothing was done at that time. On 18 July the Fort Worth Chamber of Commerce wrote to BuAer concerning the anticipated flight of the *Graf Zeppelin* to the United States, and expressed a desire that the German ship should visit Fort Worth and moor to the mast at the helium plant, last used by the *Shenandoah* in her West Coast flight four years earlier. The bureau replied that the *Graf's* visit would probably be made in late September and would end in Lakehurst. The bureau could not require Dr. Eckener to fly anywhere; the final decision would be his. The evident interest of the citizens of Fort Worth did lead BuAer on 10 August to cable the helium plant to put the mast "in shape to receive an airship as promptly as practicable," even though they added that it was doubtful that the *Graf* would come to Fort Worth. A scheduled American Legion convention on 8 October in San Antonio led the bureau to issue orders to Wiley for a flight to Texas at that time, with landing to the Fort Worth mast. A hurricane in the south, and associated bad weather, prevented flying after 10 September, and with no improvement in the weather by 27 September, Wiley commenced the overhaul scheduled before the Texas flight. Two gas cells were replaced, extra fuel was loaded, and the crew was augmented to 41 persons.

At 1825 on 6 October, the *Los Angeles* departed Lakehurst carrying 25,534 lb. of fuel, 4,525 lb. of water ballast, 1,200 lb. of oil, and 1,300 lb. of drinking water, with gas cells 86% full of helium. Eight hundred pounds of water had to be dropped as the ship climbed to 1,800 feet, setting a course for Richmond, Virginia; and at 0014 on 7 October the airship was over Richmond, where she climbed to 2,300 feet. The *Los Angeles* crossed Atlanta at 0907, and circled the city before heading west across Alabama. At 1618 she was over Mobile and at 1932 above New Orleans. The ship now proceeded in leisurely fashion through the night via Houston, intending to arrive over San Antonio in time for the American Legion parade. At 0930 on the morning of the 8th the airship arrived just as the parade was forming, and she circled the city for one and a half hours, dropping greetings at Kelly and Brooks fields of the Army Air Service. The ship then proceeded via Austin to Fort Worth, where, after some delay due to the need to valve helium and make her heavy, the *Los Angeles* made fast to the mast at 1837 before a crowd of some 25,000 people. The time in the air from Lakehurst had been 48 hours 12 minutes. Lieutenant Scott E. Peck and CBM F. J. Tobin, who had been sent on ahead to supervise the mooring, now reported aboard for duty. During the night, 19,189 lb. of fuel and 130,000 cubic feet of helium were piped on board.

The *Los Angeles*'s flight to Fort Worth had demonstrated the skillful use of pressure pattern flying by Lcdr. Wiley, the airship taking advantage of the clockwise flow of air around a huge high-pressure system in the center of the United States as she flew via the southeastern and southern states. Instead of heading straight home for Lakehurst, Wiley now took advantage of the same pattern by proceeding north and then east. At 0858 on 9 October the airship lifted off from the Fort Worth mast. At 1055 she was over Ardmore, Oklahoma, and at 1820 over Kansas City, Missouri. During the night she proceeded north across Iowa and Illinois, and at 0325 on the morning of 10 October was over Chicago. Turning east, the *Los Angeles* traveled a familiar route via Toledo and Youngstown, Ohio, to Pittsburgh. She reached pres-

sure height of 3,700 feet in the passes of the Alleghenies between Connellsville and Bedford. At 2135 she settled into the hands of the ground crew at Lakehurst, and was housed in the shed. The time in the air had been 36 hours 37 minutes. The Fort Worth flight, equaling anything achieved by the *Shenandoah*, demonstrated the professional skill, resolution, and judgment of her temporary commander, Lcdr. Herbert V. Wiley, and foreshadowed a distinguished career in airships.

On 15 October 1928, five days after the *Los Angeles* returned from Fort Worth, the German *Graf Zeppelin*, completing a 111-hour transatlantic flight, arrived at Lakehurst and was housed in the hangar alongside the *Los Angeles*, the smaller and older sister now upstaged and forgotten. The entire country had followed the flight of the *Graf* as if it were a melodrama staged for its benefit; agonized at the news that the fabric cover of the port fin had been badly damaged in going through a severe squall line west of the Azores, particularly when the airship sent a request for assistance drafted by Rosendahl; rejoiced when a second message was sent canceling the first; and had gone on to cheer and applaud as the big craft flew triumphantly up the East Coast via Washington, Baltimore, and Philadelphia to New York. Thousands mobbed the ship on her landing at Lakehurst, and Eckener was the hero of the hour. There was a ticker tape parade up Broadway, and a reception by President Coolidge at the White House. Requests poured in for the *Graf* to show herself throughout the country, particularly in Chicago. Meanwhile the *Los Angeles* was confined to her shed—and with the *Graf Zeppelin* occupying the berth on the south side of the hangar, the new mobile mast being erected and assembled between the *Los Angeles*'s nose and the west hangar door, and the blimps J 3 and J 4 stowed under her stern at the east end, she was effectively immobilized. Repairs to the German ship's fin took 12 days, and Eckener decided the season was too far advanced to show the *Graf* to the midwesterners. On 29 October he departed Lakehurst for Friedrichshafen, with Commander Maurice Pierce, Lt. T. G. W. Settle, and Lt. Charles Bauch on board.

Rosendahl resumed command of the *Los Angeles* on 29 October, with Wiley once more acting as executive officer. Relatively few flights were made, however, about 40 members of the ground crew having been transferred, so that operations were limited in less than perfect weather. More men were received on 22 November; and during the remainder of the month, a trapeze that had been built by Goodyear for receiving airplanes in flight was attached to the bottom girders of the ship at Frame 100. A mock-up of water recovery apparatus as designed for the new 6,500,000-cubic-foot ships was installed at Frame 115 on the port side, this work being done by Lt. Calvin Bolster (CC), experimental officer of the *Los Angeles*, who now appears on the ship's roster for the first time. On 4 and 6 December, flight tests were made to measure the drag of the water recovery unit. For the remainder of the month there was no flying. The #2 gas cell, the first of viscose-latex, was found badly deteriorated after only six months in service, and was replaced. A three-bladed metal propeller was installed.

On the evening of 8 January 1929, the *Los Angeles* departed Lakehurst for Florida, where the *Patoka* awaited her in the spacious St. Joseph's Bay, east of Pensacola near Apalachicola. Early in the flight #2 engine was shut down with a burned piston and a scored cylinder, but the valves in the damaged cylinder were blocked open, and the engine was put back in operation. Increasing head winds delayed the ship on her southerly flight. "During the night, one small town remained below us for several hours and actually at one time after we passed it, it drew ahead again as the strong winds even forced us astern. I do not recall ever experiencing such fierce gusts as on this occasion."[35] Early in the morning of 10 January, fog developed, and shortly before mooring to the *Patoka* at 1246 the airship passed through a wind-shift line. The flight from Lakehurst had lasted 40 hours 6 minutes. While in Florida, the *Los Angeles* made two flights over the peninsula to the south, one of them being of 39 hours 31 minutes' duration. While she was on the *Patoka* mast, heavy rain squalls repeatedly soaked the ship; and on several occasions, even when ballast and sometimes fuel were hastily released, the airship's tail was forced into the water. The much easier flight north, on 14–15 January, took only 13 hours 50 minutes, with the *Los Angeles* being carried along by a strong south–southwest wind of 50 knots.

The airship was then laid up for removal and overhaul of two engines, and for replacement of #7 cell, an old rubber one, which had been found to be leaking badly during the Florida flight. The overhaul period extended longer than expected because of the discovery of corrosion in the hull structure, which

was inaccessible when the gas cells were inflated. About 35% of the structure was cleaned and varnished; and the fuel system was cleaned because of problems with dirty gasoline. On 28 January a workman, forcing his way down between two fully inflated cells to repair a broken wire, tore a hole in #3 cell; it was deflated, removed, patched, and reinstalled. The overhaul period was completed 20 February, but foul weather kept the ship in her shed. The #3 cell was then changed, as it was leaking helium.

The post-repair flight took place on 1 March. With Herbert Hoover to be inaugurated as thirty-first president of the United States on 4 March 1929, the *Los Angeles* was ordered to participate in the inaugural parade along with the Navy's Lakehurst-based nonrigids J 3 and J 4, and the Army's TC 5 and TC 10 from Langley Field. Many heavier-than-air craft were to participate also. The *Los Angeles* left the stub mast at 0714 with the sky clear, but as she proceeded south it became overcast, light rain fell, and the visibility deteriorated. Near Washington fog developed with clouds nearly down to ground level; but a providential break near Marlboro, Maryland, revealed the four pressure airships at the rendezvous. With the smaller craft trailing astern, Rosendahl brought the *Los Angeles* over the Capitol at 1,200 feet on schedule at 1500; the visibility improved as the aerial procession passed up Pennsylvania Avenue to the White House, and then the airships found themselves in zero-zero visibility again. They dispersed, J 3 and J 4 landing at the Naval Air Station, Anacostia, to be refueled and then having to be deflated when overtaken by the ensuing storm. Little was seen of the ground between Washington and Philadelphia, and clouds forced the *Los Angeles* lower and lower as she groped her way from one landmark to another, following the Mount Holly–Lakehurst road. At the field the airship was down to 400 feet; the wind was light, so Rosendahl landed immediately, and the ship was walked into the hangar after a flight of 10 hours 45 minutes. It had been a nerve-racking day; and while the airships had been present and accounted for in the inaugural parade, only a handful of the heavier-than-air craft were in the air.

11

Los Angeles: Maid of All Work

Rosendahl's days were numbered as commanding officer of the *Los Angeles*. It was time for a change: the lean years were over, and at Lakehurst an expanded training program commenced to provide officers and men for the new *Akron*, due to complete in 1931, while a sister ship, the *Macon*, was to follow her 15 months later. Research and development projects in connection with the outfitting and equipment of the new airships became the lot of the *Los Angeles*. To direct the numerous investigations going on simultaneously in the spring of 1929, the chief of naval operations on 9 April 1929 ordered that Rosendahl be detached as commanding officer of the *Los Angeles* and be elevated to the post of commander, Rigid Airship Training and Experimental Squadron, with additional duty under the commanding officer, NAS Lakehurst, in charge of experimental projects. Wiley was to command the *Los Angeles*, while Lcdr. Vincent A. Clarke, Jr., who on 1 January 1929 already had 460 hours of rigid airship time, was to be ordered to the *Los Angeles* for duty under instruction. Upon detachment of Wiley, expected about 1 September 1929, Clarke would succeed him as commanding officer of the *Los Angeles*.[1] The big changeover took place on 9 May 1929, when Rosendahl read his orders as ComRATES and Wiley assumed command of the *Los Angeles*.

Thus, Wiley was in charge during the summer of 1929 when the *Los Angeles* was involved in the most unusual experimental program of her career—the development of airplane hook-on and release procedures. Earlier trials had been made with releasing airplanes from airships, but it remained for the U.S. Navy to develop the technique to a regular routine, greatly enhancing the military capabilities of the big rigids in the process.

The idea of carrying an airplane had intrigued the airshipmen of other countries. On 26 January 1918, the German naval Zeppelin L 35, attached to the experimental unit at Jüterbog near Berlin, had ascended with a standard Albatros D III fighter and released it to fly back to the field. The purpose was to defend the naval Zeppelins against enemy aircraft over the North Sea, but the Leader of Airships, Fregattenkapitän Peter Strasser, opposed the idea, as he preferred the airships to seek safety at high altitude. Late in the war the British experimented with carrying a Sopwith 2F.1 Camel aloft under the rigid airship R 23 at Pulham: on 6 November 1918, the Camel was released and flown to a landing by Lt. R. E. Keyes. The end of the war terminated this project. Later, when R 33 was recommissioned for some experimental work in connection with the building of R 100 and R 101, some hook-ons were made in October 1925, with the tiny De Havilland DH 53 Hummingbird.

Similarly, the first experiment in the United States was carried out on local initiative when, on 12 December 1918, the naval pressure airship C 1, based at NAS Rockaway Beach, lifted an Army JN 4 to 2,600 feet by means of a pelican hook and a wire. Here the pilot tripped the hook and flew safely to his base at Fort Tilden, New York.

In the fall of 1921, Lawrence Sperry, the head of the Sperry Aircraft Company and son of Elmer Sperry, the pioneer of gyro flight instruments, interested the Army Air Service in developing the airship–airplane combination. He believed the hook-on airplane would be useful in the Army airship mission of coastal patrol—to make a close inspection of suspicious vessels while the vulnerable airship remained at a distance, or to act as a courier ashore.

Further, his company was building a tiny single-seater biplane weighing only 862 lb. loaded—light enough to be carried by the Army's C class pressure airships of 181,000 cubic feet. Sperry made some early flight tests that convinced him that a hook-up of the airplane to the airship was feasible, and fabricated a trapeze structure to hang beneath the airship. He also designed the hook, to be attached by struts to the top of the center section of the Messenger, with a guide bar sloping down and forward to lead the hook onto the trapeze. Yet Sperry did not live to see the outcome of his inspiration; on 13 December 1923 he drowned when the engine of his Messenger failed during a crossing of the English Channel.

Not until 3 October 1924, in a demonstration at the Pulitzer Races at Dayton, was a Messenger carried aloft by an airship, when the Army's TC 5, of 210,000 cubic feet, ascended with the small biplane to be released over the crowd. The Messenger and trapeze were then delivered to Scott Field, the Army's lighter-than-air base near St. Louis. On 15 December, with the trapeze rigged to the TC 3, 1st Lt. Clyde V. Finter succeeded in hooking his tiny biplane to the trapeze on the third try—the first time an airplane had ever "landed" on board an airship. An important discovery was that just as in a wind tunnel, though on a huge scale, there was a turbulent flow of air around the body of the airship, making it nearly impossible to fly the Messenger close under the bag on a level with the trapeze; whereas if Finter flew below the trapeze and climbed to put his hook on it, he could be more sure of success. The Army, however, did not experiment further, though it was willing to give its data to the Navy, including plans for the "sky hook."

Naval interest in airship hook-ons dated back to the spring of 1925, when BuAer (as related in Chapter 8) proposed that the Shenandoah carry out such experiments. Lansdowne advocated the use of a large aircraft and offered suggestions for the design of the airplane hook and the trapeze, but of course did not live to carry out the project. Meanwhile the bureau was elaborating the 6,000,000-cubic-foot Design #60, which later, enlarged to 6,500,000 cubic feet, would be the Akron and the Macon. In 1926, the chief of naval operations, Admiral Eberle, ruled that the new airships would carry airplanes, and the Goodyear designs which won in both the 1927 and 1928 competitions incorporated an airplane hangar with door in the bottom of the hull. In mid-1926 the Bureau of Aeronautics asked Goodyear-Zeppelin to quote a price for a trapeze to handle the Vought UO-1 two-seater observation airplane weighing 2,305 lb. fully loaded. Dr. Arnstein himself took charge of the design, proposing a rectangular frame 13 feet high and 6½ feet wide, hinged at the upper end and carrying a resiliently mounted landing bar at its lower end. The

The first airplane trapeze installed at Frame 100 of the *Los Angeles* in December 1928. Hangar tests are being made with the Vought UO-1 aircraft A-6615. (U.S. Navy)

frame was to be supported by cables from the lower end to pulleys and drums in the airship both fore and aft. This would permit the frame to swing forward and absorb the landing impact, as well as allowing the frame, with the airplane attached, to be winched up against the hull. Except for a reduction in width to four feet, the trapeze finally delivered by Goodyear was essentially of this form.

The Naval Aircraft Factory was charged with developing the airplane hook, and a UO-1 airplane was delivered to the factory for this purpose. The Sperry hook was used as a model, while, in addition, two auxiliary hooks were mounted on the upper wing rear spar to be engaged by eyes on the trapeze, thereby steadying the airplane after landing.

The first flight experiments with the *Los Angeles* occurred on 11 June 1927, when a UO-1 aircraft without hook piloted by Lt. (j.g.) de Long Mills made six approaches to within about five feet of the keel in simulated hook-ons. The good control and the fact there was little relative motion served to reassure the airship personnel, who feared that the airplane might crash into the giant hull. "Plane carrying project now seems simpler," wrote Rosendahl to Moffett.[2]

The bureau signed a contract with Goodyear for the trapeze on 3 June 1927. Late in October the design was completed and the bureau authorized construction, and in December 1928 the trapeze was installed under the keel of the *Los Angeles* at Frame 100.[3] Though water ballast would have to be shifted away from this point, to compensate for the weight of the airplane, the trim would not be affected, as Frame 100 was at the center of buoyancy. Static tests revealed difficulties with the hoisting mechanism, and not until 24 June 1929 was the trapeze re-installed. Static tests were carried out in the shed on 26 June, and dynamic tests on 1 July, under the direction of the ship's experimental officer, Lt. Calvin M. Bolster (CC) USN.

At 0022 on 3 July, the *Los Angeles* took off for the first hook-on tests. At 0415, the airship headed into the wind—Wiley feeling he had to follow aircraft carrier practice, though the *Los Angeles* and the airplane were in the same medium, and there was no relative lateral motion. The plane was Vought UO-1 A-6615, and the pilot Lt. Adolphus W. ("Jake") Gorton, who had been flying since 1918 and had twice narrowly escaped death in high-speed racing-seaplane crashes while a member of the U.S. 1923 and 1924 Schneider Cup teams. Gorton was bold, skillful, and experienced; but in 15 approaches to the trapeze, he was able to make contact only four times, owing to the turbulence under the hull. The hook embodied a safety release, copied from the Sperry design, and when Gorton managed to fly the hook onto the bar, the release opened, and the aircraft dropped.

Gorton having failed to connect with the trapeze, Lcdr. Leslie C. Stevens from the bureau suggested that reversing the process might be simpler: the airship to trail a wire with a hook on the end, the airplane pilot to catch the hook and insert it in an eye on the airplane and be hoisted aboard, as in recovering cruiser float planes from the water. On 15 August Stevens, flying the newer Vought O2U "Corsair," had his chance, with a sandbag trailing from the airship simulating the hook; he had no luck at all trying to grab the swinging sandbag as his plane bobbed around beneath the airship.

Gorton himself was not discouraged. A heavier spring was incorporated in the hook's pressure release mechanism, while Gorton felt that a different type of approach would be more successful. Flying level with the trapeze, Gorton found, as had Finter, that the plane was difficult to control in the eddies and turbulence created by the huge hull, the propeller wash from #4 and #5 engines, and the openwork trapeze itself. Gorton proposed a "reverse carrier approach": where the carrier aircraft stalled out on the carrier's deck with the tail hook in the arresting wires, Gorton would climb up to the trapeze in a nose-high attitude and stall out with the hook on the bar. On 20 August, and using the reverse carrier approach, Gorton hooked on at the first try. He missed on the second attempt, but succeeded on the third and fourth approaches, after which the *Los Angeles* circled the station with the UO-1 on the trapeze. The drag decreased her speed by one knot, while she had to fly 2 degrees nose-up to carry the weight. On the next day, 21 August, Gorton made the

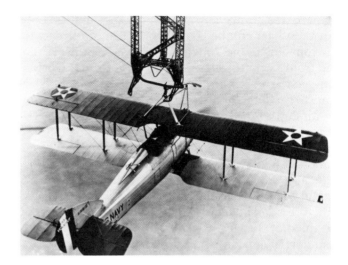

Vought UO-1 airplane A-6615 hanging on the *Los Angeles* trapeze after hook-on. (AIAA)

first landing with the *Los Angeles* flying at 40 knots "to determine if a hook-on could be made in rough air." Then Lcdr. Charles A. Nicholson, who had been handling the development of the trapeze at BuAer, had a try: after making two approaches and missing twice, he made two successful hook-ons. He was followed by Lcdr. Stevens, who made one landing without trouble. The success of these relatively inexperienced officers was not unusual; hook-on pilots assigned later to the heavier-than-air units of the big airships held that it was easier to fly an aircraft to the airship trapeze than to land on a runway, and certainly easier than to land on a carrier deck.

After Nicholson returned to Washington and reported results to Admiral Moffett, the latter made a public announcement to the press. The next step was to publicize BuAer's latest success. The National Air Races were to be held at Cleveland on 24 August–2 September 1929, and as early as 23 July Wiley had visited to arrange with officials for the *Los Angeles* to participate. The stub mast was to be shipped from Lakehurst, and would also serve as the home pylon on the field. The *Los Angeles* was to arrive on 24 August about 1500, then to clear the field and come in to land about half an hour before sunset. The race committee would provide a 200-man handling party, and she would remain moored until the following afternoon.

What better audience could Admiral Moffett want to publicize the Navy's success with the hook-on experiment than the 100,000 spectators at the National Air Races? While the *Los Angeles* followed through on her part of the program, Gorton ferried the UO-1 out to Cleveland. When the airship arrived over the field after a 25-hour flight from Lakehurst, she lowered the trapeze, and Gorton took off from the field. Embarrassingly, he failed to connect on his first three approaches, but he succeeded on the fourth. The trapeze was cranked up against the keel, and Lt. Calvin M. Bolster climbed out over the trapeze girders to the top wing of the Vought, and lowered himself into the front cockpit. The trapeze was lowered; Gorton tripped the hook, and glided down to the field. Bolster thus became the first passenger to be conveyed from an airship to the ground by an airplane.

No longer was it glamorous to land an airplane on an airship, but the experimental program had to go on. Chief Boatswain E. G. Reber, and Chief Aviation Pilot J. J. O'Brien, both attached to the Naval Aircraft Factory in Philadelphia, now took over the drudgery of flying hook-ons with the weary UO-1, and the experimental program generally. Lieutenant Commander Nicholson came up from the bureau from time to time to check on progress and to fly a few trapeze landings himself. For the first time in over a month, Reber on 8 October made approaches to the trapeze without landing. Then, on 10 October 1929, Moffett brought from Washington a distinguished audience, including Secretary of the Navy Charles Francis Adams; Assistant Secretary of the Navy for Aeronautics (since 16 March 1929) David S. Ingalls, the U.S. Navy's only fighter ace of World War I with five victories, who at this time flew himself in a Boeing F4B-1 fighter marked with his flag; and their entourage. While the official party watched enthralled from the control car, O'Brien flew the UO-1 to a successful hook-on. There were more flights by O'Brien, and on 20 May 1930 the Los Angeles participated in a presidential fleet review off the Virginia Capes. Commander Nicholson flew the Vought from the flight deck of the carrier USS Lexington to hook on to the Los Angeles's trapeze as she was passing over the heavy cruiser Salt Lake City with President Hoover on board.

Meanwhile Admiral Moffett, in the fall of 1929, had conceived the idea of the Los Angeles's carrying a glider that might be used to land an officer to take charge of mooring the airship, instead of using the conventional parachute which was more dangerous. He turned for advice to Lt. Ralph S. Barnaby, who, unique among naval aviators, had taken an early interest in gliding and soaring. The preceding summer Barnaby had trained under German instructors at the pioneering American Motorless Aviation Corporation school at South Wellfleet, Massachusetts, and on 18 August he had won the first American "C" certificate by soaring on the sand dunes of Cape Cod for 15 minutes 6 seconds in a German-built Prüfling intermediate glider. Barnaby assured the admiral that the experiment was feasible, and on his advice, BuAer purchased a Prüfling (A 8546) from the American Motorless Aviation Corporation.[4] On the morning of 31 January 1930, the Los Angeles was brought out of the Lakehurst shed, the Prüfling was attached to special fittings at Frame 100, and at 1115 Barnaby

was launched in the glider from 3,000 feet, landing on the snow-covered field 13 minutes later.

Moffett seems not to have continued his enthusiasm for the glider, and it appeared only once more in public, on the occasion of the Curtiss Marine Trophy races at Anacostia on Memorial Day, 1930. This time, however, the Prüfling was attached at Frame 120 to leave the airplane trapeze clear. Barnaby having come down with influenza, Lt. T. G. W. Settle volunteered to fly the glider in his place. Settle, a qualified lighter-than-air pilot who served as radio officer in the Shenandoah and engineering officer in the Los Angeles, had taken civilian flight training and won a pilot's license after the Navy had refused his application for heavier-than-air instruction. Further, while acting as inspector of naval aircraft at Akron, he had learned slope soaring from Wolfgang Klemperer, an early pioneer of German motorless flight who had come to America in 1924 to serve Goodyear-Zeppelin as an aerodynamicist.

During the flight south from Lakehurst, the glider attachments carried away in turbulent air and the Prüfling was damaged, suffering a five-inch hole in the starboard wing. Nonetheless, Settle climbed down into the cockpit, and at 1418, released the glider two miles southeast of the Naval Air Station at Anacostia:

The wing hole was "no help" and as I approached the leeward side of the ridge bounding the field (over the town of Anacostia) I was getting short of altitude, and good up-drafts were absent. So I casted about for a clear place to set down, and spotted a large building with ample courtyard and a wall around the compound. So I started an approach to that courtyard. There were a lot of people in the yard, and they started to clear a landing area, waving me cordially to come on in. But, in the nick of time, over the enclosure wall, I got a fine up-draft that cleared me over the trees on top of the ridge by a few feet, and I went on in to a normal landing on a runway, near the spectators. I asked someone what that building was where I had almost landed, and was told it was St. Elizabeth's.[5] I suppose nobody has ever gotten in there by glider![6]

Settle's moment of glory was brief, for immediately after the Prüfling released, Lcdr. Nicholson flew in with the UO-1 to hook on to the trapeze. Except for a few hook-ons by O'Brien in August, this demonstration at Anacostia would be the last for over a year, the basics of airplane hook-on operations with rigid airships having been worked out with the Los Angeles and the old UO-1. Procurement of operational aircraft for the big Akron and Macon was still in the future, and the types to be used had not yet been decided on.

The round-the-world flight of the Graf Zeppelin in August 1929 added to public enthusiasm for the airship, and encouraged American airshipmen. Wil-

Lt. Thomas G. W. Settle poses with the German *Prüfling* glider A-8546 at NAS, Anacostia, D.C., after releasing from the *Los Angeles* on Memorial Day, 1930. Though Vice Admiral Settle later related that there was a hole in the right wing, this photograph shows it in the leading edge of the left wing. Possibly the negative is reversed. (NASM 81-14799)

liam Randolph Hearst, the newspaper tycoon who had made the largest financial contribution to the world flight, had insisted that the journey commence in America; so on 4 August the *Graf* arrived at Lakehurst. Three days later she departed for Friedrichshafen, carrying 22 passengers including Rosendahl and Lt. J. C. Richardson as naval observers. Departing Friedrichshafen on 15 August, the big airship traversed Russia and Siberia to arrive at Kasumigaura Naval Air Station near Tokyo on 19 August. The crossing of the Pacific was made between 23 and 26 August, the *Graf* mooring to a stub mast at Mines Field, Los Angeles. From Mines Field the *Graf* proceeded to Lakehurst on 27–29 August, following the same southern route from San Diego to El Paso as that taken by the *Shenandoah* on the West Coast flight five years earlier, and experiencing her share of troubles with turbulence over the desert. At Lakehurst Rosendahl disembarked. When the *Graf* headed for Friedrichshafen on 1 September, Wiley and Lt. Roland G. Mayer were on board, while Rosendahl temporarily assumed command of the *Los Angeles* until her regular commander returned from Germany on 23 September. The world flight marked the apex of Rosendahl's relationship with Dr. Eckener, and was the prototype of the transoceanic passenger service in which Rosendahl believed until well after World War II. Indeed, Eckener's dramatic propaganda effort impressed American businessmen and might well have borne fruit if the stock market had not crashed two months later, heralding the Great Depression.

There were many local training flights in the autumn of 1929, with the *Los Angeles* towed into the shed on the mobile mast for the first time on 20 September, and flying moors to the mobile mast. Operations were restricted because of bad weather early in October; and with 90% of the outer cover six

years old, Wiley started a program of removing and replacing panels during marginal weather. The only long flight saw the *Los Angeles* proceeding to Akron on 7 November, the date of the ring-laying ceremony for the big ZRS-4, later to be christened the *Akron*. Admiral Hughes, the chief of naval operations, reprimanded Wiley for making the flight without his prior authorization or knowledge. Between 23 and 26 January the *Los Angeles* flew to Parris Island to test the new stub mast, with an excursion to Florida to calibrate the radio compass stations at St. Augustine and Daytona. On 31 March 1930, Lcdr. Clarke relieved Wiley.

The *Los Angeles* made many training flights under Clarke's command; in fact, when he was relieved slightly more than a year later, 953 hours had been put on the ship in 77 ascents. The change-of-command ceremony took place at the mooring-out circle with the *Los Angeles* at the mobile mast; immediately afterward she took off with 52 persons on board for a 10-hour 2-minute flight. During the preceding year there had been trouble with broken wires in the hull structure: the Bureau of Standards had advised that the wires were breaking from fatigue and that an increasing number of failures could be expected. Throughout this flight representatives of the Assembly and Repair Department at Lakehurst were on board taking tension readings on all accessible transverse bulkhead and shear wires for the Board of Inspection and Survey. The board found the material condition of the *Los Angeles* to be good, and felt that if the airship were operated in the conservative manner in which she had been flown in the previous years, with inspections continually made by qualified personnel, she might be serviceable for two to four years longer.

At a conference on 12 June involving Commander

Fulton, Commander Carpenter of the Operations Division of BuAer, and Captain Claude of the *Patoka*, complaints were made that the *Los Angeles* had not made adequate use of the tender even when she was available. The airship people at Lakehurst were told they "must use her or lose her," and six moorings took place soon thereafter, all at Newport.

Aside from airplane hook-ons and the glider display at Anacostia, various other experiments were made with the *Los Angeles*. To test the air drag of the flat panel type water recovery condensers planned for the *Akron* and *Macon*, the *Los Angeles* on 8 July ran tests with a simulated apparatus made by Goodyear of air bags taped against the outer cover above #3 engine gondola, inflated to measure their drag. Water was drained from the cooling system of #5 engine and replaced by Prestone (ethylene glycol); the higher operating temperatures expected with the glycol were not realized, the coolant boiling at 112°C because of absorption of water from the air.[7] With a closed system the coolant temperature was raised to 130°C, but the interior temperature in the gondola went to 140°F, prompting concern for the health of the machinists' mates. After the Prestone was drained from the engine and replaced by water, it was found that the cooling system leaked from every seal. The rubber had in fact been attacked by the ethylene glycol, and all of the seals had to be replaced. During the year a number of steel two- and three-bladed propellers were delivered, and by 10 September 1930, all four of the ship's 520-h.p. VL-2 engines were driving metal propellers. Only the #1 engine of 400 h.p. still had a wooden propeller; the bureau felt that with the higher power of the VL-2, the wooden propellers were being loaded to the limit of their strength.

An unrelated event was the departure of Rosendahl from Lakehurst in June 1930. Relieved by Captain Harry E. Shoemaker as commander of the Rigid Airship Training and Experimental Squadron, Rosendahl went to Washington to be First Assistant in the Plans Division at BuAer, where it was hoped that he could be of more value to the airship program as the *Akron* approached completion. He would not again be stationed at Lakehurst until he brought the newly completed *Akron* to the East Coast base on 22 October 1931.

More than seven years after her acceptance by the U.S. Navy, the USS *Los Angeles* participated as a scouting craft, in the fleet exercises of 1931 which were to be held near Panama in February. Not since the summer of 1925 had a rigid airship of the U.S. Navy undertaken operations with fleet units, when the *Shenandoah* had been involved in exercises with the battleship *Texas*. The *Los Angeles's* civilian status, as decreed by the Conference of Ambassadors, pre-

cluded her participation in such naval activities. Now, with the *Akron* due to complete in the latter half of 1931, it was necessary to obtain information on capabilities of rigid airships in operating with the fleet, and on possible tactics. At the instigation of Assistant Secretary Ingalls, the State Department approached the governments involved in the original procurement of ZR 3. The Navy Department emphasized that the German-built rigid would not be armed. The French and British governments had no objection to the participation of the *Los Angeles* in the maneuvers; the Japanese government did not reply to State's inquiry, a lack of action that was taken as approval.

Thus, on 15 November 1930, the *Los Angeles* was docked for extensive overhaul of structure, engines, and outer cover to extend to 15 January. At the same time a stub mast was to be erected at the Naval Operating Base, Guantanamo, Cuba, and the *Patoka* was sent south to transit the Panama Canal and await the *Los Angeles* in Dulce Bay, Costa Rica, on the Pacific side of Central America.

At 1726 on 4 February 1931, the *Los Angeles* unmoored from the mobile mast carrying 49 persons, 29,811 lb. of fuel, and 5,250 lb. of water ballast. The flight south via Cape Hatteras and the Gulf Stream was uneventful, and after 24 hours 7 minutes the airship was moored to the stub mast at Guantanamo to take on fuel and water ballast. The heavy winter flight clothing was sent ashore. At 0820 on the 6th the *Los Angeles* slipped from the mast and headed for Colon, in the evening passing over the Scouting Force including its flagship, the battleship *Arkansas*. After circling Colon, the airship followed the Panama Canal to Balboa on the Pacific side. Instead of crossing land to reach the Gulf of Dulce, Clarke headed across the Gulf of Panama to Cape Mala and then followed the coastline via Cape Maliato and Jicaron Island to Punta Burica and the Gulf of Dulce. The *Patoka* was sighted at 0420 on the 7th, but the first landing attempt at 0705 was spoiled when the stopper on the *Patoka*'s main cable carried away. The sun was rising, and superheating of the gas forced Clarke to valve helium repeatedly for a total of three minutes, releasing over 100,000 cubic feet of the precious gas. Not until 0824 was the mooring completed, 24 hours 4 minutes after the airship departed Guantanamo.

On the morning of 8 February, the *Los Angeles* cast off from the *Patoka*'s mast and retraced her course to Panama Bay. While waiting for the *Patoka* to proceed to the same destination, where the Atlantic-based Scouting Force was assembling for Fleet Problem XII, the airship cruised over the Gulf of Panama, showed herself over Balboa and Panama City, and more than once circled the offshore Perlas Islands. At 2034 on the evening of 9 February, after 36 hours 26 minutes in the air, the *Los Angeles* was moored to the *Patoka*'s mast and brought into the fleet anchorage in Panama Roads. There she remained for over two days while the ships came in—the battleship *Texas*, flying the flag of Admiral Frank H. Schofield, commander in chief of the United States Fleet; the battleship *Arkansas*, flagship of the Scouting Force commanded by Vice Admiral Arthur L. Willard; the new heavy cruisers *Northampton*, *Salt Lake City*, and *Pensacola*; the older light cruisers *Detroit*, *Milwaukee*, *Raleigh*, *Memphis*, *Marblehead*, *Omaha*, *Cincinnati*, *Trenton*, *Richmond*, and *Concord*; as well as tenders, destroyers, and nine submarines. Among the last to arrive were the big carriers *Saratoga* and *Lexington*, on the morning of 12 February.

On the afternoon of 15 February, Assistant Secretary of the Navy for Aeronautics David S. Ingalls, and Admiral Willard boarded the *Patoka*. The admiral soon departed; but at 1620 Ingalls boarded the *Los Angeles*, and a few minutes later the airship cast off. During the night the *Los Angeles* cruised in the vicinity of the assembled men of war in Panama Bay and next morning, 16 February, moored to the *Patoka* mast.

The fleet problem was due to begin on this date. The exercise was based on the assumption that "a Pacific power" was attacking both the Panama Canal and a hypothetical Nicaraguan canal with the aim of putting landing forces ashore. The "Blue" defending fleet, essentially the Scouting Force commanded by Admiral Willard, included the carrier *Lexington* and the *Los Angeles*. The attacking "Black" force under Rear Admiral Joseph M. Reeves commanding the Carrier Divisions was essentially the Battle Force, U.S. Fleet, consisting of most of the Navy's battleships proceeding to Panama from its base at San Pedro, California, and further including the *Saratoga* and the older and slower carrier *Langley*. The chief umpire was none other than the chief of naval operations, Admiral William V. Pratt, on board the battleship *California*.

At 1635 on the afternoon of 16 February, the *Los Angeles* was again airborne with 39 persons on board, including Secretary Ingalls and Commander Alger H. Dresel, who was the ship's umpire and an experienced airship officer, and 26,511 lb. of fuel and 4,800 lb. of water ballast. For several hours the airship cruised near the fleet anchorage in Panama Bay, and at 2120 she watched the *Patoka* get under way for the Gulf of Dulce. At 2210 came a message from Admiral Willard to "execute Blue Fleet Operation Plan #3-31," and the *Los Angeles* departed for her assigned search area. Proceeding on a southwest course during the night, she arrived at 0955 at Point Baker, Lat. 2° 40' north, Long. 86° 00' west, some 450 miles from the coast of Costa Rica. For six hours the airship steered

on various headings, without sighting an enemy ship. Low cumulus clouds and rain squalls formed during the afternoon, the airship passing through some without experiencing turbulence. At 1515 the uninhabited Cocos Islands, at 5° 30' north, 87° 2' west, were sighted while the airship was on a track of 18°. At 1600 the *Los Angeles* was put on a track of 54° for the Gulf of Dulce. Shortly afterward she encountered the light cruiser *Trenton* of the "Blue" force and exchanged signals. Burica Point Light was sighted at 2242, but it was 0405 on 18 February before the *Patoka* was located by the tender sending a searchlight signal. At 0700 the *Los Angeles* was secured to the *Patoka* after a flight of 38 hours 25 minutes.

There was much to be done, for the airship was expected to continue participating in the war game. Fueling was begun even before the *Patoka* anchored, 15,733 lb. being delivered by 1100; 54,000 cubic feet of helium was piped on board in the afternoon, together with 1,775 lb. of added fuel, 480 lb. of food, and 300 lb. of ice. At 1835 on the 18th the *Los Angeles* slipped from the *Patoka*'s mast carrying 39 persons including Secretary Ingalls, 27,206 lb. of fuel, and 4,700 lb. of ballast. Until 2135 the airship cruised in the vicinity of Burica Point while thunderstorms built up in the Gulf of Dulce, with occasional flashes of lightning. At 0043 on 19 February the *Los Angeles* was directed by the commander of the "Blue" fleet to "search sector 300 mile circle between radii 195 and 227 from Bahia commencing daybreak Thursday 19th for unaccounted enemy vessels." At 0140 the airship stood out to sea on a track of 200° for Rivadeneyra Shoals. Lightning and thunderstorms were seen on various bearings, and the course was changed to avoid them. While passing under squall clouds the ship encountered a down draft of 400 feet per minute. At 0545, with daybreak, the airship changed heading to port and began to fly the 300-mile circle as laid down in her orders. There was some excitement when at 0950 a large carrier was sighted, later identified as the "Blue" unit *Lexington*.[8] At 1154 a large square-rigged sailing vessel was sighted; on closing her she was identified as the *Tusitala*, five days overdue at Panama from Hawaii.[9] Shortly afterward, at 1320, the *Los Angeles* sighted a large number of ships at a distance of 30 miles and sent off a contact report; these were promptly identified as the "Black" main body, including the small carrier *Langley*. A message was sent to the commander of the "Blue" fleet: "Force previously sighted main body aircraft carrier second line latitude 5° 33' longitude 83° 30' course 090–1332." This was the first reliable report of the enemy main body received by Admiral Willard from any source, and made possible a successful attack later in the day by the *Lexington*'s aircraft. The airship altered course to close the force and obtain more detailed information, failing to notice from a distance that the "enemy" was flying off aircraft. Three of them were sighted belatedly a mile distant on the starboard quarter, and while Clarke was sending an amplified report, one plane made a bombing attack approach. Dresel ruled that the *Los Angeles* had been destroyed, and the radio was shut down in the middle of the message. Passing over the "Black" force, Clarke received a signal from Admiral Pratt, the chief umpire on board the battleship *California*, "You are sunk," followed by "pleasant voyage," a non sequitur that led the C.O. *Los Angeles* to tell Admiral Moffett, "Believe you should ask Admiral Pratt if there was any connection intended between his two signals."[10] In later maneuvers, the ZRS-5 *Macon*, for instance, after being "shot down," would be allowed to continue as "ZRS-6," or even "ZRS-7," but the *Los Angeles* was not to be resurrected. At 1523 there was a message from Admiral Schofield, the CinC U.S. Fleet, "Consider *Los Angeles* out of action during remainder of problem direct *Patoka* proceed Panama Bay and anchor approximately 3000 yards south of entrance buoys Panama Canal clear of fairway and await further instructions." Course was set for Jicaron Island, and at 0643 on the morning of 20 February the airship was moored to the *Patoka* in Panama Bay, after a flight of 36 hours 8 minutes. Secretary Ingalls left the ship for good. After loading 5,940 lb. of fuel, the *Los Angeles* unmoored for a 10-hour local flight around the Gulf of Panama to "carry out a photographic survey of the Perlas Islands."

Not until 22 February did the *Los Angeles* commence her return journey, unmooring from the *Patoka* at 0822. As before, the air was rough as she crossed the isthmus at 1,000 feet to the Atlantic side, and later four head wires were found broken at Frames 70, 85, and 160, with small holes in cells #5 and #11. A head wind of 15 to 18 knots made for a slow flight to Guantanamo. At 1740 on 23 February, Clarke weighed off for a landing to the stub mast, but changed his mind because of gusty surface winds. When these subsided, the *Los Angeles* came in and moored at 2125, after 37 hours 3 minutes in the air. Nonetheless, the rough air forced Clarke alternately to drop 700 lb. of ballast and valve helium for a total of nearly two minutes. Fuel and 72,000 cubic feet of helium were received on board, along with the heavy winter flight clothing and 300 lb. of alcohol. The broken head wires had to be replaced, and the leaking radiator of #4 engine required repair. The gusty winds continued, and on the afternoon of 26 February the wind shifted, swinging the ship to starboard from a heading of 350° to 227°, while the after car with stern carriage lifted off the ground with 12 men on the hand rails.

At 1000 on 27 February, the *Los Angeles* departed Guantanamo, proceeding via Havana, Key West, and Jacksonville, Florida, to Parris Island, South Carolina, where she moored to the stub mast on the following morning after a flight of 22 hours 43 minutes. The #4 engine car radiator was removed, but reinstalled by evening. At 2310 on 1 March the airship departed Parris Island, and at 1758 on the following evening she moored to the mobile mast at Lakehurst, where she was towed into the hangar.

Technically, the *Los Angeles*'s performance under Clarke's command had been impressive, particularly for a seven-year-old craft, for she had been away from the Lakehurst hangar for 27 days, based solely on mooring masts, and had traveled 14,500 miles in 272 flying hours. This exceeded the time away from Lakehurst, and the distance covered, by the *Shenandoah* in the West Coast flight in 1924. Previously, there had been concern about superheating effects and possible gas cell deterioration while operating in the tropics, but these problems were not unmanageable. Lieutenant George Calnan (CC), the ship's First Lieutenant, writing before the first long scouting flight on 16 February, acknowledged the loss up to then of 200,000 cubic feet of helium—some from valving and the rest from going over pressure height, either in flight or from superheating at the mooring mast during the day. With air temperatures of 75° to 86°F maximum, superheating reached 26½° while the ship was moored in the Gulf of Dulce during the day on 7 February. Gas temperature was at least 112°, possibly 120°F, in the top of the ship.

> The men who went up the climbing shaft say that you could cook eggs at the top. I feel that the cells take a punishment on these daytime rides at the mast, but I can't get any concise data to prove it. The gelatin latex cells are standing up well. That day at Dulce, when pressed together by the fingers, they had a slight tendency to stick but it was not serious. . . . The rubber cells seem to get very flexible but I can see no change in them. Some of the men seem to think that the bubbles are increasing in numbers in the skin cells and that there is a slight tendency for the seams to slip. I can see no definite indication of this to date.[11]

Calnan acknowledged that "everybody is a little tired but bearing up well all in all. Operating in the tropics is very uncomfortable especially coming from the North in the middle of winter." Clarke, however, found that a new feature had greatly improved morale: "The smoking room has been the biggest factor imaginable toward successful operation. The old complaint of stomach disorder after a long flight has disappeared and long flights are accepted with as good will as all hands used to greet short ones—dreading the long."[12] Smoking rooms, as a result, were included in the design of the *Akron* and the *Macon*.

Even before her return to Lakehurst, however, the *Los Angeles* was the storm center of a controversy concerning her effectiveness as a naval unit. As Admiral Moffett observed:

> To a comparatively small group who have had experience with airships or who have studied their possibilities, the performance of the *Los Angeles* was gratifying. To a much larger group, and this group includes a great many who have given no consideration, or only cursory consideration, to airships, the *Los Angeles* merely confirmed pre-conceived opinions that airships either are no good or are of so little practical use that their existence is not justified.[13]

Secretary Ingalls, described by Clarke as having "had the time of his life and . . . pleased and more interested than ever,"[14] was

> exceedingly gratified at the marked success attendant upon the use of the *Los Angeles* in connection with the Fleet manoeuvres, although the ship was employed in a scouting capacity only, and therefore no defense of her at all was attempted. Our experience has conclusively established that such type ships are of material value in naval operations at sea in defense of our coast. The repeated contacts with theoretically friendly ships and the final discovery of the main body of the theoretically hostile fleet attacking the Panama Canal, definitely establish the advisability, or rather the necessity, of the continued development and maintenance of lighter than air by the United States Navy.[15]

On his return, the assistant secretary asked that more simulated war exercises be arranged for the *Los Angeles* in conjunction with the *Langley* and the Scouting Force in the Atlantic. Admiral Willard felt that rigid airships, when further improved, should be the source of much valuable information at the risk of relatively few lives. Yet highly critical articles appeared as early as 25 February in the *New York Sun* and the *New York Times*, with the headline, "Naval Men Doubt Airship War Value." The *Sun* charged that "observers generally agree that the gas bag *Los Angeles* completely failed to justify confidence in dirigibles as engines of war," and "the big balloon was of little use for scouting." Much was made of her "vulnerability" and the fact that she had been "shot down." No less a figure than Admiral Pratt, the chief of naval operations, wrote to the *Times* in the airship's defense, pointing out that the papers had failed to grasp the value of negative information; he asserted that the *Los Angeles* had been injected into the problem after it had been drawn up, and that it was immaterial that she had been "shot down." Already she had delivered valuable information, while a modern, well-armed craft equipped with its own defending aircraft such as the *Akron* would be a much more difficult opponent to dispose of.

Lastly, did the hasty decisions of the various umpires take into account the fact that *Los Angeles* was inflated with helium? Unlike the German Zeppelins, she would have been difficult to set afire with machine gun ammunition, and her metal structure could have withstood some damage even from small bombs.

The fleet, however, was generally unimpressed. Admiral Schofield was strong in his "opposition to the proposed development of rigid dirigibles" on the grounds that their cost was "out of proportion" and their "appeal to the imagination . . . not sustained by their military usefulness."[16] Ingalls and Moffett continued their belief in, and support of, the rigid airship, but they all too soon disappeared from the scene—Ingalls resigning his post on 1 June 1932 (as an economy measure he was not replaced by the Hoover administration) and Moffett going down in the *Akron* on the night of 3–4 April 1933—only a few months before he expected to retire for age, after three epoch-making terms as chief of the Bureau of Aeronautics.

In view of the outcry in the papers about the vulnerability of the *Los Angeles*, and the ease with which she had been "shot down," it may be regretted that Clarke did not plan in advance how he would develop his contact with the "Black" force, and try to conceal his craft at a distance or in clouds. Yet Panama demonstrated that the World War I airship scouting methods followed were out of date when the "enemy" brought his own high-performance aircraft to sea, not only on the catapults of cruisers, but also on the flight decks of the carriers *Langley*, *Lexington*, and *Saratoga*. Despite the provision of airplane-handling facilities on board the new *Akron*, the lesson was lost on Rosendahl, her first commander. It was left for the *Macon* under Alger H. Dresel, and particularly under Herbert V. Wiley, to develop the airship as a carrier for fast scouting planes ranging far ahead while the more vulnerable dirigible remained at a distance in the background.

This was the last long flight made by the *Los Angeles*. There would be a great many local training flights, even one cruise to Parris Island on 26–27 October 1931, and such odd events as having Admiral Moffett, Assistant Secretary Ingalls, and nine influential newspapermen including Roy Howard of the Scripps-Howard Press on board on 9 June 1931 for a hook-on demonstration. After being balked by a thunderstorm on 24 July, King Prajadhipok and Queen Rambaibarni of Siam, with a royal party of 13, were taken for a flight of 7 hours 15 minutes on 27 July, which included a hook-on demonstration. On 21 April 1931, Commander Alger H. Dresel relieved Lcdr. Clarke as commanding officer of the *Los Angeles*. Neither of them knew that the old ship's active life had only 14 months left.

Meanwhile the *Los Angeles* was involved in a final chapter in the airplane hook-on saga in the summer and fall of 1931. BuAer, after considerable delay, had decided on the hook-on aircraft types for the big new *Akron* and *Macon*, and it was necessary that the pilots assigned to the heavier-than-air unit of the *Akron* get some practice before the ship entered service. The dimensions of the *Akron*'s hangar door dictated that the airship hook-on airplane should have a span of less than 30 feet, and a length of less than 24 feet. BuAer had prepared a special design for a small triplane, but funds were not forthcoming for its construction. In the meantime, with the idea of procuring a carrier fighter aircraft small enough that it would not require folding wings, the bureau on 10 May 1930 had issued specifications for Design #96 for an aircraft with a span of not more than 25 feet, a length of not more than 20.5 feet, and a gross weight of about 2,300 lb. By the spring of 1931, three aircraft built to this specification, the Berliner-Joyce XFJ-1, the General Aviation (Fokker Aircraft Corporation of America) XFA-1, and the Curtiss XF9C-1, had been delivered to NAS Anacostia for testing. The best of these was the Curtiss; but because the upper wing was at the eye level of the pilot, visibility forward and downward was considered too poor for carrier landings. Thus the upper wing was raised four inches, but, even so, Curtiss was not given a contract for the aircraft as a carrier-borne fighter. Its size suited it, however, for employment aboard the *Akron* and *Macon*, and ultimately Curtiss received a contract for six production F9C-2s. These planes, equipped with sky hooks, ultimately served aboard both of the big airships.

Meanwhile the Navy's heavier-than-air pilots were invited to put in for hook-on flying, with a remarkable response, no fewer than 41 requests for such duty being received from pilots in the Scouting Force alone. The first of them to report at Lakehurst was Lt. Daniel Ward Harrigan in February 1931, followed by Lt. Howard L. Young during the summer. As a stop-gap until the Curtiss fighters were ready, the bureau made available six Consolidated N2Y-1 biplanes—in effect, civilian Fleet 2 trainers with 110-h.p. Kinner engines, then stationed at Pensacola. These planes were fitted at the Naval Aircraft Factory with sky hooks, the first of them arriving at Lakehurst in March 1931. No flying could be done to the *Los Angeles*, however, as her trapeze had been removed after O'Brien's last hook-on 25 August 1930. It was reinstalled on 26 May 1931, and on the following day O'Brien flew some practice approaches in an N2Y. O'Brien also performed for Admiral Moffett and Secretary Ingalls on 9 June, making two hook-ons which were recorded in motion pictures for a training film. Harrigan made his first flight to the *Los Angeles*'s trapeze on 17 June, experiencing no difficulty in making ten successive hook-ons. On 18 August Harrigan again, and Young for the first time, were practicing

with two of the N2Ys with an improved hook designed by Lt. Bolster; Young made eight hook-ons with no trouble. Both officers practiced further in September, and on the night of the 29th made the first hook-ons after dark. Mechanics in the #2 and #3 engine cars of the *Los Angeles* aimed flashlights at the trapeze, and Young and Harrigan between them made 12 landings without trouble. If anything, it was easier at night because the air was less turbulent.

At last, in mid-October, the original Curtiss XF9C-1 was ready with sky hook at the Navy Aircraft Factory, and Harrigan ferried it from Mustin Field[17] to Lakehurst. On 23 October, Harrigan and Young tried the fighter prototype on the *Los Angeles*'s trapeze over Barnegat Bay. Whereas the lightly loaded N2Y had landed with the airship doing 50 knots—cruising speed—the HTA pilots asked Captain Dresel to bring the airship up to full speed—59 knots—for landing the faster and more heavily loaded fighter. Harrigan made five landings on the trapeze with no trouble, but Young, after the third hook-on, found he could not trip the hook to release. The problem was that the hook and its mechanism were suited to the little N2Y's gross weight of 1,637 lb., but when transferred to the fighter, which weighed 2,770 lb. loaded, the heavier strain stretched the cable between the pilot's release lever in the cockpit and the releasing mechanism overhead at the hook. For 35 minutes Young struggled with the balky mechanism, with no success. With the fighter's wheels hanging 23 feet 6 inches below the airship's keel, there was no way the *Los Angeles* could land with it on the trapeze. Finally Lt. Calnan decided that he would have to knock the plane off the trapeze. While Dresel stopped #4 and #5 engines, with #2 and #3 on cruising speed and #1 at half speed, Calnan climbed down the lattice girders of the trapeze to stand on the yoke and pounded with a wrench at the recalcitrant hook until it snapped open, allowing the XF9C-1 to fall clear. Back at Lakehurst a new release wire was installed, and the little fighter flew to Jersey City, where a three-day air meet was in progress and a hook-on exhibition had been announced. Four days later, during a Navy Day flight by the *Los Angeles* to Parris Island, Harrigan flew the little fighter to a hook-on over College Park, Georgia, a suburb of Atlanta.

This was the last landing made on the *Los Angeles*'s trapeze. On 18 December 1931, BuAer approved the removal of the trapeze so that it could be cannibalized by the Naval Aircraft Factory to provide a unit for the *Akron*, which had arrived at Lakehurst on 22 October but was still unable to handle the hook-on fighters. The trapeze was delivered to Lakehurst on 7 February 1932, but because the *Akron* was seriously damaged in a ground handling accident 15 days later, it was not until 3 May that Harrigan and Young made the first hook-ons to the big ship. The *Los Angeles* was supposed to get back her own trapeze in the spring of 1932, but on 9 May BuAer notified the NAF to discontinue work on it as the old ship was to be decommissioned.

Having made her first flight in August 1924, the *Los Angeles* was seven years old in August 1931, with 280 flights totaling 3,446 hours by the 31st of that month. (She would have a total of 331 flights aggregating 4,092 hours when finally decommissioned ten months later.) Her German builders had given her a life expectancy of four years when handing her over to the U.S. Navy, but the old "L.A." kept right on flying, and winning the approval of successive Boards of Inspection and Survey. Indeed, in view of her unprecedented length of service, there was no experience by which to judge how long she might be airworthy. Few indeed of the early Zeppelin airships had had long lives, least of all the ones flown in combat in World War I—though the German Navy's L 14, commissioned on 10 August 1915, and involved in 17 raids on England and 42 scouting flights over the North Sea, had flown on as a training ship after 5 April 1917. She was decommissioned 8 September 1918, after a grand total of 526 flights, and destroyed in her shed at Nordholz on 23 June 1919. The longest-lived British rigid airship, R 33, had first flown in March 1919, and was broken up in 1928; but she spent most of her career laid up and had only 800 flying hours. The small postwar commercial Zeppelins *Bodensee* and *Nordstern* survived until 1928 and 1926 in Italy and France respectively, but surely had little flying time. The *Graf Zeppelin*, most famous of all, showed how resistant the duralumin girder and wire braced structure could be to static and aerodynamic loads, fatigue, and corrosion: in service nearly nine years until laid up after the *Hindenburg* disaster in 1937, she had a grand total of 16,000 flying hours. But in 1930 she was younger than the *Los Angeles* and had only 2,320 hours by end of the year.

It was not the weaknesses of old age that ended the *Los Angeles*'s career, but politics and economy. For months after the stock market crash in October 1929, politicians and cabinet members made optimistic prophecies about the economy, President Hoover leading with assurances that "prosperity is just around the corner." Nonetheless, foreign trade declined sharply, factories shut down, more and more men were out of work, mortgages were foreclosed, banks failed, and the U.S. Treasury's surplus turned to a deficit as sources of revenue dried up. "Appropriations for national defence, the veterans' service and interest on the national debt absorbed every dollar of the national income. The Treasury deficit, which stood at $900,000,000 at the end of the fiscal year

1931, threatened to exceed $2,000,000,000 before June 30, 1932."[18] The aim of the president, the Congress, and the country, was to impose the strictest economy possible on every kind of government expenditure.

Thus, when the Naval Sub-Committee of the House of Representatives met in 1931 to consider the fiscal year 1933 appropriations, their intention was to eliminate every unnecessary expenditure. The item in the Navy's budget of $270,000 for maintenance and operation of the *Los Angeles* seemed to fall in this category—in the latter part of 1931 the new *Akron* was due to enter service, and could presumably carry out the training and experimental missions of the older craft. The $270,000 appropriation for the *Los Angeles* was thus stricken from the bill then being drafted, with the unanimous recommendation that the airship not be operated after 1 July 1932. The Navy's airshipmen protested, as did BuAer, and on 22 April 1932, Charles Francis Adams, the secretary of the navy, wrote to James W. Byrnes, the chairman of the House's Committee on Appropriations, urging that the *Los Angeles* be kept in service to continue experimental and development programs, and training of personnel, at least until the second big airship, the *Macon*, was in service. The Navy Department would not ask for reinstatement of the $270,000 appropriation, but would defray the expense of operating her through fiscal 1933 from other sources.[19]

Adams, Moffett, et al., had seriously misjudged the mood of Congress, as was made clear when Byrnes replied a few days later. Not only did he agree with the Naval Sub-Committee on withholding the $270,000, but he threatened to impound the money the Navy proposed to divert from other sources to use in connection with maintenance and operation of the *Los Angeles*:

> The bill, of course, does not specifically provide that the *Los Angeles* shall not be operated, but if there is a real desire on the part of the Navy Department and the Administration to avoid other than absolutely necessary expenditures, I am sure this possible saving of at least a quarter of a million dollars will be made.[20]

The handwriting on the wall was plain: BuAer proposed that the *Los Angeles* be placed out of commission on 30 June 1932, and be docked at Lakehurst and preserved in such a manner that she might be recommissioned at some future date.

Actually the bureau hoped the old ship might find a buyer, with some financial gain for the Navy Department. Moffett felt she might be worth $400,000 to $500,000. Quite unrealistically, Moffett believed that Goodyear might accept the *Los Angeles* in exchange for lengthening the *Macon*: this would be an oppor-

The *Los Angeles*'s next to last flight, on 23 June 1932. She is disfigured by "Experimental Distinctive Markings for Increased Visibility": All fins are chrome yellow; also after engine car and control car. Star on nose is chrome yellow edged with blue. Additional star in a circle insignia forward port and starboard, and also on top of ship amidships. (National Archives)

tunity for Goodyear to initiate commercial airship operations flying patrons of the Chicago World's Fair down the Mississippi to St. Louis and New Orleans, possibly to Miami and Havana. Paul W. Litchfield, Goodyear's president, gave a hard-boiled answer: Goodyear had dared to pioneer rigid airship construction in the United States but had lost heavily on the *Akron* and *Macon*, while the Depression made it essential that they not gamble on speculative ventures. Operating the *Los Angeles* in conjunction with the Chicago World's Fair appeared to Goodyear a highly unprofitable risk. "So far as Goodyear-Zeppelin or International Zeppelin are concerned, frankly, you must count us out of the picture."[21]

The old ship was active to the end in training flights. In September 1931, Commander Frank C. McCord replaced Lt. Scott E. Peck as executive officer; on 3 January 1933, he would become commanding officer of the USS *Akron*, and be lost in her three months later. On 1 February 1932, Commander Fred T. Berry relieved Dresel, becoming the *Los Angeles*'s last commanding officer: serving subsequently as commanding officer of NAS Lakehurst, Berry, too, would die in the *Akron*.

The last flight, of 7 hours 36 minutes' duration, took place on 24–25 June 1932. A scheduled "final" flight on 27 June was canceled because of "bad weather." Since the day was said to be excellent for flying, Hepburn Walker, himself a leading rigger and flight crew captain in wartime pressure airships, suggests the cancellation arose from a naval superstition against last flights. At 0815 on 30 June, Captain

Shoemaker read the orders of the chief of naval operations of 13 May 1932, directing that the USS *Los Angeles* be decommissioned not later than 30 June 1932, and be docked in the shed in the custody of the commanding officer, NAS Lakehurst. She was to be maintained in such a state as to be capable of recommissioning on 30 days' notice with minimum expenditure of funds and effort. The ship was hung up in the shed close to one end, so that pressure airships could be housed at the other end. Gas cells remained 15% inflated so that the ship could be completely suspended from the roof, and the floor underneath be entirely clear. Commander Berry was detached and ordered to duty as executive officer of NAS Lakehurst; Commander McCord was ordered to the USS *Akron* for duty under instruction as prospective commanding officer.

Though Rosendahl and other Lakehurst personnel hoped to see the *Los Angeles* recommissioned and flying once more, this did not happen, even after her shed mate, the *Akron*, went down at sea on 4 April 1933. Secretary of the Navy Claude Swanson, however, on 23 February 1934 authorized use of the *Los Angeles* for experimental work to as great an extent as possible in a non-flight status. BuAer solicited suggestions for such a program from Commander Dresel (C.O. of the *Macon*), Dr. Eckener, the Guggenheim Airship Institute in Akron, the Goodyear-Zeppelin Corporation, the National Advisory Committee for Aeronautics, the Metalclad Airship Corporation of Detroit, Lakehurst personnel, and so on. Rosendahl drew up a 25-page memorandum for experimental

Lakehurst in the summer of 1936. The *Hindenburg* on the mooring-out circle on the west field; the *Los Angeles*, decommissioned and with a blue band around her nose, moored out semipermanently on a new circle in the distance.

projects for the ship in flying status; moored outside the hangar; inflated and inside the hangar; and deflated and inside the hangar. The chief of BuAer, now Rear Admiral Ernest J. King, urged Admiral William H. Standley, the chief of naval operations, to consider operating the *Los Angeles* in flight for experimental purposes; but in the end Standley merely authorized experimental activity short of flying. This included inflation and mooring-out over extended periods.

As commanding officer of NAS Lakehurst, Rosendahl pushed through the appropriations needed to recondition the *Los Angeles* for mooring-out. The original railroad mast, completed in 1931 for the *Akron*, was cut down to a height suitable for the old ship, and all her subsequent dockings, undockings, and mooring-out operations involved the use of this mast. Further, preventer wiring had to be provided to hold the ship to the mast in case the mooring cone and cup failed. It was no secret at Lakehurst that Rosendahl would have been glad of an excuse to fly the *Los Angeles* once more, and with the aim of keep-

ing the tests as realistic as possible, he obtained $1,000 to purchase 18,000 lb. of fuel, oil, and antifreeze for the ballast system. By early 1935 a total of $35,396.13 had been expended on readying the *Los Angeles* for her new role, including helium charges.

Fully inflated at last with helium, and with fuel and ballast on board, the *Los Angeles*, on 18 December 1934, was undocked for the first time in two and a half years for a test of mooring equipment, and returned to her hangar six hours later. On 9 March 1935, she was undocked and moored at the mooring-out circle on the southwestern side of the field. "She will be manned and equipped for flight at all times, but she is to be flown only in the event of an emergency." Rosendahl's wish was not to be granted, for on every occasion when severe weather conditions threatened, she was hangared in good time and never had to take to the air to prevent destruction at the mast. Over the next few years, the *Los Angeles* was moored out for weeks, even months; and she was often seen in the background when her more glamorous new sister, the palatial *Hindenburg*, visited Lakehurst during 1936. A variety of experimental programs were carried out: A large oil-fired heater was used in an attempt to melt snow on top of the ship, and when this failed to do the job, brushes and sweeps were used. At one time the forward third of the silvery hull was painted sky blue in a camouflage experiment. On 13 March 1935, the old ship tried to fly by herself: a gust picked up the stern together with the weigh-off platform, stern riding car, and a section of the circular track. Preventer lines broke, with some damage to the hull structure, and the stern was free; but she was brought under control with minor damage to the after car from its being dragged over the ground. The last docking recorded in the archives (which are not complete—as she was no longer a commissioned ship of the U.S. Navy, no log book was kept) was on 18 November 1937.

There was still talk of recommissioning and flying the *Los Angeles*, as the rigid airship cause in the Navy was not entirely dead even after the loss of the *Macon* on 12 February 1935. A Board of Inspection and Survey, made up of Rear Admiral H. L. Brinser, Commander Garland Fulton, and Lcdr. R. E. Jennings, examined the old ship, and concluded that a major overhaul could put the *Los Angeles* in condition for limited service primarily as a training airship.

Whether or not the overhaul is warranted depends not alone on material questions but also on matters of policy with reference to the future of airships of this class. In view of the age of the *Los Angeles* and the short life to be expected from a rigid airship of obsolescent design and in view of the high costs involved, amounting to perhaps 20 per cent of the cost of a new airship, the Board considers such an extensive overhaul as herein outlined should not be undertaken. If the *Los Angeles* is not to be recommissioned, it is recommended that she be made available for such tests not involving flights as may be prescribed by the Bureau of Aeronautics and that upon completion of such tests, the airship and unusable parts thereof be scrapped.[22]

One consideration influencing the board was that a replacement airship—designated ZRN, 650 feet long with a volume of 3,000,000 cubic feet and able to carry three airplanes—had been authorized in 1938. In the end ZRN was not proceeded with, because of the direct opposition of President Roosevelt.[23]

The chief of naval operations, now Admiral Harold R. Stark, forwarded the report to Secretary Charles Edison on 25 September 1939, with the recommendation that the *Los Angeles* be scrapped. She was stricken from the Navy List on 24 October, but apparently work had been started earlier, as by 27 October about 40% of the outer cover had been removed and her gas cells deflated to 50% fullness. A few structural tests were performed on 4 and 5 December, which involved inflating Cell #7 with air until major failure occurred, and loading the horizontal fins at Frame 15 with about 8,000 lb. applied in 2,000-lb. increments while Cell #1 was inflated until failure occurred. Station personnel continued dismantling the hull framework, and this work was completed in 14 days with all scrap piled outside the hangar by 3 January 1940. A purchaser was found for the scrap duralumin, and it had all disappeared by the end of February. For years Admiral Rosendahl's study in nearby Toms River featured the portrait that Grace Coolidge, the *Los Angeles*'s sponsor at her christening on 25 November 1924, gave to the ship with her inscription, "Go forth under the open sky and may the winds of Heaven deal gently with thee."

Thus ended a career unique in the history of the rigid airship. The *Los Angeles* actually had the longest life of any rigid airship ever built—15 years, though only 8 were in flying status. She outlived most of her successors—R 100, R 101, the *Akron*, the *Macon*, and the *Hindenburg*. Only the *Graf Zeppelin* came close to matching her record, with a life of nearly 12 years, of which 9 were spent in flying status. And she nearly outlived the *Graf*, which together with the big LZ 130, named the *Graf Zeppelin II*, was broken up at Frankfurt am Main in the spring of 1940. Of the 161 rigid airships built and flown in the years 1900–40, two thirds—110—met violent ends, killing 748 flight crew members all told, 105 of them Americans.[24] Yet the *Los Angeles* never killed anyone. Her value to the U.S. Navy's rigid airship program was incalculable in terms of training personnel and developing such American innovations as water recovery, gelatin-latex gas cells, the stub mast and later the mobile mast with mooring-out circle, and the carriage and operation of hook-on airplanes with military capability. She was certainly seen by more people than any other American rigid. At a high political level, she even helped significantly to overcome anti-German feelings in the United States, a gain later nullified by Hitler's anti-Semitism and aggression. A thing of symmetry and beauty, she symbolized the romance and appeal of the rigid airship; and she lives on today in the memories of the men who served in her, and of those who saw her floating like a giant silvery fish in the sky.

12

Akron and *Macon*: The Long-Range Scouting Airship

The lessons learned from the crash of ZR 2, from the building and operation of the *Shenandoah* and the *Los Angeles*, and from the Zeppelin Company itself during the Era of Experimentation, were all to be embodied in an American design for a large rigid airship, inflated with helium, to carry out the U.S. Navy's requirement for long-range strategic reconnaissance in the far reaches of the Pacific Ocean. This was the goal for which Maxfield and Lansdowne had died with their men, and toward which Moffett, Fulton, Rosendahl, and many others had labored tirelessly and devotedly for many years.

As early as March 1924, Starr Truscott, in BuAer's Lighter Than Air Design Section, had put down on paper some ideas for a large scouting airship. The times were propitious: the *Shenandoah* was flying, with attendant favorable publicity; in Friedrichshafen ZR 3 was nearing completion, and the agreement between President Litchfield of Goodyear and Dr. Eckener of the *Luftschiffbau Zeppelin*, creating the Goodyear-Zeppelin Corporation, ensured the existence of an airship-building industry in the United States, with experienced German designers and engineers on its staff.[1] But as in other times and other countries, Trustcott was limited by one unalterable factor: the new ship would have to fit in the Lakehurst hangar, whose interior length and height were 804 and 193 feet respectively.

Tentatively labeled Design No. 60, Truscott's proposal was more of a concept than a detailed blueprint. The ship of course would be inflated with helium, and the volume initially was to be in the neighborhood of 5,000,000 cubic feet. Remarkably, considering that the operation of airplanes from airships was highly experimental, and the Army had just commenced using the tiny Sperry Messenger with its nonrigid airships, Design No. 60 was configured from the beginning to carry no fewer than three or more than six airplanes.[2] At this date it is impossible to determine whether the airplane-carrying feature was a pure inspiration on the part of Truscott, or whether he was influenced by other thinkers in the bureau. Moffett, and airship officers generally, took it for granted that the airship would not only make the initial contact with enemy surface forces, but would shadow them from a distance, as was done by the German Zeppelins in the North Sea in World War I. With float planes already going to sea on the catapults of cruisers and battleships, not to mention land-type single-seater fighters on board the Navy's first aircraft carrier, the *Langley*, it was clear that they would pose a threat to airships operating close to a fleet.

The news that the British government was sponsoring the construction of two 5,000,000-cubic-foot passenger airships (the later R 100 and R 101) caused Truscott to increase the volume of Design No. 60 to 6,000,000 cubic feet to obtain the same performance with helium. Length was to be 780 feet and diameter 122 feet. General design features followed Zeppelin practice with flat wire-braced main frames. Following the *Shenandoah* disaster in the fall of 1925, which demonstrated the violence of weather conditions in North America and the need for greater hull strength than heretofore anticipated, BuAer accepted the advice of Dr. Arnstein, the chief designer of the Goodyear-Zeppelin Corporation, that the so-called deep ring of triangular section would be much stronger than the conventional flat rings of Zeppelin design. Other recommendations made by Massachusetts Institute of Technology's warship design expert, Professor William Hovgaard, at the *Shenandoah* Court of Inquiry were embodied in the design:

1. A lower fineness ratio to increase the resistance of the hull structure to bending loads. This resulted in the diameter being increased to 135 feet, and the gas volume to 6,500,000 cubic feet when 95% inflated.
2. The control car built directly onto the keel structure.
3. Power plants to be enclosed within the hull structure, a practical arrangement in a helium ship.

That the Design No. 60 proposal led to the construction of the airships *Akron* and *Macon*, despite public and congressional opposition to rigid airships in the wake of the *Shenandoah* disaster, is a tribute to Admiral Moffett's extraordinary political sense, tact, skill, and ability in marshaling facts (with the able assistance of Commander Garland Fulton, now heading BuAer's Lighter Than Air Design Section) to win over the admirals on the General Board and the legislators on Capitol Hill. Moffett skilfully pleaded for the rigid airships:

> Their great radius of action, their high speed relative to surface vessels, their ability to hover, their ability to receive and transmit information promptly, and their general long-range scouting ability . . . . The rigid airship is primarily a scouting ship, the purpose of which is to travel long distances at high speed; carry observers who can see what is going on and report back by radio.[3]

BuAer's Five Year Plan, as passed by Congress in 1926, authorized the construction of two large rigid airships and an airship base on the West Coast.

BuAer expected that Goodyear-Zeppelin would receive the contract for the two large airships, but political considerations required that the Navy Department make the gesture of inviting competitive bids. The closing date was 16 May 1927, and 37 designs were submitted. Goodyear-Zeppelin offered three alternative designs and was the only firm that bid on construction. The other entries were amateurish or impractical—or, where they had some merit, their creators had no plant in which to build. But declaring Goodyear the winner with the offer to build both ships for $8,000,000 did not clear the way for a contract.

Congressional influence was brought to bear on behalf of the American Brown-Boveri Electric Company, part of a conglomerate assembled by the financial adventurer Lawrence Wilder and including the New York Shipbuilding Company of Camden, New Jersey. At a special hearing before the House Subcommittee on Appropriations, Wilder persuaded its

members that he could build airships more cheaply than Goodyear-Zeppelin: if New York Ship could fabricate surface vessels, it could readily construct rigid airships, while he seemed to believe that he could persuade the creator of the modern rigid airship, Professor Johann Schütte, to be his designer. Under pressure from Congress, Secretary of the Navy Curtis Wilbur was persuaded to schedule a second design competition with a deadline of 28 July 1928.

This time there were nine entries, but only three deserved serious consideration: Goodyear-Zeppelin's, again with three different proposals for ships of 6,500,000 cubic feet which differed from the 1927 entries; Brown-Boveri; and Schütte and Company of Mannheim, Germany. Clearly the old master had rebuffed the agents of Brown-Boveri, who had then proceeded as best they could to appropriate whatever Schütte-Lanz information they could get their hands on. In turn, Schütte, who had no facility in which to construct a large rigid airship, had entered the competition to expose Brown-Boveri. While the Brown-Boveri design presented Schütte-type triangular duralumin girders,[4] it lacked supporting calculations and stressing data, and performance claims were rated overly optimistic. The Schütte design was advanced and sophisticated, but the company no longer had a building hangar. The Goodyear Project I won the bureau's favor, and with some modifications became the design of the ZRS 4 *Akron* and ZRS 5 *Macon*. On 6 October 1928, Goodyear and naval representatives signed a contract whereby the Akron, Ohio company would build two airships for the sum of $5,375,000 for the first one and $2,450,000 for the second. The elaborate charade of "competition" put on at Congress's bidding had delayed by two years the start of construction.

While the final design of the two airships was being elaborated, Goodyear commenced work on the building shed at Akron. In contrast to the Lakehurst hangar, whose flat doors, moving laterally away from the centerline, created turbulence at the shed entrance, the Akron "air dock," streamlined in shape, had "orange peel" doors which rotated back nearly flush with the walls as they opened. The Akron shed measured 1,175 feet long, 325 feet wide, and 197 feet 6 inches high. The first arch was erected on 21 May 1929, and the hangar was essentially completed on 7 November of that year when construction of ZRS 4 officially began.

The design of ZRS 4 and 5, as evolved by Dr. Karl Arnstein in cooperation with the Navy Department, closely followed the winning Project I of the 1928 competition. The streamlined hull was 785 feet long and 132.9 feet in diameter, with a nominal gas volume of 6,500,000 cubic feet when 95% inflated. There were many innovations, representing significant departures from conventional Zeppelin practice, which Dr. Arnstein and the Bureau of Aeronautics regarded as improvements. The hull was based on 36 longitudinal girders, and of the 12 main frames, 10 were the stiff triangular section "deep" rings spaced 22.5 meters (74 feet) apart instead of 15 meters as in the German craft. Because of the increased main frame spacing, there were three intermediate frames between each main one instead of two. Instead of a single inverted-V-section keel at the bottom of the hull, there was one at the top of the ship, and two others port and starboard in the lower hull. These added extra strength to the framework, particularly in the way of the internal airplane hangar on the centerline abaft the control car. Also, the lateral keels housed the eight engines, four to a side, in their after portions. This improved streamlining compared to the external engine gondolas of the hydrogen ships. The power plants were the familiar Maybach VL-2s of 560 h.p. Each engine drove a propeller that was mounted on an external bracket, and could be rotated to provide thrust in four directions, considering that the Maybachs were reversible. Extending up the hull above each engine room, and prominently visible from a distance, were five water recovery condensers, one above the other, and flush with the hull. There were 12 gas cells of cotton fabric gas-proofed with gelatin latex in place of the traditional goldbeater's skin.[5] The control car forward was divided into three sections—the control room surrounded by windows, the chart room amidships, and a room at the rear which usually served as a smoking room. Duplicate elevator and rudder controls were fitted behind windows at the leading edge of the lower fin. There were emplacements for eight .30-caliber machine guns: three along the ship's back in the upper keel; one in the extreme tail; two in the windows of the auxiliary control position; and two in the after room of the control car.

In two respects the final ZRS 4 and 5 design differed significantly from the Project I of the 1928 design competition. The fins of Project I were long and narrow in depth, extending over 115 feet of the ship's length and firmly anchored to main frames 0, 17.5, and 35. Certain airship operators, however, objected that the lower fin was not visible from the control car, visibility being considered desirable as the lower fin made contact with the ground aft. In a revision designed to meet this objection, the fins were shortened and deepened. They were now attached only to main frames 0 and 17.5, and extended forward only to intermediate frame 28.75. At the same time the control car floor was lowered 11 inches, and the car moved aft 8 feet. In later years, especially after the loss of the ZRS 5 *Macon*, which originated in a structural failure of the upper fin, much was made of

these changes—particularly by German designers who further argued that the casualty had resulted from omission of the heavy cruciform structure that in the Zeppelins ran right through the ship from one fin to the other. Actually the deep frames in ZRS 4 and 5 should have been able to handle the aerodynamic loads imposed by the bolted-on fins; but later events would demonstrate that the deep frames were underdesigned for the loads involved. Further, the Zeppelin Company, guided by operational experience, designed the upper fin of the *Hindenburg* for a 40% higher aerodynamic load than that assumed for the ZRS 4 upper fin, based on wind tunnel observations.

Construction of ZRS 4 commenced officially on 7 November 1929, when Admiral Moffett, before 30,000 spectators, drove a golden rivet into the first main frame to be erected in the hangar. Further frames were built on the hangar floor, hoisted upright, and connected by longitudinal girders; the internal engine rooms were completed, power plants and propeller outriggers installed, the control car and fins attached, and the cotton outer cover applied and coated with aluminum dope to reflect the heat of the sun's rays.[6] On 5 August 1931, ZRS 4 was far enough completed to be christened the *Akron* by Lou Henry Hoover, the wife of the president. Half a million visitors crowded into the city for the event, lending a carnival-like atmosphere to Akron's moment of civic pride, and the ceremony was well covered by the media—that is, radio and the newspapers.

But not all the publicity was favorable; and with the passage of time, it became clear that a number of influential journals (particularly the *New York Sun*) had a consistent bias against the big airship, blowing up every mishap to catastrophic proportions. Even before her completion there were shrill cries of "sabotage" and "Communist conspiracy" deriving from the charges of publicity-seeking workmen on the ship. Denials by naval inspectors never caught up with the sensational allegations. Then, before the first flight, the newspapers made much of the fact that the *Akron* would be 22,282 lb. overweight compared to the 1928 design specifications. This was a small figure compared to her gross lift 95% inflated with helium of 403,000 lb., useful lift of 159,291 lb., and fixed weights of 243,709 lb. Furthermore, 3,532 lb. of the excess weight represented Navy-authorized alterations. The *Akron* was not the first prototype rigid airship—or aircraft, for that matter—to come out overweight compared to design estimates, but to the newspapers this was evidence of gross negligence and culpability.

Not until 23 September 1931 did the *Akron* emerge from the huge hangar for her first flight. Lieutenant Commander Charles E. Rosendahl, America's most experienced rigid airship officer, was in command,

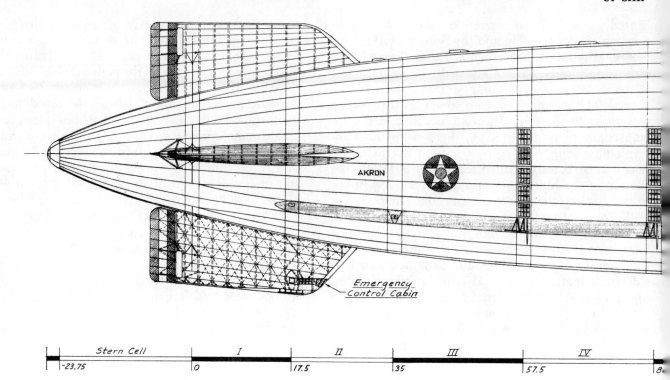

Emergency
Control Cabin

Stern Cell	I	II	III	IV
-23.75	0	17.5	35	57.5

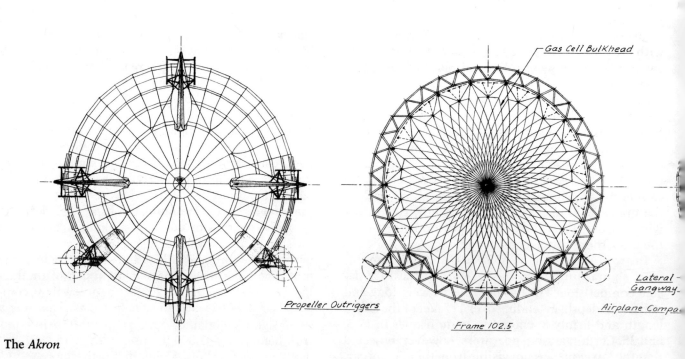

Gas Cell Bulkhead

Propeller Outriggers

Lateral
Gangway

Airplane Compa.

Frame 102.5

The *Akron*

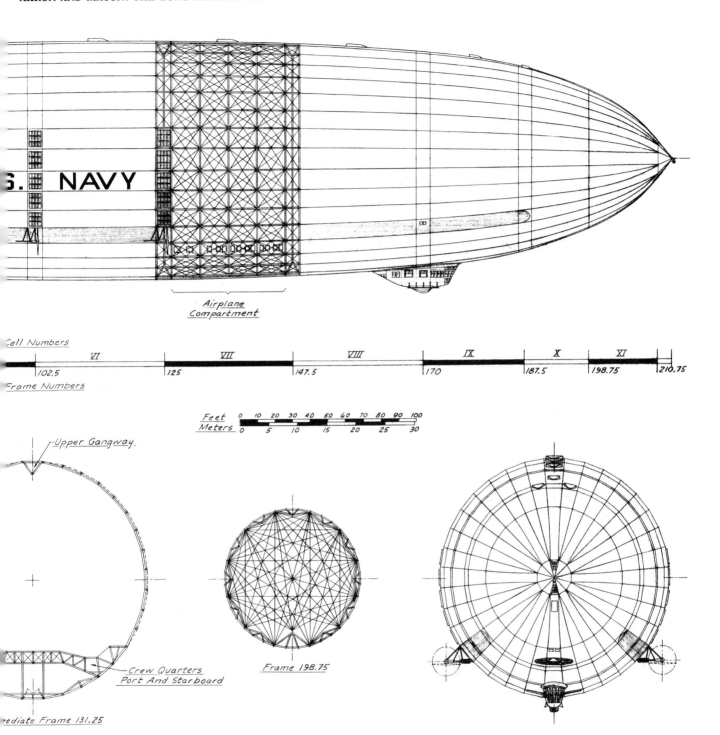

Airplane
Compartment

Cell Numbers

VI　　　VII　　　VIII　　　IX　　　X　　　XI

102.5　　　125　　　147.5　　　170　　　187.5　　　198.75　　　210.75

Frame Numbers

Feet　0　10　20　30　40　50　60　70　80　90　100
Meters　0　5　10　15　20　25　30

Upper Gangway

Crew Quarters
Port And Starboard

Frame 198.75

ediate Frame 131.25

William F. Kerka

and Goodyear-Zeppelin's and the Navy's faith in the giant ship was demonstrated by the list of distinguished passengers: Secretary of the Navy Charles Francis Adams; Assistant Secretary of the Navy for Aeronautics David S. Ingalls; Chief of the Bureau of Aeronautics Rear Admiral Moffett; the ten-member Navy Board of Inspection and Survey; President Litchfield and other Goodyear-Zeppelin officials; and Garland Fulton, Dr. Arnstein, Charles P. Burgess, and Ralph Weyerbacher. Altogether 113 persons were on board. Nine more trial flights followed, including the delivery flight to Lakehurst on 21–22 October. On her trials the Akron fell 3 knots short of her contract full speed of 72 knots, and the press again made much of her "failure." On 27 October 1931, the Akron was placed in commission at Lakehurst.

In the Akron the Navy at last had a large rigid airship specifically designed for fleet operations; and with little appreciation that she was merely a prototype for a fleet of ten such large rigids contemplated under U.S. naval war plans, an ambitious schedule of exercises had been planned to test her capabilities with the fleet. Undoubtedly the imposing mass and awesome presence of the 785-foot sky giant overly impressed surface admirals with an exaggerated estimate of the big ship's long-range capabilities; but she was not materially ready for cooperation with the fleet when first commissioned, and her personnel were creating doctrine and procedure as they went along. Furthermore, the first commanding officer lacked a clear comprehension of the urgent necessity to prove this expensive novelty to the fleet, and himself appeared fascinated with flying and showing off to the public the biggest airship in the world.

The chief material deficiency was in the heavier-than-air unit, whose role in executing the scouting mission seemed increasingly important, given the number of aircraft going to sea with the fleet. The vital trapeze, to which the hook-on aircraft would land and which would hoist them into the hangar and out again, was not ready to install when the Akron arrived in Lakehurst—an indication in itself of the lack of urgency in proving the ship's usefulness to the Navy, and the failure to have anyone in authority force her material readiness for operations at the earliest possible date. (Fulton attempted to hurry matters along, but he was only a commander in the Construction Corps, and Moffett was still enamored of publicity schemes.) The trapeze was still on board the Los Angeles when the Akron arrived at Lakehurst. It required modification to fit the larger ship, but not until December 1931 was it shipped to the Naval Aircraft Factory. On 7 February 1932 the trapeze was returned to Lakehurst, where day-and-night working schedules were instituted to get it installed. In any

case the hook-on aircraft unit was not ready either: its six Curtiss F9C-2 "Sparrowhawk" aircraft were only ordered on 14 October 1931, and not until 29 June 1932 did the first article arrive at Lakehurst. The remaining five aircraft were not delivered until September 1932. (The prototype Curtiss XF9C-1 fighter was at Lakehurst with a hook, while the Consolidated N2Y hook-on aircraft were available for training, but were of course useless for military purposes.) Harrigan and Young, the original hook-on pilots who had practiced with the Los Angeles, were still at Lakehurst, but the additional four officers needed to fill out the complement of the hook-on unit did not arrive until June and July.[7]

The Akron made some flights before the end of the year with journalists on board in a vain attempt by Admiral Moffett to obtain a more favorable press for the airship, and there had been a 46-hour endurance test flight to Mobile, Alabama, with return to Lakehurst via the Mississippi and Ohio valleys. In January she was scheduled to exercise with the cruisers and destroyers of the Scouting Force off the Georgia coast.

Deteriorating weather did not prevent Rosendahl from departing Lakehurst on the afternoon of 9 January to carry out his orders from Vice Admiral Arthur L. Willard, commanding the Scouting Force, to be off Cape Lookout, North Carolina at daylight the following morning and to search for a squadron of destroyers en route from Charleston to Guantanamo Bay, Cuba. Warned of a storm over Cape Hatteras, Rosendahl planned to proceed via Philadelphia, Richmond, and Baltimore to stay to the west of the storm center and to use its counterclockwise circulation to speed him on his way. Between Baltimore and Richmond blinding snow enveloped the big ship, and ice built up on her hull and horizontal fins to a depth of six inches in some places. It was calculated from the Akron's static condition that she was carrying over eight tons of ice through dynamic lift, but the added load did not affect her operation. During the following morning as she flew over the warm Gulf Stream, loosened chunks of ice kept falling off the hull.

With no airplanes on board, the Akron attempted to locate Scouting Force units by World War I methods. At 1240 strong radio signals from an "enemy" destroyer were heard close by; but the Akron had not yet been equipped with a radio direction finder, and the surface craft were not seen. Two of the destroyers, however, sighted the Akron ten miles away to the northwest. The airship did better on the morning of the 11th, sighting and identifying the light cruiser Raleigh and 12 destroyers. Admiral Willard felt that the Akron's performance had been promising, though her failure to sight the destroyers on the 10th was a black mark. If only she had had her full complement of aircraft, radio direction finder, and so forth!

The exercise in the Atlantic with the Scouting Force had been the preliminary bout; the main event was to be the 1932 Fleet Problem XIII in the Pacific. As early as October 1931, at the time when the *Akron* was delivered to Lakehurst, the chief of naval operations, Admiral William V. Pratt, had planned to send the big ship to the West Coast. She was to arrive there in January, thence proceed to Hawaii where she would operate from the mast at Ewa; and during February and March she would participate in Grand Joint Exercise No. 4, Fleet Problem XIII, and tactical exercises during the fleet concentration on the West Coast. It was 1924 all over again, when the commander in chief of the United States Fleet wanted the *Shenandoah* to operate for three and a half months in the Hawaiian Islands! No consideration whatever was given to logistics, and there was still no airship hangar on the West Coast.

Only in the spring of 1929 did a board of officers, headed by Admiral Moffett, inspect a number of sites for the West Coast airship station authorized in the Five Year Plan. Despite the insistent claims of fleet personnel for Camp Kearney near the fleet base at San Diego, the board had chosen Sunnyvale, about 30 miles south of San Francisco and more than 350 miles from the fleet's exercise area. Here was built a large shed with orange peel doors and streamlined shape resembling that at Akron, measuring 1,133 feet long, 308 feet wide, and 198 feet high. Not until March 1933 was the huge building completed, and Naval Air Station, Sunnyvale, Mountain View, California, was commissioned on 12 April 1933. Later, after Moffett's death in the *Akron*, the airship base was renamed Moffett Field.

The *Akron* personnel intended to participate in the fleet problem in March; the trapeze was installed on 7 February, and the prototype XF9C-1 fighter would have been carried, along with one or two of the N2Y utility craft. Sunnyvale, of course, was far from ready, and the *Akron* would have operated from the expeditionary masts at Camp Kearney, Sunnyvale, and Ewa. Had the *Akron* appeared at the exercises, the fleet might have been favorably impressed; but a fateful event on 22 February 1932 prevented her participation. While she was being brought out of the Lakehurst hangar that morning in a 6- to 14-knot cross wind, the tail tore loose from the stern beam. As the runaway airship, still attached to the railroad mast, weathervaned with the wind, the lower fin smashed repeatedly on the ground. Had it not been for the sturdy hull structure, more than the fin could

have been shattered. Embarrassingly, the accident was witnessed by four members of the House Committee on Naval Affairs, invited by Moffett to make the flight. Two of them, hostile toward the airship, felt justified in loudly and publicly proclaiming her deficiencies.

For two months the *Akron* was under repair at Lakehurst, not to fly again until 28 April. On 3 May, for the first time, Harrigan and Young made landings on the *Akron*'s trapeze, first with the N2Ys and later with the XF9C-1.

The *Akron* thus missed Fleet Problem XIII, the main feature of which, for the first time (but not the last), was an attack on Pearl Harbor by the squadrons of the carriers *Lexington* and *Saratoga* from northwest of Oahu. Could the *Akron*, scouting from Hawaii, have located the carriers and given warning of the attack? Considering her general state of readiness this would have been improbable, but success would have engendered a new respect for the rigid airship in the fleet.

The Navy Department was determined that the *Akron* should fly to the West Coast, even though the fleet problem was over. The Scouting Force, which had come through the Panama Canal, was still in the San Diego area, and she could exercise with its units. Furthermore, a successful transcontinental cruise would impress the taxpayers. Thus on the morning of 8 May the *Akron* was off for Camp Kearney, with Harrigan and Young hooking on with the XF9C-1 and one of the N2Ys after the ship was airborne. Rough weather, and at times fog, in the passes of West Texas, New Mexico, and Arizona duplicated the problems of the *Shenandoah* eight years earlier on the West Coast flight. Three days later, at 0800 on 11 May, the *Akron* was over the mast at Camp Kearney; but between a fog and the clumsiness of the inexperienced ground crew, it was 1131 before the airship's mooring cable was connected to the mast cable. Meanwhile, however, the hot sun had been expanding the helium and increasing the ship's lift; the tail rose, the engines shut down because fuel would not flow uphill, and five tons of water spilled accidentally from emergency bags in the stern. The mooring cable had to be cut, and the ship ballooned upward to 1,000 feet—carrying three men of the ground crew. Two of them lost their holds and fell to their deaths—as newsreel cameras captured the horrifying event. The third lashed himself to the lines and was hauled inboard an hour later. Not until 1900 did the *Akron* successfully moor to the Camp Kearney mast.

Rosendahl had valved a large amount of helium trying to save the lives of the men on the lines, and now the ship was heavy, with her lift sharply reduced. He could not possibly carry out his orders to

The *Akron* over the Golden Gate, San Francisco, with an N2Y aircraft on the trapeze. May 1932. (U.S. Navy)

join the Scouting Force as soon as possible; there was no helium at Camp Kearney, and to replace it, he had to proceed up the coast to the unfinished base at Sunnyvale. Once there, Rosendahl was in no hurry to get back to San Diego; flying from a stub mast, the *Akron* made "hand-waving" flights into the San Joaquin and Sacramento valleys, moored to the *Patoka* in San Francisco Bay, and showed herself to the citizens of the Northwest in a flight to Bellingham, Washington. Not until 1 June did she come south from Sunnyvale to participate in the Scouting Force exercises, leaving her planes behind.

Entering the exercise area near Guadalupe Island on the morning of 2 June, the *Akron* soon found a number of enemy cruisers, which sent off seaplanes from their catapults to attack. A similar encounter took place on the following day, a total of 13 aircraft taking off to attack the airship. The pilots flying the O2U seaplanes felt she could easily have been destroyed with bombs and machine gun fire, overlooking the fact that the *Akron* was inflated with nonflammable helium. The reaction of the surface admirals was mixed; clearly during a fleet action she stood a good chance of being destroyed, but in long-range reconnaissance westward from Hawaii she could give the commander in chief valuable information, both negative and positive.

The chief of naval operations wanted the *Akron* to stay on the coast into the summer, and then proceed east with the Scouting Force; but Rosendahl's concern for the mounting mechanical deficiencies of the ship led him to insist on returning to Lakehurst and the security of its hangar. The flight east over the mountains was difficult, and the *Akron* was four and a half days en route, including a layover at the expeditionary mast at Parris Island, South Carolina. Her crew were proud of their success in operating away from her hangar for five weeks; yet the fleet had not been impressed—but had in fact developed a conviction of the rigid airship's "vulnerability," and noted that she had participated in the maneuvers for only 2 out of the 38 days she had been away from Lakehurst.

On 22 June 1932, Commander Alger Dresel relieved Rosendahl as commanding officer, so that he could take an obligatory tour of sea duty to qualify for promotion. Dresel had volunteered for airship training in 1929, had flown on board the *Los Angeles* for a year, and had commanded her in 1931–32. He had made the *Akron*'s West Coast flight as an observer. Not only did he resist demands from Washington for "hand-waving" flights inland; unlike the previous commander, he saw the need to use the hook-on aircraft for scouting, while the *Akron* remained in the background. In developing a doctrine for the tactical employment of the hook-on fighters, the senior naval aviator of the HTA unit, Lt. D. Ward Harrigan, played a significant role. In a report prepared in December 1932, he emphasized the need for better radio communications; a "flight control officer" in the airship who would maintain a plot of the fighters' positions when out of visual contact; removal of the airplanes' landing gear (superfluous in hook-on operations) and its replacement with a long-range fuel tank; and a combination parachute and inflatable dinghy harness. Further, Harrigan urged the development of radio homing equipment, and wanted the aircraft carried outside the ship on individual "perches" in the combat zone, so they could all be released simultaneously instead of one by one through the hangar door—a slow procedure.

During the fall of 1932 the HTA unit "shaped up" in frequent local flights by the *Akron* from Lakehurst, a handicap being that because of obstructing girders in the hangar, only three of the "Sparrowhawks" could be carried (in the later *Macon* the girders were hinged, so that she could carry five aircraft). A scouting procedure devised by Lieutenant Donald M. Mackey, the "60–60" method, enabled the *Akron* to sweep a path 100 miles wide: With the airship advancing straight ahead at 50 knots, and the aircraft able to make 100 knots, a "Sparrowhawk" on either beam, heading out and back at a 60-degree angle to the airship's course, would always bear 90 degrees relative to the airship and would find her on each inboard leg. Later, with sophisticated voice radio and a reliable homing device, the little fighters covered a path 200 miles wide through the "60–60" method, each aircraft patrolling for five hours with a long-range auxiliary tank.

Dresel, already designated prospective commanding officer of the *Macon*, was relieved on 3 January 1933 by Commander Frank McCord, an experienced airship officer who had served at Lakehurst and had flown in the *Los Angeles* in 1925–27. Thereafter he had served for two years in the carriers *Langley* and *Saratoga*, then late in 1929 had returned to Lakehurst. Before taking command of the *Akron*, he had been the *Los Angeles*'s executive officer. Not absorbed in the airship as an end in itself, McCord, with his experience in the carriers, did not need to be told that he must sell the rigid airship to the fleet.

McCord set a fast pace. Immediately after the change-of-command ceremony, he set off for Florida. Based on the mast at Opa-Locka, the *Akron* proceeded to Cuba, sending Garland Fulton and three other officers down separately in an N2Y to inspect the Guantanamo area for a mooring site. In March there was a flight to Panama via Opa-Locka which kept the *Akron* away from Lakehurst for ten days. McCord also impressed everyone with his competence in handling the *Akron* when an East Coast storm with 30-knot gusts prevented her from landing at Lakehurst after a 43-hour flight. Taking a northerly course up the Hudson Valley, McCord then proceeded west over Lake Ontario and Lake Erie to get behind the storm. From Cleveland he headed east, following behind as the disturbance moved out to sea. In clearing weather, the *Akron* landed at Lakehurst at sunset after a flight of nearly 72 hours.

Yet it was in a storm that the *Akron* met her end three months later. During the day of 3 April 1933, in lowering weather, the big ship was prepared for a two- or three-day cruise along the New England coast to calibrate radio direction finding stations. Admiral Moffett came up from Washington to fly in the *Akron* as he had often done, and there were 76 people on board when the airship took off in fog at 1928 hours. Because of the fog, McCord ordered Trapnell, who was to fly one of the N2Ys on board, to stay on the ground. Though the fog extended from 300 to 1,500 feet, there was no suspicion or warning of really bad weather. In fact, a cold front accompanied by severe disturbances was approaching rapidly from the west with a thunderstorm developing over Washington and moving to the northeast.

Flying westward at first to reach Philadelphia, the *Akron* then followed the Delaware River south toward Wilmington. Here lightning flashes were seen to the south. The executive officer, Lcdr. Herbert V. Wiley, recommended flying west to get behind the storm in the "safe semicircle," but McCord had seen lightning to the west. As lightning filled the southern sky, the *Akron* steered east, and then northeast. The ship increased her altitude to 1,600 feet to stay above the top of the fog. At 2200 she went out to sea on a heading of 83° true. McCord assumed he had made his departure from Asbury Park; actually a head wind had held him back, and the *Akron* probably went out to sea at Bay Head, 11 miles south. To add to McCord's troubles, static prevented reception of one-third of the 2200 weather map, though Wiley saw a low-pressure area centered over Washington.

McCord told Wiley at this point that he intended to ride out the storm at sea, passing ahead of it as it tracked northeast; but instead the lightning became ever more vivid on all sides of the ship. At 2300 McCord reversed course to 280°, nearly due west, and an hour later lights seen below were taken to be at Asbury Park. In fact, the *Akron* was now over Barnegat Inlet, some 45 miles to the south, being seen at this time by the personnel of the Coast Guard station there as she once more headed out to sea on a course of 120°. Wiley later suggested that McCord, believing himself to be more to the north than he was, might have feared a collision with New York skyscrapers in low visibility; but more likely he believed that on the southeast course he could get behind the storm center which he believed to be moving off to the northeast.

Lightning flashes continued to fill the sky, and rain fell heavily. At 0015 the elevator man reported the ship falling rapidly. Ballast was released, the *Akron* leveled off at 700 feet, and she began to rise rapidly. A few minutes later the air became very turbulent, and again the ship was reported falling. Engine telegraphs signaled full power, and the elevators were put up to raise the nose and cause the ship to climb. The *Akron* assumed an up angle of 20 to 25 degrees. Suddenly, with 800 feet on the altimeter, there was a severe shock, like a violent gust, and the lower rudder controls carried away. Only later did Wiley realize that the shock was not a gust, but must have been caused by the lower fin and rudder striking the sea. "I was waiting for the shock of the stern hitting the water, but it never came." At 300 feet by the altimeter, personnel in the control car sighted the surface of the water, and a few moments later the USS *Akron* was down in the sea, with water pouring through her control car windows. Partly due to the lack of lifesaving equipment, partly due to the coldness of the water, the loss of life was heavy—73 dying, including Admiral Moffett and Commander McCord, while only three were saved—Wiley, the executive officer; Moody Erwin, Aviation Metalsmith 2nd Class; and Richard E. Deal, Boatswain's Mate 2nd Class.

Owing to the small number of survivors, it was difficult to determine what had caused the disaster. McCord was censured by the Court of Inquiry for "having committed an error of judgment in not setting such courses as would have kept him in the safe semicircle (to the west) of the storm, thereby avoiding the severe conditions finally encountered." Yet the low-pressure disturbance moving northeast from Washington that the *Akron* was fighting when she met her end was merely one of many along a massive cold front rapidly advancing from the west and extending up and down the entire Atlantic seaboard. McCord would have felt its unpredicted violence no matter which way he turned, though if he had gone inland the loss of life would have been small. But the storm did not directly cause the *Akron*'s destruction; and in spite of the fact that Erwin and Deal, inside the hull, saw numerous girders breaking, these structural failures occurred *after* her tail slammed into the ocean. The plain fact is that at the bottom of the last descent, the ship did not have enough "sea room" to recover, and raising the elevators to make the ship climb instead forced the lower fin into the sea. This was confirmed when divers found the lower fin on the ocean floor at a distance from the wreckage, although apparently it was still tenuously attached to the hull when the wreck sank in 105 feet of water about 30 miles due east of Little Egg Inlet. The lower rudder never was found, and obviously tore off at the moment of impact with the water.

The storm further played an indirect role through causing a false reading on the altimeter. Admiral Rosendahl suggested that in the center of the low pressure area into which the airship was flying, the barometer could have stood 0.32 inch lower than at Lakehurst, causing the altimeter to read at least 320 feet too high, and possibly even 600 feet too high. "Never was a 'non-barometric' altimeter more desperately needed than during the *Akron*'s last journey."[8]

ZRS 5, named for the city of Macon, Georgia by Jeanette Beverly Moffett, Admiral Moffett's wife, on 11 March 1933, was a sister ship of the ZRS 4 *Akron*. Naturally there were improvements reflecting experience with the prototype. In particular, better streamlining of radiators and outriggers, and efficient three-bladed metal ground adjustable propellers enabled the *Macon* to attain a maximum speed of 75.6 knots compared to 69 knots in the *Akron*. Through refinements in structure and fittings her weight empty was 8,000 lb. less than that of the *Akron*, with a corresponding increase in useful load. At the same time, she might *not* have been a sister to the *Akron*, but bigger through the insertion of an added 22.5-meter bay amidships. This would have made her the largest airship ever built, with a gas volume of 7,430,000 cubic feet, and an overall length of 859 feet, too long for the Lakehurst shed, but not for Sunnyvale. Performance would have been improved,

the range at 50 knots, for instance, being increased by 25% to 11,500 miles. But the chief of naval operations did not want to ask Congress for the additional funds.

With Alger Dresel in command, and 105 persons on board, the *Macon* made her first flight on 21 April 1933. Three more test flights followed; then on 23 June she was placed in commission at Akron by Rear Admiral Ernest J. King, Moffett's successor as chief of the Bureau of Aeronautics. A few hours later, with King on board, the *Macon* was on her way to Lakehurst.

Having graduated from Annapolis 11 years behind Moffett, and having entered aviation only in 1927, King had different ideas about the purpose and usefulness of the rigid airship. By his own admission, "he had had little direct contact with dirigibles or enthusiasm for them. Nevertheless he was unwilling ever to dismiss a potential weapon summarily, without thorough investigation."[9] During his three years as chief of the Bureau of Aeronautics, King pressed senior officers in the Fleet for "a square deal all round for the *Macon*,"[10] but his pleas were not heeded, and no long-range strategic scouting missions were arranged for her in fleet exercises.

Further trials at Lakehurst included training four of the heavier-than-air-unit pilots in landing the F9C-2s on board the airship (none of the little fighters had been on board the *Akron* at the time of her loss). Then at the end of August she was formally accepted by the Navy. With the United States Fleet on the West Coast, there was no purpose in keeping the *Macon* at Lakehurst, and on 12 October 1933, she departed for Sunnyvale, never to return. She was the last rigid airship of the U.S. Navy to fly from the East Coast base.

Dresel experienced the usual troubles in West Texas, New Mexico, and Arizona. Going through Dos Cabezos Pass between Willcox and Vail, Arizona, the *Macon* was forced up by the terrain to 6,000 feet, and because of loss of helium through the automatic valves, she was 15,000 lb. heavy—a load carried by flying dynamically at a nose-up angle of 2 degrees. On 15 October, after a flight time of 3 days 1 hour 17 minutes, the *Macon* moored to the traveling railroad mast at Sunnyvale and was moved into the hangar.

The *Macon* was on the West Coast for only one reason: As stated by the chief of naval operations, Admiral William F. Standley, to Admiral David F. Sellers, commander in chief of the U.S. Fleet, in July 1933 she was "to be employed to the fullest extent possible in fleet exercises, so that her military value could be determined."[11] Both senior officers were cool to the rigid airship, Sellers in particular exaggerating her shortcomings, while he showed no imagination or interest in setting strategic tasks for the *Macon*, which repeatedly was involved in tactical scouting in small areas. Predictably, she was usually "shot

The last word in mechanical ground handling equipment: the *Macon* being drawn out of the hangar at Moffett Field by the mobile railroad mast. The stern beam under the lower fin is not visible inside the hangar. (U.S. Navy)

down" by anti-aircraft fire or by carrier aircraft, enabling the airship's enemies to emphasize her "vulnerability."

In the first exercise in which the *Macon* participated, on 15–16 November, two F9C-2 fighters were on board, but they were not used with imagination, Dresel tending to make the initial contact with the airship and then continuing to shadow with her. In one case, one of her planes discovered the "enemy" advance force before the airship made contact. On the other hand, the *Macon* was shot down three times, twice by anti-aircraft fire and once by enemy fighters. Each time she was transformed into the "ZRS 6" or "ZRS 7" and continued to operate. The exercises showed the need to use the airplanes for scouting while the more vulnerable airship remained in the background.

In the next series of exercises on 3–5 January 1934, the *Macon* made a number of useful reports on the "enemy" fleet in a congested tactical situation, once reporting a convoy which was "wiped out" by an air strike from friendly carriers. On the other hand, she was criticized for "sheltering" over a friendly cruiser division to enjoy the protection of its anti-aircraft batteries against attack by enemy planes. On the last day of the exercise, the *Macon*'s two hook-on planes

were employed in a search pattern ahead of the airship in the "60–60" scheme. Twice the *Macon* was shot down, once by anti-aircraft fire and once by enemy fighters.

The airship participated only briefly in exercises on 20–21 February owing to bad weather, and was criticized by Admiral Sellers even though he admitted that "the weather was particularly unsuitable for all aircraft operations."[12] She made a bad impression by letting herself be "shot down" by the battleships *New York* and *Texas* when she approached them at close range in murky weather. Dresel, a conservative operator, was concerned about a threatening line squall, and for the safety of his ship he was heading for Sunnyvale even though he knew Sellers would hold it against the *Macon* that she was leaving the exercise.

In a similar crowded tactical situation near the California coast on 10 April, the *Macon* was "shot down" once by enemy cruisers, and again destroyed by a squadron of dive bombers. It was then time for her to proceed to the Caribbean, where the fleet was bound for maneuvers designed to test its ability to protect the Panama Canal against an attack by a European power. The *Macon* was to be based during the exercises at the expeditionary mast at Opa-Locka.

As usual, there was the high-altitude problem in crossing the Continental Divide. In fact, Dresel would have preferred the longer but lower-level route via the Isthmus of Tehuantepec, and the Mexican government had given permission; but Admiral Sellers decreed that the ship would proceed east by the usual route.

The result was near-disaster, the *Macon* in the process sustaining injuries that eventually proved fatal. She departed Sunnyvale on 20 April carrying 82,800 lb. of fuel and 17,100 lb. of water ballast. By early morning of the next day, over Willcox, Arizona, she was at 6,100 feet and had dropped 9,000 lb. of ballast and 7,000 lb. of fuel; yet owing to valving of helium as she went over pressure height, she was 20,200 lb. heavy. Worse was yet to come: In West Texas the heated air was unusually turbulent, with vertical gusts so violent that men in the catwalks had to hold on lest they be thrown off their feet. Yet with the ship still 15,000 lb. heavy, Dresel had to drive her at full speed on all engines to hold her in the air dynamically.[13] The combination of vertical gust loads and aerodynamic loads, increasing as the square of the speed, was too much: just after noon two diagonal girders broke and one buckled in main frame 17.5 port side, because of excessive loads on the port fin bolted to the frame at this point. Quick action by a senior chief petty officer led to the broken girders' being promptly reinforced before the damage spread farther. The ship proceeded into smoother air with six engines on standard speed, and by the evening of 22 April was at the Opa-Locka mast. Here for nine days the *Macon* remained while a Goodyear-Zeppelin repair party made more permanent repairs.

It was now realized that the structure at Frame 17.5 was weak relative to the severe loads that might be imposed on it by the fins when flying in heavy turbulence. At a later date, after wind tunnel studies and stress analyses by the Bureau of Aeronautics and the Goodyear-Zeppelin Corporation, it was decided to reinforce the main frame structure in the vicinity of all four fins. Unfortunately this work was not considered urgent and was to be "accomplished from time to time, as opportunity offers, at the discretion of the Commanding Officer,"[14] in order not to interfere with operating schedules.

In scouting with the fleet in the Caribbean, the *Macon* was handicapped by thunderstorms and poor visibility, and as usual found herself in a tactical situation with large numbers of ships in a relatively small area. Again it was demonstrated that the big airship could not approach to within visual range of a force containing a carrier without being "shot down" by the latter's massed fighter squadrons, and the two F9C-2s on board could not possibly defend her successfully, partly because they could only be launched

one by one from the hangar via the single trapeze. As a result, Dresel, acting on the suggestions of Lt. Mackey, the flight control officer, began experimenting with scouting methods that would keep the airship at a distance from the surface units. These included having two F9C-2s on station ahead, perhaps flying a "60–60" pattern across the airship's track; and for the first time, with the *Macon* using radio and other intelligence, actually controlling the distances and directions flown by the fighters through the use of voice radio. Obviously the latter method would increase the flexibility and effectiveness of the long-range scouting airship, but could not be depended on until better radio equipment was available, and a reliable radio homing beacon was developed which could infallibly bring the fighters back to the airship in an emergency.

To the annoyance of Admiral King, and the disgust of Admiral Sellers, Dresel insisted on returning to Sunnyvale before the conclusion of the maneuvers. He did not want to face once more the passes of West Texas, New Mexico, and Arizona in the thunderstorm season in July and August, and felt that the weakness at Frame 17.5 should have prompt attention. His solicitude for the safety of the Navy's only rigid airship is understandable, but left the fleet with the impression that she could only operate under ideal conditions. The *Macon* accordingly departed Opa-Locka on 16 May, and after a relatively uneventful flight of 51 hours returned to Sunnyvale.

To indicate his displeasure, Admiral Sellers sent his evaluation of the *Macon* to the chief of naval operations in June rather than in September as planned. Carelessly assembled by members of his staff,[15] it complained that she was "overweight," a fault that was true of the *Akron*, and unrealistically expected her to perform at high altitudes. She was vulnerable to weather, airplane attacks, and anti-aircraft fire, and her endurance in the operational area was only 36 hours. While admitting that the constant improvement in the airship's performance was "remarkable and commendable," and that using her for tactical scouting put her at an unfair disadvantage, he refused to suggest how she might otherwise be employed. Sellers concluded that "the USS *Macon* has failed to demonstrate its usefulness as a unit of the Fleet," and he was "decidedly of the opinion that the further expenditure of public funds for this type of vessel for the Navy is not justified."[16] For the price of another large rigid airship, Sellers argued that 30 to 40 flying boats could be purchased with an operating radius of 3,000 miles.

In a response that would have done credit to Admiral Moffett, Ernest J. King ridiculed Sellers's argument in favor of the flying boat, pointing out that a 3,000-mile radius was beyond the capability of any existing airplane. For routine reconnaissance over water more than 500 miles from base, only one aerial vehicle had the necessary performance—the airplane-carrying rigid airship. He emphasized the illogic of misusing the *Macon*, with her long-range capability, in tactical situations, and insisted that this was not her proper mission. Since Admiral Sellers had commended the *Macon*'s remarkable progress, Admiral King felt his negative summation was contradictory.

Sellers's damning conclusions about the rigid airship's military uselessness did not of course condemn it to extinction, but reinforced the prejudices of senior officers who had never believed that the big ships' expense justified the meager results obtained in operating with the fleet. And it had to be admitted that the *Macon* had not given of her best in the hands of the cautious Dresel. All this was to change drastically, however, after his replacement, on 11 July 1934, by Lcdr. Herbert V. Wiley, the only officer survivor of the *Akron* disaster.[17]

Wiley brought a new drive and purpose to the *Macon*'s activities, which resulted in part from his role as detached observer of the airship and its shortcomings during a year on board the light cruiser *Cincinnati* following the loss of the *Akron*. Under Wiley's direction, there were many innovative changes from the routine under Dresel. The hook-on squadrons came to play the chief role in scouting, while the airship, hidden below the horizon, served as carrier, radio relay station, and command center. It became routine to remove the landing gear of the F9C-2 aircraft at the start of each cruise and to replace it with a 30-gallon fuel tank. Top speed rose from 176 to 200 mph, flight time was increased to 5½ hours, and the operating radius from 175 to 255 miles. Long-range operation of the airplanes became practical and safer with the development of a foolproof low-frequency radio homing device by Dr. Gerhard Fisher, a civilian physicist, and Lt. Howard N. Coulter, the *Macon*'s communications officer. Wiley finally tried out the pilot rescue gear—a life raft on the end of a long line—and briefly experimented with the "spy basket," or sub-cloud car. This much-overrated device, allegedly used by the Germans in World War I lowered 1,000 to 1,500 feet below the airship to direct her while the ship herself was hidden in cloud, could not compare in utility with the hook-on aircraft.

Wiley promptly devised some strategic scouting schemes of his own, the first one also intended to give the *Macon* some favorable publicity. From newspaper reports and probable speeds he determined the probable course and position of the heavy cruisers *Houston*, with President Roosevelt on board, and *New Orleans*, which, en route from Panama to Hawaii, had departed Clipperton Island on 17 July. In some secrecy, perhaps because Wiley feared that the commander Aircraft, Battle Force, his superior, might refuse permission if his true intentions were known, Wiley made plans to rendezvous with the cruisers at sea. On 17 July he received permission for "a protracted flight to sea." Actually his destination was a point some 1,500 miles south of Sunnyvale, along the assumed track of the cruisers, 100 miles ahead of their estimated position at 1000 on 19 July. The flight plan, Wiley believed, closely simulated a wartime strategic scouting mission based on what information might be obtainable concerning enemy movements.

For 500 miles after leaving the California coast, the *Macon*'s navigator was able to take cross bearings from radio stations ashore with the Fisher-Coulter set. Further navigation in squally weather was by dead reckoning, but a brief glimpse of the sun at 0600 on 19 July gave a line of position only 22 miles distant from the dead reckoning plot. At 1003 Wiley turned southeast to intercept the cruisers, and two of the F9C-2s were sent on ahead. At 1145 they sighted the *Houston* and the *New Orleans*. The president and his entourage were astounded to find small fighter-type aircraft—sans landing gear!—buzzing them when the nearest land was over 1,500 miles away! They were thrilled when the *Macon* appeared and when the F9C-2s, after returning aboard the airship, dropped newspapers, magazines, and souvenir letters for the president. Wiley received a "well done" by radio from President Roosevelt. His superior officers were not pleased, however, commander Battle Force demanding an "immediate" explanation, while the commander in chief, United States Fleet, now Admiral Joseph N. Reeves, was furious at the display of "misapplied initiative." Jealousy at the *Macon*'s success in a mission that emphasized her special capabilities may have been a factor, but Admiral King was obviously pleased. The teapot tempest was forgotten when Wiley came up for selection for commander a year later. With no publicity, Wiley later repeated the scouting procedure in searching for liners and freighters on the run between Hawaii and San Francisco.

With the fleet on the East Coast until November, Wiley was free to drill his crew intensively at battle stations with the F9C-2s making dummy runs on the ship for individual battle practice. The fighters were constantly flying simulated scouting missions; the two "running boats," three-place Waco XJW-1 utility aircraft that had replaced the weary N2Ys, were frequently ferrying passengers to and from the airship. Flights were made to the Camp Kearney mast to familiarize the ground personnel with the ship, and vice versa; and at Sunnyvale Wiley preferred to leave the *Macon* on the mast overnight, rather than in the hangar. Between Wiley's assumption of command, and the return of the fleet to San Diego, the *Macon* made 14 flights for a total of 404 hours in the air. Never had any U.S. naval airship crew been drilled so rigorously and realistically for actual wartime operations.

The 7th of November found the *Macon* at the Camp Kearney mast. The fleet was steaming up the Mexican coast from Panama; the naval units on the West Coast, including the *Macon*, were to intercept it. Flying south during the night, the *Macon* at 0556 on 8 November was 100 miles south of San Clemente Island, ready to sweep a wide area down to Guadalupe Island along the enemy's westward flank. The plan of the day approximated actual wartime conditions: all officers and men would be continuously on duty from 0500 to 1600 hours, with those manning lookout and gun positions to have their meals brought to them at their stations. At this point the *Macon* was ordered by the force commander to search the enemy's eastern flank also; his patrol flying boats were grounded by fog. Sending off two F9C-2s, Wiley ordered them to rendezvous with him over Guadalupe. During the next few hours the hook-on pilots discovered and reported a division of enemy cruisers, and then the main body. Arriving at Guadalupe at 0903, the *Macon* promptly sighted the carrier *Saratoga* to the southeast, launching a flight of dive bombers to attack. Forced to await his fighters, Wiley could not run, but as the six SU-1s commenced their dive, he foiled them by a sharp turn to starboard which brought all his guns to bear. For the duration of the exercise, the *Macon*, concealed 60 miles to the south, shadowed the unsuspecting carrier with her planes. Subsequently the commander Aircraft, Battle Force, complimented the *Macon* on "her excellent scouting and the character of the radio reports by her planes." Nothing was said about the patrol planes being six hours late because of a morning fog.

The first exercise with the fleet with Wiley in command on 6–7 December 1934 was again a tactical one in a restricted area as the battleships, cruisers, and carriers proceeded from San Pedro to San Francisco. With four F9C-2s aboard, the *Macon* on 6 December had two flights of two aircraft each in the air alternately, flying east and west of the airship as she proceeded south to look for the Fleet. When the *Macon*'s lookouts discovered a battleship in the west, Wiley changed course to the northwest to circumvent the enemy, while the westward pair of fighters reported that the big ship was heavily escorted. Meanwhile the eastward pair were tracking the carrier *Lexington* and her cruiser escort. Dive bombers from the carrier made a successful surprise attack out of the sun, and the airship was ruled "shot down." As "ZRS 6" she

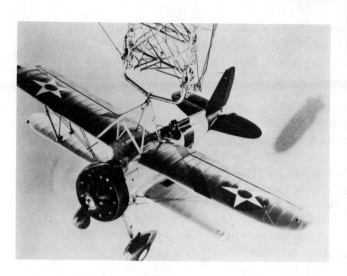

Curtiss "Sparrowhawk" F9C-2 fighter on the *Macon* trapeze. Note airship's shadow on the water below. (U.S. Navy)

continued to operate for another hour until she was again "shot down." On 7 December, operating close to the Farallons as the fleet approached San Francisco, the *Macon* and her planes tracked various "enemy" units, until 1325 when the exercise was canceled and a real search problem substituted: two catapult planes from the cruiser *Cincinnati*, Wiley's old ship, were lost, had exhausted their fuel, and were down at sea. At 1348 two F9C-2s were sent off to search to the north. At 1507 two more departed to search to the south, and within 35 minutes one of these had located the two missing *Cincinnati* aircraft and had dropped a smoke candle. The *Macon* joined her aircraft and watched as fleet surface units appeared on the horizon. The *Macon* and her planes had been first to locate the missing aircraft and were commended by commander Battle Force, while Wiley had his revenge on the *Cincinnati* aviators who had ridiculed airships in general and the *Macon* in particular.

At last there was some prospect of the *Macon* being able to demonstrate her unique qualifications for strategic scouting. Admiral King had been pressing for orders to the *Macon* for such employment, beginning with letters to commander Aircraft, Battle Force, Rear Admiral John Halligan; and the commander in chief, United States Fleet, Admiral Sellers, shortly after New Year's 1934. By the fall of 1934 he was pressuring the chief of naval operations, Admiral Standley, and had won the backing of the General Board. The fact that Fleet Problem XVI, to be staged in the spring of 1935, was to be fought west of Hawaii, made it probable that the *Macon* would scout strategically from the mast at Ewa. But first there was the matter of the weakness of Frame 17.5 as demonstrated by the damage in rough air over West

Texas in April 1934, and the reinforcement recommended by BuAer and the Goodyear-Zeppelin Corporation.

On 14 September 1934, two boxes containing 598 lb. of reinforcement parts were shipped from the Goodyear-Zeppelin plant at Akron to Sunnyvale. Wiley, however, had been setting a fast pace, and did not want to take time out for their installation. He and his officers felt that reinforcement was not necessary for operation in smooth air over the ocean. During several overhaul periods between 10 November 1934 and 10 February 1935, the reinforcing material was installed in the way of the lower fin and the two horizontal ones. Nothing had been done about the reinforcement of the upper portion of Frame 17.5 where the upper fin was attached. On the one hand, the BuAer letter of 24 July 1934 concerning the installation of the reinforcing duralumin channels had given priority to strengthening the horizontal fin attachments, where the failure had occurred in West Texas; on the other hand, the gas cells I and II would have to be deflated to give access to the upper part of Frame 17.5. This would be time-consuming, and Wiley planned to have the work done during an overhaul period in March.

Meanwhile Wiley continued training his ship's company, and further drilled his hook-on pilots in new techniques. During a 47-hour flight, on 31 January 1935, the F9C-2s flew simulated dive bombing attacks on the Macon, designed to work out defensive maneuvers, while lookouts and gun crews reported and tracked the "attackers." Homing and communications tests with the hook-on fighters signaled the progress made in the past six months: the "Sparrowhawks" were able to take accurate bearings on the Macon from 185 miles, clear voice communications were possible out to 95 miles, and Morse code transmissions were read with ease at 140 miles. On 1–2 February, further drilling took place, while complete control of the Macon was shifted from the control car to the auxiliary control station in the lower fin. All hands felt prepared in every sense to turn in a perfect performance with the fleet in scheduled exercises on 11–12 February. And beyond lay Fleet Problem XVI, for which Wiley and the hook-on pilots had prepared a surprise: nothing less than an after-dark dive bombing attack with the F9C-2s on the carrier Lexington. Night operations with the hook-on planes were now routine, while the surface carriers were then required to have their aircraft on board before dark.

In the determined hands of Lcdr. Herbert V. Wiley, the USS Macon, together with her HTA unit, had finally fulfilled the dreams of all those who had gone before, and who had seen the big rigid airship as the answer to the problem of long-range reconnaissance

in the vastness of the Pacific. Admiral Fiske in 1913 had dimly glimpsed her remarkable capacities in terms of range and endurance; Admiral Moffett in 1921 had hoped to bring the dream to fruition; but, instead, too much time and effort had been wasted on political demonstrations and "hand-waving" flights. The Macon's recent performance had re-created respect for the rigid airship. The General Board was recommending immediate construction of a 2,500,000-cubic-foot training airship that would carry three airplanes. A presidential commission had recommended that the Navy expand its airship operations; that a training airship be built immediately to replace the 11-year-old Los Angeles; and that the government subsidize the construction of two large passenger-carrying rigids for transoceanic service, a Metalclad commercial carrier of moderate size, and an East Coast passenger terminal.

Now every hope was riding on the Macon. At 0710 on 11 February 1935, she ascended into a low overcast and headed south to look for the fleet en route from San Diego to San Francisco. She was under orders from commander Aircraft, Battle Force, to use the fleet movement for training in strategic reconnaissance. Two of the F9C-2s flew out from Sunnyvale and were hoisted on board half an hour after takeoff; two others homed onto the Macon's radio beacon three hours after her departure. Soon the little fighters, with landing gear replaced by long-range tanks, were searching the Santa Barbara Channel and the fleet anchorages at Long Beach and San Diego. In the role of flying aircraft carrier, the Macon idled off Point Arguello and received the reports of her aircraft as they returned from their long missions: ComAirBatFor had enjoined radio silence. Throughout the day the little fighters tracked the fleet, reporting its composition, position, course, and speed, while the airship remained undiscovered. The last pair of scouting aircraft were recovered at 1745 and 1749. At dawn on 12 February, two F9C-2s were sent south to see if any ships were returning to San Diego, and by 1230 all four hook-on aircraft were heading north to search for the fleet off San Francisco, while the Macon followed behind. At 1330 the Macon received word from Admiral Reeves, commander in chief, United States Fleet, that she was released from the exercise. The return to Sunnyvale via Point Sur, Monterey, and the Santa Clara Valley would be routine.

The weather deteriorated, but the fog, the rain, and the low visibility were hardly a danger to the big airship. At 1704 Point Sur was almost abeam. Suddenly, without warning, the Macon was struck by an exceptionally severe gust and lurched violently to starboard. The heavy lateral force on the upper fin caused it to tear free from the ship, taking with it the top of main frame 17.5. As the upper fin disintegrated, the wreckage punctured Cells II, I, and 0 in the tail cone, and all three cells rapidly deflated. Even so the ship might conceivably have been saved, but on receiving news of the casualty from personnel in the stern, control car personnel dumped such large quantities of fuel and ballast that the stern-heavy ship, driven by her still-running engines, not only rose through pressure height, which was 2,800 feet, but continued on up to 4,850 feet. So much helium was lost through the automatic valves that the ship was no longer buoyant; thus the *Macon*'s descent into the sea 24 minutes after the casualty was inevitable. This time, however, in contrast to the *Akron* disaster, there was plenty of lifesaving equipment, the water was warm, and cruisers from the fleet were almost immediately on hand to rescue the survivors. Only 2 persons were lost of the 83 on board.

The Court of Inquiry found that the primary cause of the loss of the *Macon* was the failure of girders in the top of Frame 17.5 when overstressed by the gust load on the upper fin. Damage inflicted by broken girders cause three gas cells to deflate with a loss of lift of 30,000 to 40,000 lb. The keepers of the Point Sur Lighthouse, who were actually observing the *Macon* through binoculars at the moment of the failure, gave valuable testimony concerning the breakup of the upper fin. The investigators also concluded that no less than 32,700 lb. of fuel and water ballast had been dumped during the five minutes after the fin failure.

The panic release of ballast aft, together with the thrust of the running engines forcing the ship upward dynamically, made the loss of the *Macon* inevitable by driving her far above pressure height. In retrospect, could the big rigid, though severely damaged, have made it home to Sunnyvale? German practice would have called for the engines to be stopped at once, a weigh-off to be performed to see if the airship were light or heavy, the valving of gas or release of ballast depending on whether the ship rose or sank, and the shifting of weights forward, or even valving gas from the foremost cells, to bring her into trim. Possibly the nose-up angle would have defeated any attempt to shift weights forward, and certainly merely sending unneeded crew members into the nose, as in World War I Zeppelins, would have been inadequate. Perhaps the *Macon* could have returned to Sunnyvale at low speed, with only the lower rudder and control from the auxiliary station in the lower fin, in which case there would have been at least a brief reprieve.

As airship historian Richard K. Smith points out, following all previous rigid airship disasters in the U.S. Navy there had always been a newer and better craft coming forward.[18] After the ZR 2 crash the *Shenandoah* was under development. When the *Shenandoah* was destroyed, the *Los Angeles* was already in service. The *Macon* was nearly complete when the *Akron* was lost. But there was no successor to the *Macon* herself, and she was the last rigid airship built and flown in the United States. Her passing marked the end of an era.

13

A Final Judgment

The loss of the *Macon* in February 1935 truly marked the end of the rigid airship in the U.S. Navy. Between then and the outbreak of World War II in Europe, numerous paper programs were drawn up for naval rigid airships, some to be as large as 10,000,000 cubic feet in volume and carrying a squadron of dive bombers; and it was claimed that three such ZRCVs with 27 dive bombers would have the striking power of one aircraft carrier of the contemporary *Yorktown* class. But a month and a half after the loss of the *Macon* the first Consolidated PBY patrol flying boat made its initial flight, and it was the "Cat," and the Martin PBM, that in World War II performed the rigid airship's strategic scouting mission over the vast expanses of the Pacific Ocean, even though they lacked the rigid's capacity to remain on station for several days, and to carry sophisticated radar equipment. The "blimp" used for coastal convoy escort in that war did not correspond militarily to the big rigid airship, and was not intended for the same purpose.

Why did the rigid airship fail to find a place in the U.S. arsenal of weapons, particularly when the United States possessed a monopoly of nonflammable helium? In the light of hindsight, the adverse judgment against the rigid airship was inevitable, given the remarkable and unanticipated progress of heavier-than-air aviation in the United States in the 1920s and 1930s. As advocated by Admiral Fiske in 1913, the Zeppelin-type craft was fully evolved conceptually before World War I, and further development involved only refinements in detail and increases in size; there were no dramatic breakthroughs.

Although the rigid airship may have been a victim of prejudice in the U.S. Navy, it had its chance to demonstrate its military capabilities in the hands of Germany, whose people had made a strong emotional commitment to this impressive symbol of German technology and science. The German Army in World War I employed 43 rigid airships in night bombing raids, mostly on the Eastern Front, but disbanded the service in 1917 as the ships were too vulnerable to anti-aircraft fire and were grounded by weather much of the time. The German Navy had 68 rigids in service during the war: their best year was 1915, during which nearly $4,000,000 worth of damage was done in attacks on England, but in the following year the dream of achieving "a prompt and victorious ending of the war" through strategic bombing evaporated when seven Zeppelins were destroyed in raids on England, five with all hands. In 1915, scouting flights were made over the North Sea on 34% of the days, but thereafter the percentage declined, falling to 23 in 1918. Casualties were heavy, 40% of naval flight crew personnel being killed by enemy action or in operational accidents. The defeated enemy concealed these failures from the victors, the truth emerging only after the German Navy's archives were captured in 1945. Instead, the exaggerated claims of airship propagandists in Germany and elsewhere were believed by airship advocates in the Navy Department and even in BuAer.

Thus the big rigid airship, when compared with the flimsy and dangerous airplanes of the day, appealed to senior officers of Moffett's generation who commanded the fleets, and staffed the General Board, in the period immediately after the 1918

Armistice. While they lacked any experience, knowledge, or true understanding of aviation and its potentials, they could identify with an aerial craft longer than a dreadnought, ponderous and stately like the ships they had grown up with at sea. As in surface ships, the airship crews stood watches, four hours on and four hours off, and it was the officer of the deck who gave orders to the helmsmen in the control car, also called "the bridge." And was it not widely believed that the German Zeppelins had saved the High Seas Fleet at the Battle of Jutland, and inspected every square mile of the southern North Sea every day? Actually it was a British Admiralty document of 1917 that made the former false claim. So impressed was the Admiralty that up to the Armistice, they seriously aimed to procure 16 large rigid airships patterned after German prototypes, some of which would have been inflated with American helium for North Sea operations. As the junior partner in the war at sea in 1917–18, the U.S. Navy was much influenced by British concepts and programs. With increasing possibility of a Pacific war with Japan, and the poor performance of primitive short-range flying boats, the rigid airship was seen by senior officers as an ideal long-range scouting weapon.

In 1921 Admiral Moffett, at the age of 51, was appointed chief of the new Bureau of Aeronautics and charged with building up the Navy's air arm, which essentially was conceived of along the lines of the British Royal Naval Air Service as developed in World War I. Operations were primarily by flying boats and seaplanes from shore bases; rigid airships, when perfected, would assume the strategic scouting missions. The aircraft carrier was just appearing, the Royal Navy in July 1918 having mounted the first carrier strike in history against a land target by sending seven Sopwith "Camels" to bomb the German airship base at Tondern, where two Zeppelins were destroyed.[1] Two more carriers joined the Grand Fleet just before the Armistice. It was not Moffett, however, but Henry Mustin, Kenneth Whiting, and other qualified naval aviators who realized that high-powered, wheeled aircraft carried to sea on board carriers would be the strike weapon of the future and could in time eclipse the battleship as the final arbiter of sea power. A few years later, while the Los Angeles was making publicity flights out of Lakehurst, the 40,000-ton Lexington and Saratoga, attached to the United States Fleet at San Diego, were training air groups and developing the doctrine that would defeat Japan in 1944–45.

While the big carriers were integrated into the fleet organization, and played an increasing role in maneuvers and fleet problems, the airship's proponents failed to convince senior officers of its potential usefulness in a major war in the Pacific. This failure cannot be attributed to blind prejudice by battleship admirals, as the carriers and their attack groups were accepted in the fleet. Certainly the airships spent too much time in publicity demonstration flights, yet the problem of how to employ them was a complex one, rooted in a lack of money. Had the experimental program been more adequately funded, with more airships and men made available, and none of the pettifogging restrictions on yearly expenditures for gasoline and helium, the operators and designers would have accumulated experience more rapidly, and the big fleet airships of the Akron type would have flown earlier with a better chance to compete with airplanes.[2] Caught between the upper and nether millstones of inadequate funding versus fleet demands and expectations, Moffett rightly or wrongly saw himself forced to use the Shenandoah and the Los Angeles to generate public support for naval aviation in the heart of the country as well as along the sea coasts.[3]

Moffett persisted in his advocacy of the rigid airship, but had to deal with increasing resistance and skepticism. Unlike the situation in prewar Germany, there was no public support or enthusiasm. In fact, the airship was the target of growing hostility in the newspapers and in Congress. In a period of deflationary economy, this hostility was based originally on cost. Repeated accidents, not only to American craft but also to foreign ones, emphasized the inherent fragility and vulnerability of the type, though its proponents argued in vain that hazards always existed in pioneering any new weapon.[4] There was resistance in the Navy Department itself: Not only was there the usual bias against anything new in an environment dominated by battleship concepts; not only did the carrier advocates in BuAer regard Moffett's fascination with the rigid airship as an aberration on his part; but the offensive-minded U.S. Navy was disinterested in an aircraft that had no attack capabilities (though the ZRCV was intended to cater to this point of view). With the services starved for funds by the "business as usual" Harding, Coolidge, and Hoover administrations, the airship suffered in the fight for its share of niggardly appropriations. And not only the airship—the expansion of the Navy as a whole, and its readiness for war, were seriously impaired.

While airshipmen were fond of saying that the big rigids did not compete with airplanes, they complemented them, the competition was certainly intense when it came to dividing inadequate funds between airships and airplanes. It was frequently asserted that 40 flying boats could be purchased for one rigid airship, and this was certainly true. Inevitably the younger officers in BuAer were tempted to finance the development of a variety of heavier-than-air prototypes, expensive as they were by the standards of the day, instead of putting all their eggs in the airship basket. And the aircraft industry responded. Wood was rapidly replaced by steel tubing as a structural material; heavy water-cooled power plants disappeared in favor of lighter and more reliable radial engines, which by 1939 produced over 1,000 h.p. The picturesque biplane with its drag-producing struts, wires, and open cockpits was replaced by the streamlined, all-metal monoplane, with cantilever wing construction, retractable landing gear, enclosed cockpits, and trailing edge flaps to enable it to combine high speeds of 150 mph or more with low landing speeds. Above all, with increased power and aerodynamic refinements, the airplane's efficiency was multiplied more than fourfold: wing loading increased from the 9.7 lb. per square foot of the F5L flying boat of 1919 to 25 lb. in the PBY and 41 lb. in the PBM flying boats. But the lift of helium had not increased at all, and the airship, to increase its carrying capacity, had to increase its dimensions to gigantic size, with an upper limit being set by the measurements of the few hangars in the country. And while airplane speeds increased every year, there appeared to be a practical upper limit of about 90 mph for maximum speed of an airship. Not until the early 1930s would an operationally efficient fleet airship appear, while at the time of the *Akron*'s loss in 1933—taking with her Admiral Moffett, who had always fought for the big rigids—truly remarkable aircraft were about to appear in American skies: the Boeing 247, the Douglas DC-2 and DC-3 which would revolutionize air transportation around the world, and the Martin Clippers which opened the first transpacific commercial air service. Beyond them loomed the Boeing B-17 bomber of World War II, the big Boeing flying boats carrying 40 or more passengers across both oceans, and the first pressurized airliner, the Boeing 307.

Thus, nothing could alter the widening gap between the static performance of the big rigid airship and the spectacular technological advances of the American aviation industry. The final verdict would necessarily have been the same if Lakehurst personnel had ruthlessly dedicated themselves from the be-

ginning to preparing their giant craft for war in the Pacific; if there had been a base and hangar constructed in the San Diego area with the airship closely integrated with operations of the United States Fleet;[5] or if Congress had funded and supported Paul W. Litchfield's dream of an American transoceanic air line of giant passenger-carrying rigids. Even in the commercial field the rigid airship would have been only briefly competitive with the flying boat, and outclassed by multiengined land planes.

There remained, however, for some years a considerable group of people who had served in the big rigids, and who insistently advocated their return for commercial and military purposes. Their leader and spokesman was Vice Admiral Charles E. Rosendahl, who in World War II rose to be chief of Naval Airship Training and Experimentation during a period when the U.S. Navy operated 178 pressure airships on antisubmarine and convoy duties, not only on the Atlantic and Pacific coasts, but also in the Caribbean, the South Atlantic, and even the western Mediterranean. Rosendahl's heart, however, belonged to the rigid airship, and in books and articles he continued to bring it to public attention, and to advocate its employment by the U.S. Navy, until his death in 1977.

While the old-timers, and the younger rigid airship enthusiasts who have never seen one, today propose tasks and missions that only the rigid airship can perform, they are at a deeper level motivated by the intense emotional desire to bring back the beautiful ships in the sky. I too have known the enthrallment, the fascination, the ecstatic pleasure of watching the silver monsters passing majestically overhead, and I have envied the happy people on board, for whom many childhood dreams of magic omnipotence were being fulfilled. The unacknowledged emotional appeal of the big airships in their heyday was a strong factor in their advocacy by those who flew them; but weapons procurement cannot (or should not) be based on emotional considerations. The loss of the *Macon* in February 1935 confirmed the many opponents in the fleet, in Congress, and in the country, in their opinions as to the uselessness of the rigid airship for the Navy; and the judgment has been final.

A

The U.S. Navy Rigid Airship Detachment, Howden

First Draft Reported Howden 20 April 1920

[1]Cdr. L. H. Maxfield Commanding Officer
[1]Lcdr. V. N. Bieg Senior Engineering Officer
Lt. R. G. Pennoyer Executive Officer
[1]Lt. C. G. Little USNRF Watch Officer (navigation)
Lt. T. B. Null USNRF Watch Officer (navigation)
[2]Lt. J. B. Lawrence USNRF Watch Officer
[2]Lt. A. R. Houghton USNRF Watch Officer
Lt. W. R. Taylor (MC) Medical Officer
Lt. (j.g.) J. H. Kyger (SC) Supply Officer

[1]C. I. Aller CBM	H. Christensen CQM (D)
[3]A. F. Carlson CQM (D)	[1]R. M. Coons CMM (A)
[2]J. W. Cullinan CMM (A)	A. B. Galatian CMM (A)
[1]J. T. Hancock CMM (A)	J. J. Harrigan CQM (D)
[1]W. Julius CMM (A)	[1]M. Lay CBM
H. H. O'Claire CBM	[1]Ad Pettit CBM
[3]W. A. Russell CMM (A)	L. T. Stevens CMM (A)
[1]W. J. Steele CMM (A)	T. L. Thomas CQM (D)
F. M. Gorey CMM (A)	S. H. Knight QM1 (D)

Second Draft Reported Howden July 1920

[1]Lcdr. E. W. Coil Engineering Officer
[1]Lt. H. W. Hoyt Watch Officer
Lt. F. P. Culbert
[1]Lt. M. H. Esterly USNRF Radio Officer
Ensign (T) W. J. Medusky
Ensign (T) J. H. Hykes
Chief Machinist S. S. Halliburton
   Assistant Engineering Officer

L. K. Coleman CMM (A)	[2]C. H. Broom CMM (A)
[1]L. E. Crowl CMM (A)	J. H. Collier CCM (A)
C. M. Deem MM1 (A)	G. F. Collins EIC-R
C. A. Heckbert QM1 (D)	C. W. Frank QM1 (D)
J. A. Leonard CQM (D)	R. Jones MM1 (A)
[1]A. L. Loftin CMM (A)	E. C. Lewis CQM (D)
F. L. Peckham CQM (D)	C. J. McCarthy MM1 (A)
J. E. Waterman E1 (RA)	C. J. McCawley AMM1C
[1]G. Welch CMM (A)	F. F. Moorman CMM (A)
N. O. Walker QM1 (D)	J. F. Shields CCM (A)
B. J. Wiederkehr CY	

Reported At Various Intervals

Lt. J. B. Anderson USNRF Meteorological Officer	
T. D. Dickerson CMM (A)	W. A. Lamkey CMM (A)
C. W. Cass CMM (A)	E. S. Downs CPhM
E. M. Riley CY	J. H. Robertson CE (RA)
F. Kuback E3 (RA)	F. H. Cutler Y3
M. C. Hegel Y3	C. S. Solar MM1 (A)

[1]Killed 24 August 1921, aboard ZR 2.
[2]Killed 3 September 1925, aboard ZR 1 *Shenandoah*.
[3]Killed 4 April 1933, aboard ZRS4 *Akron*.

B

Training Flights With American Crew

Flights of R 32 1920–21

11 Aug. ⎫
26 Aug. ⎬ 34 hr. 0 min., 1,212 mi.
27 Aug. ⎭

   8 Sept. ⎫
   9 Sept. ⎪
w 21 Sept. Flight Lt. Wann 12 hr. 25 min. ⎬ 56 hr. 10 min., 1,731 mi.
w 28 Sept. Cdr. Maxfield 9 hr. 30 min. ⎭

w   8 Oct. Cdr. Maxfield 11 hr. 10 min. ⎫
  10 Oct. ⎪
w 11 Oct. Cdr. Maxfield 21 hr. ⎪
  13 Oct. ⎬ 63 hr. 58 min., 2,253 mi., "training USN & NPL flights"
  14 Oct. ⎪
c 25 Oct. "to Hornsea" 5 hr. 15 min. ⎭
w 29 Oct. Cdr. Maxfield 7 hr.
w,c 5 Nov. Cdr. Maxfield 6 hr. 30 min. "to Yoath"
w   8 Nov. Cdr. Maxfield 6 hr. 40 min.
   7 Dec. Cdr. Maxfield 5 hr. 50 min.
w,c 10 Dec. Cdr. Maxfield 5 hr. 5 min.; "practiced landings"
w   7 Jan. Cdr. Maxfield 4 hr.
b 27 Jan. with R 34
w   3 Feb. Cdr. Maxfield 5 hr.
b   5 Feb.
c   7 Feb. 3 hr. 52 min.
w   9 Feb. Flight Lt. Wann 3 hr. 50 min.
w 11 Feb. Flight Lt. Wann 4 hr. 45 min.
w,c 24 Feb. Flight Lt. Wann 6 hr. 45 min.
w 31 Mar. Flight Lt. Wann 20 min. "pay hop"
  Total recorded time 203 hr. 15 min.

c = James H. Collier logbook.
w = Norman Walker logbook.
b = Valentine Bieg letters.

Flights of R 80 1921

   c 26 Mar. 1 hr. 10 min.
   c 18 Apr. 3 hr.
w,c 12 May Flight Lt. Little 2 hr. 45 min.
   c 1 June 1 hr. 50 min.
   w 1 July Flight Lt. Little 10 hr. 15 min.
   w 5 July Flight Lt. Little 1 hr. 50 min.
   w 5–6 July Flight Lt. Little 8 hr. 50 min. (Maitland parachute jump?)
     Total recorded time 29 hr. 40 min.

C

Memorandum by Commander Settle on Problems at Lakehurst

May 31, 1939

MEMORANDUM TO CAPTAIN[1]

Pursuant to your request, following is an outline of Lakehurst history, 1923 to 1929; only the high spots will be touched. It is largely a sad story, one of temperamental personalities, publicity seeking, political manoeuvring in Washington and elsewhere, and personal and professional feuds here, all of which of course is foreign to what should go on in the Navy and is largely responsible for our failures. I believe that my outline following is impartial inasmuch as during the years in question I was practically the most junior officer here; I was never involved on either side in the various feuds here and while I differed with others professionally on many occasions these differences never became personal so far as I was concerned.

In the summer of 1923 the *Shenandoah* was nearing completion here under the industrial managership of Weyerbacher. McCrary was in command and Klein was executive. A couple of years before the R 38 (ZR 2) had been lost in England; and the *Los Angeles* was building in Germany. Heinen was here as a civilian under contract with the Navy Department and was Weyerbacher's right-hand man on the *Shenandoah* construction job. A group of wartime blimp and kite balloon officers and men were here, all of these officers being ex-temporary or mustangs. The first student officers' class had been assembled in late spring of 1923, including Pierce, Deem, Arnold, Hancock, Rosendahl, Wiley, etc., and Heinen was instructing this class in a ground school. McCrary was a

[1]Commander Jesse L. Kenworthy Jr., Commanding Officer, Naval Air Station, Lakehurst, N.J.

genial, rather easy going and capable officer with some experience in LTA and HTA, was here against his strong desires for other duty. McCrary's administration of the station was weak, and under him we had two unusually strong personalities, mutually violently antagonistic professionally and personally, Klein and Weyerbacher. Klein was executive officer and of a Naval Academy class two years senior to Weyerbacher, but the latter being a naval constructor was senior to Klein by date of commission. Weyerbacher was a brilliant officer and naval constructor, highly ambitious and aggressive, and of the type of naval constructor who desire and demand line prerogative and authority. Klein was an aggressive, ambitious, capable line officer with an excellent wartime record in a destroyer command. Klein and Weyerbacher clashed throughout their time here and both tended to "run over" and "by pass" the captain, McCrary. There was a large civilian force here and politics were rife among them. All hands were divided into two camps, the Weyerbacher and Klein camps. The *Shenandoah* was commissioned in September with a highly publicized joy ride with Secretary and Mrs. Denby and various other dignitaries and ladies. The ship then operated for four months on various ballyhoo and publicity missions; she was Admiral Moffett's particular pride; the Admiral was projecting the North Pole voyage for the following spring. She operated under the nominal captaincy of McCrary but was actually handled and run by Weyerbacher, Heinen and Mayer. In early January 1924 the North Pole project went by the board in Congress. In late January she broke away from the mast, was brought back by Heinen. Kincaid, a student officer, had a fight with Heinen in the ship and after returning to Lakehurst spilled a very unsavory story to newspapermen. This caused the lid to blow off and when the smoke blew away McCrary, Weyerbacher, Heinen and Kincaid had all gone leaving Klein in command on the station, Lansdowne coming up from Washington to command the *Shenandoah*, and Nelson as industrial manager (changed about this time to A&R Officer).

Shenandoah Second Phase. The ship was ready for service again in April 1924. The last of May the famous air circus was held here. On that afternoon Klein and Lansdowne broke over an insignificant matter; this fire was fanned by wives and immediately the station was broken up into two "armed camps," the Lansdowne and Klein factions respectively; officers would refuse to speak to those in the other camp, wives would snub the opposite ones. This situation persisted until the loss of the *Shenandoah* in September 1925. Lansdowne was a capable, experienced airship officer; he flew and handled his own ship (the only airship captain in our service who has done this, to the best of my knowledge), he was in no sense a "prima donna" and desired only to be left alone to operate the ship as a naval vessel. Admiral Moffett however insisted upon continuous ballyhoo trips and the ship's whole time practically was spent in such trips except for several weeks each in August 1924 and August 1925 during which she operated quite successfully in naval missions off the Atlantic Coast. In August 1925 Lansdowne was ordered to sea, to be detached in September. There was high tension as to who would get the ship, Hancock, executive in the *Shenandoah*, and Klein, CO of the station, being the principal candidates; this tension was accompanied by the strongest animosity on both sides. The wrecking of the *Shenandoah* in early September intervened.

Los Angeles First Phase. In the summer of 1924 the *Los Angeles* was nearing completion in Germany and Klein, station CO, went across in September to return in the ship on her delivery flight. Steele, Kraus and Klein returned in the *Los Angeles* in middle October 1924. Steele was named as commanding officer of the station and of the *Los Angeles* with Klein as executive officer of both. Steele was sickly so that Klein exercised actual command of the *Los Angeles* and station the rest of that fall and spring of 1925. 3 German officers stayed here 3 months as instructors, Flemming, Wittemann and Scherz. Nelson was 1st lieutenant and mostly handled the ship statically. Klein was an experienced sea-going officer, and with rounded experience and application would have made a good airship handler. He made one splendid landing to the *Patoka* in Bermuda spring of 1925

under bad conditions, but was inclined to be rash in his decisions. The operations of the first half of 1925 with the *Los Angeles* with Captain Steele aboard were quite similar to the Army RS-1, in which a clear cut line of authority was absent. In the fall and winter of 1925 and 1926 the *Los Angeles* was laid up with calcium chloride troubles and reaction from the loss of the *Shenandoah*. Early in 1926 Klein resigned and went into brokerage in New York, Steele went to sea in May 1926 leaving the *Los Angeles* command to Rosendahl and the station command to Captain Jackson.

Los Angeles Second Phase. From summer 1926 to summer 1928 Rosendahl was in the saddle; Captain Jackson was an earnest, intelligent officer without any LTA experience and of a weak and vassilating (sic) nature in the exercise of his command. He was only nominally in command here as Rosendahl was the real authority and continually by-passed Jackson, handling all important matters directly with Washington. A personal feud grew up between Captain Jackson and his family on the one hand and Rosendahl on the other. Station officers generally sided with Jackson and ship officers with Rosendahl, although there was not the best of internal harmony in either camp. Mayer as 1st lieutenant handled the ship while Rosendahl handled the external policies, politics and publicity. A number of successful ballyhoo missions were carried out in these two years, as for instance the Detroit flight, the Panama and Pensacola flights, the *Saratoga* landing, etc. Some creditable development was done of the stub mast and Mobile stub mast; a number of *Patoka* landings were made in various ports.

In the summer of 1928 Rosendahl went to Europe for the *Graf Zeppelin* initial voyage leaving Wiley in command of the *Los Angeles*. Rosendahl resumed active command early in 1929. Wiley did not disturb Rosendahl's general ship organization and manner of operating; Mayer continued to run the ship except that Wiley supervised ship affairs more closely than had Rosendahl.

In the period from 1925 through 1928, a number of relatively senior officers were brought in, given the usual ground school and nominal flight training, and then thrown into relatively high billets because of their rank. This was apparently at Admiral Moffett's insistence, his idea being to induct more rank into the game so that it would "draw more water" in the service. This caused a bad situation in two ways, it blocked off the possibilities of advancement in billets in the game for the more junior officers who had been here for a moderate or long time, and secondly it put officers in responsible billets for which they were not qualified by experience.

You are aware of the technical details of the *Shenandoah* break-away flight and final wrecking. The *Los Angeles* was a very lucky ship; she had quite a few close squeaks, needless ones usually occasioned by a combination of inexperience and the ballyhoo missions assigned the ship. During this period many of the recruits to the game, officer and men, came here solely for flight pay and desired to fly to the minimum extent possible and then only on hand-waving missions. The super-man publicity-conscious complex was evident in quite a few.

Respectfully,

T. G. W. Settle,
Commander, U.S. Navy
Executive Officer

D

The *Shenandoah*'s Midwest Flight Itinerary

Itinerary ordered for *Shenandoah* flight to Minneapolis by CNO, Admiral Eberle, in letter to C.O. *Shenandoah*, 19 June 1925:

Lakehurst to Minneapolis:

Lakehurst
Cleveland, Ohio
Sandusky, Ohio
Toledo, Ohio
Detroit, Mich.
Ann Arbor, Mich.
Jackson, Mich.
Battle Creek, Mich.
Kalamazoo, Mich.
Miles, Mich.
South Bend, Ind.
Chicago, Ill.
Waukegan, Ill.
Kenosha, Wis.
Milwaukee, Wis.
Madison, Wis.
Fond du Lac, Wis.
Oshkosh, Wis.
Wautoma, Wis.
Black River Falls, Wis.
Eau Claire, Wis.
Menomonie, Wis.
St. Paul, Minn.
Minneapolis, Minn.
  (landing)

Minneapolis to St. Louis:

St. Paul, Minn.
La Crosse, Wis.
Webster City, Iowa
Fort Dodge, Iowa
Boone, Iowa
Ames, Iowa
Des Moines, Iowa
Creston, Iowa
Maryville, Mo.
St. Joseph, Mo.
Kansas City, Mo.
St. Louis, Mo.
  (land Scott Field)

St. Louis to Lakehurst:

Springfield, Ill.
Lafayette, Ind.
Indianapolis, Ind.
Dayton, Ohio
Columbus, Ohio
Zanesville, Ohio
Wheeling, W.Va.
Pittsburgh, Pa.
Lakehurst

E

Airships' Performance Data and Chronology

ZR 1 USS *SHENANDOAH* (AFTER 22 MAY 1924)*

Characteristics and Performance

Air displacement of hull:		2,289,861 cu. ft.
Volume of gas cells:		2,115,174 cu. ft.
Length overall:		680 ft. 2 in.
Total height:		93 ft. 2 in.
Maximum diameter:		78 ft. 9 in.
Engines:		5 Packard 1A-1551
Total h.p.:		1,500
Main frame spacing:		10 m. (32.8 ft.)
No. gas cells:		20

Weights (95% inflated with helium):

Fixed weights:	80,226 lb.	62.2% of gross lift
Useful lift:	48,774 lb.	37.8% of gross lift
Total weight (= gross lift):	129,000 lb.	100.0% of gross lift

Speed and endurance (95% inflated with helium):

Full speed:	51 kts.
Full speed endurance:	2,250 miles
" " "	50 hours
Cruising speed:	41 kts.
Cruising speed endurance:	3,980 miles
" " "	97 hours
Crew:	54 total
"	40 flight

Significant Chronology

Construction authorized by Congress:	11 July 1919
Design prepared:	Aug. 1919–Oct. 1921
Built by:	Naval Aircraft Factory and NAS Lakehurst
Work commenced:	NAS Lakehurst April 1922
Completed ("launched"):	20 Aug. 1923
First flight:	4 Sept. 1923

*Primary source: Capt. W. H. Sitz, USMC, BuAer, Technical Note #160, *A History of U.S. Naval Aviation*, April 1925, Ch. XII, "Development of Lighter Than Air Craft."

Christened:	10 Oct. 1923
Commissioned:	10 Oct. 1923
Destroyed:	3 Sept. 1925
Formally stricken:	5 Sept. 1925
Total no. flights:	59
Total flight time:	740.09 hours
Cost:	$1,500,000

ZR 2 (R 38)*

Characteristics and Performance

Air displacement of hull:		2,960,000 cu. ft.
Volume of gas cells:		2,724,000 cu. ft.
Length overall:		699 ft.
Total height:		92 ft. 0 in.
Maximum diameter:		85 ft. 6 in.
Engines:		6 Sunbeam "Cossacks"
Total h.p.:		2,100
Main frame spacing:		15 m. (49.2 ft.)
No. gas cells:		14
Weights (100% inflated with hydrogen):		
Fixed weights:	65,400 lb.	39.5% of gross lift
Useful lift:	100,000 lb.	60.5% of gross lift
Total weight (= gross lift):	165,400 lb.	100.0% of gross lift
Speed and endurance (100% inflated with hydrogen):		
Maximum speed:		71 mph.
Normal full speed:		67 mph @ 1,755 h.p.
Full speed endurance:		5,230 miles
" " "		78.1 hours
Cruising speed:		45 mph @ 650 h.p.
Cruising speed endurance:		9,470 miles
" " "		211 hours
Static ceiling:		21,900 feet
Crew		30 flight

Significant Chronology

Purchase authorized by Congress:	11 July 1919
Design prepared:	Aug.–Sept. 1918
Built by:	Short Bros., Bedford (later Royal Airship Works)
Ordered as R 38:	Sept. 1918
Work commenced:	Feb. 1919
British Cabinet approved sale to United States:	9 Oct. 1919
U.S. agreement:	23 Oct. 1919
Completed:	7 June 1921
First flight:	23 June 1921
Christened:	—
Commissioned:	—
Destroyed:	24 Aug. 1921
Total no. flights:	4
Total flight time:	57.35 hours
Cost of construction (to British):	$1,584,000
Sale price to United States	$1,920,000

*Primary source: *Report of the Court of Inquiry into the Loss of H.M.A. R 38*, Appendix 62. Note: Performance figures were estimated in advance, and as trials were never completed, some of them probably would have proved overly optimistic.

ZR 3 USS *LOS ANGELES**

Characteristics and Performance

Air displacement of hull:	2,764,461 cu. ft.	
Volume of gas cells:	2,599,110 cu. ft.	
Length overall:	658 ft. 4 in.	
Total height:	104 ft. 5 in.	
Maximum diameter:	90 ft. 8 in.	
Engines:	5 Maybach VL-1	
Total horsepower:	2,000	
Main frame spacing:	15 m. (49.2 ft.)	
No. gas cells:	14	

Weights (95% inflated with helium):

Fixed weights:	91,030 lb.	57.6% of gross lift
Useful lift:	66,970 lb.	42.4% of gross lift
Total weight (= gross lift):	158,000 lb.	100.0% of gross lift

Speed and endurance (95% inflated with helium):

Full speed:	65 kts.
Full speed endurance:	2,825 miles
" " "	43 hours
Cruising speed:	48 kts.
Cruising speed endurance:	5,770 miles
" " "	119 hours
Crew	54 total
"	40 flight

Significant Chronology

Contract signed:	23 June 1922
Design prepared:	1922
Built by:	*Luftschiffbau Zeppelin,* Friedrichshafen, Germany
Completed:	Aug. 1924
First flight:	27 Aug. 1924
Transatlantic flight to Lakehurst:	12–15 Oct. 1924
Christened:	25 Nov. 1924
Commissioned:	25 Nov. 1924
Decommissioned:	30 June 1932
Formally stricken:	24 Oct. 1939
Total no. flights:	331
Total flight time:	4181.28 hours
Cost to German government:	$713,332
Cost to U.S. government	$150,000

*Primary source: Sitz, Technical Note #160.

ZRS 4 USS *AKRON* AND ZRS 5 USS *MACON**

Characteristics and Performance

Air displacement of hull:	7,401,260 cu. ft.
Volume of gas cells:	6,850,000 cu. ft.
Length overall:	785 ft.
Total height:	146.5 ft.
Maximum diameter:	132.9 ft.
Engines:	8 Maybach VL-2
Total horsepower:	4,480
Main frame spacing:	22.5 m. (73.8 ft.)
No. gas cells:	12
No. airplanes accommodated in hangar:	5

Weights (95% inflated with helium):

	Akron			Macon	
Fixed weights:	243,709 lb.	60.5 % of		242,356 lb.	60.1% of
Useful lift:	159,291 lb.	39.5 % gross		160,644 lb.	39.9% gross
Total weight (= gross lift):	403,000 lb.	100.0% lift		403,000 lb.	100.0% lift

Speed and endurance (*Macon* 95% inflated with helium):

Maximum speed:	75.6 kts.
Standard speed:	65.0 kts.
Standard speed endurance:	4,855 nautical miles
" " "	75 hours
Cruising speed:	55.0 kts.
Cruising speed endurance:	5,940 nautical miles
" " "	108 hours
Crew	81 total
"	60 flight

Significant Chronology

	Akron	Macon
Construction authorized by Congress:	24 June 1926	24 June 1926
Contract signed:	6 Oct. 1928	6 Oct. 1928
Built by:	Goodyear-Zeppelin Corporation, Akron, Ohio	
Work commenced:	Nov. 1929	May 1931
Christened:	8 Aug. 1931	11 March 1933
First flight:	25 Sept. 1931	21 April 1933
Commissioned:	27 Oct. 1931	23 June 1933
First planes aboard:	3 May 1932	6 July 1933
Destroyed:	4 April 1933	12 Feb. 1935
Formally stricken:	30 April 1933	26 Feb. 1935
Total number of flights:	73	54
Total flight time:	1,695.8 hours	1,798.2 hours
Cost:	$5,375,000	$2,450,000

*Primary source: Richard K. Smith, *The Airships Akron and Macon*, Appendices I and II.

F

Airship Terms

Adiabatic heating: When a gas is compressed, its temperature rises, owing to the work done on it. (The opposite is true when the gas expands.) With hydrogen the temperature of the gas changes approximately 5°F per 1,000 feet of ascent or descent; with helium the adiabatic temperature change is somewhat over 7°F per 1,000 feet. When landing, adiabatic heating of the gas could make the airship lighter than it otherwise might be.

Airspeed meter: Pitot-tube actuated, this device presented the speed through the air in miles per hour. Corrections had to be made for decreased density with increased altitude, and it did not give speed over the ground.

Altimeter: An aneroid instrument, actually a barometer measuring air pressure, this device was graduated to give the altitude in feet. Changes in barometric pressure after takeoff could produce false readings, though corrections could be obtained by radio. A drop of 0.1 in. in barometric pressure could result in the altimeter reading 100 feet too high.

Antifreeze: Alcohol was invariably used in airship engine cooling systems. In the *Los Angeles*, calcium chloride was used initially as an antifreeze in water ballast sacks, its damaging corrosive effects on duralumin not being realized at first. Later, alcohol was used as an antifreeze in the ballast sacks of U.S. airships.

Automatic valves: Spring-loaded valves in the bottom of each gas cell opened automatically whenever the internal pressure exceeded the external by 7 to 15 mm. of water, as when an airship with full gas cells ascended to a higher altitude, expanding the gas. In the *Los Angeles* the automatic valves were 500 mm. (about 19½ in.) in diameter, and weighed 11½ lb. each. There were two valves in each of the ten largest cells.

Axial cable: The *Shenandoah* was the only U.S. rigid airship so equipped. This was a stranded wire cable running through the gas cells from bow to stern of the airship, and connecting the wire bracing of all the main rings at their centers, reducing the loads on the framework if there was an inequality of pressure between adjacent cells. (Actually the axial cable was not continuous; each gas cell contained a 10-meter segment which was attached to the center bulkhead wiring of the main rings.)

Ballast: To enable the airship to ascend to higher altitudes, or to compensate for gas loss or increased loads on the ship due to rain or ice, droppable ballast was carried. In American rigid airships water was the invariable form of ballast.

Ballast sacks: Most of the ballast was carried along the keel in rubberized fabric sacks holding 2,200 lb. of water. Fourteen of these, arranged in pairs, were in the *Los Angeles* when she was delivered. Toggles in the control car were pulled by the elevator man to empty them as necessary with the time being taken with a stopwatch (in ten seconds 400 lb. of water would be released). The officer of the watch was responsible for keeping a running record of how much ballast had been released, and from which locations.

Ballonet: In pressure airships (q.v.), this was an air-filled compartment inside the main envelope which, being kept under pressure by a blower or other means, maintained a constant pressure in the large bag, regardless of changes in the volume of the gas.

Compass: Early rigid airships were steered by magnetic compasses, the gyro compasses used on shipboard being too heavy for airships. The *Shenandoah* had a 90-lb. gyro compass originally developed by Sperry for Army tanks. The *Los Angeles* was delivered with a gyro compass by Anschütz, with several repeater compasses. With these the course could be held within 3/10 of a degree instead of the 5 degrees obtainable with the magnetic compass.

Control car: The foremost gondola in the rigid airship housed the commander, the navigator, and watch officers with rudder and elevator men. In the *Shenandoah* the control car was slung beneath the ship on struts and wires, as an engine in the rear drove a propeller 18 feet in diameter. In the *Los Angeles* and later U.S. rigids, the forward engine was omitted, and the control car was built securely onto the hull. Glass and celluloid windows provided good all-round visibility except right aft. The rudder man handled the rudder wheel in the bow of the car. On

Applied aerostatics as exemplified by the elevator man's station on the port side of the control car of *Los Angeles*. Top left, under outline of the ship showing ballast bag locations, the black toggles for the emergency bags fore and aft, and the white ones for the large 2200-lb. sacks along the keel. Top right, toggles for the eight maneuvering valves in the tops of the gas cells, with the wheel to which the toggles can be attached so that all will be opened simultaneously. Bottom left, the elevator wheel with two inclinometers just above. In the V formed by the girders are (left) an American altimeter reading in 1000-foot increments, and (right) a German altimeter reading in 100-meter increments. Above, on the blackboard, the running record in chalk of water ballast at various stations, fuel consumed, and water recovered through water recovery apparatus. To left of the blackboard, the statoscope. (AIAA)

the port side of the car was the elevator wheel, with water ballast releases and maneuvering valve controls also in charge of the elevator man. A small chart table was on the starboard side of the car, with engine telegraphs overhead to transmit orders to the engine gondolas aft. Usually the sound-proofed radio cabin with transmitters and receivers was to the rear, but in the later *Akron* and *Macon* the radio room was in the keel above the control car.

Cover: In U.S. airships, this was made of cotton BB cloth weighing 2.8 oz. per square yard and printed with a dark pattern to minimize damage from ultraviolet rays. Large panels were tailored to the lines of the airship to fit between the main longitudinals and main and intermediate transverse frames, some panels being as long as 45 meters. After being laced to the girders, the panels were doped in place. Two coats of clear dope were followed by two coats of dope in which aluminum powder was suspended. After the third coat of dope, sealing strips were glued on over the lacing at the edges of the panels, and the fourth coat was applied overall.

Crew: In U.S. naval rigid airships, the crew was organized as in surface warships. There were three watches of enlisted men, but only two watches were carried on flights, the third watch being left at home. (a) *Officers*: One commanding officer, one executive officer (navigator or engineer). One navigating or engineering officer. One watch and communications officer. One watch and commissary officer. One first lieutenant in keel. One assistant first lieutenant in keel. *Desirable at times*: Aerologist. Radio officer. Medical officer. Additional watch officer. (b) *Enlisted men*: nineteen riggers, three sections of six each, plus one leading petty officer (rudder and elevator men in this group). Twenty-five engineers, three sections of eight each, plus one leading petty officer. One cook. Two radio men. *Total of regular crew*: 54 (though with only two watches on board, total of 40).

Cruciform: a heavy cross-shaped girder structure in the stern of the ship at the rudder post, which gave added strength to the rudder and elevator seatings. In the *Los Angeles*, there was a second cruciform extending into the fins 10 meters forward of the stern post.

Docking rails: Running through the sheds at Lakehurst and Sunnyvale, and for 1,500 feet out into the field on either side, the rails carried so-called trolleys (q.v.) to which the ship was made fast fore and aft by tackles, so that she was prevented from being blown sideways by the wind when entering and leaving her shed.

210

UP SHIP

Dope: a solution of cellulose nitrate or acetate in acetone, brushed onto the outer cover after it was in place, to tauten and waterproof it.

Drift: the lateral motion of an aircraft over the ground, due to wind blowing at an angle to its course. To steer a true course over the ground, the wind strength and direction must be determined.

Drift meter: device to measure drift angle and ground speed. A circle marked in degrees, or a series of radiating lines or wires, enabled the navigator to read the drift angle by observing the apparent direction of motion of the ground passing below. Ground speed was obtained by setting the instrument to the altitude shown by the altimeter, and then reading the time required for an object on the ground to move between two transverse lines.

Duralumin: name applied to a family of alloys of aluminum which are much stronger than the parent metal. Its properties were first discovered by Alfred Wilm in Germany in 1909, and it was first manufactured in Düren, Germany. Beginning in 1916, duralumin was manufactured in the United States using as samples fragments from Zeppelins brought down in Allied or neutral countries. A formula for American duralumin was:

Aluminum (minimum):	92.00%
Copper:	3.5 to 4.4%
Magnesium:	0.2 to 0.75%
Manganese:	0.4 to 1.0%
Iron:	under 0.6%
Silica:	under 0.6%

Dynamic lift: the positive (or negative) force on an airship hull, derived from driving her at an angle with the power of her engines. With a large amount of engine power, flying a ship "dynamically" could readily compensate for considerable degrees of heaviness or lightness. At full power and with an angle of 8 degrees, the *Los Angeles* developed a dynamic lift of over 8 tons.

Elevators: movable horizontal surfaces at the tail of an airship, attached to the trailing edge of the horizontal fins. Motion upward or downward inclined the ship's nose up or down, and caused her to ascend or descend dynamically.

Emergency ballast: To quickly lighten the ship at bow or stern, as in takeoff or landing emergencies, water ballast was carried in small sacks near the nose and tail. The *Los Angeles* had six sacks in the nose, and six in the tail, each containing 550 lb. of water. Unlike the large ballast sacks in the keel, the emergency bags emptied their entire contents instantly (often on the heads of the ground crew!) when the elevator man pulled their toggles in the control car.

Engine cars: small streamlined enclosures attached by struts and wires to the hull framework of the airship, designed to accommodate an engine or engines, and personnel attending them, and to provide enough space to work on the engines in case of a breakdown.

Engines: The engines used in U.S. rigid airships had the following characteristics:

Builder	Type	h.p.	rpm	Wt., lb.	lb./ h.p.
Packard	1A-1551	300	1,400	1,138	3.79
Maybach	VL-1	400	1,400	2,100	5.2
Maybach	VL-2	550	1,600	2,315	4.2

	Fuel consumption, g/hp/hr	Cylinders	Compression ratio
Packard	205	6	6.5/1
Maybach	190	12	5.3/1
Maybach	210	12	7/1

Factor of safety: the ratio between the ultimate strength of a structural member and the maximum permissible or working stress when in use. If the maximum working stress is 1,000 lb. and the structure is designed to withstand 4,000 lb. before failing, the factor of safety is 4.

Fins: vertical or horizontal stabilizing surfaces at the tail of an airship, at the trailing edges of which were attached the movable control surfaces. In the five U.S. rigid airships the fins were of thick cantilever section with a minimum of bracing.

Fixed weights: total weight of structure and other permanent installations of an airship. In a rigid airship, this included framework, bracing wires, gas cells, outer cover, gondolas, engines, fuel tanks and piping, ballast sacks, instruments, etc.

Gangway: See keel.

Gas cells: Filling the entire interior of the rigid airship when 100% full of gas, the cells were held in place by large mesh wire netting, and finer mesh ramie cord netting, which transferred their lift to the hull framework. Gas cells were made to be both light in weight and as gas-tight as possible. The usual gas cell fabric in U.S. rigid airships was HH cloth (cotton) weighing 2.00 oz. per square yard. Various gas-proofing materials were used in the U.S. ships: A rubber film was sandwiched between two layers of HH cloth, which at 8.5 oz. per square yard was unacceptably heavy and leaked up to 12 liters of hydrogen per square meter in 24 hours. One layer of HH cloth was lined with goldbeater's skin, which was made to adhere with rubber cement and then varnished; this weighed only 4.55 oz. per square yard, with only 2 liters of hydrogen lost per square meter in 24 hours. The text relates the numerous problems with "skinned fabric" cells, while in German service at least the goldbeater's skin was attractive to mice. (The German procedure involved employing glue to attach the goldbeater's skin to the cloth. The original German cells in the *Los Angeles* were made with glue and after her delivery at Lakehurst, some glue cells were procured from Germany.) The development of gelatin latex as a gas-proof film by the Bureau of Standards was a great advance; cells lined with this material were much cheaper and more durable than earlier types. The weight was 5.3 oz. per square yard.

Gas shafts: Made up of wooden hoops and netting, and about 32 in. in diameter, these extended upward between the gas cells to conduct gas from the automatic valves in the bottom of the cells to exhaust hoods along the backbone girder of the airship. One shaft served the valves of two adjacent cells; hence the number of gas shafts was roughly half the number of cells. The gas shafts were an important safety feature in hydrogen ships, and were retained unchanged in the U.S. helium ships.

Girders: Transverse frames, and longitudinal members, required to resist compression and bending loads, were built up of light girders of triangular section. These were made up of rolled duralumin channels connected by stamped X-shaped lattices and riveted. A section of longitudinal girder of the *Shenandoah* 16.4 ft. long, 14.15 in. high, and 10.63 in. wide, weighed only 10.2 lb. but could support a compression load of 4,928 lb. For the later *Akron* and *Macon*, Dr. Arnstein designed a four-sided girder measuring 5½ × 5½ in., and made by riveting four pre-stamped strips of duralumin with large lightening holes.

Goldbeater's skin: Superb gas tightness, together with light weight, was attained by lining the inside of the gas bags with goldbeater's skin, and this was the preferred gas-proofing material through most of the rigid airship era. Goldbeater's skin was the delicate outer membrane covering the cecum or large intestine of cattle, each animal yielding only one skin measuring not more than 39 × 6 in. The careful handling required in the slaughter-houses, the quantity of skins involved, and the skilled handwork needed in assembling the skins at the gas cell factory, caused the bags so made to be enormously expensive—$14,000 apiece for the cells built by Goodyear for the *Shenandoah*.

Gondola: generic name for any car or enclosure suspended below an airship, possibly derived from the fact that early Zeppelin gondolas were not only shaped like open boats, but also were intended to float on the water.

Gondola bumpers: One or two were located under each centerline gondola to cushion the shock of landing. These were rubberized air bags enclosed in a rattan framework and covered with heavy canvas.

Gravity tanks: fuel tanks permanently installed horizontally over each engine car and feeding the engines by gravity. In U.S. airships these were known as "service tanks," and there were 15 in the *Los Angeles*, three for each power car, with a capacity of 116 U.S. gallons each. While German mechanics were required to hand-pump fuel from the slip tanks (q.v.) along the keel to the gravity tanks, in U.S. rigids this work was done by retractable wind-driven centrifugal pumps, with a hand-powered "wobble pump" in reserve.

Gross lift: the total lift, under standard conditions, of the gas contained in an airship; equal to the total weight of air displaced minus the weight of the gas.

Ground crew: Initially following German practice, the U.S. Navy used large numbers of men to walk the airships in and out of their sheds, to manhandle them on the ground, and to secure them on landing. The Navy needed 157 men to ground-handle the *Los Angeles*, but with the complete mechanical equipment designed for the *Akron* and *Macon*, a dozen men could do the job.

Hangar: large building at rigid airship bases, designed to contain one or two airships each, and with large rolling doors at either end. The leeward door was always used for entry and exit except in very light winds. During the rigid airship era in the United States, only four large hangers were built, the Navy's at Lakehurst and Sunnyvale, the Army's at Belleville, Illinois, and Goodyear-Zeppelin's at Akron.

Helium: the second lightest gas known, developed for airship use in the United States, which during the rigid airship era had a monopoly of its production from natural gas. Helium has the great advantage for airship use of being nonflammable, but it weighs 11.14 lb. per 1,000 cubic feet in the pure state and has only 93% of the lifting force of hydrogen. In rigid airships the expense of helium required the installation of heavy and drag-producing condensers to recover water from the engine exhausts to compensate for the weight of fuel burned and to eliminate the need to valve the lifting gas as fuel was consumed.

Hogged; hogging: in naval architecture, a condition in which the longitudinal axis of a vessel curves upward amidships, and droops at bow and stern. Similarly in an airship, where because the lift of the large midships gas cells exceeds the local loads, the longitudinal axis of the hull tends to curve upward amidships, while the bow and stern, whose structural weights exceed the lift of the small gas cells at the ends of the ship, tend to sag downward. In this state the upper longitudinal girders are placed under tension, while the bottom longitudinal girders are loaded in compression (note that girders are much more likely to fail in compression than in tension). Opposite of sagging (q.v.).

Hydrogen: the lightest gas known, weighing only 5.61 lb. per 1,000 cu. ft. in the pure state. Although hydrogen is easily and cheaply manufactured by a variety of methods, so that it may be valved at will by a "light" airship, the Navy's Bureau of Aeronautics, after the ZR 2 crash in England, never wavered in its determination that U.S. airships should fly with helium.

Inclinometer: an instrument that informed the elevator man of the up or down angle of the airship; usually a modification of the common spirit level, with a bubble moving in a curved tube with its convex surface upward.

Intermediate frames: One or two intermediate frames were spaced at 5-meter intervals between the main frames (q.v.) to reduce bending loads on the longitudinal girders. A ring of girders circled the ship, but there was of course no transverse wire bracing.

Jampot covers: rubberized fabric covers clamped over the automatic valves to reduce the leakage of gas outward and the admission of air inward to the gas cell involved. Although they were used in flight by Captain Lansdowne in the *Shenandoah*, after her loss it was strictly ordered that they "should only be used when the airship is to remain in the shed for several days or more, and should always be removed before the airship leaves the shed."

Keel: a triangular-section corridor running from end to end of a rigid airship at the bottom of the hull, with a walkway or catwalk about a foot wide made of light plywood and covered with fabric. Heavy concentrated loads such as fuel tanks and water ballast bags were hung from sturdy box girders along the keel, and here were located bunks for the crew. In the *Shenandoah* the keel was an inverted V composed of the two bottom longitudinals of the hull and an apex girder. In the *Los Angeles* it was an upright V with the top longitudinals bearing the heavy loads. In the *Akron* and the *Macon* (which had separate staterooms for officers and men) there were three keels 120 degrees apart, a walkway in the top of the ship and two in the lower hull port and starboard containing the eight engine rooms in their after portions.

Landing lines: In making a ground landing, the airship approached the field at a low altitude and dropped from her nose two trail ropes 300 feet long, by which the ground crew hauled her down. Shorter handling lines attached to each main frame along the keel were used to hold her on the ground. So-called spiders—short lines radiating from a snatch block—enabled five or more men to haul on each handling line.

Longitudinals: The main longitudinal girders were the lengthwise strength members of the airship. In the *Shenandoah* there were 13, 12 of them triangular, 14.15 in. deep and 10.63 in. wide, while the top longitudinal was a doubled girder of W-section. The intermediate longitudinals, of which there were 12, did not extend all the way to the tail, were designed primarily to support the outer cover, and were generally lighter than the main ones, though in the *Shenandoah* the 3 lower intermediate longitudinals were designed larger than in the L 49, the German prototype, to better withstand bending loads.

Main frames: The chief transverse structural members of the rigid airships, these were polygons built of girders (13-sided in the *Shenandoah* with kingpost bracing to support the intermediate longitudinals; a more sophisticated design in the *Los Angeles* involved ten diamond-shaped trusses in a circle with heavy keel structure at the bottom, the main longitudinals at the tips of the diamond trusses, and the intermediates in the middle). The ability of the main frame to withstand the forces exerted by the lifting gas, and by the weight of the ship's structure and lading, was a basic consideration in airship design. Main frames were heavily braced with both radial and chord wires, which also served as bulkheads to prevent fore and aft surging of the gas cells.

Maneuvering valves: Fitted in the tops of certain gas cells, these enabled the commander to make the entire ship heavy, or to trim her by releasing gas from one end. The valve pulls were overhead at the elevator man's station and were handled by him. To make the ship heavy, they were opened all together for a measured time interval by attaching their toggles to the rim of a wheel ("valving on the wheel"). Maneuvering valves were installed in 8 of the 13 gas cells of the *Los Angeles* and were 19¾ in. in diameter.

Mooring mast: Realizing that the Germans' inability to walk their Zeppelins in and out of their sheds in stiff cross winds imposed a severe operational handicap, British Major C. H. Scott, in the early postwar period, devised the mooring mast, to which a rigid airship could be moored in the open, ready to take the air regardless of the wind direction and velocity. At the "high" mast developed by the British, and copied by the U.S. Navy at Lakehurst, the ship required constant attention because of changes in buoyancy, with a skeleton crew on board at all times. For this and other reasons, the U.S. Navy later developed the "low" or "stub" mast to which the airship was secured on the ground. The nose was held by the mast, while the tail, resting on the ground, swung with the wind on a circular track.

Nonrigid airship: a small pressure airship (q.v.) consisting of a rubberized fabric gas bag whose streamlined shape was maintained by gas pressure, and from which a single gondola was suspended by internal rigging.

Payload: the portion of the useful load (q.v.) that earns revenue, devoted to the carriage of paying passengers or cargo or mail; in military airships, used loosely to include bombs or armament.

Pressure airship: generic term including both the nonrigid and semirigid airship (q.v.), in both of which the shape is maintained by gas pressure; contrasts with the rigid airship, which may be (but hardly ever is) described as a "pressureless airship."

Pressure height: the altitude at which decreasing atmospheric pressure causes the lifting gas to expand and build up a relative pressure inside the cells such that the automatic valves open, and gas is "blown off." Hydrogen ships usually took off 100% full of gas and hence blew off gas from the ground up. To conserve helium, U.S. ships never took off 100% full, but with a percentage of fullness appropriate to the planned pressure height. Thus, inflated to 82.5% fullness with helium, the *Shenandoah* had a pressure height of 6,000 feet; i.e., she would not blow off gas with her cells 100% full until rising to this altitude.

Propellers: Two-bladed wooden propellers, built up of laminations of ash, walnut, and mahogany, were standard in all but the last U.S. rigid airship. In the *Shenandoah* the four geared engines drove propellers 18 feet in diameter, while the two direct-drive engines turned propellers 10 feet in diameter. The *Macon* had three-bladed all-metal Hamilton Standard ground adjustable propellers 16.3 feet in diameter.

Rigid airship: an airship with a rigid frame (usually duralumin girders) which maintained its shape regardless of whether it was inflated with gas.

Rudder: movable vertical surfaces attached to the upper and lower fins at the tail of the airship, whose motion steered the airship to port or starboard.

Sagged; sagging: in naval architecture, a condition in which the longitudinal axis of a vessel sags downward amidships, and curves upward at bow and stern. Similarly in an airship, where the longitudinal axis of the hull tends to sag downward amidships, and curves upward at bow and stern. In this state the upper longitudinals are loaded in compression, and the lower ones in tension (note that girders are much more likely to fail in compression than in tension). Sagging in an airship is unlikely to occur in practice unless there is severe loss of gas amidships, or a strong upward dynamic force under the bow as a result of the airship's flying "heavy" in a nose-up attitude. Opposite of hogging (q.v.).

Semirigid airship: a pressure airship with a rigid keel running the length of the bag, either suspended under it or faired into its underside, for the attachment of engines and gondolas, and the distribution of fuel, ballast, and other loads. This design permits the construction of airships larger than the nonrigid type.

Shear wires: hard-drawn steel wires providing diagonal bracing in all rectangular panels formed by longitudinal girders and transverse frames, taking the shear loads on the rigid hull.

Shed: See hangar.

Slip tanks: aluminum fuel tanks distributed along the keel, and contrasting with gravity tanks (q.v.) permanently installed over the engine gondolas. In U.S. practice, the fuel tanks suspended vertically on both sides of the keel were called "reserve tanks," and in the *Los Angeles* there were 60 of them, each with a capacity of 111 U.S. gallons. While all the keel tanks could be slipped or dropped through the outer cover in German ships, only 19 of the 60 tanks in the *Los Angeles* could be slipped as ballast in an emergency. It should be noted that a further 39 gasoline tanks could have been installed in the keel of the *Los Angeles* for long cruises, at the expense of water ballast.

Stall: in aircraft, a condition where an excessive angle of attack causes a loss of lift, and the aircraft falls out of control. It should be noted that while a "heavy" airship flying nose-up can stall downward like a heavier-than-air craft at 13 degrees or more nose-up, it can also "stall upward." When flying "light" and nose down, it may be inclined downward so far that the negative lift of the hull acting as an airfoil diminishes, and the excessive lift of the "light" condition will cause it to rise out of control.

Standard conditions: in U.S. airship practice, temperature 32°F, barometric pressure 760 mm., and relative humidity 0%.

Static lift: the lift of an airship without forward motion, and due solely to the buoyancy of the gas; constrasts with dynamic lift (q.v.).

Statoscope: an instrument used by the elevator man to maintain the altitude ordered by the officer of the watch. Very sensitive to barometric pressure, it could be set to the prescribed altitude, and would then register even small variations of altitude. With the statoscope the elevator man was expected to hold his altitude within ± 20 feet in good weather, and ± 50 feet in more turbulent conditions.

Supercooling: a condition (usually obtaining after dark) in which the heat of the lifting gas was radiated into the atmosphere, and the gas then was cooler than the surrounding air. Since the density of the gas was increased as it contracted with cooling, its lifting power was less. As much as −9°F of supercooling has been recorded.

Superheating: a condition (usually due to sun's heat being trapped within the hull) where the gas was warmer than the surrounding air. Since the density of the gas was decreased as it expanded with heating, its lifting power was greater. The British R 34 experienced superheating of +66°F on 4 July 1919, during her flight to the United States.

Taxying cars: low flat cars mounted on railroad wheels on which the forward and after gondolas rested when the airship was being brought out of or into the shed. The taxying cars rode on the standard-gauge track running through the centerline of the ship's berth in the shed.

Thermometer: An air thermometer was in the control car, and also a remote-reading electrical thermometer giving the interior temperature of one of the gas cells. The data provided by these two instruments were essential to determining the lift of the airship, particularly with superheating or supercooling (q.v.).

Three-wire system: Between 1917 and 1919, and before the completion of the first mooring mast at Pulham, the British moored airships in the open with three wires made fast to a mooring point under the ship's nose, and rigged to terminate in three ground anchors at the apices of a triangle that measured 550 feet to a side. This was used by R 34 during her three-day layover at Mineola, Long Island in July 1919. There were disadvantages in that while aloft on the three wires, the ship could not be supplied with hydrogen, fuel, or water ballast, nor could crews be changed.

Trim: the attitude of the airship in the air in response to static forces. When weights and lifting forces were properly balanced so that the center of gravity was located directly under the center of lift, the airship was on an even keel and said to be "in trim." If this was not the case she was "out of trim"; if the nose was inclined downward, she was "trimmed by the bow," if the tail was inclined downward, "trimmed by the stern."

Trolley: a wheeled truck pulled by hand and rolling on docking rails (q.v.). Trolleys served as attachment points for tackles made fast to the airship fore and aft when she was being moved in or out of the shed.

Turn indicator: a gyroscopic instrument that, by deviation of a needle to right or left, indicated the direction of turn when flying blind, while the degree of deviation indicated the rate of turn.

Useful lift: the amount of lift remaining after subtracting the fixed weights of the airship from the gross lift.

Useful load: the load that an airship can carry, equal in weight to the useful lift; includes fuel, oil, water ballast, crew, spare parts, passengers and cargo, or armament and bombs.

Variometer: an instrument that indicates to the elevator man the rate of ascent or descent in feet per minute or meters per second.

Water recovery: In U.S. airships filled with helium, to avoid having to valve the scarce and expensive gas as the airship became lighter through consumption of fuel, the exhaust gases from the engines were passed through condensers hung above the gondolas in order to recover the water of combustion. In theory, 145 lb. of water could be recovered for every 100 lb. of gasoline burned. In practice, the figure was 110 to 122 lb. depending on the outside air temperature. The condensed water was piped to ballast bags in the keel.

"Weighed off": the state of an airship whose lift and load have been adjusted so as to be equal, or whose excess of lift or load have become known by test. (Colloquially, if said to be "weighed off," an airship is in equilibrium, while she will otherwise be said to be "weighed off—pounds heavy," or "weighed off—pounds light.") Before leaving the hangar an airship, through release of water ballast, was weighed off so precisely that one man at each end could lift her off the trestles under the gondolas. In flight, an experienced elevator man could tell a good deal about her static condition from the "feel" of the ship, her inclination nose up or nose down, and the angle of elevator required to keep her at this inclination. Good practice demanded that before landing a ship should be "weighed off" in the air above the field. The engines were stopped or idled and the rise or fall measured on the variometer. In the *Los Angeles*, a rise or fall of 0.2 meter per second indicated she was 1000 lb. light or heavy. Gas would then be valved or ballast released to bring her into equilibrium.

Weight empty: equals fixed weights (q.v.).

G

Abbreviations

GENERAL

AIAA	American Institute of Aeronautics and Astronautics
ALUSNA	American Legation, U.S. Naval Attaché
AvOps	Aviation Section, Office of the Chief of Naval Operations
BuAer	Bureau of Aeronautics
BuC&R	Bureau of Construction and Repair
BuNav	Bureau of Navigation
BuSEng	Bureau of Steam Engineering
BuY&D	Bureau of Yards and Docks
ComRATES	Commander, Rigid Airship Training and Experimental Squadron
CC	Construction Corps
CinC	Commander in Chief
CO	Commanding Officer
CNO	Chief of Naval Operations
DELAG	*Deutsche Luftschiffahrts Aktien-Gesellschaft* (German Airship Transportation Company)
HTA	Heavier Than Air
IAACC	Inter-allied Aeronautical Commission of Control
INA	Inspector of Naval Aircraft
JANAB	Joint Army–Navy Airship Board
LTA	Lighter Than Air
NACA	National Advisory Committee for Aeronautics
NAF	Naval Aircraft Factory
NAS	Naval Air Station
NASM	National Air and Space Museum
OpNav	Office of the Chief of Naval Operations
RAF	Royal Air Force
RN	Royal Navy
SecNav	Secretary of the Navy
SIMSADUS	SimsAdmiralUS (Telegraphic address of Admiral Sims's Headquarters in London)
USNRF	U.S. Naval Reserve Force

ENLISTED MEN'S RATINGS
(a) Before July 1921

CBM	Chief Boatswain's Mate
CCM	Chief Carpenter's Mate

CE (RA)	Chief Electrician (Radio)
CMM (A)	Chief Machinist's Mate (Aviation)
CQM (D)	Chief Quartermaster's Mate (Dirigible)
CY	Chief Yeoman
E 3(RA)	Electrician's Mate 3rd Class (Radio)
MM1 (A)	Machinist's Mate 1st Class (Aviation)
QM1 (D)	Quartermaster's Mate 1st Class (Dirigible)
Y3	Yeoman 3rd Class

(b) After July 1921

ACMM	Aviation Chief Machinist's Mate
ACR	Aviation Chief Rigger
AMM1c	Aviation Machinist's Mate 1st Class
AR1c	Aviation Rigger 1st Class
BM1c	Boatswain's Mate 1st Class
Cox	Coxswain
CPhM	Chief Pharmacist's Mate
CRM	Chief Radio Man
QM1c	Quartermaster 1st Class
RM1c	Radioman 1st Class
Sea1c	Seaman 1st Class
Sea2c	Seaman 2nd Class

Notes

INTRODUCTION

1. In naval planning between the wars, ORANGE referred to Japan, BLUE to the United States, RED to Great Britain, BLACK to Germany, etc.

2. For a scholarly discussion of this thesis, see Charles M. Melhorn, *Two Block Fox: The Rise of the Aircraft Carrier, 1911–1929.*

3. For a full and thoroughly researched account, see Richard K. Smith, *The Airships Akron and Macon: Flying Aircraft Carriers of the U.S. Navy.*

CHAPTER 1

1. Douglas H. Robinson, *The Zeppelin In Combat.*

2. Ernst Lehmann and Howard Mingos, *The Zeppelins.*

3. Groos, Otto. *Der Krieg in der Nordsee*, Vols. I–V.

4. Kap. Lt. von Schiller, "The Achievements of German Airships in the World War." *Office of Naval Intelligence, Monthly Information Bulletin*, Jan. 1924, p. 26.

5. One further British rigid airship design deserves notice because of its excellence, and it was outstanding because it was German. R 31 and R 32, built by Short Brothers at Cardington, were modified copies of one of the Schütte-Lanz wooden frame ships, plans of which had been brought to England by a Swiss employee of the Mannheim firm.

6. C. P. Burgess to Bureau of Aeronautics, 26 May 1922, Garland Fulton files.

7. In 1919, the pound sterling was worth about $4.80; hence the cost of R 38 amounted to $1,920,000, which at that time was a great deal of money.

CHAPTER 2

1. Bradley A. Fiske, Aide for Operations, to SecNav, 16 July 1913, General Board files.

2. The post went in May 1915 to Admiral William S. Benson, whom time would show to be cool to naval aviation.

3. J. C. Hunsaker, *The History of Naval Aviation*, Vol. VI, *The Development of Naval Airships*, p. 1.

4. J. C. Hunsaker, "The Present Status of Airships in Europe." *Journal of the Franklin Institute*, Vol. 177, No. 6, pp. 597–639.

5. Lcdr. Frank R. McCrary, the naval inspector at the New Haven factory, reported disgustedly later that "it could hardly be called an aircraft company. It consisted of a New Haven R.R. lawyer as financial backer; an ex-Amusement Park Concession operator as manager; an Austrian who claimed to have piloted a dirigible and two German mechanics who claimed to have been members of the crew of a Zeppelin. The 'plant' was a six-by-eight office . . . and a rented boat shed." Archibald K. Turnbull and Clifford L. Lord, *History of United States Naval Aviation*, p. 85.

6. Rear Admiral Charles J. Badger to SecNav, 24 June 1916 (serial #513), General Board files.

7. Acting Chief Signal Officer to Adjutant General, 2 Oct. 1916, RG 18, CentDec Files, Bx 1053.

8. Considering that the ship's size would have been dictated by the small dimensions of the Vickers building shed at Barrow in Furness, any rigid built by them would have been incapable of flying the Atlantic. The bureau in any case held a poor opinion of Vickers's designs: "it became clear later that Vickers was still experimenting and not really in possession of sound knowledge and experience." Hunsaker, VI, p. 6.

9. Starr Truscott to JANAB, 8 Dec. 1917, RG 18, File 334.7. "Argon" was the usual code word of World War I for helium, whose intended use in airships was a secret. Other synonyms were "Currenium" and "C-gas."

10. Report to Joint Army–Navy Airship Board on Design, Construction and Use of Rigid airships in England, France and Italy, RG 18, CentDec Files, Bx 1052.

11. Joint Army–Navy Airship Board, Final Meeting, RG 72, CNO, Bx 20.

12. Naval Affairs Committee (House) Hearings, 65th Congress, 2–3 Session, 1918–19.

13. Ibid., Capt. G. W. Steele, 27 Nov. 1918. Steele had seen a British Admiralty document that stated: "from results already given of instances it will be seen how justified is the confidence felt by the German Navy in its airships when used in their proper sphere as eyes of the Fleet. It is no small achievement for their Zeppelins to have saved the High Seas Fleet at the Battle of Jutland; to have saved their cruiser squadron on the Yarmouth raid (April 25, 1916), and to have been instrumental in sinking the *Nottingham* and *Falmouth* (on August 19, 1916)." "The Uses of Airships for the Navy (British)," 20 Sept. 1917, Garland Fulton Files. None of these claims was true, but Steele and Irwin had no means of realizing this in 1918.

14. Hunsaker. VI, p. 15.

15. General Board #449, Serial 887, General Board Files.

16. See Patrick Abbott, *Airship*, for a full history of R 34 with emphasis on the transatlantic flight.

CHAPTER 3

1. In 1977 the name of the station was changed to The Naval Air Engineering Center, Lakehurst, N.J.

2. U.S. Navy Bureau of Aeronautics, *Rigid Airship Manual 1927*, p. IX–1.

3. The taxying cars derived from British airship practice.

4. Maxfield to Weyerbacher, 11 April 1921, RG 72, C&R, Bx 418.

5. Silicol was a commercial ferrosilicon (silicon 85%, iron 15%) that reacted with caustic soda to form hydrogen ($Si + 2NaOH + H_2O = NaSiO_3 + 2H_2$).

6. Weyerbacher to Chief, Bu Y&D, 24 March 1921, RG 72, Airship History, Bx 24.

CHAPTER 4

1. Ramsey (Naval Aviator #45) served in carriers in World War II, reaching the rank of rear admiral. From August 1943 to June 1945 he was chief of the Bureau of Aeronautics. Immediately after World War II he was vice chief of Naval Operations under Admiral Nimitz.

2. Craven to Ramsey, 15 Aug. 1919, RG 72, CNO, Bx 380.

3. The state of war with Germany continued until 18 Oct. 1921, when the U.S. Senate ratified a special treaty with Germany.

4. OpNav to Knapp, 26 July 1919, RG 72, CNO, Bx 263. The year's delay was to allow for completion of the Lakehurst shed.

5. Air Marshal Sir Hugh Trenchard, the chief of the Air Staff, was not prejudiced against airships, but felt obliged to get rid of them because of the heavy drain on the slim appropriations for his service. "He had to jettison liabilities to preserve the R.A.F. itself." Robin D. S. Higham, *The British Rigid Airship 1908–1931*, p. 210.

6. Conversely, the Americans willingly allowed themselves to be used in place of R.A.F. personnel, who were being rapidly demobilized, because the Americans valued the training they were receiving.

7. Knapp to OpNav, 24 Oct. 1919, RG 72, CNO, Bx 264.

8. Ramsey to Craven, 7 Aug. 1919, RG 72, CNO, Bx 380.

9. The 5,000,000-cubic-foot ship was never built or even seriously considered.

10. Knapp to OpNav, 20 Aug. 1919, RG 72, CNO, Bx 264.

11. SecNav to Knapp, 30 Aug. 1919, RG 72, C&R, Bx 418.

12. Ramsey to Craven, 30 Sept. 1919, RG 72, CNO, Bx 380.

13. Knapp to OpNav, 7 Oct. 1919, RG 72, C&R, Bx 418.

14. SecNav to Knapp, 17 Oct. 1919, RG 72, C&R, Bx 418.

15. On 29 Dec. 1917, Lansdowne had proceeded to Pulham where he trained in R 23, and he then went on 10 Jan. 1918, to Howden for further instruction. He remained at Howden until some time in February, training in R 25.

16. Benson to OpNav, 12 Jan. 1919, RG 72, CNO, Bx 265. On 1 Oct. 1919 Craven wrote to Ramsey, "Admiral Benson retired last week, and while he is a very estimable man, a splendid character, etc., there were quite a few dry eyes around here in the Aviation Section when he relinquished the chair of office." RG 72, CNO, Bx 380.

17. AvOps to Benson, 29 April 1919, RG 72, CNO, Bx 264.

18. Craven to Ramsey, 15 Aug. 1919, RG 72, CNO, Bx 380.

19. Knapp to OpNav, 7 Oct. 1919, RG 72, C&R, Bx 418.

20. Ramsey to Craven, 14 Oct. 1919, RG 72, CNO, Bx 380.

21. Knapp to OpNav, 24 Oct. 1919, RG 72, CNO, Bx 264.

22. In fact, rapid demobilization in America had likewise created a severe shortage of personnel, particularly of experienced men with aviation training.

23. SecNav to SIMSADUS, 25 Oct. 1919, RG 72, C&R, Bx 410.

24. Daniels to McKean, 25 Oct. 1919, RG 72, CNO, Bx 264.

25. SecNav to SIMSADUS, 28 Oct. 1919, RG 72, CNO, Bx 264.

26. Ramsey to Craven, 4 Nov. 1919, RG 72, CNO, Bx 380.

27. About $24,000 U.S., no small sum at a time when a seaman's pay was $21.00 per month!

28. Knapp to OpNav, 14 Nov. 1919, RG 72, CNO, Bx 273.

29. Craven to Ramsey, 1 Dec. 1919, RG 72, CNO, Bx 380.

30. SecNav to SIMSADUS, London, 23 Dec. 1919, RG 72, C&R, Bx 418.

31. Air Ministry to Force Commander, 20 Feb. 1920, RG 72, C&R, Bx 418.

32. Large amounts of hydrogen for the British airship program were produced at the bases by the Water Gas Contact process. Steam forced through a bed of hot coke at the right temperature was reduced to hydrogen and carbon dioxide. The latter gas was removed in a scrubber.

33. Air Ministry to Force Commander, 24 March 1920, RG 72, CNO, Bx 264.

34. Force Commander to Air Ministry, 31 March 1920, RG 72, CNO, Bx 264.

35. Air Ministry to Force Commander, 16 April 1920, RG 72, CNO, Bx 264.

36. Memo, Maxfield to Craven, 26 Nov. 1919, RG 72, CNO, Bx 264.

37. Chief BuNav to COs all air stations, 22 Jan. 1920, RG 19, GenCor, Bx 387.

38. For the names and ratings of members of the first draft, see Appendix A.

39. Staff Representative, London, to BuNav, 15 April 1920, RG 19, GenCor, Bx 387.

40. BuNav to all COs NAS, 27 April 1920, RG 19, GenCor, Bx 387.

41. CO Howden to CNO, 12 July 1921, RG 19, GenCor, Bx 388.

42. The (T) indicates warrant officer with temporary commission.

43. For the names and ratings of the second draft, and the ten casuals, see Appendix A.

44. John McCarthy, a member of the Howden Detachment, reflected this admiration in relating how Maitland one night had the Americans turn out to fly him to London in R 32. The Americans entered with enthusiasm into the project, but were surprised when Maitland, over the capital, jumped by parachute through a keel hatch, followed by his batman and his luggage attached to a parachute. Interview, Lakehurst, N.J., 25 June 1971. British airshipmen regarded the tale as apocryphal, but *The Airship*, Vol. I, No. 1, p. 3, relates that Maitland's last parachute jump was at night over Cardington from R 80, which at that time was based at Howden and was being used by the Americans as a training ship.

45. Occasionally it was *not* "hands across the sea": "I tried to get them to put some sort of gauge on the expansion tanks on the tops of the radiators so that the water level could be seen but nothing doing with that. King James got along without it and that was the end of it." Letter, Bieg to Kraus, 22 July 1921.

46. Lord Ventry says this was SSE-3 (two 110-h.p. Sunbeam Dyak engines) delivered to Howden 8 March 1920, for training U.S. naval personnel. She made her last flight there on 28 Oct. 1920. Letter to Robinson, 22 Nov. 1978.

47. Surviving Bieg by 24 years, Takajiro Onishi as vice admiral commanding the Japanese First Air Fleet in the Philippines in Oct. 1944, conceived and fostered the *Kamikaze* tactic, and committed hara-kiri on 16 Aug. 1945, the day after the Japanese surrender.

48. Visiting Howden in June 1920, Lord Ventry remembers the Americans flying in the big North Sea NS 7. Letter to Robinson, 6 Dec. 1978.

49. In the year 1959 some mindless bureaucrat put all the British airship log books through a shredding machine. Robin D. S. Higham, personal communication.

50. Bieg to Kraus, 13 May 1920.

51. Weekly news letter, Howden, Yorkshire, England, 10 June 1920, RG 72, CNO, Bx 186.

52. Bieg to Kraus, 13 June 1920.

53. O'Claire notebook, p. 9.

54. For a list of all known U.S. naval training flights in R 32 and R 80, see Appendix B.

55. Norman Walker logbook. R 32 flights are listed in detail in the logbooks of Norman Walker and James H. Collier, who arrived in July with the second draft.

56. Cousin of Charles A. Lindbergh's mother, and as a rear admiral, World War II chairman of the U.S. Maritime Commission, and head of the War Shipping Administration. He had replaced Captain McBride early in 1920.

57. Air Ministry to Naval Attaché, 21 Jan. 1921, RG 72, CNO, Bx 264.

58. Bieg to Kraus, 6 Feb. 1921. Patrick Abbott, *Airship*, pp. 135–42.

59. Staff Representative, London, to SecNav, 4 Feb. 1921, RG 72, CNO, Bx 264.

60. Air Ministry to Staff Representative, London, 9 Feb. 1921, RG 72, CNO, Bx 264. The Air Ministry did not mean that new gas cells would be made for L 64, merely that it would take this long to make them if desired.

61. Air Ministry to Naval Attaché, 30 March 1921, R 38 Court of Inquiry Proceedings, Appendix 45.

62. Naval Attaché to Air Ministry, 4 April 1921, ibid.

63. Letter, Shotter to Keller, 1 April 1959.

CHAPTER 5

1. Captain McBride to Chief Constructor, 26 Oct. 1919, RG 72, C&R, Bx 418.

2. Hunsaker, VI, p. 15.

3. In the later 1920s and 1930s when R 101 was built here, "Cardington" was synonymous with the airship works, but "Bedford" was generally used at the time when R 38 was under construction.

4. Force Commander to BuSEng and BuC&R, 7 Jan. 1920, RG 72, C&R, Bx 418.

5. Visiting six months later, Bieg wrote, "I had tea at Dyer's place.... He has a regular ducal palace. Great grounds, stables, gardens, and tennis court. I felt like an ant." Bieg to Kraus, 27 June 1920.

6. In fact, lift and trim trials before the first flight showed that the ship was somewhat bow-heavy even though not all the bow mooring gear had been installed. She was trimmed by not filling the two forward emergency water ballast bags at Frame 1, which contained 525 lb. of water each.

7. Report of the Court of Inquiry into the Loss of HMA R 38 (hereafter "C of I"), Appendix 4.

8. Truscott to Hunsaker, 17 May 1920, RG 72, C&R, Bx 418.

9. Burgess to BuC&R commenting on Hunsaker letters of 2 and 5 July 1920, RG 72, C&R, Bx 418. Author's italics.

10. Burgess to BuC&R, 19 Oct 1920, RG 72, C&R, Bx 418.

11. Air Ministry to U.S. Representative, London, 20 April 1921, RG 72, C&R, Bx 418.

12. Acting Secretary to SecState, 12 May 1921, RG 72, CNO, Bx 264.

13. C of I, Campbell to Director of Research, Appendix 44.

14. Pritchard memo, 11 Aug. 1921, C of I, Appendix 61.

15. Air Ministry to Commander Land, C of I, Appendix 45.

16. C of I, Appendix 12. Italics in original.

17. Higham, p. 218.

18. Commanding Officer ZR 2 to CNO, 6 June 1921, RG 72, C&R, Bx 418.

19. Maxfield to CNO, 1 July 1921, RG 72, C&R, Bx 418.

20. This matter appears somewhat obscure, and is mentioned only in R & M 775, *Report on the Accident to H.M. Airship R 38* (hereafter referred to as "R & M 775"), p. 18.

21. Memo, Dyer to Rear Admiral Nathan C. Twining, Naval Attaché, London, 15 Dec. 1921.

22. ALUSNA, London, to BuNav, 21 July 1921, RG 72, C&R, Bx 418.

23. C of I, Appendix 13.

24. Second endorsement to Maxfield report to Staff Representative, London, of 20 July 1921, RG 72, C&R, Bx 418.

25. Bieg to Kraus, 22 July 1921.

26. Griffin to CNO, 16 Aug. 1921, RG 72, C&R, Bx 418.

27. Burgess and Truscott memo, 16 Aug. 1921, RG 72, C&R, Bx 419.

28. In the end, Maxfield sent home in June Lt. Houghton, Ensigns Medusky and Hykes, and O'Claire, McCarthy, Thomas, Knight, Peckham, and Leonard. Hykes carried

with him the manuscript of a rigid airship operating manual written by Maxfield. I cannot determine that this was ever published and circulated. CO Howden to CNO, 31 May 1921, RG 19, GenCor, Bx 388.

29. Bieg to Kraus, 20 July 1921.

30. C of I, Appendix 7. Frame 13 was at the leading edge of the fins, and Frame 15 was at the rudder post, aft of which was the tail cone and gunner's cockpit, a very light structure.

31. USNAPEAN to BuSEng, 21 Aug. 1921, RG 72, CNO, Bx 264.

32. Flag *Utah* to OpNav (signed by Maxfield), RG 72, CNO, Bx 264.

33. Lt. C. A. Tinker, USNRF, to Naval Attaché, London, 10 Aug. 1921, RG 72, C&R, Bx 419.

34. C of I, Appendix 12.

35. Richard E. Byrd, *Skyward*, p. 126.

36. Appendix A indicates the members of the Howden Detachment who died in the crash. The only American survivor was ACR Norman C. Walker.

37. The actual figures were: Cell 1, 92.6%; 2, 87.3%; 3, 93.6%; 4, 92.05%; 5, 76.4% (!!); 6, 95.4%; 7, 91.6%; 8, 92.4%; 9, 92.3%; 10, 92.3%; 11, 89.7%; 12, 92.8%; 13, 90%; 14, 87.2%. Collier notebook.

38. After the crash, Coil's body was found entangled in wires at Frame 10. Shipmates were sure he had stationed himself here because he anticipated that the ship would break at this point under heavy aerodynamic loads. Part of a parachute was found on his body indicating that he had expected the worst and hoped to save his life by jumping. Flight Lieutenant Montagu's body was found a little farther aft, at about Frame 12; evidently he too feared a failure in the tail.

39. Hunsaker memo, conversation with Flight Lieutenant A. H. Wann, 4 May 1922.

40. C of I, pp. 37–38. Very probably Pannell was again handling the rudder wheel. An earlier comment by Maxfield is interesting: "Mr. Panel (sic) is a very large man and my experience with him leads me to believe that he is exceedingly hard on the controls." Maxfield to CNO, 11 April 1921, "Accident to H.M.A. R 36," Garland Fulton Files.

41. Letter, Sir Victor Goddard to Robinson, 10 May 1977.

42. I accept that two parachutes opened as the ship fell. It is remarkable that the men under them did not survive; some witnesses claimed they descended into the burning gasoline on the water.

43. Davies testimony, C of I, p. 40.

44. Wann was still hospitalized at the time the Court of Inquiry was held, and no formal statement was ever taken from him.

45. The sixteenth American body, that of British-born CMM J. T. Hancock, was sent the day before at the request of his relatives to the American cemetery in England at Forest Gate.

46. C of I, p. 1.

47. C of I, Appendix 60. Author's italics. The Board of Admiralty, headed by the First Lord, a political appointee, was made up of the respective sea lords, all senior admirals

of great experience. The controller was the sea lord directly responsible for warship procurement and construction. In meeting to discuss and approve warship designs, the Board received the advice of the chief constructor of the Navy, the head of the Royal Corps of Naval Constructors.

48. Byrd to Moffett, 27 Aug. 1921, RG 72, C&R, Bx 419. Byrd was undoubtedly reflecting the fears and concerns of his late friend Lcdr. Coil, who had stationed himself at Frame 10 for the turning trials.

49. Glazebrook was chairman of the Aeronautical Research Committee and director of the National Physical Laboratory. Petaval was chairman of the Aerodynamic Sub-Committee of the Aeronautical Research Committee, of which Bairstow and Campbell himself were members.

50. R & M 775, p. 15.

51. My late friend Oberst Martin Dietrich, the wartime German naval commander of L 71, retained his interest in airships to the end of his life in 1973. He considered that R 38 was structurally unsuited to high-speed operation at low altitude, and that the disaster had been caused by misuse of the controls.

52. R & M 775, p. 10.

53. Ibid., p. 11.

54. C of I, p. 37.

55. "Boffin": British slang for a theoretical scientist lacking practical knowledge or experience.

56. Moffett to NavIntel, 24 March 1922, RG 72, C&R, Bx 419.

57. BuAer memo, 12 Feb. 1923, RG 72, C&R, Bx 419.

58. Memo, Whiting to Moffett, 13 July 1921, General Board files.

59. Nothing in the voluminous archives even suggests what name ZR 2 would have borne had she arrived in America and been commissioned in the U.S. Navy.

CHAPTER 6

1. Taylor and Griffin to SecNav, 28 July 1919, RG 72, C&R, Bx 419.

2. Great Britain, Admiralty War Staff, Intelligence Division. CB 1265, CB 1265A, *German Rigid Airships* (Confidential).

3. Truscott memo to C&R, 29 Aug. 1919, RG 72, C&R, Bx 419.

4. On her delivery flight on 15 June 1917, L 49 had sustained major structural damage when the lower nose framework forward of Frame 170 had imploded during a descent from 11,500 to 2,600 feet, owing to lack of venting apertures for equalizing pressure inside the tightly-doped outer hull. The Americans were generally aware of the facts of this accident.

5. Admiral Taylor (BuC&R) to General Board, 18 Feb. 1920, General Board files.

6. A simple reduction gear for the forward engine, a reduction and reverse gear for the port engine, a reduction and reverse gear of the opposite hand for the starboard engine, and a reduction gear enabling the two engines in the after gondola to drive its single 19–foot propeller.

7. The German twin-engine gondola had been copied in R 33 and R 34, whose engineering personnel heartily disliked it. "A horrible contraption. It was impossible to syn-

chronize these engines, one was always pulling the other."
Letter, John Shotter to Charles Keller, 1 April 1959.

8. Letter, Campbell to Hunsaker, 4 June 1920. Campbell letter enclosed in Hunsaker to BuC&R, 8 June 1920.

9. Letter, Garland Fulton to Charles Keller, 19 Oct. 1958. Actually Burgess left over 400 design memoranda, preserved today in the Naval Air Systems Command library.

10. Burgess to BuAer, 1 Sept. 1921, RG 72, C&R, Bx 420. Author's italics.

11. C. P. Burgess, J. C. Hunsaker, and Starr Truscott, "The Strength of Rigid Airships." Journal of the Royal Aeronautical Society, Vol. 28, June 1924.

12. Charles P. Burgess, Airship Design.

13. Taylor and Griffin to SecNav, 5 Nov. 1920, RG 72, C&R, Bx 420.

14. Burgess memo on conversation with Weyerbacher, 2 July 1920, RG 72, C&R, Bx 419.

15. Truscott memo, 1 April 1921, RG 72, C&R, Bx 420.

16. Chief, BuAer to SecNav, 26 Oct. 1921, RG 72, C&R, Bx 420.

17. Memo, Moffett, to CNO, 11 Aug. 1921.

18. Aviation, 17 Oct. 1921, Vol. 11, No. 16, p. 458.

19. L 49 data, German report, submitted to BuC&R, 25 Jan. 1921.

20. C. P. Burgess, Design Memorandum #42, Comparative Weights of Airships ZR 1 and ZR 3, Nov. 1924.

21. Interview, Richard K. Smith, with Commander R. D. Weyerbacher, Booneville, Indiana, 8 July 1960.

22. Moffett to NACA, 20 April 1922, RG 72, C&R, Bx 420.

23. Presumably this refers to the small rudders fitted and the large number of turns of the helm required to move them hard over.

24. "Technical Aspects of the Loss of the USS Shenandoah." Journal of the American Society of Naval Engineers (hereafter referred to as "ASNE"), Vol. 38, No. 3, Aug. 1926, p. 491.

25. Westervelt to C&R, 13 March 1921, RG 72, C&R, Bx 420.

26. Meadowcroft visit to Chicago packing houses, 7 and 8 Feb. 1922, RG 45, subject file Bx 110.

27. NAF to C&R, 17 Nov. 1920, RG 72, C&R, Bx 420.

28. NAF to BuAer, 12 May 1922, RG 72, C&R, Bx 421.

29. U.S. Navy Bureau of Aeronautics, Rigid Airship Manual 1927, p. IX–8.

30. Clifford W. Seibel, Helium, Child of the Sun, p. 20.

31. With unconscious exaggeration, Hunsaker claimed that "this was the inception of the helium gas adventure—certainly the boldest and most romantic enterprise of applied physics ever known to the world." Hunsaker, VI, p. 8.

32. Annual Report, Secretary of the Navy, Fiscal Year 1922.

33. Aviation, 4 Dec. 1922, Vol. 13, No. 23, p. 745.

34. McCrary to BuAer, 16 Nov. 1922, Gen Cor, Bx 3843.

35. BuAer memo, 25 Nov. 1922, RG 72, C&R, Bx 422.

36. In 1924 he was also designated Naval Aviator (HTA).

37. Weyerbacher to BuC&R, 1 June 1920, RG 72, Gen Cor, Bx 5560.

38. To preserve them against corrosion, all the girders had to be varnished by hand ("about 4% of ground American Blue added to make varnish definitely visible"). This took about six hours per girder, adding 320 lb. to the weight of the ship.

39. NAF Memo, Master Schedule #13, RG 72, C&R, Bx 420.

40. NAF to BuC&R, 27 Jan. 1922, RG 72, C&R, Bx 420.

41. Weyerbacher to Hunsaker, 24 April 1922, RG 72, C&R, Bx 420. Why was the first frame an intermediate one with no wire bracing? Frame 105 was in fact exactly at the center of the ship, and when she was docked, either bow to the east or bow to the west, Frame 105 was always in the same location relative to the shed. Thus it may have had symbolic significance.

42. Weyerbacher to J. C. Hunsaker, 26 July 1922, RG 72, C&R, Bx 421.

43. Truscott memo, 8 May 1922, RG 72, C&R, Bx 420.

44. Lt. Mayer memo (NAF), 15 Aug. 1922, RG 72, C&R, Bx 421.

45. J. C. Hunsaker endorsement to letter, Dyer to BuAer, 29 April 1922, RG 72, C&R, Bx 420.

46. Commander T. G. W. Settle, "Memorandum to Captain," 31 May 1939. This is reproduced in full as Appendix C.

47. E. J. King and W. M. Whitehill, Fleet Admiral King: A Naval Record, pp. 207–11.

48. Letter, Fulton to Keller, 3 June 1960.

49. Chief, BuAer, to Chief, BuNav, 16 Dec. 1922, RG 72, C&R, Bx 422.

50. The training in free balloons, a tradition going back to McCrary and Maxfield at Akron in 1915, continued at Lakehurst to the end of the airship era. Curiously, despite its value in teaching aerostatics, it was not part of the German curriculum. Royal Naval Air Service airship pilots received free-balloon training during World War I.

51. The Packard had a bore of 6.625 in., stroke of 7.5 in., and a displacement of 1,551.24 cu. in. The experimental engines had a compression ratio of 5.5:1, the production engines, 6.5:1, and they were rated at 300 h.p. at 1400 rpm. Length overall was 66.31 in., width 31.31 in., and height 44.5 in. Dry weight was 1,138 lb., giving a weight/h.p. ratio of 3.79 lb./h.p. (The Maybach MbIVa of 1918 had a bore of 6.5 in., stroke of 7.09 in., and a displacement of 1,412 cu. in., with a compression ratio of 6.7:1. Rated at 245 h.p. at 1400 rpm at 6,500 feet, it weighed 860 lb. for a wt./h.p. ratio of 3.51 lb./h.p., and had a fuel consumption of .44 lb./h.p./hr.) The 12-cylinder Liberty, with a bore of 5 in., stroke 7 in., and displacement of 1,648.42 cu.in., had a dry weight of 844 lb., for 2.81 lb./h.p. when developing 300 h.p.

52. In the completed ship, #1, #2, #4, and #6 engines were left-handed, while #3 and #5 were right-handed. The propellers on the geared engines turned in the opposite direction, however, so the propellers, when seen from aft, turned to the right (#1, #2, #5, and #6) and to the left (#3, #4). BuAer memo, 9 Oct. 1922, RG 72, C&R, Bx 422.

53. BuAer to NAF, 30 March 1922, RG 72, C&R, Bx 420.

54. Truscott memo, 19 May 1922, RG 72, C&R, Bx 420.

55. Letter, Truscott to Fulton, 19 April 1923, Garland Fulton files.

CHAPTER 7

1. Weyerbacher memo 2 June 1923, RG 72, C&R, Bx 423.

2. BuAer to Lakehurst, 14 Aug. 1923, RG 72, C&R, Bx 423.

3. *New York Times*, 11 Sept. 1923, 19:6.

4. The Navy sank the Army, winning all four first places, the legendary Lt. (j.g.) Alford J. Williams coming in first with a record speed of 243.67 mph.

5. Moffett to Senator Spencer, 20 Aug. 1923, RG 72, C&R, Bx 423.

6. BuAer to Lcdr. Pierce and Lcdr. Mitscher, 29 Sept. 1923, RG 72, C&R, Bx 423.

7. McCrary to BuAer, 29 Sept. 1923, RG 72, C&R, Bx 424.

8. Hunsaker to Fulton, 12 Oct. 1923, Garland Fulton files.

9. Moffett to McCrary, 24 Sept. 1923, RG 72, C&R, Bx 424. With helium, ZR 1 in no way could have flown the Atlantic nonstop, particularly from east to west against prevailing head winds.

10. I have been unable to determine whether this is true in any Indian language. The translation may have been a poetic fantasy of Mrs. Denby, who came from the Shenandoah Valley in Virginia and probably suggested the name to her husband. Later rigid airships were treated as cruisers for christening purposes, and were named after cities.

11. CNO Order, 12 Oct. 1923, RG 72, Bx 424.

12. McCrary to BuAer, 24 Sept. 1923, RG 72, C&R, Bx 424.

13. *Rigid Airship Manual*, p. IX–97.

14. The crew of the *Shenandoah* was divided into three watches, though only two flew in her at a time.

15. McCrary to BuAer, 7 Nov. 1923, RG 72, C&R, Bx 424.

16. BuAer to Lakehurst, 16 Nov. 1923, RG 72, C&R, Bx 424.

17. Endorsement to McCrary to BuAer, 23 Nov. 1923, RG 72, C&R, Bx 424.

18. *New York Herald*, 16 Nov. 1923.

19. *Aviation*, 15 Oct. 1923, Vol. 15, No. 16, p. 491.

20. This was one of the great days of my life. I well remember the *Shenandoah*, proceeding west from Boston, appearing in the sky to the northeast, shining silver with the red, white, and blue star-in-a-circle insigne and rudder stripes, and the legend "U.S. Navy" amidships. I was five years old and, at the time, living in Weston, Mass. (DHR)

21. McCrary to BuAer, 22 Nov. 1923, RG 72, C&R, Bx 424.

22. John B. Lawrence memo for BuAer, 3 Dec. 1923, RG 72, C&R, Bx 424.

23. Endorsement to C.O. *Shenandoah* to BuAer, 16 Jan. 1924, RG 72, GenCor, Bx 5565.

24. BuAer (Moffett) to C.O. Lakehurst, 9 Jan. 1924, RG 72, GenCor, Bx 5565.

25. *New York Times*, 7 March 1923, 1:2.

26. Amundsen and Ellsworth, with four other men, made their attempt from Spitzbergen in two Dornier *Wal* flying boats on 21 May 1925—the first expedition by airplane in the Arctic. Both aircraft landed on the ice at 87° 50′ north when one suffered engine trouble, and after great hardship the six succeeded in flying off the ice and back to Spitzbergen in one aircraft on 15 June. Theirs, however, were not the first aircraft in the Arctic: on 11 July 1897 Salomon August Andrée and two companions disappeared on a balloon flight from Spitzbergen to the pole, not be heard from until 33 years later (when they were found

dead); and Walter Wellman made two unsuccessful ascents from Spitzbergen in 1907 and 1909 in the semirigid airship *America*, of 258,000 cu. ft.

27. *Aviation*, 17 Dec. 1923, Vol. 15, No. 25, pp. 748–49.

28. The other members were Commander William R. Furlong; Lcdrs. Ezra G. Allen and Fitzhugh Green; Mr. Gilbert Grosvenor, president of the National Geographic Society; and Lcdr. Harold T. Bartlett, as member and recorder.

29. Actually about 3,200 mi. from Teller, but only 2,400 mi. from Point Barrow on the north slope, where the tender might be based during the summer.

30. Truscott to Chief, Design Section, 8 Dec. 1923, RG 72, Airship History, Bx 35.

31. Cover sheet note on BuAer memorandum, Capt. A. W. Johnson, 24 Dec. 1923, RG 72, C&R, Bx 350.

32. M. A. Mitscher Memo, 31 Jan. 1924, RG 72, C&R, Bx 351.

33. McCrary to Moffett, 9 Jan. 1924, RG 72, C&R, Bx 350.

34. *New York Herald*, 2 Jan. 1924, 1:4.

35. *New York Times*, 13 Jan. 1924, 14:2.

36. Ibid., 20 Jan. 1924, 1:3.

37. Burgess Design Memo #31, 28 Jan. 1924, RG 72, GenCor, Bx 5570.

38. Reports on 16 Jan. 1924, Mayer Report 24 Jan. 1924, RG 72, GenCor, Bx 5570.

39. ZR 1 wireless messages on break-away flight, 17 Jan. 1924, RG 72, C&R, Bx 68.

40. Lcdr. Victor D. Herbster to President, Board of Inspection and Survey, 11 Feb. 1924, RG 72, GenCor, 1925–42, Bx 5565.

41. *New York Times*, 12 Feb. 1924, 6:1.

42. At the very end of the Zeppelin era, and after the *Hindenburg* disaster, her sister ship the *Graf Zeppelin II* was fitted with water recovery apparatus. Since she never received the helium promised by the United States, this was never tested in flight.

43. Theoretically the combustion of gasoline produced water and carbon dioxide. In practice, unburned carbon (soot) coated the inside of the condenser tubes, degrading their ability to transfer heat to the atmosphere. In the *Akron* and *Macon* era, cleaning carbon from the water recovery apparatus was considered a form of punishment.

44. *Rigid Airship Manual*, p. VIII–45.

45. Parker memo, RG 72, GenCor, Bx 5567.

46. NAF to BuAer, 7 April 1924, RG 72, GenCor, Bx 5567.

47. The other half of the helium production at Fort Worth went to the Army Air Service. During the early 1920s, the Army had six airship companies, operating two pressure airships each, at Langley Field, Aberdeen Proving Ground, and the headquarters base at Scott Field, Belleville, Ill., near St. Louis. Most of the craft were blimps of the TC class of 210,000 cu. ft., though the semirigid RS-1 of 745,000 cu. ft. was based at Scott Field. The Navy successfully blocked every effort by the Army Air Service to procure a rigid airship. See Thomas Ray, "Army Air Service Lighter-Than-Air Branch 1919–1926." *Journal of the American Aviation Historical Society*, Vol. 25, No. 4, Winter 1980, p. 301.

48. "1155 Lt. Williams took off and did special stunts.

1205 Lt. Williams landed." Logbook, NAS Lakehurst, 31 May 1924.

49. T. G. W. Settle, "Memorandum to Captain," 31 May 1929.

50. Lansdowne to Moffett, 9 June 1924, RG 72, GenCor 1925–42, Bx 5564.

51. Ibid.

52. C.O. *Shenandoah* to BuAer, 22 July 1924, RG 72, GenCor, 1925–42, Bx 5564.

53. This figure represented five railroad box cars each loaded with 500 small steel cylinders containing 140 cu. ft. of helium at 1,800 psi. Inasmuch as transport of helium from Fort Worth to Lakehurst via small cylinders was inefficient and expensive, the Navy developed special railroad cars carrying six vertical banks of five cylinders each, 18 in. in outside diameter and 40 feet long. Filled at 2,000 psi, each car transported 200,000 cubic feet of helium. In 1934 the Navy owned 12 such helium tank cars, and the Army Air Corps two.

54. In June 1925 the bureau had a portable *hydrogen* generator put on board the *Patoka* for use in emergencies. While mixing hydrogen with the helium in the airship's gas cells would have created a purification problem, the airship would at least have been able to fly back to Lakehurst with a reasonable load of fuel. In fact the hydrogen generator was never used. RG 72, GenCor, Bx 985.

55. Captain Harry E. Yarnell was commander of Aircraft Squadrons, Scouting Force, and Captain Stanford E. Moses was commander of Aircraft Squadrons, Battle Force. Both visited the *Shenandoah* while she was in Newport.

56. Lansdowne to Moffett, 6 Aug. 1924, RG 72, GenCor, 1925–42, Bx 5565.

57. Lansdowne to Moffett, 27 Aug. 1924, RG 72, GenCor, 1925–42, Bx 5569.

58. Burgess to BuAer, "Experimental Mooring of the *Shenandoah* to the *Patoka* on 8 August 1924," RG 72, GenCor, 1925–42, Bx 5565.

59. C.O. *Shenandoah* to Commander Scouting Force, Report on Scouting Problems, 16 August 1924. 21 Aug. 1924, RG 72, GenCor, 1925–42, Bx 5564.

60. Lansdowne to Moffett, 19 Aug. 1924, RG 72, GenCor, 1925–42, Bx 5564.

61. C.O. *Shenandoah* to Commander Scouting Force, Report on Scouting Problems, 16 August 1924. 21 Aug. 1924, RG 72, GenCor, 1925–42, Bx 5564.

62. Obviously Lansdowne meant here the automatic valves in the keel which were readily accessible by the keel watch during flight.

63. Lansdowne to Moffett, 19 Aug. 1924, RG 72, GenCor, 1925–42, Bx 5564.

64. Plans Division to Chief, BuAer, 9 May 1923, C&R, Bx 423.

65. McCrary to BuAer, 9 Nov. 1923, RG 72, C&R, Bx 424.

66. CinC U.S. Fleet to CNO, Employment of *Shenandoah*, 18 Aug. 1924. RG 72, GenCor, 1925–42, Bx 5564.

67. C.O. *Shenandoah* to BuAer, 2 Sept. 1924, RG 72, GenCor, 1925–42, Bx 5564.

68. Ibid.

69. CNO to CinC Fleet, 15 Dec. 1924, RG 72, GenCor, 1925–42, Bx 5564.

70. For the polar expedition, and before the helium shortage became acute, Fort Worth was to have had 500,000 cu. ft., San Diego 600,000 cu. ft., and Seattle 500,000 cu. ft. BuAer to Helium Plant, Fort Worth, 21 Jan. 1924, RG 72, C&R, Bx 351. On the West Coast flight, the *Shenandoah* took 180,000 cu. ft. of helium at San Diego outward bound and 150,000 cu. ft. on the return flight; 90,000 cu. ft. at Camp Lewis; and 220,000 cu. ft. at Fort Worth en route home. She took none at Fort Worth going out.

71. Lansdowne to Moffett, 5 Aug. 1924, RG 72, GenCor, 1925–42, Bx 737.

72. CNO Orders for *Shenandoah*, 25 Sept. 1924, RG 72, GenCor, 1925–42, Bx 737.

73. Junius B. Wood to Moffett, 24 Sept. 1924, RG 72, GenCor, 1925–42, Bx 5569.

74. Junius B. Wood, "Seeing America from the *Shenandoah*." *The National Geographic Magazine*, Vol. 47, No. 1, Jan. 1925.

75. Hugo Eckener, *Im Zeppelin über Länder und Meere*, p. 404.

76. C. E. Rosendahl, *Up Ship!*, p. 48.

77. The adiabatic temperature change with helium is 1.2 times greater than with hydrogen; thus with hydrogen in this case the temperature rise would have been only 5 degrees.

78. Junius B. Wood, "Seeing America from the *Shenandoah*," p. 42.

79. In the aftermath of the Teapot Dome scandal, Secretary Denby submitted his resignation. President Coolidge replaced him on 10 March 1924 with Curtis D. Wilbur.

80. SecNav to C.O. *Shenandoah*, 25 Oct. 1924, RG 72, GenCor, 1925–42, Bx 5564.

81. Z. Lansdowne Report on West Coast flight, no date, Garland Fulton files.

82. BuAer (Burgess) to Lakehurst, *Shenandoah*, 7 Nov. 1924, RG 72, GenCor, 1925–42, Bx 5565, File ZR-1/Fl-1. This examination must have been made during the long lay-up, but no report is to be found in the archives. Probably no significant damage was found.

83. Letter, Harold W. Lipper, Acting Assistant Director—Helium, U.S. Dept. of the Interior, Bureau of Mines, to Keller, 5 Jan. 1961.

84. Fulton to Chief, BuAer, 18 May 1925, RG 72, Airship History, Bx 17.

CHAPTER 8

1. C.O. *Shenandoah* to BuAer, 31 Dec. 1924, RG 72, GenCor, 1925–42, Bx 5565.

2. Vice Admiral Settle contributed a prescient anecdote of Lansdowne from the summer of 1925: "One day the ship and handling lines were ready and manned, and standing by in the Lakehurst shed for a wind-lull to undock. I was Communications/Radio Officer and was leaning on the sill of a portside window of my 'radio shack.' Just below me, standing on the hangar deck, Lansdowne and several other officers were chatting. Glancing up at the strut-wire suspensions of the control-radio car, Lansdowne remarked casually (partly jocular, partly serious), 'some day this control car is going to break away and fall free.' This flashed through my mind on September 3 when the Ava news came." Letter to Robinson, 31 July 1977.

3. C.O. *Shenandoah* to BuAer, 16 Sept. 1924, RG 72, Gen-Cor, 1925–42, Bx 5564.

4. In the Imperial German Navy, the Leader of Airships, Fregattenkapitän Strasser, discouraged the use of the maneuvering valves as they might stick open, and insisted that a "light" ship be made heavy by being driven over pressure height to release gas from the automatic valves in the keel.

5. Actually helium did not leak out of the automatic valves in the bottom of the gas cells, but air did leak inward, contaminating the lifting gas and diminishing the gross lift.

6. C.O. *Shenandoah* to BuAer, 15 Dec. 1924, RG 72, Gen-Cor, 1925–42, Bx 5564.

7. BuAer to C.O. *Shenandoah*, 28 May 1925, RG 72, Gen-Cor, 1925–42, Bx 5565. As a result of the final modification made in June 1925, the *Shenandoah* had: automatic valves on Cells #4, #5, #8, #9, #12, #13, #16, and 17; maneuvering valves on Cells #4, #6, #7, #10, #11, #14, #15, and 18.

8. BuAer to C.O. *Shenandoah*, 13 June 1925, RG 72, Gen-Cor, 1925–42, Bx 5564.

9. Owing to the exhaustion of the Petrolia field, helium production thereafter dropped steadily to 3,373,072 cu. ft. in fiscal 1929, after which the situation was changed by the much larger Cliffside field coming into production at Amarillo, Texas. Letter, Lipper to Keller, 5 Jan. 1961 (Chap. 7, n. 83). The Helium Company of Louisville, Ky., a private firm, provided 7,000,000 cu. ft. between 1927 and 1929 from gas wells in Kansas and Colorado, after which the government refused to buy further from them.

10. Fulton to Chief, BuAer, 18 May 1925, Airship History, Bx 17.

11. Letter, CNO to C.O. *Shenandoah*, 16 June 1925, RG 72, Airship History, Bx 18.

12. Letter, CNO to C.O. *Shenandoah*, 19 June 1925, RG 72, Airship History, Bx 18. See Appendix D for names of the 43 cities involved.

13. C.O. *Shenandoah* to CNO, 15 June 1925, RG 72, Airship History, Bx 18.

14. First endorsement, C.O. NAS Lakehurst to CNO, 15 June 1925, RG 72, Airship History, Bx 18.

15. Second Endorsement, CNO to Chief, BuAer, 20 June 1925, RG 72, Airship History, Bx 18. Author's italics.

16. A note by Truscott on the cover sheet reads, "County fair stuff instead of real work." RG 72, GenCor, 1925–42, Bx 5564.

17. Fabric secondary condensers were installed inside the outer cover above #5 engine car. These would eventually have been fitted to all the water recovery units.

18. C.O. *Shenandoah* to BuAer, Carrying Airplanes on *Shenandoah*, 21 Aug. 1925, RG 72, GenCor, 1925–42, Bx 5564.

19. C.O. *Patoka* to BuAer, 23 July 1925, RG 72, GenCor, 1925–42, Bx 5564.

20. Statement of Rear Admiral C. F. Hughes, Morrow Board Hearings, 1925, p. 1025.

21. Only after 1927 was the *Texas* fitted with a catapult.

22. C.O. *Shenandoah* to CNO, 10 Aug. 1925, Operations 6 July to 1 Aug., RG 72, File ZR 1/A4. Considering that all this armament would have added nearly 1,000 lb. in weight, at the expense of range, Lansdowne's recommendations were more theoretical than practical.

23. C.O. *Shenandoah* to CNO, Report of Gunnery Practice, 26 Aug. 1925, RG 72, GenCor, 1925–42, Bx 5564.

24. C.O. *Shenandoah* to CNO, Towing Experiments, *Shenandoah* and *Patoka*, 29 Aug. 1925, RG 72, GenCor, 1925–42, Bx 5564.

25. Rosendahl to BuAer, 14 Aug. 1925, RG 72, Airship History, Bx 18.

26. C.O. *Shenandoah* to CNO, 4 Aug. 1925, RG 45, Subject File, Bx 109.

27. "Technical Aspects of the Loss of the USS *Shenandoah*" (ASNE), p. 687.

28. CNO to C.O. *Shenandoah*, 11 Aug. 1925, RG 45, Subject File, Bx 109.

29. At 0400 Eastern Standard Time the ship's clocks were set back one hour to correspond to Central Standard Time.

30. Rosendahl to SecNav, Loss of the *Shenandoah*, 21 Sept. 1925, RG 72, GenCor, Bx 5570.

31. Mayer testimony, ASNE, p. 509.

32. Weyerbacher, not realizing that the manifold had been tied off, expressed his concern about the matter to Garland Fulton. "The practice would be all right if you went over pressure height on an even keel, but when inclined such as reported, it would seem a most dangerous procedure. The more you go into the subject, you come to the conclusion that dangerous pressures existed." Weyerbacher to Fulton, 25 Sept. 1925, Garland Fulton files.

33. Figures for altitude, and rate of ascent and descent, in preceding paragraphs were taken from a recording barograph recovered from the wreck. A re-drawn copy of this tracing appears on pp. 106–7.

34. Rosendahl to SecNav, Loss of the *Shenandoah*.

35. Mayer testimony, ASNE, p. 510.

36. The four elevator cables, and two upper rudder cables, were found intact in the stern section abaft Frame 70. *New York Times*, 26 Sept. 1925, 1:6, p. 7.

37. Rosendahl, *Up Ship!*, p. 79.

38. The *Shenandoah* tragedy, in which five officers had died and they had survived, bound Rosendahl, Mayer, and Bauch in a special relationship terminated only by the death of Bauch in an auto accident in 1930. Led by Rosendahl, the three fought to defend their dead commander before the Court of Inquiry from blame for the loss of the *Shenandoah*, and later the three served together in the *Los Angeles*.

39. They were found on 10 Sept. about ten miles off the island of Kauai, having sailed 450 miles after being forced down by fuel exhaustion on 1 Sept. For a full account, see Dwight R. Messimer, *No Margin for Error* (Annapolis: Naval Institute Press, 1981).

40. *New York Times*, 4 Sept. 1925, 4:6. Brought up in a patrician family, Betsy Lansdowne was trained to suppress her feelings. At the same time she was only 23 years old, the mother of a little girl not quite 3, and stepmother to a 9-year-old boy. To have the shattered body of the 36-year-old husband whom she loved and depended on shipped home from Ohio in a coffin labeled "not to be opened" would have overwhelmed a much older woman. As she was the widow of the *Shenandoah*'s commanding officer, her grief and distress were exposed to public gaze through the

relentless hounding of newspaper reporters. Other women were left alone to mourn in private. Lewis Hancock's widow, Joy Bright, a year older than Betsy, had lost her first husband, Lt. Charles G. Little, in the ZR 2 disaster. Both women later made lasting marriages, and Joy Bright Hancock became a captain USNR and director of the WAVES in World War II.

41. Vice Admiral Charles E. Rosendahl, personal communication. For many years the *Shenandoah* safe was a familiar sight in the admiral's study.

42. *New York Times*, 10 Sept. 1925, 4:3.

43. *New York Times*, 11 Sept. 1925, 8:1–3.

44. Hall testimony, ASNE, p. 514.

45. Summary by Commander S.M. Kraus, ASNE, p. 678. Donald Woodward points out that everyone in the court overlooked the fact that the inflation manifold was still tied off between Cells #8 and #9. With the ship nose-up before the final break, Cell #8 would have been filled by gas from the after cells flowing forward through the manifold. Letter to Robinson, 10 Sept. 1977.

46. Because of rumors that the jampot cover on the automatic valve of Cell #13 had never been removed, the cell was brought into court on the day that Querheim testified. The jampot cover was in place, but had been ripped.

47. The overpressure experiment with Cell #18 of the British R 32 on 27 April 1921 (p. 25) is relevant. Though the cell ultimately was pressurized to 30–32 mm. of water, it did not rupture, but its expansion caused 24 girder fractures in the longitudinals in the bay, with numerous shear wires being pulled out. The cell of course could hold more gas than its legend volume in the ship by expanding into a spherical shape without rupturing, but the radial loads on the longitudinal girders would exceed their structural limits.

48. Nor did L 49, from which she was copied, though the shear wires had first appeared in the earlier ships of the L 30 class.

49. Whittle testimony, ASNE, p. 577.

50. Burgess testimony, ASNE, pp. 542, 540.

51. Hovgaard Technical Argument, ASNE, p. 646.

52. Ibid., p. 639.

53. Ibid., p. 644.

54. *New York Times*, 23 Sept. 1925, p. 11, 1:7.

55. Bureau of Standards Report, ASNE, p. 522.

56. Anderson testimony, ASNE, p. 581.

57. The testimony at the Court of Inquiry led many members of the public to believe that Lansdowne was convinced that his ship would be lost if she were sent to the Midwest in September. If he could have correctly anticipated the extraordinary vertical currents that destroyed the *Shenandoah* over Ohio, Lansdowne surely would not have insisted on the drastic reduction in the number of automatic valves.

58. Dr. Karl Arnstein, interview, Akron, Ohio, 1955.

59. Colonel Hall had embarrassed the Navy by charging that the *Shenandoah*, "notoriously slow, had tried to escape the approaching storm, but, unable to make headway against the terrific wind, was sucked slowly into the vortex of a line squall to certain destruction." He believed she might have escaped disaster if she had retained the sixth engine. *New York Times*, 25 Sept. 1925, p. 10, 1:1.

60. Only two parachutes were carried to drop personnel if necessary to organize and direct a ground handling party.

61. "Brief Submitted by Interested Parties," ASNE, p. 678.

62. "Findings of the Court," ASNE, p. 691.

63. Ibid., p. 691.

64. Ibid., p. 683.

65. Flying with helium appears to have been undertaken with little advance realization of the problems involved. Hydrogen inflation would have increased useful lift and range by 40%, eliminating the added weight, drag, and plumbing problems of water recovery—though this option was taken out of the hands of BuAer after the fiery crash of the *Roma*. However, the 29 survivors of the *Shenandoah* owed their lives to helium; had she been inflated with hydrogen, she surely would have burned in the air with all hands.

66. It will be remembered that because of weather-related problems, the German Navy's Zeppelins in World War I flew scouting missions at sea on an average of only one day in four. Robinson, *The Zeppelin In Combat*, p. 350.

CHAPTER 9

1. Testifying before a House committee, Major Oscar Westover, then the assistant to the chief of Training and War Plans Division, astounded congressmen by asserting that within eight or ten years the Army expected to be able to transport a regiment—6,000 men—in one airship! "Helium Gas," Hearing before the Committee on Public Lands, House of Representatives, 67th Congress, 4th Session, December 1922.

2. As late as 1933, General Mitchell held that the rigid airship was useful as a bomber. U.S. Congress Joint Committee, Hearings, Investigation of Dirigible Disasters, 73rd Congress, 1st Session, 1933.

3. The Scott Field hangar was 810 feet long, 206 feet wide, and 178 feet high. Construction commenced on 25 Sept. 1921. Letter, Merle Olmsted to Robinson, 5 Aug. 1977.

4. Memo, Col. Wm. N. Hensley, Jr., ASA to Director of Air Service, "Report of Operations Abroad," 14 April 1920, RG 72, CNO, Bx 154.

5. Davis to Milstaff, 17 Sept. 1919, RG 18, CentDec Files, Bx 1053.

6. Davis to Milstaff, 3 Oct. 1919, RG 72, CNO, Bx 154.

7. Whereas the prewar rate of exchange was 4.25 marks to the dollar, these figures indicate a rate of 33.3 marks to the dollar.

8. It was later alleged that a twin-engine power car seen by American officers in Friedrichshafen had been built for LZ 125. Probably this car was built before the Armistice for the earlier L 100.

9. SecNav to SecWar, 26 May 1920, RG 72, CNO, Bx 165.

10. SecWar to SecNav, 17 June 1920, RG 72, CNO, Bx 165.

11. Weyerbacher interview, Booneville, Ind., 8 July 1960.

12. It will be remembered that the U.S. Senate refused to ratify the treaty, a state of war with Germany then continuing until Oct. 1921.

13.

	U.S.	Italy	Gt. Britain	France	Japan	Belgium
1st part			L 71	L 72		
2nd part	L 65*	L63*	L 64	L 52*	L 42*	L 41*
	L 14*	L 61	L 56*	LZ 113	L 37	L 30
		LZ 120				

*Destroyed by German airship crews, 23 June 1919.

14. While the actual value of the mark declined weekly owing to inflation, the theoretical "gold mark," used in computing Germany's obligations to the victorious Allies, retained its prewar value of 4.25 to the dollar.

15. *Luftschiffbau Zeppelin* to Foulois, 13 June 1921, Garland Fulton files.

16. Published works persistently but incorrectly refer to ZR 3 as the "reparations airship." Garland Fulton always insisted that her procurement had nothing to do with the reparations payments assessed against Germany under the Versailles Treaty; her construction at the expense of the German government represented *compensation* for the two Zeppelins L 65 and L 14, which had been awarded to the United States under the Versailles Treaty, and which had been destroyed at Nordholz on 23 June 1919.

17. SecState to American Ambassador Paris, 5 Aug. 1921, RG 18, CentDec Files, Bx 1053.

18. SecNav to SecState, 19 Sept. 1921, Garland Fulton files.

19. SecNav to SecState, 14 Oct. 1921, Garland Fulton files.

20. SecState to Ambassador, Paris, 9 Nov. 1921, Garland Fulton files. Author's italics.

21. Ambassador Paris to SecState, 16 Dec. 1921, Garland Fulton files.

22. Garland Fulton files.

23. Though the actual designer of ZR 3, and the designer of all Zeppelin Company airships since L 30 of 1916, was Dr. Karl Arnstein, a Bohemian-German Jew!

24. Eckener statement, 10 Jan. 1922, Garland Fulton files.

25. Letter, Upham to SecNav, 14 Jan. 1922, Garland Fulton files.

26. Letter, Moffett to Fulton, 18 Feb. 1922, Garland Fulton files.

27. Cable, ALUSNA, Berlin, to NavIntel, 19 Jan. 1922, Garland Fulton files.

28. Cable, American Embassy, Paris, to Dept. of State? 14 Feb. 1922, Garland Fulton files.

29. The 31,665 gold marks in addition represented the U.S. share of war material confiscated and destroyed in Germany by the IAACC.

30. Upham to SecNav, 16 Jan. 1922, Garland Fulton files.

31. Letter, Dyer to Upham, 26 Jan. 1922, Garland Fulton files.

32. Pennoyer returned to the United States late in 1923 to join the training staff at Lakehurst.

33. Published statements claim that Fulton and Weyerbacher signed for the United States. The actual signatories were Dr. Eckener for the Zeppelin Company and Captain Upham for the United States.

34. In August, Fulton and Pennoyer were joined by Lt. Karl Schmidt of the Construction Corps.

35. Weyerbacher Interview, Booneville, Ind., 8 July 1960.

36. Garland Fulton, "Notes on Personalities," 15 Dec. 1922, Garland Fulton files. Arnstein did in fact leave Friedrichshafen following completion of ZR 3. Anticipating that the Zeppelin Company might not survive, Eckener, Colsman, and Lehmann, in Oct. 1923, entered into an agreement with Paul W. Litchfield and William C. Young of the Goodyear Tire and Rubber Co., which led to the founding of the Goodyear-Zeppelin Co. of Akron, Ohio. North American rights to the Zeppelin patents, and Zeppelin engineering and operating experience, were to be conveyed to the American firm. In Oct. 1924, Dr. Arnstein sailed for America to become chief designer of Goodyear-Zeppelin, taking with him 12 other Zeppelin Company engineers.

37. Actually the new ship was only the 116th built by the *Luftschiffbau Zeppelin*. Six German naval Zeppelins ordered during the war were not completed, while four designs proposed in 1919 were never built.

38. The detachable passenger accommodation idea was dropped at an early date.

39. Letter, Fulton to Keller, 27 May 1959.

40. Notes from Garland Fulton's diary as INA, Garland Fulton files.

41. Letter, Moffett to Beehler, NavAtt Berlin, 10 May 1922, Garland Fulton files.

42. Letter, Chief BuAer to Chief Air Service, War Department, 29 June 1922, Garland Fulton files.

43. Letter, *Luftschiffbau Zeppelin* (Dr. Eckener) to Major Geiger, 23 Dec. 1922, Garland Fulton files.

44. "Notes for a conference with the INA regarding strength data by Lehmann," 23 Jan. 1923, Garland Fulton files.

45. Ibid. Italics in original

46. Ibid.

47. Ibid.

48. Letter, Moffett to Vissering, 24 Feb. 1923, Garland Fulton files.

49. Letter, Fulton to Moffett, 5 March 1923, Garland Fulton files.

50. Letter, Fulton to Moffett, 6 March 1923, Garland Fulton files.

51. Letter, Fulton to Hunsaker, 27 March 1923, Garland Fulton files.

52. Letter, Moffett to Fulton, 16 April 1923, Garland Fulton files.

53. Letter, Fulton to Keller, 3 July 1959.

54. Letter, Hunsaker to Fulton, 29 March 1923, Garland Fulton files.

55. *Aviation*, 16 Oct. 1922.

56. Letter, Fulton to Moffett, 26 Feb. 1923, Garland Fulton files.

57. Letter, Upham to Moffett, 1 March 1923, Garland Fulton files.

58. Memo, Hunsaker to SecNav re ZR 3 airship, 10 March 1923, Garland Fulton files.

59. *Aerial Age*, April 1923.

60. *Washington Post*, Sunday, 24 June 1923.

61. Letter, SecNav to SecState, 6 July 1923, Garland Fulton files.

62. Note that unlike all other Zeppelins, the rudder post and main cruciform in ZR 3 were not at Frame 0. This resulted from a late change in the basic hull design, when wind tunnel tests showed that the fins and rudders would be more effective if moved forward 5 meters from their original location on the hull.

63. *Aviation*, 27 Nov. 1922, Vol. 13, No. 22, p. 716.

64. ZR 3 Progress Report, 20 Nov. 1922, RG 72, CNO, Bx 313, file Progress Reports.

65. *Maybach Motorenbau* G.m.b.H., Friedrichshafen, *Maybach Flugmotor Bauart MbIVa 260 p.s. überverdichtet*, p. 24.

66. "History of VL-1 Engines with Reference to their Installation in ZR 3," May 1924, CNO Correspondence, 1917–25, RG 72, Bx 326.

67. Ibid.

68. Memo, Pennoyer to Halsey, 13 Sept. 1923, Garland Fulton files.

69. Letter, Hunsaker to Fulton, 20 Sept. 1923, Garland Fulton files.

70. "History of VL-1 Engines: List of VL-1 Engine Troubles."

71. Letter, Moffett to Fulton, 10 May 1924, Garland Fulton files.

72. "History of VL-1 Engines: List of VL-1 Engine Troubles."

73. Letter, Fulton to Burgess, 7 Aug. 1924, Garland Fulton files.

74. Though as will be seen, ZR 3 personnel had serious problems with burned-out connecting-rod bearings due to carbon deposits. This led to the requirement that each engine be completely disassembled and overhauled every 150 hours.

75. This was the German Navy's Zeppelin L 72, renamed and commissioned in the French Navy. The *Dixmude* had made a number of spectacular flights from the base at Cuers near Toulon in the latter part of 1923. One record flight, extending into the Sahara, lasted 118 hours 41 minutes. She was destroyed with all hands—50 persons—when she exploded in a thunderstorm off the south coast of Sicily on the night of 20–21 Dec. 1923. Zeppelin Company personnel had advised her commander, Lt. de Vaisseau Jean du Plessis de Grenedan, that L 72 was very lightly built for high-altitude flying and should not be flown heavily loaded at low altitude. German opinion was that she was unsuited for long-distance flying and had been mishandled by being flown into the thunderstorm.

76. Garland Fulton participated in all the earlier flights, but not the *Deutschlandfahrt*.

77. A. Wittemann, *Die Amerikafahrt des ZR III*, p. 87.

78. Hugo Eckener, "Der Amerikaflug des ZR III," in Hans Hildebrandt (ed.), *Zeppelin Denkmal für das deutsche Volk*, p. 366.

79. Letter, Fulton to Keller, 3 July 1959.

CHAPTER 10

1. Notes—Prospective Uses ZR 3 (no date), Garland Fulton files.

2. Board on Employment of ZR 3, 14 Nov. 1924, RG 72, GenCor, Bx 5572, File ZR 3. The matter of lengthening ZR 3 had come up even before her completion. The Zeppelin Company before the contact was completed had mentioned the possibility, and Fulton had agreed that "structurally a 15 meter lengthening should be entirely within reason and a 30 meter lengthening should not be unreasonable." In the first case, ZR 3 would have been 707.5 feet long with 3,061,900 cu. ft. volume 100% full; in the second case, 756.7 feet long with 3,361,760 cu. ft. Politically of course it was out of the question in 1923 because of the 70,000 cu.-meter limitation set by the Conference of Ambassadors in approving the ship's construction. This limitation was cited later when it was proposed to lengthen ZR 3 in the United States, and the ship was never lengthened despite the obvious advantages. Notes on possible major changes in ZR 3 to meet special conditions of service, 15 Nov. 1923, Garland Fulton files.

3. The American Investigation Corporation, founded in 1921 for the purpose of establishing commercial airship lines in the United States, showed some interest, but backed off after the *Shenandoah* disaster.

4. In Jan. 1925, it was hoped to have enough helium to inflate the *Shenandoah* also by March. Actually it was not until 2 Nov. 1931, that two American rigids flew simultaneously—the *Los Angeles* and the new *Akron* over Washington, Baltimore, Philadelphia, and New York City.

5. Ever since the "new Navy" of the 1880s, U.S. cruisers have been named for cities, and this was the case with ZR 3's successors also. The *Los Angeles* (CA 135) and the *Macon* (CA 132) of World War II were heavy cruisers.

6. BuAer to NAF, 16 Sept. 1924, RG 72, GenCor, Bx 5585, file ZR 3/F28.

7. Memo for C.O. Lakehurst from Wm. Nelson, 24 Nov. 1924, RG 72, GenCor, Bx 5585, File ZR 3/F28.

8. BuAer to CNO, 10 Dec. 1924; CNO endorsement 15 Dec. 1924; RG 72, GenCor 1925–42, Bx 5564, File ZR 1/A4.

9. It was the German Captain Hans Curt Flemming who sprang to the engine telegraphs to give the vital order in the nick of time. Letter, Vice Admiral T. G. W. Settle to Robinson, 24 Feb. 1978.

10. Rosendahl, *Up Ship!*, p. 59.

11. C.O. *Los Angeles* to CNO, 30 July 1925, RG 72, GenCor, Bx 5576, file ZR 3/A4-3.

12. BuAer to CNO, 13 May 1925, RG 72, GenCor, Bx 5576, File ZR 3/A4.

13. C.O. Lakehurst to CNO, 23 June 1925, RG 72, GenCor, Bx 5587, file ZR 3/F45.

14. Telegram C.O. Lakehurst to OpNav, BuAer, 9 June 1925, RG 72, Airship History, Bx 18.

15. Summary of Maybach VL-1 and VL-2 engines procured for the *Los Angeles*: #110001, 110002, 110003, 110004, 110005, delivered with ship; #110007, 110008, spares delivered 12 Dec. 1924; #110009, 110010, delivered Sept. 1926; #110026 delivered 9 Nov. 1927; #110027 delivered 5 Dec. 1927; #110038 delivered summer 1930. The last three were VL-2s.

16. Steele to CNO, 10 May 1926, RG 72, GenCor, Bx 5582, File ZR 3/F1 8.

17. Letter, Fulton to Keller, 7 Feb. 1960.

18. BuAer to C.O. *Los Angeles*, 17 March 1926, RG 72, GenCor, Bx 5572, file ZR 3/A4.

19. C.O. *Los Angeles* to BuAer, Helium Situation, RG 72, GenCor, Bx 5572, file ZR 3/A4.

20. The airship, operating at altitude, could calibrate the stations to seaward more efficiently than surface ships, while only the airship could calibrate the segment of the circle inland.

21. The only other airship to moor at the Ford mast was the large Army semirigid RS-1, on 18 Sept. 1926.

22. C.O. *Los Angeles* to BuAer, 9 Dec. 1926, RG 72, GenCor, Bx 5585, File ZR 3/F20.

23. Letter, Harold W. Lipper, Assistant Director—Helium, U.S. Dept. of Interior, Bureau of Mines, to Keller, 5 Jan. 1961.

24. ZR 3 operations, Rosendahl to CNO, 16 May 1927, RG 72, GenCor, Bx 5572, ZR 3/A4.

25. Rosendahl to Moffett, 14 June 1927, RG 72, GenCor, Bx 5572, File ZR 3/A4.

26. Moffett to C.O. *Los Angeles*, 17 June 1927, RG 72, GenCor, Bx 5584, File ZR 3/F20.

27. Admiral Rosendahl told me that seven photographs were taken in all, but that the first and last ones, which I have never seen, showed the ship practically horizontal. (DHR)

28. Letter, Rosendahl to Moffett, 26 Aug. 1927, RG 72, GenCor, Bx 5572, File ZR 3/A4 v. 2.

29. Ibid.

30. Garland Fulton, "Airship Progress and Airship Problems." *American Society of Naval Engineers Journal*, Vol. 41, No. 1, Feb. 1929.

31. I am indebted to Mr. Hepburn Walker for detailed information in this paragraph. Letter to Robinson, 20 Oct. 1977.

32. *New York Times*, 28 Jan. 1928, 1:5.

33. Rosendahl, *Up Ship!*, p. 129.

34. Ibid., p. 129.

35. Ibid., p. 115.

CHAPTER 11

1. BuAer to BuNav, 13 April 1929, RG 72, GenCor, Bx 5573, File ZR 3/A4.

2. Rosendahl to Moffett, 14 June 1927, RG 72, GenCor, Bx 5572, File ZR 3/A4.

3. At Army request, the original specifications for ZR 3 called for "two reinforced points . . . in the keel capable of supporting concentrated weights of not less than 2500 lb. each," showing that the Army was thinking of carrying airplanes though such employment was not publicized in view of the "commercial" character of the ship. The Zeppelin Company objected successfully on account of the added structural weight, but Fulton pointed out that "by omitting fuel and ballast from Ring 100, this point . . . can support up to three tons without difficulty." INA Friedrichshafen to Chief, BuAer, 23 Nov. 1923, Garland Fulton files.

4. The *Prüfling* glider was designed by Alexander Lippisch and Fritz Stahmer and built in Kassel, Germany, by the *Rhön-Rossitten Gesellschaft*. It was 32 ft. 8 in. in span, 17 ft. 9 in. long; gross weight was 400 lb., and glide ratio 15:1. It was in this craft that Lt. Ralph S. Barnaby, in Aug. 1929, made the first "C" badge flight, of 15 minutes 6 seconds, by an American. The *Prüfling* was written off on Labor Day,

1931, at Akron, when the tow hook failed to disengage from the wire on tow. Lt. Rodney Dennett was seriously injured in the resulting crash. (Information from Capt. Ralph S. Barnaby USN Ret.)

5. St. Elizabeth's Hospital, the federal government institution for the mentally ill in the District of Columbia.

6. Letter, Vice Admiral T. G. W. Settle to Robinson, 14 April 1977.

7. Pure ethylene glycol boils at 197.2°C.

8. The *Lexington* and the *Saratoga*, otherwise identical, were distinguished for recognition purposes by a broad horizontal black band at the top of the funnel (*Lexington*) and broad vertical black bands on both sides of the funnel (*Saratoga*).

9. This beautiful full-rigged ship, built in 1883 and bearing the Polynesian name of Robert Louis Stevenson, was operated regardless of expense between 1923 and 1932 by James A. Farrell, the president of the United States Steel Corporation. She was laid up in the Hudson River in 1932.

10. V. A. Clarke to Admiral Moffett, 22 Feb. 1931, Garland Fulton files.

11. Letter, Lt. George C. Calnan (CC) to Garland Fulton, 16 Feb. 1931, Garland Fulton files.

12. V. A. Clarke to Moffett, 22 Feb. 1931, Garland Fulton files.

13. "Notes by Moffett about 1932," Garland Fulton files.

14. Clarke to Moffett, 22 Feb. 1931, Garland Fulton files.

15. Rosendahl, *Up Ship!*, p. 118.

16. Quoted in A. K. Turnbull and C. L. Lord, *History of United States Naval Aviation*, p. 281.

17. The field at the Naval Aircraft Factory in Philadelphia, named for Captain Henry C. Mustin USN, Naval Aviator #11.

18. *Encyclopedia Britannica*, 1958 ed., Vol. 22, p. 848A.

19. Charles Francis Adams, SecNav, to Hon. James W. Byrnes, Chairman, Committee on Appropriations, House of Representatives, 22 April 1932, RG 72, GenCor, Bx 5573, File ZR 3/A4.

20. James W. Byrnes to SecNav, 28 April 1932, RG 72, GenCor, Bx 5573, File ZR 3/A4.

21. Litchfield to Moffett, 11 Feb. 1932, RG 72, Bx 5587, File ZR 3/L4.

22. Report of Board of Inspection and Survey (ZR 3), 6 Jan. 1939, RG 72, GenCor, Bx 5580, File ZR 3/F3.

23. Richard K. Smith, *The Airships Akron and Macon*, p. 167.

24. Sixteen in ZR 2, 14 in the *Shenandoah*, 73 in the *Akron*, 2 in the *Macon*.

CHAPTER 12

1. See Chap. 9, n. 36.

2. Initially, the airplanes were intended to defend the mother ship from attack by enemy aircraft, but with operational experience, it was realized that they could extend the airship's range of vision in the reconnaissance role.

3. HR 9690, "To Authorize the Construction and Procurement of Aircraft and Aircraft Equipment in the Navy and Marine Corps," etc., p. 1624, Garland Fulton files.

4. Recognizing the shortcomings of wooden girder construction, Schütte had spent two years in wartime ex-

perimenting with girders built up of duralumin tubing. One rigid airship with duralumin girders was in the early stage of construction at the Armistice in 1918.

5. Actually in the *Akron* as delivered, only half the gas cells were of gelatin latex, and the other half of rubberized cotton. The gelatin latex, however, was so successful that it was used in all the cells of the *Macon*.

6. Clear dope was used on the strakes over the lateral keels, to permit light to diffuse through the cover for internal illumination. This produced a curious effect as though the hull at this point was angled outward.

7. Lt. Frederick M. Trapnell, and Lts. (j.g.) Harold B. Miller, Robert W. Larson, and Frederick N. Kivette.

8. C. E. Rosendahl, *What About The Airship?*, p. 123.

9. King and Whitehill, *Fleet Admiral King*, p. 256.

10. R. K. Smith, *The Airships Akron and Macon*, p. 109.

11. Ibid., p. 103.

12. Ibid., p. 113.

13. German practice was to minimize aerodynamic loads in rough air by dropping ballast and slowing the engines. In the *Macon*'s case, however, Admiral Rosendahl pointed out that Dresel, flying through twisting canyons, needed high speed to control his ship, while he could not drop more fuel as he might not be able to reach Opa-Locka. Lastly, "we thought those ships were so strong that they could take anything." Interview, Toms River, N.J. 8 May 1971.

14. Smith, p. 145.

15. Airshipmen felt they had been victimized by Commander Holloway H. Frost of Sellers's staff. In an otherwise excellent book on the Battle of Jutland (*The Battle of Jutland*, United States Naval Institute, Annapolis, Md., 1936), Frost had gone out of his way to ridicule the performance of the German Zeppelins.

16. Smith, p. 125.

17. Dresel was made commanding officer of NAS, Sunnyvale.

18. Smith, p. 162.

CHAPTER 13

1. Robinson, *The Zeppelin in Combat*, p. 319.

2. "Aeroplanes breed like rabbits, airships like elephants," observed Charles G. Grey, the waspish editor of the British journal *The Aeroplane*.

3. Questioned on this point in 1976, Admiral Rosendahl, who read the introduction and outline for this book, still felt Moffett had no choice, considering Billy Mitchell's agitation to take over naval aviation, and the indifference of Congress and the public to the Navy's need for its own air arm.

4. The painful loss of so many experienced personnel out of such a small organization severely handicapped progress. Beyond doubt, the airship cause would have gone forward more rapidly and favorably if Maxfield, Lansdowne, McCord, and the hundred other men who perished with them in ZR 2, the *Shenandoah*, and the *Akron* had survived. Although Moffett was due to retire for age in Nov. 1933, he would have continued to wield great influence as the elder statesman of naval aviation.

5. With benefit of hindsight, it is apparent that it was a major error of policy not to have constructed a fully equipped airship base in southern California. This would have avoided the detrimental isolation of Lakehurst and Sunnyvale. The airship commanding officer would have been a frequent visitor on board the fleet flagship, and there would have been a fruitful exchange of knowledge with the fleet staff leading to realistic and worthwhile participation in exercises, perhaps even a more favorable attitude by the commander in chief.

Bibliography

ORIGINAL SOURCES

This work is primarily based on extensive research by Charles L. Keller in the National Archives, principally Record Group 72. All available documents were abstracted concerning the procurement of ZR 2, the activities of the Howden Detachment, and the loss of that ship; the construction and operation of the ZR 1 *Shenandoah*; and the negotiations leading to the procurement of the ZR 3 *Los Angeles* from the Zeppelin Company, and her operation by the U.S. Navy.

Furthermore, the late Captain Garland Fulton USN, who between the years 1918 and 1940 served first in the Aviation Section of the Bureau of Construction and Repair, and later in the Bureau of Aeronautics as head of the Lighter Than Air Design Section, made available to the authors a quantity of material concerning his activities, particularly as inspector of naval aircraft, Friedrichshafen, in 1922–24. Captain Fulton's papers are now held by the Naval Historical Foundation at the Washington Navy Yard.

BOOKS

Patrick Abbott, *Airship*. New York: Charles Scribner's Sons, 1973.

Charles P. Burgess, *Airship Design*. New York: Ronald Press Co., 1927.

Richard E. Byrd, *Skyward*. New York: G. P. Putnam's Sons, 1928.

Hugo Eckener, *Im Zeppelin Über Länder und Meere*. Flensburg: Verlagshaus Christian Wolff, 1949.

Great Britain. Admiralty War Staff, Intelligence Division. CB 1265, CB 1265A, *German Rigid Airships* (Confidential). London: Ordnance Survey, Feb. 1917.

Otto Groos, *Der Krieg in der Nordsee*, Vols. I–V. Berlin: E. S. Mittler u. Sohn, 1921–25.

Robin D. S. Higham, *The British Rigid Airship 1908–1931*. London: G. T. Foulis & Co. Ltd., 1961.

Hans Hildebrandt (ed.), *Zeppelin Denkmal für das deutsche Volk*. Stuttgart: Germania-Verlag G.m.b.H., 1925.

J. C. Hunsaker, *The History of Naval Aviation*. Typescript, 1923, retyped and mimeographed by Charles L. Keller, 1960.

E. J. King and W. M. Whitehill, *Fleet Admiral King: A Naval Record*. New York: W. W. Norton Co., 1952.

Ernest Lehmann and Howard Mingos, *The Zeppelins*. New York: J. H. Sears & Co., 1927.

Maybach Motorenbau G.m.b.H., Friedrichshafen, *Maybach Flugmotor Bauart MbIVa 260 p.s. überverdichtet* [1918]. (Engine handbook)

Charles M. Melhorn, *Two Block Fox: The Rise of the Aircraft Carrier, 1911–1929*. Annapolis: U.S. Naval Institute, 1974.

R & M 775, *Report on the Accident to H.M. Airship R 38*. London: H. M. Stationery Office, 1922.

Report of the Court of Inquiry into the Loss of H.M.A. R 38, 1921.

Douglas H. Robinson, *The Zeppelin In Combat*. London: G. T. Foulis & Co., Ltd., 1962.

Charles E. Rosendahl, *Up Ship!* New York: Dodd, Mead & Co., 1931.

Charles E. Rosendahl, *What About The Airship?* New York: Charles Scribner's Sons, 1938.

Clifford W. Seibel, *Helium, Child of the Sun*. Lawrence: The University Press of Kansas, 1969.

Richard K. Smith, *The Airships Akron and Macon: Flying Aircraft Carriers of the U.S. Navy*. Annapolis: U.S. Naval Institute, 1965.

Archibald K. Turnbull and Clifford L. Lord, *History of United States Naval Aviation*. New York: Yale University Press, 1949.

U.S. Navy Bureau of Aeronautics, *Rigid Airship Manual 1927*. Washington, D.C.: U.S. Government Printing Office, 1928.

Anton Wittemann, *Die Amerikafahrt des ZR III*. Wiesbaden: Amsel-Verlag, G.m.b.H., 1925.

ARTICLES

William A. Althoff, "The Decommissioned *Los Angeles.*" *Journal of the American Aviation Historical Society*, Vol. 23, No. 2, Summer 1978, pp. 103–11, and Vol. 25, No. 1, Spring 1980, pp. 29–41.

C. P. Burgess, J. C. Hunsaker, and Starr Truscott, "The Strength of Rigid Airships." *Journal of the Royal Aeronautical Society*, Vol. 28, June 1924, pp. 327–448.

Garland Fulton, "Airship Progress and Airship Problems." *Journal of the American Society of Naval Engineers*, Vol. 41, No. 1, Feb. 1929.

Thomas Ray, "Army Air Service Lighter-Than-Air Branch 1919–1926." *Journal of the American Aviation Historical Society*, Vol. 25, No. 4, Winter 1980, pp. 301–313.

Kap. Lt. von Schiller, "The Achievements of the German Airships in the World War." *Office of Naval Intelligence, Monthly Information Bulletin*, Jan. 1924, pp. 26–48.

"Technical Aspects of the Loss of the USS *Shenandoah*," *Journal of the American Society of Naval Engineers*, Vol. 38, No. 3, Aug. 1926, pp. 487–694.

Junius B. Wood, "Seeing America from the *Shenandoah*." *The National Geographic Magazine*, Vol. 47, No. 1, Jan. 1925, pp. 1–47.

Index

236

UP SHIP

Mooring (cont.)
    Stub mast, 147, 154, 155, 156, 158,
        160, 165, 167, 168, 170, 184, 200
    Tail drag, 145, 148, 151
    Three-wire mooring, 6, 15, 24, 27, 148,
        150
Moses, Capt., 92, 95
Müller, Hermann, 9
Mustin, Capt. Henry C., 194, 228n17

Narragansett Bay, 86, 102, 148
National Advisory Committee for Aero-
    nautics, 55, 58–59, 147
National Physical Laboratory, 25, 35,
    38–39, 43–44
Naval Aircraft Factory, 7, 13, 49, 51, 56,
    59, 60, 63, 64, 66, 69, 70, 82, 83,
    140–41, 146, 150, 164, 166, 172, 173,
    182
Navigation, Bureau of, 22–23, 40, 42, 70,
    136
Nelson, Lcdr. William, 109, 112, 201
New Orleans, USS, 189
Newport, R.I., 86–87, 103, 143, 144, 148,
    156, 157, 160, 168
New York, USS, 89, 187
Niblack, Adm., 46
Nicholson, Lcdr. Charles A., 165–66
Nicholson, W. F., 37
Nordholz, Germany, 3, 116, 119, 123,
    173
Norfleet, Cdr. Joseph P., 15, 62, 101
Null, Lt. Telford B., 22, 46

O'Brien, Chf. Aviation Pilot J. J., 166,
    172
O'Claire, CBM Harry H., 24, 219n28
Old Plantation Flats, 148, 150, 156, 158
Onishi, Takajiro, 24, 219n47

Palmer, Lt(jg) Carlton D., 82, 87
Panama, 142, 158, 168–71, 185, 190
Panama Canal, 168–71, 183, 187
Pannell, John, 39, 43–45, 220n40
Parker, Humphrey F., 82–83, 90
Parris Island, S.C., 171, 172
Patoka, USS, 78–79, 86–89, 99–103, 141–
    43, 148, 150, 156, 158, 160, 162,
    168–70, 184, 201, 223n54; mast
    height increased, 144
Patrick, Gen. Mason M., 72, 126
Payne, Naval Constructor, 30, 47
Peck, Lt. Scott E., 158, 161, 174
Peckham, ACR Frank L., 70, 219n28
Pennoyer, Lt. Ralph G., 22–24, 46–47,
    111, 124–25, 135, 226n32, 226n34
Petaval, Sir J. E., 47, 220n49
Phelps, Adm. William W., 97
Pierce, Cdr. Maurice, 68, 70, 72, 80–81,
    111, 139, 142, 147, 161, 200
Potter, Cpl. Walter, 45, 46
Pratt, Adm. William V., 169–71, 183
Princess Matioka, 22
Pritchard, Flt. Lt. John Edward
    Maddock, 36–40, 42–48
Pulham, England, 4, 11, 15, 18, 20, 22,
    23, 24, 26, 27, 28, 43, 44, 46, 49, 75–
    76, 82, 117, 163

Quernheim, AMM1c A. C., 111, 113,
    225n46

Raleigh, USS, 169, 182
Ramapo, USS, 78–79
Ramsey, Lcdr. DeWitt C., 17–21, 30, 62,
    218n1(4)
Reber, Chief Boatswain E. G., 166
Reeves, R. Adm. Joseph M., 169, 189,
    191
Rigid Airship Training and Ex-
    perimental Squadron, 163, 168
Rittenhouse, Lt. David, 84
Robertson, Gunner, 80
Robinson, Theodore Douglas, 142
Robison, Adm. Samuel S., 92
Rodgers, Cdr. John, 110
Roosevelt, Franklin Delano, Asst. Sec-
    Nav, 7, 11, 13; President, 176, 189
Roosevelt, Theodore, Jr., 72, 85
Rosendahl, V. Adm. Charles E., 68, 86–
    88, 90–94, 101, 104–13, 140, 143,
    144, 147–48, 150–64, 167–68, 171,
    174, 175–77, 179–84, 186, 195, 200–
    201, 224n38
Royal Airship Works, Bedford, 24, 30–
    31, 34, 36, 43, 124, 219n3
Russell, ACMM W. A., 109, 113

Sabatier, Naval Constructor, 51, 56
Salmond, Air Vice Marshal Sir John, 47
Salt Lake City, USS, 166, 169
Saratoga, USS, 115, 157–58, 169, 171,
    183, 185, 190, 194, 200, 228n8
Scales, R. Adm. Archibald H., 73, 81
Schiller, Hans von, 138, 154, 160
Schmidt, Lt. Karl, 136–37, 226n34
Schnitzer, CRM George C., 108
Schofield, Adm. Frank H., 169–71
Schütte, Dr. Johann, 3, 55, 178, 228n4(12)
Scott, Major George H., 24, 47, 49, 74,
    76
Scouting Force, 168–69, 171, 172,
    182–84
Seely, Gen. J. E. B., 18, 21
Sellers, Adm. David F., 186–90
Settle, Cdr. T. G. W., 151–52, 159, 161,
    166, 202, 223n2
Sheppard, Lt(jg) Edgar W., 105, 109
Shevlowitz, AMM1c Joseph, 108–9, 113
Shoemaker, Capt. Harry E., 168, 174
Short Bros., Cardington, 5, 9, 19, 30, 117
Sims, Adm. William S., 10, 19
Sperry, Lawrence, 163–64
Spratley, AMM1c William H., 108
Squier, Lt. Col. George O., 8–9
Standards, Bureau of, 9, 59, 82–83, 112,
    146, 167
Standley, Adm. William H., 175, 186,
    190
Steam Engineering, Bureau of, 23, 29,
    31, 34, 40, 50–51, 70, 124
Steele, Capt. George, 11, 101, 105, 110,
    137–38, 140–42, 144–47, 201
Stevens, Lcdr. Leslie C., 165
Strasser, Freg. Kap. Peter, 119, 163
Sunnyvale, Calif., airship shed, 183
Sutton Pippard, Dr. A. J., 47

Swanson, Claude, SecNav, 174
Sykes, Gen. Frederick, 27

Taylor, R. Adm. David W., 7–10, 15, 16,
    29–30, 35, 40, 42, 50–51, 55, 57,
    59–60
Texas, USS, 100, 101, 102, 103, 113,
    168–69, 187
Thomas, Flt. Lt. Godfrey Maine, 23, 43,
    45–46, 76
Tinker, Lt. Clifford A., 42–43, 46
Tobin, CBM F. J., 72, 161
Towers, Cdr. John T., 111, 137
Trapnell, Lt. Frederick M., 185
Trenchard, Air Marshal Sir Hugh, 37,
    43, 46, 218n5(4)
Trinity, USS, 47
Trinkle, E. L., Gov. of Virginia, 101
Truscott, Starr, 9, 10, 13, 35, 41–42, 49,
    50–51, 54, 56, 69, 75, 76, 78, 79, 87–
    88, 90, 102, 177
Twining, Adm., 40, 42, 46, 49

Upham, Capt. Frank P., 122–24, 130,
    140, 150, 226n33
Utah, USS, 42–43, 46

Van Nostrand, Maj. P. E., 42
Versailles Treaty, 116–20, 129
Vickers, 4, 5, 6, 9, 10, 27, 60, 117
Vissering, Harry, 119–20, 124, 127–29,
    135
Vyvyan, Air Marshal A. V., 46

Walker, ACR Norman O., 27, 45–46,
    220n36
Wallis, Sir Barnes, 4, 5, 27, 55
Wann, Flt. Lt. Archibald H., 24–25, 37,
    39, 43, 45–48, 65, 220n44
Warner, Edward P., 148
Westover, Maj. Oscar, 126, 225n1
Weyerbacher, Cdr. Ralph D., 7, 16, 42,
    51, 56, 58, 63–68, 70–75, 77–82, 119,
    125, 182, 200–201, 224n32, 226n33
White, Cdr. Newton H., 37, 46
Whiting, Cdr. Kenneth, 49, 194
Whittle, Lt. G. V., 112
Wilbur, Curtis D., SecNav, 110, 111,
    140, 158, 178, 223n79
Wiley, Lcdr. Herbert V., 68, 147, 154,
    158–61, 163, 165, 167, 171, 185,
    189–91, 200–201
Williams, Lt. Alford J., 67, 84
Willard, V. Adm. Arthur L., 169, 171,
    182
Wilm, Dr. Alfred, 8, 59
Wilson, Woodrow, President, 7, 120
Wittemann, Anton, 138, 140, 201
Wittmundhaven, Germany, 3, 116, 120
Wood, Junius B., 90–92
Wood, Lcdr. R. F., 62
Wyatt, Lt. Ben H., 92

Yards & Docks, Bureau of, 9, 13–15, 154
Yarnell, Capt. Harry E., 157
Yorktown, USS, 193
Young, Lt. Howard L., 172–73, 182, 183

Zahm, Dr. Albert F., 56